ISRAEL
and the Occupied Territories
THE ROUGH GUIDE

KU-175-271

THE ROUGH GUIDES

OTHER AVAILABLE ROUGH GUIDES
**NEW YORK, MEXICO, CALIFORNIA, PERU,
FRANCE, SPAIN, CHINA, KENYA, PORTUGAL,
MOROCCO, EASTERN EUROPE, TUNISIA, YUGOSLAVIA,
SICILY, BRITTANY & NORMANDY, PARIS, VENICE,
SCANDINAVIA, CRETE, GREECE, AMSTERDAM,
ITALY, GERMANY and IRELAND**
FORTHCOMING TITLES INCLUDE
**BRAZIL, BERLIN, GUATEMALA & BELIZE, HOLLAND,
BELGIUM & LUXEMBOURG and THE PYRENEES**

ROUGH GUIDE CREDITS

Series Editor: Mark Ellingham
Editorial: Martin Dunford, John Fisher, Jack Holland
Production: Susanne Hillen
Typesetting: Dan Goldstein and Greg Ward
Design: Andrew Oliver

ACKNOWLEDGEMENTS

Special thanks go to Dr Uri Davis for his advice, encouragement and infinite patience; and to the many others who have contributed their valuable time and expertise to this effort: Dr Hassan Amun and Yahya Dabbah in Deir al-Assad; Salman Fakhreddin in Majd al-Shams; Rizeq Petro and staff at *Attic Tours* in Jerusalem; Sleiman Nofal and staff at the *Regents Hotel* in Jerusalem; Leah Tsemel, Michael Warshawsky and members of the AIC; Michael Lowry; Ronit and Nawaf; Mahmoud and Helen Huwari; Anita Vitullo and Sama'an Khouri; Mohammed Daoud and family; the IGTO, particularly Michael Gidron in Jerusalem and the staff in Eilat; Nuri al-Uqbi and members of the SPBR in Beersheva.

Much gratitude goes to Gila for her superb artistry and Paul Cossali for invaluable work in Gaza. Last but certainly not least: thanks to John Richardson for pulling the project out of deep waters, to John Fisher for breathing life into it, to Mark Ellingham for solace and comfort, to Jane Foxworthy for injections of sanity, to Bob Cumming and Karen Phillips for crisis management, and to Adam Jukes for shoring up the banks.

Extract from *The Gun and the Olive Branch* © David Hirst 1983, by permission of Faber & Faber.
The Ecology of Jerusalem by Yehuda Amichai from Selected Poems (Penguin; © Chana Bloch and Stephen Mitchell 1986) reproduced by permission of Penguin Books and Olwyn Hughes.
Extract from *Israel – A Victory Wasted* © Amos Kenan by permission of Amos Kenan.

Illustrations by Ed Bryant and Gila

Published by
Harrap-Columbus, Chelsea House, 26 Market Square, Bromley, Kent BR1 1NA.

Typeset in Linotron Univers and Century Old Style.
Printed by Cox & Wyman, Reading.
464p.
Includes index.

British Library Cataloguing in Publication Data
Eber, Shirley
  Israel and the Occupied Territories: the rough guide.
  1. Israel. Visitors' guides.
  I. Title. II. O'Sullivan, Kevin
  915.694'0454

  ISBN 0–7471–0105–1

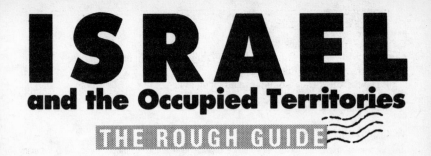

ISRAEL
and the Occupied Territories
THE ROUGH GUIDE

WRITTEN AND RESEARCHED BY
SHIRLEY EBER
and
KEVIN O'SULLIVAN

with an additional account by
Paul Cossali

Edited by John Fisher
with John Richardson and Shirley Eber

HARRAP-COLUMBUS ■ LONDON

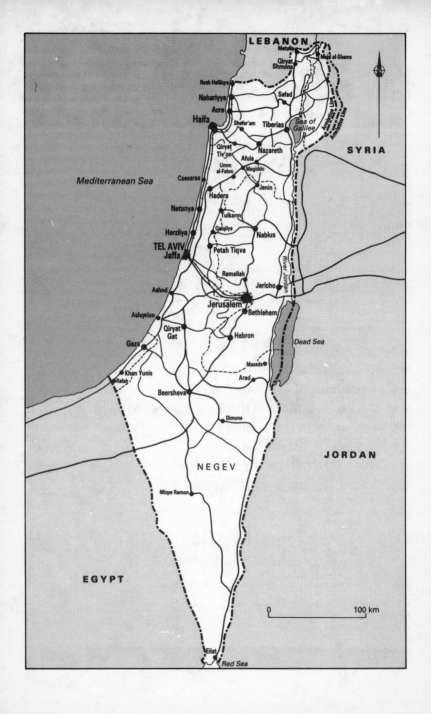

CONTENTS

Introduction *vi*

PART ONE BASICS   1

Getting There (3)/ Red Tape and Visas (7)/ Costs, Money and Banks (8)/ Health and Insurance (9)/
Information and Maps (10)/ Getting Around (12)/ Sleeping (15)/ Eating and Drinking (18)/
Communications – Post, Phones and Media (23)/ Opening Hours and Holidays (25)/ Entertainment (28)/
Trouble, Police and Security (30)/ Sexual Harassment (31)/ Gay and Lesbian Life (32)/ Work (33)/
Directory (36).

PART TWO THE GUIDE   39

- **1   JERUSALEM 41**
- **2   THE WEST BANK 132**
- **3   TEL AVIV AND THE SOUTH COAST 194**
- **4   HAIFA AND THE CENTRAL COAST 242**
- **5   GALILEE AND THE NORTH 286**
- **6   TIBERIAS AND THE PANHANDLE 321**
- **7   THE GOLAN HEIGHTS 346**
- **8   THE GAZA STRIP 356**
- **9   NEGEV, THE SOUTH AND EILAT 369**

PART THREE CONTEXTS   411

The Historical Framework 413
Religion in the 'Holy Land' 421
Books 427
Writers on Israel and Palestine 432
Language 442
A Hebrew and Arabic Glossary 446

Index 448

INTRODUCTION

T he size of modern-day Israel and the occupied territories of the West Bank, Gaza Strip and the Golan Heights, and their relatively small population, come as a surprise. In stark contrast to the volume of international attention that the place receives, it is physically very small. Within the 'green line' that separates Israel from the territories occupied in 1967, the population is a little over four million, of whom about 17 per cent are Palestinian, while that of the occupied territories is one-and-a-half million. Yet few countries arouse such intense emotions or as much media coverage, positive or negative. And still fewer excite as much controversy. In many ways, Israel is a unique country: sanctioned by a UN resolution to partition Palestine into two states, the Israeli state that was forged out of the flames of war in 1948 still has no official borders, and the problems then created remain to this day.

Israel is also unique in the central position it occupies for the adherents of the three major monotheistic religions; for **Jews**, it is the Promised Land given to them by God; for **Christians**, it is the birthplace and home of Christ the Saviour; for **Muslims**, it contains the site from which the Prophet Mohammed ascended to Heaven. Members of all three religions often lay claim to the land, or various parts of it, as of 'divine right'. Indeed, this coastal strip of the Middle East has been fought over since biblical times, and conquered time and time again. Today, monuments to its troubled past are juxtaposed with monuments to its troubled present – from medieval Crusader fortresses to fortress-like modern settlements; from imposing mosque minarets to glass-fronted skyscraper megastores; from Middle Eastern bazaars to fast-food takeaways; from socialistic agricultural plantations to nuclear plants; from lush fertile plains to arid lunar-type deserts; from towering snow-capped mountains to the lowest point on earth. It is a country with a distinct Mediterranean flavour and a vibrant outdoor life but where the streets empty when Dallas in on TV; where Hebrew and Arabic are the official languages, but where everyone speaks English, or French, German, Russian, Rumanian, Polish, Yiddish, Ladino, Spanish ... where black-robed orthodox Jews destroy adverts showing scantily-clad women, while the beaches of Eilat are almost as cosmopolitan as those of the South of France.

Above all, Israel is unique in that this small strip of land, only 20,000 square kilometres, is claimed as the homeland of two peoples: Palestinians and Israelis. Those Palestinians who remained within the 'green line' live mostly in the north of the country and, despite being citizens of the state, an undeclared apartheid makes them disadvantaged in terms of education, employment, housing and social services. The Palestinians in Israel, whether Muslim, Christian or Druze, have their own language (Arabic), customs, traditions and history, and political, cultural and religious institutions. And since 1967, when Israel occupied the Palestinian West Bank and Gaza Strip, their isolation from the rest of the Arab world, and particularly from their fellow Palestinians in these areas came to an end. The feeling of solidarity has grown in the years following the 1967 war, and particularly during the recent Palestinian **intifada** against Israeli rule in the occupied territories, which is now the focus of international attention.

Israeli society is itself far from homogeneous. The obvious political problems aside – there's a wide gulf between left and right, secular and orthodox – there's also a growing divide between Ashkenazi (European) and Sephardi (Oriental) Jews, in effect a class division. Politically and financially Ashkenazi Jews dominate Israel, but increasingly the Sephardi majority are finding their voice, a voice which is distinctively Middle Eastern.

Yet another curious aspect of the country is that, despite all the upheavals and conflict, it is still possible to travel in substantial areas and see and experience nothing of them. You can, if you want, sit in the cafes of **Tel Aviv**, walk up Mount Carmel in **Haifa** and sunbathe on the beaches of **Eilat**, and imagine you're on the Costa Brava. In **Jerusalem**, the highlight of any visit and the heart of the conflict, it's a bit more difficult to take such a blinkered approach, but plenty of people still manage it. However, if you don't go into either the occupied **West Bank** or the **Gaza Strip**, you will have passed on an opportunity to see an aspect of Israel that the authorities would rather you didn't. Few Israelis nowadays, apart from settlers, soldiers and those in solidarity with the *intifada*, venture into the occupied territories, but it is still relatively safe for foreign visitors do so (see West Bank and Gaza chapters). In any case, most people will want to cross the 'green line', if only to float on the salt waters of the **Dead Sea**, visit Jesus' birthplace in **Bethlehem**, set foot in **Jericho**, the lowest and oldest city on earth, or ski on the slopes of **Mount Hermon**. Others might want to go for a dose of reality, an alternative to the biblical 'Holy Land' trail.

As it is, many of the religious sites are disappointingly commercialised or steeped in controversy. In Jerusalem the rivalries between Christian denominations reduce what should be the greatest Christian shrine in the world, the **Church of the Holy Sepulchre**, at times almost to the level of farce. Here and everywhere you'll find rival churches each pushing the claims of their own sites where various biblical events are supposed to have taken place. Where rival religions are concerned, the disputes can be more serious: as at the Muslim **Dome of the Rock**, which Jews claim as the site of Solomon's Temple, and whose supporting wall is the Western or **Wailing Wall**, site of Jewish pilgrimage from all over the world. Other places – **Nazareth** for example – it is rampant commercialism which takes the gloss off the biblical associations.

Nonetheless, there are simply so many important religious sites that in the end it's impossible not to find what you're looking for somewhere. And for those interested in ancient **archaeology** there are magnificent compensations in the abundant remains of Jewish, Muslim, Crusader, Herodian, Roman and even earlier civilisations almost everywhere you go. The age of Herod, with magnificent fortresses and palaces at **Herodion**, **Masada** and **Caesarea**, is particularly well represented. But legacies of almost every conceivable age can be found somewhere, from the Bronze Age settlements of the **Negev Desert** to superb medieval cities at Acre, Safad or Jerusalem.

For **nature** lovers, there's an astounding assortment of flora and fauna, and some very beautiful and varied landscapes – underwater coral reefs and desert caves, pine forests and nature reserves, terraced mountains and planted valleys, beaches and oases, olive and orange orchards and cotton fields. Since the land lies on a major route of migration, it's also a paradise for bird-watchers.

And, of course, there's the great **climate**: at any time of year, it's possible to bask in the sun somewhere in the country. In **winter**, Eilat and Tiberias are favourite resorts, and even the Jerusalem sun can be warm during the day. But if you do go during that season, be warned that in mountainous areas it can snow, and it almost certainly will rain by the bucketful. Since neither the architecture nor the facilities are geared to the cold and wet, this can be as miserable as the worst European winter. In **summer**, the only problem is how to cool off. It's a season when you'd do best to steer clear of the more humid coastal region and head for higher and drier places inland. **Spring**, though, is definitely the best time to come, when the country is a blaze of flowers and greenery and the weather is temperate enough to make touring enjoyable just about everywhere.

CLIMATE CHART

Average Maximum Temperatures (°C)

	Jan	Feb	Mar	Apr	May	Jun	July	Aug	Sept	Oct	Nov	Dec
Jerusalem	11	14	16	21	25	27	29	30	28	26	19	14
Tel Aviv	18	19	20	22	25	28	30	30	31	29	25	19
Haifa	17	18	21	25	25	28	30	30	30	27	23	18
Tiberias	18	19	22	27	31	35	37	37	37	32	26	20
Eilat	21	23	26	31	35	37	40	40	40	33	28	23
Dead Sea	20	22	25	32	34	37	39	39	36	32	27	22

THE INTIFADA

The Palestinian **intifada** or popular uprising against the Israeli occupation of the West Bank and Gaza Strip began on December 8, 1987, sparked off by a road accident in Gaza. Eighteen months later more than 600 Palestinians had died, hundreds more had been injured, 38,000 held for up to 18 days without access to a lawyer and over 4000 held under administrative detention (without charge or trial) for up to a year. Despite Israel's attempts to suppress the uprising, however, it shows no sign of abating.

The intensity and unaninimity of the *intifada* may be new, but in historical terms it is merely the continuation of Palestinian resistance. From 1936–1939 the **Palestinian Revolt**, primarily against the British Mandate authorities, began with a six-month general strike. The **Palestine Liberation Organisation** and its military arm the **Palestine Liberation Army** were established in 1964, and following the 1967 war the Palestinian guerilla movement organised widespread insurrection against the occupation. As well as armed action, there has been continual non-violent protest. **Strikes**, **sit-ins** and **demonstrations** in the occupied territories were common in the late 1970s, and in 1982, when the Israelis tried to impose a 'civil administration', deposed lawfully elected local mayors and increased their settlement effort, Palestinian civilian protest led to a **three-month uprising**. Ever since, protests have grown steadily in scale and intensity.

Although it is predominantly the youth – the **shabiba** – that run the *intifada* (indeed 70% of the entire Palestinian population is under 30), Palestinians of every age, sex and social class are actively involved: school-children and their parents confront the Israeli army in the streets; demonstrations take place in practically all refugee camps, towns and villages, some of which have declared themselves 'liberated zones' where public para-military parades are held and which even the army does not enter. Resistance does not only involve the sort of protest that hits the headlines, though, but also the establishment of alternative Palestinian institutions, from universities to trade unions and newspapers, and the organization of **popular committees** to provide social and health care, Even the traditionally conservative merchant class has set up shopkeepers' committees to observe strikes and opening hours; doctors, lawyers and other professionals have lowered or cancelled fees and offer free advice; and agricultural committees offer technical advice, tools and seeds to the public.

The intifada has, on the whole, been remarkably disciplined, thanks perhaps to its clandestine but highly organised **United National Leadership**. Its main weapons are strikes and demonstrations, a boycott on Israeli goods, the withdrawal of labour from Israeli industry and the withholding of taxes. The effect on Israel has been marked: it has had to increase its military presence in the occupied territories from 5000 to 70,000 and has doubled the period of reserve duties. Economic losses from this, from the labour boycott and from the drop in tourism, have been considerable. The *intifada* has also caused a political move towards the right in Israel: a number of influential Israelis, including members of Knesset, now openly call for the 'transfer' – the mass deportation – of Palestinians to neighbouring Arab states.

Alongside the strengthening of the right, however, is a parallel growth of those calling for withdrawal from the occupied territories, talks with the PLO and a two-state solution. In 1988, over 150 retired Israeli army officers formed a Council for Peace and Security advocating withdrawal and even the Chief-of-Staff told a parliamentary committee that the uprising could not be crushed because it was a national struggle. In March 1989, Israeli Intelligence was advising the government that the uprising could not be ended 'without talking to the PLO'. Just as worrying to the Israeli authorities is the rise in nationalism of its Palestinian citizens, many of whom have been arrested in incidents related to the *intifada*.

The **demands** of the *intifada* are clear: the withdrawal of the Israeli army from centres of Palestinian population; the lifting of martial law; the release of prisoners and return of deportees; compensation for deaths and injuries; free local elections and permission for local members of the Palestine National

Council, the Palestinian government-in-exile, to attend its sessions abroad; the lifting of economic restrictions on Palestinian development; and an end of settlement activity. The ultimate goal is the establishment of an independent Palestinian state under the leadership of the PLO, to be arrived at through negotiations in an international peace conference at which Israel and the PLO would have equal status.

Quite how far the *intifada* will affect you, as a traveller, in **practical terms**, is hard to predict. The short answer at the moment is surprisingly little. Tourists still routinely visit all the major sites of the West Bank – though they nowadays do so mostly in day trips from Jerusalem or elsewhere – and are certainly not the target of any deliberate hostility. Tourism is important to the Palestinians too. Obviously, though, you might be affected by strikes, which hit restaurants and above all public transport in the occupied territories, and you'd be unwise to drive through any occupied area in a car with Israeli number plates, even a rented one. Basically you should treat every situation with extreme sensitivity, and always seek local advice before setting out, to avoid winding up somewhere in the middle of a demonstration, or being stranded by an extended strike.

HELP US UPDATE

We've gone to a lot of effort to ensure that this edition of the Rough Guide to Israel and the Occupied Territories is completely up-to-date and accurate. However, given the volatile politics of the region, it's impossible to tell how the situation may change, and the possibilities for travel may well differ from those we've given. Any suggestions, comments, or corrections toward the next edition – even just a post-card detailing a change in opening hours – would be much appreciated. We'll credit all contributions, and send a copy of the new book (or any other Rough Guide, if you prefer) for the best letters. Send them along to: The Rough Guides, 149 Kennington Lane, London SE11 4EZ.

PART ONE

THE

BASICS

GETTING THERE

Despite the intifada and the fact that Israel is rarely out of the news, it remains a popular tourist destination. But as tourism has dropped considerably (by 15% in 1989), it should be possible to pick up some cheap tickets, particularly in low season. Much the easiest and quickest way to get to Israel is to fly direct, but it is also possible to get there by travelling overland to Greece and then taking a ferry to the port of Haifa.

FLIGHTS

Flights to and from Israel are regular and relatively inexpensive. From London you can fly either to Tel Aviv or Eilat in around five hours, and there are also regular flights to Tel Aviv (and charters to Eilat) from regional British airports. Tel Aviv is the more popular destination, but package deals to Eilat can be very attractively priced, particularly in the winter. If you intend travelling during the main Jewish holidays (Passover or Jewish New Year) or Christian holidays (Christmas or Easter), you'll need to book well in advance.

Scheduled fares with *British Airways* (65–75 Regent Street, London W1R 7HG; ☎01-897 4000 for information) or with Israel's national airline *El Al* (185 Regent Street, London W1R 8BS; ☎01-437 9255) range from just over £250 to £300 return, according to season. These tickets are valid for a minimum stay of six days and maxi-

mum of two months. Both companies also offer a one-year open ticket, club class only, for over £900. It is not advisable to try to get into Israel with a **one-way** ticket unless you can show convincing evidence of your intention to leave again (a ticket home from Egypt, for example) or plenty of money to support yourself and buy a ticket home.

Charter fares range from around £150 to £270, dependent again on the season, but also on factors such as the operator (most common are *Dan Air* and *Sun Dor* from Gatwick, *El Al* from Heathrow) and which day of the week you fly. Most charters are for a limited period only, usually two or three weeks, and your date of return cannot be changed. Some companies, however, do offer a yearly or six-monthly open return for £200–250 (*WST Charters* are one: book through *STA Travel*, on ☎01-938-4362). If you do this, it's advisable to book your flight back from Israel as early as possible to avoid getting stuck because the planes are all full.

The best flight deals – including scheduled seats for considerably less than the official fares – can be found above all among the adverts in the weekly *Jewish Chronicle*. Also worth checking are the London **listings magazines** such as *Time Out*, *City Limits* and *LAW* or, nationally, the small ads in the *Sunday Times* and *Observer*. If you are a **student** or **under 26**, it's worth investigating special fares offered by the airlines and by the specialist operators listed below: you should save £10–20 on the regular adult fare.

Note that on top of any quoted fare you'll be expected to pay Israeli **departure tax** – currently around £7.50 – which is payable when you buy the ticket.

TRAVEL OPERATORS AND PACKAGE DEALS

Almost any High Street **travel agent** can sell you a package holiday in Israel, but there are also numerous specialists offering rather more interesting packages. **STA Travel** (86 Old Brompton Road, London SW7; ☎01-937 9921; for other addresses, see their ad at the back of this book) and **Campus Travel** (52 Grosvenor Gdns, London SW1; ☎01-730 3402/8111) are reliable student/ youth orientated agents, both of them offering a range of discount flights (not only for students) and organised tours. Travel agents specialising in charter/package deals to Israel include *Uniglobe* (3 Caxton Walk, off Charing Cross Road, London WC2 8PW; ☎01-379 5959); *Goodmos* (9/13 St. Andrew Street, Holborn Circus, London EC4 3DH; ☎01-353 8682); *Peltours* (Mappin House, 4 Winsley Street, London W1N 7AR; ☎01-580 0372); *AMG Travel* (70 Edgware Way, Edgware, Middx.; ☎01-958 5636); *Homtel* (Suite 604, Triumph House, 189 Regent Street, London W1R 7WF; ☎01-437 2892); *Speedwing Holidays*

(Westworld, Westgate, Ealing W5 1XP; ☎01-991 2999); *Ipale* (92 West End Lane, London NW6; ☎01-328 8431) and *Pullman Holidays* (31 Belgrave Road, London SW1V 1RB; ☎01-630 5119).

All these operators offer cheap all-in **package deals**, with return flight and hotel accommodation included. The cheapest of these are generally to Eilat, midweek off-season, starting from around £180 for a one-week stay. Your local **IGTO** (Israeli Government Tourist Office) also stocks a range of brochures from

AIRPORT PROCEDURE AND SECURITY

Security is an obsession in Israel, and your first experience of it will be at the airport of departure, especially if you are travelling with an Israeli airline. The standard questions before the baggage check are whether you packed your own luggage, if it was with you all the time, whether anybody gave you anything to take, whether you're carrying any weapons, for self-defence or otherwise. You may also be asked why you're going to Israel, if you've been before, whether you know anyone there, where you intend to go etc. Whilst most of the questioning can be justified on grounds of security, the aggressive tone of some of the Israeli personnel can be intimidating. Your passport may be taken away for a time, particularly if it has stamps in it from Arab countries considered hostile (Libya, Syria and Iraq for example), and you may then be faced with another set of questions from a different security officer. Young back-packers (especially, it seems, those who are not Jewish) generally get given the hardest time of all. Once you've received security clearance and are on the plane, **arriving** in the country is usually no problem.

Leaving, however, can be an even more stressful experience. As well as the same standard questions that are asked when entering, you are often required to give a detailed description of your visit, where you stayed and who you met, particularly Arabs. Again, young travellers get the heaviest treatment, which can mean up to an hour's questioning, a complete and thorough baggage check (like squeezing out toothpaste tubes), sometimes followed by a strip-search. If you're carrying any 'opposition' literature or publications, even those that are quite legal in the country, they may be confiscated, or taken away and photocopied. Occasionally people are held up so long by the security palaver that they miss their flights.

Check-in and -out

Because of the tight security checks, pre-departure formalities for those **going** to Israel take longer than for most other destinations. You must get to the airport 2½ hours before the scheduled departure time of your flight, and since the check-in closes well in advance of departure, late arrivals are simply not allowed onto the plane. At Gatwick the check-in area is in a separate section, together with the flights to Ireland.

When **leaving** Israel, be sure to confirm your flight with the airline concerned at least 72 hours in advance. This is not only to make sure you have a seat, but to check that the flight is still going when it's supposed to – airlines, particularly the cheapies, seem to change their departure times at short notice (usually to an unearthly hour of the morning). Again, you have to check in at Ben Gurion Airport a full 2½ hours in advance. If you're flying with *El Al* you can check in your luggage the evening before at their offices in Jerusalem (Shopping Centre, 49 Yirmiahu Street, corner of Jaffa Road), Tel Aviv (El Al Town Terminal, Arlozorov Street) or Haifa (80 HaAzma'ut Street) and it will be taken directly to the plane. You get your seat allocation and boarding card and need only turn up at the airport one hour before departure.

travel firms offering a variety of holidays: kibbutz accommodation, self-drive, holiday apartments, nature trips and combined itineraries including one or more of Jordan, Egypt and Turkey. Among the more interesting of these are the camping/trekking trips organised by *Explore Worldwide*, who also include Jordan and Egypt in some of their itineraries (*Explore Worldwide (RGI)*, 7 High Street, Aldershot, Hampshire; ☎0252-319448).

A quite separate range of packages is offered by companies who specialise in guided **Christian pilgrimages** to the 'Holy Land'. *Sharon Tours* Catholic Pilgrimages (c/o *ATS World Travel*, 106 Seymour Place, London W1H 5DG; ☎01-724 5533) offer nine-day trips from around £500–600; *Star Tours* (93 Church Road, Hove BN3 2BA; ☎0273-29080) include combined trips to Israel and Jordan (from £420 to £750); *Inter-Church Travel* (Freepost, PO Box 58, Folkestone, Kent CT20 1YB; ☎0800 300 444) offer pilgrimages ranging from £360 for nine days to £670 for a twelve-day Christmas tour. Others include *Holy Land Christian Tours* (Bedfordia House, Prebend Street, Bedford MK40 1QP; ☎0234-49540), *Orientours* (87 Regent Street, London W1R 8LS;

☎01-434 1551), *Jericho Tours* (Bonser Road, Twickenham, Middx.; ☎01-744 1268) and *Trust Travel* (42 Baldwin Street, Bristol BS1 1PN; ☎0272-273554) for student study tours.

OVERLAND: THE GREEK CONNECTION

Genuine overland travel to Israel may look possible on the map, but in fact is barely feasible, and calls for a major expedition. If the endless roads through Turkey weren't bad enough, you then have to pass through Syria and Lebanon – and the Syrians will not want to encourage you to go to Israel. There are no trains.

In practice, then, overland travel means getting to Greece, and continuing by ferry from there.

TRAINS

There are basically two **rail routes** from London to Athens, either of which takes around three and a half days with the minimum of stops en route. The cheaper one is London–Paris–Venice–Belgrade–Athens, but the last leg of this journey, through Yugoslavia, is interminably hot and crowded. The alternative route, down through

BEN GURION AIRPORT

All international flights – except those to Eilat – operate through **Ben Gurion International Airport**, approximately halfway between Tel Aviv and Jerusalem just outside the town of Lydda (Lod). There are regular connections from here to all the major centres.

Tel Aviv

An *El Al* airport bus leaves Ben Gurion for the terminal in **Tel Aviv** every hour 6am–10pm and at other hours according to flight arrivals. *United Tours* operates an hourly bus service (#222) between the airport, the terminal and the Palace Hotel (HaYarkon Street) 4am–midnight. *Egged* buses leave for Tel Aviv every fifteen minutes 5am–11pm. The journey takes about twenty minutes.

Returning **to the airport**, *El Al* buses leave from the terminal on Arlozorov Street half-hourly 4.30–10am and 2–4pm, hourly 10am–2pm and 4pm–10pm; departures between 10pm and 4.30am depend on flight schedules. *Egged* buses leave from the central bus station every fifteen minutes 5am–11.30pm, *United Tours* depart hourly from the Palace Hotel.

Jerusalem

Egged buses leave the airport for **Jerusalem** every twenty minutes 7.15am–6pm. *Nesher* shared taxis (*sherutim*) depart frequently, as soon as the car is full; tickets cost $10 and the journey takes about 45 minutes.

Heading back, *Egged* buses leave the central bus station every twenty minutes 6.15am–7pm. If you want to share a taxi, book in advance through *Nesher Taxis* (21 King George Street; ☎02-227227).

Haifa

Egged buses leave for **Haifa** every twenty minutes 7am–6pm. The journey takes around 1½ hours. To return to the airport *Egged* buses leave the central bus station every 45 minutes 7am–6pm, or you can get a *sherut* taxi from *Aviv* (6 Nordau Street; ☎04-666333).

France and Italy, crossing over to Greece by ferry, is well worth the small extra expense.

If you're under 26, the cheapest way is to get an **InterRail Pass** (currently £139 from *British Rail* or any travel agent), which allows a month's free rail travel on all European railways (half-price within Britain). There is also a **Senior Citizen InterRail** for anyone over 65. If you need longer than these passes allow, a **Eurotrain** ticket (again under 26 only) is valid for two months and allows as many stopovers as you choose along a pre-specified route: details from *Eurotrain*, 52 Grosvenor Gardens, London SW1 (☎01-730 8518). A single to Athens is just over £100, return just under £200. **Standard rail tickets** cost around 25% more: details from the *British Rail European Travel Centre* (Victoria Station, London SW1; ☎01-834 2345) or from any decent travel agent.

COACHES

If price is your only object, then **coaches** – from around £50 one-way, £95 return – are the cheapest way of getting to Piraeus for the connecting ferry to Israel. Be warned that the journey – around 3½ days, with twenty-minute stops every five or six hours – is at best tedious and uncomfortable, and if things start to go wrong can become a nightmare. Again you'll find details in the ads in the back of *Time Out* or *LAW*, but to avoid the worst it's worth spending a few pounds extra on a reputable company. Among these are *The Miracle Bus Company* (408 Strand, London WC2; ☎01-379 6055) and *Eurolines*, the latter operated by *National Express* and other international bus companies (details from your local *National Express* coach terminal, or any travel agent).

DRIVING OR HITCHING

Taking a car to Israel doesn't really make sense – it would almost certainly cost less to hire a car there as part of a fly-drive deal – but it can be done. There are two basic routes to Athens for the ferry, each of them around 1900 miles, or at least two days non-stop driving: one is via Yugoslavia, the other down through Italy and across on the ferry from Brindisi or Otranto to Patra. The AA can advise on the best routes, and on the legal requirements for all the countries you'll pass through.

Hitchers should allow at least a week to reach Athens: the best hope is to cross on the ferry to Ostend or the Hook of Holland, plugging directly into the major European through routes and avoiding the Channel ports and Paris, two of Europe's most notorious hitching black spots. Again the Italian route, though slower, is infinitely more pleasant: being stranded by the roadside in Yugoslavia is not a pleasant experience.

FERRIES

The chief **shipping companies** operating passenger and car ferries between Piraeus and Haifa are *Stability Line* (11 Sachtouri Street, Piraeus, ☎01-4132392; and through *J. Caspi*, 76 Derekh HaAtzma'ut, Haifa, ☎04-674449) and *Afroessa Lines* (1 Harilaou Tricoupi Street, Piraeus, ☎01-4183777; and through *Mano Passenger Lines*, 39/41 Sderot HaMeginim, Haifa, ☎04-351631). Both companies have boats sailing from Piraeus every Thursday and Monday throughout the year; one-way costs range from £43 (deck, low season) to £153 (4-berth cabin with private bath, high season), plus another £9 port taxes, exclusive of meals. Return tickets run from around £80 to £250: students or anyone under 26 get a 20% discount. The trip takes at least 48 hours, generally with stops at either Iraklion (Crete) or Rhodes, and Limmasol (Cyprus).

For further information and reservations, contact *Viamare Travel* (33 Mapesbury Road, London NW2 4HT; ☎01-452 8231), who can also book you on 3-day cruises: Limassol–Haifa–Limassol or Limassol–Port Said–Limassol, or a 4-day cruise, Limassol–Haifa–Port Said–Limassol. Other agents in Britain are *Cyprus Travel* (42 Hampstead Road, London NW1; ☎01-387 7854) and *Zenon Travel and Tours* (15 Kentish Town Road, London NW1; ☎01-485 9555). In Israel, the main agent is *Jacob Caspi* (1 Rehov Ben Yehuda, Tel Aviv, ☎03-658784; 4 Rehov Yani, Jerusalem, ☎02-247315; 76 Derekh HaAtzma'ut, Haifa, ☎04-674449).

RED TAPE AND VISAS

On arrival in Israel, you will be asked to fill in an **entry card** which you hand over with your passport. Half of it will be torn off and the rest returned to you. You must keep this returned portion safe to hand back when you leave; losing it can make the departure procedure even longer and more tiresome than it already is. If you intend to use your current passport for visiting an **Arab** country, you can ask the Israeli passport official for your visa to be stamped onto the entry card rather than in your passport (no Arab country, with the exception of Egypt, will allow you in if your passport shows that you have been to Israel). Israeli officials are prepared to do this, but make sure you say so the moment you hand over your passport, otherwise it may be too late.

Israeli **departure tax** is now included in the price of the airline ticket, which should have a stamp confirming payment; check that yours has one. There is no Israeli departure tax required at either the Rafah (Rafiah) or Taba borders into **Egypt**. Be warned that stamps from these border crossings may be taken by other Arab countries as evidence that you have been in Israel, and consequently prevent you entering: Egyptian officials will insist on stamping your passport.

A transit tax is required when crossing the **Allenby Bridge** into **Jordan**. This revenue stamp can be bought at any post office in Israel as well as at the bridge. If your trip has started in Jordan then you can cross from Jordan to Israel and back pretty much at will (because as far as the Jordanians are concerned you are not crossing an international border, but entering the occupied West Bank); if you start in Israel you can cross to Jordan but will have great difficulty trying to return to Israel (mainly because to cross back into Israel you are required to fill in a form on which you have to write your point of entry to Jordan; you cannot put Israel, you cannot put the West Bank – because it's not a separate country – and you'll have no Jordanian stamp to back up a claim that you entered anywhere else). You must have a **Jordanian visa** and a **permit** to cross the bridge: these you should obtain from a Jordanian embassy before travelling, as you cannot get them in Israel. In Britain the Jordanian Enbassy is at 6 Upper Phillimore Gardens, London W8 (☎01-937 3685).

Citizens of the UK, USA, Australia, New Zealand and most EEC countries (with the exception of Germans born before 1928) need only a valid passport for entry into Israel: a visa will be stamped into it when you enter the country. However, it must be a full passport (temporary British Visitor's Passports are not acceptable) with at least one month remaining on your date of departure from Israel. For further information, contact the Consular section of an Israeli Embassy: in Britain this is at 2 Palace Green, London W8 (☎01-937 8050).

Visitors are usually allowed to stay in the country for three months from the date of arrival. An **extension**, which generally requires your passport to be stamped (see below), can be obtained for a small fee from any district office of the Ministry of the Interior. The main offices are in Jerusalem (Generali Building, Rehov Shlomzion Hamalka; ☎02-228211), Tel Aviv (Shalom Meyer Tower, Visa Department, 9 Rehov Ahad Ha'am; ☎03-651941/657758) and Haifa (Government Building, 11 Hassan Shukri; ☎04–667781). Remember that it is illegal to **work** on a tourist visa, despite the fact that many people do and the police and immigration authorities generally turn a blind eye.

COSTS, MONEY AND BANKS

COSTS

Over the years the Israeli economy has been dogged by hyper-inflation – a massive 445% in 1984. Since 1985, when stiff measures were brought in under a comprehensive economic stabilisation programme, inflation has settled down to an annual rate of around 20 per cent. Transport and basic foodstuffs are relatively cheap, but taken as a whole there's no denying that Israel is an expensive place to live or travel. A night in a hotel can cost anything from £7 to £15 and up; a light meal between £5 and £10. You can save a great deal by buying some of your own food from the markets, or relying on the ubiquitous street stalls selling *falafel* or *hummus*, and by camping occasionally, but even so don't expect to survive on much less than £15 a day – over £20 if you expect to stay in hotels and eat in restaurants all the time.

The Israeli economy is closely linked to the US dollar – huge American loans effectively prop the whole thing up, and the States is by some way the country's biggest trade partner. At one time the Israeli government even considered abandoning the **shekel** and adopting the dollar as the country's currency. They didn't, but even so prices, particularly for more expensive goods or upmarket hotel accommodation are frequently quoted in dollars. In tourist areas, many shopkeepers will accept dollars more readily than they would shekels. For this reason, and because of the relative instability of the shekel (inflation may alter the shekel price, while the dollar value remains relatively consistent), the prices quoted in this guide are in **dollars**.

MONEY

The official Israeli currency is the **New Israeli Shekel** (NIS). Notes come in denominations of NIS5, 10, 20, 50 and 100. One *shekel* is divided into 100 *agorot* which come in 1, 5, 10, 50 and NIS1 coins. The New Israeli Shekel replaced the old shekel (IS) in 1985 (NIS1 = IS100), and before that the Lira; you may occasionally come across people who still refer to prices in the old currency. Among Palestinians on the West Bank, the **Jordanian dinar** is still widely used, and prices are sometimes referred to in this currency. There are no restrictions on the amount of **foreign currency** you take in or out of Israel, nor are you compelled to change any set amount on arrival. Since the shekel is virtually worthless outside Israel it's best not to change too much at a time – you can change shekels back into hard currency before you leave (up to a maximum of $100), but expect to lose around ten per cent in doing so. Most people will advise you to take **dollars** to Israel, and certainly they're easier to use than any other currency (see below), but pounds or any other major European currency can also be freely changed at banks and with many money changers. Current exchange rates are published daily on the penultimate page of the *Jerusalem Post*. At the time of writing the exchange rate was a little over NIS3 to £1, NIS1.8 to US$1.

The easiest and safest way to carry money is as **travellers' cheques**, widely accepted by banks, money changers and at shops and hotels in the more touristed areas. Most travellers' cheques are accepted, though to avoid any inconvenience it's best to opt for the more well-known ones such as *Thomas Cook*, *American Express* or *Barclays*. **Eurocheques** are not widely accepted, though some shops do take them. Major **credit cards** – *Visa*, *Mastercard/Access* and *American Express* – are also accepted (though rarely at the cheaper places) and are useful for extra expenses such as car hire. You can also get cash advances from banks with a credit card – and *Visa* offers cash dispenser machines if you know your *PIN* (Personal Identification Number).

BANKS (AND ALTERNATIVES)

When inflation was at its peak it made sense to bring notes into the country, so as to take advantage of the widespread – and very open – **black market**. Today, however, the exchange rate for hard currency on the black market is only marginally higher than the official bank rate. The market still exists (through money changers in East Jerusalem and on Lilienblum and Shenkin streets in Tel Aviv) but although you can haggle to try and get the rate up, it's probably more valu-

able in saving you time – a minute's wait rather than up to half an hour at a bank – than money. You'll need banknotes to take advantage of this.

On arrival, you'll find 24-hour **exchange facilities** at the airports and ports: at Ben Gurion Airport the bank is just beyond passport control and the baggage retrieval area and before you go through customs. Israeli banks have branches in all towns. **Banking hours** are: Sunday, Tuesday and Thursday from 8.30am to 12.30pm and 4 to 5.30pm; Monday and Wednesday 8.30am to 12.30pm; Friday and eve of holidays 8.30am to noon. Branches in the big hotels tend to open longer, more convenient hours.

HEALTH AND INSURANCE

MEDICAL PROBLEMS

No **vaccinations** are required to enter Israel but, particularly if you intend travelling on, it's wise to check that you're up-to-date with polio and tetanus boosters, and perhaps to have a typhoid-cholera jab. Diseases such as hepatitis are rare but not unknown: *gamma-globulin* is an effective preventative, but for the best advice contact your local doctor before leaving.

Hazards you're more likely to confront include **stomach upsets** and problems of overexposure to sun and sea. To avoid the worst varieties of the former it's advisable to wash fruit and vegetables, and to bring anti-diarrhoeal medication (like *Arret* or *Lomotil*) for when the precautions

fail. A good barrier **suntan lotion** is essential for protection against sunburn, as even a hazy Middle Eastern sun can burn fiercely. They are available in Israel, but much more expensive than at home. Drink plenty of fluids, keep up your salt intake to avoid dehydration and wear a hat against **sunstroke** – surprisingly easy to suffer while sightseeing during the summer months. **Mosquitos** can also be a problem during the summer; to avoid getting bitten, take a mosquito repellant with you – especially if you intend to camp or sleep on the beach. If you're sleeping indoors, you can buy a small anti-mosquito device to keep the pests away (see "Directory").·

Tap water is safe to drink throughout the country or you should always be able to get the locally produced mineral water. It is inadvisable to drink from streams and wells unless they're clearly supplies of drinking water.

If you do have any minor medical problems you should go to a **pharmacy** (*mirkachat* in Hebrew; *saydaliyyeh* in Arabic) where you will almost certainly find someone who speaks English. Pharmacists are well-trained and usually helpful. For more serious complaints, go to a **doctor** (they virtually all speak English). If you're taken seriously ill or are involved in an accident, dial ☎101 for an ambulance. There is some form of hospital or clinic in even the smallest of places to which you can go in an emergency, and the standard of care is generally very good, but expensive.

INSURANCE

Investing in some kind of **travel insurance**, for medical and other emergencies, is an essential precaution. Most travel agents or insurance brokers should offer adequate policies for about £25 per month, to cover not only medical expenses but also loss or theft of baggage. One of the best is an *ISIS* policy from *Endsleigh* (97 Southampton Row, London WC1; ☎01-436 4451) or *STA* (addresses under "Getting There").

To claim medical expenses on your return, you will need to keep receipts for everything spent on treatment or drugs: to claim for lost or stolen goods you'll need a letter from the local police or a copy of their report. Persuading them to write it in English can save hassle when you present your claim to the insurance company back home.

INFORMATION AND MAPS

In a country of so much political tension, where and from whom you get your information can very much determine what you get out of your trip. On the Israeli side, information for tourists is available in abundance – tourism being an important source of income, and propaganda being an important part of the battle for (Western) hearts and minds. On the Palestinian side, with few facilities and fewer funds, information is rather harder to come by.

ISRAELI TOURIST OFFICES

The **Israeli Government Tourist Office (IGTO)** produces and gives away a vast collection of pamphlets, leaflets and maps of every kind, published in English and every major European language. These include glossy pamphlets on the principal towns and resorts, lists of hotels and *kibbutzim*, guides to archaeological sites and study programmes. Since all of these are widely available in Israel, there's not much point schlepping them with you, though you might want to study some before you leave.

Within the 'green line' (and in Bethlehem on the West Bank) there are **IGTO offices** in virtually every major town (addresses are detailed in the Guide). These dispense more detailed local information as well as free Israeli listings magazines such as *Hello Israel*, *This Week in Israel* and *This Week in Jerusalem*. The IGTOs will also help recommend restaurants or accommodation and have information about free tours and events. There are IGTO offices in: Acre, Allenby Bridge, Arad, Ashqelon, Bat Yam, Beersheva, Ben Gurion Airport, Bethlehem, Eilat, Haifa, Jerusalem, Nahariyya, Nazareth, Netanya, Rafiah (Rafah), Rosh Hanikra (Ras Naqura), Safad, Tel Aviv and Tiberias.

ALTERNATIVE INFORMATION

None of the officially recognised Israeli tourist offices, in or outside the country, will exactly encourage you to visit the **occupied territories** – even journalists have been prevented from entering certain areas where the army is in force. As long as the *intifada* continues, many of the Israeli-organised tours to Palestinian sites (Jericho, Hebron, Nablus etc) are likely to be suspended. Nevertheless, you can and should go to the occupied territories to see the situation for yourself, preferably in the company of someone (Palestinian or Israeli) known and accepted by the local Palestinian community. On one level this is simply because the West Bank, in particular, has some of the most beautiful countryside and fascinating sites you'll see. On quite another plane, such a visit can be both illuminating and valua-

Israel Government Tourist Offices abroad
include:

BRITAIN 18 Great Marlborough Street, London
W1V 1AF (☎01-434 3651).

CANADA 180 Bloor St West, Toronto (☎416-
964 3784).

DENMARK Vesterbrogade 6C, København
(☎11-96-79).

EGYPT 6 Ibn al-Malik, Giza, Cairo (☎729-734).

FRANCE 14 Rue de la Paix, Paris (☎4261-0197).

GERMANY Westendstr. 4, Frankfurt (☎069-
720157).

NETHERLANDS Wijde Kapelsteeg
2, Amsterdam (☎020-249-325).

SWEDEN Sveavagen 28–30, Stockholm (☎08-
213386/7).

USA 350 Fifth Avenue, New York, NY (☎212-
560-0650).

ble: your presence a mark of solidarity which may
at least temporarily have an effect in curbing the
brutality of the Israeli military. You will also
contribute simply by acting as a witness and
reporting what you've seen when you return
home.

Since the Palestinians do not, as yet, have
their own Ministry of Tourism, sources of **information from a Palestinian point of view** are
limited. However, the Palestine Liberation
Organisation (PLO) is now recognised by more
countries than recognise Israel, and has accred-
ited embassies, delegations or offices in all major
European, American, African and Asian capitals.
For information on visiting specifically Palestinian
institutions and places of interest, or on working
in Palestinian refugee camps, villages and towns
(see also section on work), a good first step is to
write to your local PLO office or phone to make
an appointment.

There are also numerous Palestine **solidarity
and support groups** whose members are knowl-
edgeable and often have first-hand experience to
share with prospective visitors. Most will be
happy to offer advice, provide or suggest background reading material and recommend people
and places to visit in line with your particular
interest.

Within Israel and the occupied territories,
various Palestinian (and some Israeli) institutions
will be able to offer advice on the advisability or
otherwise of visiting certain areas. It's best to
phone before going along to see them, since they
are primarily concerned with issues more pressing
than those of tourism; but genuine enquiries are
always welcome and the usually hard-pressed
staff will often prove extremely helpful and
welcoming. Many of these organisations are
listed in the relevant chapters, above all in
Jerusalem where most are concentrated, but the
main ones are listed below. East Jerusalem travel
agents, too numerous to list, will also be knowl-
edgeable about travel to the occupied territories.

MAPS

If information is controversial in Israel, **maps** are
even more so. According to Israeli law, it is forbidden to print maps that show the borders that
divided Israel from the West Bank (the 'green
line'), Gaza Strip and Golan Heights until 1967. So
if you're using a map supplied by the IGTO or
bought from an Israeli bookstore, you literally
won't know where you are. According to these,
the West Bank is now Judaea and Samaria and an
integral part of Israel. But even if the actual

Palestine solidarity groups in the UK
include:

PLO, 4 Clareville Grove, London SW7 5AR
(☎01-370 3244).

*The Centre for the Advancement of Arab-British
Understanding (CAABU)*, 21 Collingham Road,
London SW5 0NU (☎01-373 8414).

Friends of Bir Zeit University (FOBZU), 21
Collingham Road, London SW5 0NU (☎01-373
8414).

London Friends of Palestine, 21 Collingham
Road, London SW5 0NU (☎01-373 8414).

Palestine Solidarity Campaign (PSC), BM PSA,
WC1N 3XX.

Palestine Trade Union Federation, PO Box 196,
WC1X 0AT (☎01-724 2358).

Jerusalem and Peace Service, 1A Highbury
Grove Court, Highbury Grove, London N5 (☎01-
226 7050).

Alternative sources of information in Israel and the occupied territories include:

Al-Fajr, 2 Hatem al-Ta'ie Street, East Jerusalem (☎02-281035).

Palestine Press Service, 10 Salah al-Din Street, East Jerusalem (☎02-280147; closed since the *intifada*).

Arab Tour Guides Union, PO Box 19413, East Jerusalem (☎02-281941).

Arab Studies Society, PO Box 20479, East Jerusalem (☎02-281012/273330/273341; closed since the *intifada*).

Mennonite Central Committee, 79 Nablus Road, East Jerusalem (☎02-282834).

Alternative Information Centre, 14 Koresh Street, Jerusalem (☎02-241159).

Hanitotz/Shirara Collective, 14 Koresh Street, Jerusalem (☎02-221614).

---

border-posts are no longer there, the boundaries are still very much in existence – and reinforced by the *intifada*. It is essential to have a map that shows the border, as much for your own safety as anything else. One of the best road maps is that produced by *Hallwag*, sold at many bookshops or from *Stanfords* (12–14 Long Acre, London WC2E 9LP; ☎01-836 1321) or *McCarta* (122 Kings Cross Road, London WC1; ☎01-278 8278).

Maps of **Jerusalem** showing the 'old' border are particularly hard to find, although some bookstores in East Jerusalem still have a stock of old and rather picturesque Jordanian tourist maps of the city dating from pre-1967. The *Hallwag* map

(above) also has a map of Jerusalem showing the borderline. *Carta's Historical Atlas of Jerusalem* also includes a map of Jerusalem between 1948 and 1967.

Another excellent map, though more of historical than practical interest, is published by the *Arab Studies Society* (see address above). It shows the present international borders, the armistice lines, the borders according to the 1947 Partition Plan, the distribution of Palestinian towns and villages in 1945, and the Jewish settlements that have since been established. In London, you can buy a copy from *Jerusalem and Peace Service* (also above) for £5.

GETTING AROUND

Much the most common means of transport within Israel is the bus. Almost the entire country is well covered by an extensive bus network: distances are short and fares still relatively cheap. Most intercity buses are air-conditioned. Second most popular and convenient way of getting around is the *sherut* or *service* taxi, slightly more expensive than buses but faster. These shared

taxis connect all the major towns frequently, generally setting out as soon as a car-load of people has gathered. A railway runs along the coast from Nahariyya and Haifa in the north to Tel Aviv, and inland from Tel Aviv to Jerusalem – but it's really worth taking only as a curiosity. Driving yourself in a hire-car may be worthwhile in the remoter parts, hitching can be slow and tedious. As for internal flights, while they do connect all the major centres, distances are so short that they're rarely worth it.

BUSES

The **bus system** in Israel is well developed, efficient and frequent. Most services start around 5am and run until 11.30pm. On Friday and the eve of holidays, services end about one hour before the start of the sabbath or the holiday. In Haifa and Nazareth, there is a partial bus service on the sabbath and holidays. Arab buses in East

Jerusalem, the West Bank and Gaza Strip run every day.

The main Israeli bus company, **Egged**, operates throughout the country. It is advisable to buy your ticket in advance from the ticket kiosks in the bus stations, especially on less frequent bus routes (eg Eilat to Jerusalem). Prices, subsidised by the Israeli government, are very low – you can expect to pay no more than $5 on intercity journeys lasting 2–3 hours; Jerusalem to Tel Aviv, a journey of one hour, costs around $3. On presentation of a valid **International Student Identity Card (ISIC)** students can obtain a 10% discount on all intercity routes.

You can also buy *Round-About* **bus passes** that allow unlimited travel anywhere in Israel. A 7-day ticket costs $44, 14 days $69, 21 days $89 and 30 days $99. These are available from all main *Egged* offices, but you'd have to be travelling more or less permanently to make the saving worthwhile.

Bus tours are another way of getting around. Organised tours range from visits to archaeological and biblical sites, to desert tours and scenic trips. The main companies running sightseeing tours are *Egged* (head office: 15 Rehov Frishman, Tel Aviv; ☎03-242271-6), *Galilee Tours* (42 Ben Yehuda, Tel Aviv; ☎03-5466343) and *United Tours* (113 Rehov HaYarkon, Tel Aviv; ☎03-298181). Their itineraries are advertised in the free listings magazines such as *Hello Israel, This Week in Israel* and in the weekend edition of the *Jerusalem Post.* You can also pick up the companies' brochures at IGTOs.

ARAB BUSES

The West Bank and Gaza Strip are served by an extensive network of Arab buses, most of which are based at the Damascus Gate Bus Station in East Jerusalem. Although the buses themselves tend to look somewhat run down, their services are regular, efficient and cheaper than *Egged* where both run the same route. Other advantages are that they reach parts that the other buses don't; they run every day of the week; they won't be the target of stones (unless thrown by settlers); you won't have to share your seat with an Uzi machine gun; and chances are you can get into a conversation with Palestinian passengers. The disadvantage is that they get held up at army roadblocks and, because of curfews and other restrictions imposed by the military, their services generally stop before sunset.

TAXIS

The main rival to the buses are **sherut** (Israeli) or **service** (Palestinian) **taxis** – generally sevenseater Mercedes which operate along set interurban routes. Individual fares are about 10% more expensive than the price of the bus but the taxis are faster, more comfortable and more convenient in that the driver will drop you off where you want along the route and may agree to take you on to your particular destination in town for an extra charge. They also run on the sabbath and holidays when there are no intercity buses. However, the driver will not set off until the car is full and on some routes (and on the sabbath and holidays), this can mean a tedious wait. On the main intercity routes, like Jerusalem–Tel Aviv, you rarely have to wait more than a few minutes. You can also hail a *sherut* or *service* on the road, particularly in remoter areas. If there is room, the driver will stop to pick you up and will charge you a fare according to the distance.

Taxi stands in town are usually located near the central bus station (but see the "Travel Details" at the end of each chapter). Some towns also have internal *sherut* taxi services; in Tel Aviv, for example, there are mini-buses along main streets which charge a set fare and drop you off where you want. This system also operates in the Gaza Strip where four-seater Peugeots provide the transport.

Regular **private taxis** are not cheap; drivers must by law operate the taxi meters, but many object to doing do and will try to get you to accept a set fare – invariably higher than what it would be on the meter. Particularly at peak times, they will often simply drive off it you don't accept their price. Always try to establish the fare before you get in the cab to avoid unpleasantness at the end. You can threaten to report them (to the IGTO or the police), as what they are doing is illegal, but this often only makes them more aggressive. They must in any case give you a receipt if you ask and this will have their number on it. Israeli taxi drivers in general have a reputation for neanderthal chauvinism: **women** passengers in particular risk being hassled or propositioned. If you're travelling alone, sitting in the back rather than beside the driver can keep the conversation to a minimum – friendly chat may be interpreted as an invitation. In Jerusalem, Israeli taxi drivers will often refuse outright to take you to the east side, or will agree to drive you there and then come on heavy, particularly about the fare even if it's been agreed beforehand.

TRAINS

The **railway network**, such as it is, runs along the coast from Nahariyya through Acre and Haifa to Tel Aviv and from Tel Aviv to Jerusalem. The trains are slow, antiquated and few and far between, but it can be a pleasantly relaxing way to travel. The journey from Tel Aviv to Jerusalem is particularly picturesque. Another incentive is that tickets are cheap, and students get a 25% discount on production of a valid ISIC card. Seats can be booked in advance; all trains have a buffet car; there is no service on the sabbath or on Jewish holidays.

The main railway stations are located at: Jerusalem, Kikar Remez (☎02-717764); Tel Aviv, Rehov Arlosorov (☎03-254271); Haifa, Bet Galim (☎04-531211). A full railway timetable is available from all these stations.

DRIVING AND CAR HIRE

In general Israeli roads are good, and **driving** can give a great deal of extra flexibility to what you can do, especially in remoter areas like the Negev. But **hiring a car** isn't cheap. To do so you need a valid international driving licence or the national driving licence of a country acceptable in Israel (UK included), written in English or French.

Local **car rental companies** are generally better value than the big ones: *Eldan Car Hire* is widespread in Israel, with prices starting from around £85 to £120 a week, depending on the season. This is generally 20–25% cheaper than the likes of *Avis, Hertz, Europcar* or *National*, but it's always worth looking around to see what special discounts are on offer. Car rental in Eilat, a duty-free zone, is about 10% cheaper than anywhere else in the country, the only drawback being that you usually have to return the car to Eilat. You can rent **motorbikes** from two firms:

Distance Between Major Towns And Cities (in kilometres)

	Beersheva	Eilat	Haifa	Jerusalem	Tel Aviv	Tiberias
Acre	227	474	23	177	118	56
Ashdod	90	333	136	72	41	176
Ashqelon	63	306	151	75	56	191
Beersheva	–	243	208	83	113	248
Bethlehem	76	319	168	10	73	169
Eilat	243	–	451	326	356	432
Ein Gedi	106	232	210	78	153	179
Gaza	44	288	172	128	77	212
Haifa	208	451	–	158	95	70
Hebron	48	291	195	37	100	190
Herzilya	125	368	83	75	12	123
Jericho	161	287	155	35	98	124
Jerusalem	83	326	158	–	63	159
Lod	98	341	112	50	18	152
Masada	90	216	226	94	169	195
Netanya	145	388	63	95	32	103
Ramallah	98	341	140	15	75	150
Tel Aviv	113	356	95	63	–	135
Tiberias	248	432	70	159	135	–

Otzma B'tnua Mehira (46 Rehov HaAliya, Tel Aviv; ☎03-834105) and *Bikerent* (New Tourist Centre, Eilat; ☎059-76663).

If you're taking **your own car**, you must have valid international insurance (Green Card from your insurance company) and driving licence. You can keep your car in the country for a period of one year only

THE RULES OF THE ROAD

In Israel you drive on the right-hand side of the road: the country has one of the highest road accident rates in the world, and drivers are very aggressive, so be careful until you get used to it. By law, seatbelts must be worn outside city limits but are not required inside. The speed limit in built-up areas is 50kph (31mph) and 80kph (50mph) on open roads unless otherwise stated. These and other regulations tend to be poorly signed (except on the main roads) and ignored in any case by most Israelis: at unmarked junctions, priority is to the right.

HITCHING

Hitchhiking is not as common a practice as it once was in Israel, and is increasingly dangerous. There have been several cases of hitchhikers being attacked, robbed and worse. Priority is generally given to soldiers, although many drivers will also stop for tourists. To get a lift, hold out your arm with your forefinger pointing down to the ground – thumbs up is a rude sign. **Women** should definitely not hitch alone; two together

might be okay, but be sure to ask the driver where he is going before you reveal your destination. Apart from ensuring that he's actually going somewhere and is not just 'on the make', the procedure also gives you a brief time to get an impression of the driver. Don't hitchhike at night and try not to get dropped in the middle of nowhere.

The same general guidelines apply to hitching in the West Bank and Gaza Strip though the hazards, especially since the *intifada*, are if anything even greater. Palestinians will stop for you as long as they don't think you're an Israeli, and won't be very impressed if you ask to be dropped off at a Jewish settlement. Jewish settlers will stop as long as they don't think you're a Palestinian, and won't be impressed if you want to go to a Palestinian refugee camp or village. Whenever possible, you're better off getting a bus.

FLIGHTS

The Israeli airline *Arkia* operates a number of **internal flights** between Eilat, Jerusalem, Tel Aviv and Rosh Pinna. Tickets start at about $30 single, although the country's so small that they're only worth the expense if you're exceptionally pressed for time. For further information, contact *Arkia Israeli Airlines*, Sde Dov Airport, Tel Aviv (☎03-424266). A number of other companies operate **charter flights** for three to ten passengers to various parts of the country. Ask at travel agents or the IGTO.

SLEEPING

Accommodation in Israel is overpriced in comparison to most of its Mediterranean neighbours. While most of the large cities

do have some cheaper alternatives, hotels and hostels in more out-of-the-way places tend to charge a small fortune for a bed. During the main Jewish holidays (Passover and New Year), accommodation is scarce in coastal resorts such as Tel Aviv, Tiberias and Eilat; Jerusalem and Bethlehem are booked out at Christmas and Easter. At these times it's advisable to book well in advance, although you can usually find a bed somewhere less popular.

The availability of accommodation is not only directly linked to religious holidays but to political events in the country. The *intifada* has hit Israeli tourism hard, particularly in the US market. But there are still plenty of visitors at the larger hotels in the coastal resorts, as well as those wanting to work on *kibbutzim*.

HOTELS

Israeli **hotels** follow the usual system of star ratings: at the bottom end of the range, you can expect to pay £6–15 for a single room in a one- or two-star hotel, £12–25 for a double. Check whether the price includes **breakfast** – this is often a buffet including salads, eggs, milk products (yoghurt, cheese etc), olives and bread, as well as fruit juices and tea or coffee. A good breakfast, even if the hotel is a little more expensive, can be a money-saver as you can tank up for the rest of the day.

You should also check the availability of **hot water** – many hotels run their hot water systems from solar heaters which provide masses of hot water in the summer, but less in the winter. The hot water supply should then be boosted by electricity, but many hoteliers are reluctant to spend the money. The staff are unlikely to tell you that there isn't any so it's a good idea to ask to see the room before you agree to check in – and to test the water at the same time.

Students may well be entitled to a **discount**, which again is always worth asking about. At slack times a little bargaining over the price rarely goes amiss – low season (October–May, excluding the main Christian and Jewish holidays) is when you can get the best discounts. Locations of the cheaper hotels are detailed in the Guide: in general terms the area around a bus station is always a good bet, though it may also be the local 'red-light' district.

HOSTELS AND OTHER ALTERNATIVES

Private hostels, found primarily in the main tourist destinations, fall somewhere between official youth hostels (see below) and cheaper hotels. They can vary wildly in terms of facilities and atmosphere – the best are considerably better than cheap hotels, the worst can be awful – but they're almost always the cheapest of all places to stay.

Prices vary according to location, time of year and demand, but in general allow £3–5 for a bed in dormitory accommodation, £4–10 for a private room. Some hostels offer mattresses 'under the stars', usually on the roof, from about £1.50. If it's hot, mosquitos and early dawns

apart, this alternative can make for a better night's sleep than a stuffy room indoors. Most hostels are informal places, usually offering some sort of communal cooking and eating facilities. One or two are notorious for thefts and harassment of women, so it's a good idea to take a walk around and suss out the atmosphere before you book in. Places that offer a safe for you to leave your cash and passport, and those that have night curfews, are probably more secure than those that don't. Many also have segregated accommodation, which offers greater security to women on their own.

Official **youth hostels** tend to be more regimented: there are 31 throughout the country belonging to the *Israel Youth Hostel Association* (IYHA). These are usually well-run, clean and cheap – expect to pay around £4–7 a night, with a saving of £1 or so if you are a member of the *International Youth Hostel Federation*. A list of hostels can be obtained from the *IYHA* (3 Dorot Rishonim, Jerusalem; ☎02-222706/227439/ 221648) or from IGTO offices. Both private and official hostels make good places to meet up with fellow travellers, and many will have noticeboards offering ride-shares, work and items for sale.

The IYHA also run tours called '*Israel on the Youth Hostel Trail*'. These 7-, 14-, 21- or 28-day tour packages include accommodation, breakfast and dinner, unlimited bus travel, entrance to 31 national parks, free membership card to 24 museums and an information pack.

HOSPICES

Christian hospices generally offer facilities much like those of the better hostels for similar prices, but they're geared primarily to Christian pilgrims and usually located in areas of interest to such visitors – Jerusalem, Bethlehem, Nazareth, Tiberias and Haifa. Many have pretty austere regimes – very early curfews, for example – but they can also be wonderfully peaceful and relaxing. Among the best are the *Church of Scotland Hospice* in Tiberias and *St. George's Hostel* in Jerusalem, both in beautiful old buildings with a relatively informal atmosphere.

Hospices cater mainly for pilgrim groups and are therefore heavily booked at Christmas and Easter. Individual travellers are unlikely to get a room without a reservation at these times, and some will not accept lone visitors whatever the time of year. Accommodation is in single, double, three-, four-, or six-bed rooms, offering breakfast, half-board or full-board. A list of hospices can be obtained from the *Christian Information Centre* (Omar Ibn al-Khattab Square, Jaffa Gate, Jerusalem; ☎02-287647), and from the *Israel Tourist Administration, Pilgrimage Youth and Student Dvision* (24 King George St, Jerusalem; ☎02-240141).

KIBBUTZ INNS

Kibbutz inns have mushroomed in recent years as *kibbutzim* look for alternative ways of bringing in income. A few still offer very basic, hostel-style accommodation, but the majority are now much more upmarket, luring visitors with a range of attractions from mountain climbing, water sports and horse-back riding to hot springs for health cures and accommodation for the (Jewish) observant.

The kibbutz inns have their own rating system similar to that employed by the hotels: a few get no stars at all, the majority are three- and four-star. Details of the kibbutz inns (there are 28 around the country) are given in the relevant sections of the Guide, but for a complete list, or to make reservations, contact the *Kibbutz Hotel Association* (90 Ben Yehuda St, Tel Aviv, ☎03-246161).

APARTMENTS AND FAMILY LIFE

If you're planning a longer stay, and especially if you can find people to share with, **renting an apartment** can be an economical option. Purpose-built holiday and time-share apartments, ranging from modest to luxurious, are available in all the touristy areas and can be booked in advance through companies such as *Homtel* (189 Regent Street, London W1R 7WF, ☎01-437 2892; 333 Dizengoff Street, Tel Aviv, ☎03-289503; 3 Ben Sira Street, Jerusalem, ☎02-244539). In Israel you could also try looking through the ads in the weekend edition of the *Jerusalem Post* – though these are likely to want you to stay for a month at least.

Shorter term – one night at a time if you want – many local IGTO offices also run an accommo-dation service which allows you to **stay in an Israeli home**. The idea is to give travellers the chance to meet 'average' Israelis, but of course it's pot luck who you'll end up with. The price of this type of accommodation starts at around £7 a night.

CAMPING

There are **campgrounds** spread throughout the country, and in the summer months camping can be a really tempting alternative. It also allows you to stay in remoter places where there are no hostels or hotels, although most campsites are accessible by bus. Many sites offer tents for hire, or cabin or caravan accommodation if you don't have your own tent, though inevitably this is more expensive. Basic prices range from £1–3 depending on the facilities offered: washing, electricity, restaurant and stores, telephone, picnic and campfire areas, swimming pool (on site or close by) and 24-hour guards. Some of the better sites have a safe in which you can keep your valuables. A 7-, 14-, 21- or 28-day voucher entitles you to stay overnight at 16 sites, includ-ing breakfast and unlimited bus travel. This is available from the *Israel Camping Union* (PO Box 53, Nahariyya; ☎04-923366/925392) along with general information and a list of recognised sites; a camping leaflet is available from any IGTO.

Camping outside the official sites is a cheap alternative which is fairly widely done, though you need to exercise caution. There are often small communities of freelance campers sleeping on the more isolated beaches in summer – during the winter it's a different story. The authorities will usually turn a blind eye to it as long as tents are not in full view of paying hotel guests and campers don't cause too much trouble by being noisy, untidy, stoned, drunk . . . How-ever, you need to be vigilant with your valuables and careful of your own safety – don't camp alone or miles away from civilisation (or in the occupied territories). Mosquitos and other assorted nippers can be a pest, but the human (male) species are often even more bothersome.

EATING AND DRINKING

In a country of two often warring peoples, food is one area where the cultures have markedly converged. Much of the food considered typically Israeli, such as the 'national dish' – falafel – is actually Arab in origin. Likewise, humus, tahina, shishlik, kebab, and many of the other foods you'll come across on your travels, are eaten throughout the Middle East.

Which is not to say that food is free from contention: an important part of the *intifada* is the Palestinian boycott of Israeli products, which began with cigarettes but has now been extended to include food and other products. Palestinians now only buy Israeli goods which are essential and not otherwise produced by the Palestinian sector, choosing, for example, fruits from Jericho and Gaza rather than from *kibbutzim*, milk and milk products such as *labaneh* and yoghurt made in Palestinian dairies rather than from *Tnuva*, and soft drinks made on the West Bank.

RESTAURANTS

For such a small country, an amazing number of **restaurants** offer an extraordinary variety of different types of food: from traditional Palestinian/Arab or traditional Jewish European to North and South American, Ethiopian, North African or Yemeni. But of course, the more unusual and 'exotic' the restaurant, the more you're likely to have to pay. The price of a meal

might range from £5 in the cheapest places, to a full £25 a head in a fancy 'international' restaurant.

The smaller **Palestinian** restaurants frequented by local people are invariably the cheapest option. These restaurants often specialise in one dish, or type of dish only. You'll find places that have little else other than *humus* or grilled chicken, for example, served with side-salads and *pitta* bread. Other establishments will only serve sweets – *kanafeh, baklawa* etc – while coffee houses do not usually have any food at all. To get a full meal this way, there's nothing more enjoyable than going on a 'food crawl' round several of them – also an excellent way of getting to know an area, taking breathers between sites. For a hearty and rather more restful meal, larger Palestinian restaurants serve the sort of cooked food traditionally eaten at home: this usually consists of a selection of starters or *meze*, a main (generally meat) dish, dessert of 'oriental' sweets or fruit, followed by tea or coffee.

Israeli restaurants at the cheaper end of the range will serve the same basics as Palestinian restaurants – *humus, falafel, tahina* and aubergine dishes, along with basic meat and vegetable meals. The fare at other restaurants varies with their ethnic basis: **Hungarian** locales will serve such traditional dishes as goulash or blintzes; at **Eastern European** restaurants, you can get gefilte fish, borscht or chicken soup with knaidels (dumplings) and other specialities thought of as traditionally Jewish in London or New York. If you fancy something a bit different and altogether spicier, **Yemeni** and **North African** restaurants are the places to try.

Most, but not all, Israeli restaurants serve **kosher** food, supervised by the religious authority or *Beth Din*. Those that are kosher will have a sign to that effect in the window or on the menu. This means, amongst other things, that meat and dairy dishes are kept separate. Remember that **pork** is prohibited according to both Jewish and Muslim dietary law, although it is available in some non-kosher Israeli restaurants and Palestinian ones owned by Christian Arabs.

Vegetarians can eat well in Israel. The staples of the local diet – *humus, falafel* and so on – are based on beans and pulses, and salads,

COMMON FOODS AND RESTAURANT TERMS

BASICS

English	Arabic	Hebrew		English	Arabic	Hebrew
Bread	khubez	lekhem		Honey	'asal	dvash
Butter	zibda	khem'a		Meat	lahmeh	basaar
Eggs	beid	beitzim		Fish	samak	dag
Cheese	jibneh	gvina		Fruit	fawakeh	peirot
Oil	zeit	shemen		Vegetables	khudaar	yerakot
Pepper	filfil	filfil		Bottle	anineh	bakbuk
Salt	meleh	melach		Glass/cup	kas	kos
Sugar	sukar	sukar		Fork	shawkeh	mazleg
Tea	shai	tay		Knife	sikineh	sakeen
Coffee	ahwa	cafay		Spoon	mala'a	capeet
Water	mai	mayim		Table	tawla	shulkhan
Milk	haleeb	khalav		The bill	al-Hissab	HaKheshbon

SNACKS

Boureka Puff pastry pie covered with sesame seeds and stuffed with cheese, spinach or potatoes.

Falafel Spicy deep-fried balls of ground chickpeas, usually served in pitta bread with salad.

Ful Cooked Egyptian brown beans served with spices and olive oil, or with *humus*.

Humus Chickpeas ground to a smooth paste, mixed with tahina, spices and garlic and served with olive oil, or with *snobar* (pine kernels), or with minced meat.

Msabaha Whole cooked chickpeas covered with tahina paste.

Tahina Smooth sesame seed paste, mixed with spices and garlic.

SALADS

Ba'adunis Tahina mixed with fresh coriander.

Labaneh Sour white cream cheese served with green olive oil.

Muttabal Baked aubergines mashed with tahina.

Tabbouleh Burghul (cracked wheat) mixed with finely chopped onions, mint, lemon and garlic.

BREAD

Pitta Round, flat, hollow bread, either for dipping or for stuffing with salads, *falafel* etc.

Ka'ak Ring of bread covered with sesame seeds, eaten with *za'atar* (ground thyme), hard boiled eggs, cheese or *falafel* stuffed with onions.

Mana'ish Flat bread baked with *za'atar*.

Bagels Hard and shiny rolls, eaten alone or as a sandwich.

Chala Traditional plaited loaf eaten on *shabbat*, made with eggs.

Matza Unleavened bread, eaten during the week of Passover.

DRINKS

'Asir loz Almond juice.

Tamar hindi Sweet, heavy tamarind juice.

'Asir tamar Date juice.

'Asir bortu'an Orange juice.

'Asir tuffah Apple juice.

Shai bi-na'ana Tea with mint.

Shai bi-maramiya Tea with sage.

Ahwa bi-hel Arab coffee with cardamom.

Sahlab Sweet hot milk, served with coconut and raisins.

olives, dairy produce and eggs are served in abundance. For self-caterers, the markets are packed with superb fresh fruits and vegetables, and a variety of breads, Jewish and Arab – *pitta*, *ka'ak* and *bagels*, for example. And although there are few specifically vegetarian restaurants outside the largest cities, kosher **dairy restaurants** always have a wide variety of meat-free dishes.

Typical **breakfasts**, as provided in most hotels and *kibbutzim*, are hearty affairs which may take a bit of getting used to: they are usually **buffets** serving an almost infinite variety of fare, such as salads of chopped tomatoes, cucumbers, green peppers and onions, accompanied by eggs, cheese, yoghurts, olives and pickles, fresh bread and fruit juices, tea and coffee. Working people will often breakfast on a bowl of *humus* on their way to work. **Lunch** is traditionally the main meal of the day, while **supper** is a light affair. For fresh fish, the best places are by the sea: Tiberias, Eilat, Gaza and Jaffa.

SNACKS AND TAKEAWAYS

You'll save a great deal of money, and also come across some of the more interesting tastes, if you eat **street food** at least some of the time. There are stalls and markets everywhere, dishing out a wide variety of delicious snacks. Most common, and arguably best, is the staple **falafel**, spicy balls of ground chickpeas usually served in a sandwich of flat round pitta bread. *Falafel* is available on practically every street corner and in every bus station. At most stalls or kiosks, you can help yourself to a variety of salads and dressings of *tahina* (sesame paste) or chilli sauce. One whole pitta with 6–8 balls costs around £1 and you can keep refilling your bread with salad until you're full. Some places offer half portions too, though this seems increasingly rare.

Another tasty and filling snack to munch on the move is **ka'ak**, a delicious freshly-baked ring of hot sesame bread, traditionally eaten with *za'atar* (crushed thyme) and olive oil, or with a large onion-stuffed *falafel* ball or a hard-boiled egg. And of course there are **bagels**, shiny and hard with an almost infinite variety of fillings.

Shawarma – slices of pressed, skewered lamb stuffed into pitta with salad and optional chilli sauce – also makes a convenient meal, as can a sandwich of **humus** and salad in *pitta*

bread. In restaurants, a bowl of *humus* is dressed with fresh green olive oil and served with a helping of brown *ful* beans, chickpeas or *snobar* (roasted pine kernels). It should be accompanied by a side plate of pickles, onion and fresh green peppers, which look innocent enough but can be lethally hot. If you're charged extra for this or the pitta bread, change to another location next time.

Other foods available on the street include **bourekas** – pies of flaky pastry stuffed with cheese, spinach or potatoes – **hamburgers** (the Israeli chain is called *McDavid's*), **hot dogs** and slices of **pizza**. In season, charcoal-grilled or boiled **corn on the cob** (*doura* in Arabic, *tiras* in Hebrew), sold out of huge vats in the streets, bears no comparison to the anaemic stuff we get in Europe.

For nibblers, there is a wonderful variety of nuts, seeds and pulses – peanuts, pistachios, almonds, sunflower and melon seeds, chickpeas, broad beans etc – which you can buy from stalls and shops in 100-gramme bags and which also serve to replace the valuable salt lost in the summer heat. All of these are collectively known (in Arabic) as **bizr**.

In the outdoor **markets**, you'll find a huge range of fresh produce. **Fruit** is especially good and ranges, depending on the season, from the common orange and other citrus fruits to honey- and watermelons, and to the more exotic like fresh figs and dates, parsimon (*afarsimon*), pomegranates (*rimonim*) and cactus fruit (*sabra*) – these should only be handled after the thorns have been removed, but to save the bother, buy them already peeled from a street vendor. At all costs, resist the temptation to pick one yourself off a nearby bush unless you want to spend the next week picking the thorns out of your hand.

Fresh **vegetables**, for salads and cooking, are also plentiful in season and, like fruit, are cheapest and freshest from the open-air markets. From **supermarkets** or local grocery stores, you can buy a variety of delicious milk products, such as yoghurt, *eshel*, *shamenet* or *leben* – yoghurt and cream derivatives. Palestinian *labaneh* is a delicious, salty, sourish cream cheese that, eaten with olive oil and a side dish of pickles, lemon, garlic, olives, chilli peppers and onions (or some of these), can be a meal in itself.

For those unconcerned about carrying a few extra kilos back home – around their waists – *halva*, a mouthwatering sweet basically made of

Common Foods And Restaurant Terms
(continued)

PALESTINIAN SPECIALITIES

Shawarma Slivers of pressed, skwered lamb usually served in pitta.

Shishlik Pieces of lamb grilled on a spit over charcoal.

Kebab Meat minced with coriander and spices, grilled over charcoal.

Kubbeh Minced meat enclosed in a case of *burghul* (cracked wheat) and deep fried.

Kibdet djaj Chicken liver fried or cooked on charcoal.

Djaj meshwi Grilled chicken.

Musakhan Chicken soaked in olive oil, baked with onions and a lemony, red-coloured spice (*sumak*) on a bed of pitta.

Djaj mahshi Chicken roasted with a stuffing of rice and *snobar* (pine kernels), almonds or meat.

Cusa mahshi Courgettes stuffed with above stuffing.

Beitinjan mahshi Stuffed aubergines.

Waraq dawali Stuffed vine leaves.

Ma'lubeh Layers of meat or chicken, vegetables and rice, served 'upside down'.

Fasulia Haricot beans and minced meat cooked in tomato sauce.

Bamia Okra and minced meat cooked in tomato sauce.

Ruz Falastini Rice cooked with fine pasta, fried *snobar* and saffron.

Mujadara Rice cooked with lentils, pasta, cumin and pepper, served with fried onions, yoghurt and salad.

Sfiha 'Pizza', usually Armenian, baked with minced meat, tomatoes and onions.

Ftireh Three-cornered pie stuffed with meat or spinach.

JEWISH SPECIALITIES

Gefilte fish Sweet and sour minced fish balls.

Borscht Beetroot soup eaten hot or cold, sometimes with potatoes.

Knaidels Matza dumplings, maybe stuffed, usually eaten in chicken soup.

Kreplach Ravioli type envelopes of pasta, stuffed with minced meat and eaten in (chicken) soup.

Cholent Stew of lamb and/or chicken, beans, barley, potatoes and vegetables cooked slowly overnight.

Blintzes Pancakes, usually stuffed with sweet cheese.

Latkes Grated potato mixed into pancakes with egg and flour and deep fried.

Schnitzel Lamb, veal, chicken or turkey steaks dipped in batter and fried.

Goulash Meat, usually beef, stew cooked with sweet paprika and pepper.

Kugel Savoury potato and onion mix, or sweet noodles and raisins, baked in the oven.

Kasha Cracked buckwheat usually served to accompany meat instead of rice or potatoes.

Farfel Short cut macaroni, cooked with onion and meat stock.

SWEETS (Palestinian)

Atayef Pancakes stuffed with walnuts, pistachio nuts, raisins or cheese, eaten in the evenings during Ramadan.

Kanafeh Soft cheese cooked on layer of orange coloured shredded or crumbled pastry, served hot with very sweet syrup.

Baklawa Layers of pastry stuffed with nuts, covered in syrup.

Burma Sweet shredded pastry stuffed with pistachios.

SWEETS (Israeli)

Sofganiot Doughnuts eaten especially around Channuka.

Hamentashen Three-cornered pastries stuffed with poppy-seeds, eaten on Purim.

crushed sesame (and sometimes with chocolate and/or pistachios), can be great eaten as a sandwich in *pitta* bread but is positively an experience on a chunk of *chala* – yeast-and-egg bread traditionally eaten on *Shabbat* in Jewish households. Not to be missed either are the wonderful range of East European-type **cakes** (cheese, poppyseed, apple *strudel*) and Palestinian **sweets**, particularly *kanafeh* – sweet cheese on a layer of crumbly pastry and drenched in syrup – and the other irresistible goodies such as *burma* (made with pistachios) or *baklawa*.

One final thing to look out for are the various **specialities** produced for religious holidays – and also shortages at such times. During the eight days of **Passover** (*Pesach*), for example, bread is virtually unobtainable in Israel, particularly in the more orthodox areas (though you will find it in Arab shops). Doughnuts (*sofganiot* in Hebrew) are traditionally eaten in quantities around *Succot*, while during the fast of **Yom Kippur**, the Day of Atonement, you may find it hard to find anything to eat at all. Likewise, during **Ramadan**, the month of fasting for Muslims, Arab-run restaurants are shut until sunset. Don't miss one food with which this fast is traditionally broken in the evenings: *atayef*, or pancakes stuffed with pistachio nuts or sweet cheese and covered in syrup.

DRINK

The most common alcoholic drink in Israel is locally produced, lager-type **beer**, which is freely available. You'll also come across local **wines** (mostly produced under the *Carmel* label, and drinkable if unexciting) and **spirits**. The best and most popular of these is aniseed-based *araq* which is usually drunk diluted with water and ice (if available), and in bars or restaurants may be accompanied by a range of snacks – nuts, pickles, pieces of carrot or cucumber.

By far the best thirst-quenching non-alcoholic drinks are freshly-squeezed **fruit juices**: orange, grapefruit, lemon, or less expected tastes like bitter-sweet almond juice or the very sweet, brown tamarind (*tamar hindi*), which is rumoured

to have aphrodisiac properties. Unfortunately, it's becoming more and more difficult to find fruit juice stalls as the market is gradually taken over by synthetic, sugared drinks like the ubiquitous *Coca-Cola* and *Seven-Up* (these, at least, are generally better than their locally produced counterparts).

Tea and **coffee** are drunk everywhere, and sitting in an outdoor café watching the world go by remains one of the undoubted pleasures of the country. Tea in Israeli establishments usually consists of a meagre bag dunked in a cup of hot water, whilst in most Arab coffee-houses you can still get a whole pot or glass of refreshing *shai bina'ana* – mint tea. Coffee in Israeli cafes may be *Nescafé*, *café afuch* (with milk), cappucino or *botz*, where the coffee grounds are left to settle at the bottom of the glass. Arab coffee (*ahwa arabiya* or even *ahwa turkiya* – Turkish coffee) comes flavoured with *hel* (cardamom) and is drunk black, strong and sweet from tiny cups; if you're lucky, you may even get your future read from the grounds left at the bottom. The coffee can be ordered very sweet (*ziyyada*), medium (*mazbout*), with a little sugar (*ariha*) or plain (*saada*). As bitter, unsweetened coffee is commonly served to guests at funerals, it is probably considered a little strange to order one but then foreigners are a little strange anyway!

A word on Arab **coffee-houses**: as in the Middle East in general, cafés are traditionally the exclusive domain of men, who will sit for hours playing cards or backgammon (*tawla* or *sheshbesh*) and smoking waterpipes (*sheesha*). In some, women are tolerated, if not exactly welcomed, but in the main they will be tourists or 'foreigners'; it is still comparatively rare to find Palestinian women in the more traditional cafés. But there are many places where women are happily accepted and can even sit alone without too much hassle; however, if you're unsure about going in to a more out-of-the-way place, take a look to see whether there are any other women inside or not. The best bet is the cafés of hotels, at tourist sites or recreation centres, but wherever you are, if you're alone, some male is bound to make a play.

COMMUNICATIONS – POST, PHONES AND MEDIA

MAIL

The **postal service** to and from Israel is notoriously slow and unreliable; postcards and letters to Europe take upward of ten days, to the US a couple of days longer, while parcels often fail to reach their destination at all. Make sure Israel has diplomatic relations with the country to which you're sending mail – you can post letters to Egypt but to no other Arab country in the Middle East. As post offices are often crowded, it's worth buying a block of stamps once you get to the counter, or get them from a hotel or a stationery or souvenir shop. The cheapest letters are pre-stamped **aerogrammes**, sold at all post offices, many large hotels and gift shops.

Parcels can be sent a number of ways: by sea, airmail or by the more expensive airmail express (although this seems not to arrive any faster than airmail). Packages should be tied well with string and left open at the corner for security checks. You must also take your passport for identification when you post a parcel.

Mail from the **occupied territories** (including East Jerusalem) has to go through the Israeli postal network and so takes longer. For a speedier service, post your letters from an Israeli post office.

If you want to **receive mail** in Israel you can have it held for you at most main post offices. Letters should be addressed to you, preferably with surname in capitals, to **poste restante**, followed by the name of the town. Again, use Israeli post offices rather than ones in the West Bank or Gaza if you want your mail to get through. You will need your passport for identification when collecting your post.

Main post offices are **open** all day 8am–6pm, branch offices 8am–12.30pm and 3.30–6pm. Friday hours are 8am–1pm or 2pm; all post offices are closed on Saturday and holidays.

Telegrams can be sent from post offices and hotels, or by dialling ☎171.

PHONES

Telephones generally work well for international calls or between large towns, but less well between smaller places. Phone lines to the occupied territories are very often 'out-of-order' for inordinate periods of time.

There are **public telephones** in the streets and at post offices, bus stations and some shopping centres. The **tokens** (*assimonim*) which are needed to operate them can be bought at post offices, some tobacconists and newsstands or at bus stations from the *assimonim* sellers. They cost 10 *agorot* each and it's worth having ten or so with you in the event of having to make an urgent phone call, or in the more likely case that the phone you choose is malfunctioning and gobbles up your tokens. If you do have any left, you can always sell them back at bus stations before you leave. Hotels, cafés, restaurants and some shops will let you use their private phone, and charge you according to the meter, more expensive than token phones. Some public phones take the recently introduced **phonecards** available from the same outlets as *assimonim* and useful if you want to try to make an international call from a pay-phone.

You can make direct **international telephone calls** to most countries by dialling 00 for an international line, followed by the country code (44 for the UK), then the area code (minus its initial zero) and the number. You can also go via the international operator (☎18). For overseas **collect calls**, dial ☎03-622881. Long-distance and overseas calls can be booked at your hotel (usually more expensive) or at main post offices between 9am and 6pm.

Most main post offices and hotels will carry an English-language telephone directory or *Golden Pages*, or you can ask information (☎14) for a number. The international operator can obtain telephone numbers abroad.

News is an Israeli obsession, and everywhere you go you'll see people devouring it from the TV, the papers and the radio. If you're in a bus or taxi, chances are the driver will turn up the volume for the hourly news broadcasts, particularly if there has been an incident somewhere in the area.

TELEVISION

Even if there hasn't been any dramatic development, the hour between 9 and 10pm is not a good time to phone your Israeli acquaintances, as they're more than likely to be glued to the Hebrew-language TV news programme. Israel has two government-controlled **television** channels which transmit, among other things, English-language films and programmes from the UK and US (*Yes, Prime Minister* and *Dallas* have cult status here).

Jordan Television has a foreign-language channel, showing French programmes until 8pm and English-language shows and films from then until midnight. The news, which always begins with the latest on the Jordanian royal family, is broadcast in English at 10pm.

In the north of the country, it is possible to pick up **Middle East TV**, a Christian-evangelist station transmitted from southern Lebanon. In the vicinity of the Golan Heights, **Syrian TV** can also be viewed.

RADIO

News in English is broadcast four times a day on **Israel radio**: 7am for a news summary, 1pm for a news and features programme, 5pm for news headlines and 8pm for another summary. These can be picked up on 576, 1170 and 1458kHz. The **BBC World Service**, best received on 1322kHz, has newsreels at 2pm, 5pm and 9.15pm GMT. **Voice of America**, on 1260kHz, has news on its breakfast show at 5–6am and 8–9am, and at 5pm and 11pm. **Jordanian** and **Egyptian** radio both broadcast news in English at various times of the day.

Kol Israel (Voice of Israel) has five radio stations offering talk shows, commentary, news

and music ranging from classical to rock. Its army station, *Galei Zahal*, serves up an almost continual diet of decent pop music. **Radio Jordan** also plays a good selection of pop, rock and country music, although its DJs get rather tedious at times.

A couple of months after the start of the *intifada* (December 1987), a Palestinian radio station – the **Voice of the Intifada** -began transmitting from 'somewhere in the Middle East'. It broadcast the latest news of the *intifada*, as well as commentaries, analyses and nationalist songs. Not surprisingly it is now jammed by the Israelis, but it is still around and you may be able to pick it up for a few minutes when the Israeli jammer falls asleep.

NEWSPAPERS AND MAGAZINES

Since Israeli society is a multi-lingual one there is a wide selection of local and international newspapers and publications available in a variety of languages, at newsstands or in branches of *Steimatzky's* bookshop.

Locally, there are seven major Hebrew daily **newspapers**, a number of Arabic dailies and many weekly, bi-weekly and monthly journals. The main English-language daily is the **Jerusalem Post**, on sale throughout the country. This independent newspaper, with a daily circulation of around 60,000, covers the main events in Israel and around the world. It has a liberal stance and makes interesting reading, reporting widely on events in the occupied territories and containing opinion pieces that reflect attitudes on both the right and left of the Israeli spectrum. The **weekend supplement** carries comprehensive listings of events, including cinema, theatre and TV programmes for the coming week, as well as advertisements for talks, tours and walks. A second supplement, **In Jerusalem**, contains articles on local and other issues. The daily edition contains shorter TV, radio and cinema listings.

The other English-language newspaper to read is the Palestinian weekly **Al-Fajr**, published in East Jerusalem. Within the limits imposed by the Israeli censor, this offers wide coverage of events in the occupied territories and political analysis reflecting the Palestinian point of view. *Al-Fajr* (The Dawn) is widely available in East Jerusalem and in the occupied territories and is essential reading for anyone interested in the local political scene.

Until it was closed down by the Israeli authorities during the *intifada*, a second English-language Palestinian publication – **Al-Awdah** (The Return) – was published in East Jerusalem by the **Palestinian Press Service**. If the magazine or the office are ever allowed to reopen, it's worth looking them up for information on what's happening and for a Palestinian perspective on current events.

Other essential reading for what is really happening in the occupied territories and within the Israeli left includes: *News from Within*, a monthly bulletin of news and analysis, *The Other Front* (both published by the **Alternative Information Centre** and available on subscription or from their office at 14 Koresh Street, Jerusalem; ☎02-241159), *Newsletter on the Freedom of the Press* (from the Hanitotz/Shirara collective, 14 Koresh Street, Jerusalem, ☎02-221614) and *The Other Israel*, issued by the

Progressive List for Peace, also available on subscription (PO Box 956, Tel Aviv, ☎03-5565804). *New Outlook* (9 Gordon Street, Tel Aviv; ☎03-236496) provides an interesting view of current affairs from a left-Zionist viewpoint.

Israeli-produced English-language **magazines** include: *Eretz*, a glossy quarterly that focuses on the history, culture and wildlife of the country and often has articles which offer interesting alternatives to the usual tourist trail; *Israel Scene*, a pro-establishment monthly dealing with social and political issues; *Israel Review*, very middle of the road, and *The Israel Defence Forces Journal*.

Most major **British**, **American** and **European newspapers**, as well as magazines such as *Newsweek*, *Time* and *The Economist*, are available at newsstands and shops in all the larger centres. The *Middle East*, published in the UK, is sometimes available, as is *Middle East International*.

OPENING HOURS AND HOLIDAYS

Most shops and businesses are open 8am–1pm and 4pm–7pm, although many now stay open right through the day and on into the late evening, especially in tourist areas. Jewish-owned shops close early – around 2pm – on Friday, the start of *shabbat*, and on the eve of holidays, and are closed on Saturday and some religious holidays (see below). Muslim-owned shops and offices may be closed on Friday and other religious holidays and Christian-owned ones on Sunday and Christian festivals. Whilst this is all very confusing, it does mean that in such 'mixed' areas as Jerusalem you are bound to find something open on one day of these long weekends, although you should check before traipsing off miles to see a site that may be closed.

The situation has become more complex since, as a result of the *intifada*, all **Palestinian** shops and offices in the West Bank, Gaza Strip and East Jerusalem (including the Old City) have been observing a half-day protest strike and are open only in the morning. Total strikes of one, two or more days, to mark national days (see below) or to protest a particular Israeli outrage, are also common.

Banks opening hours are Sun, Tues and Thur 8.30am–12.30pm and 4–5.30pm, Mon and Weds 8.30am–12.30pm, Fri and eve of holidays 8.30am–noon. **Archaeological sites** and **National Parks** run by the National Parks Authority (NPA), are open April–Sept 8am–5.30pm, Oct–March 8am–4.30pm, closing one hour earlier on Friday and eve of holidays, two hours earlier on the eve of Passover and high holy days. **Museums** follow the general patterns outlined above, but are harder to generalise about: details are given in the relevant chapters.

The times of Sunday and other holiday **church** services can be obtained from the *Christian Information Centre* (Omar Ibn al-Khattab Square, Jaffa Gate, PO Box 14309, Jerusalem; ☎02-287647). Unless otherwise stated, **mosques** are open to the public at all times except during the five daily prayer periods and on Fridays and holidays. **Synagogue** prayer times are morning and evening daily, with sabbath services beginning at sunset on Friday and throughout Saturday. At all these places of worship, whether during prayer times or otherwise, decorous behaviour and modest dress is expected (and usually enforced), particularly for women – head covering in all three places is

JEWISH HOLIDAYS

	1989	1990
Pessach	Wed 19 April–Wed 26 April	Tues 10 April–Tues 17 April
Shevu'ot	Fri 9 June	Wed 30 May
Rosh HaShana	Sat 30 Sept, Sun 1 Oct	Thu 20 Sept, Fri 21 Sept
Yom Kippur	Mon 9 Oct	Sat 29 Sept
Succot	Sat 14 Oct, Sat 21 Oct	Thu 4 Oct, Thu 11 Oct
Simhat Torah	Sun 22 Oct	Fri 12 Oct
Yom HaAzma'ut	Wed 10 May	Mon 30 April

MUSLIM HOLIDAYS

	1989	1990
Leilat al-Miraj	Sat 4 March	Wed 22 Feb
Ramadan	Fri 7 April–Fri 5 May	Tue 28 March–Tue 25 April
Eid al-Fitr	Sat 6 May	Wed 26 April
Eid al-Adha	Thu 13 July	Mon 3 July
Al-Hijra	Wed 2 Aug	Sun 23 July
Mawlid al-Nabi	Wed 11 Oct	Sun 1 Oct

PALESTINIAN HOLIDAYS

Fatah Day	January 1
Jerusalem Day	February 22
International Women's Day	March 8
Land Day	March 30
Deir Yassin Day	April 19
Israeli invasion of Lebanon	June 4
1967 war	June 5
Black September	September 18
Balfour Day	November 2
UN Palestine Day	November 29

recommended although rarely strictly imposed. Men should remove head covering in church, but definitely put one on in a synagogue (and sites such as the Wailing Wall in Jerusalem). Shoes should be taken off when entering a mosque – canvas slippers or coverings are often provided at the door.

HOLIDAYS

All of the above opening times are regularly thrown out by a bewildering array of **public** and **religious holidays**. Given that there are three major religions (and numerous subdivisions within them), you can be sure to run up against at least one date when something you want to see is shut.

An additional complication is that since Jewish and Muslim holidays are dated according to a **lunar** calendar, they fall on different days of the **Gregorian** calendar (our western one) in each year. Above, we have given the dates of Jewish and Muslim holidays for 1989/1990: to calculate the dates further, you have to subtract 10 days per year.

The Jewish and Muslim years are also dated from different starting points: whereas the Gregorian (Christian) one begins from *Anno Domini* (The Year of our Lord), the **Jewish calendar** starts from the creation of the world (said to be the equivalent of 3760BC), and the **Muslim calendar** begins from the *hijra*, the Prophet Mohammed's flight from Mecca to Medina, in 622AD. To confuse matters even further, **Christian** holidays are celebrated on different dates by different denominations – Catholics and most Protestants use the same 'western' dates, the Greek Orthodox Church calculates according to the Julian calendar (13 days later than the Gregorian) and the Armenian Church operates a further 12 days on. Thus Christmas is celebrated by the western churches on December 25, by the eastern on January 7, and by the Armenians on January 19.

The **Jewish high holy days**, when everything including public transport shuts down, are *Rosh HaShana*, the New Year, followed ten days later by the fast of *Yom Kippur*, the Day of Atonement. *Succot*, five days after Yom Kippur, recalls the period after the exodus from Egypt spent in the desert; the week-long period ends with *Simhat Torah*, the celebration of the giving of the law. *Hannuka* commemorates the victory of the Maccabees and the rededication of the Temple in 164BC. The festival of *Purim* celebrates Queen Esther saving her people in Persia, and the *Pessach* (Passover) week recalls the Exodus from Egypt. Two weeks after the end of Passover is *Yom HaAzma'ut* when Israelis celebrate their independence, preceded the day before by *Yom HaZikaron* or Remembrance Day, for those who died in the Holocaust and during Israel's numerous wars. *Shevu'ot*, or Pentecost, is the harvest festival celebrating the giving of the Ten Commandments. *Tisha B'Av*, the Ninth of (the month of) Av, is another solemn remembrance day mourning the destruction of the First and Second Temples.

Muslim holy days start with *Al-Hijra*, the Islamic New Year, commemorating the flight of the Prophet Mohammed from Mecca to Medina. The feast of *Mawlid al-Nabi*, commemorates the Prophet's birth; *Leilat al-Miraj* is the night on which the Qur'an was revealed to the Prophet. The month of *Ramadan* is the most notable Muslim holiday, with fasting from dawn to dusk and much celebration at night. *Eid al-Fitr* marks the end of Ramadan and the breaking of the fast; *Eid al-Adha* recalls Abraham's attempted sacrifice of his son – Isma'el, according to Muslim belief – and the end of the *haj* (pilgrimage to Mecca) season.

Of the main **secular Palestinian holidays**, *Fatah Day* marks the founding, in 1965, of what is today the largest grouping within the Palestine Liberation Organisation, FATAH – an acronym for Haraket liTahrir Falistin. *Jerusalem Day* is marked throughout the Muslim world to commemorate the Israeli occupation of the third holiest Muslim site. *Land Day* recalls the murder of Palestinians defending their land in 1976, and the 1948 massacre of the inhabitants of *Deir Yassin* (see p000) is similarly commemorated on April 19 each year. *Black September* marks the massacre of Palestinians by Jordanian forces in 1970 as well as that by the Phalangists in Lebanon during the Israeli invasion of that country in 1982. *Balfour Day* recalls the 1917 Balfour Declaration, in which the British Foreign Secretary promised the Jewish people a homeland in Palestine.

ENTERTAINMENT

As you might expect in such a multi-cultural country, there is a wide variety of entertainment – music, film and theatre – to cater for practically all tastes. Most of it, naturally enough, will be in Arabic or Hebrew but on the whole you can enjoy it anyway. There's music virtually wherever you go – blaring from record shops and stalls, from car radios or from the increasingly prevalent video screens in outdoor cafés. The Israeli film industry's product is mixed in quality, and may or may not be subtitled, but the cinema is arguably worth visiting for the experience alone. There are also regular theatre productions which, for non-Hebrew or Arabic speakers, pose even more of a problem, but there's usually something on in English and again, it can be interesting to spend an evening at a play even if you barely understand a word.

MUSIC

The **Israeli** music scene has diversified greatly in recent years. In the early days, it consisted mainly of **folk** that reflected the 'pioneering' spirit of the country and which reached a climax with Israel's victories in 1967. Since then, this sort of nationalistic sentiment has begun to give way to more mellow music, such as that of the old Dylanesque master, **Arik Einstein**, or the gentle tones of **Yudit Ravitz**. Today's younger

musicians, however, have joined the age of the synthesiser to produce sounds not dissimilar from those in the west – there are even home-grown punk and heavy metal bands. With the growing protest movement, there is a parallel development on the music scene – most notably the songs of **Si Hyman** who shocked Israeli society with her recent condemnation of the army's actions in the occupied territories in *Shooting and Crying*.

The other significant development in Israeli music, once dominated by Ashkenazi/western players, is the 'coming out' of Sephardi musicians who are no longer embarrassed by their Arab heritage but are singing it loud and clear. Among their number is **Ofra Haza**, now internationally known for her updated traditional Yemeni tunes, **Haim Moshe**, whose distinctly Arabic music, sung in Hebrew, blares out from bus stations all over the country, and the group **HaBreira HaTivit**, who play a mix of Arab and 'oriental' music.

If it's genuine Arab music that interests you, there's no shortage of wonderful stuff to be listened to and bought in the *souq*. Local Palestinian talent abounds with such groups as **Sabreen**, **In A'id Rifaqi**, **Yo'ad** and the ever-popular **Marcel Khalifeh** reflecting Palestinian resistance and aspirations for independence, and more recently, songs of the *intifada*. Occasionally (but these days rarely), you may be lucky to catch a live concert and join in with the hand-clapping and spontaneous dancing. Music is an intrinsic part of Palestinian culture and even though joyful events such as weddings are nowadays muted, you may still get the chance to catch popular and live music if you're invited to attend.

Music from other Arab countries is also available everywhere: if you like it you'll get as much as you want on any journey in a *service* taxi – if you don't you'll get it anyway. Most of it is Egyptian – the great and eternal **Om Kulthoum** or **Mohammed Abd al-Wahab** or **Farid al-Attrash** – or the sweet tones of the Lebanese singer, **Fairuz**.

Western **popular** music too can be heard everywhere – the likes of Michael Jackson and Abba have a mass following here – but there are some local radio stations that play more interesting stuff. Occasionally, big-name bands or individuals visit the country – Ziggy Marley, Dire Straits, B.B. King and Bob Dylan number among recent visitors – until someone tells their managers that playing in a country widely criticised for its human rights record may not be that good for business.

As for **classical** music, there is a wide choice of concerts and **festivals** at which top-rate international and Israeli orchestras (such as the reputable Israel Philharmonic) and soloists perform. The three major cities – Tel Aviv, Jerusalem and Haifa – all have major concert halls (see the relevant sections) as well as **chamber music** venues. Information can be found in the weekend edition of the *Jerusalem Post*, in the listings magazines or from any IGTO.

FILM

Like the music scene, the Israeli cinema is beginning to show signs of maturing and facing up to reality. Although much of what is made is pure pulp, there are some more challenging and controversial offerings by Israeli filmmakers like Amos Gitai. Films such as **Beyond the Wall**, **The Tale of the Lamb**, **Avanti Poppoli** and **The Last Summer** deal with such issues as prison conditions, Palestinian-Israeli relations, the 1973 war and army conscription, and are well worth looking out for.

There is no **Palestinian** film industry as such, but there are a whole range of excellent films, mostly documentary, produced by both Palestinian and foreign filmakers. There's more chance of seeing these at home, but the Jerusalem *Cinematheque*, for example, does have a fairly broad repertoire. **Michel Kleifi**, a Palestinian currently living and working in Belgium, has made several notable films about Palestinian life under occupation, including **Fertile Memory** and **Wedding in Galilee**. Others are too numerous to list here but include Antonia Caccia's excellent **On Our Land** (about Umm al-Fahm) and more recent **Voices from Gaza**. If you're interested in films about Palestine and the present-day conflict, the organisations listed in the "Information" section will be able to help.

THEATRE

There are four main **Israeli** theatres: the national *Habimah* and *Cameri* theatres in Tel Aviv, the *Khan* in Jerusalem and the civic theatre in Haifa.

Almost all of their productions will be in Hebrew – for English plays you'd do better to check out the smaller theatre clubs and minor venues (see the *Jerusalem Post* for English language listings). If you think you can handle Hebrew theatre, try for a performance of more 'controversial' playwrights such as Hanoch Levin, or Joshua Sobol whose *Soul of a Jew* and *Ghetto* caused a stir in Israel's theatre world.

Naturally enough, Israel is one of the best places (along with New York) to see the sort of **Yiddish** theatre that was once performed by the Jewish communities in the ghettos of Europe. Again, if you don't have the language, you'll miss the subtle, linguistic jokes, but you can still pick up on the more slapstick humour and, above all, the great *kletzmer* music and songs – Yiddish melodies traditionally played by itinerant musicians on instruments like violins and trumpets that could be carried around.

Palestinian theatre is also worth going to see, curiously enough for a similar reason: namely, the sort of audience participation that it encourages. There is only one fixed venue in the occupied territories: *Nuzha al-Hakawati* in East Jerusalem (see *Jerusalem* chapter), but plays, folklore festivals and dance are often performed in the Palestinian universities of Bir Zeit, Bethlehem or Najah (in Nablus) when the Israeli authorities allow them to open. The most famous Palestinian theatre group is **al-Hakawati**, who have presented such pieces as *Mahjoub Mahjoub*, *Slaves Go West* and *The Story of the Eye and the Tooth* in many European cities, but there are many other lesser-known groups who play wherever and whenever they are not prevented from doing so by the censor or the military authorities. Inside the 'green line' (in Nazareth or Haifa, for example), you may be lucky to catch a performance of *Return to Haifa*, a play adapted from the novel of the same name by Palestinian writer Ghassan Kanafani (who died in an Israeli car-bombing in Beirut).

FOLKLORE

One further form of entertainment which you may be offered as part of an Israeli tour, or thrown in with a package deal, is an 'authentic' **folklore evening** – held regularly at many of the larger hotels, and occasionally in more genuine and impromptu fashion in city parks or cultural centres. Since indigenous folklore can hardly be said to exist in a state a mere 41 years old, these are generally a mixture of song and dance originating from various other traditions, with elements of East European (Polish, Hungarian, Russian), Greek and Arabic cultures. The shows may also contain 'bellydancing', suitably commercialised for western tastes. Hotel events are invariably sanitised and dull, but the others can be fun, especially if you are into audience participation.

Palestinian folklore, by contrast, is a living tradition, with song and dance still an essential element of local weddings and festivities. However, it is not uncommon for *dabke* dance groups to be arrested and accused of making political propaganda or for the cultural week at Bir Zeit University to be closed down. With restrictions increased during the *intifada*, your best bet for seeing Palestinian folklore is in a village or town within the 'green line'.

TROUBLE, POLICE AND SECURITY

You'll already have experienced Israeli security on entering the country, and it's a concern which is no less noticeable once you've arrived. You must keep your personal belongings with you at all times – parcels, packages and baggage left unattended may be reported to the police as suspicious and will be confiscated or detonated by the bomb squad. If you notice an unguarded package, you should report it: to the bus driver, storeowner, hotel staff or whoever else seems relevant. Also be prepared to have your bags checked constantly, especially at entrances to museums, large stores, supermarkets, cinemas and post offices.

TROUBLE

If you travel in the occupied territories there is a possibility – not a likelihood for foreigners, but a real possibility nonetheless – of being caught up in serious **trouble**. Confine your visit to areas within the 'green line' and it's unlikely that you will even notice, let alone come across, any clashes or disturbances – other than fisticuffs between taxi drivers on a sweltering summer's day.

On the beach at Tel Aviv or the Dead Sea or in Eilat you are as far away from the **Israeli-Palestinian conflict** as you would be sunning yourself on the Costa Brava. Even in Jerusalem, geographically and politically at the heart of the problem, it is possible to see, hear and meet nothing – if you try very hard. But when your guide tells you that the *souq* in East Jerusalem is closed for a 'Muslim holiday', don't be fooled. Israeli soldiers are around everywhere, particularly now during the *intifada*, stopping, checking

and harassing Palestinians. And, of course, in the West Bank and Gaza Strip, violent clashes, beatings and tear gas are commonplace. Many areas, particularly refugee camps, are regularly clamped under curfew for extensive periods, with army road-blocks and checkpoints set up along highways to control passage in and out of Palestinian towns and villages.

If you get caught up in a confrontation, or go on a demonstration in solidarity, it is unlikely that as a foreigner you will be detained. The most that's likely to happen is that you'll be asked to produce evidence of your identity, so you must carry an **ID card** or **passport** with you when travelling in the occupied territories. That said, however, Israeli soldiers have been known to shoot at or beat up or break/confiscate the cameras of even *bona fide* journalists – Palestinian, Israeli or foreign – so you take your chances if you want to stick around. If you are detained, contact your **consulate** or a **lawyer** as soon as you can (or pass word to someone else to do so).

More mundane ways of coming into conflict with the authorities include getting caught with **drugs** or being drunk. You would be foolish to do either anywhere in the country, but particularly in the already tense occupied territories, where you risk your own neck and that of others too.

Dope, although widely available, is illegal. Being caught with dope for personal use is not a serious offence, but dealing or possessing larger quantities is likely to get you deported. If you are picked up by either the army or the police, you'll probably be bundled off to spend at least one not too pleasant night in a cell. As in all such situations, you have the right to remain silent and are allowed a phone call to your consulate or a lawyer.

Less seriously, anything that might be interpreted as **immodest or disrespectful behaviour** could bring trouble from the authorities or locals. Generally speaking this is an extremely conservative society, and while sunbathing topless may be normal on the more cosmopolitan beaches around Tel Aviv, for example, showing any sort of flesh at all in orthodox areas of Jerusalem may invite hostile reaction. Public displays of affection are frowned on by religious Jews and Muslims alike, and people who drive through ultra-orthodox areas on *shabbat* will find their car being stoned by locals, and at all religious sites you are expected to keep yourself well covered – no shorts or bare shoulders. **Photography** can also be contentious. Before you start snapping away at people (especially Orthodox Jews), inside synagogues, churches or mosques, or taking pictures of anything which could be regarded as a security installation (airports etc), try to ask permission.

POLICE AND ARMY

The army is everywhere. The sight of fully-armed khaki-clad **soldiers** (most of whom look as if they should still be at school) at bus stations, hitching along the highways or walking through the streets is a common and, until you get used to it, shocking one. Within the 'green line', however, they're generally off-duty and probably making their way home or to base or on an outing.

Day-to-day authority in these areas (and as far as Israel is concerned, this includes East Jerusalem) rests with the regular **police**, who are recognisable by their navy-blue uniforms and flat caps. Israeli police are little different from police anywhere: helpful if you're a tourist (and especially female) who's got lost (and if they happen to speak English); reasonably co-operative if you've been robbed (especially if you're female); and decidedly unfriendly if you're breaking the law. If you do need to report a crime – a robbery, mugging or attack – go to the nearest police station, where hopefully someone will be sympathetic. Women who have been sexually attacked or raped should first contact a **rape crisis** centre (see "Sexual Harassment" below) for advice and someone to accompany you to a police station to file a report.

The so-called **border guards**, who wear military uniform and distinguishing green berets, are officially part of the police force, but considerably less pleasant. Their role is often interchangeable with that of the army: after recent world condemnation of the army's handling of the *intifada*, some units were withdrawn and replaced by border guards, to create the impression that Israel was listening to and complying with public opinion. The border guards, however, have long been notorious for their brutality towards Palestinians (most recently, they were responsible for the massacre of Palestinians in the West Bank village of Nahalin), so keep your distance.

SEXUAL HARASSMENT

Israelis, men and women alike, and to a lesser extent Palestinians, have a direct approach to human relations that visitors with an 'English reserve' can find disconcerting and intrusive. Mostly, it's curiosity that prompts personal questions from total strangers: get into a *service* or *sherut* taxi and by the end of the journey, your fellow passengers are likely to know more about you than your mother does! Once you've got used to this and feel relaxed enough to respond in kind, it can be really rewarding – and certainly if you go around brushing off all overtures you'll miss out on real friendship and potentially some of the best experiences of your travels.

Where such lively, genuine interest stops and **harassment**, sexual or otherwise, begins is not easy to define. Much depends on your own tolerance level. That said, both Israeli and Palestinian society are solidly heterosexual and family oriented – why anyone should choose not to marry and have loads of bouncing kids, or travel in the company of someone of the same sex (or worse still alone!), seems to be a source of mystery. It also means that life is male-dominated and sexist: women, particularly 'unattached' ones, are generally regarded as fair game.

There is little you can do about this, unfortunately, except to be aware of differences in **culture and customs**, that people in some areas are more religious and conservative than in others, and to dress and behave accordingly – in the ultra-orthodox Jewish quarter of Mea She'arim in Jerusalem, for example, there are wall-notices warning women not to display bare arms and legs, but in other places, the only way you find out is by hostile reactions. It's worth bearing this in mind at all religious sites and in such towns, for example, as Hebron or the Old City of Jerusalem. Coming off the bus from Eilat or your kibbutz and strolling around in shorts and bikini top is asking for trouble.

Most sexual harassment, however, is of the low-key variety – constant, extremely annoying and frustrating, but rarely very threatening. Every other Middle Eastern male appears to regard any female, particularly one on her own, as an object to be 'hunted', and harassment on the street ranges from penetrating stares, to wolf-whistles, to the sort of noises one would use to call a dog to heel, to kerb-crawling, following and propositioning. In short, it's difficult for any woman to be alone and enjoy a stroll, a coffee or a view by herself. Taxi drivers are also notorious – what you may take as friendly conversation, he may regard as an open invitation, although it's unlikely to get very heavy as he has his job to look out for. One way of keeping this to a minimum is to sit in the back of the cab rather than beside him.

This sort of verbal pestering is particularly heavy on the beach, where even if you're engrossed in a book or are firmly attached to your headphones, you're likely to be approached by some macho-man and asked where you come from, if you're married, where you're staying, what you're doing tonight etc. There is, of course, no easy solution to the problem. Refusing to respond may put your suitor off so that he'll leave and go hassle someone else; or it may make him even more determined, aggressive and possibly even hostile. If you do decide to answer back, politely or otherwise, this will probably be taken as some sort of interest, and the effect may be the same – either way, you'll have lost your place in the story or missed that song you particularly liked.

At its worst, sexual harassment can take the form of physical assault – the incidence of **rape** is on the increase, and the best advice that can be given is to take the same sort of precautions and avoid the same sort of situations that you would at home: dark and lonely streets, hitching alone (or even with another woman) particularly at night, sleeping on isolated beaches or accepting invitations from men you barely know. Even women soldiers in the Israeli army have been officially banned from hitching. In the worst event, there are several 24-hour **rape crisis** numbers that you can call for counselling and advice and for someone to accompany you to the police to file a complaint: they include Jerusalem ☎02-245554, Tel Aviv ☎03-234314/234819 and Haifa ☎04-382611.

GAY AND LESBIAN LIFE

Male homosexuality only ceased to be illegal in Israel in 1988 – after years of pressure from the *Citizens' Rights Movement* – and attitudes still tend to be puritanical, especially given the country's vociferous and influential religious lobby. According to the Old Testament 'If a man also lie with mankind, as he lieth with a woman, both of them have committed an abomination: they shall surely be put to death; their blood shall be upon them.' (*Leviticus 20;13*). Such attitudes are not uncommon among the orthodox even today.

Gays are not helped either by societal values, Arab and Jewish alike, which place heavy emphasis on marriage, family life and children. Most are forced to remain firmly in the closet. In the army, gays will usually lose their security rating and are frequently transferred to lower ranks or urged to leave. The army's attitude is not seen as unusual in Israel. Within Arab society, the usual pressures are exacerbated by the fear of brutal treatment by Israeli authorities.

Lesbians find themselves in a slightly different situation. Sexual relations between women are not mentioned by the Bible, and nor have they ever been proscribed by law – for the simple reason that the homosexuality law, like many others, was a product of the British legal system (which fails to accept the possibility of lesbianism) left over from the British Mandate. However, the pressure on women to conform, to marry and have children, is even greater than on men; and attitudes towards lesbians even more outdated.

AIDS, too, has affected life here as it has everywhere else. As elsewhere, it is on the increase, and as elsewhere has helped to reinforce reactionary attitudes, and undone many of the advances made by the gay community. A volunteer AIDS task force has been set up which, in concert with the Ministry of Health, runs an information hotline and AIDS centres around the country. But since positive tests must be reported to the Ministry, many gays are afraid to take advantage.

In purely practical terms, **as a traveller**, you'll find the coastal cities and resorts – Tel Aviv and Eilat especially – infinitely more tolerant than smaller places or the interior. The *Society for the Protection of Personal Rights* (PO Box 16151, Tel Aviv 61161), Israel's only significant gay organisation, runs *Israel Hospitality*, which provides information and an advice line for tourists (☎03-455166/221721; private homes, so don't call late), and a gay and lesbian switchboard, *The White Line* (☎03-625629), which operates on Tuesday, Thursday and Sunday evenings from 7.30 until 11.30pm.

WORK

Although working in Israel on a tourist visa is illegal, many visitors do it and the authorities generally seem to turn a blind eye. The most common type of unofficial work is in bars, nightclubs and cafés in the big coastal resorts: Tel Aviv, the Sea of Galilee, and especially Eilat.

It is also possible to work legally: most commonly on kibbutzim and moshavim, less commonly on archaeological digs and workcamps.

KIBBUTZIM AND MOSHAVIM

The **kibbutz** is probably the world's most famous communal society. Originally conceived as collective agricultural settlements, owned and administered communally by their members, and with members' children communally raised, few survive with their ideals intact. Most have lost their romantic, pastoral and 'pioneering' character and have diversified their income with the introduction of plastics and computer factories and processing plants to supplement their dwindling resources. More significantly, however, many now depend on hiring cheap outside labour for their survival. A **moshav** is a smallholders' cooperative village, centred around the family unit, which pursues its private interest whilst contributing to the collective.

Although work on the kibbutz is supposed to be done by its members, hiring external labour is a common practice. Palestinians (who cannot become members) are employed at very low wages, whilst **foreign volunteers** work in return for food, accommodation and almost no wages at all. It may be exploitation, but the fact remains that working on a kibbutz is a unique kind of experience and enables you to stay abroad at very little cost. Bear in mind, however, that your regime may be a fairly strict one and that since you won't be able to take time off when and as you choose, you'll have to save your sightseeing for later. Many *kibbutzim* are aware of this and arrange some day-trips out for their volunteers; others provide *ulpanim* – Hebrew-language courses – on half-days.

Living conditions in the first kibbutzim were pretty basic but nowadays many are well equipped with the latest technology, entertainment facilities and swimming pools. The normal deal is that apart from food and accommodation, you will get a small payment of around £10 per month and some other allowances such as razors, soap, cigarettes etc. The work schedule is either six hours six days a week, or eight hours five days a week. The type of work you will be given

KIBBUTZ INFORMATION OFFICES

UK

Kibbutz Representatives, 1A Accommodation Road, London NW11 8ED (☎01-458 9235).

Kibbutz Representatives, 11 Upper Park Road, Salford, Manchester, M7 0HY (☎061-795 9447).

Academic Travel/STA, 86 Old Brompton Road, London SW7 (☎01-937 9921).

Project 67, 10 Hatton Garden, London EC1N 8AH (☎01-831 7626).

Australia and New Zealand

Israel Information Centre, Jewish Centre, 61 Woodrow Avenue, Yokine, W.A. 6060, Australia.

Kibbutz Programme Desk, Wellington Jewish Community Centre, P.O. Box 27-156, Wellington, NZ.

Israel

Takam, United Kibbutz Movement, 82A HaYarkon Street, Tel Aviv (☎03-655207). Open Sun–Thur 8am–3pm, Fri 8–11am.

HaKibbutz HaArtzi, 13 Leonardo De Vinci Street, Tel Aviv (☎03-435262). Open Sun–Thur 8am–2pm, Fri 8am–noon.

HaKibbutz HaDati (religious kibbutzim), 7 Dubnov Street, Tel Aviv (☎03-257231); open Wed 8am–1pm, other days by appointment only.

---

depends on the economic base of your particular kibbutz. In general, the tasks are divided into three main groups: service work – kitchens, laundry and childrens' homes; farm work – citrus fields, banana and date plantations, vineyards, poultry and livestock; and factory work – usually involving packing or making components. Volunteers with special skills may get more interesting opportunities.

Volunteers on a moshav either live in separate accommodation (2 or 4 to a cabin) or are placed with a family and expected to join in their social and cultural life. In return for your labour, you will get board, lodging and a small wage of perhaps £50–80 per month.

There are several ways to go about **finding work on a kibbutz or moshav**, the most common of which is to approach the kibbutz or moshav representative in your home country who will arrange you a place before you leave. You will need two letters of reference and a medical certificate to prove that you are up to working. You also have to pay £50 to register, for which you get medical insurance, a kibbutz representative to meet you on arrival, and transport to the kibbutz. Some offices offer a package which includes kibbutz placement, return airfare and insurance cover for around £300. If you do it this way you are committed to staying on the kibbutz for a minimum period, generally five or six weeks, and you cannot choose the one you want to work on – it's up to the kibbutz to pick you. There is also an age limit: 18–32 for a kibbutz, 18–35 for a moshav.

You cannot work on a kibbutz if you return to Israel from a trip to Egypt – in case you've picked up some nasty sort of bug that will prevent you working – so slog yourself to death first and then go and enjoy yourself at the Pyramids.

To apply from home, write to the relevant office with a stamped addressed envelope, asking for an application form. Most kibbutzim are aligned to the various political movements in Israel so although you have no choice, you may want to know the tendency of the one you're going to work in. For more information on the various kibbutzim consult *Kibbutz Volunteer* by John Bedford (Vacation Work, 9 Park End Street, Oxford; £4.95), a detailed book on volunteering. For further information and application forms, contact your local IGTO or the addresses listed.

You can also apply directly to the central kibbutz offices **in Israel**. This should give you more say in where you end up, although you may find that the kibbutz you want to go to is booked, particularly in the busy summer months between June and August. Each kibbutz movement has its own central office; if there are vacancies, you will be interviewed and, if offered a place, will be expected to make your own way to your designated kibbutz. At the interview, you must produce: a valid passport; an insurance certificate covering medical expenses, personal accidents and loss of possessions; a medical fitness certificate; two letters of reference and, if possible, a letter of recommendation from the kibbutz representative in your own country.

Finally, you can offer your services **directly** to a kibbutz or moshav. It's fairly unlikely that you'll be accepted on this basis, but if they need someone there is a chance. So if you run across a kibbutz on your travels that particularly appeals, there's no harm in trying.

WORKCAMPS

A number of Palestinian towns and villages, both inside the 1948 borders of Israel and in the occupied territories, run **workcamps** in which volunteers are invited to participate. The aim of the workcamps is twofold: firstly, because of the shortage of funding, many basic manual tasks, such as road laying, rock and rubbish clearing, painting and building need to be done; and secondly, participating in the workcamps is an expression of solidarity and affords an opportunity to meet, work and talk with Palestinians.

Most of the workcamps are held in the summer, particularly during July and August. Volunteers are supplied with **food** and **accommodation**, either with families or in communal quarters such as a school or campsite. You have to pay your own travel and insurance and provide your own spending money. In some cases, such as

the **Bir Zeit International Workcamp** (see below), you also have to pay a \$40 registration fee. Work is usually allotted to small groups of participants on a daily basis and, depending on what needs to be done, you can have a choice in the matter. But it's important to bring light workclothes and strong shoes, as well as sunglasses and a hat or scarf. After a hard day's work, there's often a full programme of entertainment – either laid on or provided by participants.

The best-known workcamp in the West Bank is the one run by Bir Zeit University. Although this and all other Palestinian universities, colleges and schools have been closed by the Israeli authorities since the beginning of the *intifada* in December 1987, the workcamps are still being held (at least for the time being). Other workcamps are regularly held in Nazareth, Jaffa, Umm al-Fahm, Deir al-Assad, Shafr Amr, Majd al-Shams, Kufr Kana and Acre. You are advised to apply from the UK before you leave if you wish to volunteer.

Below are some organisations you can contact for further information and/or application forms for workcamps; they will also be able to help in arranging or advising on other sorts of volunteer and non-volunteer longer term work, such as teaching, medical aid, research or field work.

WORKCAMPS

Applying in the UK

World University Service (WUS), 20 Compton Terrace, London N1 2UN; ☎01-226 6747 (for Bir Zeit Workcamp).

Friends of Bir Zeit University (FOBZU), 21 Collingham Road, London SW5 ONU; ☎01-373 8414.

Universities Education Fund for Palestinian Refugees (UNIPAL), 20a Plantation Road, Oxford, OX2 6JD; ☎0865-241537.

Witness for Palestine, 20 Dartmouth Park Hill, London NW5 1HL; ☎01-263 7187.

Medical Aid for Palestinians, 29 Enford Street, London W1H 1DG; ☎01-723 7766.

United Nations Association International Service (UNAIS), 3 Whitehall Court, London SW1; ☎01-930 0679.

Applying direct

Nazareth: *Human Rights Association*, PO Box 215, Nazareth 16101 (☎06-555340); Nazareth Municipality, 606 Street, Nazareth (☎06-570911/573504).

Jaffa: *League of Jaffa Arabs (al-Raabita)*, 2 Ma'or Ainayim Street, Jaffa (☎03-812290; ask for Abeer).

Umm al-Fahm: *Al-Hadaf Cultural Centre*, P.O.Box 169, Umm al-Fahm (☎06-352915).

Deir al-Assad: *Deir al-Assad Progressive Front*, Deir al-Assad, Galilee (☎04-987078).

Majd al-Shams: *Association of University Graduates in the Golan Heights*, Majd al-Shams, Golan Heights (☎06-981624).

Beersheva: *Association for the Support and Defence of Beduin Rights in Israel*, 37 Hativat HaNegev, PO Box 5212, Beersheva (☎057-31687).

Taybeh: *Taybeh Cultural Centre*, Taybeh, The Triangle (☎052-61496; for information only).

ARCHAEOLOGICAL DIGS

At any one time there are dozens of **archaeological explorations** going on in Israel, and many of them accept volunteers during the summer. They are sited all over the country, from Tel Dan in the north and Tel Dor on the Mediterranean coast to Tel Arad and Timna in the Negev. Volunteers must normally be over 18. The names and addresses of the individual directors of excavations can be obtained from any IGTO or the Department of Antiquities and Museums, Ministry of Education and Culture, PO Box 586, Jerusalem (☎02-278502/3). You should apply early in the year to be certain of a place, but if you're lucky you may get onto a dig once you're in Israel.

If you don't feel like spending the best part of your holiday digging, you can get your hands dirty for just a morning with the *Dig For A Day* programme run by *Archaeological Seminars*, 11 Shonai Hallachot, PO Box 14002, Jaffa Gate, Jerusalem (☎02-273515). It will cost you around £9 to work on a site.

DIRECTORY

ADDRESSES Town and street signs are almost invariably written in Hebrew and English, with Arabic included for 'mixed' or Palestinian areas. English can be used for addressing mail; the word for street or boulevard (Rehov or Sderot) is often left out and the house number is put after the name, eg Allenby 27. In older towns there is often confusion caused by the fact that the Israelis have renamed all the streets: local Palestinian residents generally continue to use the original Arabic names, while signs and maps say something else altogether.

AIRPORT TAX Departure tax is paid when you buy your ticket: check that yours is stamped.

ALCOHOL Locally produced spirits – *arak* (an aniseed-flavoured drink similar to *ouzo*), vodka, brandy, whisky and rum – and wines are cheap and popular, though the taste and after-effects are not always that pleasant. There are a couple of good locally made wines, cheap from supermarkets and stores. Neither Palestinians nor Israelis are big drinkers and rowdy drunkenness in public tends to be the domain of foreigners.

ARCHAEOLOGY A 14-day pass ($12) is available which gives free access to all the major archaeological sites and parks: contact the *National Parks Authority*, 3 Het Street, HaKirya, Tel Aviv (☎03-252281). For information on joining an archaeological dig, see "Work" (p.00).

BAGGAGE Because of the security risk, there are virtually no left-luggage offices anywhere in Israel. For the same reason, you must keep your bags with you at all times – any unattended baggage is likely to be surrounded by the army and exploded!

BARGAINING is the name of the game in the *souq* – aim to knock the price down by a third. But you have to persist and perhaps even walk away a few times. You can also bargain for accommodation in some hotels and hostels, depending on how business is at the time. In shops, stores and restaurants, prices are usually marked and fixed.

BEACHES Apart from those around the Sea of Galilee, beaches are free. In Tel Aviv, there is one separate-sex beach area. Topless bathing is accepted on some beaches, but it is not the norm – and can lead to hassle. It's inadvisable to use the beach along the Gaza Strip unless you're with local Palestinians. Beaches at the Dead Sea are stoney but well-used by sun- and health-seekers. The sea itself is ghastly, but try it once for the experience!

BRING Barrier suntan lotion, sunglasses, batteries for audio and photographic equipment, and film, are all expensive in Israel, and a hat and an alarm clock are worthwhile extras. Mosquito repellent is essential, although you can buy an electric gadget which heats up an anti-mosquito pellet and keeps the pests away for the whole night. The vapour it gives off is virtually odourless and non-irritant. If you plan on trekking in the desert, a water bottle is essential.

CIGARETTES Local cigarettes are less than a third of the price you pay for a pack in the UK. International brands (*Marlboro, Kent, Camel, Rothmans* etc) are also available everywhere – more expensive than the local ones but still cheaper than in western Europe. One outcome of the *intifada* is a boycott of Israeli goods in general and particularly of Israeli cigarettes. Palestinians in the occupied territories smoke either foreign or Palestinian brands like *Imperial, Alia* or *Farid.*

CONTRACEPTIVES Condoms are available over the counter from chemists; the pill can be had only on prescription, so bring a sufficient supply.

CUSTOMS Official regulations state that you can bring in duty-free: ½ litre of perfume, two litres of wine, one litre of other alcoholic beverages, 250 grams of tobacco or cigars or 250 cigarettes, and gifts up to $125 in value. However, no-one seems to attach much importance to these, and if you're searched, it's more likely to be for drugs or weapons.

ELECTRICITY The electric current in Israel is 220 volts AC, which means that most British appliances will work fine if you have an international adaptor to fit the local plugs.

EMBASSIES AND CONSULATES Almost all foreign embassies are in Tel Aviv, since few countries acknowledge the status of Jerusalem as capital. Most western countries, however, also maintain consulates in Haifa, Jerusalem (East and West) and Eilat. Addresses are given under the relevant cities.

EMERGENCIES Ambulance ☎101, Police ☎100, Fire ☎102. For local numbers, see the relevant chapters.

KIDS Palestinians and Israelis alike dote on children and travelling with them is fine. Baby needs – food, disposable nappies, medication etc – are widely available in supermarkets and shops, and many hotels and hostels either have family rooms or will put in an extra bed. Remember, though, that it's very hot during the summer – children need lots of fluids and protection from the sun – and, in some regions, very cold in the winter.

LAUNDERETTES The larger towns all have a couple of self-service launderettes, but they're not all that common: most people do their own washing at home, particularly as the warm weather means that clothes dry in no time at all. You can get washing done at most hotels and some hostels have washing machines for residents. There are also laundries.

SWIMMING POOLS Practically all Israeli towns have municipal swimming pools and sports centres which are relatively cheap. *Kibbutzim, moshavim* and settlements usually have them too, although the use is often restricted to members, residents or volunteers. Most of the large hotels have swimming pools open to non-residents, but these are expensive.

TAMPONS are available, but expensive. Bring your own supply.

TIME Israel is two or three hours ahead of Greenwich Mean Time, depending on whether summer time (introduced despite the bitter protests of the orthodox lobby) is in force. In other words it's usually two hours ahead of Britain. In the occupied territories, the Unified Leadership of the *Intifada*, rather than have it imposed by the Israeli authorities, has brought in Palestinian summer time one month earlier.

TOILETS Public toilets are not particularly widespread, and where they do exist are often unpleasant, particularly in bus stations. Bring your own toilet paper.

VAT Value-Added Tax (15%) for items bought at recommended stores is refundable at the airport when you leave, or can be sent by cheque to your home address if you leave the country from anywhere else. Ask for a VAT refund form when you make your purchase.

WATER Tap water is generally okay to drink, and local mineral water is cheap and available almost everywhere.

PART TWO

THE

GUIDE

LEBANON

TIBERIAS
AND THE
PANHANDLE

THE GOLAN
HEIGHTS

GALILEE
AND THE
NORTH

Mediterranean
Sea

THE COAST, HAIFA
AND NAZARETH

SYRIA

THE WEST
BANK

TEL AVIV AND
THE SOUTH
COAST

JERUSALEM

THE GAZA STRIP

NEGEV,
THE SOUTH
AND EILAT

JORDAN

EGYPT

0   100 km

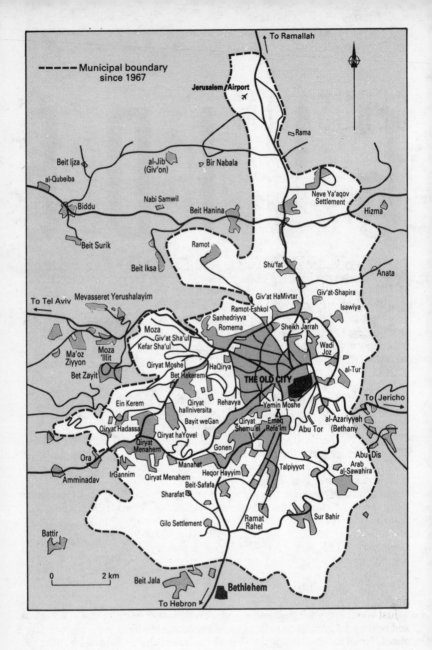

To Ramallah

Municipal boundary since 1967

Jerusalem Airport

Rama

Beit Ijza

al-Jib (Giv'on)

Bir Nabala

al-Qubeiba

Neve Ya'aqov Settlement

Biddu

Nabi Samwil

Beit Hanina

Hizma

Beit Surik

Ramot

Beit Iksa

Shu'fat

Anata

To Tel Aviv

Mevasseret Yerushalayim

Giv'at HaMivtar

Giv'at-Shapira

Ramot-Eshkol

Isawiya

Sanhedriyya

Moza

Romema

Sheikh Jarrah

Giv'at Sha'ul

Wadi Joz

Kefar Sha'ul

Ma'oz Ziyyon

Moza 'Illit

Qiryat Moshe

HaQirya

Bet Zayit

Bet Hakerem

THE OLD CITY

al-Tur

Ein Kerem

Qiryat haUniversita

Rehavya

Yemin Moshe

To Jericho

Bayit weGan

Qiryat Shemu'el

Emeq Refa'im

al-Azariyyeh (Bethany

Qiryat Hadassa

Abu Tor

Qiryat haYovel

Gonen

Abu Dis

Ora

Qiryat Menahem

Manahat

Heqor Hayyim

Talpiyyot

Arab al-Sawahira

Amminadav

IrGannim

Qiryat Menahem

Beit-Safafa

Sharafat

Sur Bahir

Gilo Settlement

Ramat Rahel

Battir

0   2 km

Beit Jala

Bethlehem

To Hebron

CHAPTER ONE

JERUSALEM

*Ten measures of beauty gave God to the world: nine to Jerusalem and one to the
remainder*
*Ten measures of sorrow gave God to the world: nine to Jerusalem and one to the
remainder*

Talmud

E very visitor to Israel goes to **JERUSALEM**. Each carries with them
their own baggage of preconceived ideas, religious or political. And
yet each is almost certainly surprised by what they find. For all its
fame (or notoriety) Jerusalem is a small town; provincial in many
ways, conservative and weighed down with history. But it also offers an enormous amount to see, whether you're interested in ancient history, religion or
contemporary politics. Above all, Jerusalem is where you really feel the pulse,
because it is where Israel meets Palestine. The 1967 front-line may no longer
exist in physical form, but the political, legal and cultural divisions are still
very tangible.

Jerusalem also straddles a real geographical frontier. Perched high in the
Judaean Hills 800m above sea level, it is where the fertile planted fields, olive
groves and settled villages of the coastal plain and the Judaean foothills to the
west meet the harsh desert of the Jordan Valley to the east. Palestinian *fellahin* and Beduin meet their urban compatriots in the markets and shops of
East Jerusalem while Israeli farmers (from their kibbutz and *moshav* homes
in the foothills) use similar facilities in the west.

All the media coverage that Jerusalem, and particularly the **Old City**, have
been receiving during the Palestinian *intifada* has created the impression
that the town is bigger than it really is. And there is no doubt that its political
and religious importance weigh heavily upon it. The Old City, home to tens of
thousands of people, is tiny and bulging at the seams. Around it Jerusalem
has been rapidly expanding over recent years, with the pre-1967 'middle-
aged' city around it covering several square kilometres – east and west – and
new tentacles pushing out ever further into the occupied territories with
rings of high-rise fortress Jewish settlements.

Just about everything about Jerusalem is disputed: from its historic origins
and religious significance to its modern borders and official legal and political
status. Israel has declared it the eternal **capital of the Jewish state**, but this
is a status recognised only by Israel and the odd South American dictator-
ship. So while the Israeli Knesset (parliament) and most ministries are in
Jerusalem, virtually all foreign embassies are in Tel Aviv. Meanwhile for

Palestinians, however difficult their day-to-day life here, Jerusalem is the central focus of all commerce, culture, political life and above all aspiration.

Jerusalem, then, is schizophrenic. For Palestinians and Israelis alike, it is the pre-eminent city, but they live a very different reality within it. Israelis used to insist that Jerusalem was a united city where you could walk freely enjoying the Old City *souq*, take a sabbath stroll on the boulevards of West Jerusalem or visit the historic sites. The Palestinian *intifada*, however, has exploded this complacency. Israelis may still enjoy a European-style life in their part of the city, but they have virtually given up visiting the east. Palestinians, meanwhile, bring their part of the city to a standstill at noon every day and periodic one- and two-day general strikes, one of the main weapons in their struggle for self-determination. The Israeli soldiers lounging in the cafés of the west side of the city are probably on leave – in the east, they're on duty.

Religion and community

Jerusalem is one of the chief centres of all three great monotheistic religions, Judaism, Christianity and Islam. And nowhere has worship of the same God provoked more conflict than in this 'holy' city. To **Jews**, Jerusalem is the place where Abraham prepared to sacrifice his son Isaac; the City of David where the Ark of the Covenant resided; where the Temple stood; and where the Messiah will appear. For **Christians**, Jerusalem is where Christ preached his ministry, was crucified, buried and rose from the dead. To **Muslims**, Jerusalem is where Abraham attempted to sacrifice Ishmael, the third most holy place after Mecca and Medina, and the site of the revered al-Aqsa mosque, where the Prophet Mohammed stopped on his night flight from Mecca and from where he rose to heaven.

Nowhere is the dividing line between **theology and politics** more blurred than in Jerusalem. Religious quotations are the stock-in-trade of reactionary politicians of all three faiths. The Zionist justification for settlement in the occupied territories, for example, relies on the Old Testament promises made by God to the patriarch Abraham. Some Western Christians support these claims through their own messianic theologies. Muslims' belief in the sanctity of Jerusalem is a driving imperative behind the Palestinian and Arab desire to see the city liberated. Fundamentalists of all three creeds are more extreme still: they each have separate visions of the city as the centre of a theocracy in which there is no place for unbelievers. The Israeli Tourist Board's choice of the golden cupola of the Dome of the Rock, a holy Muslim site, to advertise the Jewish state is perhaps the greatest irony of all: the commercial worth of its overwhelming beauty for once overriding religious and political considerations.

Apart from the obvious Palestinian-Israeli division, Jerusalem contains a number of other **communities**, and a multitude of sub-divisions within the major ones. **Palestinians** are predominantly Sunni Muslim. About one tenth of them are Christians, however, belonging to Assyrian, Greek Catholic, Greek Orthodox, Coptic, Franciscan or Protestant denominations. **Israelis** may be ethnically Ashkenazi or Sephardi, orthodox or secular. Of the smaller groups, perhaps the most significant are the **Armenians**, traditionally concentrated in the Old City south of Jaffa Gate. Communities associated with the various monastic orders are also of long standing. **Ethiopian** Copts and **Greek** priests attached to the Orthodox community can easily be spotted as they go about their business. Immigrants, too, have brought with them many national characters: the names of some neighbourhoods, such as the German Colony in West Jerusalem or the American Colony in the east, betray the nationality of their early settlers, though these are now by-and-large heterogeneous. The multitude of tourists, religious pilgrims and other foreigners studying or working in the city all add their part to the confusion.

Overshadowed as they are by the central conflict, **disputes** between and within these communities are also an enduring feature of Jerusalem life. Arguments between various Christian sects over the stewardship of sites they hold sacred stretch back hundreds of years (see especially the Church of the Holy Sepulchre), and fights between orthodox and secular Jews are just as bitter. The ultra-orthodox would like to impose strict religious observation on all Jews and are willing to take to the streets to add muscle to their demands. Saturday drivers run the risk of having their cars stoned in orthodox Jewish neighbourhoods and, in recent years, more and more areas have been unilaterally declared no-go zones. They also try to stop Saturday film-shows, forcibly close restaurants and cafés and stop archaeological digs. In the mid-1980s orthodox vigilantes razed virtually every bus shelter displaying advertisements of an overtly sexual nature.

Holidays and strikes

All these religious differences leave their mark on life in the city. On Friday afternoon and Saturday, for example, Jewish **West Jerusalem** closes up completely. In **East Jerusalem**, many Muslim-owned shops are closed on Fridays and Christians generally take Sunday off. With three separate sets of religious **holidays** to take into account (not to mention the differences in calendar between eastern and western Christian churches), there's a good chance that something you don't want to miss will be closed for at least part of your stay.

Politics also leaves its mark on commercial life. Israel closes for most national holidays, and Palestinians frequently mark their national occasions and protest against the occupation with **commercial stoppages** – those will be the days when Israeli officials and tour guides will tell you 'it's a religious holiday', but won't be able to name which one. Since the *intifada* all shops and institutions in East Jerusalem close at midday and mark certain occasions – the start of the *intifada*, Land Day, Balfour Day or a particular incident such as the recent massacre at Nahalin – with total one- or two-day strikes. These are determined by an underground command, whose communiques are widely distributed and even the Israeli press has taken to publishing synopses. The sites and shops you want to visit in the Old City and East Jerusalem are now only possible to see in the morning. In the afternoon and evening, these areas become a virtual ghost town.

Jerusalem in History

Jerusalem cannot even be confident of its own name. One theory is that it derives from **Ur Shalem**, the City of Shalem, a Jebusite deity. Others claim that the name is really **Ur Shalom**, the City of Peace. But whatever else Jerusalem may be, it is hardly peaceful. Like the rest of the country, the city has suffered a series of conquests, destructions and massacres.

The site of Jerusalem has been settled since the early **Bronze Age**, circa 2600BC, but since it was never on a trade route its importance was always more strategic than commercial. Ancient Jerusalem is first mentioned in the twentieth century BC on Egyptian figurines, and among the documents discovered in the royal archives in Tel al-Armana (in Egypt) were six letters written on clay tablets and sent by the Canaanite ruler to the pharaohs of Egypt. The hill fortress of the **Canaanite Jebusites** withstood the bloody invasion of the Israelite tribes led by Joshua in 1200BC. **David**, the next important Israelite military leader, captured the city 200 years later and declared it the capital of the united kingdom of Judah. His federation of the twelve Israelite tribes broke up on the death of his son, Solomon. In 586BC, the **Babylonians** demolished the city and **Solomon's Temple**, driving the population into exile in Babylon. The citizens of Judah, now called Jews, were allowed to return from Babylon in 538BC by Jerusalem's new Persian ruler Cyrus, and to build the **Second Temple** (515BC). Throughout these conquests, the indigenous Canaanites continued to live in and around the city.

In 332BC, Jerusalem surrendered to **Alexander the Great**. He was succeeded by his general, **Ptolemy**, whose dynasty collapsed in 198BC after bitter feuds with the **Seleucids** (descendants of another of Alexander's generals). The **First Revolt** of 167BC, in protest at the increasing Hellenisation of the city and the introduction of the institutions of a civil society, was spearheaded by the Jewish priestly caste led by Judas Maccabeus.

By 63BC, Jerusalem had fallen to **Rome** and twenty years later **Herod the Great** was installed as king of Judaea. Herod adopted the Jewish faith and, around 20BC, restored the Second Temple. There followed a long period of popular opposition to Roman rule that met with harsh reprisals. **Jesus of Nazareth** was one of the many who died. In 70AD, Emperor Titus ordered Jerusalem and the Temple destroyed. A **Second Revolt** in 132AD culminated in Emperor Hadrian flattening the city completely and building **Aelia Capitolina** on its ruins.

The conversion of the Romans to **Christianity** in 313 opened a 300-year period of almost uninterrupted Christian hegemony over the city, which ended when **Caliph Omar Ibn al-Khattab** took Jerusalem without bloodshed in 638. Under the **Omayyad** Caliphs (660–750) Jerusalem flourished, and from this period important buildings survive: Al-Aqsa Mosque and the Dome of the Rock above all. During **Abbasid** rule (750–969), Jerusalem became a religious focal point for Christian and Jewish pilgrims and was home to several prominent Muslim Sufi scholars. At the beginning of the **Fatimid** period (969–1071), the first recorded complaint against the tourist trade was made by local historian, al-Muqqadasi, who wrote that Jerusalem was being overrun by pilgrims. By the time the first Muslim Period was brought to an end with the capture of the city by the **Crusaders** in 1099, Jerusalem was divided into four naturally formed residential quarters – Christian, Muslim, Armenian and Jewish. The general outlines of the Old City date from the Crusaders' 88-year rule and many of their buildings are still in use. A less appealing legacy of the Christian Kingdom of Jerusalem was its religious intolerance: Jews were burned alive and the Muslim population slaughtered or expelled. Muslims and Jews were not permitted to live in the city.

Jerusalem was restored to Muslim rule, and to a degree of religious tolerance, by the legendary **Salah al-Din al-Ayyubi** (Saladin) in 1187, who allowed Christians to remain in the city, or to leave unharmed, and Jews to return. By the end of the Ayyubid period in 1248, however, Jerusalem was of minor political importance, being part of a Syrian province whose capital was Damascus. The **Mamluks** (1248–1517) have left their mark architecturally, with beautiful buildings, including mosques, schools and hospices, throughout the Old City. Several new markets were added, the city's fountains and water supplies were repaired and construction started outside the city walls. Again, though, Jerusalem had little political importance, and when the Mamluk dynasty was succeded by the **Ottoman Turks**, the centre of power in the Middle East shifted to Europe.

Sultan Suleiman the Magnificent (1537–1541) refortified the city and built the walls you see today. He further improved the city's water system, installed the drinking fountains (*sebil*) still visible in many parts of the Old City and lent his support to religious and teaching establishments. For over three hundred relatively peaceful years, Jerusalem remained a provincial outpost of a vast empire: Christian travellers in these years described the city as a ghost town, dusty and dilapidated.

By the **nineteenth century**, the Ottoman empire had become so moribund that it could mount no serious resistance to the burgeoning economic and political strength of the northern and western European states. Under a system of 'capitulations', foreign powers investing in the city were free virtually to do as they liked. The European powers vied with each other to gain a foothold as they waited for the 'sick man of Europe' to die. New areas, with names like the Russian Compound and the German Colony, sprouted outside the city walls. Many of the educational and religious institutions which still exist today – Schmidt's Girls' School, the Alliance Francaise and St. George's Anglican Cathedral – were founded at this time.

The twentieth century
By dint of double dealing backed with military muscle, the **British** obtained control of Jerusalem, along with the rest of Palestine, when the 'sick man's' possessions were carved up after World War I. Apart from the legacy of conflict, the British left one significant and positive physical mark on the city. The first civil administrator, Ronald Storrs, declared that all new buildings in the city should be made from local stone. The expansion of the city outside the walls continued, as both Palestinian Arabs and new Jewish immigrants constructed residential quarters spreading out from the Old City.

When Britain washed its hands of the mess it had created following World War II, the **United Nations Partition Plan** of 1947 declared Jerusalem a *corpus separatum*, open to both the Jewish and Arab states. By the end of the **1948 war**, however, the city was occupied by Israeli troops in the west and the Jordanian Arab Legion in the east. Jerusalem retained its spiritual significance, but temporal power centres moved elsewhere. For Israel, despite the moving of the administration, West Jerusalem became a frontier town, and Tel Aviv and the coastal region the economic and cultural centre. The east side of the city retained its importance to Palestinians during Jordanian occupation, but administrative and financial power in the 'united kingdom of Jordan', declared in the early 1950s, was centred in Amman.

In June 1967, East Jerusalem and the Old City were **occupied** by the Israeli army. Two weeks after the end of the war, Israel unilaterally annexed East Jerusalem and declared the city the 'eternal, united capital of Israel'. Today, Jerusalem still awaits final resolution of the divisions of 1948. For all Israel's talk of 'eternity' the international community does not recognise its jurisdiction. Most western countries still maintain consulates in the east serving the occupied territories and the Palestinians see the city as the capital of their future independent state. To preempt this, Israel has expanded the municipal boundaries to the very edges of Bethlehem to the south and Ramallah to the north and ringed the Arab city with three bands of settlements. These fortress-like suburbs are physical evidence of the immense problems which need resolving before the 'city of peace' can begin to live up to its name.

ARRIVAL AND ORIENTATION

Jerusalem is a beautiful city, full of tangible history (both past and in the making), teeming, alive, frustrating and complex. Allow plenty of time for a visit: you'll need it to see the place, and because the city can be exhausting, especially in summer, which is hot and dry. Winters at Jerusalem's considerable altitude, on the other hand, are extremely cold, especially since heating is inadequate in most buildings. It may snow around January and February and it periodically buckets down with rain between November and March.

On a further practical note, bear in mind that Jerusalem is a conservative town, where 'western' norms of **dress and behaviour** can cause offence. Beachwear or revealing attire are frowned upon and if you dress 'immodestly', you can expect problems, especially in the Old City and the orthodox Jewish quarter of Mea She'arim. **Language** is also a source of contention. It's best to practise your Hebrew on Israelis and Arabic on Palestinians. If you confuse the two, Israelis are likely to be hostile and Palestinians to charge you more. If in doubt use English.

Getting your bearings

In terms of getting about, it's easiest to see Jerusalem as two small towns, East and West Jerusalem. The **east side** centres on the **Old City** and the streets around it. Virtually everything you are likely to visit on this side of town will be within easy walking distance of your hostel or hotel. In the **west**, which is most likely where you'll arrive, all roads lead to Jaffa Road. As tourist

BUS 99 AND OTHER CITY TOURS

The easiest and most comfortable way to get a sense of the layout and size of the whole of Jerusalem is to take a round trip on Egged's **Bus 99** – a particularly good idea if you're short of time. The original route covered 34 of the city's chief points of interest in two hours, but the Palestinian *intifada* has effectively prevented the bus from going to at least three areas – Damascus Gate, Salah al-Din Street and the Mount of Olives. The bus now only stops at other sites in East Jerusalem 'on the advice of the police'.

The bus starts at the Egged bus terminus (Beit Tannous) at Jaffa Gate. The first part of the trip should circle the Old City, but whether the bus indeed follows this route depends on what is happening that day. From Jaffa Gate, it goes via **New Gate** (for Notre Dame) to **Damascus Gate** (Zedekiah's Cave and Garden Tomb) before turning up **Salah al-Din** Street to the former **Mandelbaum Gate** (Turgeman House) and past **Ramot Eshkol** to **Ammunition Hill**. From here it climbs **Mount Scopus** (Hadassa Hospital, British War Cemetery) and heads on to the **Mount of Olives**, descending to **Saint Stephen's (Lion's) Gate** (Via Dolorosa) where it turns south along the city walls to **Dung Gate** (Western Wall, al-Haram al-Sharif, City of David), passes **Mount Zion** (Coenaculum, Dormition Abbey) and returns to Jaffa Gate. The second part of the route covers West Jerusalem. From **Jaffa Gate**, the bus drives up **King George Street** (Heikhal Shlomo) to the **town centre** (City Tower), and then on past the **Central Bus Station** to the **Hebrew University** on Givat Ram and the **Knesset**. Nearby are the **Israel Museum** (Shrine of the Book) and the **Monastery of the Cross**. Passing the **Holyland Hotel** (model of Jerusalem), it continues to **Mount Herzl** and **Yad Vashem** (Holocaust Museum), returning to the centre of town via the **Jerusalem Theatre**, **Van Leer Institute** and **Islamic Museum**. The last two stops are at the **Liberty Bell Garden** (Yemin Moshe, windmill) and the **YMCA** (King David Hotel, Herod Family Tomb).

Along the way the driver provides a running **commentary**, which may be in Hebrew if the majority of passengers are Israeli. When buying or booking your ticket, it's advisable to check that the commentary on your bus will be in English. A **single tour** ticket costs $2.50, a **one-day** ticket is $10 and a **two-day** ticket $12. Although the tour is designed so that you can either stay on for the whole trip or get off whenever you want and pick up the next bus, you are advised not to break the journey because buses are usually full and you may end up waiting hours for the next one or catching a taxi back. You're better off using the tour as a way of identifying the particular sites to be visited later – to which you can either walk or take a city bus or taxi. The circular line runs Sun–Thur 9am–5pm, Fri and eve of holidays 9am–2pm, leaving once an hour, on the hour. Tickets can be bought on the bus, but it's worth reserving in advance as buses can get full and there are better ways to spend an hour than waiting in the unshaded bus terminus. It is also advisable to take something to drink (and eat) if you don't intend stopping en route.

For **information and reservations** call in at the Reservations Centre, 11a HaMeasef Street (☎02-531286), *Egged Tours*, 44a Jaffa Road (☎02-224198, 223454), the *Egged Central Bus Station*, 224 Jaffa Road (☎02-534596, 551868) or the *Egged Jaffa Gate Terminal* (☎02-247783, 248144). Other organised tours of Jerusalem are legion. There are **walking tours** run by the *Society for the Protection of Nature in Israel* (SPNI), 13 Heleni HaMalka Sreet (☎02-222357), **biblical tours** accompanied by mules (*Arod Tours*, 12 Yoel Salomon St; ☎02-233822), walks around the **Old City ramparts** (*IGTO* or ☎02-224403/4), **bicycle tours** (☎02-816062) and many others. Details can be found in the free magazines *Your Jerusalem* and *This Week in Jerusalem* available in hotels, travel agencies and tourist offices.

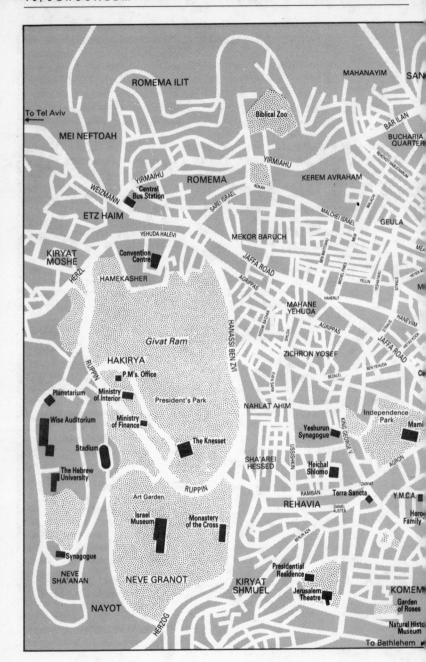

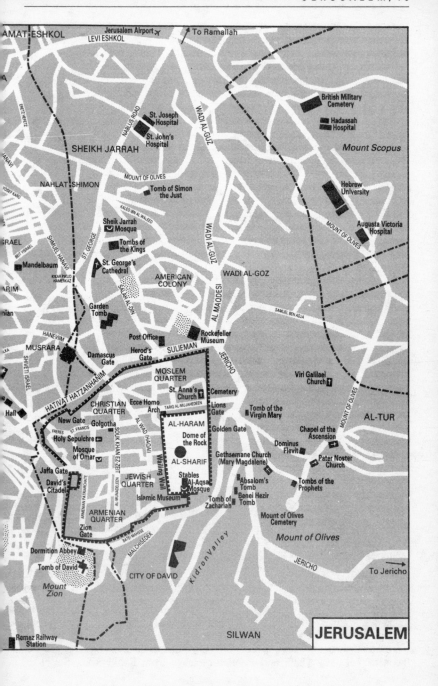

AMAT-ESHKOL

Jerusalem Airport ✈ → To Ramallah

LEVI ESHKOL

British Military Cemetery

St. Joseph Hospital

St. John's Hospital

■ Hadassah Hospital

SHEIKH JARRAH

Mount Scopus

NAHLAT SHIMON

MOUNT OF OLIVES

Tomb of Simon the Just

Hebrew University

KALED BIN AL WALEED

Sheik Jarrah Mosque

WADI AL-GUZ

MOUNT OF OLIVES

Augusta Victoria Hospital

Tombs of the Kings

St. George's Cathedral

AMERICAN COLONY

WADI AL-GOZ

Mandelbaum

KIKAR PIKUD HAMERKAZ

SALAH AL-DIN

Samuel Ben Adja

Garden Tomb

AL MADDESI

ISRAEL

HANEVIIM

Post Office

Rockefeller Museum

MUSRARA

Herod's Gate

SULIEMAN

JERICHO

Viri Galilaei Church ✝

Damascus Gate

MOSLEM QUARTER

MOUNT OF OLIVES

AL-TUR

HATIVAT HATZANHANIM

St. Anna's Church ✝

Cemetery

Hall

CHRISTIAN QUARTER

Ecce Homo Arch

TARIQ AL-MUJAHEDEN

Lions Gate

Tomb of the Virgin Mary

Chapel of the Ascension

New Gate

Golgotha

AL-HARAM

Dome of the Rock

Golden Gate

Dominus Flevit

FRERES ST. FRANCIS

Holy Sepulchre

SOUK KHAN EZ-ZEIT

AL WAD (HAOAJ)

Pater Noster Church

Mosque of Omar

AL-SHARIF

Gethsemane Church (Mary Magdalene)

Jaffa Gate

Walling Wall

JEWISH QUARTER

David's Citadel

ARMENIAN PATRIARCHATE

AL-MUGHRABI

Stables Al-Aqsa Mosque

Absalom's Tomb

Tombs of the Prophets

ARMENIAN QUARTER

Islamic Museum

Tomb of Zachariah

Benei Hezir Tomb

Zion Gate

BATU MANISE

MALCHISEDEK

Mount of Olives Cemetery

Dormition Abbey

Mount of Olives

Tomb of David

Kidron Valley

JERICHO

CITY OF DAVID

→ To Jericho

Mount Zion

Remez Railway Station

SILWAN

JERUSALEM

NABLUS ROAD

WADI AL-GUZ

attractions tend to be widely scattered in the suburbs, however, you'll need to get to know the public transport system here.

The **Old City** must be the focus of any visit to Jerusalem. Within its walls lives a bustling community which you should spend time getting to know. Stroll about and experiment. There's something interesting around most corners and although initially it may look like a maze, you'll always find your way back to a main thoroughfare or find someone who will be willing to help you. You'll definitely want to see the great monuments of the three religions: the **Haram compound**, the **Church of the Holy Sepulchre** and the **Wailing Wall**. Between them, you can't help but pass through the real Jerusalem of vaulted markets, cafés and sweet shops, craft workshops and small stores.

Beyond the walls, the modern commercial centre of **East Jerusalem** fans out (northwards) from Damascus Gate along Nablus Road and Salah al-Din Street. Money changers, bookshops, travel agents, restaurants and hotels are situated here. East of the Old City lies the **Mount of Olives**, south the **City of David**.

To the west, you can walk from the main post office on Jaffa Road into downtown **West Jerusalem**. Here you'll find shops, swish European-style cafés, the main airline offices, banks, the visa office, cinemas and what little nightlife there is in the city, centred around the pedestrian precinct at Ben Yehuda. From Jaffa Road or King George Street buses run to sites like Mount Herzl, the Israel Museum and Yad Vashem.

There are two main **Israel Government Tourist Offices** (IGTOs) in Jerusalem where you can get free city maps and information on events and accommodation: these are at 24 King George Street (☎02-241281) and just inside Jaffa Gate (☎02-282295/6). The **Christian Information Centre** at Jaffa Gate (PO Box 14308; ☎02-287647) has information on city bus lines, opening hours of Christian and other places of interest in Jerusalem, a list of Christian guest houses and hostels and a varied bookshop.

Points of Arrival

If you are entering the city **by bus** directly from **Ben Gurion airport** or from any other part of pre-1967 Israel, you will arrive at the **Egged Bus Station** in Jaffa Road at the northern entrance to West Jerusalem. There are several buses a day between most Israeli towns and Jerusalem. All *Egged* buses stop early on Friday afternoon and resume on Saturday after sunset or on Sunday morning. To get from the bus station to the centre (south-east along Jaffa Road) or to the Old City, cross the main road by the underpass and take bus #13 or #20 to the centre and Jaffa Gate; #23 or #27 to Damascus Gate. For other routes, see the box below: a bus map is available at *Egged* offices.

Sherut taxis are quicker than buses and run every day, though they're considerably more expensive and charge extra on the sabbath. The intercity *sheruts* from the airport and Israeli towns terminate in the centre of West Jerusalem, in Rabbi Kook Street (off Jaffa Road, near Zion Square). *Sherut* taxis to Tel Aviv, Haifa and Beersheva leave from Rabbi Kook Street or

MAIN BUS ROUTES IN JERUSALEM

From Egged bus station (West Jerusalem):

To Damascus Gate: #23 & #27.

To Jaffa Gate via Jaffa Road and Zion Square: #13 & #20.

To King George Street: #8, #9 & #31.

To Israel Museum: #21.

To Mount Scopus: #9, #28 & #23.

To Railway Station: #6, #7, #8 & #30.

To Islamic Museum: #15.

To Yad Vashem/Mount Herzl: #13, #18 & #20.

From Damascus Gate Station (East Jerusalem):

To Jaffa Gate: #21, #22 & #23.

To Railway Station: #21 & #22.

To Mount of Olives: #75.

To Bethlehem: #22.

To Hebron: #23.

To Jericho: #28.

From Nablus Road (East Jerusalem):

To Ramallah: #18.

To Mount Scopus: #82.

To Sheikh Jarrah: #71.

Shamai Street, also near Zion Square. For a *sherut* to Ben Gurion airport, contact *Nesher Taxis* (see "Listings"). These will pick you up from wherever you are staying.

Entering West Jerusalem these taxis all follow the bus route and will let you off at any point along the way: they may agree to take you direct to your destination as a 'private' passenger, but will charge you extra. To avoid unpleasant hassles do your bargaining before starting out. For a **private taxi** ride drivers should, by law, operate the meter but many take strong exception to being asked. Tourists are officially advised to report any complaints to the police or the IGTO; drivers' licence numbers are displayed inside the cab. Israeli taxi drivers have a reputation for chauvinism even more extreme than most: remember this if you are a woman or if your destination is Arab East Jerusalem.

If you enter the city from the West Bank or from the Gaza Strip on an **Arab bus** (daily services), you will arrive in East Jerusalem at either the Damascus Road or Nablus Road bus stations, both very near the Damascus Gate and Herod's Gate entrances to the Old City. *Service* taxis coming from and going to the occupied territories (for Bethlehem, Hebron, Jericho, Ramallah, Nablus and Gaza) use the **Musrara taxi station** in Prophets Street just opposite Damascus Gate. Private taxis are available at the taxi stands beside both Damascus and Herod's Gate and, as with Israeli taxis, make sure either that the meter is turned on or establish how much the fare will be before you get in. For taxis to the **Allenby Bridge**, contact the *Abdo* office near Damascus Gate (see "Listings").

Jerusalem's local **airport** (*Atarot*) is on the road to Ramallah at Kalandiya. It handles only expensive internal flights daily to most main Israeli centres – and since other forms of transport are so cheap and efficient, it's only worth considering a flight if you want to get to Eilat in a hurry.

Trains are a more promising option. From the **Kikar Remez railway station** (☎02-717764; buses #5, #6, #7, #8, #21, or #30), a single daily train heads down to (and up from) Tel Aviv and Haifa. The journey is slow but much more picturesque and relaxed than going by bus or taxi, leaving Jerusalem at 4pm to arrive in Tel Aviv (Bnei Brak) at 6.03pm (via Beit Shemesh, Ramla and Lod). It continues via Netanya and Hadera, reaching Haifa Central at 7.31pm. On Fridays and eve of holidays, departure from Jerusalem is at 11.30am. A one-way ticket to Tel Aviv costs $3 ($2 for students); to Haifa, $5.50 ($4.50 students).

Accommodation

There are plenty of budget **hotels and hostels** in Jerusalem, but the city is chock-a-block with visitors particularly around Christmas, Easter and the other big religious holidays. Since the *intifada* occupancy has dropped off – though you still have to compete with foreign journalists and TV crews! – but it's still best to book in advance at peak times. If you can't find accommodation in the city, you can always stay at Ramallah or Ein Karem. There's a school of thought that considers these places pleasanter anyway, particularly during the heat of summer.

Unless you are a particularly good sleeper, have a very strong constitution or are very broke, it may be worth spending a bit extra for a good bed in pleasant surroundings. The noise and bustle of the city, the summer heat and so much to see can be exhausting. Many places have interior courtyards or gardens, ideal for retreating from the world outside, and those housed in old Arab buildings are generally cool and airy, the high vaulted architecture purpose-built. Even in the heart of the Old City there are oases of calm.

The best of the **cheaper accommodation** is almost all Palestinian-owned. Since the Israelis have not allowed Palestinians to build or complete hotels since occupation, all of these are at least twenty years old. There's no government tourist office to advise on accommodation in East Jerusalem, but if you have problems, commercial tourist offices can help. What follows is just a selection of the better hostels and hotels.

The **Christian Information Centre**, Omar Ibn al-Khattab Square, Jaffa Gate (☎02-287647) has a list of specifically Christian accommodation in Jerusalem and other centres: of the 25 listed for Jerusalem, around half are in the Old City or nearby. Most are impeccably clean and quiet, and there's usually a curfew which, although sometimes inconvenient, means that you can be assured of a good night's sleep. As well as separate rooms, some offer dormitory accommodation which may be for women only.

The Old City

In terms of atmosphere and proximity to the sights, the Old City is certainly the place to stay, and it's here that you'll find many of the more comfortable, old-fashioned possibilities. Thanks to the labyrinthine streets and inadequate street lighting, parts of the Old City can be unnerving after dark, so learn your way home before you start to explore too far.

Near Jaffa Gate

Lutheran Hostel (☎02-282120). Ideally placed in St. Mark's Road near Jaffa Gate, smack in the centre of the Old City but away from the busy *souq* area, this is arguably the best place to stay of all, with a beautiful courtyard garden. A dormitory bed costs just over $5 per person (20 beds for men, 40 for women) in an underground vaulted cellar, kitchen facilities and hot water. Breakfast is around $5. It closes at 10.45pm and during the day between 9am and noon. There is also a guest house charging $27 B&B per head or $35 full-board. It is popular throughout the year so book in advance.

Christ Church Hostel (☎02-282082). Another restful hostel, built around a courtyard attached to the oldest Anglican church in the Middle East, in Omar Ibn al-Khattab Square opposite David's Citadel. Two rooms for women, two for men, six per room; four-bed dormitory accommodation. $8 per person with 'English' breakfast. Dormitory closes 10am–4pm, main gate shuts at 11pm. No kitchen facilities. Accommodation is also available in the *Christ Church hospice* – 26 private rooms with toilets and showers for $23 per head B&B in a double room. Very peaceful, cloistered, respectable atmosphere.

New Imperial Hotel (☎02-282261). A huge hotel right by Jaffa Gate, built in 1883 and now owned by the Orthodox Patriarchate. The sixty rooms with shower, bath and hot water, have clearly seen better days, but they're clean if shabby. High season $12 per person, $40 for room for four B&B, $10 low season. Kitchen and huge, cool, high-ceilinged dining room, clearly too big to maintain.

Petra Hotel, David Street (☎02-282356). Once one of the most popular locations in the Old City though its fortunes are now somewhat in decline. Charges should be around $4 per person, but you can bargain. The roof-top rooms are the best, with a great view of the Old City.

Jaffa Gate Hostel. Beside the Christian Information Centre, the Jaffa Gate Hostel has dormitories for 2–6 people at around $6 per head; private rooms for 2–3 people cost $10. Breakfast is an extra $1. Hot water, kitchen facilities, outside showers and two sitting rooms are included, along with a midnight curfew, but the place is pretty pokey and basic and the dorms have no windows. Sleeping on the roof, for around $2.50, is the best deal.

New Swedish Hostel, 29 David Street (☎02-854980). Used to have a bad reputation (as the *Swedish Hostel*) for harassment of women, but should be better under new management. $3.50 per person, students 10 per cent discount. If you stay for seven nights and pay in advance, you get the seventh night free. Free tea and coffee, clean sheets. Bunk beds, 18 to a room or 12 to a room upstairs with mattresses on the floor for women only. Friendly atmosphere.

Mr A's, 27 Girges Street (☎02-283982). Peaceful, quiet and good value (a bed for just over $2, a mattress just under), offers kitchen facilities, showers, laundry and a small inner courtyard, all just off Greek Patriarchate Road. Closes 9am–1pm. Curfew 10pm.

Joc Inn Youth Hostel, 21 Aqabat al-Khanka (☎02-282865). A homely atmosphere in the Christian Quarter of the Old City, with clean sheets, hot water and breakfast on request. It has the dubious advantage of being on the same premises as the *Joc Inn Tearoom* which blasts constant pop/rock music and is popular with roving kibbutz volunteers and local (male) talent on the lookout for some excitement.

Old City Youth Hostel, 1 Ararat Street (☎02-288611, follow the signs from St. Mark's Road). This Israeli YHA hostel is housed in a beautiful restored Arab building and is invariably crowded with schoolkids and soldiers. Beds are $4.50 per person, breakfast $3, dinner $4.80. Check in 5–8pm; Check out 7–9am. Hostel closes 9am–5pm.

Near Damascus Gate

Funduk al-Arab (☎02-283537). A Palestinian run youth hostel, right in the middle of the *souq* on Khan al-Zeit, with great views. A dormitory bed here costs $3 for students, $3.50 non-students; double room $6 for students, $6.50 non-students. Free coffee, tea and kitchen facilities, three showers and three bathrooms. Curfew midnight, but open all night if you ring.

New Hashemi Hostel, 73 Khan al-Zeit (☎02-284410). A few doors down from the latter, newer and brighter but a little more expensive at $7 per person without breakfast. Rooms with 2, 3 or 4 beds have private bathrooms.

Al-Ahram Youth Hostel, Al-Wad Road (☎02-280926). By the 3rd Station of the Cross on the Via Dolorosa . A 'private' room with 2 or 3 beds costs $15 per room. Sharing in a room for 5 is $4 per person, sleeping on the covered roof $3. With a small kitchen and cosy sitting room, the place has a good communal feel. Curfew 11pm in winter, midnight in summer.

East Jerusalem

East Jerusalem, within walking distance of the Old City gates, offers almost as much atmosphere and more in the way of amenities, as well as being extremely good value. Note, however, that like the Old City, it closes down at midday and completely on strike days during the *intifada*.

Near Damascus Gate

Faisal Hotel, 4 Prophets Street (☎02-282189). Good views of the Old City walls, Damascus Gate and Dome of the Rock, but only if you can stand blaring music and early morning traffic noise. $4 per person in dormitory rooms, $10 in double rooms, without breakfast: kitchen facilities, hot water and balcony. Curfew midnight.

Palm Hotel, 6 Prophets Street (no telephone). Run by Christian 'believers'. Single-sex rooms with 2–6 beds cost $4 per head; $3.50 for a mattress on the floor. Private rooms for married couples $12. Rooms with 6 beds are a bit cramped; one sheet per bed is provided but an additional sheet costs extra. Hot water showers, kitchen, sitting room, pretty lounge with glass roof and lots of plants. Curfew midnight, check out 10am. Residents must leave the hostel between 10am and 1pm.

New Raghadan Hostel, 10 Prophets Street (☎02-282725; opposite the service station). A throwback to hippy days with a ramshackle sitting room and rather dismal 'dining room'. Often difficult to find anyone at reception. Rooms with 2 and 3 beds cost $4 per head, double rooms $10, trebles $12, all without breakfast. Most have a private bath and toilet and are pretty basic. Sheets and hot showers are available, as are facilities for cooking and leaving baggage. Five new rooms on the roof, with maybe a restaurant/ snack bar, are planned. Curfew 11pm.

Ramsis Youth Hostel, 20 Prophets Street (☎02-284818). Clean and friendly, though the rooms are rather cramped. $4 per person in a six-bed room, $5 in room with three beds, $6 in room with two: kitchen, dining and sitting room, and facilities for washing and drying clothes.

Jerusalem Hotel, 4 Antara Ben Shaddad Street (☎02-283282). Just off Nablus Road near the bus station and opposite the Garden Tomb: old and a bit run down, but the rooms are clean and spacious. $10 per person, $12 with breakfast, with possible reductions for students. Showers and toilets in modern rooms of 2, 3 or 4 beds. The garden is great for summertime breakfast, the large dining room downstairs good for winter.

YMCA (Aelia Capitolina), 29 Nablus Road (☎02-282375). Expensive at $25 single B&B, $42 double, but cool and airy, and the modern 'oriental' lounge, with its brass coffee tables and sofas, is a good place to rest. The snack bar offers tea, coffee, soft drinks, sandwiches etc at around $1 for members, $1.50 for non-members.

YWCA Wadi Joz (☎02-282593). Not quite as splendid and a bit more out of the way, but equally comfortable and provides secure surroundings for women. $24 single, $36 double, B&B.

St. George's Cathedral Hostel (Anglican), 20 Nablus Road (☎02-283302). Built in cloister style around an attractive garden, the hostel has many rooms with private bathrooms from $17 per person B&B, $22 half-board. It has a calm, 'family' atmosphere and is about 10 minutes' walk from Damascus or Herod's Gates.

American Colony Hotel, 1 Louis Vincent Street, off Nablus Road (☎02-282421/2/3). The most beautiful hotel in Jerusalem. It's expensive, but the buffet breakfast is generous enough to stuff yourself for the rest of the day. If you can't afford to stay, you can still visit the inner garden (open until midnight for light meals and drinks), have a meal in the poolside restaurant (10am–midnight) or spend an evening in the cellar bar (open till 1am). The swimming pool is free to guests, but costs about $15 per day for visitors.

New Regent Hotel, Zahra Street (☎02-282700). All rooms in this newly redecorated hotel have private toilets and showers, but avoid those that face onto the stuffy inner court-yard: plain breakfast served in panoramic rooftop dining room/lounge. From $16 B&B single in low season to $28 in high season.

Holyland Hotel (east), Haroun al-Rashid Street (☎02-284841). Large, comfortable hotel with spacious rooms, each with private bathroom. Generous buffet breakfast and a bar. From $26 B&B low season to $40 high.

Salah al-Din Street

There are several hotels in the commercial heart of East Jerusalem on Salah al-Din Street, all of which are adequate if rather dull.

Rivoli Hotel (☎02-284281). $20 B&B single, $32 double.

Metropole Hotel (☎02-282507). $15 single, $20 double.

Capitol Hotel (☎02-282561/2). Rather more luxurious, with a pretty flower garden and cocktail lounge, carpeted rooms. $25 B&B single, $34 double.

Mount of Olives

Mount of Olives Hotel (☎02-284877/8). A rather splendid place at the top of the Mount of Olives next to the Chapel of Ascension, 15 minutes' walk through the Garden of Gethsemane to the Old City. Clean and spacious. $15 per head B&B, $22 half-board and $27 full-board.

West Jerusalem

West Jerusalem has comparatively little inexpensive accommodation, and what there is can't touch the east side for atmosphere. The Israelis, however, have cornered the market in modern, middle-to-top quality hotels, and you may also find rather more life in the evenings. If you can afford, and want, fitted carpets, 'international cuisine' (and Kosher food) stay here. The IGTO can give you a full list of one- to five-star hotels or can arrange for you to stay in an Israeli home. The following is a selection of the smaller hotels and hostels.

Hotel Zefania, 4 Zefania Street (☎02-286384/272709). Singles $12–15, $6 per person in room of four. No breakfast, but kitchen facilities available.

Geffen Hotel, 4 HaHavatselet Street (☎02-224075/225754). $15 single, $40 room for four. Kitchen facilities, no breakfast.

Hotel Nogah, 4 Bezalel Street (☎02-661888). Singles $12, doubles $16.

Ron Hotel, 42a Jaffa Road (☎02-223471/246377). Singles $28, doubles $34; possibly cheaper in winter. Comfortably boring (newly furnished with private bathrooms) but central to West Jerusalem and within walking distance of the Old City.

YMCA (pronounced 'imca' in Hebrew), King David Street (☎02-227111). Splendid but distinctly upmarket hotel with a terrific view from its landmark tower.

Bernstein Youth Hostel, 1 Karen HaYessod Street (☎02-228286). The official IYHA youth hostel, a bit of a way out and 11pm curfew. Members $8, non-members $9; breakfast and other meals available.

Outside Jerusalem

If you'd rather stay outside the city confines, the following are a couple of easily accessible possibilities. For accommodation in Ramallah, see the *West Bank* chapter.

Ramat Rahel Kibbutz (bus 7 from Jaffa Gate). Elegant hotel/guest house ($23 up) with fancy coffee bar (around $3 per cup!), lounge etc. Often busy because it's used as a conference centre.

Ein Karem Youth Hostel, Ein Karem (☎02-416282; bus #17 from Jaffa Road bus station). Cool and quiet, away from the bustle of Jerusalem, but the walk up the hill from the Virgin's Spring is steep, and can feel even more so with a heavy rucksack. $11 per person B&B, YHA members $9.50; 10–12 beds per room and some bungalows for three.

THE OLD CITY

The walled **Old City** is in every sense the heart of Jerusalem. The religious and historical sites bring in the tourists; the alleys and busy markets with cafés, restaurants and sweetshops on every corner, deserve equal time. Above all, though, it is the people who give the place its unique atmosphere. If you can shrug off the semi-professional tourist hustlers, ordinary Palestinians are open, friendly and helpful.

The **religious monuments** are well known. Less obvious is the fact that the Old City is one of the best-preserved medieval **Islamic** towns in the world. Its present shape dates mainly from the time of Salah al-Din (1187AD) who recaptured the city from the Crusaders and initiated a building programme that was continued and expanded by the Mamluk sultans (1248–1517AD). During this period mosques, Quranic schools (*madrasa*), Sufi hostels (*khanqa*), living quarters for holy men (*zawiya*), orphanages (*makatib aytam*), hospitals, drinking fountains (*sebil*) and pilgrims' hostels (*ribat*) were built.

The Old City was under Jordanian rule from 1948 until the June war of 1967 when it was taken by the Israelis and annexed to 'united' Jerusalem. In look and feel it remains distinctly Palestinian, but it holds within its walls two realities, two visions of the future. The walled complex of **al-Haram al-Sharif** (The Noble Sanctuary) and the busy streets around it are the focus of the Palestinian presence and aspirations. For Jews, this complex is called the **Temple Mount**, and the **Wailing Wall**, which adjoins it, is a centre of prayer and pilgrimage.

Exploring

On most maps, the Old City is divided into the **four traditional quarters** and *al-Haram*. The Muslim quarter lies in the northeast section, the Christian quarter in the northwest, the Armenian quarter in the southwest and the Jewish quarter in the southeast. *Al-Haram al-Sharif*, with its collonades and gardens, occupies a vast area – 140,900 square metres, or almost one-fifth of the Old City – between the Muslim and Jewish quarters, its eastern wall overlooking the Kidron Valley opposite the Mount of Olives. The division into quarters seems to have developed around a thousand years ago, but it was never a rigid system: members of all faiths and communities lived alongside each other throughout the city. After the 1967 conquest, however, the Israelis expelled all non-Jews from the Jewish Quarter on the grounds that it was 'Jewish'. Since the 1970s, Jewish settlers have been forcibly occupying parts of the other quarters too.

An excellent way of getting an **overview** of the Old City before plunging into its maze is to walk around on top of the magnificent crenellated **walls** (9am–5pm, Fri and eve of holidays 9am–3pm). Built by Sultan Suleiman the Magnificent between 1537 and 1540, these run for four kilometres around the city and are broken by seven gates. The best starting point for the walk is Jaffa Gate, from where you can follow the ramparts northward to New Gate, turn east past Damascus Gate and Herod's Gate and then south to St. Stephen's or Lion's Gate. Alternatively you can begin from Damascus Gate, or head south from Jaffa Gate to Zion Gate and from there eastward almost as far as Dung Gate.

Of the seven **gates**, Jaffa – the main entrance from West Jerusalem – and Damascus – from the East – are the busiest. Dung Gate and St. Stephen's Gate give best access to the Wailing Wall and the Via Dolorosa respectively. The other three offer the best opportunity to get lost, if such is your wont.

Jaffa Gate or Bab al-Khalil

The main western entrance to the Old City, **Bab al-Khalil** is very much a tourist gate. Appropriately, perhaps, the actual portals were destroyed in the late nineteenth century to give free access to the touring German kaiser and his entourage: this is still one of the few ways to drive into the Old City. The shops around the gate are purely for tourists, and the hustlers eagerly await the chance to relieve you of your money and/or peace of mind.

Once through the gates, **Omar Ibn al-Khattab Square** opens up. The large Israeli police and border guard station on the right (the *Ishleh*) sets off its atmosphere perfectly. Opposite is a seedy late-night "pizza" bakery, haunt

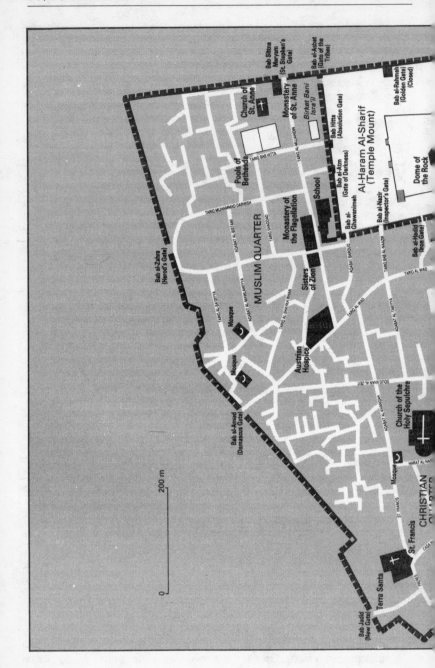

Bab Sitna Maryam (St. Stephen's Gate)
Bab el-Asbot (Gate of the Tribes)
Bab al-Rahmeh (Golden Gate) (Closed)
Church of St. Anne
Monastery of St. Anne
Birket Bani Isra'il
Bab Hitta (Absolution Gate)
Al-Haram Al-Sharif (Temple Mount)
Pools of Bethesda
TARIQ BAB HITTA
Bab al-Atm (Gate of Darkness)
Dome of the Rock
TARIQ MUHAMMAD DARWISH
School
Bab al-Nazir (Inspector's Gate)
Monastery of the Flagellation
Bab al-Ghawanimeh
Bab el-Zahra (Herod's Gate)
ADABAT AL-BISTAMI
TARIQ SHA'DAD
ADABAT AL-MAWLAWIYYA
MUSLIM QUARTER
Sisters of Zion
TARIQ AL-SA'DIYYA
TARIQ AL-SHAYKH RIHAN
ADABAT BARDUQ
TARIQ BAB AL-NAZIR
Bab al-Hadid (Iron Gate)
Mosque
TARIQ AL-WAD
TARIQ AL-WAD
ADABAT AL-TAKIYYA
Austrian Hospice
Mosque
200 m
SOUQ KHAN AL-ZEIT
Bab al-Amud (Damascus Gate)
ADABAT AL-KHANQA
Church of the Holy Sepulchre
0
ST. FRANCIS
HARAT AL-NASARA
Mosque
Terra Santa
St. Francis
CASA N...
FRERES
CHRISTIAN QUARTER
Bab Jadid (New Gate)

THE OLD CITY

Single Gate (Closed)

Archaeological excavations

Mount Moriah

Al-Aqsa Mosque

•al-Kas

the Chain

Triple Gate (Closed)

Double Gate (Closed)

Bab al-Silsileh

Bab al-Sikineh (Chain Gate)

Western Wall

Islamic Museum

Bab al-Magharibeh (Morrocans' Gate)

Archaeological excavations

Bab Harat al-Magharbah (Dung Gate)

Bab al-Mathara (Gate of the Ablutions Place)

SOUL A...

DARAF AL-AYN

ABU MADYAN

Crusader Church

ADABAT AL-KHALONIYA

TARIQ BAB AL-SILSILEH

AQABAT MADYAN

(MISGAV LADACH)

Yad Ben Zvi

JEWISH QUARTER

Four Sephardic Synagogues

BATID MIDAN

Yeshivat Hakotel

Archaeological excavations

TARIQ AL ...

SOUK AL KHAWAJAT

SOUQ AL-ATTARIN

SOUQ AL-LAHHAMIN

SOUK AL-HUSUR

HAARAT AL-YAHUD (JEWISH QUARTER RD.)

TARIQ BAB AL-NABI DA'UD (IHARAD ST.)

Redeemer

Mauristan

Church of St. John the Baptist

KNUTT DAUD (DAVID ST.)

ST. MARK

Assyrian Convent

The Cardo

ARMENIAN QUARTER

ARARAT RD

ST. JAMES

Armenian Convent & St. James Church

Armenian Seminary

of Omar

Pool

(CHRISTIAN QUARTER RD.)

Citadel

OMAR IBN AL-KHATTAB SQUARE

Police Station al-Qishleh

Armenian Garden

TARIQ HARAT AL-ARMAN (ARMENIAN PATRIARCHATE RD.)

Bab Nabi Da'ud (Zion Gate)

IGTO

LATIN PATRIARCHATE

Bab al-Khalil (Jaffa Gate)

Seminary

of off-duty Israeli patrols and other shady characters. Directly inside the gate, on the left, is the **IGTO** (☎02-282295/6) where you can get information, leaflets and maps, and diagonally across the square is the **Christian Information Centre** (CIC) (☎02-287647; Mon–Fri 8.30am–12.30pm and 3–6pm, Sat 8.30am,–12.30pm). Next door to the CIC are the Anglican Hospice (see "Accommodation") and **Christ Church**. The church was built in 1842 under the supervision of the first Anglican bishop of Jerusalem, Michael Solomon Alexander, a rabbi who converted to Christianity. The cool, airy church reflects this Jewish influence, with a wooden screen inscribed with the Lord's Prayer in Hebrew as a centrepiece.

Leaving the gate behind, the main Tariq Suweiqet Alloun (now called **Khutt Da'ud, David's Street**) runs east through the main market area and into Tariq Bab al-Silsileh (Chain Gate Street) which continues in turn to the al-Haram compound. First, however, on the right just inside Jaffa Gate, is one of the city's best known sites, the Citadel or Tower of David.

The Citadel

Beautifully excavated, with all the periods of its development clearly marked, the **Citadel** or **Tower of David** (☎02-283273/283394) is well worth taking time to explore (Sept–May Sat–Thur 10am–5pm, June–Aug 10am–7pm, Fri 10am–2pm; admission $5). Despite the name, its distinctive tower is actually the minaret of a mosque built in the Ottoman period and has no connection whatever with King David.

The **site** is undeniably historic, though, a strategic position on the western hill of the Old City which has been fortified by every ruler of Jerusalem since the second century BC. Herod the Great strengthened the old Hasmonean walls by adding three new towers, and the historian Josephus tells us there was an adjoining **palace** 'baffling all description', remains of which have been excavated in the Armenian garden to the south. This palace was the Jerusalem residence of the Roman Procurator (whose HQ was in Caesarea) until it was burned down in the Jewish Revolt of 66AD. When Titus razed the city in 70AD, only one of Herod's three towers – *Phasael* – remained standing. During the Byzantine period (second to fourth century) this Herodian tower acquired the name **David's Tower**.

Under Muslim and Crusader rule the citadel was gradually built up, but it acquired the basis of its present shape in 1310 during the rule of the Mamluk Sultan Malik al-Nasir. Suleiman the Magnificent later constructed a square with a monumental gateway in the east. The **minaret**, a prominent Jerusalem landmark, was added around 1635–55.

Allow yourself a good couple of hours to wander around and see all the remains – including a **wall** from the Hasmonean period, a **Roman cistern**, the ramparts of the **Omayyad citadel** which held out against the Crusaders in 1099, the base of a large round tower and Crusader pillars. A pamphlet clearly outlining a **guided walk** around the Citadel is obtainable from the ticket office outside or from the bookshop inside. From the tower in the southeast corner there are good views over the excavations inside and the Old City outside, as well as into the distance south and west.

A recent addition to the Citadel is the **Museum of the History of Jerusalem** which combines the physical setting of the building with archaeological remains and findings from the site. Particular historical periods are represented in eleven separate arched chambers, using a variety of means such as reproductions, models, dioramas, holograms, computerised graphics and animated video film. A 14-minute introductory film describes the history of Jerusalem from the point of view of a Jerusalem stone; the tour starts from the Canaanite period, through the First and Second Temple periods, to the late Roman and Byzantine period, to the Arab, Crusader and Ayyubid period, the Mamluk and Early Ottoman periods, the Mandate and 'Divided City', ending in the 'reunification' of Jerusalem in 1967.

There are three main tours on offer: an **exhibit** tour of the museum, an **archaeological** tour of the remains uncovered on the site, and a **panoramic** tour with views of the Old and New cities from the Citadel towers. There is also a special tour for visitors with limited time. Portable tape-recorders and cassette guides in English are available for rent at the entrance.

A **Sound and Light Show** (Sat–Thur 8.30pm, summertime 9.30pm; $5; a combination ticket for the museum and the show costs $7.50) tells some of the Citadel's history. Alternatively, a half-hour multi-screen film – *Shalom Jerusalem* is shown in the basement by the western gate. The first 25 minutes of the film runs through the history of Jerusalem from the time of David, emphasising the city's Judaeo-Christian heritage: the last five minutes show how Israel is 'developing' the city by building settlements (in English Sun–Fri at 8.30am, 10.30am, noon, 12.30pm, 2.30pm, 4pm, 6pm and 6.30pm. Last show Fri and eve of holidays 12.30pm).

The Armenian Quarter

Armenian Orthodox Patriarchate Road, to the right as you leave Omar Ibn al-Khattab Square, leads into the **Armenian Quarter** – a city in miniature. There have been Armenians in Jerusalem since before the Byzantine period, and as early as the seventh century there were seventy Armenian monasteries in Palestine. Today's 4000-strong community maintains a separate language, alphabet and culture and is the heart of the Armenian diaspora.

Armenia, situated in what today is eastern Turkey and southwestern USSR, was the first state to accept Christianity as its religion in 301AD. It lost its sovereignty in 1375 when the Kingdom of Lesser Armenia (Cilicia) fell to the Mamluks of Egypt, later coming under the rule of the Seljuk Turks and eventually succumbing to the Oghuz (Osmanli) Turks who moved into Asia Minor from Central Asia. Today the **Armenian Soviet Socialist Republic** gives a semblance of linguistic, cultural and economic autonomy to its inhabitants, but territorially Soviet Armenia covers only ten per cent of the historic kingdom. There are Armenian ethnic enclaves above all inside the Azerbaijan Soviet Socialist Republic, especially in the mountainous area of Karabagh. Their struggles for union with the rest of Armenia have in recent years made world news.

In Turkey, Armenian culture and political aspirations were actively suppressed. As the Ottoman Empire crumbled, the Armenians became pawns in the Europe-wide power struggles and were victims of several massacres as the Turks attempted to maintain their grip at the end of the nineteenth century. Hundreds of thousands were killed or exiled. During World War I, Turkish policy escalated from pogroms to genocide. Using the pretext that they constituted a fifth column, Armenians in the Ottoman army were disarmed and imprisoned. In 1915, prominent intellectuals and national leaders were rounded up and the entire population forced into concentration camps and systematically murdered. Before 1914, there were two million ethnic Armenians living in Turkey. After the war, the figure was barely 100,000. (With perhaps half a million refugees.)

The Armenian Compound

As you enter the quarter, a high wall on the right encloses the **Armenian garden**, in the grounds of which is the **Armenian seminary**. The road narrows into a short tunnel, at the end of which is a door leading into the **Armenian Compound or Convent** (*Deir al-Arman*), home to some 1000 Armenians. Within its confines you'll find St. James Cathedral, the Armenian Library and Museum, the Armenian school and the Convent of the Olive Tree.

Saint James Cathedral, dedicated to Jesus' brother (the first Bishop of Jerusalem), is one of the most attractive churches in Jerusalem. Its rich carpets, carvings, paintings and countless golden lamps make the church positively glow with light and colour. At the entrance are pieces of wood and bronze – *nakus* – which were used to announce prayer times from the ninth century when the ringing of church bells was prohibited. The cathedral itself dates from the eleventh century and was expanded by the Crusaders, but there was a church here as early as the fifth century.

In the peaceful, open courtyard of the compound are the St. Tarkmanchatz Armenian school; the **Armenian or Gulbenkian Library**, which contains over 50,000 publications, half of them in Armenian; and the **Mardigian Museum of Armenian Art and History** (Mon–Sat 10am–4pm). The museum reflects the role of the Armenian community in the history of Christianity. Thousands of objects are arranged in thirty rooms – formerly the living quarters of Armenian seminary students – around an ochre-stone courtyard dotted with cypress trees. Those on ground level, looking out over the tombstones of an overgrown cemetery, provide the historical and cultural background. The first room illustrates the Armenian problem through maps and commentaries. The second records the Armenian presence in Jerusalem, with Roman and Byzantine mosaics believed to have been made by Armenian artists. Beyond are two rooms of photographs of the nineteenth century Armenian Patriarch of Jerusalem, providing a charming record of the city and the Armenian Quarter at the time (even today many of the photography shops in east Jerusalem are run by Armenians) and a group of charcoal sketches of destroyed Armenian churches in the Soviet Union and Turkey. Also on display are the first woodcuts of the Jerusalem printing press, established in 1833 for liturgical books.

Upstairs, with views over the cityscape of Jerusalem and the surrounding hills, are mosaics, manuscripts and copperware. There's a collection of eighteenth-century yellow, white and sky-blue tiles from northwest Turkey as well as the more familiar blue tiles which predominate in Jerusalem; metalwork from the seventeenth century – long graceful shapes and intricate filigree artefacts; and other rooms with ritual objects such as jewelled crosses, mitres and embroidery. In the last room, in a gilded frame, is a painting of Mount Ararat, symbol of the Armenian homeland and struggle for survival. The most important and attractive exhibits, however, are the jewel-encrusted, brilliantly-coloured, illuminated manuscripts.

Still in the compound, the beautiful **Convent of the Olive Tree** (*Deir al-Zeitouneh*), where Jesus is said to have been tied during the scourging before the crucifixion, is also known as the **House of Annas** after the father-in-law of Caiaphas, the high priest under whose authority Jesus was condemned. The small chapel was built around 1300 in classical Armenian style; in one corner is the stone which, according to Luke (19:40), 'would have cried out had the disciples not praised God'.

The exit from here, through a low gateway and narrow street, up a flight of steps, brings you back out into Armenian Orthodox Patriarchate Road, close to Zion Gate. Backtrack a little and you'll find St. James' Road leading into the residential area. On the left, down Ararat Street, you can savour the delights of *sfiha* – a spicy, mincemeat 'pizza' – baked before your eyes at the **Armenian bakery**. Further down Ararat, under the arched and winding street, is a small pottery studio selling distinctively decorated plates and other ceramics, and a little further on you'll find the **Assyrian Convent** on the right. The Syrian Orthodox Community, whose living language is Syriac, is one of the smallest Christian sects in Jerusalem, established here since the end of the sixth century. They claim that **Saint Mark's Church** (9am–noon and 3.30–6pm; ask for the key), inside the convent, is on the site of St. Peter's first church, where the Virgin Mary was baptised and where the Last Supper was eaten (a claim to rival the *Coenaculum* on Mount Zion). At the bottom of Ararat Street, the market is to the left, the Jewish quarter to the right.

Damascus Gate or Bab al-Amud

Damascus Gate is the largest, the most elaborate and the most heavily defended of the Old City's seven gates. It is also the only one to have been excavated. The excavations (Sat–Thur 9am–5pm, Fri 9am–3pm) are to the left as you face the gate from outside the wall. A smaller archway, 1400 years older than the present gate, can be seen at a lower level. This was built by the Emperor Hadrian in the second century BC as part of his new town of *Aelia Capitolina* and is the only surviving arch of a triple triumphal gateway. Through Hadrian's arch you reach a pavement of huge irregular stones, the second-century Roman plaza that was the beginning of the Cardo. In the middle stood a column (shown in a hologram; it originally bore Hadrian's statue and later, in Byzantine times, a cross) from where the distance to Damascus was measured. To this day, the Arabic name of Damascus Gate is

Bab al-Amud, the Gate of the Column: in Hebrew it is known as Sha'ar Shechem (Nablus Gate) as it stands at the start of the ancient road heading north.

From the Roman plaza a corridor leads into a large room where stairs ascend through one of the towers flanking Damascus Gate up onto the city wall: there are magnificent panoramas from the top. The vaulted room was once used for olive oil production, and the remains of an olive press are on view – it lent its name to one of the main thoroughfares from here, *Souq Khan al-Zeit* (the Market of Inn of the Oil).

The steps leading down to the present gate form an amphitheatre and are a great place to sit and watch the people going in and out. It really buzzes on Fridays and Jewish holidays when thousands of Muslims and Jews pass through on their way to prayer. Traditionally, though not while the *intifada* continues, during *Ramadan* the gate is decorated with bright lights and the whole area is awake till late at night. Around the gate stalls offer tasty snacks, local sweets and newspapers; kids will try and sell you wholesale quantities of chocolate bars, chemical-tasting Israeli cola briefly cooled on blocks of ice, or anything else they can pick up cheap and reckon you'll buy dear; and, as the gate is the main entrance for Muslims going to pray at al-Aqsa, there are always a number of beggars. You can test the political temperature of the Old City by watching the Israeli patrol permanently at Damascus Gate to see how many Palestinians they stop. If things are really hot they, and their colleagues stationed on the walls over the gate, will be carrying gas canisters and riot sticks as well as the ubiquitous assault rifle. If they're using them, don't go in.

The gate's angled entrance, designed to break the path of potential attackers, leads into the main north–south artery of the Old City. Immediately inside are a number of money changers which offer competitive rates for foreign currency and travellers cheques. On the left is a large café, another good place to sit and enjoy the crowds while you wait for whoever you've lost. Inside, this place remains the domain of male card and *shesh-besh* (backgammon) players, but it's welcoming nonetheless and the management are protective of their customers. The cafés opposite and in the modern piazza are newer, less traditional and more expensive. Other shops and stalls at the entrance sell *ka'ak*, *falafel*, great *kanafeh* and assorted snacks.

Souq Khan al-Zeit

About 50m from Damascus Gate the road forks. To the left, Tariq al-Wad leads into the heart of the Muslim quarter (see below). Right, **Souq Khan al-Zeit** separates the Muslim and Christian quarters. It's the busiest shopping street in the Old City – exciting if you're just looking around, frustrating if you want to get somewhere. Boys pushing heavily-loaded barrows (the main form of transportation in the market) give you only one warning before running you down. If you hear a voice yelling "Alo, 'Alo, 'Alo, hit the wall! Everything from nuts, to clothes, to spices, to electrical equipment, to cassettes, to shoes, to pots and pans can be found here. If the shop you're in doesn't have it, the owner's brother a few doors down certainly will (or at least something very like it). Women from surrounding villages, their produce laid out on the ground, face running battles with the market authorities who constantly try to move them off elsewhere. The fruit and vegetables they'll sell you are guaranteed to have been in the ground, or on the tree, that morning, and have been carried into the city in enormous creaky bags and groaning cartons. This is a great place to experiment with tastes you can't get at home.

About halfway down, the street crosses the **Via Dolorosa** and the irresistible force of everyday chaos meets the immovable object of religious fervour. The only way to get through the jam is to slipstream a boy with a suitably large barrow. Souq Khan al-Zeit runs into Souq al-Attarin, a covered market area. To the right, where the two join, is the heart of the Christian Quarter.

The Church of the Holy Sepulchre

The vast and rambling **Church of the Holy Sepulchre** (4.30am–7pm in winter, 4.30am–8pm in summer; modest dress required, no shorts or sleeveless shirts) is just about the first thing you'll encounter if you approach the Christian quarter this way. As the traditional site of **Christ's crucifixion, burial and resurrection** it is one of the most venerated shrines in Christendom, and the centre of Christian worship in Jerusalem. The last five **Stations of the Cross** (see "Via Dolorosa" p.71) – the 10th station, where Jesus was stripped of his clothes, the 11th, where he was nailed to the cross, the 12th, where he died on the cross, the 13th, where his body was removed from the cross, and the 14th, his tomb – are all within the church. Each of these five stations is marked with a decorated altar: the first four all on the **Hill of Calvary** enclosed inside the church, the fifth, Jesus' tomb, beneath it.

The earliest known Christian church on this site dates from before 66AD, but the area was levelled by the Roman Emperor Hadrian who raised a temple to Aphrodite here in 135AD. Its present significance was established by **Queen Helena**, who visited the country in search of traces of Jesus' ministry, identified the site as the location of his crucifixion and burial, and claimed to have found the **True Cross** in an underground cave here. Her son, the Byzantine Emperor Constantine, built a church on the site which was completed in 348AD. The authenticity of the claim that this is where Jesus is buried rests on the assumption that, in biblical times, Calvary was sited outside the city walls, where Jewish burials had to take place. The controversy over the real site of Jesus' tomb centres on whether or not this site was within or outside the walls. Anglicans, for example, believe he was buried in the Garden Tomb outside the present city walls.

The Byzantine church was destroyed by the Persians in 614 and restored two years later by the Greeks. The Muslim Caliph Omar Ibn al-Khattab declined to pray in the church when he accepted the surrender of Jerusalem in 638AD on the grounds that his Muslim followers would want to convert the building into a mosque if he did so. 'Such generosity', notes O'Connor, 'had unfortunate consequences; had the church become a mosque it would not have been destroyed by the Fatimid Caliph Hakim in 1009'. Ninety years later, in 1099, the church was the target of the invading European Crusader armies, who built the structure you see today. They completed restoration in 1149AD. The church was again damaged by a fire in 1808, allegedly started by a drunken monk who then tried to douse it with *aqua vitae*.

Interdenominational wrangles

Today, the church is frankly a mess. The enormous space is permeated with the din of repairs and the hum of tourists and pilgrims, and filled at prayer times with a cacophony of rival chants. Since the *intifada*, with fewer tourists, some semblance of peace does occasionally descend on the Holy Sepulchre, but if you're expecting a place of harmony and meditation, you are still more likely to find it in the market outside.

The main reason for this is **competition** between Christians. The Holy Sepulchre is shared by six communities: the Latins, Greek Orthodox, Armenian Orthodox, Syrian (Jacobite) Copts and Abyssinians, who co-habit on an uneasy 'cold war' footing, their activities controlled since 1757 by a ruling on the **status quo** which regulates who can do what and when in the church. Each controls certain areas of the building and exercises the liturgy at different times of the day or night, others are permitted only certain ceremonies on special occasions.

Repairs are especially problematical. Restoration work following the 1927 earthquake has only recently been completed following thirty years of interdenominational wrangling, resolved in a 1958 works agreement, and a further thirty years of construction. Even the smallest of works can be a major source of contention, as those carrying them out can then lay claim to the area involved. Larger renovations can be performed only through collaboration – which is rarely forthcoming. In 1954, a Common Technical Bureau was set up for renovating areas used by all groups. One project involved the demolition and rebuilding of a wall behind three pillars in the Rotunda. One pillar is square and belongs to the Greek Orthodox who are renovating it. The other two are Corinthian and belong to the Armenians who are restoring theirs. Behind the wall is a recess controlled by the Armenians but used by the Copts, another disputed zone.

Perhaps the most obvious symbol of this interdenominational competitiveness is the **Stone of Unction or Anointing** immediately inside the entrance. Although the limestone slab beneath is held in common by the six denominations, each insists on their own lamps hanging over it. According to the Greek tradition, the stone marks the spot where Christ was removed from the Cross. Catholics, however, believe he was anointed here before burial. The wall behind was purpose-built for Greek icons. To the left is the Armenians' **Stone of the Three Women** where Jesus' mother Mary, her sister and Mary Magdalene stood by the Cross (but see *Stabat Mater* below).

Calvary

The site of the crucifixion – **Calvary** or **Golgotha**, the place of the skull – is to the right of the Stone of Unction, up a steep flight of stairs. At the bottom, Crusader kings were buried inside the richly decorated Greek Orthodox **Chapel of Adam**, where legend has it that Adam's skull was discovered. At the top are three altars, the Roman Catholic **Altar of the Crucifixion** and

Stabat Mater (where Mary stood at the foot of the cross), and the more glittery Greek Orthodox one under which a silver-inlaid hole marks the spot where **Christ's cross** stood. Two other discs indicate the placement of the thieves' crosses.

Jesus' Tomb

To the left of the Stone of Unction you'll see the **Rotunda**, the only part of the church (apart from some of its foundations) that corresponds to Constantine's original structure. Eighteen massive columns support a dome 11m above the ground: below, in the centre of the Rotunda, stands the tomb monument, the **Holy Sepulchre** itself, built over the rock burial chamber after the fire of 1808. The place is a glittering jumble, decorated with no less than 43 lamps provided by the various denominations. You enter the sepulchral chamber through an anteroom, the **Chapel of the Angel**, that contains the stone on which the angel sat to tell of Christ's resurrection (*Matthew 28:1*). The marble tomb room itself is tiny – it can hold only four people at a time – so be prepared to wait.

The rest of the church

Behind the Holy Sepulchre is the **Chapel of the Copts** where another part of the rock tomb can be seen. Opposite, in fourth-century Constantinian walls, is the **Syrian Jacobite Chapel**: a low door behind it leads into a Jewish burial chamber dating from the first century. On the opposite side of the Rotunda is the main Crusader church, known as the **Katholikon**, which now belongs to the Greek Orthodox Church. Its main feature is the marble basin under the dome, the *omphalos* or Navel of the World.

The cave where Queen Helena, assisted by a Jew named Judas, found the True Cross, nails and all, in a former cistern, is at the east end of the church. The domed twelfth-century Armenian **Chapel of Helena** is one of the most attractive places in the church, its rock walls covered with crosses scratched by medieval pilgrims. From here thirteen narrow steps (in the right-hand corner) lead down into the **Crypt of the Finding of the Cross** itself.

The Ethiopian village

There have been **Ethiopians** in Palestine since the fourth century, forming one of the oldest expatriate Christian communities anywhere. Traditionally, they had a presence in five holy sites, including the Church of the Nativity in Bethlehem and the Grotto of David on Mount Zion, but they were evicted from the Church of the Holy Sepulchre by 'the big five' when their documents were lost in the 1808 fire. Since then they have occupied a cluster of mud huts on the roof. Whatever the Ethiopian monks may feel about this, to an outsider they appear to be better off in the calm silence and beautiful surroundings of this veritable African village, than in the chaos downstairs. To visit them, head from the church into the market, turn first left into Souq Khan al-Zeit and climb the stairs to the **Coptic Patriarchate** on the left. A small door at the end of the street opens onto the 'village'.

Some twenty Ethiopian monks live here, but even this sanctuary is the subject of a legal wrangle with the Egyptian Copts who also claim title to this part of the roof. The Coptic Church of Egypt has ruled that no Egyptian pilgrims will visit Jerusalem until the conflict is settled.

The **rooftop village**, *Deir al-Sultan* (Monastery of the Sultan), is directly above the Chapel of St. Helena; its monks speak Amharic, the national tongue of Ethiopia, and fasting plays a major part in their life. Members of the community eat only vegetables during the forty days preceding Christmas (January 6 and 7 in their calendar). During ceremonies, the monks wear velvet robes and floor-length capes, embroidered in gold and silver with the Lion of Judah and the Star of David: they regard King David as the father of their church, which they claim was founded by King Menelik, the son of King Solomon and the Queen of Sheba. Cymbals and other traditional instruments used in the temples of Pharaonic Egypt are played during the Christmas service which lasts until 2am – it's well worth going if you're around at this time of year. After the service a meal is taken and in the morning all the participants journey to Bethlehem to worship in the Grotto of the Nativity.

The Christian Quarter

The Church of the Holy Sepulchre aside, the **Christian quarter** is relatively thin (by Jerusalem's standards) on specific 'sights'. South of the Holy Sepulchre is an area known as the **Mauristan** – you'll approach the church from this direction if you come from Jaffa Gate and David's Street. The name, Persian in origin, means hospital or hospice and the area was once crowded with lodging houses for pilgrims and travellers. Today you'll find a complex of churches and other religious-oriented institutions around the Mauristan, which is now a Greek bazaar known as **Souq Aftimos**. Its shops are crammed with tourist paraphernalia, gold and leather goods above all.

Charlemagne founded the enclave in the early ninth century, and although it was damaged in 1009 by the 'mad' Caliph Hakim, many of the buildings were later restored by a group of traders known as the **merchants of Amalfi**. They erected three important churches: St. Mary la Latine (now the Lutheran Church of the Redeemer; Mon–Sat 9am–1pm and 2–5pm); St. Mary la Petite (where the ornate fountain now stands); and the oldest church in Jerusalem, St. John the Baptist, in the southwest corner of the square.

Saint John the Baptist, clearly signed off Christian Quarter Road, is nowadays below street level. The church is the focus of the order of St. John's Hospitallers, familiar to British visitors in their modern manifestation as the St. John's Ambulance Brigade. For the conspiratorially minded, they are also at the centre of many of the Machiavellian theories of secret sects pedalled by pop academics. In this role they are accused of/credited with controlling the world in league with the Rosicrucians and Freemasons (among others). The widely available book *The Holy Blood, The Holy Grail* is one of the latest additions to this scholarship. As for the church itself, the two small bell towers are later additions to an eleventh-century building.

The **Church of the Redeemer** as you see it now was built by Crown Prince Friedrich Wilhelm, who bought the site during a visit in 1869 after the original building had fallen into decay. From the church tower you can trace the outlines of the Constantinian Holy Sepulchre and see as far as the Mount of Olives and Mount Zion. For traces of the original church, look at the medieval northern gate, decorated with the signs of the Zodiac and the symbols of the months.

Opposite the Church of the Redeemer, the **Alexandra Hospice** houses the church of the **Russian Orthodox** commmunity. The church itself can be visited only once a week (Thursday at 7am) when mass is held for the soul of the Tsar: beneath it, however, are **excavations** (Mon–Sat 9am–1pm and 3–5pm) which have uncovered sections of the Herodian city's second northern wall. These remains indicate that Calvary was indeed outside the city walls (see above). There are also remnants of a triumphal arch from the time of Hadrian which may have led into the Forum of *Aelia Capitolina*.

Not far away, down past the entrance to the Holy Sepulchre the **Mosque of Omar** commemorates Caliph Omar's prayers in the courtyard of the Holy Sepulchre in 638AD. The Dome of the Rock is often (mistakenly) called the Mosque of Omar, but this is the real one. To the north of the church lies a sister mosque, **Khanqah Salahiyya**, originally a Sufi hospice. According to O'Connor, '. . . the mid-point of a line drawn between the minarets falls approximately at the entrance of the tomb of Christ in the Holy Sepulchre'. This arrangement, he believes, 'was intentional, but its purpose remains obscure'.

Bab al-Jadid or New Gate

Bab al-Jadid, at the northwest corner of the Old City, was constructed to create access between the Christian quarter within the city walls and new Christian properties outside them. It opens into one of the quieter parts of the Old City and can thus make a good starting point for your own explorations.

On the right inside the New Gate is the **Ecole des Frères** (Christian Brothers' School). Turn left past this, and Tariq al-Frere will eventually lead you up to Souq Khan al-Zeit and the Via Dolorosa. To the right, Tariq al-Jawalida leads past the *Knight's Palace Hotel* and the **Latin Patriarchate and Seminary**. Beyond here, on the corner of Tariq al-Qaddis Butrus (St. Peter's Street) stands the **Casa Nova Hospice**: follow the street along (Latin Patriarchate Road) and you'll come to Jaffa Gate.

One of Jerusalem's most prominent landmarks, the white stone **Notre Dame de France**, rises immediately outside the gate. Built in 1887 by the Assumptionist Fathers, this massive building, with its central doorway topped by two towers, houses the offices of the papal representative to the city, a church, a monastery and an up-market hotel with East Jerusalem's finest (only) French restaurant – genuine French restaurant prices too. Among the shops which front the street is a Catholic Advice Centre. In the 1948 war, Notre Dame was right on the border (New Gate itself was closed between 1948 and 1967) and was an important Israeli observation post. High on the hill, the building looks most impressive at night when it is floodlit.

Saint Stephen's Gate and the Via Dolorosa

Saint Stephen's Gate, on the eastern side of the Old City (*Egged* bus #43 from Damascus Gate), marks the start of the Via Dolorosa. In a city where everything seems to have at least two names, St. Stephen's Gate can boast at least four. The eponymous saint is said to have been martyred nearby: it is also commonly known as **Lion's Gate** after the pair of stone lions on either side of the entrance, and in Arabic as either **Bab al-Ghor** (Jordan Valley Gate) or **Bab Sittna Maryam** (Gate of Our Lady Mary). The latter stems from the belief that the Virgin Mary was born in a house just inside. This is the way into the Old City if you're coming from the direction of the Mount of Olives, across the Kidron Valley. Once inside, **Tariq al-Mujahidin** (Freedom Fighters' Street), which becomes the Via Dolorosa, heads through the Muslim Quarter to end at the Church of the Holy Sepulchre in the Christian Quarter.

The **Church of St. Anne** (Mon–Sat 8am–12pm and 2.30–6pm in summer, 2–5pm in winter; ☎02-283285), named for the mother of Mary, stands within a large walled compound to the right of the street. Supposedly the site of Mary's birth, it's a small church, but one of the most beautiful and simple Crusader monuments in the country. It was built in 1140 over the ruins of a Byzantine church, which had itself been constructed over an even older shrine. The inscription above the door shows that Salah al-Din converted it into a *madrasa* in 1192, and it remained in Muslim hands until 1856, when the Ottoman rulers donated the church to French Catholics in gratitude for support during the Crimean War. The fortress-like basilica has elements of French and Muslim styles, with beautiful frescoes on the walls. Inside, stairs lead into the ancient crypt which stands on the site of the house of Mary and her parents Joachim and Anne. Here are remains of mosaics and columns dating from Byzantine times.

In the grounds to the northwest are the ruins of two great pools constructed around 200BC to supply water to the Temple. The water of the **Pools of Bethesda** was believed to have medicinal qualities, and here Jesus cured a man who 'had an infirmity thirty and eight years' (*John 5:1–13*). Excavations show the remains of five porches referred to by St. John, with the small natural caves nearby adapted as baths for the thousands of sufferers. A detailed plan on the extensive site explains all. There is a small museum containing objects found during excavations which rarely seems to be open; the guardian, however, has the key.

The first street on the left past St. Anne's, Tariq Bab Hitta, brings you to al-Haram's **Bab Hitta** (Absolution Gate). On its left is the now-filled pool known as **Birket Bani Isra'il** (Pool of the Sons of Israel). The second street on the left, Tariq al-Malik Faisal or Tariq Bab al-'Atm, leads into the Haram compound at **Bab al-'Atm** (Gate of Darkness). Along this street are two fine examples of Mamluk architecture: the **Madrasa al-Dawadarrya** with striking double vaulted gates; and **Madrasa al-Sallaniyya**, noted for the decorations suspended above its coloured facade. Straight ahead lie the first stations of the Via Dolorosa.

Via Dolorosa

According to Christian tradition, the **Via Dolorosa** (Way of Sorrow or Way of the Cross) is Jesus' route from Pilate's judgement hall to Golgotha, the site of the crucifixion. Along this route are fourteen stations of the Cross, each commemorating an event in the gospel narrative. These fourteen stations are a relatively new innovation. In Byzantine times, Christian pilgrims followed a similar path but did not stop on the way. By the eighth century, the route had moved: beginning at Gethsemane on the Mount of Olives, it headed south to Mount Zion and then doubled back around the Temple Mount to the Holy Sepulchre. A split within the Latin church in the Middle Ages meant that for a period there were two rival routes: the group with churches to the west went westward, those with property to the east, eastward. From the fourteenth to the sixteenth centuries, the route followed that of the Franciscans, starting at the Holy Sepulchre. By then, there were eight stations. Meanwhile, a tradition of fourteen stations, marking the order of events in the gospels, was developing in Europe. So as not to disappoint European pilgrims to Jerusalem the difference was made up. Some of the present stations were located as recently as the nineteenth century.

Whether the Via Dolorosa as followed now corresponds to historical reality is still a matter of controversy. **Anglicans** believe Jesus would have been led north, towards the Garden Tomb. **Dominican Catholics** set out from Jaffa Gate where, at Herod's palace, Pontius Pilate usually stayed when he came from Caesarea to police the crowds on Jewish feasts. If he did condemn Jesus here, the path to the crucifixion would most likely have gone eastward along what is now David Street, north (left) at the Triple Souq and then west to the Holy Sepulchre. All this seems to matter little, however, to the crowds of pilgrims that walk the path, particularly during Easter Week.

Today's Via Dolorosa is a busy shopping street and although most of the stations are marked by plaques, they can be difficult to spot, particularly when the route enters the *souq* proper. If you want to be sure to locate all fourteen stations, it's worth your while joining an organised party – the main Friday procession (at 3pm) is led by the Franciscans. For information about alternative tours, ask at the *Christian Information Centre* or at regular tourist agencies. All tours start from the newly renovated **Pilgrims' Reception Centre**, about 300m inside St. Stephen's Gate.

The Stations

The **first station of the cross** is at **Madrasa al-Omariyya**, which is held to be the site of the **Antonia Fortress**, where Jesus was condemned by Pontius Pilate. Steps on the left of the street lead into the courtyard of the *madrasa*, which is still used as a school (open Fridays, Muslim holidays and during lunch break). The building overlooks the whole of al-Haram compound and from the steps in the south, you can view the area for yourself. For the **second station** you have to backtrack and cross the road to the **Franciscan monastery** (Mon–Sat 8am–12pm and 2–6pm in summer; 1–5pm in winter). The **Chapel of Judgement**, where Jesus was sentenced to crucifixion, is on the left. On the right, with a beautiful stained glass window behind the altar, is the **Chapel of the Flagellation** where Jesus was beaten by Roman soldiers.

The next turning on the left, Tariq Bab al-Ghawanimeh, leads to the north-western gate of al-Haram – **Bab al-Ghawanimeh**. Spanning the street just past this junction is the arch of **Ecce Homo** ('Behold the man'; *John 19:5*), where Pontius Pilate is said to have stood and mocked Jesus when he was brought out wearing a crown of thorns. The arch, part of a gate dating from the time of Hadrian, was given its name in the sixteenth century. Part of the original gate can still be seen behind the altar in the **Convent of the Sisters of Zion**, better known as the Ecce Homo church (Mon–Sat 8am–12.30pm and 2–5pm). Below the church are large pieces of the **Pavement of Justice** (*Lithostratos*) where Jesus was tried: the grooves carved in its stone surface are variously explained as channels for rainwater (see the huge subterranean cistern below) or as a device to prevent horses slipping. It is agreed, however, that the squares, triangles and other scratch marks on the slabs were made by game-playing Roman soldiers.

The **third station**, where Jesus fell for the first time under the weight of the cross, is left on Tariq al-Wad, marked by a relief sculpture above the door of a small Polish chapel. The Armenian **Church of Our Lady of the Spasm** commemorates the **fourth station**, where Mary stood and watched her son go by. Inside you can see the outline of a pair of sandals, said to be Mary's footprints, on the remarkable fifth-century mosaic floor. From here, the journey is less of a spiritual odyssey and more an obstacle race. The shops along the route are tourist-oriented, and shopkeepers and street traders try their best to lure the pious from their prayers, taking the exercise every bit as seriously as their predecessors did at the time of the actual event. The frequent stops of pilgrims and tour guides add to the already frayed tempers and congestion on busy and narrow streets.

The **fifth station** is on the corner of a narrow stepped street, right off al-Wad. A 'handprint' on the wall of the first house on the left is attributed to Jesus as he leant against it. At this station, the cross was given to Simon of Cyrene. The Via Dolorosa now climbs steeply to the **sixth station** at the **Church of Saint Veronica**, who wiped Jesus' face. The image of his face was imprinted on the handkerchief she used and is said to have cured Emperor Tiberius of an illness. The cloth, known as the *Sudarium* or *Veronica*, is now kept in St. Peter's in Rome: the name Veronica itself may be a corruption of the Latin **vera icon** (true picture).

At the junction with Souq Khan al-Zeit, a Franciscan chapel marks the **seventh station**, the place of Jesus' second fall. Across the market street, up the steps of Aqabat al-Khanka, the **eighth station** is opposite the *Station VIII Souvenir Bazaar*. A cross and the Greek inscription NIKA on the wall of the **Greek Monastery of Saint Charalambos** mark the spot. Here Jesus consoled the lamenting women of Jerusalem.

After this, the Via Dolorosa seems to lose itself. Doubling back and turning right on Khan al-Zeit, the **ninth station** is some distance down on the right, up a flight of 28 stone steps that lead to the Coptic Patriarchate. A Roman pillar here marks Jesus' third fall. On the right is the **Queen Helena**

Church, and beyond the steps is the **Ethiopian Compound** on the roof of the Chapel of St. Helena in the Holy Sepulchre. The **tenth to fourteenth stations**, inside the Church of the Holy Sepulchre, have already been covered (see p.65). To get to them, you have to go round to the main entrance of the church: back onto Souq Khan al-Zeit, right into Souq al-Dabbagha and on to the end of the street.

The Muslim Quarter

The **Muslim Quarter**, stretching down from Damascus Gate to *al-Haram al-Sharif*, is the largest of the four quarters and the commercial and financial centre of the Old City. It is particularly rich in buildings in the Islamic style and is well worth exploring: you will have to take the initiative, however, as most tours, guides and tourist literature underplay Jerusalem's Islamic character and Arab history. Perhaps the most striking omission is the tomb of Sharif Hussein bin Ali, the leader of the Arab Revolt in World War I.

Islamic architecture
If you are particularly interested in the buildings here, you may be able to get some help from the architectural department of the **Waqf** (Islamic Trust). The *Waqf* administers Muslim property, educational and religious institutions, and welfare and charitable projects for the community. The Trust does not have the facilities to organise tours for visitors, but should be able to point you in the right direction (*Waqf Department of Islamic Architecture*, Tariq Bab al-Hadid; ☎02-289961). Another source is the excellent book *Mamluk Jerusalem* by Michael Burgoyne, published in London by the World of Islam Festival Trust.

Islamic buildings, unlike those built in European styles, do not turn their best faces to the world. Their most attractive features are inside, or around internal courtyards. But since there are few public buildings in the quarter into which you can wander alone, you will generally have to be satisfied with street facades – some of these are truly splendid. In Jerusalem buildings which elsewhere would merit special status as architectural or historic monuments are now homes for local families. This is partly because of the housing shortage, but also because if they are left empty or as historical attractions, there is a real risk that they will be taken over. The Israeli groups which have already grabbed houses in the quarter make no secret of their aim to drive all Palestinians out of the Old City.

The Mamluks
Most of the best preserved Islamic buildings are grouped around the northern and western wall of al-Haram and most date from the **Mamluk period** (1248–1517AD). At the start of this period, Jerusalem was part of the Syrian province whose capital was Damascus, but in 1376 its status was raised and its governor appointed directly from the Mamluk capital, Cairo. This increased importance was reflected in the construction of many beautiful buildings all over the city and the restoration of existing ones. Scores of

colleges, hospices and mausoleums were built in Jerusalem, characterised by the use of red, white and black stone and distinctive arched entrances.

The Mamluks are probably unique in political history in that they were a dynasty of slaves, of different races and nationalities, who formed a military elite governing an alien territory. The Mamluk sultans managed to get rid of the remnants of the Crusader forces from their Syrian-Egyptian territories and checked the advance of the Mongols from Asia. These military successes were all the more remarkable given that the rulers were frequently overthrown and that there seems to have been an almost constant condition of intrigue and conspiracy in the ruling elite, compounded by the lack of an agreed line of succession: the throne went to the strongest. In their 250-year dynasty, there were over fifty separate reigns (some sultans ruling more than once). This helps to further explain the number of fine Mamluk buildings in Jerusalem: prominent members of previous regimes were often exiled to the city when power changed hands.

Mamluk buildings are noted for the lightness of their design and the use of striped masonry. The Kufic lettering and geometric arabesques which are now familiar features of Muslim decoration were developed by the Mamluks. Other common artistic flourishes include elaborate bronze work on doors, carved wooden pulpits, beautiful mosaics, stained glass and the use of precious stones to emboss Qurans.

Much important historical information about Jerusalem comes from the great fifteenth-century jurist and historian, **Mujir al-Din al-Ulaymi,** who was born in the city on October 23, 1456 and eventually became chief qadi (religious judge) of Jerusalem. His five-volume history of Jerusalem and Hebron, published in 1495, describes the sacred sites, details the history of the city in Islamic times, provides a topographical and historical commentary, contains a compendium of the biographies of notables and scholars and includes a chronicle from 1468–95. Mujir al-Din died in 1522 and is buried at the foot of the Mount of Olives. Although it has never been available in full in a European language, al-Din's work (along with the official documents of the Haram and the Ottoman regime) remains the major source for most histories of the city.

Three small streets in the shadow of *al-Haram* – Souq al-Qattanin, Tariq Bab al-Hadid and Tariq Bab al-Naazir – give a good impression of the varied styles and shapes of Islamic architecture, as do the quarter's two chief thoroughfares, Tariq al-Wad and Tariq Bab al-Silsileh.

Tariq Bab al-Silsileh or Chain Gate Street

In Mamluk times, Jerusalem's main street was **Khutt Da'ud** (David Street) which runs from the western gate of the city (Jaffa Gate), to the principal gate of *al-Haram*, Bab al-Silsileh (Chain Gate). The eastern end of the thoroughfare, beyond the central market, is called **Tariq Bab al-Silsileh** (Chain Gate Street). It crosses the central Tyropoeon Valley (*al-Wad*) on a wide bridge which dates from Herod's time and which was rebuilt in the early Islamic period. The eastern part of this bridge is known to westerners as Wilson's Arch (see p.83).

Along Tariq Bab al-Silsileh hospices, important Quranic schools (*madrasas*) and markets were established. By the late fourteenth century, the part nearest *al-Haram* had acquired architectural distinction and some fine examples of Mamluk buildings have survived here. Since the western end of the street borders the **Western Wall piazza**, it has today become one of the focal points of conflict between Jewish settlers and Palestinians. Many of the buildings, particularly on the south side of the street, have been seized and turned into either look-out posts or Jewish religious seminaries (*yeshivot*).

At the top of the street, at the west wall of *al-Haram*, the twin, green-painted gates of **Bab al-Silsileh** and **Bab al-Sikineh** (Knife Gate) stand in a vaulted porch which forms the western side of an open courtyard. The structure in front of the doors was a well, and set back from the street in the north wall is a small arched doorway, the entrance to the Madrasa al-Baladiyya. Built in 1380 as a mausoleum for Sayf al-Din al-Ahmadi, governor of Aleppo, this now houses al-Aqsa Library along with a number of private homes.

To the west of *al-Baladiyya*, a simple but distinctive arched recess leads to the main entrance of the **women's hospice**, the *Ribat al-Nisa'*, just one of the many institutions founded by Emir Tankiz al-Nasiri. A celebrated Mamluk ruler, al-Nasiri was appointed governor of Damascus in 1312 and became ruler of all Syria before being deposed in 1340. He was noted for his public works and support for religious institutions, founding *caravanserais* and public baths in Damascus, Jerusalem and elsewhere. One of his most impressive legacies is the three-storeyed **Madrasa al-Tankiziyya**, opposite the women's hospice on the south side of Bab al-Silsileh. Its striking portal is decorated with black-and-white mosaics over which is an inscription:

In the name of God, the Merciful, the Compassionate. This blessed place was erected, in the hope of God's reward and His forgiveness, by his noble excellency Sayf al-Din Tankiz, servant of al-Malik al-Nasir, in the year 729 (1328–29AD).

The original *madrasa* has undergone several transformations in its history. In the mid-fifteenth century, tribunals were held here and by 1483 it had become the seat of the town *qadi*. From the nineteenth century until the early days of the British Mandate, it was Jerusalem's law court. Later it became the residence of the head of the Supreme Muslim Council, Haj Amin al-Husseini. The Jordanians used the room building as a secondary school during their occupation, and the Israeli army seized it after 1967. A large sign nailed to the mosaic lintel now proclaims it the 'Western Wall Lookout of the IDF', so you'll have to be very resourceful to gain entrance. The building has its own entrance into *al-Haram*, giving the Israeli army open access to the whole site. Across Tariq Bab al-Silsileh where the street leaves the courtyard, is **al-Sa'adiyya**, the *Turba* (tomb) of Sa'ad al-Din Mas'ud, a chamberlain in Damascus during the reign of Mohammed Ibn Qalawun (who restored the mosaics and dome of the Dome of the Rock). His chamberlain's tomb was built around 1311. The street facade has a doorway decorated with red and black arabesques and an unusual coloured marble frieze: to the right of the entrance are two grilled windows framed with red and black stone. A little further to the west is another tomb, the **Turba of Turkan Khatun**. According to one story this is the grave of a Mongol princess who died in

Jerusalem while on a pilgrimage to Mecca around 1352. The two windows overlooking the street facade are bordered by red and cream stone: above each is a large grey stone elaborately carved with palms and stars.

On the same side of the road a stepped street, Daraj al-Ayn, leads down to Tariq al-Wad. Immediately west of the junction, and overlying the valley below, is **al-Jaliqiyya**. Baybars al-Jaliq was one of the leaders who drove the Mongols out of the country in a 1281 expedition. He died outside Ramla in 1307 and was buried in Jerusalem in accordance with his last wishes. The beautiful calligraphy above the iron grille that opens into the tomb chamber is a funerary inscription giving the name and date of the occupant. On the south side of the street, almost directly opposite *al-Jaliqiyya*, is the **madrasa of Siraj al-Din al-Sallami**. The main feature of the facade is an archway blocked with large stones with a small stone window at its centre.

The market area

From here on the buildings are difficult to identify, their facades increasingly covered with gaudy tourist junk. At the start of the market proper, a beautiful carved wooden *mashrabiyya* at the level of the first floor juts out over the north side of the street. It is part of the **Madrasa al-Taziyya**, built in 1362 by the Mamluk Emir Sayf al-Din Taz. Taz rose from the position of cup-bearer to Sultan al-Malik Mohammed to become governor of Aleppo, but was arrested and imprisoned in Alexandria after a palace plot in 1358. This fall from grace left him with a relatively plain memorial, its only elaborate decoration a large grilled window built in red and cream stone with a dedicatory inscription on the lintel. The upper storey window is typical of nineteenth-century Ottoman construction and is believed to have replaced an earlier Mamluk *mashrabiyya*. The building, identified by a modern sign reading 'Antiquities From Jericho Shop', is now a private home.

Next door to it is **al-Kilaniyya** which has been described as both a *turba* and a *madrasa* and is thought to have been erected in 1352. According to Mujir al-Din, 'it is named after the Haj Jamal al-Din Pahlavan . . . known as the son of the Lord Kilan'. On either side of the domed and carved entrance are decorative grilled windows, the easternmost of which is blocked up. If you step back into the small street opposite (Aqabat Abu Madyan which leads back down into the Western Wall piazza) you can get a view of the whole of the splendid three-domed building, recently renovated by the *Waqf*. Its central and eastern domes rest on octagonal drums, while the western one has a 16-sided drum.

Opposite, on the corner of Aqabat Abu Madyan, is the **Turba of Barka Khan**, built between 1265 and 1280. Emir Barka Khan was commander of the Khwarizmians, a Tartar tribe that reached Gaza in 1244, but whose power was broken two years later in a battle at Homs (Syria). Barka Khan was killed during this battle. The original building, erected during the Ayyubid dynasty (1187–1247), was extended by the Mamluks in 1390. In 1900, a library of some 12,000 books and manuscripts was collected by Sheikh Raghib al-Khalidi in what had been used as the family mosque. After 1967, Jewish settlers acquired a house overlooking this **Khalidi Library**, between it and the Western Wall piazza, turned it into a *yeshiva*, and have kept up a campaign of continual harassment ever since. There have been several attempts to break into the library and garbage has been dumped in its court-yard. On New Year's Eve 1987, disciples of the extremist *Gush Emunim* leader Rabbi Moshe Levinger smashed their way in, but were eventually evicted by the police. The settlers are worried that the Khalidi family will renovate the building and open it as a centre of Palestinian heritage: an appli-cation for a renovation permit was granted by the Israeli authorities in 1987 after a four year delay. The priceless books and manuscripts, which include a *Quran* given to a member of the family by Salah al-Din, have been removed to safety and are being catalogued.

On the western corner of the same junction, the **Tashtumuriyya** is a particularly magnificent example of Mamluk architecture. Built in 1382, it houses the domed tomb of Emir Tashtumur and his son Ibrahim. Tashtumur was a noted Islamic scholar who is also said to have had an inclination towards poetry and music: he was the First Secretary of State to Sultan Sha'ban until the latter was assassinated, and governor of Safad in the Galilee from 1380 to 1382. The building he erected was in use as a *madrasa* until the end of the sixteenth century. The high arched entrance, up a flight of stairs, is decorated with black and white mosaics. To the right, the square decora-tive windows of the mausoleum boast sills embellished with fine examples of marble mosaic work.

You are now in the heart of the central market. Just before the junction of Tariq Bab al-Silsileh and Souq al-Khawajat, on the right, is an elegant vaulted passageway leading into the Mamluk *caravanserai* known as **Khan al-Sultan**. Built in 1386AD under Sultan Barquq (1382–1399), it is a typical medieval urban *caravanserai*. Here merchants stayed while they sold their goods to local retailers: the chambers on either side of the vaulted market hall were used to store merchandise, while the rooms on the upper floor were the merchants' lodgings. The great barrel-vaulted chamber at the end of the passageway on the west side of the main hall (or possibly the large court-yard at its northern end) were used to stable animals. The *khan* is currently being restored by the *Waqf* who plan to turn the rooms on the ground and first floors into workshops.

Tariq al-Wad

Tariq al-Wad, forking left as you leave Damascus Gate, is the chief route from East Jerusalem to *al-Haram* and the Wailing Wall, cutting across the Via Dolorosa on the way. It's also an area of some tension, where several build-ings have been seized by Israelis (among them Ariel Sharon, the former defence minister and architect of the 1982 invasion of Lebanon).

At the Damascus Gate end of the street are a series of cafés and tourist shops, and, immediately to the left of the fork, a small all-night **bakery**. Traditionally this provided bread and baking facilities to the neighbourhood from open wood-burning ovens; nowadays, they have branched out and cook small pies and pizzas for hungry visitors. As you continue down the street the emphasis on tourism goes on, with souvenir shops, cafés and hostels.

The architecture on al-Wad itself is not especially exciting: about 100m down, at the corner of the Via Dolorosa, the **Austrian Hospice** is an impressive landmark, the last hospital in the Old City until it was closed in the mid-1980s. Beyond, approaching *al-Haram*, the market peters out and the street becomes quieter and darker; in the side streets running off to the left here, in the shadow of *al-Haram*, are some particularly fine buildings.

Tariq Bab al-Naazir or Inspector's Gate Street

Tariq Bab al-Naazir, which runs from al-Wad to Bab al-Naazir (Inspector's Gate) is also known as Tariq Bab al-Habs (Prison Gate Street) as there was a prison here until the Mandate. Many of the Palestinians who live here are the descendants of African Muslims who came to Jerusalem on pilgrimage (in Ottoman times, al-Haram was protected by predominantly Sudanese guards). The building with the columned entrance, first on the right just outside the gate, houses the administration of the **Supreme Muslim Council**. The facade was constructed during British rule; the interior is an interesting example of how traditional styles influenced later designers. The Supreme Muslim Council administers the affairs of the community in the occupied territories and, in the absence of other local representative bodies, has acquired an exaggerated importance in appointing functionaries and in administration. The Council holds the keys to the vaults under *al-Haram* and sometimes gives visitors permission to enter them.

Next door is one of the earliest Mamluk buildings in Jerusalem, **Ribat Ala al-Din al-Basir**. A pilgrims' hospice founded by the eminent Emir al-Basir (who was superintendent of both the Jerusalem and Hebron *harams*), it has an arched gateway with stone benches (*mastabas*) on either side and a founding inscription (1267) above the small entrance. The cells around the inner courtyard, typical of the other hospices you may have seen, became real cells when the place was used as a jail by the Turks. On the right of the courtyard, now full of shacks, is al-Basir's burial chamber.

Opposite the hospice is **Ribat al-Masuri** with two finely decorated windows that belong to a large main hall. The monumental entrance arch of distinctive red and cream stone opens into a large and impressive vaulted porch, whose inscription states that it was built in 1282 by Sultan al-Masur Qalawun. The Sultan also built a *Sufi* and pilgrim hospice and hospital in Hebron and a number of fine buildings in Cairo. This *ribat*, also used as a prison until 1914, nowadays houses members of Jerusalem's African community.

Tariq Bab al-Hadid or Iron Gate Street

Tariq Bab al-Hadid, parallel to the south, connects al-Wad with Bab al-Hadid (Iron Gate). **Ribat al-Mansuri**, on the north side of the street, is typical of the many small hostelries which dotted the city in Mamluk times. Al-Mansuri, a governor of Tripoli, financed its construction in 1293: the low square door is set in a shallow arched recess and flanked by stone benches;

beyond, a long passage leads to an open courtyard around which rented rooms were grouped. It is now a family home.

Opposite the hospice, behind the red and white stone arch, is the cruci-form **Madrasa al-Arghuniyya** (1358), around whose inner vaulted courtyard are Argun al-Kamili's tomb and that of **Sharif Hussein**, leader of the **Arab Revolt**. Hussein, the Sharif of Mecca, led the Arabs against the Turks in World War I after being given assurances of support for the foundation of an independent Arab state: at much the same time as Britain and France were conspiring to carve the area up between them.

A simple cream-coloured arch, originally part of the Arghuniyya, now leads into the **Madrasa al-Khatuniyya** to the east. Through it, a long vaulted passage opens into a courtyard enclosed by cells, an assembly hall and a domed chamber tomb. On the other side of the entrance is **Madrasa al-Muzhariyya** (1480), a college built by Abu Bakr Ibn Muzhir who was one time head of the Chancery Bureau in Cairo. Ibn Muzhir, who came from a Nablus family, left his mark all over the Arab world, financing two public fountains in Mecca, a *ribat* and *madrasa* in Medina and another in Cairo. Here, the tall entrance arch of red and yellow stones is decorated with black and white mosaics and, to the left of the doorway, a pair of identical iron-grilled windows are finely embellished with red and cream stone on grey marble. The inner courtyard is surrounded by rooms once used by students, but which are now family homes.

Opposite the Muzhariyya, beside Ribat al-Mansuri and partly built over it, is the **Madrasa al-Jawhariyya**. The Jawhariyya, which was also a hospice, traditionally housed important visitors to Jerusalem. One of the two *qadis* sent from Cairo in 1475 to mediate in the dispute over a collapsed synagogue (see p.84), received a delegation of the Jewish community at his lodgings here. It is now the administrative offices of the *Waqf Department of Islamic Archaeology* and is therefore more accessible than other, residential, build-ings. If you are interested in more information about the area, this is the place to ask.

The lane on the left, just before Tariq al-Hadid enters a short tunnel, leads to Souq al-Qattanin. If you continue straight down, you'll return to al-Wad.

Souq al-Qattanin or Cotton Merchants' Market

Of several new markets added to Jerusalem during the Mamluk period, the best known is **Souq al-Qattanin**, linking al-Wad with Bab al-Qattanin in the western wall of al-Haram. Designed as a commercial centre by Sultan al-Nasir Mohammed and Tankiz al-Nasiri, the covered *souq* was built in 1336–37 with shops down its length and monumental entrances at each end. There are living quarters above the shops and the original market had two public bath houses and a *khan*. By the nineteenth century, however, the market had fallen into decay and although it was restored by the *Waqf* and reopened in 1974, it is still unfinished.

Behind the iron gates about halfway down the south side of the market is **Hammam al-Shifa**, one of two surviving Mamluk bath houses which the *waqf* have plans to restore. **Khan Tankiz**, further down behind the heavy red gates, is also being renovated. The open domed rooms off the central entrance will be workshops, since pre-1967 plans to turn the *khan* into a folk museum have had to be abandoned. **Hammam al-Ayn**, on the corner where Souq al-Qattanin meets al-Wad, gives a much clearer picture of how the public bath houses operated. The entrance opens into spacious changing rooms from where bathers moved through cold and warm rooms to the hot room. The bathing rooms, heated from beneath, are domed and the roofs perforated with patterns of small openings through which shafts of daylight penetrate, giving a beautifully soft and surreal light. You may be able to visit if you can persuade the doorman to let you in.

The Jewish Quarter

The **Jewish Quarter** is located in the southeast sector of the city, bounded by Tariq Bab al-Silsileh (Chain Gate Street) to the north and Suq al-Husur (Habad Street) to the east. In the time of King Hezekiah (700BC), this was one of the wealthiest parts of Jerusalem but in 586BC its defensive wall and towers were destroyed by the Babylonians. Luxurious palaces rose again under the Maccabean and Hasmonean dynasties (167–63BC) but were razed (along with the rest of the city) by the Roman armies of Titus in 70AD. The Jewish population was expelled from Jerusalem after the Second Jewish Revolt (135AD) and although Jews were allowed to return in the fifth century it was a further 500 years, scarred by the slaughter of Muslims and Jews at the hands of the Crusaders, before the rule of Salah al-Din in 1187 introduced a tolerance that enabled the Jewish community to flourish. Still later, Jews fleeing the Spanish Inquisition emigrated to Jerusalem, bringing with them the skills of medieval Spain.

Severely damaged during the **1948 war**, the quarter was not redeveloped until the Israeli occupation of the Old City in 1967. Since then, with massive private and government funding, it has been extensively excavated, restored and expanded. The contrast with the other quarters is stark. With its newly paved and lighted streets and tarted-up houses, this is once again a chic and expensive area. The architects have struggled to maintain the intrinsic dignity of the buildings, but somehow it all seems rather sterile and anonymous. Craft boutiques, art galleries and studios have 'ambience'; the rest of the city has life.

Jewish Quarter **residents** are, in the main, religious and extremely nationalist settlers – Rabbi Kahane is very popular here. Apartments are expensive and many of them are used as summer bases by expatriate Americans. It is also dotted with *yeshivot* whose students are predominantly North American 'born-again' Jews. If you are Jewish (or look it), and preferably male, you may be invited to attend a lecture or spend a sabbath at one of them.

Since propaganda is everything, the quarter is clearly signposted and practically all the sites have explanatory notes and diagrams – you can get an excellent picture of the physical development of Jerusalem through the ages here. There are two **information centres**: the *Jewish Quarter Information Centre* on Tiferet Yisrael Street, and *Archaeological Seminars* (34 Habad

Street; ☎02-282221). The latter organise two-hour guided walking tours of the Old City, including the City of David and the excavations below al-Haram; tours begin at 8.45am, Sunday to Friday. Most sites in the Jewish Quarter are closed on Friday afternoon, Saturday and Jewish holidays, but these are good times to walk around and watch the activity at the Western Wall.

Bab Harat al-Magharbeh or Dung Gate

Dung Gate, in the southeast corner of the Old City, is the only city gate leading directly into the Jewish quarter, as well as being the most direct approach to the Wailing Wall and al-Haram al-Sharif. Most Israeli tours enter the Old City here, so the approach to the gate looks like (and basically is) a giant car park. It is easy to approach, though, on *Egged* bus #1 or #38 direct from the main bus station. The name **Bab Harat al-Magharbeh** (Gate of the Moorish Quarter) derives from the fact that the area immediately inside it was traditionally inhabited by North Africans: Dung Gate recalls the time when Jerusalem's garbage was carted through here before being dumped into the Kidron Valley. In Hebrew it is known as **Sha'ar HaKotel** – (Western) Wall Gate.

On the right just inside the gate, on the southern side of Mount Moriah, lies the huge and impressive maze of the **Ophel Archaeological Gardens** (Sun–Thur 9am–5pm, Fri 9am–3pm), which seem to encompass the whole of Jerusalem's turbulent history in one confined area. You can see remains of structures ranging from the tenth century BC, the time of Solomon, to the sixteenth-century reign of Sultan Suleiman the Magnificent; above all, a majestic 100m-wide flight of stairs that led pilgrims up to the Hulda Gates entrance of the Temple precincts. Other finds include the ruins of a vast public building from the First Temple period, sections of Robinson's Arch (see below) and a Byzantine residential quarter, including a two-storey house with mosaic floors. There are also Muslim buildings: an administrative complex from the Omayyad period (661–749AD) including the caliphs'

PALESTINIANS IN THE JEWISH QUARTER

The Jewish Quarter was made *Arabrein* after 1967. In an infamous **Supreme Court decision** Judge Haim Cohen (currently president of the Israeli Civil Rights Association) ruled that the authorities could keep the area free of non-Jews *"because they have three other quarters"*. His decision is of no use, of course, to Palestinians defending their homes from settler expansion into other parts of the Old City.

One of the most poignant cases was that of **Muhammad Burkan**. He was thrown out of his family home in the mass evictions, and when the Jewish quarter development company put the house up for sale he tried to buy it back. But he failed and it was in relation to his appeal through the Israeli courts that Judge Cohen made his ruling. Burkan's trials, though, did not end with the loss of his rights in the Old City. He built a new home outside Jerusalem on land owned by relatives. When the Israelis put up Pisgat Ze'ev, the third in the suburban settlement rings to the north of the city, Burkan's new house ended up in the middle of a roundabout! Not many tourists visit Pisgat Ze'ev, but as a monument to discrimination and hypocrisy it takes some beating.

palace, and a tower built by the Fatimid sultans (969–1071AD) repaired by the Crusaders, the Ayyubids and the Mamluks. These were lucky to survive. The excavations, begun in 1968, were led by the late Israeli archaeologist, Professor Mazar, and according to the Israeli newspaper *Ha'aretz* (Oct 16, 1987):

> *During the excavations important Muslim buildings were "surprisingly" discovered. The question was what to do with them . . .Yigal Yadin is reported to have said: "Why bother? No one knows. Let's get rid of them and continue to the periods that interest us." What did Mazar do? Until the issue was leaked to the press, he was almost persuaded by Yadin. Emotionally he was on Yadin's side; practically, he understood it was not scientific.*

The Western or Wailing Wall

From Bab Harat al-Magharbeh there's a direct approach to the quarter's proudest monument, the **Western or Wailing Wall**, one of the most sacred of Jewish shrines. In Jewish tradition it is the Western Wall (*HaKotel HaMa'aravi*) of the Second Temple. The wall is also sacred to Muslims for whom it is the place from which the Prophet Mohammed rose on his night journey to heaven. In Arabic, the wall is known as *al-Burak* after the prophet's horse. In reality, the wall is part of the retaining wall built to support the mount above: the massive stones of its lower part bear all the hallmarks of Herod the Great's building style and were erected in 20BC. The upper part was rebuilt during the Muslim period using smaller stones.

Even though it was never actually part of the Temple but only its support, the wall has significance for Jews who come here to lament the destruction of the temples – hence the **Wailing Wall** – and to tuck prayer notes into its crevices. Among ultra-orthodox sects reverence of a wall made of stone is shunned as tantamount to idol worship; you only have to observe devotees walking away from it backwards to see their point of view! Prayer at the wall is fervent, particularly on Friday evenings and Jewish holidays. Jewish people come from all over the world to hold bar mitzvah services for their sons in front of it, and Israeli army units use the esplanade in front of the wall for swearing-in ceremonies.

The wall is treated as a synagogue and divided into two sections; the smaller part on the right reserved for women, the larger one for men, with a metal railing separating the prayer area from the esplanade. Recently, clashes between 'liberal' Jewish women, mostly Americans, and orthodox men objecting to their vociferous prayer services, have taken place here. All bags are searched at the entrances (Dung Gate, Tariq Bal al-Silsileh and Tariq al-Wad), modest dress is required, smoking is forbidden and no photography is permitted on the sabbath or Jewish holidays. Men must cover their heads if they wish to approach the Wailing Wall: the guards will lend you a skull cap if you don't have one.

Historically, the right of Jews to pray at the wall was guaranteed by the **status quo** – the agreements reached between the three faiths predominant in the city. With the rise of Zionism, however, the religious significance of the wall acquired a more political bent. During the British Mandate period, the

Zionists held demonstrations at the wall and tried to acquire *Waqf* property nearby. In 1928, Jewish worshippers attempted to introduce a partition screen at the wall, but were prevented from doing so by the Mandatory authorities. Matters came to a head on August 25, 1928, when Jewish nationalists (led by Jabotinsky) called for 'revolt and insubordination'. Ensuing clashes between them and the Muslim population left 29 Jews and 38 Arabs dead and scores wounded.

Before Israeli occupation only a narrow alley separated the wall from the nearest houses. Paintings, prints and old photographs capture the intimacy of the devout at prayer while around them non-Jews go about their daily business. Today there's a vast open **esplanade** in front of the wall, the site of the former **Magharbeh Quarter** which was bulldozed in June 1967. Meron Benvenisti, a respected Israeli historian and writer, former deputy mayor of Jerusalem and founder/director of the West Bank Data Project, described the events:

> *Saturday, June 10, 1967, the families occupying the houses in the Quarter were informed that they would have to evacuate the buildings within three hours. Only a few managed to take all their possessions with them. Bulldozers . . . began to topple the one- and two-storey houses by floodlight. By morning a space of more than one acre had been cleared in front of the Wall . . . it turned out that the bulldozer operators had also mistakenly demolished some houses not originally scheduled for removal. It was then decided to demolish the entire Mughrabi Quarter.*

Over 600 Palestinians were made homeless as the result of this one 'mistake'.

Underneath the arches

To the north of the wall, an arched passageway leads from the new Western Wall plaza to Tariq al-Wad. The tunnel is one of the vaults under the ancient bridge that carries Tariq Bab al-Silsileh from west to east across the town's central valley, al-Wad. The bridge is known to westerners as **Wilson's Arch** after the archaeologist Charles Wilson who discovered it in 1868. The vaults were cleared of debris in 1977 and today are mainly used as synagogues. Some parts date from the fifteenth to sixteenth century, some from the Second Temple period and others from the Ommayad period (seventh to eighth century). There are also the remains of a Roman-Byzantine street and a pre-Herodian room. Signs on both sides of the tunnel indicate excavated periods.

High on the southern end of the Western Wall are the remains of the fifteen-metre-high **Robinson's Arch**, thought to have been the first of the series of arches that formed the monumental bridge over the valley and connected the western part of the city with the Haram mount. Beneath it archaeologists have uncovered parts of a paved street containing cells which served as shops. Stoneware, weights, first-century coins and Herodian pottery have been unearthed here.

To the right of the wall, up a ramp, **Bab al-Magharbeh** (Moors' Gate) leads into the al-Haram sanctuary. A large sign warns observant Jews against entering the area since, during the time of the Temple, only high priests were allowed to enter the 'Holy of Holies'.

Jewish Quarter Road

The other main approach to the Jewish quarter is via Jewish Quarter Road, which runs south from the central *souq* area. About halfway down stands the **minaret** of the Mosque of Sidi Umar, which dates from around 1397, was damaged by sniper fire in the 1967 war and repaired in 1974. Beside it are the Rambam and Hurva **synagogues**, both built on the remains of a Crusader church. **Rambam**, the oldest synagogue in the quarter, was founded by the famous medieval scholar Rabbi Moshe Nachmanides, who came from Spain to Jerusalem in 1267. In 1474, following a heavy rainfall, it collapsed and after a long and involved dispute, was demolished but later rebuilt on the intervention of Sultan Qaytbay.

All that remains of the **Hurva** (Ruins) synagogue is an incongruously new arch spanning what used to be the central hall. The construction of the synagogue was begun in 1700 by Rabbi Judah the Hassid, a member of one of the first organised groups of *Ashkenazi* Jewish immigrants to Jerusalem. Building stopped on the rabbi's death but was restarted under Ibrahim Pasha in 1836. Eventually completed in 1857, it was destroyed by the Jordanians after 1948.

Next to the synagogues is the **Jewish Quarter Centre or Museum**, which for a small fee offers a 15-minute slide show on the history of the quarter from biblical times to the present, emphasising the loss of the Jewish quarter to the Arab Legion in 1948 and its recapture in 1967. Across the road, the **Old Yishuv Museum** (6 Or HaHayim St; ☎02-284636; Sun–Thur 9am–4pm) is a restored complex containing synagogues and exhibition rooms showing aspects of Jewish life in the Old City from the mid-nineteenth century to World War I.

The Cardo

The most interesting of the quarter's archaeological sites is the **Cardo Maximus** on the west side of Jewish Quarter Road more or less opposite the minaret. This was the colonnaded main street of Hadrian's *Aelia Capitolina* (132–135AD) and continued to be the principal throughfare of the Byzantine city (later being used by the Crusaders as their main market). At the open southern end of the excavated section, below the present street level, are **Hasmonean** city walls and remains of buildings of the **First Temple** period. The street then runs on underground, its highlight a reproduction of the famous sixth-century mosaic **Madaba Map**. This map, discovered on the floor of a church in Madaba in Jordan, depicts the towns and cities of the whole country. Jerusalem is shown with a main street running from Bab al-'Amud (Damascus Gate) in the north to the southern Nea Gate of *Aelia Capitolina*. Diagrams and covered archaeological exhibitions along either side of the route describe other historical periods. In an effort to divert trade from the Arab shops in the Old City, the vaulted northern end of the Cardo (open and lit up at night) now contains expensive gift shops and art galleries, generally deserted.

Four Sephardi Synagogues

The recently restored **Four Sephardi Synagogues** (HaKehuna Street), three metres below street level to the south of here, are arguably the most famous in Jerusalem. Originally built in the seventeenth century, and once the centre of Jewish community life, they remain the religious heart of Jerusalem's Sephardic community: it was here the Jews of the Old City gathered and finally surrendered in 1948. They were built deep below ground level because of a regulation which forbade their roofs rising above those of surrounding buildings.

The **Rabbi Yohanan Ben Zakkai Synagogue** is named after the first-century sage who is said to have taught his pupils on the site. Its twin Arks are decorated with a bright blue and gold mural. The **Emtza'i (Central) Synagogue**, the smallest of the four, and the **Stambouli (Istanbul) Synagogue** – so called because many of its congregation came from Turkey – stand alongside each other. The latter has a gilded seventeenth-century Italian Ark and a four-columned *bima* (platform). The oldest of the four synagogues, **Eliyahu HaNavi** (Elijah the Prophet) (Sun–Thur 9am–4pm, Fri 9am–1pm), takes its name from the belief that this was where the prophet prayed on *Yom Kippur* (the Day of Atonement). The chair at the entrance replaces the one on which he is said to have sat and inside there's a magnificent hand-carved wooden Ark, of sixteenth century Italian craftsmanship.

Elsewhere in the quarter

From behind the Hurva synagogue, Tiferet Yisrael Street leads past the facade, now strangely topped by ugly grey cement, which is all that remains of the nineteenth-century Tiferet Yisrael or **Nissan Bak Hassidic synagogue**. Nearby is the Jewish Quarter Information Centre and further along the street, down towards the Western Wall, one of the most remarkable sites in the Jewish Quarter, the **Burnt House** (9am–5pm; ☎02-287211). The remains of one of the houses torched during Titus' destruction of the city in 70AD, this has an entrance corridor, four rooms, kitchen and bathing pool, all of which can be clearly made out. It belonged to the priestly Kathros family – the name was engraved on weights uncovered in the basement – and among the more gruesome finds was the skeletal arm of a woman who apparently died struggling to escape the fire. A **sound and light show** (in English at 9.30am, 11.30am and 3.30pm) vividly re-creates the destruction.

Next to the Burnt House are new excavations of the Herodian city, while across the road, on Misgav Ladach Street, stands a twelfth-century complex consisting of a hospital, a hospice and the church of **Saint Mary's of the Germans**. The Crusader church was built as a pilgrim centre and run by German members of the order of St. John.

From here, broad stone steps lead to the Western Wall piazza. On the right, halfway down, is the newly rebuilt **Porat Yosef Yeshiva**, designed by Israeli architect Moshe Safdie and the largest in the quarter. Continuing down the steps you get a great view of the Western Wall, with the golden

Dome of the Rock and the silver dome of al-Aqsa behind and the Mount of Olives as background. On a clear day, this view can even take in the Dead Sea beyond.

Another of the area's sprouting *yeshivot*, **Yeshivat HaKotel** (Western Wall yeshiva) can be found on Batei Mahasse Street on the south side of the quarter. In its basement are the remains of the huge basilica built by Justinian in 543AD: the **Nea** or **New Church** that is clearly marked on the Madaba Map. All that remains of it is the southern apse, projecting outside the city walls, while in the courtyard are carved columns and other masonry thought to be part of a Hasmonean palace.

Between the two *yeshivot*, at 35 Misgav Ladach Street (corner of Hagittit Street), is the new **Siebenberg House archaeological museum** (Sun–Thur 9am–5pm, Fri 9am–1pm; 45-min guided tour in English at noon; ☎02-282341/ 287969). Finds beneath the house include a Hasmonean cistern, sections of a water conduit which may be part of the lower aqueduct that once conveyed water from Solomon's Pools to the Temple and arrowheads used to defend the city against the Babylonians in 586AD.

In the northern sector of the Jewish Quarter is the **Yad Ben-Zvi Institute** (Plugat HaKotel). The institute, founded in memory of Yitzhaq Ben-Zvi, second president of Israel, teaches and researches the history of Jewish communities. A recent project is a model of Jerusalem at the time of the First Temple, based on rather scanty evidence. An adjacent room houses exhibitions on burial customs and ancient scripts. The institute, according to its director, is 'not a tourist site but an educational centre', catering mainly for groups. Individual visitors, however, are admitted (noon, 12.30pm, 2pm and 4pm; admission $2) for talks on the model with a slide show.

Opposite the institute, a flight of steps leads down into an excavated area. Here a massive section of the **first wall**, dating from the eighth to the seventh century BC, has been revealed, part of the wall that once ringed the City of David, the Temple Mount and the Upper City. Adjacent to it was an eight-metre-high tower. Arrowheads found here again date from the Babylonian siege of Jerusalem in 586BC.

Al-Haram al-Sharif

At the dawn, when the light of the sun first strikes the dome and the drum catches the rays, then is this edifice a marvellous sight to behold, and one such that in all of Islam I have not seen the equal . . .

Al-Muqaddasi, 985AD

Al-Haram al-Sharif, the Noble Sanctuary to Muslims and the Temple Mount for Jews, graces a great esplanade above the city. The vast open expanse, shaded by greenery and dominated by the gold and mosaic Dome of the Rock, is an extraordinary oasis of calm in the heart of this crazy city. You'll have seen the **Dome of the Rock** from various vantages around and outside the Old City, and in images of Jerusalem around the world, but to enter is something else. The compound is dotted with people preparing for prayer or simply strolling around, sitting, talking or reading in the forecourt, with kids playing and tourist groups wandering about. You can come here just to see the architectural wonders – a visit of an hour or two – or spend longer relaxing away from the heat and crush outside. The Christian theologist Alfred Guillaume, in his book *Islam*, compared the atmosphere here to that in the Church of the Holy Sepulchre: 'A Christian who, like the writer, goes from a visit to the Church of the Holy Sepulchre with its warring, noisy, competitive sects to the peace and devotion of the Great Mosque of Jerusalem cannot but be saddened and chastened to find in the one what he was looking for in the other.'

Apart from the mosques, there are scores of lesser Islamic monuments in the sanctuary area – *mastabas* (raised platforms), *mihrabs* (prayer niches) and *sebils* (fountains) – as well as the library of al-Aqsa and the fascinating Islamic museum. **Access to the compound** is free and the area is open every day except Friday from 8am till sunset, except during the five daily prayer times: for the most important areas, the Dome of Rock, al-Aqsa and the Islamic Museum, you'll have to get a ticket from offices near Bab al-Naazir or Bab al-Magharebeh. Entry to non-Muslims is permitted only through four of the gates – **Bab al-Ghawanimeh** (Gate of the Beni Ghanim family), **Bab al-Naazir** (Custodian's Gate), **Bab al-Silsileh** (Chain Gate) and **Bab al-Magharebeh** (Moors' Gate) – though you can leave through any gate.

The whole Haram area is under the supervision of the Islamic *Waqf*, (trustees) whose offices are just outside Bab al-Hadid (Iron Gate). As for all religious sites, dress should be modest. Shoes must be removed before entering mosques, and eating, drinking and smoking are not allowed.

Some history

Mount Moriah, on which the complex stands, is the traditional site of the holy rock where **Abraham** prepared to sacrifice his son (Isaac according to Judaism and Christianity, Ismael according to Islam). Here Solomon is believed to have erected the **First Temple** in 960BC to house the Ark of the Covenant which his father, David, had brought into Jerusalem. Solomon's temple was burned to the ground by the Babylonians in 586BC. Whether it actually stood here, however, is open to question: according to one Israeli academic, Gaalya Cornfeld, if the temple had been gutted by fire, remains of ashes would have been buried in the surrounding earth. But there are none. Based on his readings and research, and encouraged by the late and respected Israeli archaeologist Benyamin Mazar, Cornfeld believes that Solomon erected his Temple above the houses on the plateau of Mount Zion.

The **Second Temple**, consecrated in 515BC, rebuilt by Herod in 20BC and destroyed by Titus in 70AD following the first Jewish Revolt, was sited here, though few traces survive. The Western Wall and Solomon's Stables under al-Aqsa Mosque are thought to date from the time of Herod. Thanks to the comprehensive account of Josephus (*Antiquities 15:380–425*) and the measurements detailed in the *Mishnah*, a model of how Herod's temple might have looked has been constructed and can be seen in the *Holyland Hotel* (p.110). After the Second Revolt in 135AD, Jerusalem was again razed to the ground and subsequently Hadrian erected a temple to Jupiter on this site.

The Byzantine Christians used the area as a dump and it was in this state that the first Muslim Caliph, Omar Ibn al-Khattab, found it when he accepted the surrender of Jerusalem in 638AD.

According to the *Quran*, **Mohammed** flew from Mecca to Jerusalem in a single night on his horse, al-Burak. On reaching Jerusalem, in the company of the archangel Gabriel, the Prophet of Islam prayed at the **Holy Rock of Abraham** and from it ascended to heaven on a staircase of light, returning to Mecca before dawn. It was towards Jerusalem, venerated by the followers of Islam, that Muslims first directed their prayers (the first *qibla*) before Mecca became the main centre of the faith.

When Mohammed's successor, the Caliph Omar, was met by Patriarch Sophronius of Jerusalem, he asked to be taken to the Holy Rock. The Patriarch instead took him first to the Church of the Holy Sepulchre. After eventually finding the rock under a rubbish dump, Omar ordered the place cleaned and built a small mosque at the southern end of the sanctuary. Bishop Arculfus, a Christian visitor of 670AD, described it as '. . . a square house of prayer . . . of boards and large beams on the remains of some ruins'. Omar's mosque, now al-Aqsa, marks the spot where Mohammed tethered al-Burak. The Umayyad Caliphs (661–749AD) built the first great monuments: the Dome of the Rock in 691AD and al-Aqsa mosque in 705–715AD.

The Dome of the Rock

Tradition has it that the purpose of **Caliph Abd al-Malik Ibn Marawan** in building the golden-domed mosque in 691AD was, in part, to put the relatively new religion of Islam on an equal footing with its predecessors, Judaism and Christianity, and to detract from the Church of the Holy Sepulchre. The Jerusalem historian, al-Muqaddasì, writing in 985AD, states: 'and in like manner the Caliph Abd al-Malik, noting the greatness of the Church of the Holy Sepulchre and its magnificence, was moved lest it should dazzle the minds of the Muslims and hence erected above the Holy Rock a dome which is now to be seen there.' Abd al-Malik is said to have employed 52 official cleaners to wash the mosque with a mixture of saffron, musk and ambergris in rose water before prayer times.

The octagonal **Dome of the Rock** (*al-Qubbat al-Sakhra*; 8–11.30am, 12.30–2.30pm and 3.30–4pm, closed Fridays and Muslim holidays; ☎02-283313), which the Crusaders mistakenly named the Mosque of Omar, dominates the peaceful sanctuary. With its landmark golden dome, dazzling mosaics and exquisite, mathematically perfect proportions, it is justifiably considered one of the wonders of the modern world. The inner circle around the rock is formed by 12 marble columns and 4 piers supporting the patterned golden dome, in which are set 16 stained glass windows that allow in a soft greenish-blue light. This circle is surrounded by 2 octagons, the first formed by 16 columns and 8 piers, the second by the outer walls.

Under the rock is a cave containing two small shrines to Abraham and al-Khadr (Elijah) beneath which, in the Bir al-Arwah (Well of Souls), spirits are said to await Judgement Day. Hairs from Mohammed's beard are kept in a shrine next to the rock which is opened once a year on the 27th day of

Ramadan. Mohammed's footprint and the imprint of the hand of the archangel Gabriel, who restrained the rock as it tried to follow the prophet up to heaven, can be seen on the underside of the rock.

The beauty and complexity of the interior and exterior **decoration** of the Dome of the Rock defy summary. There is no one point where you can stand and take in the whole. You will be drawn round the building again and again, captivated here by the intricacy of tiles, there by the play of soft light filtering through the stained glass windows onto rings of Arabic calligraphy, arabesques and small arches. The large barren rock at the centre seems incongruous amid all this splendour. Above it the drum and dome are decorated by bands of predominantly gold and green glass, mother-of-pearl and gold sheet mosaics. These are the oldest of the decorations, dating from the time of the original designers. Most of the patterns consist of stylised vegetation laid out symmetrically and divided by lines of calligraphy and friezes. The ceilings of the ambulatories are patterned with abstract designs in gold, russet and green interspersed with octagons and circles.

Outside, the walls are faced with marble slabs topped with glazed green and blue tiles, and the outer face of the drum is similarly tiled. The present designs, a combination of Quranic inscription, geometrical shapes and vines and flowers, were originally commissioned by Suleiman the Magnificent in the sixteenth century. They have been repeatedly renovated and repaired since, most recently in 1963. The **dome** was covered with anodised aluminium in the 1960s, lighter than the lead covering that had been causing structural damage to the building, and cheaper than the gold which supposedly once kept out the elements before being melted down to pay the caliph's debts.

Al-Aqsa Mosque

Glory be to him who carried his servant by night
from the Holy Mosque to the Farthest Mosque
the precincts of which We have blessed . . .

Quran, Sura 17

Simpler and less grandiose than its sister, the silver-domed **Masjid al-Aqsa** – the Farthest Mosque (8–11.30am, 12.30–2.30pm and 3.30–4pm; closed Fridays and Muslim holidays; ☎02-283313) – is altogether calmer and cooler, its atmosphere more conducive to quiet meditation.

Inside it seems relatively modern, as it was substantially restored between 1938 and 1942. Throughout its history, indeed, the mosque has been constantly damaged by earthquakes and continually rebuilt. The original structure, erected around 715AD by Caliph al-Walid, son of Caliph Abd al-Malik, was destroyed in 747AD. When it was restored in 780AD under the next Caliph, Mohammed al-Mahdi, it had twenty aisles instead of the seven that exist today. In 985AD, Al-Muqaddasi described the mosque as having fifteen doorways in the north wall and eleven in the eastern wall, and an interior with 280 columns set in twenty rows. Damaged in the earthquake of 1016AD, the mosque re-emerged with five gates in the north and ten in the east, with an enamelled pulpit and beautifully carved roof. The present structure is essentially that of Caliph al-Zaher Li-Izaz Dinillah who rebuilt it after yet another earthquake in 1033AD.

In 1099, the Crusader leader Godfrey de Bouillon set up his headquarters here. On its west side he built his armoury – the beautiful arched buildings now used as the **Women's Mosque** and the **Islamic museum** – and the mosque became a church, its dome topped with a cross. The underground vaults, living up to their traditional name of Solomon's Stables, housed Crusader horses. The military order of the **Knights Templar**, founded in 1118, was named after the complex, known by the Crusaders simply as the Templum.

Salah al-Din removed the Templar constructions from the west side of the mosque, decorated the beautiful *mihrab*, and from Aleppo brought the famous cedar-wood *minbar* (pulpit), inlaid with ivory and mother-of-pearl, that was destroyed in the fire set by a Messianic Christian in 1969.

Entering al-Aqsa today, you pass through the impressive arched main doorway into the **central aisle**, the widest of the seven, which has a beautiful carved and painted roof supported by massive columns of pale marble. To the west of the *minbar* are two small prayer niches dedicated to Moses and Jesus. The exquisite green, gold and blue mosaic work of the dome, which has been described as the most beautiful in al-Haram, was also commissioned by Salah al-Din in 1189. The motifs are similar to those in the Dome of the Rock and it has been suggested that the original artists were ordered to make copies. The dome is supported by four arches and inset with seven of the mosque's 121 stained glass windows.

Outside the main northern entrance a flight of steps leads down into **Solomon's Stables**, a labyrinth of massive pillars and arches where it has been suggested that sacrificial animals were housed in the days of the Second Temple. A long vaulted passage leads from here to the blocked **Double Gate**

Lesser structures

A further nine domes can be seen within the Haram complex. Northwest of the Dome of the Rock is the **Dome of the Ascension** (Qubbat al-Miraj). Its original date is unknown, but it was restored in 1200AD. Between here and the Dome of the Rock, the **Dome of the Prophet** (Qubbat al-Nabi), was built on eight marble columns around 1845. Just east of the Dome of the Rock, at the exact centre of the compound, the **Dome of the Chain** (Qubbat al-Silsileh) is an 11-columned monument variously explained as a scale model for the Dome of the Rock or as the Treasury of the Haram; its name derives from a legend that those who held onto a chain hung from the roof during Solomon's time were struck dead if they told a lie.

There are also seven **fountains**, the most impressive of which is the **Sabil of Sultan Qaytbay**, west of the Dome of the Rock in front of the al-Aqsa Library. It takes its name from the sultan who restored it in 1482. Directly south of the Dome of the Rock, in line with al-Aqsa Mosque, is the fountain for washing before prayer known as **al-Kas** (The Cup) which originally drew its water supply from springs near Hebron. You approach it through one of

THE THREAT TO AL-HARAM

For the aesthete there is nothing in Jerusalem to equal the experience of al-Haram. Muslim visitors will obviously have it at the top of their itineraries, and believers of other faiths have drawn spiritual inspiration from the compound. Politics, however, casts a lengthening shadow. In **1967**, Israeli soldiers flew their flag in triumph from the Dome of the Rock and the army rabbi called for the reconstruction of the Temple. Wiser counsel prevailed at that time, and guarantees were extended to the *Waqf* that supervision of al-Haram would remain theirs. The military retained the keys to several of the locked gates, however, and *Waqf* control has never been accepted by certain sections of Israeli society. As **fanaticism** has grown in Israel so have the movements to destroy the Muslim shrines.

This political extremism is exemplified by the self-styled **Custodians of the Temple Mount** who stage frequent demonstrations and prayers outside al-Haram. They have also managed to infiltrate the area in recent years and demonstrate with army protection. More sinister groups and individuals prefer direct action. An Australian Christian set fire to al-Aqsa in 1969 causing extensive damage. An Israeli soldier opened fire on worshippers and the Dome of the Rock in the early 1980s. Several people were killed when other soldiers fired on protestors and over 80 bullets damaged the drum and dome. Others have died in the suppression of demonstrations in and around al-Haram, especially since the start of the *intifada.*

In 1981 a group of Israelis were detained outside Jerusalem with a large cache of **explosives** and other military equipment. At their trial it was revealed that they planned to destroy al-Aqsa and the Dome of the Rock as a prelude to the establishment of a new Temple. Other explosives caches have been discovered in religious seminaries in the Jewish Quarter, where several schools are training seminarians to become priests in the reconstructed temple.

Less drastically, the activities of **archaeologists** burrowing around the edges of al-Haram are causing concern for the structural integrity of the buildings above. In one case *Waqf* employees clearing out a basement came across a tunnel; following it back they emerged in a building occupied by settlers. In the furore which followed, it was revealed that the settlers were carrying out their own search for evidence of the Temple.

Thus far the Israeli campaign for the destruction of al-Haram has been studiously unofficial. The military and Jerusalem municipal officials have confined themselves to piecemeal adjustments in the 1967 agreement. But Palestinians, victims for a century of Zionist *faits accomplis,* are understandably less charitable than the western media in their interpretations of incursions.

the archways at the top of the eight stairways leading to the platform of the Dome of the Rock. This arch is the *minbar* of Judge Burhan al-Din, built in 1388.

The **gates to the haram** are also well worth investigating. In the **north wall** are Bab al-Atim (Gate of Darkness), Bab Hittah (Gate of Remission), the Minaret of Asbat and Bab al-Asbat (Gate of Tribes). The arcades, originally built by the Crusaders, were restored in 1213. The **east wall** is pierced by al-Bab al-Zahabi (Golden Gate), a two-arched construction comprising Bab al-Rahmeh (Gate of Mercy) and Bab al-Taubeh (Gate of Repentance), and you can also see the Kursi Suleiman (Solomon's Throne). In the south wall are the Single Gate, Double Gate and Triple Gate (all sealed) and the Minaret of al-Fakhriya (1278). Along the **west wall** are the main points of entry: Bab al-

Magharebeh (Moors' Gate), with the twin Bab al-Silsileh (Chain Gate); Bab al-Salem (Gate of Peace); the Minaret of the Chain; Bab al-Matarah (Gate of Rain or Ablution); Bab al-Qattanin (Gate of the Cotton Merchants); Bab al-Hadid (Iron Gate); Bab al-Naazir (Custodian's Gate); and Bab al-Ghawanimeh. Also along this side of the compound are a minaret and arcades dating from the fourteenth century.

The Islamic Museum

The **Islamic Museum** (8–11.30am, 12.30–2.30pm and 3–4pm, closed Fridays and Muslim holidays) was originally established in 1923, four years before the Palestine Archaeological Museum, and is therefore the oldest museum in Jerusalem. It is housed in two historic buildings, one Mamluk, the other Crusader, to the west of al-Aqsa Mosque, buildings so much in harmony with the rest of the Noble Sanctuary that you barely realise you're entering a secular building. Between the museum and the mosque are dozens of column capitals from the numerous phases of the latter's history, beginning with the building erected in the early eighth century by the Ommayad Caliph al-Walid.

Inside, **exhibits** range from tiny flasks for kohl eye make-up to giant architectural elements from mosques. The first display is of porcelain cups from the Far and Near East – the locally produced ones inscribed with angular fifteenth-century Kufic script. Inscribed brass mosque seals, glassware from early Islamic times, filigree incense burners and coins can also be seen. The larger objects include exquisite gilded and enamelled mosque lamps from the Hebron area dating from the thirteenth century, a large jewel-encrusted Hand of Fatima, and a collection of decorated guns, swords and daggers from the seventeenth and eighteenth centuries.

The **manuscript section**, which has some rare medieval and Ottoman copies of the *Quran*, including an eighth-century version ascribed to the Prophet's great-grandson, is another of the highlights. Look out for the case containing a huge leather box with silver decorations, which holds a medieval *Quran* of gazelle skin donated to al-Aqsa by the Moroccan Sultan Abd Allah ben Abd al-Haq.

The exhibits in the **second building** are much larger. Among them are exceptionally rich religious vestments of silk and gold, silk panels of calligraphy and fragments of al-Aqsa's seventeenth-century prayer-rug. There are also stone friezes and balustrades from the Crusader era, when al-Aqsa was the headquarters of the Knights Templar, decorative cypress wood panels from the original eighth-century mosque, and the burnt remains of the great cedar wood, ivory and mother of pearl *minbar* that was given to the mosque by Salah al-Din in 1187. Other objects include ancient stained glass, a fourteenth-century crescent from the Dome of the Rock, the magnificent Crusader wrought-iron screen that surrounded the Holy Rock from the twelfth to the twentieth century, remains of mosaic and ceramic walls from the Dome of the Rock, a nineteenth-century cannon which was fired to mark the start of the fast during Ramadan, and huge copper kettles from the soup kitchen established for the poor by the wife of Suleiman the Magnificent.

EAST JERUSALEM

Beyond the confines of the Old City, **East Jerusalem** is the victim of its time. Anywhere else it would be a fairly pleasant, not particularly notable small town. But this small town has had capitalhood thrust on it in an age when the occupation will not allow it to expand into the space it needs to fulfil this role properly. So the overwhelming first impression is one of crowds. National newspapers, charities, businesses and administrations all vie for office space. Shops and restaurants shoulder each other aside. Regional and local transport systems tie each other in knots in the congested streets. And the seekers of God or Mammon cram pavements already overcrowded with schoolkids, market traders, men seeking work and the military trying to keep a lid on it all.

The town grew up around the turn of the century, with its main arteries fanning out north and east from the Old City. Of the two chief commercial thoroughfares, **Nablus Road** has the offices and institutions, **Salah al-Din Street** the shops. Between them are a selection of both, with the bus station thrown in to make the journey hazardous. The further away from the Old City you are, the quieter it gets. **Al-Zahra Street**, the third biggest of the East city centre, has a couple of hotels, what few 'chic' restaurants the city has to offer, and a far less frenzied atmosphere. Tourist sites are scattered through the commercial and residential quarters; they're easiest visited a few at a time to make a break from the intensity inside the walls.

Unfortunately, East Jerusalem is too small (and too congested) to bus or taxi around, but just big enough to make walking about an exhausting experience. Allow yourself plenty of time and have lots to drink.

Outside the walls

The first few sites can be found almost immediately outside the Old City walls. The entrance to **King Solomon's Quarry**, whose workings descend 200m deep beneath the Old City, is on Sultan Suleiman Street, between Damascus and Herod's Gate. Although it's unlikely that King Solomon actually quarried stones from here to build the First Temple, material was being removed and used for important public buildings in Jerusalem right up to the beginning of this century. The quarry is also known as **Zedekiah's Cave**, for it was allegedly used as an escape route to Jericho by King Zedekiah (597–587BC) as he fled from the Babylonians. The well-lit, stepped descent (Sun–Thur 8am–4pm, Fri 8.30am–2pm) plunges deep under the Old City, and although there's not actually much to see, it's a distinctly strange experience – not one for the claustrophobic.

A short walk from here, hidden away down an unmarked alley off HaNevi'im (Prophets') Street between *Ramsis Youth Hostel* and a building bearing a sign reading *International Christian Committee*, is one of the most beautiful mosaics in the country – all the more splendid for the sense you get of having discovered it all on your own. Inside the vine-hung entrance of a simple residential house, a sad-looking old man sitting beside an equally sad-looking collection box will unlock the door of the **Armenian Convent of Polyeucte** (7am–5.30pm) and let you peek at the **Mosaic of the Birds**. This brilliantly coloured and delicate mosaic floor, all that remains of the fifth- to sixth-century convent, was discovered in 1894 when the foundations of the house were dug. Beneath an inscription, 'To the memory and salvation of the souls of all Armenians whose names are known by God alone', the tendrils of a huge vine each encircle a different bird while two enormous peacocks guard the nine-petalled vase from which the vine grows. The mosaic is thought to be one of the first monuments to the unknown soldier; beneath it is a grave containing the bones of Armenian warriors.

A monument to more recent history is the **Tourjeman Post** (1 Chail HaHandasa Street; Sun–Thur 9am–3pm; ☎02-281278 for group visits and guided tours), a distinctive pink-stone building which was a private Palestinian house belonging to the Baramki family until they were evicted by the Israelis in 1948. They are now refugees in Ramallah. From 1948 to 1967, the house they left behind became a frontier post, separating Israeli and Jordanian forces and overlooking the former **Mandelbaum Gate** crosspoint, through which UN personnel, diplomats, pilgrims and convoys to the Israeli Hebrew University enclave on Mount Scopus were allowed to pass. During the fighting of 1967, the building was badly damaged (the bullet holes are still visible) but today it has been transformed into an educational museum designed to show parties of Israeli schoolkids and soldiers 'what a divided city looks like'.

In the upstairs lookout room is a useful, building-by-building **model of Jerusalem** with the borders as they were. A 17-part exhibition of photographs, maps and documents portrays the history of Jerusalem from Palestine under the British to the 'reunification' of the city in 1967. Although the titles above the pictures are displayed in Hebrew, English and Arabic, the detailed commentaries alongside are in Hebrew and English only. The explanation of the museum attendants was that 'Palestinians don't come here because they consider it a museum of occupation!' A four-minute film without commentary shows the events of 1967 from an Israeli point of view.

Nablus Road

As its name implies, **Nablus Road** is the main thoroughfare from Jerusalem to the north of the West Bank. At its Damascus Gate junction, the road is narrow, dusty and congested with one-way traffic pouring into the city, but once free of the crush it widens out into far calmer and cooler surrounds with a few noteworthy sites.

As you head out from the Old City, the first site of interest is the **Garden Tomb** (Mon–Sat 8am–12.30pm and 2.30–5.30pm). On a visit to Jerusalem in 1883, the British General Gordon (of Khartoum 'fame') identified this as the real site of Christ's burial. Picturing Jerusalem as a skeleton, with the Dome of the Rock as the pelvis and Solomon's Quarries as the ribs, he posited that the hill to the north of Damascus Gate was the Golgotha or 'place of the skull' referred to in the gospels. The tangible result of his hypothesis today is a beautiful garden of flowers and shrubs, pools and streams: a refreshingly tranquil spot to rest. First laid out by a group of Anglicans in 1892, and now run by the *Garden Tomb Association* from London, it contains an unspectacular two-chambered tomb dating from around the first century AD.

Another fine product of the British imperial/religious love affair with this former possession is **Saint George's Anglican Cathedral**, a short distance further up Nablus Road at the corner of Salah al-Din Street. A perfect little church, dotted with wall-plaques in commemoration of British personnel who died during or since the Mandate period, it is used by the Palestinian Anglican community as well as by English-speaking visitors. The church is typically British colonial, an idealised view of the little parish church that is forever England: the school magazines of St. George's School adjoining the church enshrine the pre-1948 cricket results of the sons of wealthy Palestinians. In short, it is another monument to the failed attempt to give the 'natives' the trappings of an English public school education while depriving them of the power for which their Anglo-Saxon counterparts were groomed. The Crusader-like compound, built in 1899, also houses a **hostel** (see "Accommodation") in an exquisite inner courtyard garden.

The **Tomb of the Kings**, on the opposite corner of Salah al-Din Street and Nablus Road (8.30am–5pm), is so called because it was once thought to be the burial site of the kings of Judah. Now it is believed to be the family vault of the royal family of Adiabene, an independent state within the Babylonian empire whose queen, Helena, along with her son Izates, converted to Judaism. In Jerusalem on a pilgrimage in the first century, the queen decided to stay and, according to the historian Josephus (*Antiquities 20:95*), her son ordered her bones 'buried at the pyramids which their mother had erected . . . three furlongs from the city of Jerusalem'. A wide flight of time-worn steps descends into a vast open courtyard in which is a covered porch carved into the rock. A minute entrance on the right of the porch, once closed and hidden by a rolling stone, leads into an underground labyrinth of burial chambers and passages. Take a torch if you want to explore.

Museums

The imposing **Palestine Archaeological Museum** (PAM), on the hill more or less opposite Herod's Gate, was planned and built in 1927 under the British Mandate and is one of the richest and most fascinating museums in the country. Now renamed the **Rockefeller Museum**, its remarkable collection (Sun–Thur 10am–6pm, Fri and Sat 10am–2pm; tickets for Saturday must be bought in advance – see Israel Museum; ☎02-282251) starts in the Stone Age and ranges all the way through to the present day.

Some of the most notable **exhibits** are Bronze Age skeletons and weapons, finds from Egypt and Mesopotamia, Roman sarcophagi, Romanesque sculptures from the Church of the Holy Sepulchre, Greek and Byzantine pottery and eighteenth-century wood carvings from al-Aqsa Mosque. Also on display are parts of the walls, ceilings, facades and plasterwork of **Hisham's Palace** in Jericho. While most of the exhibits are well labelled, you may notice that some have had their descriptions removed: this is the censor's work, history being a security issue in Jerusalem. More notoriously, the famous **Dead Sea Scrolls** were looted from the PAM as part of the spoils of the 1967 war and are now rehoused in the Israel Museum – an act of vandalism denounced by the international academic community. As a result, the scrolls are not accepted abroad for temporary display, much to the Israeli government's chagrin. For more detail on individual pieces, ask at the desk for a **guide to the museum**; these frequently sell out, but if they have the attendant should lend you one to help you around.

As you browse, take a look at the **building** which houses the museum – a massive rectangular structure with a distinctive octagonal turret, built around a courtyard pond complete with water-lilies. There are panoramic views of Mount Scopus and the Mount of Olives from its grand entrance, with the northwest corner of the Old City wall at eye-level.

The **Palestinian Arab Folklore Centre** (*Dar al-Tifl al-Arabi*) in Obeid Ibn Jarrah Street (☎02-283251/273477) is the nearest thing Palestinians have to a national museum, a small five-room collection devoted to preserving the national culture and heritage. The thick-walled window arches of this 200-year-old house provide a setting for life-size mannequins displaying Palestinian dress and occupations, and there are displays of jewellery, cloths, pottery and metal, all hand-labelled in English and Arabic. A detailed, coloured catalogue is available, and the centre is well worth a look, but the collection is a private one, so call in advance to make an appointment.

The Mount of Olives

The **Mount of Olives** rises some 100m to the east of the Old City across the Kidron Valley. Green, fertile and nowadays dotted with more churches and shrines than olive trees, its summit affords a magnificent view of the whole of Jerusalem with the sealed Golden Gate of the Old City and, in the other direction, of the Judaean desert, the Jordan valley and the Mountains of Moab. In the Old Testament, the Mount of Olives is mentioned as the place where David mourned the death of his recalcitrant son Absalom (*II Samuel 15:30*),· and the mountain is also closely associated with Jesus who, according to the Gospels of Luke and Mark, used to walk over the hill from Bethany to Jerusalem. On its slopes, 'He beheld the city and wept over it' (*Luke 19:41*) and here, in the Garden of Gethsemane, he was arrested. At the summit, beacons were once lit to herald the new moon and inform Jerusalemites of the start of a new lunar month.

The best way to see the Mount of Olives is to **start at the top** and work your way down. Wear sensible footwear as the path is steep and slippery, and leave the best part of a day for the visit (but not Sunday when many of the sites are closed). To get to the top, catch one of the many *service* taxis plying the Old City–Kidron Valley–al-Tur route, or take bus #75 from the Damascus Gate bus station or #27 from the Israeli bus station off Nablus Road. The fit and foolhardy may prefer to walk. From the Palestine Archaeological Museum take the road that plunges east, down into the Kidron Valley, and then climbs steeply past the Islamiyya College, the new Mormon University, the *Palace Hotel* on the left and the *Commodore Hotel* on the right, to the village of **AL-TUR**, right at the top.

Al-Tur

From the bus stop in al-Tur walk past the *Mount of Olives Hotel* (on your left) and you'll come to the miniscule **Mosque or Chapel of the Ascension** from where, Luke says, Jesus 'was carried up into heaven' forty days after the Resurrection. There has been a church on the site since 390AD, but the small and rather disappointing building here today was erected by the Crusaders, and converted into a mosque by Salah al-Din in 1198, with a *mihrab* added in 1200. Muslims also venerate the ascension of Jesus. The rock inside the octagonal shrine is marked with the footprint Jesus left as he ascended.

The small **burial crypt** next to the mosque has something for everyone: Jews believe it contains the grave of the seventh-century prophetess **Hulda**; Christians that it is the tomb of the fifth-century saint **Pelagia**, and Muslims that **Rabi'a al-Adawiyya**, an eighth-century holy woman, is buried there. East of here is the White (Czarist) **Russian monastery and church** with its landmark tower crowning just about the highest point in Jerusalem. If you manage to get permission to visit, the view from the top of the six-storey bell-tower, from which the village takes its name (*al-Tur* = the tower), is truly spectacular. The head of John the Baptist is said to have been found here.

Across the road from the Ascension Mosque, past a grove of ancient olive trees, **Pater Noster Church** (Mon–Sat 8.30–11.45am and 3–4.30pm) is set in an enclosed garden and built over a cave in which Jesus preached on the ultimate conflict of good and evil leading to the end of the world (*Matt 24:1–25*). The original **Eleona Basilica** (Basilica of Olives), built under the direction of Queen Helena, was destroyed by the Persians in 614AD. The Crusaders, believing this to be the place where Jesus taught his disciples the Lord's Prayer, built a new church on the site and gave it its present name. The building dates from 1894, when the site was under the care of Carmelite nuns. Inside, a short flight of stairs from the south side of the open courtyard leads to the tomb of the Princesse de la Tour d'Auvergne who bought the property in 1868 and who had the Lord's Prayer inscribed in 62 languages on tiled panels in the entrance and cloister.

The road along the crest of the hill takes you towards the grand **Intercontinental Hotel**, built under the Jordanians, which offers *the* view of Jerusalem. This is the spot for the 'sunset over Jerusalem' shots your neighbours will expect you to bring back, though to get them you will have to elbow yourself some lens room among the busloads of tourists and their retinue of aspiring young 'tourist guides'. Postcards, prayer beads and wooden camels are on offer here, or you could have your photo taken on a real camel.

Heading down

As you set off down the mountain, the **common grave** of 48 soldiers who died in the 1948 war, and who were reinterred here shortly after the occupation, lies to your right. The vast **Jewish cemetery** just beyond is symbolic of the belief that when the Messiah comes, entering Jerusalem through the opened **Golden Gate** opposite, all the Jews buried here will be resurrected. This may come to nothing, however, as the Muslim cemetery, laid out beneath the Golden Gate across that supposed path, is believed by some to be a conspiracy to block the way of the Messiah who, as a member of the Cohen (priest) caste, will be forbidden by Jewish law to enter the ritually impure ground of a graveyard.

The **Tomb of the Prophets** (Sun–Fri 9am–3.30pm), to the left, is the traditional resting place of the last three Old Testament prophets: Hagai, Malachi and Zakariah. The 100-metre-long semi-circular outer corridor contains fifty tombs, whilst the inner tunnel was used for prayers. The keys to this 3000-year-old catacomb have been held for generations by the Othman family who live next door; the present key-holder, Harbi, will gladly light your way and give you a detailed guided tour of the tombs (for a 'donation' of one shekel) and may invite you into the family home for a cup of coffee. Ask at the house if all seems quiet.

The path from here down to the Franciscan Church of **Dominus Flevit** (The Lord Wept) gets steeper and more slippery; if you are exhausted and look it when you arrive, the doorman at the entrance to the grounds will sit you down on his chair and press glasses of cold fresh water on you till you revive. To the right inside the grounds (7–11.30am and 3–5pm) are the excavations of four burial chambers with Hebrew inscriptions, dating from 100BC to 300AD. The church, built over the remains of a fifth-century monastic chapel, was designed in 1955 by the Italian architect Anton Barluzzi in the shape of the tear shed by Jesus as he foresaw the fate of Jerusalem (as well he might!). Its exquisitely simple form hides a more elaborate interior. The arched wrought-iron grille window above the altar, framing the golden Dome of the Rock in the distance, is an image you'll have seen on many a postcard.

The next stop, halfway down the time-worn path, is the White Russian **Church of Saint Mary Magdalene** (Thur and Sat 9am–noon and 2–4pm, Sun 10am–noon), the seven golden cupolas of which are another of Jerusalem's most distinctive landmarks. Erected in 1885 by Czar Alexander III in the old Russian style, its crypt holds the remains of his mother, killed in the Russian Revolution of 1917.

The **Church of All Nations** (8.30am–noon and 2.30–6pm), so named because its construction in 1924 was financed by twelve different countries, is also known as the Basilica of the Agony. Another of Barluzzi's designs, the church is built over the ruins of two others: the *Egeria* dating from around 380, and a Crusader basilica of around 1170. The rock in the nave, where Jesus is reputed to have prayed, belongs to the fourth-century church. Parts of the Byzantine mosaic floor are visible inside, and there's a striking modern Byzantine-style mosaic arch above the entrance. All of this stands in the **Garden of Gethsemane** (though the Church of Mary Magdalene, above, also claims that distinction), where traditionally Jesus prayed the night before he was arrested. The garden itself, said to be 2000 years old, is full of flowers and ancient gnarled olive trees, from one of which Judas may have hanged himself.

The **Gethsemane Souvenir Shop**, to the right a little up the hill, is a welcome source of cold drinks and provides tables outside where you can sit and recover. Nearby is the tomb of the Arab historian **Mujir al-Din al-Ulaymi**, who died in 1522 and whose detailed work is an invaluable source of information on the city of his time (see p.74).

At the bottom of the Mount of Olives, the **Tomb of the Virgin** (Mon–Sat 6.30–11.30am and 2–5pm) lies to the right of the path. Writers of the late sixth century describe a church here in which Mary was supposedly entombed. By the time the Crusaders arrived, however, all they found were ruins. In 1130 the church was rebuilt by Benedictines, Franciscans took it over after the Crusaders left, and since then Greeks, Armenians, Syrians, Copts, Abyssinians and Muslims have all had shares in it. To the right of a twelfth-century flight of 45 marble steps is the tomb of the Crusader Queen Melisande who died in 1161; opposite is the vault of members of King Baldwin II's family and in the centre is a Byzantine crypt partly cut out of the rock, which used to be decorated with paintings. Mary's stone tomb lies to the right. Further along the *mihrab* gives the direction of Mecca; the site is also venerated by Muslims since, on his night journey from Medina to Jerusalem, the Prophet Mohammed is said to have spotted a light over Mary's tomb.

A short distance from the tomb is the cave where the disciples rested while Jesus prayed and where Judas kissed him. The **Grotto of Gethsemane** (8.30–11.45am and 2.30–5pm, Sun and Thur 2.30–3.30pm) has been frequently restored and contains traces of Byzantine mosaic floors, three new altars and frescoes.

The Kidron Valley

At the foot of the Mount of Olives, the **Kidron Valley** runs southwest past Mount Ophel to join the Valley of Hinnom south of the Old City, its east side dotted with ancient cemeteries. On the modern road there are three prominent monuments, the most elaborate of which is the curious bottle-shaped **Tomb or Pillar of Absalom**, dating from the first century AD. Nearby is another tomb identified from its Hebrew inscription as that of the priestly **family of Hezir**, whilst the third, with its pointed roof standing away from the rock, is the **Tomb of Zachariah**. Another notable monument, thought to date from the ninth to the seventh century BC, is the monolithic **Tomb of Pharaoh's Daughter** in the Palestinian village of SILWAN on the opposite side of the Kidron Valley.

Mount Ophel

The oldest part of Jerusalem, inhabited since the Early Canaanite period, lies on **Mount Ophel** directly south of Mount Moriah and the Dome of the Rock. On its eastern slope, Canaanite graves – the earliest evidence of human habitation in this area – were excavated by the English archaeologist Kathleen Kenyon in the 1960s: her books on the subject are still the seminal works. An eighteenth-century BC wall of massive stones is thought to be the remains of

a citadel, the ancient defences of the Jebusite city that enabled it to avoid
destruction at the hands of Joshua. It was finally conquered some 200 years
later by King David, who brought the Ark of the Covenant into the city (*II
Samuel 6*) and made Jerusalem the capital of his kingdom of Judah.

The Spring of Gihon

At the foot of Mount Ophel is the **Spring of Gihon**, the ancient lifeblood of
Jerusalem and probably the reason that the Jebusites built *Ur Shalem* here in
the first place. During the Assyrian seige in 700BC, King Hezekiah
constructed elaborate tunnels to cut off the attackers' water supply and
protect the city's own. This he did by blocking off the original spring and
diverting its waters down to the west side of the City of David (*II Chr 32:30*)
and along an underground tunnel beneath the wall of the city, to emerge at
the **Pool of Silwan** or Siloam (*Shiloah* in Hebrew) within the city walls. The
tunnel was carved out by two teams of rock hewers working simultaneously
from both ends. The non-claustrophobic can walk by candle-light, knee-deep
in water, through the narrow, eerily impressive 512-metre-long tunnel as
it twists and turns through the hillside, and emerge blinking into daylight at
the Silwan Pool (where Jesus is said to have healed a blind man). Near the
middle of the tunnel you can see where the two teams of diggers almost
missed each other (Sun–Thur 9am–5pm, Fri 9am–3pm).

Warren's Shaft

A short way into the tunnel, at the right-angle bend to the left, a wall blocks a
channel which leads to the bottom of a vertical shaft. Known as **Warren's
Shaft** after its nineteenth-century discoverer Charles Warren, this is thought
to have been driven through the rock by the Jebusites even earlier than
Hezekiah's tunnel to ensure their water supply. It may also have been the
shaft used by David's emmissary Joab to penetrate the city's defences (*II
Samuel 5:8*). If you don't fancy getting wet, this feat of aquatic engineering
can be experienced rather more comfortably from the top. Up there, there's
an entrance at the foot of the City of David excavations, through a renovated
Turkish building housing a small exhibit of pottery found at the site and a
model of the Warren's Shaft water system. Colour photographs depict
Captain Warren's expedition and the present excavations. From the exhibition room, a stupendous rock-hewn tunnel descends to the mouth of the shaft
– an incredibly deep well from where, if it's quiet enough, you can hear the
distant gurgle of the running Gihon spring water. A plan, maps and books in
the entrance hall explain all (Sun–Thur 9am–5pm, Fri 9am–1pm).

The City of David

The **City of David Archaeological Garden** (daily 9am–5pm) occupies the
upper slopes of Mount Ophel. Twenty-five strata of settlement have been
revealed since excavations were begun in 1978, including the impressive
remnants of Jerusalem's 'Upper City', where the wealthy lived in luxury.
From the signposted path you look over the stone walls of the base of the
Canaanite Citadel which served the ancient Jebusite town until its conquest
by King David. There are remains, too, of the 18-meter-high stepped-stone

foundations of **David's Fortress**, and of buildings destroyed in the Babylonian conquest of 586BC. One of these is the self-explanatory **burnt room**, another seems to have been a public archive – 53 clay seals (*bullae*) were found in it. Explanatory signs and diagrams along the path describe each structure's significance. The site excavations have over the years been the subject of passionate protests by orthodox Jews against what they regard as the violation of ancient Jewish graves that may be here.

If you are exhausted after all this, the *David City Rest House* (subtitled *Under Green Trees*) is nearby. Here you can sit in the shade of olive and lemon trees, have a lemon or mint tea, coffee or ice-cream and look out over the Kidron Valley to the Palestinian village of SILWAN.

Mount Zion

They that trust in the Lord shall be as Mount Zion which cannot be removed but abideth for ever.

Psalm 125:1

Irremovable, as the psalm says, it might be, but that did not prevent **Mount Zion** being separated from the rest of the Old City to the south. Until the eleventh century it was inside the city walls, as can be seen from the famous Map of Madaba. But when Sultan Suleiman the Magnificent ordered the walls rebuilt in the mid-sixteenth century, his engineers somehow left Mount Zion outside – for which, it is said, they paid with their lives. Between 1948 and 1967 Mount Zion was in the Israeli section of Jerusalem, but although this is strictly West Jerusalem, it's logically explored at the same time as Mount Ophel.

You can start **from the top**, leaving the Old City through Zion Gate, or **from the bottom** following the road round from Dung Gate. Another alternative is to exit from Jaffa Gate, head south along the Hebron Road and left up the hill opposite the Sultan's Pool.

The mountain is traditionally associated with King David, who is said to be buried here, and with events in the life of Jesus and his disciples, particularly the Last Supper. Its most prominent landmark is the black, conical roof of the **Dormition Abbey** (daily 8am–noon and 2–6pm) at the top of the hill. This white stone building (erected in 1900) is the traditional site of **Mary's death**, in a dark crypt decorated with twelve columns and with pictures of famous Old Testament women. The main church, with its ornate icons and imposing circular mosaic floor, the Madonna and Child on a gold background, glows with a golden light. The remains of the mosaic floor of the old basilica are kept under a glass cover in the courtyard but the reflection off the glass makes them virtually impossible to see. There's a cafeteria serving light refreshments and a bookshop with a selection of maps and (mostly religious) literature.

Down the hill to the right, virtually in the shadow of the Abbey, is the **Coenaculum** – the Room of the Last Supper (8.30am–sunset, closed Fri afternoon). Don't expect a room of the dimensions depicted in Leonardo da Vinci's famous painting: the room is square and small, and hardly seems as if it would have been large enough for Jesus and his disciples to have sat around a table for the Passover feast. Whether there would have been room or not is hardly an issue, however, because beautiful and peaceful as it is, the room is in fact a Crusader construction, with characteristic Gothic arches. It was part of a Franciscan monastery until 1552 when it was turned into a mosque by the Ottomans. The roof reveals a fascinating juxtaposition of church steeples and minarets, and another fabulous view across the Kidron Valley to the Mount of Olives and beyond.

Beneath the Coenaculum is the room where Jesus washed the disciples' feet after the last supper. In true Jerusalem style, not enough that the top part of the building is holy to Muslims and Christians, this room leads into another that traditionally contains the **Tomb of David**, a blue-draped cenotaph in an otherwise bare chamber (Sat–Thur 8am–6pm, Fri 8am–2pm, closes one hour earlier in winter). According to the Book of Kings (*I Kings 2:10*) David was buried on the eastern hill of the city; this room, well to the south, was declared his burial place in the tenth century AD. Its importance to Israelis increased between 1948 and 1967 when, with the Old City in Jordanian hands and the Western Wall out of bounds, the tomb became an alternative site of Jewish pilgrimage.

Through the medieval cloisters you reach the memorial **Chamber of the Holocaust** (Sun–Thurs 8am–5pm, Fri and eve of holidays 8am–2pm). Its walls are covered with plaques commemorating over 2000 Jewish communities destroyed by the Nazis, and there is also a chilling collection of holocaust relics: bars of soap made from Jewish bodies, and objects (lampshades, bags, jackets) made from destroyed Bibles. The Chamber also contains an exhibition on contemporary anti-Semitism and, in the main hall, a black stone memorial etched with the names of all the concentration camps.

Nearby is the **King David Museum** (Sun–Thurs 8am–6pm, Friday 8am–2pm), which 'would like you to experience his home town . . . to retrace his steps and to learn a little about him'. Established in 1950, it's a curious Aladdin's Cave of a place, with a hotch-potch of donated, found or collected exhibits including artefacts claiming to come 'from the Tomb of David' (which has never been located), archaeological finds from Mount Zion, and collections of Judaica such as *Torah* cases and *menorot* (ritual candelabras). At the bottom of the hill, beside the parking lot, the *Harp of David* restaurant is a handy stop for refreshment.

On the eastern slope of Mount Zion, outside Dung Gate, stands the curiously shaped, white-stone **Church of Saint Peter in Gallicantu** (Mon–Sat 8.30–11.45am and 2–5.30pm). Jesus is believed to have been imprisoned here by the High Priest Caiaphas and this is also the site where Peter three times denied knowing him, thereby fulfilling the prophecy 'Before the cock crows, you will have denied me thrice' (*Matthew 26:75*). In the garden, steep Roman steps lead down to the Gihon Spring whilst in the basement of the 1931 church are cellars dating from the time of Herod. The building itself is rather ugly, but the view from the balcony, over the City of the David and the valleys of Jerusalem, is another great one.

WEST JERUSALEM

West Jerusalem – the New City to Israelis – is indeed a relatively new place, its first Jewish settlers having moved out from the Old City little over a hundred years ago. But in the ensuing years, and especially since 1967, it has grown tremendously, with concentric rings of settlements expanding its bounds. Today, West Jerusalem is in flux, reeling under two connected pressures: religion and an explosion of property prices. Already an expensive place to live, Jerusalem is seeing property prices soar even ahead of inflation. Older neighbourhoods close to the centre of town are becoming 'yuppified' as prices take them beyond the reach of working people, a process fuelled by the influx of religious zealots, many of them from the United States. Over the past few years secular residents have gradually been moving out, if they can, as area after area has fallen. 'Economic refugees' – pushed out by price rises – often move to the government-subsidised settlement suburbs; 'cultural refugees' – fleeing the aggressive conservatism which brings dress codes and driving restrictions in its wake – generally quit for the coastal plain.

Geographically, West Jerusalem falls into two sections: those parts of the city which developed as part of the organic expansion of Jerusalem from the mid-nineteenth century, and the explosion of new settlement suburbs thrown up to tighten Israeli control of the city following the 1967 occupation. Both are worth a visit if you're an amateur historian; the former, however, are infinitely more aesthetically pleasing than the latter. Residents claim with some justification that the neighbourhoods in each part of the city each have their own distinctive characters. A short visit is not long enough to properly explore many of these, but it's certainly worth a try. The neighbourhoods are all easily accessible on regular buses from Jaffa Road or King George Street: some are worth exploring in their own right, you'll pass through others on your way to the scattered sites of interest.

In the centre there are three basic types of **pre-1967 suburb**: former Arab areas from which the original inhabitants were expelled such as Katamon, Baka and Talpiot; long-established expensive Jewish enclaves like Rehavia; and traditionally working class zones like Mahane Yehuda. **Baka**, between the German Colony and the Bethlehem Road, still has some of the feel of a Palestinian village, its original houses now highly desirable residences. **Mahane Yehuda**, behind Jaffa Road past King George Street, has a totally different character. Built to house Jewish immigrant workers, its chaotic maze of streets is crammed with minute houses of wildly differing character and little if any architectural integrity. The market here is famous both for the wealth of its produce and for the neanderthal chauvinism of the stall holders; if you're to the left of George Bush or Margaret Thatcher, don't get into political discussions here. The **Nahla'ot** area, just south of Mahane Yehuda, is a predominantly Sephardi neighbourhood with students and artists moving in for cheap accommodation. Its narrow alleys are crowded and poor, but full of life and fascinating to wander around. The contrast with the stolid respectability of nearby Rehavia is striking.

The city centre

For the tourist, the area around **Jaffa Road** as it heads away from Jaffa Gate *is* West Jerusalem. The main **post office**, the **Jerusalem Municipal Tourist Office, buses** to most suburbs, *sherut* taxis to the coast and all the big shops are concentrated here, and virtually every **bar, cinema** and **club** in Jerusalem is within walking distance. At night it may not exactly buzz, but there is definitely a gentle hum.

The pedestrian precinct of **Ben Yehuda**, a short way up Jaffa Road off **Zion Square**, is packed with cafés, restaurants and snack bars of every description. Once a rather old-fashioned shopping area, it is rapidly being swallowed up in the rush to build ever more garish American-style hamburger, pizza and ice-cream parlours, and has become the haunt of buskers, of jewellery craftspeople, flower and newspaper vendors, and a sort of 'Speakers' Corner' where some viciously racist Israelis hold forth on the merits of expelling all the Arabs, closing Palestinian universities and jailing non-Jewish partners of 'mixed' relationships. It is perpetually teeming with people, particularly on Friday afternoons before Jerusalem is closed down for shabbat and on Saturday night.

Ben Yehuda runs on to meet King George Street at the large *Hamashbir* department store. Here a distinctive and somewhat incongruous clock-arch and column marks the site of the **Talitha Kumi Building**, an orphanage and Arab girls' school that stood here from 1822 to 1901. The new **City Tower** houses shops and offices and one of the few escalators in Jerusalem; under it is a sort of flea-cum-crafts market that's interesting, but not cheap.

Next to the City Tower is a small park where open air concerts are occasionally held. The **Israeli Government Tourist Office** is further down King George Street on the same side, while off the top end of the park you'll find the **Artists' House** (12 Shmuel HaNagid Street; ☎02-223653; Sun–Thur 10am–1pm and 4–6pm, Fri 10am–1pm, Sat 11am–2pm). The building is owned by the *Jerusalem Artists' Association* and usually has attractive exhibitions and displays of original work, as well as frequent concerts and lectures. Its pleasantly relaxed café is *the* place to see and be seen if you're of an artistic bent, the haunt of Israeli and Palestinian leftists and liberals.

Much less relaxed is the **Museum of the Potential Holocaust** on Ussishkin Street, one street over to the west. This curious institution is perhaps the clearest example in the country of the symbiotic relationship between Zionism and western racism. The museum is run by the Israeli *Kach* movement and is designed to show US Jews that anti-Semitism will engulf them at any moment and that they should pack up and move to Israel rather than join the hopeless struggle against racism at home. It contains large numbers of leaflets and other publications from US racists to reinforce this point. Tours are guided by a party apparatchik every half-hour or so and no independent viewing is allowed. *Kach* is a growing movement in Israel and visitors interested in politics should consider witnessing their pitch. Be aware, however, that they are racists, extreme even by Israeli standards: if you're not and you can't keep your mouth shut, argument will surely follow. By paying the entrance fee you'll also be contributing to party coffers.

Further down King George Street the municipal gardens and **Independence Park** stretch off to the left. This huge open space runs from behind the *Plaza Hotel* almost as far as the Old City: the road which runs through it, from Hillel Street to Gershon Agron Street, is the city's gay cruising ground. At the eastern end, where the trees and undergrowth begin, is the pre-1948 Muslim cemetery, **Mamilla**, a corruption of the Arabic *Ma'man Allah* (God's place of safety). But even the dead are not safe here. There are dozens of vandalised graves and sarcophagi, many of them plastered with concrete to obliterate the Arabic inscriptions. Among them is the square dome of the **Zawiyya Kubakiyya**, the tomb of Mamluk Emir Aidughi Kubaki who was buried here in 1289AD. He was governor of Safed and Aleppo before being exiled to Jerusalem. In the centre of the graveyard is the **Mamilla Pool**. Now disused, this is typical of the cisterns excavated to supply water to the medieval city. Opposite the graveyard in the southeast corner of the park is the impressive old **Waqf building**, now confiscated and used as government offices. The Arabic inscription betraying its origin is still visible.

Mamilla Road, which runs from here back down to Jaffa Gate, was once the commercial centre of West Jerusalem. From 1948 to 1967, however, it formed the Israeli-Jordanian border and fell into irreversible disrepair. Current plans envisage reviving the street as a modern commercial complex – hopefully some of the old buildings will be preserved. One of these, the **Stern House**, has a plaque commemorating Theodor Herzl's visit to Jerusalem in the winter of 1898 to meet with Kaiser Wilhelm II. If the place is still standing, it's worth calling in at its tiny 'museum' of yellowed photographs and newspaper cuttings and at the antique shop that once had a wonderful, dusty collection of old postcards.

The Russian Compound

The first turning on the right off Jaffa Road after the central post office leads to the **Russian Compound**. Legend has it that the Assyrian army camped on this site when preparing to attack Jerusalem in 700BC, and that here too Titus planned to destroy the city. The land was bought by Czar Alexander II in 1860 to provide services and accommodation for the 20,000 or so Russian pilgrims who visited the city every year around the turn of the century. The impressive green-domed **cathedral** and Russian consulate were completed by 1864: the compound as a whole, which also sheltered hospices for men and women, a hospital and consulate, was once virtually a walled city in its own right. Nowadays the complex houses law courts and a notorious police station (**al-Muscobiyya**) denounced as a torture centre in the 1977 *Sunday Times* expose. Interrogations of Palestinian detainees still take place there and you can often see knots of people waiting outside to be allowed to visit their relatives.

At the back of the compound, in what was a prison under the British, is the **Hall of Heroism** (Sun–Thur 9am–4pm, Fri and eve of holidays 10am–1pm; ☎233209; buses #18, #20, #5 and #6), a museum dedicated to Jewish paramilitary activity during the Mandate period and later. There are exhibits around the gallows commemorating eight Jews executed by the British and a proud list of terrorist outrages committed against Palestinian civilians in the city, of bombs planted on buses and in public places. The number of dead is carefully recorded, though the list stops short of 1948 and therefore does not include (for example) the Deir Yassin massacre (see p.127). Also canonised in the museum are the two Israeli agents executed in Cairo in 1954 for planting bombs in a US cultural centre.

Mea She'arim

Behind the Russian Compound, or up Prophets' Street from Damascus Gate, located at the crossroads of Strauss and Malchei Israel Streets is the district of **Mea She'arim**, the quarter of the ultra-orthodox *haredi* community. Some, particularly the members of the *Neturei Carta* movement, do not acknowledge the State of Israel which, until the Messiah comes, they regard as profane. Their neighbourhood, founded in 1875, retains a curiously East European feel: many of its beared and sidelocked male residents still dress in the Jewish fashion of sixteenth-century Poland, replacing their long black caftans and round felt hats with fur-trimmed ones (*shtreimals*) on holidays. Women wear long-sleeves and either wigs or head scarves. There are synagogues, *yeshivot* and shops selling religious items everywhere, and signs in the district ask visitors – particularly women, but not excluding men – to dress modestly. This is a request to take seriously: photography here can also give offence, as can smoking on *shabbat*, when the whole area is closed to traffic. Buses #1, #2, #11 and #29 all pass through.

Yemin Moshe

King David Street, which runs from Mamilla Street south, can boast two of the most impressive buildings in West Jerusalem. The **YMCA West**, whose imposing tower and cupolas are Jerusalem landmarks, was built by the same company that constructed the Empire State building. The small museum, bell tower and magnificent lobby are well worth visiting. It offers all the usual facilities and is an occasional classical concert venue. Opposite is the grandiose **King David Hotel**, the poshest in the city. It was the British HQ during the mandate period and was partially destroyed by an *Irgun* action in 1946, but later restored. Behind the hotel, down a narrow alleyway (Abu Sikhra Street), **King Herod's Family Tomb** can be visited. The beautifully constructed four-chambered tomb is empty, and it is not clear who was originally interred here, but it clearly dates from the correct period.

Up the hill from the tomb is **Mishkenot Shaananim** (Dwellings of Tranquillity), the first Jewish quarter to be built outside the Old City. The cloister-like living quarters, with a turret roof and Star of David over the entrance, were constructed in 1860 with money bequeathed by Judah Touro, a resident of New Orleans. Sir Moses Montefiore, the British philanthropist, was appointed executor of his will and subsequently bought the adjoining land, when the area became known as **Yemin Moshe**. Its red-roofed town houses and cottages built of Jerusalem stone are some of the loveliest, and most expensive, houses in Jerusalem. The area's most striking monument is the narrow stone **windmill** that Montefiore built to provide flour for the settlement, although it was never actually used for this purpose. It served as an important Israeli observation post in 1948 and now houses a small museum (Sun–Thur 9am–4pm, Fri 9am–1pm) dedicated to Montefiore's life and work, with photographs of Jerusalem from the mid-nineteenth century.

In the park opposite the windmill, **Liberty Bell Garden** houses a replica of the original American bell (a traditional symbol of US liberties). An olive tree, torn from a patch of confiscated land in the West Bank, has been replanted here and dedicated to peace by the Israelis (and a member of Martin Luther King's family) over its owners' protests.

The valley below Yemin Moshe, opposite the Old City between Mount Zion and Jaffa Gate, is the site of the **Sultan's Pool**. The sultan in question was Suleiman the Magnificent who repaired the 170m by 67m reservoir in the sixteenth century while rebuilding the Old City walls. The pool today is dry and, as the **Merrill Hassenfeld Amphitheatre**, is one of the biggest venues for outdoor concerts (rock and otherwise) in the country. On the road to the south of the pool, the **Cinematheque** is Israel's premier film centre: it offers a varied programme of 'quality' films and its vegetarian café/restaurant is second only to the Artists' House as a liberal watering hole.

Talbieh

West of the Liberty Bell Garden, along Jabotinsky Street, the former Palestinian area of **Talbieh** is another one with beautiful houses and gardens. The **L.A. Mayer Memorial Institute for Islamic Art** (2 HaPalmach Street; Sun–Thur 10am–1pm and 3.30–6pm, Sat 10am–1pm; tickets for Saturday must be bought in advance; ☎02-661291; bus #15) is a well laid out and attractive museum. The objects on show – pottery, glass, calligraphy, miniatures, woodwork, textiles, jewellery and ivory carving – are from Egypt, Syria, Iraq, India and, above all, Iran and date mainly from the seventeenth and eighteenth centuries. It is certainly impressive, but the omissions are in some ways more remarkable than the exhibits. Indigenous Palestinian culture is ignored altogether and in its 'orientalist' approach the museum might as well be in Paris or London as in the Middle East.

Nearby, on HaNassi Street, is the **President's Residence** which can be visited on irregular open days (check at the IGTO), and beside it the **Van Leer Institute** (Albert Einstein Square; ☎02-667141). The institute is a non-political organisation which was founded in 1956 'to serve as an intellectual centre for the study of social problems'. It organises workshops, lectures and conferences as well as public opinion surveys, and publishes a variety of interesting and topical books in English (such as *Can the Palestinian Problem be Solved*, *If Peace Comes*, *Every Sixth Israeli*) and others in Hebrew. The institute building has a vast library of over 20,000 books, a cafeteria and attractive garden, and a concert hall where a series of chamber music concerts are held. Enquire at the reception desk for information. The **Jerusalem Theatre** (see "Nightlife") is nearby.

Givat Ram and the Israel Museum

The hill of **Givat Ram** marks the western extent of the older parts of West Jerusalem. Of several sites worth exploring, the best known is the prestigious **Israel Museum**. The museum is, in fact, a collection of separate exhibitions: three of them, the Samuel Bronfman Museum of Biblical Archaeology, the Bezalel National Museum and the Children's Museum are housed in the main building. The Billy Rose Garden of Sculptures and the Shrine of the Book are apart.

The **Samuel Bronfman archaeological museum**, on the left of the main lobby, has a well-arranged collection of finds from the Canaanite to the biblical periods. Its Jewish Ethnography section displays the material culture and folk art of the different ethnic groups living in Israel: adjacent is an exhibit of the jewellery and costumes of various Jewish communities around the world. The Jewish Ceremonial Art exhibit upstairs has a large collection of treasured pieces of Judaica from all over the world. It includes, at the end of the wing, a reconstructed sixteenth-century synagogue from Italy, and a tabernacle from West Germany that survived the Nazi destruction.

The **Bezalel National Museum** contains a permanent display of modern art which includes Cezanne, Gauguin, Picasso and van Gogh. Its children's section has an auditorium and workshops for 6–18 year-olds to experiment with painting, modelling or photography. Outside, the **Billy Rose Garden** continues the artistic theme, with important works by sculptors including Rodin, Picasso and Henry Moore. It's illuminated on Tuesday nights.

The showpiece of the museum, however, is the **Shrine of the Book**, built to house the **Dead Sea Scrolls** after they were removed from the Palestine Archaeological Museum. Its distinctive white dome is shaped like the lid of one of the jars in which the scrolls were discovered. The scrolls (see Qumran) are believed to have been written by the Essenes, a monastic sect who inhabited the area around Qumran where they were found. The manuscripts are some 2000 years old, and the oldest of them, the complete Book of Isaiah, is a full thousand years older than any other biblical text in existence. On the lower level other ancient scripts are housed, including letters and documents dating from the Second Revolt of 135AD. There are also some interesting domestic finds, such as house keys, utensils and glassware, that provide an insight into the everyday life of the period.

Opening hours for the main museum (☎02-698211) are: Sunday, Monday, Wednesday and Thursday 10am to 5pm, Tuesday 4 to 10pm; Friday and Saturday 10am to 2pm; guided tours in English are on Sunday and Wednesday at 11am, Tuesday at 4.30pm; or of the Shrine of the Book on Sunday at 1.30pm and Tuesday at 3pm. **Admission** to the museum only is $2; to both museum and shrine, $3.50, students $1.60. Student annual membership, for $10, allows unlimited access to the Israel Museum, Palestine Archaeological Museum (Rockefeller), Tel Aviv and Haifa Museums. Tickets for Saturday and holidays must be bought in advance. **Buses** #9, #24 and #28 all pass close by.

Monastery of the Cross

Below the Israel Museum is the striking **Monastery of the Cross** (Sat–Thur 9am–5pm, Fri 9am–1.30pm; ☎02-667121), a massive pink-stone building topped by a dome and clock-tower. It was founded in the eleventh century on the site of a fifth-century church, in the place where legend has it that the tree from which Jesus' cross was made grew. The monastery was once the centre of Georgian religious and cultural activity in the country, but has been Greek Orthodox since the seventeenth century. Both Georgian and Greek inscriptions can be seen in the church.

The courtyard, shaded by peach and lemon trees and vines, is overlooked by the wooden doors of 400 monks' cells, but the only resident now is the Superior who will welcome you and show you around. A massive metal-plated, wooden door leads into the church, in the shape of a Greek cross, with a central dome supported by four hefty square pillars. The walls are covered with frescoes, many of them three or four hundred years old, showing events in the life of Christ, Old Testament figures and early Christian saints. Behind the altar screen separating the sanctuary from the main body of the church (as in all Orthodox churches), a small shrine marks the traditional site of the tree from which the cross was cut.

The Knesset

Whilst you're in this area, you could also drop in on an often raucous debate in the Knesset, Israel's parliament, housed in a twenty-year-old building opposite the Israel Museum (Mon and Tues 4–9pm, Wed 11am–1pm; ☎02-554111; buses #9 or #24). In front of the entrance stands the symbol of the State, the seven-branched *menorah* (this one donated by the British parliament) and a flame on a small monument, burning in remembrance of those fallen in battle. Prominent in the entrance hall is the image of the founder of political Zionism, Theodor Herzl. Guided tours of the building, taking in **Chagall's triple tapestry and mosaics**, leave on Sunday and Thursday regularly from 8.30am until 2.30pm. Take your passport along to buy a ticket for the visitors' gallery.

Mount Herzl

The **tomb of Theodor Herzl**, the 'Father of Zionism', adorns a large pleasant park on **Mount Herzl**, west of Givat Ram (summer 8am–6.30pm, winter 8am–5pm; buses #13, #17, #17a, #18, #20, #23 and #27). The road to the left leads to a small **museum** (Sun–Thur 9am–5pm, Fri 9am–1pm; ☎02-531108) devoted to Herzl's life and work. As well as the usual documents, books and photographs, the museum contains the study in which he wrote his famous *Alt-Neuland* (Old-New Land); Herzl's study was transported piece by piece from Vienna to be reconstructed here. Also in the park is the tomb of Vladimir Jabotinsky, mentor of the *Irgun*, and other Zionist leaders such as Golda Meir and Levi Eshkol. On the northern side of Mount Herzl, with a magnificent view of the Judaean Hills, Israel's war dead are buried in the **Jewish Military Cemetery** (8am–6pm). The place is particularly busy on the eve of Israeli Independence Day (May 14) and on national and religious holidays.

Yad Vashem

Adjacent to Mount Herzl on **Har HaZikkaron** (the Mount of Remembrance), **Yad Vashem** (Sun–Thur 9am–4.30pm, Fri 9am–1pm; ☎02-531202; buses #13, #18, #20, #23 and #27) is Israel's most important memorial to the six million Jews annihilated in the holocaust, an extremely disturbing and moving experience. The path from the entrance leads along the **Way of the Righteous**, which honours those gentiles who helped the Jews, to the **Ohel Yiskor**, the Hall of Remembrance. This sombre, tent-shaped chamber has the names of 21 concentration camps engraved into its stone floor, and an eternal flame burning above a casket of ashes from the cremation ovens.

A permanent exhibit of documents and photographs, 'Warning and Witness' traces the rise of the Nazis and depicts the horrors of their regime. A new **art museum** displays paintings produced by inmates of the concentration camps and of survivors or artists using the holocaust as their theme. The camp artists were given paper and drawing implements by the Nazis in order to produce art forgeries or sanitised representations of the camps for propaganda purposes. Most of the works are sombre, but a section devoted to children's art adds colour and optimism to the exhibition.

Outside, the aluminium **Wall of Holocaust and Heroism** is a large four-part mural, symbolising extermination, resistance, emigration to Israel and strength. The **Hall of Names** records over two million of those Jews murdered during the Nazi regime. **Janusz Korczak Park**, with gardens in which to stroll, is named after the Polish teacher who voluntarily went to Treblinka with his students.

Holyland Hotel

For an excellent overview of what Jerusalem might have looked like in Herodian times, the **model of the ancient city** in the gardens of the **Holyland Hotel**, southwest of the centre on the road to Ein Karem, is well worth a visit (daily 8.30am–5pm; ☎02-630201; buses #21, #23 and #27). The detailed model, which will take an hour or two to take in properly, is made to a scale of 1:50 with materials used at the time: marble, stone, copper, iron and wood. Herod's palace at Jaffa Gate can be seen, with its three large towers and fabulous adjoining garden, along with the various markets and the Temple. Measurements for this were based on the descriptions of Josephus Flavius and those in the *mishnah*. To the north of the Temple are the Antonia Fortress and the Pool of Bethesda.

Jabal al-Muqabbar (Mount of Evil Counsel)

Southwest of the city, the **Mount of Evil Counsel** is so called because, in Christian tradition, it was here that the Sanhedrin decided to turn Jesus over to the Romans. Its Arabic name – the Hill of Proclamation – derives from the tradition that it was from here that Caliph Omar Ibn al-Khattab first caught sight of the holy city and proclaimed the greatness of Allah in 638AD.

On the top of the hill stands a palatial building, surrounded by a garden complete with bandstand, which could be nothing other than the official residence of the British High Commissioner during the Mandate. Ever since, it has been known as **Government House** (*Armon HaNatziv* in Hebrew). After 1948 the area was a demilitarised zone and served as the HQ of UN observers; it was taken by the Jordanians on the first day of the 1967 war but captured by Israeli forces later the same day. Today it serves as the headquarters of the United Nations Emergency Force (UNEF) and United Nations Disengagement Observer Force (UNDOF). It is also the site of the **Haas Promenade**, whose view of the Old City rivals that from the Mount of Olives. The recently constructed walkway is lined with open-air cafés and ice-cream bars; the romantic view and the gardens below make it a popular lovers' haunt.

Nearby is **Ramat Rachel kibbutz** (bus #7 from the central bus station; #21, #22 or #23 from Damascus/Jaffa Gates) on the site where, traditionally, the pregnant Mary paused on her way to Bethlehem. The ruins of a seventh-century BC royal palace and a fifth-century monastery have been found here. The kibbutz itself was founded in 1916 and was on the firing-line in 1948. Apart from its fruit and vegetable farms, the kibbutz sports a vacation club, swimming pool (entrance for the day, about $7), an elegant but expensive hotel/guest house (upwards of $23) and an air-conditioned lounge where you can take a break from your wanderings.

Mount Scopus

Mount Scopus overlooks Jerusalem from the northeast, just beyond the Mount of Olives (reached through Wadi Joz, on buses #4a, #9, #23 or #23a from the city centre). It is a hill which has always been of vital strategic importance, and although physically in East Jerusalem, it is spiritually – and in recent history – a part of the west.

The **Hebrew University** and **Hadassah Hospital** (tours in English, Sun-Fri 9am, 10am, 11am and noon) were both erected here before 1948, and Mount Scopus remained under Israeli control after the war, an isolated enclave maintained by fortnightly convoys under UN protection. Between 1948 and 1967 the hospital and university were moved out, but they returned to much expanded grounds after the occupation, and have been joined by vast new government buildings: virtually all Palestinian presence has been removed.

The mammoth university campus, constructed like a fortress, gives the impression that, should the need arise, the whole thing could disappear underground at the touch of a button. There are guided tours of this campus (Sun–Thur at 11am) and the one at Givat Ram (Sun–Thur 10am). Call ☎02-882819/882821 for further information. On the eastern edge of the grounds is an **amphitheatre** where concerts and plays are held, and which also offers magnificent views of the Old City, the Judaean Hills, the Dead Sea and the Mountains of Moab. The **biblical garden** at the top of Mount Scopus, founded in the 1920s, contains samples of flora mentioned in the Bible such as saffron, sesame, figs and almonds. It is tended much as it would have been in those times, though with the unbiblical assistance of mechanical water sprinklers. On site is a reconstructed watchman's hut like those that stood on every farm in the area. (Buses #9, #28 and #27a.)

Nearby is the **Augusta Victoria Hospital** with its distinctive square tower. Built in 1910, it was named after Kaiser Wilhelm's wife and was used as the residence of the British governor general after World War I. It now serves as the UNRWA hospital for the West Bank. There is also an immaculately kept World War I **British War Cemetery**.

Around the city: the settlements

There are upwards of eighteen **settlements** built in three rings around Jerusalem. Precise calculation is difficult because of arguments over the city's boundaries – Israel unilaterally expanded Jerusalem to the gates of Ramallah/al-Bireh and Bethlehem immediately after the 1967 war, and since then there has been further encroachment on the lands of Beit Jala and Beit Sahour by Gilo settlement. Ma'aleh Adumim, on the other hand, is technically in the occupied territories even though it was specifically designed to provide cheap housing for Jerusalemites from the older suburbs.

The settlements themselves are fortress-like and uninviting, and it's difficult to look at them without imagining rifles poking through the slit windows. Inside, however, many are genuinely attractive: investment in the infrastructure has been massive and this is reflected in paved, tree-lined streets and community facilities. You will be struck, though, by the fact that many of the apartments are unoccupied. Few of the settlement suburbs have any life during the day as most of the inhabitants work elsewhere, and nightlife consists of a bus to town or hanging around on street corners.

Gilo

GILO, on the road to Bethlehem, is probably the easiest settlement to visit (bus #30, #31 or #32). Apart from the fact that it's all built on confiscated land, Gilo is noted for the 'fantasia' approach of its architects: different parts look as if they've been taken from the sets of Snow White or Thunderbirds. Inside the settlement there are still at least two Palestinian families, whose embattled homes you'll spot immediately – they're the only ones over twenty years old. A visit will be both appreciated and educative.

At the foot of the hill on which Gilo stands, back towards the city, is the Palestinian village of **Beit Safafa**, through the centre of which the 1948 border once ran.

Ein Karem

Seven kilometres southwest of Jerusalem, **EIN KAREM** (Spring of the Vineyard; bus #17 or #17a from Jaffa Road), is vastly more attractive, a former Palestinian village now repopulated by Jewish settlers. Surrounded by terraced hills dotted with olive and cypress trees, the quiet village is ideal for a day trip or an overnight stay (see "Accommodation") and makes a refreshing change from the bustle of the city. The beautiful old stone houses are now mostly inhabited by Israeli artists and sculptors; there are several art galleries to visit and a variety of good restaurants.

The name goes back to biblical *Beit HaKerem*, whose inhabitants rebuilt Jerusalem after the destruction of 70BC, and this is also the traditional birthplace of John the Baptist, the city of Judah mentioned by Luke (*1:39–40*) as the place of the house of the Temple priest Zachariah, John's father. On the site of the home the **Church of Saint John the Baptist** (Mon–Sat 8am–noon and 3–5pm, Sun 9am–noon and 3–4pm; ☎02-413639) was built in 1674, though what you see combines remnants of many periods: a statue of Venus in the church courtyard shows that the place was venerated in the Roman period; mosaic fragments belong to a Byzantine floor; and there are also remains of a Crusader building. Inside, the church is decorated with seventeenth-century paintings and six square pillars divide the hall into three aisles, the central one ending at a delicate green wrought iron decorative gate behind which is the high altar of St. John. To the right is the altar of John's mother Elizabeth, and on the left steps lead into a natural cave, held to be the **Grotto of the Nativity of Saint John**.

On the slope of the hill south of Ein Kerem, the **Church of the Visitation** (9am–noon and 3–6pm; ☎02-417291), completed in 1955, is another of those designed by Antonio Barluzzi. It commemorates Mary's visit to Elizabeth when she was pregnant. In it is a natural grotto which once contained a small spring, and in front of the grotto are remnants of houses, some of which do indeed date back to Roman times. In the Byzantine period the grotto became a place of worship, and later the Crusaders built a large two-storeyed church over it, with a smaller one in front. After the Crusaders left their churches collapsed and the area was bought by the Franciscans in 1679 and restored. The lower church is adorned with large frescoes, the upper one has a painted ceiling in fourteenth-century Tuscan style. The courtyard is lined with ceramic tiles bearing the *Magnificat* (Mary's hymn of thanksgiving) in 42 languages.

At the bottom of the hill, a small mosque marks the site of the **Spring of the Virgin**. It is this spring that gives the village its name: *'Ayn* or *Ein* – spring; *Kurum* or *Karem* – vineyard). Little water remains in the well today, most of it being used for vines and crops. Beside the well is the **Targ Music Centre** where weekly chamber music concerts are held.

Not far from Ein Karem, the new **Hadassah Medical Centre**, founded in 1951 when the Mount Scopus site was abandoned, is famous for the twelve **Chagall windows** in its synagogue (Sun–Fri 1.30–4pm; ☎02-416333; bus #19 or #27). The windows were designed by Marc Chagall and presented to the hospital in 1982. Each is dominated by one main colour and depicts one of the twelve sons of Jacob. A guided tour (Sun–Fri 8.30am, 9.30am, 10.30am, 11.30am and 12.30pm; Friday tours must be booked in advance) in English covers the windows in exhaustive detail and includes a film about the Hadassah.

THE FACTS

Food and drink

You could spend weeks in Jerusalem eating well and healthily without ever
going into a restaurant. Breads, cheeses and yoghurts, pickles, olives, fresh
vegetables and fruit are freely available and cheap. Freshly pressed juices
and other traditional Palestinian drinks can be had on almost any street
corner, especially in the east. Café and street stall foods like *humus, falafel,*
corn on the cob, nuts and pulses and sweets are available everywhere. But
the restaurants are good, too – in the east for excellent value traditional
Middle Eastern foods, in the west for their extraordinary variety. Even if you
are living on a tight budget, try to have at least one better restaurant meal.
Meze and the more elaborate meat and baked dishes need to be tried.

A booklet called *Jerusalem Menus*, listing the menus of thirty of Jerusalem's
restaurants, together with their address, phone number and opening times, is
available free of charge at hotels and tourist offices. The restaurants range in
price and type – from Argentinian to Yemenite.

East Jerusalem

You could, if so inclined, spend most of your time in East Jerusalem stuffing
your face and not see anything at all. There are hundreds of **food stalls,
cafés** and **restaurants**, only a few of which (easy enough to avoid) cater
exclusively for tourists. The following list is by no means exhaustive, and if
you smell something inviting coming from a hole in the wall, or a café
kitchen, give it a try.

As a result of the *intifada*, everything is closed after midday and a strike
may mean a total shut-down on one or more days of your visit. It might be a
good idea to keep some basic supplies – fruit, bread, cheese – at your hotel
for such an eventuality. During *Ramadan* main meals are taken after
sundown.

Humus and Falafel

Small café-style places tend to be specialised in East Jerusalem. You can
rarely go into a **café** and get food or into a **humus** place and get coffee
(although in the latter the owner will be pleased to send a small boy out to
get you a cup if you want). Traditionally *humus* is the worker's breakfast and
many places (especially at the bottom of Prophets Street) serve it only in the
mornings: bread and pickles are included in the price. The best **falafel** comes
from hole-in-the-wall sandwich places: the gap opposite the Salah al-Din
Street post office and the place on the right at the top of Souq Khan al-Zeit are
particularly good.

Linda's (Via Dolorosa, off Souq Khan al-Zeit) is a small, three-table place, good for
humus with *snobar, ful, tahina* or alone: can get very crowded, especially on Saturdays.
Helpings are generous, with small salad of onions, peppers, pickles.

Abu Shukri (Tariq al-Wad, near Via Dolorosa. Open daily 8am–7pm). A very famous *humus* joint whose service has suffered from its popularity, but the *humus* remains good and there's a pleasant garden round the back.

Al-Amal (next door to the *Pilgrim's Palace Hotel* by the bus station on Sultan Suleiman). *Humus* and staples are delicious although a bit over-generous with the olive oil. Cheapest in town.

Abu Walid's (St. George's Street opposite *St. George's Hotel*). Good *humus* and *shawarma* as well as some more unusual Palestinian dishes.

George's (above *Abu Ali* in the alley between Salah al-Din and Asfahani Street). Great *humus* etc, but famed for its *fatta*, a very substantial dish made from chickpeas and bread.

Cafés

Traditional **Palestinian cafés**, still very much male preserves, can be found on Sultan Suleiman Street next to the bus station, at the bottom of Salah al-Din Street opposite the post office, and inside Damascus Gate on the left. There's a superb **fresh fruit juice** place on Sultan Suleiman, between Herod's and Damascus Gates.

Moonshine (Latin Patriarchate Road, just inside Jaffa Gate). Clean, new 'Israeli-style' pub serving everything from coffee to beer to toasted sandwiches, to the accompaniment of loud music and young hustlers.

Princes Cafeteria The best of three cafés in the new area just inside Damascus Gate: quiet, handy for the market and open every day 8.30am–8pm.

Snack bars

Abu Ali (in the passage between Salah al-Din and Asfahani Street). In a basement beneath a small sign, *Abu Ali* always has a wide variety of hot dishes available. You go into the kitchen to choose what you'll have – excellent stuffed vegetables.

Ash-Shuleh Grill (Salah al-Din, corner of Asfahani Street; ☎02-272751). Very good for light, satisfying breakfast, lunch or supper: sandwiches, salads and light meals.

'Ala Bali (opposite *Holyland Hotel*, Rashid Street) sells excellent *humus, shawarma* etc.

There are dozens of other basic **snack bars** like these, including an excellent place on Salah al-Din Street opposite Zahra Street, and others on Al-Masudi street and Rashid Street.

Bakeries and 'Pizzas'

Bakeries are mostly open 24 hours, and their ovens are also used by the neighbourhood to bake things they cannot do at home. Some have branched out from the traditional Palestinian bread products into baked savouries, particularly those with access to the late-night tourist market.

Green Door, Mohammad Ali Pizza Bakery (first left on Tariq al-Wad). Open 24 hours for 'pizzas' baked in an open wood-fired oven. Great for late-night snacks.

Musrara Bakery (Prophets Street, opposite the service station). Open 24 hours for fresh *ka'ak* and 'pizza'.

Armenian Bakery (Ararat Street, Armenian Quarter. Open Wednesday and Saturday only). Delicious, spicy Armenian *sfiha*.

Cafeteria Basti (Tariq al-Wad, opposite the Austrian Hospital). Open daily till midnight for tasty home-made pizzas.

Restaurants

Umayyah Oriental Restaurant (Sultan Suleiman Street, opposite Herod's Gate; ☎02-282789/283542). The best in town with specialities such as *musakhan* or stuffed pigeon as well as the usual *meze*, salads and sweets (and alcohol). Open daily till late.

Jerusalem Star Restaurant (32 Tariq al-Wad; ☎02-287175). Large air-conditioned restaurant, newly refurbished. Usual salads and grilled meats, elaborate *meze* of 18 dishes.

Mata'am al-A'ilat (77 Souq Khan al-Zeit; ☎02-283435). Long-established place serving a wide variety: salads, kebabs, fish, sweets, drinks, and a good value fixed menu. Open 9am–9pm daily.

Other good places for substantial meals include a cheap, unnamed chicken grill on Souq Khan al-Zeit, for spit-roast chicken with wonderful garlic sauce; *Philadelphia*, *Dallas* and another chicken grill in Zahra Street; *Ali Baba* and *Petra* in Rashid Street; and the very expensive (but very good) restaurant in the *National Palace Hotel* on Zahra Street.

Stalls and shops

The greatest concentration of *ka'ak* sellers (most also sell *falafel* and baked eggs) and other **street stalls** is around Damascus Gate, but they can also be found at most main intersections. A snack is never more than a few minutes away. The best place to **shop**, for staples like fruit, nuts, olives and traditional cheeses, is in Souq Khan al-Zeit, where you can put together a magnificent picnic. *Ja'far Sweets*, on the right coming from Damascus Gate, sells delicious *kanafeh*, *burma* and other sweets. Western-style **supermarkets**, which supply all the joys of home (including alcohol which is not quite so freely available here) can be found on Sultan Suleiman by the bus station, at the bottom of Nablus Road, on Salah al-Din Street and in al-Zahra Street.

West Jerusalem

You can get (almost) anything you want in West Jerusalem from *humus* and *falafel* to the most obscure Asian dishes. The Americans have brought with them hamburger and pizza joints (the case of the kosher cheeseburger regularly appears as a controversy in the press), while earlier waves of immigrants established Hungarian and traditional East European Jewish places. Sephardi Jews brought dishes from other parts of the Arab world, the Latin Americans had tortilla-makers in their suitcases, and trendy entrepreneurs have turned their hands to everything from obscurantist vegetarianism to the most odd self-created mushes. Restaurants which describe themselves as 'Israeli' usually have basic Palestinian dishes plus a limited selection of Jewish cuisine from the rest of the globe. Cakes, sweets and drinks tend to be European, but copied very well in the better places. On the streets, **bagels** are ubiquitous.

Restaurants go in and out of fashion (and business) with astonishing rapidity, so what follows is a list of the more reliable cheap places.

Ben Yehuda and around

The pedestrianised area of **Ben Yehuda Street** has no end of cafés selling the same basic menu of coffee, tea, cold drinks, cakes, ice-cream and snacks.

Between here and Jaffa Road, Lunz Street and Dorot Rishonim are also developing rapidly, with new places – including several pizzerias and a good Chinese fast-food joint – opening all the time.

Atari. Right in the middle of Ben Yehuda, *Atari* used to be *the* place to go, but these days there's little to choose between any of the cafés. Prices at all of them are on the high side, but it's a pleasant place to sit.

Café Rimon (Lunz Street at the junction of Dorot Rishomin). One of the plushest of the cafés: *Café La Riviera*, nearby, serves excellent croissants for breakfast.

Heffner's Deli (4 Lunz Street, next to *Café Rimon*). Wide selection of good value US-style Jewish cooking, popular with young Americans. Opposite is the self-explanatory *Burger Ranch*.

Ketsef Ice-Cream Parlour (Ben Yehuda). Good ice-creams and milk-shakes from $1 upwards.

Liber Vegetarian Restaurant (10 Ben Yehuda). Variety of salads and hot main meals. Good value.

Ta'amon (corner of King George and Hillel, 8.30am–9pm). Cheap place for breakfast and snacks but now rather run-down.

24-hour coffee house and bakery (31 Jaffa Road). Perenially popular for late-night snacking or breakfast: bagels with cream cheese, cheese cake, croissants etc.

Yoel Salomon and Rivlin streets

Also just off Jaffa Road, Yoel Salomon and Rivlin streets, and the surrounding alleys, offer a quieter alternative to Ben Yehuda. Many of these places are older **bars** which also serve food, ideal for your ageing hippies who can't take the bright lights.

Rock Bar (Salomon Street). Hot, noisy, garish decor and younger clientele than most. Pricey cocktails as well as beer and simple, salad-type food.

Off the Square (6 Yoel Salomon). Dairy restaurant serving yoghurt soup, salads, pies, to largely religious Jewish clientele.

Good Vintage Pub. Noisy, youngish, cellar bar with usual drinks, average prices.

Rasputin's (Rivlin Street). Slightly fancier restaurant – chilli con carne and spaghetti – with occasional live music.

Chocolate Soup (Rivlin Street). Really does sell chocolate soup along with other 'delicacies'. Music and decor is late 1960s Notting Hill.

The Tavern (Rivlin Street next to above). Probably the first of the Jerusalem pubs, an institution of sorts which has barely changed in the last twenty years. Attracts a strange mixture of 1960s people clinging to their youth, youngsters who seem to look on them as exhibits in a museum, kibbutz volunteers and tourists going over the top, soldiers with automatic weapons to add a touch of menace and people with musical instruments imposing themselves over the general melee. The pattern on which all the other bars around here seem to have based themselves.

27 Jaffa Road. The place for the young kibbutzniks: an alley with a plethora of pubs, bars, restaurants teeming with off-duty soldiers and noisy crowds. There's little to choose between the *Taj Restaurant*, *Little Pub*, *Lalo's Pub*, *Pinni's Pub* or *Isaac's Pub*.

HaSha'on (*The Clock*, at the bottom of Rivlin Street). Cool and sophisticated bar with prices to match.

Katie's Restaurant (Rivlin Street opposite *HaSha'on*). Fancy, very expensive restaurant, excellent food.

Mahane Yehuda

Apart from having West Jerusalem's cheapest and best **produce market**, the Mahane Yehuda district is also packed with very popular, cheap **oriental restaurants** serving appetising snacks and meals. **Agrippas Street** has dozens, almost all of them open late. A popular eating place which is similar in the downtown area is run by a sephardi Elvis Presley fan on Heleni HaMalka Street, off Jaffa Road. His place is a shrine to the king, the food good and reasonably priced – try the *shakshuka*.

Others

Because sitting in cafés is about eighty per cent of West Jerusalem nightlife and entertainment there are good places throughout the New City. The following are among the best.

The Pie Shop (Don't Pass Me By) (33 Jaffa Road, corner 4 Nahalat Shiva; 2pm–midnight; closed Friday, reopens Saturday night after sunset). Serves, as you might expect, pies in every imaginable guise, as well as cocktails and other drinks in an easy-going atmosphere. Occasional live music.

Kamin Garden Restaurant (4 Rabbi Akiva Street, off Hillel Street, opposite *Jerusalem Tower Hotel*; ☎02-234819; open daily 9.30am–4am). Three-course meals (soups, vegetable pies, meat, salads etc), without wine, around $15. Nice place just for coffee and cakes, but beware of the mosquitos in the summer!

Beit Ariela (8 Rabbi Akiva Street; ☎02-248408). Restaurant and art gallery in a beautiful restored Arab house. Good value breakfasts and sandwiches, rather pretentious.

The Pie House/HaZtrif (5 Horkenus Street). Classy joint with excellent salads and elaborate sandwiches as well as more substantial food. Moroccan couscous every Tuesday and Friday costs $11.50.

Home Plus (Horkenus Street, between HaVatzelet and Helena HaMalka). Looks and sounds like a furniture shop but is in fact a café selling varieties of ice-creams, sweets and desserts.

Artists' House (12 Shmuel HaNagid Street). Comfortable bar and restaurant open until late. Great atmosphere.

Cinemateque Café (Hebron Road, closed Friday and Saturday). Vegetarian restaurant with terrace overlooking the Valley of Hinnom. Live music once or twice a week. Reasonable prices.

Nightlife

Jerusalem, East or West, is not the place for exciting **nightlife**. If it's pubs, clubs or discos you want, then Tel Aviv is the place to be. Many Jerusalemites will take a *sherut* or drive to the coast for an evening out, especially at the weekend when, thanks to the lobbying of religious pressure groups, West Jerusalem comes to a grinding halt on Friday afternoon and only partially reawakens on Saturday night. Tel Aviv, by contrast, comes to life on Friday night and has the additional attraction of the following day at the beach.

Nightlife in **West Jerusalem**, then, consists of a film, concert or play, or a drink in a bar at one of the larger hotels or in a 'pub'. Many of the latter have already been covered in the "Food" section, but in any event this sort of action is not hard to find: simply follow the hordes of young Americans wheeling from bar to bar in the city centre. On cool summer evenings, it's pleasant simply to go for a walk, or watch the **sound and light show** at the Citadel by Jaffa Gate. Virtually all of the listings below refer to West Jerusalem.

East Jerusalem, under the unending attention of the military, becomes a virtual ghost town at night. Before the *intifada* it was still possible to stroll through the Old City at night or walk on the ramparts. What nightlife there is, however, is restricted to a play or performance at Nuzha/Al-Hakawati Theatre (see "Palestinian Culture", below), or a drink or meal in one of the fancier hotels (poolside at the *American Colony Hotel* is particularly pleasant; the YMCA and *Intercontinental* are also promising).

For up-to-date **listings** and information on events in Jerusalem, see *Your Jerusalem, This Week In Jerusalem*, or the Friday supplement of the *Jerusalem Post*. The various tourist offices also have lists of events and entertainment in the Jerusalem region.

Film

West Jerusalem has no shortage of **cinemas** and of the seventeen or so in town, one or two will probably be showing films worth seeing. Most of them are pretty noisy – the Israeli public go in for audience participation – their wooden seats are generally uncomfortable, and the films have a tendency to break down or even have their reels shown in the wrong order. All of which, if you get into it, can add greatly to the sense of occasion. As movie-going is a popular form of entertainment, cinemas get very crowded and it's advisable to start queueing for tickets in good time.

Films are usually **subtitled** in Hebrew, English or French – depending on the original language – but Hebrew language films may not be subtitled at all or may have Arabic or French titles, so check before you go. The *Jerusalem Post* Friday supplement has the fullest and most up-to-date cinema listings. If you want more comfort (and quality) the *Cinemateque* (Hebron Road; ☎02-724131) shows three or four different films daily, and is also a fashionable place to hang out. Quality movies are also shown at the *Israel Museum, Jerusalem Theatre* and *Binyanei HaUma*, and **French films** feature regularly at the *Alliance Francaise* (8 Agron Street; ☎02-227167).

Music

There's a fair choice of **music** venues in Jerusalem, but even so the scene could hardly be described as exciting. In clubs and bars you'll hear predominantly **folk** (Israeli), **jazz** (sometimes excellent) and home-grown **rock** talent (usually mediocre). As well as the bars and pubs mentioned in the "Food and drink" section, many of which host occasional live acts, promising venues include the *Khan Theatre* (2 Kikar Remez, near the railway station; ☎02-718281/2/3) which puts on concerts both in the auditorium and in its own nightclub; *Tzavta* (38 King George Street; ☎02-227621); and the *Artists' House* (12 Shmuel HaNagid; ☎02-223653). All three of these are interesting cultural centres in their own right, and all have reasonably priced café/restaurants. *Pargod* (94 Bezalel Street; ☎02-231765), the YMCA (King David St; ☎02-227111), the *International Cultural Centre for Youth* (ICCY; 12a Emek Refaim;

☎02-664144) and the *Gerard Behar Centre* (11 Bezalel Street; ☎02-242157) are
also worth checking out. **Open-air concerts**, classical and popular, are also
held, particularly in summer, at the **Sultan's Pool** opposite Jaffa Gate.

Classical music and **opera** lovers are generally better served.
Jerusalem's main concert-hall is **Binyanei HaUma** (opposite Egged bus
station; ☎02-222481) and concerts are also staged at the *Jerusalem Sherover
Theatre*, the *Jerusalem Theatre* (☎02-667167), *Dormition Abbey* (Mount Zion;
☎02-719927), the *YMCA* (26 King David Street; ☎02-227111) and *Ticho House*
(7 HaRav Kook Street; ☎02-245068). The *Van Leer Institute* (Albert Einstein
Square; ☎02-667141) sometimes holds chamber music concerts. The **Church
of the Redeemer** (Mauristan Street; ☎02-282543) holds weekly concerts.

For all of the above, and rare more offbeat performances, look out for
advertising wall posters as well as in the usual listings.

Theatre

Most **plays** by Israeli authors are, naturally enough, written and performed in
Hebrew but there is some English language drama in Jerusalem, and if you
have any understanding of Hebrew, the theatre may offer a more challenging
night out – especially works by such controversial playwrights as Yehoshua
Sobol (*Ghetto*), Shmuel Hasafri (*The Last Secular Jew*) or Shmuel Amid
(*Roommates in Jerusalem*). The *Jerusalem Theatre* (☎02-667167), the *Wise
Auditorium* (Hebrew University), the *Khan Theatre* (☎02-718281), the *Gerard
Behar Centre* (☎02-242157), *Tzavta* (☎02-227621) and *Pargod* (☎02-231765)
may all host dramatic performances and some of them also put on **dance**.
Again the *Jerusalem Post* has the fullest information.

Some of the larger hotels, including the *Hilton* (☎02-536151), *Moriah* (☎02-
232232), *King David* (☎02-221111), and *Laromme* (Jabotinsky St; ☎02-697777)
also have auditoriums where various events are staged, though these are
usually tourist-oriented or 'folkloric' shows.

Talks

Public **talks and lectures** are a significant feature of Jerusalem life, and you
may find people urging you to attend some, especially those aimed at attracting prospective (Jewish) immigrants to the country. Others, like those at the
Hebrew University Forum (*Centre for Conservative Judaism*; 2 Agron Street;
☎02-227463) or *Zionist Confederation House* (Emile Botta Street, Yemin
Moshe; ☎02-245206), are of a religious nature, and there are also occasional
meetings and seminars run by liberal/left Israeli organisations, such as *Peace
Now*, which attempt to deal with current political concerns. Again, for current
information, see the *Jerusalem Post* and other publications.

Palestinian Culture

Israeli occupation has ensured that most Palestinian cultural activity goes on
behind closed doors, not always readily accessible to visitors. In recent years,
however, there have been a series of successful conferences and events

(International Women's Day celebrations, for example), poetry readings and concerts organised by trade and womens' unions, cultural associations and academic bodies. It is well worth keeping an eye on *Al-Fajr* English-language newspaper for details.

One institution, however, has succeeded in keeping Palestinian culture visible in Jerusalem, the **Nuzha/al-Hakawati Theatre**, the first Palestinian arts centre in the country (al-Nuzha Street off Nablus Road, up an alleyway beside the *Nuzha* cinema; ☎02-288189). Opened in May 1984, the cultural centre puts on a regular programme of plays, folklore evenings, films, exhibitions, conferences and other events. It is also used as a rehearsal and teaching centre by actors and the complex includes a music workshop run by one of the top Palestinian songwriters and composers. Despite having suffered constant closures by the Israeli military authorities in its short history, and the detention of artists, performers and musicians, it remains an active and vital meeting place. A small café, open all day, serves snacks and drinks and is a good place to meet Palestinians, whether you're going to a show or not.

East Jerusalem Information

Information from the Israeli point of view is easy enough to find from any tourist office or through the media – but East Jerusalem and the occupied territories are less well served. There are, however, a number of Palestinian institutions concerned with the press, freedom of speech and welfare. The primary task of the people working there is, naturally, to be concerned with Palestinian issues rather than with tourists or visitors, but most are more than willing to help out with information or advice. If you do want to visit any of the organisations below, try to phone before doing so.

Al-Fajr, the sole English-language Palestinian newspaper, is published in rather spartan and chaotic offices in a squat building (2 Hatem al-Ta'ie Street; ☎02-281035) up the hill from the YWCA. Sister to the Arabic language *Al-Fajr* daily founded in 1972, the weekly English edition began in April 1980. Although the journalists there are usually busy, they are always ready to talk to interested visitors and are an invaluable source of information, particularly if you want to travel to the occupied territories. Apart from the newspaper itself, which can be bought at most newsstands and bookshops in East Jerusalem, al-Fajr also produces a pocket diary full of useful historical and practical information. The diary includes details of research, educational, human rights, charitable and social institutions in the occupied territories and pre-1967 Israel. If you are a trade unionist, professional or active in the women's movement, it will also give you contacts for your Palestinian counterparts.

The **Palestine Press Service** (PPS; 10 Salah al-Din Street; ☎02-280147) is an agency which provides visiting and resident foreign journalists with up-to-date information on events in the occupied territories. It also publishes two magazines, one in English, the other in Arabic, both called *al-Awdeh* (the Return). The PPS has been frequently closed by the Israelis and has been shut down since the *intifada*.

More directly involved organisations include **The Palestine Human Rights and Information Campaign** (PHRIC; al-Masudi Street; ☎02-287077) which documents human rights violations in the occupied territories and produces a number of excellent, informative studies and publications. The **Palestine Centre for the Study of Non-Violence** (al-Nuzha Building; ☎02-285061) is a small outfit promoting non-violent resistance to the occupation. It too is less than popular with the Israeli authorities, and its director, Mubarak Awad, was deported in June 1988.

The headquarters of the **United Nations Relief and Works Agency for Palestine Refugees** (UNRWA) are on the Nablus Road on the way to Ramallah (☎02-282451–6). The agency provides education, health and relief services to 2.1 million registered Palestinian refugees and can provide you with literature full of facts and figures, and advice on visiting refugee camps. Their tours are generally only open to people who have a good reason for wanting to visit a camp. As a UN agency, UNRWA employees are diplomatic and studiously non-controversial.

There are a number of libraries where you can get access to books on various aspects of the country's history and conflict. The *al-Fajr* diary (see above) contains a comprehensive list. The **Arab Studies Society** (behind Orient House in al-Nuzha Street) also has a comprehensive library which is mainly used by Palestinian students and researchers. Its English-language section is small but its selection is excellent. It has also been closed down by the Israeli authorities during the *intifada*.

Listings

Airlines *Arkia*, 9 Heleni HaMalka (☎02-225888); *British Airways*, 33 Jaffa Rd (Bet Yoel) (☎02-233111); *El Al*, 12 Hillel St (☎02-233334/5); *TWA*, King George St, 5th Floor, Migdal Ha'ir (☎02-241135/6).

Airport For travel to Ben Gurion Airport, phone *Nesher Taxis*, 21 King George St (☎02-227227/231231) for advance seat in a shared taxi ($10) or *Egged* buses (see below). Evening before baggage check-in for those travelling with *El Al*, at new *El Al* Terminal near Central Bus Station (49 Yermiyahu Street; Sun–Thur 1–11pm, Sat evenings and holidays one hour after sunset).

Archaeological Digs For information, contact the *Department of Antiquities and Museums, Ministry of Education and Culture*, PO Box 526, Jerusalem (☎02-278602/3).

Banks Most are located on Jaffa Road or in Ben Yehuda, King George and Hillel streets. Opening times: Sun, Tue and Thur 8.30am–12.30pm and 4–5.30pm; Mon, Wed and Fri 8.30am–noon. Most hotels will change money outside these hours, as will East Jerusalem money changers, who are often quicker and may offer better rates.

Books *Steimatzky's* (39 Jaffa Road; ☎02-223654) has the largest collection of English books. Several second-hand bookshops can be found in the streets round about.

British Council Next door to the East Jerusalem YMCA (Nablus Road; ☎02-282545) the British Council houses a library and a reading room where you can catch up on the international news with English papers and magazines. It's a little bit of the British Empire that hasn't quite realised that the sun has definitely set.

Camping *SPNI*, 13 Heleni HaMalka St (☎02-222357) for equipment and information.

Car Rental *Avis*, 22 King David St (☎02-249001) and 19 Salah al-Din (☎02-281020); *Budget*, 14 King David Street (☎02-248991/2/3); *Eldan*, 36 Keren Hayesod (☎02-636183/699093); *Ar Car*, 6 Pines St (☎02-384889); *Europcar*, 68 Jaffa Road (☎02-248464); *Eurotour*, 36 Keren Hayesod (☎02-661749/663392); *Visa Car*, 23 Hillel St (☎02-223440/227117); *Yourent*, 5 Pines St (☎02-383943/383883).

Churches The *Christian Information Centre* (Jaffa Gate; ☎02-287647) has a complete list of churches and times of services.

Cinemas Jerusalem has around 20 cinemas, most showing foreign films subtitled in Hebrew and English or French. See the *Jerusalem Post* for programmes and addresses.

Citizens Advice Bureau 5 Zichron Yacov, Romema (☎02-522290), and 11 Hillel St (☎02-222096).

Consulates UK, Tower House, HaRakevet St (☎02-717724) (West) and 19 Nashashibi Street, Sheikh Jarrah (☎02-282481) (East); **USA**, 18 Agron St (☎02-234271) (West) and 27 Nablus Road (☎02-282231) (East).

Dentists Emergency treatment is available at weekends and on holidays from the *Magen David Adom* (☎101, or in East Jerusalem ☎02-282495). Hadassah (Ein Karem) has an emergency room, daily 4–10pm. There are several private clinics at the bottom of Salah al-Din Street or call the *Department of Dentistry* (Ministry of Health, 20 King David Street; ☎02-247471) for referrals.

Egged *Egged* bus station, 224 Jaffa Road (Romema District; ☎02-534596/551868); *Beit Tannous* Jaffa Gate terminal (☎02-247783/248144); *Egged Tours*, 44a Jaffa Road (Zion Square; ☎02-24198/223454). Reservations centre (Bus #99), 11a HaMeasef Street (☎02-531286).

Emergencies For ambulance call ☎101; Fire ☎102; Police ☎100; First Aid from *Magen David Adom* (☎101 or in East Jerusalem at Dung Gate ☎02-282495); 24-hour rape crisis line (☎02-245554/810110).

Events Recorded what's on information, Sun–Thur after 6pm, Fri after 2pm; ☎02-244197; *This Week in Jerusalem*, published by IGTO; *Your Jerusalem*, IGTO; *Hello Israel*, IGTO; *Jerusalem Post* weekend supplement; *Kol Ha'ir* (Hebrew) newspaper. Some East Jerusalem events are advertised in *Al-Fajr*.

Flights 24-hour information service, all flights (☎03-9712484); arrivals only, all flights (☎03-381111); *El Al* reservations and departure confirmation (☎03-625252).

Hiking Information *Society for the Protection of Nature in Israel* (SPNI), 13 Heleni HaMalka St (☎02-222357); *Nature Reserves Authority*, 78 Yermiyahu St (☎02-536271); *Neot Hakikar*, 36 Keren HaYesod (☎02-699385/ 636494).

Hospitals *Maqassed* (Mount of Olives; ☎02-288133), *Hadassah Hospital* (Mount Scopus ☎02-818111; Ein Karem ☎02-427427).

Laundry There are self-service launderettes at Ramat Eshkol Shopping Centre (☎02-820230) and at the Hebrew University, Mount Scopus Campus. In East Jerusalem there are dozens of inexpensive laundries, ask for the nearest one at your hotel or hostel.

Money Changers There are numerous money changers on Salah al-Din Street and at Damascus Gate, all offer competitive rates.

Mosques Prayer times are as normal.

Newspapers and Magazines The best newsstand in Jerusalem is at the bottom of Nablus Road, opposite Damascus Gate: it carries a comprehensive selection of local and foreign publications. Local publications include English editions of *Al-Fajr*, available at most news outlets in East Jerusalem, the *Jerusalem Post* and *Al-Awdeh*, an English magazine available in East Jerusalem when it's not banned.

Pharmacies *Alba Pharmacy*, 42 Jaffa Road, Zion Square (☎02-23703); *Balsam*, Salah al-Din (☎02-272315); *Dar al-Dawa*, Herod's Gate (☎02-282058); *Kupat Holim Klalit*, Romema (☎02-523191); *Shu'afat*, Shu'afat Road (☎02-810108). Lists of late-night chemists are published in the *Jerusalem Post*. There are two homeopathic chemists on Jaffa Road opposite Mahane Yehuda.

Phones Information ☎14; Time ☎15; Overseas information ☎195; Overseas collect calls ☎03-622881; Overseas operator ☎18; Telegrams ☎171; Auto alarm ☎174. 24-hour daily fax and Telex service ☎02-244737. Tokens for public phones are available at post offices and some news stands. Main international telephone office at 1 Koresh Street behind the post office.

Post Offices West Jerusalem main office on Jaffa Road (Sun–Thur 8am–6pm, Fri 8am–1pm); East Jerusalem main office in Salah al-Din Street. Branch offices are usually open 7–10am and 3.30–6pm. Express mail service ☎02-231162/3. Stamps can also be bought from stationers, souvenir shops, bookshops and large hotels.

Post Restante Unless otherwise specified, will be delivered to the Jaffa Road post office.

Railway Station Kikar Remez (☎02-717764).

Shopping The *souqs* of the Old City and the Mahane Yehuda produce market should fulfil most everyday needs, and the Old City is also cluttered with junky souvenirs, as are the streets of West Jerusalem with more arty tourist shops. For something slightly less obvious, however, try the *Palestinian Needlework Centre* (79 Nablus Road; ☎02-828834/828433), a self-help project run by Mennonites selling fine Palestinian embroidery. The *Boys Town Shop* in Masudi Street sells similar articles and also Palestinian glass, brass and pottery. The *Palestinian Pottery Factory* produces and sells finely glazed and distinctively patterned ceramics. Palestinian pickles are also an unusual souvenir – look out for the distinctive silver, green and black packages produced by the Palestinian Women's Organisation.

Sport The YMCA on King David Street (☎02-227111; bus #5, #6, #15 or #18) has a football stadium, athletic grounds, tennis courts and other sports facilities. The East Jerusalem YMCA (Nablus Road; ☎02-282375/6) has similar, less extensive, facilities.

Student Travel *ISSTA*, 5 Eliashar Street (☎02-231418) for student discounts on flights and other travel.

Swimming There's a municipal pool in West Jerusalem at 13 Emek Refa'im (☎02-632092; buses #4 or #18). Most big hotels will let you pay to use their pools, but it's generally expensive.

Synagogues A list of synagogues and service times is available from the IGTO.

Taxis All private taxis ('specials') are governed by meters which operate according to Tariff 1 from 5.30am to 8.59pm and Tariff 2 from 9pm to 5.29am. The driver must put the meter on at the start of the journey and must give you an electronically printed receipt on request. To complain, contact the nearest IGTO, or the police, with the driver's licence number. Taxi firms include: *Abdo Taxis* (☎02-283281) to the Allenby Bridge; *Beit Hanina Taxis* (☎02-259621); *City Taxis* (☎02-284482/283242); *Damascus Gate Taxis* (☎02-288800/282744); *Imperial Taxis* (☎02-282504); *United Taxi & Travel Service* (☎02-286941/284641).

Tours and Travel Agents *Egged Tours*, 44a Jaffa Road (Zion Square; ☎02-24198/223454); *Galilee Tours*, daily bus tours to Egypt, 3 Ben Sira St. (☎02-246858/231223); *Mazada Tours*, to Egypt and the Far East, 20 Shlomzion Hamalka St (☎02-244621); *Neot Hakikar*, 36 Keren Hayesod (☎02-699385, 636494) for Sinai and Negev safaris and tours to Egypt; *United Tours, King David Hotel*, King David St (☎02-28188); *Yehuda Tours*, 23 Hillel St (☎02-227740); *Society for the Protection of Nature in Israel*, 13 Heleni HaMalka St (☎02-222357); *Tour Va'aleh* (World Zionist Organisation), tours to the West Bank, 3 Ben Yehuda St (☎02-246522, 202346) Sun–Thur 8am–2pm, Fri 8am–noon; *Etzion Tours* (☎02-931387); *Gershon Tours* (☎02-241433, ext. 2613). Seven-seater minibuses with a licensed guide can be hired privately: details from IGTO offices.

Tourist Information *Israel Government Tourist Office* (IGTO), 24 King George Street (☎02-241281/2; Sun–Thur 8am–6pm, Fri 8am–3pm); Jaffa Gate (☎02-282295/6; Sun–Thur 8am–4pm and Fri 8am–3pm, Sat and holidays 10am–2pm). *Municipal Tourist Information Office*, 17 Jaffa Road (☎02-228844; Sun–Thur 8am–6pm, Fri and eve of holidays 8am–2pm). Recorded information on events in Jerusalem (☎02-241197) Sun–Thur after 6pm, Fri after 3pm. *Christian Information Centre*, Jaffa Gate, PO Box 14308 (☎02-287647). *Voluntary Tourist Service*, Jaffa Gate (☎02-288140; Sun–Fri 8.30am–1pm) and in larger hotels including the *King David, Hilton, Plaza, Holyland* (west), *Diplomat* and *Ramada Shalom*, Sun–Thur 6–8.30pm.

Tourist Visa Extensions *Ministry of the Interior*, Binyan Klal, 1 Shlomzion HaMalka St (☎02-245561/228211).

Jerusalem to Tel Aviv

The journey from Jerusalem to the coast is a fast one, on a major highway that cuts through countryside of interest more for its historical and strategic importance than for the few sites along the way.

Just a few minutes' drive out of the centre of Jerusalem, to the right of the road a little below you, you'll see the deserted houses of **LIFTA**. This was a wealthy Palestinian village, owning virtually all the land between the built-up area and Mount Scopus, earning a living from the olive groves growing there. The Jerusalem quarter of **Romema**, behind the bus station, was established on land bought from Liftans in 1921. In 1948, the village was destroyed by Israeli forces and the people dispersed: most of the inhabitants built new homes in the Mount Scopus area (then on the other side of the border). The settlement of **Mei Neftoah** was erected over much of the former village.

After 1967, to prevent the Palestinians returning to their homes, squads of soldiers were sent round to destroy the roofs of whatever habitable buildings were left. Meanwhile, significant portions of what remained of Lifta's land and many of the former inhabitants' new homes on Mount Scopus were lost to the new Hebrew University buildings and the French Hill settlement alongside it.

Al-Qastel (Kastel)

From Lifta to Latrun, the landscape still bears the marks of generations of Palestinian farmers. The steep-sided hills are ringed with terraces which provided subsistence for the thousands of peasant families who were expelled to refugee camps. Useless to Israeli mechanised farmers, they are left as a monument to their absent owners, or planted with non-economic Aleppo pines (Israelis call them Jerusalem pines).

Signposted to the left on the way out of Jerusalem is **KASTEL** (al-Qastel). It was here that Palestinian irregulars were defeated by British-armed Zionist forces in the decisive battle in the Jerusalem region of the 1948 war. Abd al-Qader al-Husseini, the ablest Palestinian commander left in the country after the British had expelled most leaders in the 1930s, died as his forces were surrounded. There is a Crusader castle on the peak of the hill and a memorial to the Israelis who died in the battles.

Latrun

Some 20km out of Jerusalem, the highway begins to descend steeply into the Judaean foothills. An opening in a gorge at this point is known in Arabic as **Bab al-Wad** and in Hebrew as **Sha'ar HaGai** (Gate of the Valley). It was the scene of fierce battles in the 1948 war – look out for the rust-coloured trucks and army vehicles left by the roadside as memorials. Control of the gorge was vital for the Israeli forces attempting to maintain a grip on the west part of Jerusalem. It was through here that all their supplies had to pass. To the west, the Latrun corridor was under Arab control, so a circuitous bypass, which became known as the 'Burma Road', was opened to get around it.

DEIR YASSIN

As you leave the city on the Tel Aviv highway, the outer suburb of **Kfar Sha'ul** (bus #11, #15, #15a, #16, #29) lies off to the south of the road. Today, it's notable only as the home of the Government Hospital for Mental Diseases. But the village which used to stand here, **DEIR YASSIN**, is for Palestinians one of the most emotive symbols of their struggle.

At 4.30am on April 10, 1948, Deir Yassin – which had co-existed in relative harmony with its Jewish neighbours – was woken by a 132-man force of *Irgun* (a group headed by Menahem Begin) and *Stern* (then jointly run by Yitzhaq Shamir). In an operation which the raiders called 'Operation Unity', 254 people, two-thirds of the inhabitants, were massacred.

Survivors described how villagers were lined up against the wall and shot at close range, how pregnant women had their stomachs cut open, how babies were butchered, how the attackers looted and raped, walked through houses with Sten guns and grenades, and finally dynamited them. A British officer who carried out investigations at the time confirmed these eye-witness accounts of sexual and other atrocities. One first-hand account was provided by Meir Pa'el, then a young *Palmach* commando:

> *It was noon when the battle ended and the shooting stopped. Things had become quiet, but the village had not surrendered. The Etzel (Irgun) and Lehi (Stern) irregulars left the places in which they had been hiding and started carrying out cleaning up operations in the houses. They fired with all the arms they had, and threw explosives into the houses. They also shot everyone they saw in the houses, including women and children – indeed the commanders made no attempt to check the disgraceful acts of slaughter. I myself and a number of inhabitants begged the commanders to give orders to their men to stop shooting, but our efforts were unsuccessful. In the meantime, some twenty-five men had been brought out of the houses; they were loaded into a freight truck and led in a 'victory parade', like a Roman triumph, through the Mahaneh Yehuda and Zikhron Yosef quarters (of Jerusalem). At the end of the parade they were taken to a stone quarry between Giv'at Sha'ul and Deir Yassin and shot in cold blood. The fighters then put the women and children who were still alive on a truck and took them to the Mandelbaum Gate.*
>
> (Quoted in *The Gun and the Olive Branch* by David Hirst)

Menahem Begin, in his book *The Revolt*, described this and other well-documented accounts as 'lying propaganda let loose about Jewish atrocities', but nevertheless admitted that the terror spread by 'the legend of Deir Yassin helped to carve the way to our decisive victories on the battlefield . . . in particular in the saving of Tiberias and the conquest of Haifa'.

News of the Deir Yassin massacre spread like wildfire to Palestinian communities all over the country, helped on occasion by Zionist militias and the Israeli army broadcasting 'Deir Yassin, Deir Yassin' from loudspeaker trucks. In the ensuing panic, many thousands fled their homes and became refugees. In spite of all that has taken place since then, the Deir Yassin massacre remains one of the most shocking in its brutality: it is still commemorated by an annual Palestinian holiday, **Deir Yassin Day**.

From 1948 to 1967 this was the main road from Jerusalem to the coast: since 1967 the Latrun road, cutting through a jutting corner of the occupied West Bank, has once again become the route of the highway.

The strategic road junction at **LATRUN**, on the southern fringe of the Ayalon Valley, is crucial to the conquest and control of Jerusalem. A list of those who have fought over it reads like a who's who of the country's history. Here Joshua slaughtered the Amorites ('and the sun stood still, and the moon stayed until the people had avenged themselves upon their enemies' *Joshua 10:13*); Judas Maccabaeus defeated the Syrians in 161BC; the Roman Fifth Legion camped for two years before the attack on Jerusalem in 70AD; Arab armies established a large military camp in the seventh century; and the Crusaders built a fortress to guard the road to Jerusalem.

In World War I the British took Latrun, and in World War II they set up prisoner-of-war camps here for captured Germans and Italians, later using the same camps to detain members of the Jewish underground. At the outbreak of war in 1948, the police fort and military positions were occupied by the Jordanian Arab Legion, thus blocking the road from the coast to Jerusalem until an alternative route – the 'Burma Road' above – was opened. The police fort and the Latrun corridor were captured by the Israelis on the first night of the 1967 war. A major new road now circles north from Latrun towards Ramallah, to provide access from the Jewish settlements on the West Bank to the coast.

The famous **Latrun police station** is now an Israeli army post, with a tank perched on top of a platform pointing in the direction of Jerusalem. On the hillside opposite is the **Latrun Monastery** (Mon–Sat 7.30–11.30am and 2.30–4.30pm; ☎08-220065), established in 1861 as a rest station and inn for Christian pilgrims travelling the rough road to Jerusalem. When the road was paved and there was no longer any need to stay at the inn, it was sold to French Trappist monks who built the present monastery in 1926. Set within beautifully tended gardens, olive groves and vineyards, the monastery is home to 25 monks who are famous for their liqueurs, wines (on sale for $2–4) and honey. From the monastery there's a clear view of the lay of the land and the strategic importance of the place.

On the summit of the hill above the monastery is a twelfth century **Crusader fortress**, built by Flemish knights to guard the road from Jaffa to Jerusalem. The name Latrun is a corruption of the name of this fortress – *Le Toron des Chevaliers* (Tower of the Knights). Since the sixteenth century, Christian tradition has wrongly identified this as the birthplace of the **good thief** (*boni latronis*) who was crucified alongside Jesus. The remains of the castle's arches, huge columns, underground passages and outer walls can still be seen.

To get to Latrun, take bus #404 or #433 from the central bus station and get off at the **Latrun interchange**, about twenty minutes from Jerusalem. For the monastery, follow the signs to Ashqelon under the bridge.

Emmaus and Canada Park

On the other side of the junction from the monastery, on the Ramallah road, is the site of **Emmaus**, the possible location of the appearance of the resurrected Jesus (*Luke 24*). Below the large white monastery, now used as the French Centre for Prehistorical Research (large and fearsome guard dogs proclaim the area out-of-bounds), are the ruins of the Emmaus Basilica (9am–

4pm). Here are the remains of a Crusader church, built over an earlier Byzantine basilica. The delicate-coloured mosaics are thought to have been the floor of a Roman villa.

A little further along the road you come to **Canada Park**, a wooded recreation centre created by the Israelis over the ruins of three Palestinian villages, **Yalu**, **Beit Nuba** and **Amwas** (which preserved the biblical name Emmaus). The villages were destroyed on the orders of Moshe Dayan in 1967 – with the strategic excuse of securing the Latrun corridor – and their inhabitants expelled. The site is now owned by the Jewish National Fund, and is undeniably beautiful, though the only references to the history of the place are from the safely distant past, like the preserved **Roman bath house** which, according to the plaque, '. . . illustrates the opulence and prosperity of Emmaus in the Roman-Byzantine period'. The park provides horse riding, picnic areas and a campsite with an **observation point** in the centre which looks out over the central and western Ayalon Valley, Ramle and the coastal plain and the foothills of the West Bank. The **Valley of Springs** once supplied agricultural and drinking water to the residents of Amwas; along its course are old graves and winepresses. Maps of the area are available in the reception area or from IGTO or JNF offices.

The story of the razing of the villages was told by the well-known Israeli columnist, Amos Kenan, in a report written in June 1967.

The commander of my platoon said that it had been decided to blow up the three villages in the sector – Yalu, Beit Nuba and Amwas. For reasons of strategy, tactics and security. In the first place to straighten out the Latrun 'finger'. Secondly, in order to punish these murderers' dens. And thirdly, to deprive infiltrators of a base in future.

One may argue with this idiotic approach which advocates collective punishment and is based on the belief that if the infiltrator loses one house, he will not find another from which to wait in ambush. One may argue with the effectiveness of increasing the number of our future enemies – but why argue?

We were told it was our job to search the village houses: that if we found any armed men there, they were to be taken prisoner. Any unarmed persons should be given time to pack their belongings and then told to get moving – get moving to Beit Sira, a village not far away. We were told also to take up positions around the approaches to the villages in order to prevent those villagers who had heard the Israeli assurances over the radio that they could return to their homes in peace – from returning to their homes. The order was – shoot over their heads and tell them there is no access to the village.

The homes in Beit Nuba are beautiful stone houses, some of them luxurious mansions. Each house stands in an orchard of olives, apricots and grapevines, there are also cypresses and other trees grown for their beauty and the shade they give. Each tree stands in its carefully watered bed. Between the trees lie neatly hoed and weeded rows of vegetables.

In the houses we found a wounded Egyptian commando officer and some old men and women. At noon the first bulldozer arrived, and ploughed under the house closest to the village edge.

With one sweep of the bulldozer, the cypresses and the olive-trees were uprooted. Ten or more minutes pass and the house, with its meagre furnishings and belongings, had become a mass of rubble. After three houses had been mowed down, the first convoy of refugees arrives, from the direction of Ramallah.

We did not shoot into the air. We did take up positions for coverage, and those of us who spoke Arabic went up to them to give them the orders. There were old men hardly able to walk, old women mumbling to themselves, babies in their mother's arms, small children, small children weeping, begging for water. The convoy waved white flags.

We told them to move on to Beit Sira. They said that wherever they went, they were driven away, that nowhere they were allowed to stay. They said they had been on the way for four days now – without food or water; some had perished on the way. They asked only to be allowed back into their own village, and said we would do better to kill them. Some had brought with them a goat, a sheep, a camel or a donkey. A father crunched grains of wheat in his hand to soften them so that his four children might have something to eat. On the horizon, we spotted the next line approaching. One man was carrying a 50-kilogram sack of flour on his back, and that was how he had walked mile after mile. More old men, more women, more babies. They flopped down exhausted at the spot where they were told to sit. Some had brought along a cow or two, or a calf – all their earthly possessions. We did not allow them to go into the village to pick up their belongings, for the order was that they must not be allowed to see their homes being destroyed. The children wept, and some of the soldiers wept too. We went to look for water but found none. We stopped an army vehicle in which sat a Lieutenant-Colonel, two Captains and a woman. We took a gerry-can of water from them and tried to make it go round among the refugees. We handed out sweets and cigarettes. More of our soldiers wept. We asked the officers why the refugees were being sent back and forth and driven away from everywhere they went. The officers said it would do them good to walk and asked "why worry about them, they're only Arabs?" We were glad to learn that half-an-hour later they were all arrested by the military police, who found their car stacked with loot.

More and more lines of refugees kept arriving. By this time there must have been hundreds of them. They couldn't understand why they had been told to return and now were not being allowed to return. One could not remain unmoved by their entreaties. Someone asked what was the point of destroying the houses – why didn't the Israelis go live in them instead? The platoon commander decided to go to headquarters to find out whether there was any written order as to what should be done with them, where to send them and to try and arrange transportation for the women and children, and food supplies. He came back and said there was no written order, we were to drive them away.

Like lost sheep they went on wandering along the roads. The exhausted were beyond rescuing. Towards evening we learned that we had been told a falsehood – at Beit Sira too the bulldozers had begun their work of destruction, and the refugees had not been allowed to enter. We also learned that it was not in our sector alone that areas were being 'straightened out'; the same thing was going on in all sectors. Our word had not been a word of honour, the policy was a policy without backing.

The soldiers grumbled. The villagers clenched their teeth as they watched the bulldozers mow down trees. At night we stayed on to guard the bulldozers, but the entire battalion were seething with anger; most of them did not want to do the job. In the morning we were transferred to another spot. No one could understand how Jews could do such a thing. Even those who justified the action said that it should have been possible to provide shelter for the population, that a final decision should have been taken as to their fate, as to where they were to go. The refugees should have been taken to their new home, together with their property. No one could understand why the fellah should be barred from taking his oil-stove, his blanket and some provisions.

The chickens and the pigeons were buried under the rubble. The fields were turned to desolation before our eyes, and the children who dragged themselves along the road that day, weeping bitterly, will be the fedayeen of 19 years hence. This is how that day, we lost the victory.

Israel – A Victory Wasted

travel details

Egged buses from Jaffa Road

To Ben Gurion Airport (every 30min 6am–8pm; 30min); Tel Aviv (15min 5.30am–11.30pm; 45min); Latrun/Ramla (15min 6am–7.30pm; 20/ 40min); Ashqelon (30min 6am–6pm; 1hr); Ashdod (7 daily; 1hr); Haifa (40min 6am–8pm; 3hr); Netanya (30min 6am–8pm; 2hr); Nahariyya (3 daily; 3hr 30min); Jericho/Tiberias (12 daily; 40min/3hr 30min); Afula/Nazareth (3 daily; 3hr/ 3hr 15min); Qiryat Shmona (6 daily; 5hr); Neve Zohar (Dead Sea) (6 daily; 3hr); Ein Gedi/Masada (6 daily; 2/3hr); Hebron/Beersheva (30min 6am–8.30pm; 1/2hr); Qiryat Gat/Beersheva (30min 6am–8.30pm; 1hr 20min/2hr); Eilat (6 daily; 5hr).

Arab buses

Arab bus timetables may be disrupted by the *intifada*; it is best to travel in the morning.

From Damascus Gate
Bethlehem (every 15min; 30min); Hebron (10min; 1hr); Jericho (20min; 40min); Bethany (30min; 10min).

From Nablus Road
Ramallah (every 15min; 35min); Nablus (30min; 1hr 30min); Beit Hanina (15min; 15min).

Train

From Jerusalem to **Tel Aviv**, departs Sun–Thur 4pm, Fri 11.30am (2hr).

CHAPTER TWO

THE WEST BANK

I f you look for the **West Bank** on the maps supplied by bookshops, tourist offices or hotels in Israel, you won't find it. Not only has the border –
the 'green line' that separated Israel of 1948–1967 from the territory of
the West Bank which it occupied in 1967 – officially vanished but, under
Israeli legislation, it is illegal to print or publish a map showing the border.
Where the West Bank used to be, there is now what Israel calls **Judaea and
Samaria**. Apart from East Jerusalem and its suburbs, no *formal* annexation
has taken place; that would be in clear contravention of international law and
would presumably create a worldwide furore (even if the international
community remains passive about the annexation of 'the holy city').
Nevertheless, for Israel's rulers the area is de facto annexed and is an inte-
gral part of *Eretz Israel* ('Greater Israel'). Marked on the map or not, the West
Bank remains central, both geographically and politically, to the Palestinian-
Israeli conflict.

Comprising an area of about 5000 square kilometres on the western bank
of the Jordan River, the West Bank is bordered to the north by the fertile
Marj Ibn 'Amer Plain in the centre of the Galilee, by the Naqab (Negev)
desert in the south, and by an arbitrary 1949 armistice line to the west. This
zone came under Transjordanian control following the war of 1948, and when
King Abdullah annexed the West Bank to Transjordan in the early 1950s, his
kingdom was renamed Jordan. The West Bank remained under Jordanian
control until it was occupied by Israel in the June war of 1967 and has been
under **military administration** ever since. The present size of the
Palestinian population of the West Bank is difficult to assess as the Israelis
are the only ones in a position to undertake a proper census and for them the
West Bank does not exist. Educated estimates, however, are that around one
million Palestinians live here, including around 126,000 in East Jerusalem,
many others in the region's twenty refugee camps.

A major part of the conflict in the West Bank concerns the ownership and
control of **land**. Fifty-two percent of the West Bank is now in Israeli hands,
obtained by direct confiscation under the pretext of security, or by purchases
legitimate and otherwise. Over 115 **Jewish settlements** have been built on
this land, a process that began immediately after the 1967 war when the
Labour government evicted thousands of Palestinians from their homes and
land in Jerusalem and the Jordan Valley and used the *Nahal* (an army pioneer
unit) and the kibbutz movement to establish 'defence' outposts which evolved
into civilian settlements. Labour policy was to grab as much land as possible
for future annexation: further settlements, based on quasi-religious pretexts,
soon followed. The **Gush Emunim** (Bloc of the Faithful) movement, which
holds that 'there is no such thing as an Arab home or an Arab piece of land in
Eretz Israel', has spearheaded these unashamedly ideological settlement
moves.

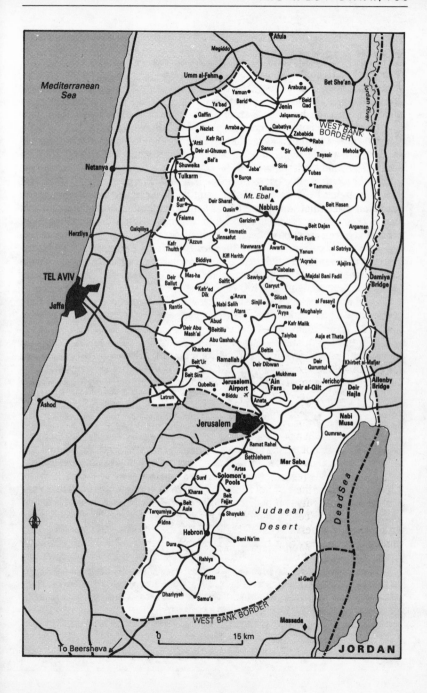

Mediterranean
Sea

Afula
Megiddo
Umm al-Fahm
Arabuna
Bet She'an
Yamun
Barid
Jenin
Beid
Qad
Ya'bad
Jalqamus
Qaffin
Arraba
Qabatiya
Nazlat
Kafr Ra'i
Zababida
Raba
'Attil
Sanur
Sir
Kufeir
Tayasir
Mehola
Deir al-Ghusun
Shuweika
Bal'a
Jaba'
Siris
Tubas
Netanya
Tulkarm
Burqa
Talluza
Tammun
Kafr
Sur
Deir Sharaf
Qusin
Mt. Ebal
Nablus
Beit Hasan
Falama
Garizim
Beit Dajan
Argaman
Herzliya
Qalqiliya
'Azzun
Immatin
Jinnsafut
Beit Furik
al Satriya
Kafr
Thulth
Hawwara
Awarta
Yanun
'Ajajira
Kifl Harith
'Aqraba
Damiya
Bridge
Biddiya
Sawiya
Qabalan
Majdal Bani Fadil
Deir
Ballut
Mas-ha
Salfit
Qaryut
TEL AVIV
Kafr'ed
Dik
Arura
Siloah
al Fasayil
Jaffa
Nabi Salih
Sinjil
Turmus
'Ayya
Mughaiyir
Rantis
Atara
Kafr Malik
Deir Abu
Mash'al
Abud
Beitillu
Taiyiba
Auja et Thata
Abu Qashsh
Kharbata
Beitin
Deir
Quruntul
Khirbet al-Mafjar
Ramallah
Beit'Ur
Deir Dibwan
Beit Sira
Mukhmas
Jericho
Allenby
Bridge
Qubeiba
Jerusalem
Airport
'Ain
Fara
Deir al-Qilt
Deir
Hajla
Latrun
Biddu
Anata
Ashod
Jerusalem
Nabi
Musa
Ramat Rahel
Qumran
Bethlehem
Mar Saba
Artas
Solomon's
Pools
Surif
Beit
Kharas
Fajjar
Beit
Aula
Shuyukh
Tarqumiya
Idna
Judaean
Desert
Dead Sea
Hebron
Bani Na'im
Dura
Rahiys
Yatta
al-Gedi
Dhariyyeh
Samu'a
WEST BANK BORDER
Massada
To Beersheva
15 km
JORDAN

WEST BANK
BORDER

Jordan River

0

In recent years, Israeli official thinking has grown closer to that of *Gush Emunim* and other fanatical groups like *Kach*. When Likud came to power in 1977, the **settlement policy** changed from 'land without people' to 'land regardless of people' and priority was given to settling areas of high Palestinian population density, particularly in the northern part of the West Bank. All major Palestinian centres are now ringed by Jewish settlements and isolated from each other by a strategic road network. The aim was to have 100,000 settlers living in the occupied West Bank by 1985 but, despite massive state subsidies allocated for settlement, funds from Zionist organisations abroad and financial incentives offered to prospective settlers, the total to date is around half that number.

From the outset, the **Israeli occupation** and its iron fist policy was met with Palestinian resistance, and the struggle of the Palestinians against the occupation has been constant. Israeli policy aims at the smashing of any manifestation of independence and hundreds of **military regulations** have been introduced to control every aspect of daily life. Apart from shootings and detention, deportation and the destruction of Palestinian homes are common punishments. Palestinian universities are regularly closed, trade unions are subject to harassment or 'illegalised', publishing houses are shut and newspapers censored. Meanwhile armed Jewish settlers are regarded as patriotic heroes in Israel – to such an extent that during the *intifada* they have even shot Israeli soldiers without being arrested or disarmed.

AVOIDING TROUBLE

As a foreigner you are immune from the worst of the West Bank's troubles: you're unlikely to be harassed or detained by the army at a roadblock, though you'll probably to be asked to show identification, and to justify your presence. On the other hand, if you are walking around an area that is under **curfew**, you clearly run the risk, at the best of being picked up, and at the worst of being shot. If you're participating or caught up in a **demonstration**, you will be subject to tear-gas, rubber and plastic rounds and live bullets like everyone else.

If you are **detained** for whatever reason make sure those taking you are aware that you are a foreigner (show them your passport and demand access to your consul); this should ensure that you are not maltreated. You are not obliged to say anything (according to Israeli law) but given that Israeli troops have almost limitless authority it may be better to try and talk your way out in the first instance, and the best way to do that is to maintain that you are a tourist, accidentally caught up. Make sure that those detaining you know you will be reporting the incident to the media and your government representatives (and make sure you do so when you are freed).

In the unlikely event of your being held for longer than a few hours demand access to a lawyer (as well as all of the above). Your camera may be taken and film exposed; there is nothing you can do about this, but make sure you get all your belongings back before leaving. As soon as possible after your release, write down what happened to you to be used as the basis of an affidavit which you can swear either at *al-Haq* or *PHRIC*. Go to Jerusalem and make the rounds of the media and the consulate and press them to take action to publicise your case. Sad but true, one foreigner gets far more attention than a thousand Palestinians.

Given the political situation, it may seem inappropriate to visit **historical and archaeological sites**. But in the light of the Israeli attempt to rewrite Palestine's history, such visits can themselves be positive political acts. To the south, barely half an hour from Jerusalem, **Bethlehem**, the birthplace of Jesus, is the chief draw for Christians: beyond lies **Hebron** where the biblical patriarch, Abraham, is said to be buried. In the east is the ancient oasis and city of **Jericho**, while **Nablus** in the north is 'the uncrowned queen of Palestine'. For all the biblical significance of the region, however – and Old Testament references are thick on the ground – these places are first and foremost living Palestinian towns, where a visit will tell you a great deal more about 1988AD than 1988BC. Since there is no Palestinian Ministry of Tourism or Antiquities to vaunt its national heritage, many of the sites lack the sort of facilities you'd find elsewhere in the country.

Another good reason to visit is simply to add your physical presence as **witness**. Army road blocks, demonstrations and confrontations are part of daily life here, but by and large the Israelis are very concerned to preserve what's left of their image abroad and are therefore reluctant to inconvenience anyone with a white skin and a western passport, so you'll be relatively free to travel around. Reports of what you have seen should be passed on to human rights organisations (*Amnesty International, al-Haq, Association for Civil Rights in Israel* etc), welfare bodies (*Red Cross, UNRWA*) or the media. The presence of a foreigner has frequently been a restraining influence on the excesses of the Israeli army. Photographs are powerful proof to back up your account, although the Israelis do not take kindly to their activities being documented in this way.

Israelis will advise against **visiting the West Bank** other than on Israeli-organised tours. These will not only give you a one-sided view but will also block any contact you might otherwise have with Palestinians. They are easy, however, and will take you to places you otherwise might not get to, or want to get to. By far the best way to travel, though, is to go in the company of a local Palestinian resident. If you are open to it, it is not difficult to make genuine friends and possibly be invited home. Otherwise, you can simply visit sites and towns on the West Bank by bus – almost all are easily handled as day-trips from Jerusalem, at least when transport is running normally. It is as well to keep abreast of the news and to seek advice from Palestinian sources (*al-Fajr* etc) before setting out.

Travelling around the West Bank is theoretically straightforward, as there are frequent and regular **bus services** as well as plenty of local and inter-city *service* taxis that are faster and only marginally more expensive. Watch out, though, for **stoppages and strike days** which might leave you stranded. Public transport invariably stops early (most buses at around dusk) and as many areas are clamped under dusk-to-dawn curfews, you'll need to check the time of the last return bus unless you plan to stay overnight.

We have assumed that you will be visiting the West Bank from Jerusalem and this chapter is structured accordingly. Of course you may end up in Hebron on your way from the Negev, or in Nablus travelling down from the Galilee. Public transport will not be a problem, but reading this section backwards might be!

THE SOUTH

The southern half of the West Bank, south of Jerusalem, has two major centres in **Bethlehem** and **Hebron**, connected by a single main road which continues to Beersheva in the Negev. Along this route and just off it are scores of sites reflecting the area's biblical and historical traditions, and many others – settlements, Palestinian villages and refugee camps – redolent of more current events. The western shore of the **Dead Sea** also falls in this region, of course, but since this is one of the main routes south to Eilat, it's covered in that chapter rather than here.

The road south from Jerusalem, along the spine of the **Judaean Hills**, may be faster now than it was for the ancient biblical figures, but it probably looks very similar: the vineyards, olive trees and rolling hills would all be familiar to Abraham if he passed this way today, though the forbidding concrete of the Israeli settlements which also line the route would not be. **Heading for Bethlehem**, the #23 bus route from Jaffa Gate in the Old City initially follows the 1967 border before passing into Israeli territory through the Jewish suburb of **Talpiot** and past **Kibbutz Ramat Rahel**. The road then crosses back into occupied territory at the Monastery of **Mar Elias** (below), an important Jordanian border post until 1967. From here it descends through semi-rural countryside towards Bethlehem, with the curious mound of **Herodion** looming in the distance at the fringe of the **Judaean Desert**, and the purple **Moab Mountains** of Jordan beyond. The journey to Bethlehem is less than 10km, but a couple of places en route make breaking your journey worthwhile.

Mar Elias

Midway between Jerusalem and Bethlehem, on the saddle of a hill giving a panoramic view of Bethlehem and Herodion, stands the silver-domed Greek monastery of **Mar Elias**. According to one tradition the prophet Elijah slept here; another holds that a Greek bishop of Bethlehem, Elias, was buried here in 1345. Yet another version places the sepulchre of St. Elias, an Egyptian monk who became Patriarch of Jerusalem in 494, on the site. Whatever its true origins (the original date is uncertain, but the buildings were restored by the Crusaders), the monastery did hold the tomb of a Bishop Elias up to the seventeenth century. It was an agricultural community, its monks cultivating such crops as olives and grapes, and upholding the virtue of labour.

Today, Mar Elias is believed to answer the prayers of barren women and ailing children. It is a popular site for pilgrimage and, before making their entry to Bethlehem on the **Christmas Day procession**, the Patriarchs traditionally pause here to be received by the notables of the area.

Near Mar Elias is a field covered with millions of small pebbles which gave rise to a parable on the consequences of telling lies. One day, goes the story, a man was sowing chickpeas in the field when Mary (according to other versions it is Jesus) passed by and asked him: "What are you sowing there, my friend?" "Stones", the man answered. "Very well, you will reap stones", was the reply. When the sower came to gather his crops, he found nothing but petrified chickpeas in his **Field of Grey Peas**.

Opposite the field is the **Tantur Ecumenical Institute**, originally a hospice built in 1876. The institute, which houses a large and impressive library, was established in 1964 to promote understanding between the Churches.

Rachel's Tomb

As the Jerusalem road approaches the northern edge of Bethlehem, it passes the traditional burial place of the biblical matriarch **Rachel**. According to the *Book of Genesis (35:19)* '. . .Rachel died and was buried in the way to Ephrath which is Bethlehem. And Jacob set a pillar upon her grave; that is the pillar of Rachel's grave unto this day'. There has been a succession of synagogues on the site: the simple building which houses the tomb today was erected by the Ottoman Turks in the 1620s, although the dome over it was rebuilt by Sir Moses Montefiore in 1841. Revered by Jews, the place is also holy to Muslims, as a cemetery of the Beduin Ta'amre tribe lies in the grounds. From 1948 to 1967, the site was under the protection of the Islamic *Waqf* and was open to Jewish worshippers. Today it is under permanent guard by Israeli soldiers (Sun–Thurs 8am–5pm, Fri 8am–1pm. Admission free).

During construction work near Rachel's Tomb in 1904, a **Roman aqueduct** was uncovered. Inscriptions on the stones date the structure to 195AD. Nearby is an even older aqueduct attributed to the time of Pilate.

Bethlehem University

At Rachel's Tomb the road divides; the left fork leads directly to Bethlehem while the right one skirts the northern side of town and continues south towards Hebron. To visit **Bethlehem University**, take the Hebron road and ask the *service* driver to let you off at the small side road on the left. The university is a short walk up the hill.

The university is one of the most important of Bethlehem's many charitable and educational institutes. Opened in 1973, it was established after Pope Paul VI, on a visit to the Holy Land in 1964, called for the foundation of new institutions to improve the quality of life for the people of the area. One of the specific priorities cited was a university for young Palestinians in their homeland. Bethlehem University, with faculties of art, sciences and business administration, and professional schools of nursing, education and hotel management, has grown from an initial enrolment of 78 students to some 1500, well over half of whom are women. Directed by the Catholic Order of the Brothers of Christian Schools, it has been frequently closed down by the Israeli authorities after demonstrations against the occupation, and like all Palestinian educational institutions, has been shut since the start of the *intifada*.

Bethlehem

You Bethlehem Ephrathah, the least among the clans of Judah, from you shall come forth for me one who is to be ruler in Israel . . . (Micah 5:2)

BETHLEHEM, surrounded by gorges, fertile terraces and fields supplying grain, olives and grapes, straddles two plateaus just to the south of Jerusalem. Being the birthplace of Christ has thrust this small, rose-coloured city onto a world stage. But don't expect too much holiness. Modern Bethlehem is a major tourist attraction, with all the accompanying commercialism that this implies. Romantic as it sounds, **Manger Square** in the centre of town is in fact a giant parking place, barely able to cope with all the cars, taxis and tour coaches wanting to cram in. And sitting in one of the cafés around the square, your attention is more likely to be caught by the Israeli flag atop the police station or the gun-toting soldiers than by church spires or minarets. The massive and modern town hall, the countless souvenir shops and the camera-clicking tourists all add to the disillusion.

What real charm Bethlehem has is to be found in the side streets away from the centre and the pilgrim sites. The town and the *souq* can at their best be a heady mix of ancient and modern, where you can find anything from plastic utensils to hand-woven rugs, where sophisticated students from Bethlehem University cross paths with priests, nuns and Beduin traders. When you tire of visiting the sites, wander around and find a local coffee-shop to sit and watch the world go by.

The biblical tradition

Bethlehem is thought to have been inhabited since the Stone Age and occupies a place of some prominence in the **Old Testament**. Jacob's wife Rachel died on her way here; it was in Bethlehem that Boaz fell in love with Ruth; their son Obed ' . . . became the father of Jesse, who was the father of David'; and the young David himself tended his flocks here until selected by the prophet Samuel to take over from King Saul as king of Israel ('Now he was ruddy and withal of beautiful eyes and goodly to look upon. And the Lord said: "Arise, anoint him; for this is he"' *I Samuel 16:12*). Isaiah prophesied that the Messiah would be a descendant of Jesse and David ('And there shall come forth a rod out of the stem of Jesse and a branch shall grow of out his roots' *Isaiah 11:1*).

Members of the **house of David** lived in the foothills of the Galilee and were known as *Natzoreans* (from the Hebrew *netzer*, branch): they gave their name to the village Nazara, later to become the town of Nazareth. **Mary and Joseph** were Natzoreans, and part of their reason for coming to Bethelehem was in order to fulfil the ancient prophecy of Mica that this would be the birthplace of the Messiah. A contributory reason for their move was that Emperor Augustus had ordered a census to help streamline his taxation system: 'And Joseph also went up from Galilee, out of the city of Nazareth, into Judaea, unto the City of David which is called Bethlehem; because he was of the house and lineage of David; to be taxed with Mary his espoused wife, being great with child' (*Luke 2:4*). Once in town they were famously

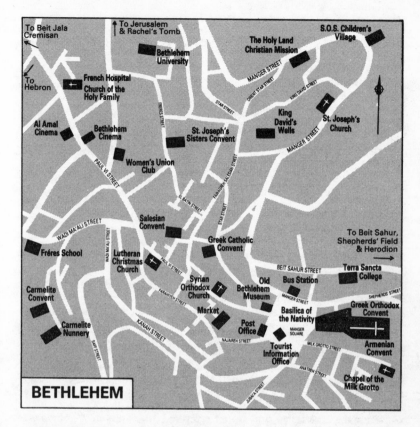

To Beit Jala Cremisan

↑ To Jerusalem & Rachel's Tomb

S.O.S. Children's Village

The Holy Land Christian Mission

Bethlehem University

MANGER STREET

To Hebron

French Hospital Church of the Holy Family

STAR STREET

ORIENT STAR STREET

KING DAVID STREET

St. Joseph's Church

King David's Wells

FRERES STREET

Al Amal Cinema

Bethlehem Cinema

St. Joseph's Sisters Convent

MANGER STREET

Women's Union Club

PAUL VI STREET

FAWAGHA SALESIAN STREET

EL BATIN STREET

STAR STREET

WADI MA'ALI STREET

WADI MA'ALI STREET

Salesian Convent

Greek Catholic Convent

To Beit Sahur, Shepherds' Field & Herodion →

Fréres School

Lutheran Christmas Church

PAUL VI STREET

BEIT SAHUR STREET

Terra Sancta College

SHEPHERDS' STREET

Carmelite Convent

FARAHYEH STREET

Syrian Orthodox Church

Old Bethlehem Museum

Bus Station

MANGER STREET

KANAH STREET

Market

Post Office

Basilica of the Nativity

Greek Orthodox Convent

Carmelite Nunnery

SAFI STREET

NAJAIREH STREET

MANGER SQUARE

Tourist Information Office

MILK GROTTO STREET

Armenian Convent

ANATREH STREET

JUBHA STREET

Chapel of the Milk Grotto

BETHLEHEM

unable to find lodging for the night ('as there was no room for them in the inn' *Luke 2:7*) and so the baby was born and laid in a manger – probably actually a cave in the back area of a house. Many Bethlehem houses are still built in this way, backing onto the rocks.

The exact location of **Christ's birthplace** is, however, a matter of bitter dispute. None of the early New Testament sources make any mention of the town and the commonly accepted version of Jesus' conception and birth comes from the Gospels of Matthew and Luke, written some 75 to 80 years after the event. Matthew is thought to have based his account on information about Jesus' childhood which he obtained from relatives in the Nazarene village of Kokhaba (Village of the Star) in the Galilee. Luke may have consulted Jesus' cousin, Simeon Bar-Kleopha. And both would also have heard (at least second-hand) some of the reminiscences of Mary, passed down through the first Christian community on Mount Zion in Jerusalem, among whom she lived until her death around 50AD.

Bethlehem gained the importance it holds for Christians today following the **Edict of Milan** of 313AD, by which the Emperor Constantine legalised

Christianity. Only then were Christians able to emerge from their clandestine status. Constantine's mother, Queen Helena, embarked on a pilgrimage to the Holy Land in 326AD to investigate three sites which had been revered since the early days of Christianity – the site of Jesus' burial at Golgotha, the Cave of the Disciples on the Mount of Olives and the **Grotto of the Nativity** in Bethlehem. The identification of this latter site is due, in large measure, to the Roman Emperor Hadrian. In order to suppress any Jewish-inspired messianic movement following the Bar Kokhba Revolt (132–135AD), Hadrian paganised all known Judaeo-Christian holy places, such as the Temple and the Holy Sepulchre in Jerusalem. Over the Grotto of the Nativity he planted the **Grove of Thammuz**, a shrine dedicated to Adonis. Far from deterring Christians from revering the site, it was thus affirmed as the birthplace of Christ. In 339AD, Helena instigated the construction of a church, the **Basilica of the Nativity**, on the spot.

Bethlehem in History

During the **Byzantine** period, Bethlehem was a walled city with two towers: it figures in the famous map of Mabada and in the accounts of early pilgrims. The city was damaged in the Samaritan Revolt of 529AD, but the Emperor Justinian (527–565AD) repaired its walls and buildings and ordered Helena's original church to be rebuilt '. . .of such splendour, size and beauty that none even in the Holy City should surpass it'.

By 600AD, many monasteries and churches had been erected in the now flourishing town. In 614, when the **Persian** invaders destroyed many of the sanctuaries in the land, the Basilica of the Nativity was one of the few saved. How this happened was described in a letter from the Jerusalem Synod of 838AD. Having reached Bethlehem, the Persians ' . . . were greatly surprised to discover a representation of the Magi from Persia. Out of reverence and respect for their ancestors they decided to honour these sages by sparing the church. And this is how it has survived until this day'.

During the **Muslim period**, the sites revered by the two other 'religions of the book', Judaism and Christianity, were protected. In 638, Omar Ibn al-Khattab prayed towards Mecca in the southern apse of the Church of the Nativity: the **Mosque of Omar** with its fine minaret opposite the church commemorates this gesture. With the **Crusader** invasion of 1099, Bethlehem was captured by Tancred. It became the site for the crowning of Crusader kings, above all the great coronation of Baldwin I in 1100, and enjoyed royal favour. Salah al-Din's forces recaptured Bethlehem in 1187, but the Ayyubid Sultan Malik al-Kamil returned Bethlehem to the Crusaders in 1229, and they held it until they were finally ousted from the country in 1291.

It remained an extremely small town, however. At the turn of this century, the **population** numbered 8200 and by 1922 it had actually decreased to 6650. The fact that 30,000 people live here today is largely due to the influx of Palestinians made refugees with the establishment of the Israeli state in 1948. Today these refugees represent some sixty per cent of the inhabitants.

Tourism and pilgrimage have also brought growth, and are an important source of income for Bethlehem. The town owes much of its prosperity to the manufacture of religious objects made from olive-wood, mother-of-pearl and coral, and is renowned too for the beautifully delicate glass products which you can watch being made in the town's workshops. Bethlehem also has a long tradition of skilled stonemasons, working the high quality stone that comes from quarries in the vicinity of the town.

The modern town of Bethlehem contains a plethora of chapels and religious institutions representing every shade of Christianity. Egyptian Copts, Armenians, Assyrians, Greek Arabs, Catholics, Protestants, Anglicans and Lutherans all have their own churches and worship in their own ways. Thus, **Christmas** is celebrated three times in Bethlehem: on December 25th by the Catholics and other western churches; on January 6th by the Armenians who keep to the Eastern calendar; and on January 7th by the Greek Orthodox and other eastern churches who follow the Julian calendar.

The Church of the Nativity

The Bethlehem skyline is an amazing array of architectural forms, old and new, oriental and occidental, towers and belfries, domes and spires, houses of worship of all kinds. But it is the **Church of the Nativity**, entered from Manger Square, which still holds pride of place.

Descriptions of the church by pilgrims throughout the centuries support the theory that the present structure is basically the original building from the time of Constantine, as enlarged and restored by Emperor Justinian. It is thus one of the oldest churches in the world, though not one of the most beautiful. The complex was later expanded by the addition of several chapels and monasteries: on the south side, churches and monasteries belonging to the Armenian and Greek Orthodox churches adjoin the ancient basilica; at the northern end is the Franciscan hospice and monastery, and the Church of St. Catherine. Inside, the competing groups maintain a precarious co-existence through an intricate schedule of worship. Control of the church has more than once led to physical warfare, most significantly when Napoleon III, who considered himself successor to the French Crusader King Louis IX, declared the entire church complex French property in 1852. This brought him into conflict with Russia which supported the rights of the Eastern Orthodox Church, and was one of the chief causes of the Crimean War.

The forbidding, fortress-like church has three **entrances**, two of them bricked up and the third small, out of scale with the importance of the interior. In fact this main door of Justinian's church was once grand (you can still see traces of the original arch) but it was lowered by the Crusaders during the Middle Ages and further restricted during the Ottoman era to prevent mounted horsemen from entering the church. The vestibule behind the entrance leads directly into the main hall of the basilica, which is divided into a central **nave** and two aisles by golden-coloured columns of local stone. The surviving mosaics on the side walls and floor, dating from the restoration of 1165–69, show how splendid the church must once have been.

Two sets of stairs on either side of the altar lead down into the **Grotto of the Nativity**, the site where Jesus is said to have been born. A fourteen-pointed silver star embedded in white marble marks the exact spot: it was installed by the Catholics in 1717, removed by the Greeks in 1847 and replaced by the Turkish government in 1853. It bears the inscription: *Hic de Virgine Maria Jesus Christus natus est* – Here Jesus Christ was born to the Virgin Mary. Of the fifteen lamps burning around the recess, six belong to the Greeks, five to the Armenians and four to the Latins. In another corner of the grotto, down three steps opposite the Altar of the Nativity, is the **Chapel of the Manger** where Christ was laid ('And this shall be a sign unto you; ye shall find the babe wrapped in swaddling clothes, lying in a manger' *Luke 2:21*). Facing the manger is the **Altar of the Adoration of the Magi**.

The Church of Saint Catherine

A small door in the north wall of the basilica leads to the tranquil medieval cloister in front of the Franciscan **Church of Saint Catherine**. This church, where Christ is said to have appeared to St. Catherine of Alexandria, was built in 1881, incorporating remains of Crusader buildings discovered during construction. It's a far lighter, airier space than the main basilica: it is from here that Midnight Mass on Christmas Eve is televised and beamed worldwide. The daily procession of Franciscan Fathers from the church to the Basilica (at noon, or 1pm during daylight saving) is well worth watching or taking part in – it's one of the few times when an air of solemnity seems to take hold of Bethlehem.

From the church, medieval stairs lead down into a complex of caves and tombs linked to the Grotto of the Nativity (although there's no public access from one to the other). The main altar in this impressive subterranean complex is devoted to **Saint Joseph**, the father of Christ. Here he had a dream in which an angel appeared, warning him to flee to Egypt to safeguard the child Jesus from Herod's anger. Nearby is the **Chapel of the Innocents**, commemorating the children who were slaughtered by Herod after the Holy Family had left ('Then Herod . . . sent forth, and slew all the children that were in Bethlehem, and in all the coasts thereof, from two years old and under' *Matthew 3:16*).

In the same complex is the **Tomb of Saint Jerome**, a Dalmatian priest who arrived in Bethlehem from Rome in 386AD and secluded himself in a cave near the Grotto of the Nativity to study the Bible. Here he began a translation of the Old Testament from Hebrew to Latin which, as the **Vulgate**, was to become the official Bible of the Roman Catholic Church for the next 1500 years. Jerome died in 420AD, and his tomb lies in a cave which also contains the remains of two of his followers, St. Paula and her daughter Eustochium, who founded a convent nearby. The cell where St. Jerome executed his mammoth task is now a chapel.

The Armenian Monastery

To the south of the forecourt of the Church of the Nativity lies the **Armenian Monastery**, most of which dates from the Byzantine and Crusader periods. Once a major centre for Armenian hermits, later full of seventeenth-century scribes copying and illustrating Bibles, the monastery now houses only six monks and provides community services for Bethlehem's 300 Armenians. The water of the well facing the arched entrance is believed by pilgrims to have curative properties.

The grand colonnaded hall in the arched vaults of the monastery – described by pilgrims as 'St. Jerome's University' – is thought to have been used by St. Jerome as a lecture hall, and there are stables in the basement which housed the horses of the pilgrims and devotees who stayed at the monastery. The monastery church is decorated with magnificent blue Armenian tiles and three wood-sculptured altars; there's also a famous baptismal font and an eighteenth-century painting depicting the Baptism of Christ. From the roof of the monastery you get a unique panoramic view of Bethlehem and its terraced surroundings.

Sites around the town

Five minutes' walk southeast of Manger Square, along Milk Grotto Street, you'll find the **Milk Grotto Church** or **Women's Cavern** (daily 8–11.30am and 2–5pm). One version of the story behind the site has it that the Holy Family hid here during the Slaughter of the Innocents: alternatively they made a hurried stop here during the flight to Egypt, and in the rush Mary let a drop of her milk fall to the ground whilst she was nursing, turning the rock from red to white. Christians and Muslims alike have since believed that the rock increases a nursing mother's milk and fertility. European pilgrims used to chip off tiny pieces of the rock to take home as souvenirs – the earliest record of such 'vandalism' is from the seventh century. The influence of Italian art on the facade of the church is evident, and can also be seen in many of the icons inside, mostly depicting a curiously fair-skinned, blonde Virgin. The cave-like interior, dominated by a golden statuette of Mary, has a sky-blue roof and is a wonderfully cool and serene escape from the summer heat outside.

King David's Well, in King David Street off Manger Street, marks the site where David's followers broke through Philistine lines in order to fetch him drinking water from the well ('O that someone would give me water to drink from the well of Bethlehem which is by the gate!' *Samuel 23:13–17*) which he then offered as a sacrifice to God. The three large cisterns are the only monument in Bethlehem to the famous king who was born here – apart, that is, from the **King David Cinema** (☎02-742939) nearby. This presents four daily showings (at 10.30am, 2pm, 5pm and 8.30pm) of a two-hour film entitled *Jesus . . . the man you thought you knew*. According to the blurb, this 'was made over five years in the Holy Land' and 'checked for accuracy by more than 200 eminent scholars': what's more, it will 'move you to tears, applause and shouts of joy'.

Alternatively, the **souq** up the stairs along Paul VI Street, past the impressive **Syrian Orthodox Church**, offers more earthly delights and is as yet surprisingly untouched by the ravages of tourist commercialism. The **Bethlehem Folklore Museum** (or Old Bethlehem Museum; Mon–Sat 10am–noon and 2.30–5pm), on the left before you reach the Syrian church, is much underestimated and well deserves a visit on the way. Established in 1971 by the *Arab Women's Union* with the aim of protecting a threatened Palestinian cultural heritage, the Union has collected popular household articles and displays them in a traditional house: there's a reconstructed *diwan* (living room) complete with *bsat* (carpets) and *kanoon* (brass stove) and a kitchen with pottery, wood, brass and straw utensils. As it has grown, the project has become more ambitious and added a permanent exhibition of local embroidered clothing and traditional jewellery of coral, gold and silver. A small showroom upstairs sells exquisite examples of local hand-embroidered items, made at home by local women.

Practicalities

Bethlehem's **Tourist Information Office** (☎02-742591) is on Manger Square, diagonally opposite the police station, next to the Municipality.

The cheapest **food**, as ever, comes from the various *falafel* stands that surround Manger Square and Manger Street. There are also several good restaurants close by, the nearest being the *Granada Grill Bar* (☎02-742810), a small, modern place in the New Commercial Centre behind the Municipality. Nearby are the *St. George* (☎02-743780) and *Al-Andalus* (☎02-743519) restaurants, and *Al-Atlal* on Milk Grotto Street. All of these have similar good value menus: meat, *shishlik*, *humus*, accompanied by salads and rice. The *Da'ana Bakery*, on Star Street past the Bethlehem Museum, bakes pitta, flat bread and gigantic pancakes to supplement with provisions from supermarkets.

As far as **rooms** go, Bethlehem is not the cheapest of places to stay, but there are a handful of reasonable **hotels and hospices**. Accommodation around Christmas and Easter is very hard to find, so unless you've booked you're almost certainly better off staying in Jerusalem and day tripping to Bethlehem. Many hotels put their prices up at these peak times, whilst in the summer months when business is slack you may be able to bargain prices down.

Franciscan Convent Hospice (Milk Grotto Street east of Manger Square; ☎02-742441). Run by nine 'White Sisters' – *Les Soeurs Franciscaines de Marie* – this is not strictly a hotel but can offer a place to sleep and is particularly welcoming to women. Prices are from $12 to $15 with breakfast, depending on whether the room has a shower or not; dormitory space for women costs around $6. The place is absolutely quiet and spot-lessly clean, with a great view of the Judaean desert beyond. Curfew at 9pm, extended at Christmas time.

Al-Andalus Guest House (south side of Manger Square; ☎02-741348). Ten rooms, seven with three beds and three with two. The hotel, on the first floor, is clean and adequate and charges $15 per person with breakfast, $10 without.

Palace Hotel (next to Basilica of the Nativity; ☎02-742798). Two-star hotel, clean and simple in pleasant surroundings: all rooms with bath, many with balconies. $17 double, $10 single, without breakfast.

Handal's Hotel (Jamal Abd En-Nasser Street, off Paul VI Street; ☎02-742494). A fancier hotel, but comfortable. $20 single, $29 double.

St. Joseph's Hospice (Manger Street, north of Manger Square; ☎02-742497). Run by hospitable Syrian Catholics; $12 single, $24 double, with breakfast; some rooms with private baths, negotiable $3 for floor space. Often booked up by pilgrims and youth groups.

Bethlehem Star Hotel (El Batin Street; ☎02-743249). Three-star hotel near the centre of town, modern and friendly. $19 single, $29 double.

Bethlehem Grand Hotel (Al-Madbassah Street, off Paul VI; ☎02-741440). Twenty luxurious rooms.

Ramat Rahel Compound (☎02-715712; bus #7). A scenic spot halfway between Bethlehem and Jerusalem. $4 per person **camping**; $9 for bed in bungalow for two; $16 for singles in adjoining hostel. Cool off in kibbutz pool for $1.50.

Around Bethlehem

Within easy reach of Bethlehem are a number of smaller sites worth exploring, all of them quickly and easily accessible on local buses. First, and closest, is the Palestinian town of Beit Sahur, barely a kilometre from the Church of the Nativity along Shepherds Street.

Beit Sahur and the Shepherds' Field

BEIT SAHUR, set in an idyllic landscape of olive groves and corn fields, has origins going back to the Bronze Age. Its modern economy is strangely split between the futuristic and the traditional: in October and November every year, the olive-picking season, the usual population of around 8000 is swelled by hundreds of people from surrounding villages who come to process their harvest at Beit Sahur's oil presses, some of them modern, but most seemingly centuries old; more recently, Beit Sahur has gained a reputation as a high-tech manufacturing centre, the West Bank's 'silicon valley'. It is also a place of fine churches – the Latin Patriarchate has a church with a very ornate altar, built in 1859, and there are two Greek churches – and of beautiful, multi-storeyed villas. Bus #47 from Bethlehem, from the stop by the police station in Manger Square, will bring you straight to the centre of town.

The main reason most people come is to visit the **Shepherds' Field**, ten minutes' walk away (take the first left at the far end of the village). Since the seventh century at least, this has been identified as the site where the angel of the Lord visited the shepherds and told them of the imminent birth of the Saviour in Bethlehem ('And this shall be a sign unto you; ye shall find the babe wrapped in swaddling clothes, lying in a manger' *Luke 2:12*). Several rival sites claim to mark the exact spot, with the weight of tradition centring on two: one in the care of the Greek church, the other maintained by the Franciscans.

The new **Greek church** was erected near the traditional site of the Grotto of the Shepherds, where a monastery once stood, dating originally from 670AD. A subterranean chapel here, with frescoes and traces of a Byzantine mosaic pavement, marks the scene of the apparition. The Franciscans' site, known as **Siar al-Ghanam**, or sheepfold, may have an even longer ancestry. Excavations have revealed a vast monastic settlement, cisterns and grottoes, and there are remains of a Byzantine church from as early as the fourth century. The modern, tent-shaped Franciscan **Church of the Angels** – another of those designed by Barluzzi – is built over a cave in which the shepherds are supposed to have lived. Inside, the altar is decorated with fifteen panels depicting various scenes from the Annunciation to the arrival of the Holy Family in Egypt. The figures are, as ever, curiously fair-skinned and closer inspection of the sheep, particularly their tails, reveals a distinctly non-Middle Eastern breed of animal.

Nearby are the remains of a watch-tower, the **Tower of Edar** or Tower of the Flocks, said to be the tower mentioned in *Genesis (35:21)*. This is also yet another contender for the setting of the apparition of the angel to the shepherds.

Another field in the fertile plain just outside Beit Sahur is identified as the **Field of Ruth**. Here Boaz saw her gleaning in the field, which later he bought and married Ruth.

Beit Jala

Two kilometres west of Bethlehem is another Palestinian town worth visiting – **BEIT JALA**. Here the great attraction is *Nahle Ka'aber's* unassuming restaurant near the municipal square. It specialises in barbecued chicken, which comes accompanied by exquisite garlic salad, sizzling chilli sauce, *humus, baba ghanoush* (aubergines in *tahina*), Arab salad and charcoal-warmed pitta bread. The restaurant does a brisk trade with visitors from Bethlehem and Jerusalem, and the village itself, surrounded by greenery and raised on a hillside above the plain, has long enjoyed a reputation as a summer resort. The restaurant apart, it's famous for its delicious apricots, for the distinctive brocaded dresses of its inhabitants and for its expert stone-masons. There are four churches in Beit Jala, the most attractive being the Greek Orthodox church of St. Nicholas with its square tower and glittering silver dome.

Passing right through Beit Jala to the top of the hill – the view from the summit is spectacular, with the greater part of Jerusalem visible – a road descends to the **Monastery of Cremisan**, renowned for the wine produced by its Salesian monks, who also run a farm. The monastery houses a high school and an impressive library. Also not far from Beit Jala is the village of AL-KHADER, traditionally famous for its stone-quarries, where the **Church of Saint George** is a popular centre of pilgrimage. The entrance to the town is marked by a distinctive stone arch.

Herodion

Ten kilometres southeast of Bethlehem, on the summit of an extraordinary flat-topped, cone-shaped hill ('. . . in the shape of a woman's breast' according to the Roman historian Josephus) lies **HERODION**, perhaps the most outstanding of all Herod's architectural achievements (Sat–Thur 7.30am–6pm, Fri 7.30am–5pm. Entrance $1.50, students $0.75). Built around 30AD as a secure refuge from his enemies, it is said also to be Herod's burial site. Josephus describes the elaborate funeral procession that brought his body here from Jericho, but archaeological surveys have so far failed to discover his tomb. After Herod's death, this strategic fortress 800m above sea level was one of the last strongholds to fall to the Romans in the Jewish Revolt of 66–70AD, conceding only after the destruction of Jerusalem. As at Masada, its defenders took their lives before the Romans could. During the Second

Revolt in 132–135AD it was again a Jewish redoubt, with the labyrinth of underground water tunnels used as fortifications. The remains of three Byzantine chapels with rich decorative mosaic floors show that the site continued to be inhabited during the fifth and sixth centuries. Later, the Crusaders (or Franks) made their final stand here before being ousted by the Muslims, giving the hill one of its alternative names – **The Mountain of the Franks**. To Arabs it is known as *Jabal al-Faradis*, the Mount of Paradise.

The mound on which the fortress and main palace lie is artificial: the top of the hill was flattened, and the resulting earth thrown up to form massive defensives. The original ascent, according to Josephus, was from the north via '200 steps of the whitest marble'. Traces of these can still be seen, but today the way up is on a winding path, a fifteen-minute climb from the southwest. The glorious fortress and palaces which once stood on the summit are long gone, but excavations have uncovered a circular enclosing wall with four round watchtowers which once guarded Herod's living quarters, and the remains of a bath house, hot baths, arcades, synagogue, and an immense banqueting hall. Perhaps the most striking aspect once you're up here, however, is the view. Bethlehem and Jerusalem are spread out to the north, in the other direction is the bare expanse of the Judaean desert, with the Dead Sea beyond.

Down below at the **base of the mound**, excavations have revealed a pool built by Herod, once filled with water diverted here from Solomon's Pools. Surrounding the pool is a reconstructed parade of colonnades; a nearby amphitheatre and pleasure garden are currently being explored.

Herodion can be reached by **bus** from Bethlehem or Beit Sahur, and some of the Bethlehem–Beit Sahur buses continue in this direction. Egged bus #38 to the nearby Jewish settlement of TEKOAH passes the access road to Herodion. A *service* taxi from Bethlehem costs about $10 for a round trip.

Monasticism in the Judaean Desert

In the desert beside his birthplace, Jesus is said to have fought his greatest battle: here he was led into the wilderness 'to be tempted of the devil' after forty days and nights of fasting. Now as then, the arid wilderness of Judaea rolls eastward from Bethlehem to the Jordan Rift Valley and the Dead Sea, a furnace of white light in the morning, iron red at sunset. To the early monks who followed in Jesus' footsteps, the harsh climatic conditions were symbolic of the evil powers which threatened the human spirit and had to be fought.

Monasticism in the Judaean Desert actually predated Jesus. The Prophet **Elijah**, believed by some to have been the first true monk, wandered in the desert for forty days and nights without food. From the fifth century on, with the country in the hands of Christian rulers in Byzantium, the example set by Elijah and Jesus began to be followed by Christian monks. Until then, the centre of Christian monasticism had been in Egypt. These **first monks**, most of whom came from Cappadocia in Central Turkey, Asia Minor and Armenia in quest of perfection and solitude, chose to live at the limits of human nature. They occupied the most remote desert gorges and caves, surviving on roots dug up with trowels. Yet these ascetics were also active scholars and many stories of the saints and martyrs were recorded here. The monastic settlements that sprung from these beginnings played a leading role in the development of Christian liturgy and dogma, and monasticism in the west can also be seen as developing from these early desert institutions.

On the eve of the Persian invasion in 614AD, the Judaean Desert was a maze of monasteries. Two of them, St. Theodosius and Mar Saba, still stand a few miles from Bethlehem.

The Monastery of Saint Theodosius
Saint Theodosius, about twelve kilometres east of Bethlehem, is the larger and more easily accessible of the two. Theodosius himself was a monk from Cappadocia who was staying in Jerusalem when he was divinely directed to seek out a cave where the Three Wise Men from the east had rested after paying homage to Jesus in Bethlehem. Here, in 476AD, he founded a monastery which at one time housed 693 Greek, Georgian, Armenian and Slavic monks within a fortified compound with four churches.

This monastery, along with virtually all the others, was destroyed by the invading Persians. The building that stands today was constructed by the Greek Orthodox Church at the turn of the century on the ruins of the Byzantine complex. It incorporates the remains of an old Crusader building and today, continuing the fifteen-century tradition, is inhabited by a dozen Greek monks. Inside, eighteen steps bring you down into the white-walled burial cave of the founder, St. Theodosius, who died at the age of 105. In a cave recess is a cluster of skulls of monks with crosses between their eye-sockets.

Mar Saba
It's a further six kilometres from St. Theodosius to the Greek Orthodox monastery of **Mar Saba**, a bumpy but negotiable road. Amid the total wilderness along the way, and the silence if you stop, you get some idea of what it was that brought the original hermits here. The immense and spectacular monastery, with its girdle of walls and towers, is a thrilling shock when it suddenly comes into view in the midst of this wasteland.

Built into the rock face of a gorge overlooking the Kidron River, Mar Saba represents a way of life unchanged since the time of Constantine. The founder, **Saint Saba**, came from Cappadocia in the fifth century. Originally, he settled in a cave in the Wadi al-Nar (Wadi of Fire) in the Kidron Valley, supplied with water and herbs by the local Beduin. Many legends grew up around him: according to one, St. Saba entered his cave to find it occupied by a lion. Without blinking, he said his prayers and fell asleep. But after the lion had twice dragged him out of the cave, the fearless saint assigned him a corner of the grotto and, apparently happy with this compromise, the two lived together happily ever after. Another, Androclean version of this legend has it that the saint pulled a splinter out of the foot of a limping lion who, out of gratitude, followed him faithfully the rest of his life.

It was not only lions that followed him. So many disciples flocked to his side that the grottos of the valley were soon overflowing and, to solve the housing problem, he founded the monastery in 482AD. Some versions of this story have it that the Virgin Mary appeared to the saint in a vision, instructing him to build the monastery. St. Saba lived here to the age of 94, and is said to have exerted great influence on the emperors of the time, including Justinian. Thus the monastery enjoyed imperial patronage: in its heyday it is said to have housed five thousand monks and was the focal point for six smaller monasteries nearby. Although Mar Saba was twice destroyed and its monks slaughtered in the seventh century, it rapidly recovered and by the eighth century was home to many prominent scholars. Of these, the most celebrated was **Saint John of Damascus**, a Greek theologian whose writings here in defence of the use of icons (at the time of the *iconoclasm* unleashed by emperor Leo II) and on the Orthodox faith were an important contribution to early Christianity.

The **monastery** of Mar Saba is immense. It has 110 cells, although today it only houses ten monks. As you enter you come into a paved courtyard, at whose centre is a green-domed octagonal chapel, the original resting place of St. Saba. His remains were carried off to Venice in 1256 by the Crusaders and were only returned to their rightful place in 1965, at a time of rapprochement between the Catholic and Orthodox churches. They lie now beneath an elaborate canopy in the main church, whose incense-laden interior is one of the most beautiful in the Middle East. A profusion of rare icons, many of them said to possess miraculous properties, cover its high walls; above all a representation of the Day of Judgement, with the Deity enthroned amongst angels and a gigantic figure weighing souls beneath. On one side, the 'minister of punishment' stands in flames whilst in the background the dead rise from their graves. Another memorial to the founder is the grotto on the southern side of the monastery, adjoining which is the **Lion's Grotto**. In a chapel adjoining these early hermits' caves are once again stored the skulls of monks killed in the Persian invasion: the tomb of St. John is here too, although his remains were removed to Russia when the Russian church rebuilt the monastery in the early nineteenth century.

Although Mar Saba is reputed to have had a long tradition of hospitality to strangers – and apparently even lions – **women** have never been allowed to enter. This regulation persists today, so women visitors must be satisfied with a glimpse of the chapel and buildings from a nearby two-storey tower, the so-called **Women's Tower**. By way of doubtful compensation, there is a superb view of the gorge 180m below, dotted with hermits' cells and cave sepulchres.

Bus #60 runs from Manger Square in Bethlehem to the Palestinian village of UBEIDIYIA; the last return leaving at 3.30pm. St. Theodosius is on a rise to the left of the road overlooking the village (ring for admittance), and from here you'll have to walk the final six kilometres to Mar Saba. Hitching, although possible, is difficult as traffic is sparse. A round trip in a *service* taxi should also be possible to arrange – for around $13. Be sure to take drinking water to avoid dehydration in the desert air and to dress appropriately both for the monasteries and for the searing sun.

Bethlehem to Hebron

If Abraham returned to travel the road from Bethlehem to Hebron today (a mere forty minutes by bus), the vineyards, the olive trees and the rolling fertile hills would probably all be reassuringly familiar. Less welcoming, though, the concrete Israeli settlements and the high, barbed-wire fence surrounding the Palestinian refugee camp of **Dheisheh** a few kilometres south of Bethlehem. The fence was erected by the Israeli authorities on the pretext of preventing Palestinian protesters from throwing stones at Israeli vehicles and troops, and is all the more shocking for the concentration camp images it evokes. Dheisheh is one of the largest refugee camps in the area. Established in 1949, it has over 6000 residents, and facilities including a health centre, schools, a youth activities centre and kindergarten. As in other camps, with many of the men either in Israeli jails or working abroad, the task of supporting the family falls to the women who have little choice but to work as underpaid labour in Israeli factories or service industries.

Solomon's Pools

About four kilometres out of Bethlehem, in a small valley surrounded by tall trees, are three huge rectangular cisterns known as **Solomon's Pools**. Although tradition attributes these to King Solomon, the pools almost certainly date from the time of Herod, and may have been conceived by Pontius Pilate. Three great pools of rock and masonry here hold about 160,000 cubic metres of water: they are constructed in steps, each six metres above the next, to enable the water to be carried as far as Jerusalem by force of gravity. The pools also supplied Herod's fortress and palace at Herodion. The system was in use as recently as 1947, and along much of the route from Bethlehem to Jerusalem original terracotta piping can still be found lying around. Near the pools are the remains of a Crusader fortress, **Qal'at al-Burak** (Castle of the Pools), built to defend the water source and maintained for this role through centuries of Arab rule.

Access to the pools is from a side road off the main highway. A little further, this road descends Wadi Artas to the picturesque village of **ARTAS**, whose name derives from the Latin *hortus* (garden). In the village is the convent and church of the Sisters of Notre Dame du Jardin, and below it the **Monastery of Hortus Conclusus** at the edge of huge gardens supposedly inspired by the *Song of Songs (4:12)*: 'A garden locked is my sister, my bride,/ a garden locked, a fountain sealed'. The *hortus conclusus* is symbolic of virginity, and an emblem of the Virgin Mary.

Settlements

After some thirteen kilometres, the road enters the disputed area controlled by the **Gush Etzion** settlement movement, whose developments were among the first to be built after the occupation. The Israelis claimed the land because there had been Zionist outposts in the area before 1948 – though similar rights do not, of course, apply in reverse for Palestinians driven out of Israel.

High on a hill dominating the left of the road lie the massive white concrete buildings of the Israeli settlement city of **EPHRAT** – the 'showpiece' of the seventeen settlements included in the Gush Etzion group. Ephrat, built in 1979 on land confiscated from the Palestinian village of al-Khader, has a population of 3–4000, most of them immigrants from South Africa and America. Settlers can buy a government-subsidised villa here for as little as $70,000.

Other settlements abound in the area. Opposite Ephrat is the barbed wire boundary of **ELAZAR**, a religious moshav established in 1975. Turning left at Ephrat, a minor road leads eastward to the Palestinian village of **TEKO'A**. The village is dominated by the Israeli settlement of TEKOAH, and by the new and growing settlement of **EL DAVID**, founded in 1982. All three lie under the shadow of the towering mound of **Jabal al-Faradis** (Mount of Paradise) on which stands Herodion. A little further on, to the right, another road leads to **KFAR ETZION**, a religious settlement that was the first to be established in the West Bank after 1967. **ALON SHVUT**, another religious settlement of 250 families established in 1970, is the regional centre of the Etzion Bloc, with a hilltop site commanding views of both Hebron and Jerusalem. Here a side road to the right leads to another religious settlement, **ROSH ZURIM**.

Palestinian villages

The Palestinian village of **SURIF**, six kilometres west of Kfar Etzion, is home to the **Surif Women's Embroidery Cooperative**, a profit-sharing enterprise that provides village women with a degree of economic independence. The 300-member cooperative was originally set up under the auspices of the Mennonite Central Committee in 1950, but is now completely autonomous. Samples of their very fine hand embroidery can be seen at the Mennonite Centre in Jerusalem.

As you continue on the main road, the beauty of the countryside testifies to the fertility and productivity of the soil here: abundant vineyards dot the area, producing the delicious and distinctive-tasting grapes for which Hebron is famous. The Palestinian town of **HALHUL** sits on a hill to the left of the road, less than five kilometres from Hebron. Just outside the village is the **mosque of Nabi Yunus** which, according to Muslim tradition, is built over the grave of the prophet Jonah. Later Jewish writers mention a tradition that the prophet Gad was buried here. Halhul also has a large, new wholesale vegetable market, financed by a US charity. It took American government intervention to wring permission to build this from the military authorities, and even then administrative delays prevented construction until senior American politicians intervened personally. Halhul has a history of refusal to cooperate with the occupation and its mayor, Muhammad Milhem, was deported by the Israelis in 1981 following an incident in Hebron: he now lives in Jordan, a leading international campaigner for Palestinian rights.

On the final approach to Hebron, the road passes numerous **glass factories** – *Holy Land Ceramics* on the left, *Al-Salaam Glass and Pottery Factory* on the right – where local glass-blowers produce the famous blue glass objects sold in the bazaars of Jerusalem. Here you can observe the whole fascinating process from beginning to end and can choose from a vast range of jars, vases, glasses, plates, baubles, bangles and beads at prices up to sixty per cent lower than in the markets. The glassblowing skills are reputed to have been brought to Hebron in the fifteenth century by Spanish or Venetian Jews fleeing religious persecution.

Halfway between Halhul and Hebron, a signpost points to one of the two sites purported to be the biblical **Mamre**, where God appeared to Abraham and told him that he would have a son, Isaac. A large oak tree marks the spot. Christians also identify this place as the site where the Holy family rested on their way back from Egypt. The church that was built here in the seventh century was notable enough to have appeared on the famous mosaic map at Madaba. Nowadays, however, there is little to see beyond the overgrown lower walls of an undated enclosure and the foundations of a fourth-century Constantinian church at the eastern end of the site. Russian monks have a small monastery here, built in 1871, behind which is a tower commanding a magnificent view extending to the sea.

Hebron

All the country around Hebron is filled with villages and vineyards and grounds bearing grapes and apples . . . Its equal for beauty does not exist elsewhere, nor can any fruits be finer.

Al-Muqaddasi, 985AD

HEBRON – known as **Khalil al-Rahman** (or al-Khalil) in Arabic and **Qiryat Arba** or **Khevron** in Hebrew – is one of the oldest towns in Palestine, and indeed has some claim to being among the oldest continuously inhabited places anywhere. Regarded as holy by Muslims, Jews and Christians alike because the patriarch **Abraham** is buried here, you'll find precious little that is holy about the place today. Of all the West Bank towns, it is here in Hebron that the Israeli **occupation** is at its most tangible. Jewish settlements built on confiscated Palestinian land form a stranglehold around the city and fanatical religious settlers have taken over buildings and whole areas in the centre under the protection of the Israeli army. The Palestinians of the Khalil region – *khalaileh* – have always enjoyed a popular reputation for a certain hard-headedness and doggedness*. This quality is nowadays manifested as *sumud* – steadfastness – in the face of the occupation.

Modern Hebron is the chief town of the southern half of the West Bank, with a population of around 40,000 and a *souq* that is the commercial centre for traders from fifty or so surrounding villages. It is also the largest indus-trial centre in the West Bank. The grapes produced here are converted into jam and a kind of molasses; dozens of quarries export stone and marble to Arab countries and sell to the building trade in Israel and the West Bank (most of the facing on Jerusalem buildings comes from the area between

---

*They are also the butt of local jokes in the same way as the Irish in England: Q – Why does a *khalaili* sleep with his *hatta* on? A – So that when he wakes up, he knows where his head is.

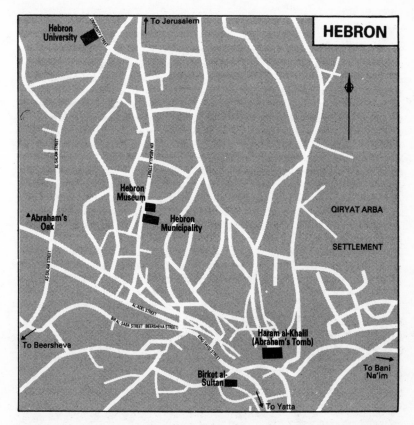

Bethlehem and Hebron); and the traditional crafts of glass- and pottery-making and tanning have been adapted to factory production. There are also a lot of plastics, furniture and shoe-making workshops. All this enterprise is tenuous, however. Palestinians can only operate in the margins of the Israeli-controlled economy. Mass-produced Israeli goods are allowed free access to the West Bank market; military orders and the occupation administration prevent Palestinians from investing in modern factories which would compete with the Israelis and from selling their products in Israel. Exports are also tightly controlled.

It's an observant and traditional town, which means Hebronites are gener-ous and hospitable, but also that you should dress and behave conservatively if you don't want to cause offence. Although clashes between armed settlers or Israeli soldiers and the local Palestinian population are a fact of life, sympa-thetic tourists are welcome; if you come with an Israeli tour, however, you will be whisked around the main sites and have little contact with the modern reality of Hebron.

History

The *Book of Numbers* (*13:22*) states that Hebron was built seven years before Zoan in Egypt, which would date its foundation at 1720BC. Excavations on the site of Jabal al-Rumeideh, however, show that it was inhabited by the Canaanites as early as 2000BC. According to Muslim tradition, it dates from the beginning of time; Adam and Eve lived out their days here after their expulsion from the Garden of Eden.

The Old Testament name for Hebron was Qiryat Arba, or the **Village of the Four**. The four in question, according to one legend, were giants who fell from heaven after a revolt against God. Another, more down to earth, explanation, is that the name derives from the four Canaanite tribes who lived in the town. Religious authorities say that it comes from the four biblical couples – Abraham and Sarah, Isaac and Rebecca, Jacob and Leah, Adam and Eve – said to be buried here. Whatever the facts of the matter, the city was certainly well established by the time **Abraham** and Sarah passed this way and pitched their tent by the oaks of Mamre. The Book of Genesis describes Sarah's death and Abraham's purchase from the sons of Heth of the Cave of Makhpela as a sepulchre for her and the rest of his family.

As the gateway to the settled northern highlands from the sub-desert southern region, Hebron has always been strategically important. When, 700 years after Abraham, **Moses** led the Israelite tribes out of Egypt, it was to the Hebron area that he sent his first reconnaissance mission. His spies returned, describing the land around Hebron as 'flowing with milk and honey'. As proof of the land's fertility, they brought back a branch with one cluster of grapes which were so succulent they had to bear it between two on a staff (*Numbers 13:23*) – the image is today the emblem of the Israeli Government Tourist Office. The spies further reported that 'the people be strong that dwell in the land, and the cities are walled and very great' (*Numbers 13:28*). It was left to Moses' successor Joshua to conquer Hebron and other areas of Canaan in 1200BC. The *Book of Joshua* (*10:37*) chillingly recounts that when he took Hebron he 'destroyed it utterly, and all the souls that were therein'.

After the death of King Saul, **David** ruled over Judah from Hebron for seven years. Around 1000BC, having subdued the northern tribes, he moved the capital of his united kingdom to Jerusalem. Later, Hebron briefly became the headquarters of David's rebellious son Absalom (*2 Samuel 15:10*). The first Hasmonean king, John Hyrcanus, took the city in 134BC.

Herod contributed to the city's prominence by building the basis of the massive **Haram al-Khalil** that houses the tombs of the biblical patriarchs and matriarchs. In 70AD, as a result of the Jewish Revolt, Hebron was destroyed, and afterwards Jews were banned from living in the rebuilt city. Under Muslim rule, from the seventh century, the town became known as Khalil al-Rahman (Beloved of the Merciful) – nowadays shortened to al-Khalil. The site is not only revered by Muslims for its connection with Abraham and the other Old Testament figures but also because, according to Islam, the *haram* was visited by the Prophet Mohammed on his night flight from Mecca to Jerusalem. Under Muslim rule, Hebron became an important centre of commerce and pilgrimage and Jews were once more allowed legal residence.

The **Crusaders** conquered Hebron in 1100AD, changed its name to Castellum, and again banned Jews from living there. The Mamluks (1248-1517AD) reversed the Europeans' discriminatory ruling and allowed Jews to reside in the town that by then had become a district capital – although only Muslims were allowed access to the *haram*. During the Mamluk period, a Muslim custom known as **simaat** evolved. *Simaat* (literally, a cloth on which food is served) is a meal of a kind of porridge made from cracked wheat and butter: this was served daily at the *haram* to pilgrims and the town's poor in remembrance of Abraham's generosity and hospitality.

As well as being a city of pilgrimage with a thriving market, Hebron has also had its share of agricultural, industrial and political fame. In Medieval times, Hebron-area apples and grapes were exported to Egypt, and Hebronites gained their continuing reputation as the best viticulturalists in the Middle East. Contemporary sources cite the town as an important centre of the gunpowder industry too. Later, Hebron's trading and strategic importance was enhanced when Napoleon's advance up the Mediterranean coast from Egypt forced regional trade inland.

During the **British Mandate**, Hebron, as the base of powerful traditional leaders, was naturally prominent in Palestinian opposition. During the 1929 upheavals, 67 Palestinian Jews were killed by a mob and the rest of the 2000-strong community left the city. The American journalist, Vincent Sheehan, wrote at the time: 'Hebron was one of the four holy cities of Judaism and had had a small, constant Jewish population since medieval days. These were not Zionists at all ... and had nothing to do with the Zionist excesses and had lived in amity with their Arab neighbours up to that day. But when the Arabs of Hebron heard that Arabs were being killed by Jews in Jerusalem ... they went mad.'

Things have continued to be tense virtually ever since, as **Jewish settlers** pursue access to sites they consider rightfully theirs. Immediately after the 1967 war, the calm in Hebron was destroyed when Rabbi Levinger moved into a city hotel (see Qiryat Arba below). This was the first hostile act in the battle between settlers and the locals which has continued ever since.

Like most large towns in the occupied territories, Hebron municipality is run by the Israeli army. The Palestinian mayor, Fahd Qawasmeh, elected in 1976 (the last vote the Israeli army has permitted Palestinians), was deported in 1980 along with Mayor Muhammad Milhem of Halhul and Sheikh Tamimi, the Hebron qadi, following the Daboyah attack (see below). Qawasmeh's deputy, Mustafa Natshe, was also removed from office and replaced by a junior Israeli army officer. Services, already in a parlous state because of military restrictions, have since deteriorated further. Nowadays social, cultural and health services are in the main provided by voluntary and charitable societies such as the Red Crescent Society which runs kindergartens and clinics.

There are two major **higher educational institutions** here: Hebron Polytechnic and Hebron University, both of them potential flashpoints which have been closed for much of the *intifada*. The polytechnic was founded in 1978 and has over 250 students who study civil engineering, architecture, electronics, mechanics and computer sciences. Hebron University, originally a *shari'a* (Muslim religious college), was established in 1971 and today enrols over 2000 Palestinian students. Two bodies unique to Hebron are the Hebron Graduates' League and the Scientific Research Centre, both of which carry out postgraduate-type research into the history, sociology, economy and culture of Hebron and the surrounding villages. They can be useful sources of further information about the Hebron area.

The town

Arriving by **bus** or *service* taxi from Jerusalem (Arab bus #23 and taxis leave from Damascus Gate), you'll be right in the centre of town, in the commercial district of Bab al-Zawiyeh. Hebron bus station was confiscated by settlers as part of their expansion plan, and when the municipality was taken over by the army they dropped the city-sponsored appeal to the Israeli high court against the removal of the bus station.

The Haram al-Khalil, which houses the Cave of Makhpela and Abraham's tomb (see below), is well signposted and in any case its physical bulk dominates the town: by following the main road that leads around the western end of the *souq*, you should have no trouble finding it. On the way, however, the older part of the city that huddles around the *haram* is definitely worth exploring, especially the **market** with its arched roofs and maze of alleys. The shops and stalls here sell everything from pottery, olivewood and glass to dried and fresh fruits (try the delicious Hebron peaches when in season), spices and trinkets of every description. It is also a good place to pick up bargains in local jewellery and metalware – though watch out for the difference between traditional hand-made goods and the mass-produced items which are increasingly replacing them.

The best way into the *souq* is to turn west from the clock-tower junction by Bab al-Zawiyeh. A few metres down, on the left side of the narrow road, is the bright and cheery *al-Arabi al-Wahid* **restaurant**, an excellent place for an authentic Palestinian lunch – or simply to rest over a mint tea. Further into the market area, you come to a junction: the right fork leads uphill into David Street and continues around the outside of the market; the road left, Ma'amun Street, goes into the heart of the old market area. Either route brings you face to face with just what the occupation really means in Hebron.

On David Street, the first and starkest evidence is the **Daboyah building** on the left, now renamed Beit Hadassah. Occupied by Jewish settlers from the nearby settlement of Qiryat Arba, Beit Hadassah is surrounded by barbed wire and guarded by armed Israeli soldiers. The residents go about their daily business brandishing submachine guns. It was an attack on the Daboyah building, in which six settlers died, that gave the Israelis the pretext to smash the municipalities in the Hebron region and greatly expand settlement in the city. A little further along the street is another house occupied by settlers, **Beit Shneyerson**. This and other occupied buildings are easily spotted by the Israeli flags fluttering on the rooftops. If the other side of the street looks strangely empty, it's because the Palestinian houses and shops that once stood there have been demolished by the military authorities. Further along David Street, yet another occupied building faces you opposite the improvised car park. Known as Beit Romano, only the top floor has been taken to date, whilst the Palestinian shopholders below continue to trade.

Along **Ma'amun Street** you reach a section of the market at the back of the Daboyah building where a high wire fence patrolled by soldiers blocks off the entrances to the shops. Customers who want to go into the stores must either face the humiliation of being searched and asked for identity papers, or else carry out their purchases over the fence. If you feel inclined to show solidarity – and want to know what it feels like to have a squad of troops permanently stationed outside your door with the express purpose of bankrupting you into leaving your home – then go and buy something, even if it's only a packet of chewing gum.

David Street continues around the outside of the southern side of the *souq*. A small passageway left brings you directly to another hotspot. Smack in the centre of the Arab market, the old **Jewish Quarter** is now being rebuilt under the watchful eye of two army lookout towers. You can walk into the area, around the handful of houses already inhabited by settlers, and climb up onto a rooftop for a bird's-eye view of the destruction of Arab houses below. From this area, you can either continue to explore the market or return to the main street. At the fork in the road, go left to get to the *haram*. To the right is **Birket al-Sultan**, a large, disused reservoir; beside it David reputedly hanged the murderers of Saul's son Ishbosheth. The place is now used, perhaps fittingly, as a rubbish tip.

al-Haram al-Khalil

The outstanding sight of Hebron is undoubtedly the **Haram al-Khalil**, or **Tomb of the Patriarchs**, a heavy rectangular building that encloses the Cave of Makhpela. Monolithic and austere, dwarfing everything else in Hebron, it looks more like a fortress than a tomb. This initial impression is confirmed by the heavy presence of armed Israeli soldiers supervising the prayers of the faithful within. Conflicts between settlers and the local Muslim community over the right to pray in the precincts have been bitter since 1967. Using a combination of military muscle, armed vigilantism and biblical claims, settlers first established the 'right' to pray in the mosque. This has subsequently been expanded until today large areas have been converted into synagogues presided over by the Israeli army. The stated aim of the settlers is to evict Muslims from the mosque altogether.

According to Arab legend, the massive stones of the walls, built without mortar, were laid by Solomon with the help of *jinns* or spirits. The construction of the walls and the pavement of the *haram*, however, bear the unmistakeable stamp of Herod the Great. Additional Crusader and Mamluk structures combine to make it one of the most impressive ancient monuments in the West Bank outside of Jerusalem.

If the basis of the building is undeniably Herodian, inside it is hard to work out what exactly is what, so many ages and religions have left their mark. First came a Byzantine church, erected in 570AD and converted into a mosque in the seventh century with only minor alterations. A small synagogue was later built adjacent to the mosque. Damage sustained during a severe earthquake in 1033 was not repaired until after the Crusader conquest in 1099. In place of the mosque and adjacent synagogue, the Crusaders left yet another of their churches. This in turn was converted into a mosque by Salah al-Din. Around 1318 the Mamluks added the adjoining Djaouliyeh Mosque (whose minarets tower above the walls), the Tomb of Joseph and the small mosque in the eastern corner of the complex. From the thirteenth century Jews were only allowed to the seventh step leading to the burial cave.

Entrance to the complex is up the Mamluk stairway on the northwestern wall of the edifice. This leads via a passageway into the spacious **Djaouliyeh Mosque** with its slender columns and calm interior. An entrance in the Herodian wall brings you into a courtyard. Here octagonal rooms to the right contain the fourteenth-century **cenotaphs** of Jacob and Leah; the two rooms housing the cenotaphs of Abraham and Sarah across the courtyard have doubled as synagogues since 1967. The embroidered cloths that shroud the cenotaphs all bear a legend similar to that found on Abraham's: 'This is the tomb of the prophet Abraham, may he rest in peace'.

Passing between the two rooms, you enter **al-Is'haqiyyeh** or the **Great Mosque**. Central to the mosque are the cenotaphs of Isaac and Rebecca, which in their present form date from 1332. The geometric sheets of marble and the inscribed frieze decorating the walls are contemporary. Remarkable stained glass windows beautifully soften the light inside. The medieval entrance to the **Cave of Makhpela**, below, lies to the right of a magnificent carved wood *minbar*. One of the finest examples of its kind, the *minbar* was made in 1091 for a mosque in Asqalan (Ashqelon) and was donated to the *haram* by Salah al-Din a century later. Beside it is the *mihrab* facing Mecca. The cave itself is closed to the public, but in an area of the mosque to the right, now taken over by Jews, is an opening through which written prayers are dropped down into it.

The small **Mamluk mosque** in the southeastern corner of the *haram* is reserved for women. In one corner, a shrine holds a stone bearing the footprint Adam is said to have left on his way out of the Garden of Eden. The exit is again through the Herodian wall, via a mosque housing what Muslims believe is the cenotaph of Joseph – Jewish tradition places his final resting place in Nablus.

The *haram* is **open** Sun–Thur 7am–7pm, Sat 11.30am–7pm; the main mosques are closed to non-Muslims during the five daily prayer times, on afternoons during Ramadan and on Fridays; passage through the surrounding hallways and synagogues is unrestricted. Right next to the tomb is a newly-built Hebron Settlers' Gift Shop where the tourist buses conveniently stop, presumably to encourage people to buy souvenirs from here rather than from the Palestinian shops nearby or from the *souq*.

The municipal museum

You pass the little-frequented **municipal museum** (Sun–Thur 8am–2pm) on the left as you enter Hebron on the Jerusalem road. An unassuming establishment next door to the equally unremarkable Hebron *baladiyyeh* (municipality), it was established under Jordanian rule and now contains a small and rather dusty collection, mainly of local archaeological finds from the

Canaanite to the Islamic period. What makes it more interesting are the bizarre extras and interesting curios that have inexplicably found their way in – the plastic flowers in a cabinet in the inner room, a fallen road sign, and assorted other objects that no-one has had the heart to throw away.

Across the road is the Hebron **Graduates' League**, which could easily be combined into the same visit.

Qiryat Arba

In the view of some latter day Jewish zealots, the fact that according to the Bible Abraham bought the Cave of Makhpela means that both it and Hebron are Jewish possessions for all time. Of the 24 settlements in the region, **Qiryat Arba**, right on top of Hebron, is the most concrete expression of this thinking. It is the biggest settlement, has received the blessing of successive ruling parties since occupation began, is headquarters of several extreme right-wing movements (during its last council election the contest was between *Kach* and *Tehiya* fanatics) and has been given a carte blanche to expand its borders by all means at the disposal of the inhabitants.

The name of Qiryat Arba, the biblical name for Hebron, was revived by the founding members of *Gush Emunim*. The movement was started by militant members of *Bnei Akiva*, the youth wing of the National Religious Party, and led by Rabbi Moshe Levinger. In 1968, they moved into a hotel in the centre of town and were given the settlement behind the ridge about one kilometre northeast of the Cave of Makhpela as their price for moving out. Massive government and World Zionist Organisation funding flowed in, and Qiryat Arba exploded throughout the surrounding neighbourhoods. Palestinian fields, gardens and occasionally homes were taken over by the settlers as they constantly moved the boundary fence outwards.

This situation was 'regularised' by the 1977 *Likud* government which has now made all Palestinian development anywhere near the settlement subject to a settler veto. The place is now a city of around 5000, mainly American-born Jews.

South of Hebron

Heading south from Hebron, the main road follows the spine of the Judaean Highlands for some distance before descending sharply to the drier Negev fringe and continuing on to Beersheva. The annual rainfall decreases dramatically the further south you travel and this has a marked effect on both landscape and population density, with villages well distanced from each other.

The Palestinian village of **SAMU'A**, 23km south of Hebron, is noted for its distinctive and exquisite woven carpets as much as for some interesting archaeological remains. To get to the village, follow the sign to the right on the main Hebron–Beersheva road. The centre of the village is right at the T-junction at the top of the hill. Some 200m past the excavations of the old synagogue, a modern two-storey building houses the Samu'a Charitable Society and doubles as a school in the mornings. If you ask for Ustaz Ya'oub, he will be happy to take you to see the **rugs** being made. The rug-making programme which he heads was started in 1984 as an income-generating project for the women of the village. The rugs are of three types: wine-red with a thin white stripe, striped the colours of the Palestinian flag – green, red, white and black – and multicoloured. They're not cheap, being finely woven of pure wool, but they are good value.

Samu'a is the site of biblical **Eshtemoa**, one of the villages with which David shared the spoils of a campaign against the Amalekites (*I Samuel 30:28*). A room beside the remains of a fourth-century synagogue is said to have once contained a treasure of silver and gold, perhaps David's gifts to the villagers. The synagogue stands beside the village mosque, and has a *bima* (raised platform) in the centre of the north wall, three niches that are believed to have held Scrolls of the Law and other ritual objects, and a mosaic floor.

An almost identical synagogue, in a much better state of preservation, can be seen in nearby **KHIRBET SUSEYA**, at the end of a dirt track leading from the Yatta–Samu'a road. This dates from the fifth century and preserves, within walls several metres thick, an attractive and complete mosaic floor, with three distinct geometrically patterned panels. The niche above the plastered benches was added as a *mihrab* in the time of Salah al-Din, when the synagogue became a mosque.

A somewhat erratic bus service to Samu'a leaves from the stop near the Patients' Friends Society in Hebron, a trip of about 25 minutes; *service* taxis run more frequently.

Dhahriyyeh

The last West Bank village on the main Hebron–Beersheva road, 20km south of Hebron, is **DHAHRIYYEH**, named after the thirteenth-century Sultan Baybars al-Dhahr, the leader who finally drove the Crusaders out of Palestine. The Wednesday morning livestock market here is still a genuinely functional part of the economic lives of local Beduin and villagers (unlike, for example, the Beduin market in Beersheva), and a fascinating slice of traditional life. Nevertheless, a visit won't take long unless you have an overriding interest in goats. A former British Mandate police fort, which later became a Jordanian Legion post, overlooks the market place. The old border, now invisible, is about 10km south of the village.

In Dhahriyyeh the effects of the occupation are once again widely felt. The Israelis have tried hard to maintain control by the manipulation of traditional *mukhtars* (clan chiefs) and regularly remove councillors who make 'the wrong decisions'. The village also has a chronic water problem and the wells regularly run dry. In the past this annual crisis was solved with the help of Hebron – water would be shipped in from the city in large tankers. When the Israeli military took over they demanded full payment for the service and Dhahriyyeh went several weeks without reasonable supplies. Cholera, typhoid and other diseases are now an annual threat when the water runs short.

Buses run regularly from Hebron to Dhahriyyeh, where you should be able to pick up onward transport on the Jerusalem–Beersheva run. **Hitching**

is no problem, either, as the road is fairly busy. From Beersheva, the early morning Jerusalem bus arrives in Dhahriyyeh in time for the market: at this time the route is often shrouded in a heavy, damp mist that makes it feel more like the Yorkshire moors than a Middle East sub-desert.

THE NORTH

There are two main routes out of Jerusalem into the northern part of the West Bank. The central road runs up through **Ramallah-al-Bireh** to **Nablus**, both of them important places historically and politically, where branches connect **Tulkarm** and **Jenin**. The northeastern road drops dramatically through the stark Judaean desert to **Jericho** on the floor of the Jordan rift valley. From here, you can carry on up the valley to the **Sea of Galilee** and **Tiberias**, or head south to the **Dead Sea**; the **Allenby Bridge** over the river to **Jordan** is just beyond Jericho.

The two routes could not provide a more extreme contrast. The Jericho road runs through bare hills laced with goat runs, where the only sign of life is the occasional Beduin herder, harrying the flocks to consume the sparse vegetation. The central route positively bustles in comparison. The bulk of the population of the West Bank live in the towns, camps and villages along the central highway, and between these are cultivated arable fields. Beyond them, the same olive trees that cover the south clothe the stepped slopes of the hills.

The road to Ramallah is always busy. Palestinian traffic runs through the suburbs of **Beit Hanina** and **Ram**, and past the refugee camps of **Qalandia** and **Shu'afat**. There's a great deal of Israeli movement, too. All the land up to al-Bireh city limits was annexed to Jerusalem in 1967, and the traffic to the triple ring of settlements around the eastern side of the city is supplemented by hitchhiking soldiers and settlers heading further north.

The road doesn't offer much in the way of **sights**, but you'll be struck by the gaudiness of many of the stores and the imaginative character of much of the architecture. The north Jerusalem suburbs are home to most of the city's expatriates and to the Palestinian middle classes – many of them now reliant on the profits of businesses abroad or the remittances of family members working in the Gulf and elsewhere.

Because Palestinian investment is positively discouraged by the Israelis, much of the cash has gone into construction and the rest into buying consumer durables. The marble-faced, mini-palaces with their clutches of Eiffel Tower TV aerials match north Tel Aviv homes in their studied kitschness. The grocery shops sell a wide variety of imported comestibles and if you just can't get by without designer clothes or overpriced electrical goods, you'll find all your pocket can run to in Beit Hanina.

The high-fenced, barrel-barricaded **refugee camps** make an extraordinary contrast, and the fortress-faced **settlement** apartment blocks and drab factory and warehouse units do nothing to alleviate the cacophony of architectural styles. Opposite the airport, above **Qalandia**, stands the half-finished palace of King Hussein of Jordan. It has been left untouched since 1967 despite being confiscated by the Israeli military in the early 1980s in a fit of republican pique when Hussein passed *in absentia* death sentences on Israeli-backed *Village League* gunmen.

Ramallah

RAMALLAH, with its twin town of **al-Bireh**, is 16km north of Jerusalem. Built across several hills some 900m above sea-level, it is famed for its pleasant, cool climate and pollution-free air. Until the coastline was built up in the early part of this century, it is said to have been possible to see the lights of ships anchored off the port of Jaffa, 45km to the west.

During the twelfth century, French Crusaders built a stronghold – **Ramelie** – here. The remains of a Crusader tower, *al-Tira*, can still be seen in the old section of the city where there are earlier remains from the Hellenic and Byzantine periods. The Crusaders also built a small church in Ramallah that was later converted into a mosque. The new mosque on the site was built in 1960.

Modern Ramallah is said to have been first settled around 1550 by Rashed Haddad and his older brother, Christians fleeing from al-Karak in what is now Jordan. Many Ramlawis (as the people of Ramallah are known) still claim descent from the Haddad family, and the majority are Christian. Nowadays the population stands at around 25,000, but many more Ramlawis live abroad: the Ramallah Society in the USA is the largest single Arab-American organisation. The US connection is a visible one; there are a number of fast food cafés in the town, modelled on American lines, and probably more gas-guzzlers per head of population than even the average American town.

Emigration from Ramallah began in the early 1900s when people left to make their fortunes elsewhere, intending to return to buy land and build houses. By 1946, 1500 of Ramallah's 6000 residents had gone. The 1948 war increased the total population, but at the same time provided a further impulse to emigration. When the Israeli forces took Lydda, Ramleh and surrounding coastal villages, their inhabitants escaped eastward; by 1953, the influx of refugees into Ramallah had doubled the population. The town couldn't cope and shortage of work, money and basic facilities led to a renewed exodus. Large numbers of skilled workers, craftspeople and professionals left first for Arab countries and later for America.

Ramallah at one time was known as 'the Bride of Palestine', and its temperate climate made it a favourite summer resort for Arabs from Jordan, the Gulf region and Lebanon. The town used to host dance and folklore festivals in the summer and its thriving hotels, hostels and restaurants were famous throughout the Middle East. All this came to an end with the Israeli occupation in 1967. Nowadays, only three hotels remain open and are frequented mainly by visiting expatriate Ramlawis, by Palestinian honeymoon couples from other parts of the country and by a few tourists. But the cool summer climate, the physical proximity of Jerusalem and the relatively peaceful, tourist-free atmosphere still make it an ideal break for a night or two.

In terms of modern Israel, however, Ramallah's reputation is based on its leading role in **resistance** to the occupation. The town has paid a high human price, and before you go you should check on the latest situation – it is frequently under curfew. Just about the only local source that has been allowed to remain open is *al-Haq* (PO Box 1413, ☎02-952421), an affiliate of the Geneva-based *International Commission of Jurists* which researches and lobbies on legal issues concerning the occupation and has a number of English language publications. *Al-Haq* is located in a large office building on the right of al-Tira Street

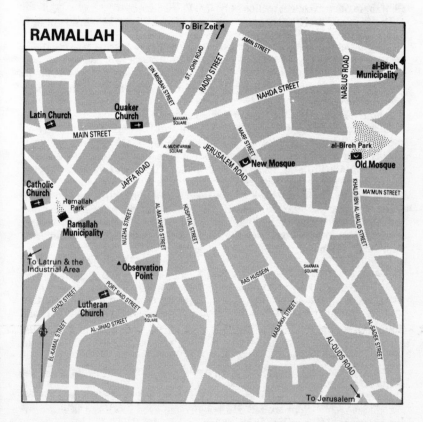

The town

Ramallah is the easiest of places to get around; all the town's seven main streets radiate out from **Manara Square**, the roundabout in the middle of town. Everything you need is within walking distance of the *manara*, so if you find yourself going further than a few hundred metres you're almost certainly lost. **Buses** almost all stop at the central bus station right on the *manara*, and *service* **taxis** will drop you at one of a variety of points, none more than a couple of minutes away.

Having got here, you'll find that the refreshing climate and the excellent food really are the attractions. If you want to go sightseeing, you'll need to get out into the surrounding villages. The **food**, however, justifies the trip on its own. Ramallah is renowned for its **muntazaat** – outdoor restaurant parks – where you can join Palestinian families enjoying an afternoon or night out over *mezeh* and a bottle of *araq* or a delicious full-course meal. These *muntazaat* are mostly to be found along **Jaffa Road**, off **Mughtaribiin Square**, and all of them offer excellent menus of typical Palestinian food.

The first, and perhaps the most famous, is *Naoum's* on the left side of Jaffa Road. The second, *al-Bardouni* (☎02-95141; open daily till midnight), with a pretty garden full of flowers, real grass (a rarity in the Middle East) and two beautiful stone fountains, offers a veritable *mezeh* feast of 55 plates – meats, vegetables, *humus*, twenty different salads etc – for around $17.50, enough to stave off the hunger of five or six people. For an extra $7.50, a litre of *araq* goes down very nicely.

A little further along the road is the smaller and marginally cheaper *Plaza Pension and Muntaza* (☎02-952020; open till 2am), where you can feast on *musakhan*, kebab or *shishlik*, or sit in the white-pebbled courtyard and sip a whisky, beer or *araq* with an accompaniment of salads. This is also the cheapest of the **places to stay**, its rooms with 2, 3 or 4 beds, and showers, ranging from $5 to $9 per person, with reductions for students or those staying longer than a week. Continuing down Jaffa Road you'll come to a second hotel, *Miami Pension* (☎02-952808), which charges $24 for two people, $15 for one and also offers reductions for longer stays. This place has a bar, but no restaurant. Across the road from the *Miami* is the splendid *Muntaza Baladiat Ramallah* (Ramallah Municipality Gardens; ☎02-952835; daily 9am–midnight), so named because it is on the corner of the road in which Ramallah Municipality stands. The large circular garden is shaded by ivy, vines and bougainvillea, the tables set in flowery niches or under parasols.

The third, and by far the grandest place to stay in Ramallah, is the *Qasr al-Hambra* (☎02-952226), half a mile north of the *manara* along Radio Boulevard on the road to Bir Zeit. Set back off the main road in a pine-tree garden, this magnificent four-storey building was built as a family home in 1926 and remodelled as a hotel in the 1940s. In its heyday in the Forties and Fifties it was popular with Arab, Jewish and British officials alike, and King Abdullah of Jordan himself is said to have stayed here. It still exudes an aura of old-fashioned luxury, with beautiful tiled floors and verandahs, and can be exceptional value: from around $14 per person, even lower out of season if you're prepared to try a bit of negotiation.

Around Ramallah

Getting out of Ramallah and into the villages around – whether it is to explore the religious sites such as **Nabi Samwil** or the secular pleasure of a debate at **Bir Zeit University** – is well worth the effort, if only to enjoy the country-

side. Most places are served by buses from the central bus station and by
service taxis. Drivers will drop you on the main road at the entrance to the
villages, from where you can walk or hitch the final leg. The only likely problem is getting back, when you may have a long wait for the next transport to
pass.

The nearest place to Ramallah is **AL-BIREH**; the two are now so closely
bound together that the only people who can say for certain where one ends
and the other begins are employees of the two municipalities and residents
under administrative town arrest who can be detained if they inadvertently
stray over the city limits. Al-Bireh is the working town which offsets
Ramallah's more casual ambience, with pharmaceutical and light engineering
industries. There's no real reason to come here, especially as you'll see it
anyway as you travel around the area.

Nabi Samwil

About thirteen kilometres southwest of Ramallah, beyond the airport on a
mountain top 890m above sea level, is a site traditionally held to be the tomb
of **Nabi Samwil** – the prophet Samuel. Although the large, turreted building
has for hundreds of years been the centre of pilgrimage and worship for
Jews, Christians and Muslims alike, it has little to do with Samuel who was
actually buried in Rama. Nevertheless, in the darkened cellar is a cloth-
covered tomb venerated as Samuel's. How the tradition came about is
unknown, but it was well established by the sixth century and – history
notwithstanding – it is still adhered to today.

The Crusaders, approaching Jerusalem in 1099, caught their first glimpse
of the holy city from here and, to express their delight, named the place *Mont
de Joie* – **Mountjoy**. They built a church on the traditional burial site in 1157,
the graceful, painted arches and buttressed walls of which are incorporated
into the mosque that was put up in 1911. This mosque became in turn a
Jordanian Legion camp guarding access to Arab Jerusalem until taken by the
Israelis in 1967.

The mountain-top village, also called NABI SAMWIL, is built around the
mosque, whose minaret affords an extensive view over the hills of Jerusalem
and Bet El, and, on a clear day, even the Mediterranean and the mountains of
Jordan. There is free access to the minaret except during times of prayer.
Nearer at hand the village overlooks the Jewish settlements of RAMOT, built
in 1973, to the south, and GIV'ON, established in 1977, to the north. You can
get to Nabi Samwil either direct from Ramallah or by taking one of the Egged
buses from West Jerusalem to the settlements and walking up the mountain.

Al-Jib (Giv'on)

A couple of kilometres to the north lies the picturesque Palestinian village of
AL-JIB, site of biblical Gibeon whose inhabitants tricked Joshua into making
a pact with them against the Canaanites (*Joshua 9*). It was to prolong the
battle with the five kings outside Gibeon that Joshua uttered his famous
command: 'Sun, stand thou still upon Gibeon; and thou, Moon, in the valley

of Ayalon' (*Joshua 10:12*). In the seventh century BC, the city became prosperous through its production of wine: 63 wine cellars have been discovered, each capable of storing 42 large barrels of wine. The city was finally destroyed by the Babylonians in 587BC.

Al-Jib today is worth visiting to see the excavations of Gibeon, and especially the excellently preserved **ancient water system**. Near the village cemetery is a great, rock-hewn pool, over 11m in diameter and 10m deep. Winding steps lead down to the bottom of the cistern, whose supplies of water would have sustained the Gibeonites through extended siege. Entrance into the pool is from an opening at the back of the nearby tel. With the aid of candles or flashlights, you can descend right to the heart of the ancient city, thought to be over 3500 years old.

The original water system served Al-Jib until very recently: a tunnel brings the water from the spring in the centre of the hill to the pool, from where it was piped to a series of taps. Another tunnel descends from inside the ancient city wall to the pool, denying water to attackers while making it available to inhabitants under siege. The worn steps and polished sides show how frequently they were used, as do the smoke-darkened niches where oil-lamps once stood. Wine and olive presses and potsherds inscribed with the word 'Gibeon' have also been found on the site.

To reach the site, take the Biddu road from the village and walk up the hill to the 'parking lot'. From here a rough path leads to the excavations.

Tel al-Nasba

Much closer to Ramallah, just three kilometres to the south, **TEL AL-NASBA** was once an Israelite centre and the capital of Judah. Here in the Bible it is known as **Mizpeh** – the Israelites defeated the Philistines (*1 Samuel 7*) after Samuel had sacrificed on their behalf, and here Saul was proclaimed first king of Israel (*1 Samuel 10*). Perhaps surprisingly, it is not one of the most exciting archaeological sites: a wall and a gate from the period of the kings of Judah has been excavated and you can also see a palace cellar complete with wine jars, a cloth-dyeing plant, temples and the ruins of a Crusader church.

East of the Jerusalem road

All of the places above lie to the west of the Ramallah–Jerusalem road. The sites on the east side are rather smaller. **TEL AL-FUL** (Giv'at Shaul), some 11km from Ramallah, overlooks the ancient Land of Benjamin, the Dead Sea and the Hills of Moab. It was the birthplace of King Saul, hence the modern Hebrew name of the settlement – **Giv'at Shaul**, the Hill of Saul. Near the tel is the Palestinian village of **Shu'afat**, believed to be the site of **Nov**, the city of the temple *kohanim* (priests). The Palestinian refugee camp at Shu'afat houses over 5500 people: it was built in 1965 to accommodate 3000 Palestinian refugees who were living in unsatisfactory shelters in the Mu'askar Camp in Jerusalem's Old City.

Nearby is the Palestinian village of **ANATA**, the site of Roman and Byzantine *Anatot*, where the remains of a Byzantine church can still be seen. This was another town of the *kohanim* and the birthplace of the Prophet Jeremiah. A little further out, at **HIZMA**, are prehistoric graves known to the locals as *Qubur Beni Israel* – tombs of the tribe of Israel. To the east of Hizma, **AIN FARA** is identified by some as biblical Parah (*Joshua 18:23*) or Ephrata.

RAM, some 6km from Ramallah near the airport, may have been the biblical **Rama**; home, birthplace and burial site of the Prophet Samuel. Others think it might be **Harama**, where the Prophetess Deborah lived. Whatever the truth, modern Ram is a sleepy dormitory suburb for Palestinians working in Jerusalem, and speculation about its origins are best entertained in a *service* as you speed by.

East of Ram, a side road leads to the Palestinian village of **MUKHMAS**, which dates originally from the Iron Age. This is probably the site of **Michmash** where Saul and his son Jonathan fought against the Philistines. The remains of Roman and Byzantine settlements have been found here. Just south of Mukhmas is the village of **JABA**, the biblical **Geva**. The prophet Benjamin prophesied that the boundaries of Jerusalem would extend as far as here. Since 1967 they have done.

Ramallah to Nablus

The journey from Ramallah, or Jerusalem, to Nablus is worth making if only for the ride. The road climbs, dips and winds across spectacular landscapes of terraced hills planted with olive and fig trees. The rich browns and reds of the densely cultivated fields, scattered with hillside villages whose houses are in cooler tones of white, blue and green, are at their best in spring and very early in the morning or, better still, in the red and purple glow of sunset.

Most visitors travel the road to Nablus by *service* or bus without stopping. But if you are going by car, or you're in no hurry and prepared to wait for the next bus or *service* to come along, there are a few stops along the way that may be of interest. Most villages will, at the very least, have somewhere where you can buy a cold drink; given the grand prix style of most of the driving on the road it's worth resting a while to regain sanity and enjoy the peace of the countryside.

Beitin (Bet El)

Shortly after Ramallah, a minor road turns off east, towards Jericho. A couple of kilometres down this road lies **Bet El**, where archaeologists have uncovered strata from the earliest Canaanite period to that of the Second Temple (the time of Herod) and beyond. The site is identified with the biblical Bet El where Abraham, on his way south from Shechem (Nablus) 'built an altar unto the Lord' (*Genesis 12:8*). From here Lot looked out over Jordan on his way back from Egypt and, on the hill called **Jacob's Ladder**, Jacob dreamed he saw a ladder reaching up to heaven with angels ascending and descending. In the time of David, the Tabernacle and the Ark of the Covenant were set down at Bet El and the Prophet Samuel is said to have held court here. In the second century BC there was a fortified post and later a Byzantine church and Crusader castle.

Nowadays, **BEITIN** is a pretty village set in a valley, but there's little evidence of any of this history. The houses are painted blue and lavender and the village is surrounded by almond, fig, peach, apple and olive orchards. The minaret of its mosque, most unusually, has glass windows to keep out the wind. It's also known in modern Israel for less happy reasons. There is a refugee camp here and a Jewish settlement, **BET EL**, which houses the headquarters of the Israeli civil administration. The settlements of Bet El A and Bet El B, where the luxury homes of Jerusalem commuters are contained within barbed wire fences, were built in the late 1970s in the first flush of *Likud* expansionism.

From Beitin, a road leads to **Tel Bet El**, a cult centre in the period of the Judges, where you can see the excavated remains of temple foundations. On the nearby tel of the biblical **Ai**, one of the earliest conquests of Joshua when he overran Canaan, remains have been found of enormous Bronze Age fortress walls and two early temples, as well as Iron Age buildings.

Further along the Jericho road is the settlement of **OFRA**. This, the first of the *Gush Emunim* settlements, was built on Silwan land in 1975 and houses approximately 100 families. They are mainly orthodox and if you are going to visit it is advisable not to drive there on the sabbath.

Bir Zeit

Back on the main road, the **Jalazoun refugee camp** lies to the left just after the Jericho turn-off. Because of the proximity of the army base and the settlements there are frequent clashes here; yellow number plated cars are prime targets when tension is running high.

The town of **BIR ZEIT**, 20km north of Ramallah to the east of the road, is perhaps the preeminent modern centre of the Palestinian national struggle. The unprepossessing town is little more than a village; it has gained its reputation because of the **University** which bears its name. Bir Zeit was established first as a school in the 1920s by the formidable Nasser family; it acquired university status in the 1970s.

Its history is one of struggle to promote excellence in education in the face of almost constant harassment from the Israeli military. It has been closed for most of the duration of the *intifada*, but if it is open it's well worth spending a day there meeting students and learning about the current situation. The **Public Relations Department** is located on the new campus which is set off the road about 2km south of town. There is frequent transport from the old campus in the centre. The new campus is worth visiting in any case, its Gulf-financed buildings among the finest examples of modern Arab architecture in the country.

Expect to be questioned about your reasons for visiting Bir Zeit. Settlers and military personnel in plain clothes have made frequent attempts to provoke incidents by infiltrating the campus and students are naturally suspicious in the first instance. In the summer (when open) Bir Zeit University runs a series of **open classes** in Arabic and Palestinian sociology and history, and two or three international **workcamps**. There is probably no better way to get a real understanding of life in the occupied territories than volunteering for a workcamp: details can be obtained from the PR department by writing to the university (and see "Work" in the *Basics* section).

Sinjil, Shilo and the north

Past Bir Zeit the road passes through **SINJIL**, the Arabic form of St. Giles, a French monk who lived here in Crusader times. Off to the right, high on the hill above the **Shilo Valley** is the settlement of **SHILO**. Its foundation was something of a *cause célèbre* in 1978, when *Gush Emunim* settlers engineered a confrontation with the *Likud* authorities by illegally setting up the first settlement of the period with no ostensible 'security' reason behind it. Until 1978, settlements had always been built on land initially held by the military – even if later they expanded into the fields of neighbouring villages. At the entrance to Shilo is a famous sculpture erected by **Peace Now** as a monument to peace.

Shilo settlement is situated on land belonging to TURMUS AYA across the valley. In the twelfth century BC, the Ark of the Covenant was set up at **Shiloh** (*Joshua 18:1*), and here Samuel was called to become a prophet (*1 Samuel 3*). Shiloh was destroyed when the Philistines captured it in 1050BC, but excavations have revealed that it was reoccupied and inhabited up to Roman times. Near the **Pilgrim's Church** at the southern end of the site are two tomb complexes dating from the Roman period; there are also two fifth century Byzantine churches with mosaic floors and two Muslim sanctuaries, *Weli Yetin* and *Weli Sittin* (which may have originally been a synagogue).

As the road winds on towards Nablus it is worth stopping at the roadside café at the top of **Jabal Batin** to enjoy the breathtaking view down into the **Valley of Dotan** and the village of LUBBAN SHARQIYEH, famous for its incense and tobacco. The village is a possible site of biblical **Lebonah**. In the valley there are several ruined *khans*, wayside inns which housed travellers and their livestock. After descending into the valley, the road winds its way back up to the twin peak of **Jabal Rahwat** and from there runs on towards Nablus.

At the last minute the road swings round to the west, so that you approach the city with two great hills on either side: **Mount Gerizim** on the left, **Mount Ebal**, higher but further away, on the right. Entering Nablus, you pass first the largest Palestinian refugee camp in the region, **BALATA**, whose 11,000 residents come originally from about 65 villages, now destroyed, in the Lydda, Ramleh and Jaffa area. The Israeli army maintains permanent bases at the entrance to the camp and has strongholds inside: there are, therefore, frequent clashes, but visitors wanting to see Balata for themselves and meet camp residents are welcomed. Visits can be arranged through the UNRWA information officer in Nablus. After this comes another army post and prison built originally by the British – at the very gates of the city.

Nablus

Nablus, Shechem, Neapolis, about which nineteenth-century pilgrims enthused: 'the whole valley filled with gardens of vegetables, and orchards of all kinds of fruits, watered by fountains, like a scene of fairy enchantment . . . Here the bulbul delights to sit and sing, and thousands of other birds unite to swell the chorus. The inhabitants maintain theirs is the most musical vale in Palestine . . . .' But the chords lilting now come from Farid al-Attrash and Fairouz, on radio waves from afar, not to speak of the tooting of car horns in the main streets down below. One can almost, but not quite, forget the Occupation, with its frequent patrols in khaki jeeps and armoured cars.

Simon Louvish, *City of Blok*

In antiquity **NABLUS** (and before it the biblical town of *Shechem*) lay astride an important crossroads, where the main north–south trade route met a road from the coast to the Jordan Valley. Lying 63km north of Jerusalem, the 'uncrowned Queen of Palestine' is still an important place, the largest city on the West Bank outside Jerusalem, with a predominantly Muslim population of 120,000, including a small community of some 250 **Samaritans**. Surrounded by fertile fields primarily used for growing olives – the backbone of the regional economy – and situated between the historic mountains of **Gerizim** and **Ebal**, Nablus is at the centre of Palestine and forms the southernmost tip of the area called the Triangle, with Tulkarm to the northwest and Jenin directly north.

Although Israelis prefer to call Nablus by its biblical name of **Shechem**, the town which developed into present-day Nablus was founded only in 72AD; ancient Shechem lies just outside. The extensive destruction of Nablus in an earthquake in 1927 means that everything you'll see in the city is relatively modern. It's a place to visit for its historical and political significance – and to make forays to nearby sites – rather than for its beauty or antiquity. Tourist facilities are barely developed at all, but it can still be an enjoyable place to stay, its rooflines picked out with blue and green domes, and a crowded local *souq* to add atmosphere.

Above all, Nablus is worth visiting to get a real feel for present-day Palestine. It has been prominent in resistance to foreign rule for centuries and during the current *intifada* has frequently been under curfew and the scene of sporadic violent clashes with Israeli troops. Like most Palestinian towns, however, once you get past the occupation road blocks you'll find a warm welcome. As elsewhere in the occupied territories, sensitivity to the situation of people living under occupation is called for, but genuine interest will most often be met by genuine hospitality and welcome. Before you set out, however, check on current developments in Jerusalem.

History

Scarcely anything remains of the 'New City' of **Flavia Neapolis** that Titus built in 72AD in honour of his father, Flavius Vespasian; what little survived the centuries was destroyed in the 1927 earthquake. In the early centuries of Christianity, Neapolis was the scene of constant strife between the local Samaritan and Christian populations. The **Samaritan revolt against Rome** in 529AD was put down with severity by Justinian and most of the Samaritans were expelled. In 636 the Arabs took the town, changing its name to Nablus: it has been predominantly Muslim ever since.

The only brief disturbance to this dominance came under the **Crusaders**. Tancred's army conquered Nablus in 1099AD and they held the city until the arrival of Salah al-Din in 1187. During this occupation they built a number of churches, including one on the ruins of a Byzantine church at **Jacob's Well**. It is speculated that the **Great Mosque** (*al-Jami'a al-Kabir*) at the eastern end of the city was also once a Byzantine basilica, originally dedicated to **John the Baptist**, who baptised people by immersion in the nearby springs. Other sources, however, claim that the mosque is built on the site of a **Samaritan synagogue** of similar date. With their keen eye for strategic positions, the Crusaders also built a fortress on the top of **Mount Gerizim**.

Nablus' modern reputation rests on the business acumen of its leading families. They have dominated the agricultural economy of the region for centuries, as well as controlling trade and manufacturing. During the eighteenth century, the inhabitants of Nablus were among the most prosperous in the country, depending for their wealth on wheat and olives. Olive oil **soap** has always been the one of the main products of Palestine and there were famous factories in Gaza, Ramle and Hebron. But *Nabulsi* soap is still the best, renowned for its purity and exported throughout the markets of the Middle East.

During the **British Mandate**, Nablus was a centre of Palestinian resistance to Zionist immigration. It was here in 1936 that a National Committee was first set up; similar bodies were soon formed in all the towns and large villages of Palestine. The committee was crucial in rallying opposition and in calling for the General Strike of 1936. Collectors of British socialist trivia might also be interested to know that veteran SWP leader Paul Foot's uncle was military governor during the 1930s, and that present-day Nablus is twinned with the Scottish city of Dundee.

For a time after the Israeli occupation in 1967, it was from the Old City or *qasbah* of Nablus that PLO leader **Yasser Arafat** organised resistance networks. Today, Nablus still maintains its radical reputation; it is home to former elected mayor Bassam Shaka'a who was deposed by the Israelis in 1981 after losing his legs in an assassination attempt by Israeli extremists the year before. The **Al-Najah National University** which overlooks the city is the largest in the occupied territories: it has been closed for much of the period of the *intifada*.

Since 1967 Nablus has declined economically. Its exports are restricted while subsidised products from Israel have flooded the market, closing its famous match factory and other small industries. Today no less than 41 Israeli settlements ring Nablus, which, because of its radicalism, has been singled out by the Israelis – the local electricity generating company has been specifically targeted and subjected to swingeing taxation in a blatant attempt to drive it out of business.

In the immediate vicinity of Nablus, there are four **refugee camps**: Balata, at the entrance to town on the Jerusalem road; Askar, on the main road out towards Amman; Fara'a, to the northeast of Nablus near Ein Fara'a; and Camp No. 1, to the west of Nablus on the Tulkarm road. Visits can be arranged through the local office of UNRWA (United Nations Relief and Works Agency; Palestine Street, off Hussein Square; ☎053-70202). Al-Fara'a is also the site of an infamous detention centre opened in 1982 when Israeli jails could no longer accommodate the numbers being detained. It soon gained a reputation for brutality and after representations by international human rights and humanitarian organisations to get the place closed, the military took the unusual step of trying and sentencing some of the most vicious torturers. The place, however, remains open.

Practicalities

The journey from Jerusalem to Nablus on the **bus** (from the bus station in Nablus Road in East Jerusalem) takes about two and a half hours; the *service* taxis are quicker, but cost almost twice as much. Either will drop you in al-Hussain square, or just off it in **Merkaz Tijari Street**. On the square, the unassuming looking *al-Alamain Restaurant* (☎053-74677) is one of the best places in Nablus to get a good meal. Upstairs, it's always crowded with local customers, sure proof of the quality of the food.

If you want to **stay** in Nablus there are half a dozen decent hotels and pensions, all of which charge much the same. They include *Pension Ramses* (85 Assakia Street, one block south of the Municipality off al-Ghazali); the one-star *Palestine Hotel* (4 Shwetri Street, 700m down Ghirnata Street to the end, then right onto Shwetri; ☎053-70040); *Al-Istiqlal Pension* (Hitteen Street; ☎053-72925); *Al-Arabi Pension* (New Commercial Street; ☎053-75135); and *Al-Farah Pension* (Easter Gate; ☎053-70107).

Seeing the city

From al-Hussain Square, the way to the *souq* and the Old City lies along Merkaz Tijari Street, a route lined with shops selling a mouth-watering selection of Palestinian sweets such as *baklawa* or *burma* stuffed with pistachios or almonds. Above all you should try *kanafeh*, a sweet-cheese pastry, served warm, for which Nablus is renowned. *Bsais Kanafeh Shop*, where a quarter kilo (*awiyeh*) costs around $1, has a particularly good reputation.

The second street on the right off Merkaz Tijari will bring you into the **souq**. At its centre is **Manara Square** where there is an impressive mosque, al-Nasser; non-Muslims are not allowed in. The *souq* itself is well worth exploring, though. Far less touristy than Jerusalem, it offers a wonderful escape from the heat and traffic outside. The **Great Mosque**, al-Kabir, on the eastern edge of town, is said to stand on the spot where Joseph's brothers presented Jacob with the bloodstained coat of many colours, to persuade him that his youngest son was dead. Again, it is not normally open to visitors.

You can also explore, in the west of town, the cramped **Samaritan quarter** or Haret al-Samira (see Mount Gerizim below), but most of the other specific 'sights' of Nablus lie beyond the city limits, especially on the slopes of Mount Gerizim.

Jacob's Well

Jacob's Well (Mon–Sat 8am–noon and 2–4pm) is not far from the refugee camp of Balata, off the main road as it approaches Nablus: you reach it through the village of ASKAR, biblical **Sychar**. The 35-metre-deep well, stands on the land that Jacob bought from Hamor for 'a hundred pieces of silver' (*Genesis 33:19*). It was here that Jesus, 'being wearied with his journey', rested and asked a Samaritan woman to draw water from the well for him to drink. The well has since become an object of pilgrimage and its waters are believed to have miraculous properties.

Today it stands behind bright blue metal doors within the walled complex of a Greek Orthodox Monastery. A church was built over the well as early as 380, but this was destroyed in the Samaritan revolt of 529. The Crusaders rebuilt it, but it fell into decay again and further attempts at reconstruction have never been completed. There is, however, a beautiful small chapel sheltering the well, its walls hung with icons and paintings of Jesus and the Samaritan woman. Ring the bell outside the gates to get in and be shown around.

Joseph's Tomb

A little to the north of Jacob's Well, **Joseph's Tomb** is one of the three sites (the other two are the Tomb of the Patriarchs in Hebron and the Temple in Jerusalem) to which specific claim has been laid by Zionist fanatics using 'biblical purchase' as the pretext. It is allegedly part of the land bought by Jacob (see above), but why the settlers don't also claim Jacob's Well, on the same plot, is unclear, although it may be to do with the fact that it lies on church property. The cloth-covered sarcophagus said to contain the bones of Joseph is housed in a small, white-domed and entirely unspectacular building, guarded by decidedly bored-looking Israeli soldiers.

Shechem

The road beyond Jacob's Well heads northwest between Mounts Ebal and Gerizim, passing Balata on the right, and the mound of Tel Balata. Here, east of the modern city of Nablus, is the ancient Canaanite town of **Shechem**.

The site was first settled by Chalcolithic people around 4000BC, although the town appears to have been founded in the nineteenth century BC. By the time **Abraham** and his family migrated from **Ur** in his native Iraq, forded the Jordan River, travelled up the beautiful Wadi Farah (Nahal Tirza) and arrived here on his first entry into the land of Canaan, the city was already flourishing (*Genesis 12:6*). By the sixteenth century BC it was a powerful city state.

After the Israelite invasion of 1200BC, **Joshua** gathered all the tribes of Israel to Shechem (*Joshua 24:1–4*) to consolidate their faith and unity. It became the first capital of the breakaway northern Kingdom of Israel (*I Kings 12*), but under King Omri the seat of government was transferred to the newly-founded city of Samaria in the ninth century BC (see Sebaste/Samaria below). After Samaria was destroyed in the Assyrian invasion in 722BC, Shechem regained some importance and, in 300BC, a temple was built on Mount Gerizim to rival that of Jerusalem. Internecine rivalry during the time of Hasmonean king John Hyrcanus, led to the destruction of both town and temple in 129BC.

The town revived somewhat until it was destroyed by Vespasian in 67AD during the First Revolt against Rome. According to Josephus, a large number of Samaritans gathered on Mount Gerizim and prepared to resist the Romans. The mountain was put under siege by Vespasian's forces and around 11,000 Samaritans were killed. With the foundation of Flavia Neapolis (Nablus) Shechem faded from the historical record. It was finally destroyed in 529AD during the **Samaritan revolt**.

At **the site**, the main gate between the defensive walls is where business was carried out and news was exchanged. Guards would have been posted in the adjacent barracks to keep a look out for potential trouble. The remains of the walls around the entrance to the site are believed to date from between 1650 and 1550BC. To the other side of the gate, another complex between the inner and outer defensive walls represents a private temple of three rooms: an antechamber, a square room containing an altar, and a third, rectangular room. The large temple in the reconstructed courtyard nearby is thought to have been for public worship.

Mount Gerizim and the Samaritans

Mount Gerizim and **Mount Ebal**, 881m and 940m respectively, dominate views of Nablus. They are strikingly different in appearance: Gerizim green and tree-covered, Ebal for the most part bare, grey rock. Traditionally this was the work of God as passed on by Moses – 'I set before you a blessing and a curse . . .. And it shall come to pass when the Lord thy God hath brought thee into the land whither though goest . . . that thou shalt put the blessing upon mount Gerizim, and the curse upon mount Ebal' (*Deuteronomy 11:26–29*). But since Mount Gerizim faces north and has a great deal more shade than its south-facing sister, there may be a rather more scientific explanation of the phenomenon.

Mount Gerizim is held sacred by the **Samaritans**, who believe it to be holy because its peak was above The Flood. They call it *Har HaKedem* (The Early Mountain) because it is believed to predate even the Garden of Eden. And to add to its mystique, dust taken from here was used in the creation of Adam. The Samaritans are an ancient sect whose history dates from the Assyrian invasion of Canaan in 722BC. The second Book of Kings relates that Shalmaneser, the king of Assyria, 'came up throughout all the land, and went up to Samaria . . . and carried Israel away to Assyria . . .' (*II Kings 17:5–6*). Those Israelites who were not expelled but remained behind in Samaria came to be known as Samaritans.

When the Israelites returned after 550BC, now called Jews after their home in Judaea, they accused the Samaritans of intermarrying with Assyrians and Babylonians, and adopting pagan customs. For their part, the Samaritans claimed to be the true adherents of Mosaic Law and rejected that part of the Old Testament written in exile in Babylon. The animosity between the Samaritans and the Jewish orthodoxy was so fierce that Jews on pilgrimage to Jerusalem from the Galilee would go the long way round, via Jericho, rather than pass through 'pagan' Samaria. Hence the surprise of the Samaritan woman at being addressed by a Jewish preacher, Jesus, at Jacob's Well.

The Samaritans today speak Arabic and some Hebrew, but their religious services are conducted in the ancient Samaritan language. Throughout the Middle Ages, there were many flourishing Samaritan communities both in Palestine and in neighbouring countries, nowadays just two small groups remain: in Nablus and in Holon near Tel Aviv.

The Samaritan community is a hierarchical one, led by a High Priest. Whilst orthodox Judaism uses the Babylonian Bible as its scripture, the Samaritans recognise only the first five books of the Old Testament – the Pentateuch – and the Book of Joshua (which they hold to have been written by Abishua, a contemporary of Joshua). They are also at variance with mainstream Judaism on other points; they maintain that Mount Gerizim, rather than Mount Moriah in Jerusalem, was the site of Abraham's sacrifice of Isaac. Orthodox rabbis say that Samaritans can only be accepted into the 'community of Israel' when they reject Mount Gerizim and recognise Jerusalem as the site of the most holy mountain. Another point of controversy is the site of Joshua's altar; whereas the scriptures maintain the site to be Mount Ebal (*Joshua 8:30*), the Samaritans point to twelve rocks on Mount Gerizim as Joshua's altar.

The Samaritans celebrate the feasts of Passover, Pentecost and Tabernacles in strict accordance with biblical injunctions. The congregation spends the entire week of Passover on the summit of Mount Gerizim; here seven lambs are sacrificed on the altar (*mizbeah*). The lambs are afterwards spitted, then put into a pit (*tannur*) heated with twigs and branches, to be roasted as the Bible decrees. After the midnight meal, all the remains are burned in the altar depression. The sacrifice is nowadays held on a plateau on the mountain, south of the tarmac road from Nablus. To witness the ritual, you can join one of the tourist buses bringing visitors from Jerusalem and Tel Aviv, hire a taxi for around $10 or make the long hike up the mountain.

Just beyond the plateau, a dirt track leads to the northern peak, **Tel er-Ras**, on which once stood the Samaritan temple. Built in the fourth century BC, it is thought to have been destroyed by John Hyrcanus in 129BC. Roman coins minted in 159AD show a temple on the summit, linked to the city by a long flight of steps. According to some, the temple was dedicated to Zeus; other sources say it is the Emperor Hadrian's temple to Jupiter. Guided by the illustration on the coins, archaeologists unearthed a large platform on which a temple once stood, as well as 65 steps cut into the rock of the mountain following the precise line shown.

The **view** from the top of Mount Gerizim is spectacular. Over fifty kilometres to the west lies the Mediterranean, thirty kilometres to the east the Jordan Valley. From **Mount Ebal**, the view is even better, with Safad and the peaks of Mount Hermon to the north, Jaffa, Ramle and the sea to the west.

Sebaste

In the Samarian Hills, 13km northwest of Nablus, lies the royal city of **SEBASTE** or **Samaria**. Samaria was the third capital of the ancient Kingdom of Israel, succeeding Shechem at Tel Balata (see above) and Tirzah (Tel al-Farah). King **Omri** (876BC) bought the hill of Samaria from Shemer for two talents of silver (*I Kings 16:24*), and built a new city; partly because of its superior strategic situation, but also perhaps to eradicate the memory of the civil strife which had plagued the final years of Tirzah. The new capital stretched over some 25 acres, and its name later came to denote the whole area. Today, the Israelis use the name Samaria for the northern West Bank to denote that they consider it theirs.

Omri's son **Ahab** (871–852BC) consolidated his father's work with extensive building, and expanded the kingdom through numerous military victories. His downfall is attributed to the influence of his Phoenician wife, the infamous Jezebel. ('But there was none like unto Ahab, which did sell himself to work wickedness in the sight of the Lord, whom Jezebel his wife stirred up' – *I Kings 21:25*.) This 'wickedness' included building temples to Jezebel's pagan deities, Baal and Astarte, which incurred the wrath of the prophet Elijah who promptly appointed the army commander Jehu as king. Jehu, however, could not sustain his rule and at one stage was forced to pay tribute to the more powerful Assyrian kingdom.

Some semblance of order was restored in the reign of **Jeroboam II** (784–748BC), when the borders of the kingdom were temporarily extended as far as Damascus. But the emergence of a powerful and decadent aristocracy signalled internal weakness, as foretold by the prophets Hosea and Amos. From 743BC onwards, the city and the kingdom came under increasing pressure from the Assyrians and, after a three year siege, both finally fell in 722BC. Thirty thousand people, about a third of the population, were deported and would become known as the 'ten lost tribes'. Those who remained became known as **Samaritans** (see above).

Under the **Persians** (550BC), Samaria became a provincial capital. Alexander the Great later populated the city with his Macedonian soldier-settlers and expelled the Samaritans to Shechem after the assassination of one of his representatives. Samaria remained under Hellenic influence until the advent of the Hasmonean dynasty and the destruction of the city by John Hyrcanus.

In the latter part of the first century AD, Herod restored the city to much of its former glory in his usual grandiose style, renaming it **Sebaste** (Greek for Augustus) in tribute to his Roman patron, Caesar Augustus. Here he installed foreign mercenaries, celebrated his marriage to the doomed Mariamne and executed two of his sons. In the second century, Septimus Severus granted Sebaste the status and privileges of a Roman colony in an attempt to reduce the influence of Shechem, whose population remained hostile to Roman rule. All periods of occupation are represented among the hill-top ruins, set among encroaching olive groves, but the bulk of what you see dates from Septimus's reconstruction of the Herodian city.

Village and site

Nine kilometres along the main Nablus–Tulkarm highway, at the Palestinian village of DEIR SHARAF, a road leads off right to Jenin. Along this road, there are two signposted turnoffs to the right: the first leads to the Palestinian village of **SEBASTIYA** which lies a little to the east of the ancient site; the second steeper route goes directly to the site. There is a direct *service* from Nablus to the centre of the village.

The village square is dominated by the huge buttressed walls of a once-magnificent Crusader cathedral. From Byzantine times, this site was said to be the place where John the Baptist's head was buried, and the Crusader church (1160) was built over an earlier church. The tradition was continued by Salah al-Din who transformed the Crusader building into a mosque – it is a nineteenth-century rebuilding of this, the **Mosque of Nabi Yaha** (John the Prophet), that stands here today.

Within the courtyard, a stairway in the small domed building leads down into a subterranean cave. Among the six burial niches here, two are said to be those of the prophets Elisha and Obadiah. Elisha spent much of his life in Samaria and Obadiah is said to have hidden 100 prophets here, feeding them on bread and water. From the mosque, there's a great view of the village and the surroundings. An open-air café opposite will provide refreshments before you set out along the steep path that leads up through the village to the ruins of Sebaste.

The ten-minute walk up from the village brings you into the site at the huge Roman **forum**. This now doubles as a car park surrounded by shops, their owners patiently awaiting the next coachload of tourists: the restaurant on the right serves delicious Palestinian food to revive you after you've exhausted yourself at the site. The western end of the forum is littered with columns and capitals from a collapsed portico, beyond which was a raised **basilica**. From the northern end of the basilica, a trail leads around to the stepped remains of the Roman **theatre**. Alongside is a Hellenistic tower, considered the finest example in the region (which is more of a comment on the devastation which has been visited on these sites than the quality of the tower).

On the summit of the hill is what was perhaps the last building erected here, Herod's **Temple of Augustus**, restored at a later date by Septimus Severus. Nothing much of the temple survives except for low walls, the wide entrance steps and a few large fragments of columns and capitals. Sections of the Israelite palace walls, which provided the foundations for Herod's temple complex, have been excavated a few yards to the south and show the skill of the builders employed by Omri and Ahab. Finds here include a temple to Baal and a figure of Astarte, confirming the biblical accounts of Ahab's reign.

The path that circles the temple is still strewn with pottery shards that play an important part in dating various levels. South of the summit is the small Byzantine **Church of St. John,** on the site of the discovery of the head of John the Baptist (before it was buried below). Here, according to Christian tradition, Herod held the infamous party at which Salome danced and demanded the Baptist's head. The granite columns were introduced in the eleventh century to support a dome over the structure. The Greek Orthodox church encased them in masonry in the twelfth century and built a chapel over the crypt.

The approach to the site from the second, steeper road leads to the remains of the **west gate**, Roman on Israelite foundations, and the Roman city **wall**, whose scale gives some idea of the former size of the city. At the entrance are two impressive watchtowers, the bases of which are Hellenistic. From here you can follow the line of a **colonnaded street** on which some of the estimated 600 columns still stand. About halfway along, just down from the Byzantine church, the foundations of several one-room **shops** have been unearthed, suggesting there was a bazaar area here during Roman times.

It's an impressive site, but perhaps the most attractive aspect is the rural atmosphere. There's no hint of the over-groomed sterility of many similar sites – here the ruins are dotted amongst olive groves that are still tended by Palestinian farmers. It makes getting around a little harder, but it gives the place a feel of reality too often missing elsewhere.

Jerusalem to Jericho

The forty-minute trip eastward from Jerusalem to Jericho is truly spectacular. Starting at 800m above sea level in Jerusalem, the road plunges down through stark and dramatic desert landscape to the oasis of Jericho at 250m below sea level, the lowest city on earth. It's a serpentine route through the white limestone hills of the Judaean sub-desert. During the summer, these are usually pretty stark, but after a winter storm the hills can briefly burst into a glorious display of flowers and colour. There are small Beduin encampments on either side of the road, some of black or brown goat's-hair tents, others predominantly shacks of wood and corrugated iron, reflecting the Palestinian Beduin tradition of combining settled and nomadic life-styles, depending on economic circumstance. The hills are scarred with goat tracks only centimetres wide, showing both the agility of these essential animals and the distances they have to forage in this environment.

As far as **public transport** goes, there are frequent Arab buses (#36) and local Egged buses (#43) from Jerusalem's Damascus Gate bus station to Bethany. For Jericho, there are the usual *service* taxis from both Damascus and Jaffa Gates. Both Arab and Egged buses also run: Egged services, from the Jaffa Road station, call at the settlements, bypassing Bethany to join the road at Maale Adumim; Arab buses from East Jerusalem follow the main road as outlined below.

Bethany

Leaving Jerusalem, the road sets out through the Kidron Valley below the Mount of Olives, passes the village of Silwan, and then swings east to **BETHANY**. Bethany is known in Arabic as **al-Azariyeh**, a form of the Greek Lazarion or place of Lazarus. It was here that **Lazarus** was resurrected (*John 11:1–44*), that Jesus went with his disciples after the events of Palm Sunday (*Mark 11:11*), and that Jesus' feet were anointed with precious ointment at the house of Simon the Leper before he was betrayed by Judas (*Mark 14:3–9* and *Matthew 26:6*).

Today it's a rather nondescript village stretched out along either side of the main road. You could drive through without noticing anything special about the place at all, but if you turn off by the souvenir shops on a sharp right-hand bend in the road, a lane leading up the eastern slope of the Mount of Olives, will bring you to no less than six churches and a mosque.

Chief of them is the modern, cruciform **Franciscan Church** (7am–noon and 2–5.30pm), marking the site of the **Tomb of Lazarus**. This was built in 1954 – designed, like many in Jerusalem, by the Italian architect Antonio Barluzzi – and within its grounds are preserved numerous earlier structures. On the left as you enter the courtyard are remnants of the mosaic floors of the earliest church at the site, built in the fourth century and destroyed by an earthquake. These are preserved under trapdoors adjacent to the walls of a fifteenth century church, in turn razed by the Persians in 614AD. Under Crusader rule, the church was rebuilt and reinforced – note the stone buttresses as you descend from the street into the courtyard. To this, a large abbey complex was added by the Crusader queen Melisande in 1138, and a chapel was erected over the tomb of Lazarus. Through its wheat and olive-oil production, the abbey became one of the wealthiest in the Crusader kingdom – a mill and oil-press can be seen in one of the remaining rooms accessible from the church courtyard. By the end of the fourteenth century, the **Al-Ozir Mosque** had supplanted the Crusader chapel, and it is here that you now find the tomb: from street level 22 rough stone steps descend into a dank cave with three rather uninspiring burial niches – hardly worth risking a sprained ankle.

Perhaps to show that ancient sectarian rivalries are still alive and well, a **Greek Orthodox Church** was built up the street as recently as 1965. It's an attractive building, with a pale blue dome, but its gates appear to be permanently padlocked. To the left of the crossroads is a ruined tower known as the **Castle of Lazarus** which is thought to be the site of the House of Simon the Leper. This too belongs to the Greek Orthodox Church, but it was once part of a nunnery founded in 1138 by Millicent, the wife of Fulk, Crusader king of Jerusalem. The **House of Mary and Martha**, where Lazarus was raised from the dead, is east of the tower. A little further up the mountain are the excavations of ancient Bethany or **Bet Anania**, which have revealed evidence of habitation from the sixth century BC to the fourteenth AD.

Turning right at the crossroads by the Greek church, a track winds between the houses of the Palestinian village of ABU DIS. It emerges beside the high-walled Franciscan monastery and chapel at **Bethphage**. From here you can look down into the wadi that was the ancient Bethany–Jericho road. Bethphage itself was the starting point of Jesus' triumphal entry into Jerusalem on Palm Sunday, and from here the contemporary **Palm Sunday procession** begins. The chapel was built in 1883 on the remains of a medieval church commemorating Jesus' meeting with Martha and Mary, the sisters of Lazarus. Inside the chapel is the **Stone of Meeting**, which the Crusaders believed was the block on which Jesus stepped to mount his donkey when he set out for Jerusalem. They were apparently oblivious of the fact that little help is needed to mount indigenous Palestinian donkeys, which are considerably smaller than their own massive war horses. Beautiful medieval paintings on the stone depict scenes from Jesus' life.

From Bethphage, the road descends into the Wadi al-Hod (Valley of the Watering Place). **Hod al-Azariyeh**, known as the Apostles' Spring, is the only well between here and the Jordan Valley and is where the travelling apostles are believed to have stopped to drink.

The Good Samaritan and Maale Adumim

Around 10km from Jerusalem, a sixteenth-century Turkish *khan* to the right of the road marks the spot where the Good Samaritan took compassion on an injured traveller (*Luke 10:30–36*). Known both as *al-Khan al-Ahmar* (Red Inn) because of the colour of the soil in the region and as the **Inn of the Good Samaritan**, it is insubstantial and easy to miss, despite its romantic sounding name. Before the advent of modern means of transportation this was a lively meeting place where travellers stopped to refresh themselves and their mounts. Today, what refreshments there are are served in a conveniently placed 'Beduin' tent outside the *khan*. The most interesting feature of the nondescript building is the notice on the door announcing: 'Because of technical difficulties the place will be closed on Saturdays and festivals'.

The hill above the inn is the probable site of biblical Adummim (*Joshua 15:7*), through which the border of the tribe of Judah ran; on the top is the ruined castle of **Qala'at ed-Dum** (Castle of Blood). The present day Jewish settlement of **MAALE ADUMIM** here hits the eye like a sledge-hammer. Established in 1978 and now classified as a city, it is the largest of the sixteen Jewish settlements in the Jerusalem area: plans are for a total population of 30,000, and for the whole settlement to be incorporated into metropolitan Jerusalem.

Maale Adumim was the centrepiece of the second phase of the *Likud* settlement campaign. Earlier settlements in the heart of the West Bank were massively funded but not on the whole popular, attracting mostly ideologues and political extremists. The second phase – suburban settlements within commuting distance of Jerusalem or Tel Aviv – provided super-cheap housing in places where more people were prepared to live. Having purchased their homes, these people clearly have a financial stake in the continuation of Israeli control. By succeeding in populating settlements on this scale, the government effectively ruled out a US-bankrolled buy-out of the sort which accompanied the Israeli withdrawal from Egyptian territory. The fact that the first wave of apartments in these settlements was put up for sale at the same time as the media was full of stories about the fantastic sums given to Sinai settlers to evacuate can only have helped encourage would-be settlers.

Beyond the *khan*, the road begins its descent into the **Wadi al-Rummaneh** (Valley of the Pomegranates). To the left, side roads lead to the Monastery of St. George and Wadi Qelt and the small Israeli agricultural settlement of MIZPE YERIHO. Eleven kilometres from Jerusalem, the point where you have reached sea level is marked by a sign – a descent of 800m (2600 feet) so far.

Wadi Qelt and the Monastery of Saint George of Koziba

Wadi Qelt, a natural rift in the hills with high, sheer rock walls, carves a deep and dramatic crevice for 35km between Jerusalem and Jericho. Once part of the main highway, it was in frequent use as such right up to the end of the Ottoman period. Monks have inhabited this awesome place for 1600 years, initially in caves and rock-hollowed niches, later building monasteries

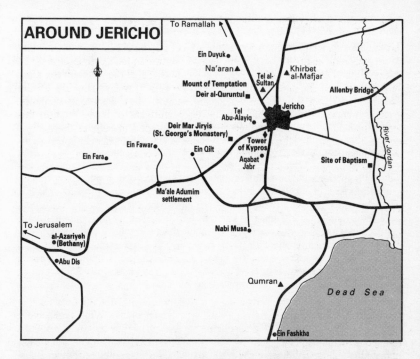

AROUND JERICHO

To Ramallah

Ein Duyuk
Na'aran ▲
Mount of Temptation   Tel al-   ▲ Khirbet
Deir al-Quruntul   Sultan ▲   al-Mafjar
                                                        Allenby Bridge
                        Tel   Jericho
                        Abu-Alayiq
Deir Mar Jiryis
(St. George's Monastery) ■   ♦ Tower
Ein Fawar   Ein Qilt   of Kypros
Ein Fara   Aqabat   Site of Baptism
                        Jabr

Ma'ale Adumim
settlement

To Jerusalem
al-Azariyeh
(Bethany)   Nabi Musa

Abu Dis

                Qumran ▲
                        Dead Sea

Ein Fashkha

River Jordan

and hermitages throughout the wadi. Three perennial springs enabled the monks to survive here and also traditionally provided Jericho with fresh water. The monasteries flourished above all between the fourth and seventh centuries, the main period of desert monasticism (see p.147): only the **Monastery of Saint George** of Koziba survives.

The easiest and most common route to St. George's is from the main Jerusalem–Jericho road. A large orange signpost some 6km from Maale Adumim points the way, an easy walk down of about fifteen minutes: coming back up, however, can be quite a slog. An enterprising seller has set up shop on the main road here, with a monopoly on juices and ice-creams. He does a flourishing trade and so can and does charge above the odds – but as you'll probably be gasping by the time you get back, there's little point in complaining and even less in arguing.

Alternatively, you can **hike** along the Wadi, either for the whole 35km from Jerusalem to Jericho, or just for part of the way. The walk needs to be undertaken seriously: make sure there are at least three in your party, let someone know where you're going and take lots of liquids with you. This is especially important in summer, but even in the winter the temperatures can be in the seventies Fahrenheit. Head covering is also essential. The easiest short walk is to take the Israeli bus to Mitzpe Yeriho and follow the track which gives an awesome panoramic view of the limestone and chalk crags that wall Wadi Qelt.

Along this last route, you'll see the remains of a turn-of-the-century flour mill at the bottom of the track. This is still inhabited by a Beduin family who traditionally are responsible for the upkeep of the aqueduct next to it. A mile or so along the path of the aqueduct, you come to the perennial spring of **Ain Qelt**: an astonishing torrent of water gushing out of bare and apparently lifeless limestone rock. The spring is fed by the winter rains from around Jerusalem and Bethlehem which collect in huge aquifers (strata of porous rock below ground) and eventually pour out through a fault into the wadi. The other two springs, Ain Fara and Ain Fuwar, are above Ain Qelt in the upper Qelt canyon. This water is unsafe to drink, but people do swim in it – the pools are waist deep, even in summer.

Retracing your steps toward the mill, a small ceramic plaque in the cliff sings the praises of the nineteenth-century builder of the aqueduct. This is only the latest in a succession of major water engineering projects here. To the right, the impressive arch of an eighth-century Umayyad aqueduct crosses a smaller wadi, and the surrounding hillsides are littered with traces of Hasmonean, Herodian and Roman **aqueducts** in which you can go for a paddle – but take care as the flow of water can be considerable. Just after passing some large caves on the far side of the wadi, the aqueduct traces a large horseshoe to the left. Here it is better to head down to the floor of the wadi and to follow the dry, rather rocky river bed for a mile or so until you reach the monastery.

Above a beautiful garden of olive, palm and cypress trees, the magnificent Greek Orthodox **Monastery of Saint George of Koziba** (Mon–Sat 8am–4pm in winter, 8am–5pm in summer) is carved out of the rockface, clinging to the canyon walls like a fairytale fortress. It is an extraordinary sight. One of the oldest in the country, the monastery was originally a *laura* or spiritual centre for the hermits of the region who came here for divine liturgy. Towards the end of the fifth century it was converted into a monastery by John of Thebes, and in the following century it became known as St. George (*Mar Jiryis* in Arabic) under the leadership of St. George of Koziba. The prophet Elijah is said to have stayed at this place on his way to the Sinai, and here St. Joachim was informed by an angel of the Virgin Mary's conception.

The present building was reconstructed between 1878 and 1901, following the design of a Crusader restoration of 1179. Until it was destroyed in the Persian invasion of 614AD, the monastery housed scores of monks and was famed for its hospitality to travellers en route to such distant places as Damascus and Baghdad. Today, only ten monks remain and visits are mainly confined to two **chapels** within the monastery complex. The principal chapel is dedicated to the Virgin Mary. The interior, hung with a multitude of golden lamps and dominated by a double-headed Byzantine eagle in black, white and red mosaic, is so ornate that it feels more like being inside Aladdin's cave than a church. That feeling is heightened by an exceptionally rich array of paintings and icons, most of which date from the 1901 restoration. The smaller of the two chapels, with a sixth-century mosaic floor that marks it as part of the oldest section of the monastery, is dedicated to Saints George and John. It has a delightful, domed, sky-blue roof and an altar dominated by glowing icons of the twelve Apostles. In one corner is a gruesome display of the skulls of fourteen monks, and the recently discovered mummified remains of another, who were martyred in the Persian destruction.

A display of a very different kind can be enjoyed from the **roof** of the monastery. Laid out before you is a landscape of startling contrasts; the lush green of the monastery garden and the natural vegetation in the wadi, complete with palm trees, set against a backdrop of sheer, bleached rock, is nothing short of fantastic. The whole is enhanced by an awesome silence (if there aren't too many tourists around) that is broken only by the gurgle of spring water far below.

Continuing **from the monastery to Jericho**, you can cross to the opposite cliff and take the road or stay on the north side of the wadi and follow a well-graded trail for forty minutes along the line of the Herodian aqueduct. The wadi emerges into the Jordan Valley at two hills that were once surmounted by the Hasmonean fortresses of **Taurus** and **Thrax**. Herod refortified the fortress of Taurus to provide himself with a safe retreat from his nearby winter palace and renamed it Kypros (see below) after his mother. This is thoroughly ruined, so you're probably better off saving your climbing energy for somewhere else – there are far better examples of Herodian architecture at Herodion and Masada, for example. The course of the wadi continues past Herod's palaces (see below), whence a dirt road brings you to the main highway, a couple of kilometres further

Nabi Musa

Back on the main road, just before the final descent into the Jordan Valley, a signpost to the right points to **Nabi Musa**. This, according to Muslim tradition, is where Moses is buried, and the complex of domes set against the rolling dunes of the desert – Islamic architecture at its simple best – is definitely worth making a detour to see.

The **tomb of Nabi Musa** (the prophet Moses) has been a site of annual **pilgrimage** since the time of Salah al-Din. The main body of the present shrine, however, was built by Mamluk Sultan Baybars in 1269. Rooms were later added to house pilgrims and, in 1475, the hospice was extended to its present size. The Ottoman Turks further restored the building around 1820. To counterbalance the influx of Christian pilgrims to Jerusalem during the Holy Week at Easter, they encouraged a week-long pilgrimage to the site.

Traditionally, the pilgrimage was a time for celebration and relaxation. The procession to Nabi Musa set out from Jerusalem under the leadership of the Mufti; along the way the pilgrims sang, played drums, flutes and lutes and danced the *debkeh*. At the shrine the pilgrims lived either within the complex or in tents, and entertainment was laid on constantly: traditional story-tellers in the coffee shop, shadow theatre, cards and backgammon, as well as horse-racing and jousting.

The gathering of so many Palestinian Muslims was always a potentially significant event, forging links between people from different parts of the country. Delegations from Hebron, villagers from the north and city dwellers from Jerusalem, Nablus and other towns would gather and spend a week together at the festivities. During the 1920s and 1930s, this potential power was marshalled into **demonstrations** against increasing Zionist encroachment in Palestine. In 1930, for example, the British army was called in a vain attempt to quell tens of thousands of demonstrators gathered at the Nabi Musa pilgrimage. In an attempt to defuse this sort of political resistance, the Nabi Musa celebrations were banned by the British Mandate authorities in 1937, and the annual pilgrimage was resumed only in April 1987, when some 50,000 Palestinians attended after a break of fifty years.

You'll find the place cared for by a family who will gladly show you around. There is no entrance fee, but contributions are welcomed. You will be shown the beautifully simple and serene **mosque**, with a white domed roof, glazed green *mihrab* and painted green wooden *minbar*. Inside the mosque, in a small room to the right of the entrance, is the stone **mausoleum** of the prophet. Do not miss the view from the top of the minaret which displays the whole complex below, the desert hills beyond, the Jordan Valley and purple hills of Moab in the distance to the east. The cemetery outside was used mainly for Muslims who died during the festival. Muslim legend identifies two of the tombs here as being those of Moses' shepherd, Hassan er-Ra'i, and the prophet Mohammed's wife, Aisha.

On leaving Nabi Musa, you'll shortly come to a fork in the road. Left leads to Jericho, right to the Jordan valley and the Dead Sea.

Jericho

The revolutionary step forward was the discovery that wild grains could be cultivated . . . the growth of fixed settlements became possible . . . . From this, all civilization is derived. It is in the inception of this revolution that Jericho takes a great place . . .

Dame Kathleen Kenyon, *Digging up Jericho*

JERICHO, the 'City of Palms', lies low in the south Jordan Valley, 10km northwest of the Dead Sea and 7km west of the Jordan River. This sleepy, rather ramshackle West Bank town is the archetypal desert oasis, a thriving agricultural settlement based on plentiful local springs. Rich in date palms and other tropical fruit and vegetables, Jericho is also famed for its medicinal plants and spices. At 250m below sea level, it is the lowest town on earth. According to some archaeologists, it is also the oldest.

There are, then, dozens of fascinating historical sites. These apart, modern Jericho is a thriving town of some 7500 inhabitants whose balmy winter climate has long made it a favourite resort. Tourism declined dramatically after the Israeli occupation of 1967, when visitors from the Arab world stopped coming, and has fallen off further since the *intifada*: tourists nowadays rarely stay longer than a day. If you have the time, Jericho deserves more than this: the history is absorbing, and the atmosphere, with numerous outdoor cafés and excellent restaurants, refreshingly laid-back.

The oldest city on earth

The name Jericho derives either from the Hebrew for 'moon' – *yereah* – or from *reah*, the fragrance of flowers. The former refers to an ancient moon cult thought to have once been practised in the region. Jericho's known history stretches back almost 12,000 years. From the earliest times its perennial spring, Ein al-Sultan, would have enticed mesolithic nomadic hunters to camp by its abundant waters before resuming their trail. The oldest of some twenty successive **settlements** excavated here dates back to around 8000BC, when a rectangular stone building was raised, probably a cult centre for these nomadic peoples. Over the next thousand years or so, a permanent settlement with a defensive wall became established, marking the change of its inhabitants from wandering hunter-gatherers to settled food-producers. As far as Kathleen Kenyon – the archaeologist who did much of the most important work at the site – is concerned, this effectively makes it the world's oldest civilisation: village settlements known elsewhere are almost two thousand years younger, and the pyramids, the first major stone constructions in the Middle East, went up four thousand years later.

This city was eventually destroyed – whether by war or natural disaster is unknown – and some time after 6000BC was reinhabited by a different people, makers of simple pottery. After a brief move to a different site in the Wadi Qelt in the fifth millennium (perhaps because the water source moved), the city was re-established here, with a new city wall. This ancient site, today known as **Tel al-Sultan**, was a flourishing **Canaanite** centre as early as 3000BC. Around 1200BC, Joshua and the invading Israelites, after crossing the Jordan River, reduced the city to rubble – 'and the walls came tumbling down', as the song tells it. Later in the Bible Ahab reconstructed the city, and Elisha purified the water of the spring. Jericho became an administrative centre under the Persians in 550BC but thereafter declined: under Alexander the Great (332BC), an area to the south (again near Wadi Qelt) became a royal estate, its warm winter climate making it an ideal retreat from the cold of Jerusalem and the highlands.

Jericho was visited by **Christ** several times; here, he restored the sight of a blind beggar (*Luke 18:34–43*) and on Jabal Quruntul, the Mount of Temptation, he spent forty days in meditation. In the Byzantine period, the centre of population shifted from Tel al-Sultan to the site of the present town.

In **Roman** times the Hellenistic estate continued in use. It was given to Cleopatra by Mark Anthony, and Herod the Great is said to have initially leased the oasis from her, though later it was given to him by the Emperor Octavian. Herod laid out new aqueducts to irrigate the fields and to supply his fabulous winter palace at Tulul Abu al-Alaiq. Another magnificent palace was built here in 724AD by the Ummayad Sultan Hisham Ibn Abd al-Malik. His hunting palace at Khirbet al-Mafjar is one of the most outstanding surviving examples of the Islamic architecture of the period. During the Middle Ages, the conquering **Crusaders** introduced sugar production to Jericho. They renamed it 'New Jericho' and erected a church in commemoration of the Temptation of Christ on Jabal Quruntul.

In **modern times** the introduction of fruit production following World War I brought new wealth to Jericho, now as part of British Mandate Palestine. After 1948, it was held by Jordan as part of the West Bank; 185,000 Palestinian refugees from coastal territories captured by Israel flooded into the area. Three refugee camps were erected: 'Awawme, housing 120,000 persons; Ein al-Sultan with a population of 20,000; and Aqabat Jaber with 45,000. In the wake of the Israeli occupation of the West Bank in 1967, most of these refugees were again displaced, many of them escaping across the Jordan River. 'Awawme today stands empty whilst the population of the other two is much reduced. Ein al-Sultan now has a population of around 700, whilst Aqabat Jaber is 'home' to some 3000 survivors and decendants of the initial wave of refugees.

Arrival

Buses to and from Jerusalem run hourly until around 5pm; *service* taxis generally continue later, till 7 or 8pm, depending on demand. Arriving in Jericho by either means you'll be dropped just off the main square. On the square are the Israeli-run *baladiyyeh* (municipality) and police station; just off it you'll find the **post office** (Amman Street), hospital (Salah al-Din Street) and main **bank** (Ein al-Sultan Street).

Jericho has the easy-going atmosphere of a small desert town and its streets hold few secrets. Its inhabitants are accustomed to and indulgent of the bus-loads of visitors who sweep in and out in the space of a few hours. Those who hang around a bit longer, long enough to tune in to the relaxed pace and intimacy of the town, will inevitably discover an altogether different place. The best time of year to visit Jericho is in the warm winter months (September–April), avoiding it in summer when the temperature often soars into the 40s (over 100°F).

Most of Jericho's historical attractions are some distance apart, and outside the main town, and one of the best ways to see them is to **hire a bicycle**. Three bike shops in Moscobia Street, just east of the *baladiyyeh*, will rent you a bicycle for around $0.60 an hour. The owner of the first on the right, Mohammed Ibrahim Judeh, may ask for a student card or passport by way of security. His sliding rates are only slightly cheaper than those of his immediate neighbour, Darajat Hawayeh, or Fakhri Abu Khater's across the road.

Food and accommodation

Like all West Bank towns, Jericho has its share of small *humus* and *falafel* joints. What is special about Jericho, however, is the exceptional range and flavour of locally-grown fresh vegetables and seasonal **fruit**. They taste like nothing you've ever tasted before. If you don't feel like having a full meal, you can do no better than buy a *falafel* sandwich or an oven-fresh *ka'ak* and some fruit to go with it. For a generous helping of *humus* or *ful*, try *Nabil's Restaurant* (Jerusalem Road, opposite Jericho Hospital). The recently opened *Al-Manara Al-Jadid* (in the main square) serves delicious grilled chicken, salads and bread.

The fruit may be good, but the **outdoor restaurants** are even better. People come here from all over the West Bank simply to eat (especially on Fridays) and to listen to some of the best musicians in the area. Most of the restaurants are strung out along Ein al-Sultan Street between the centre of

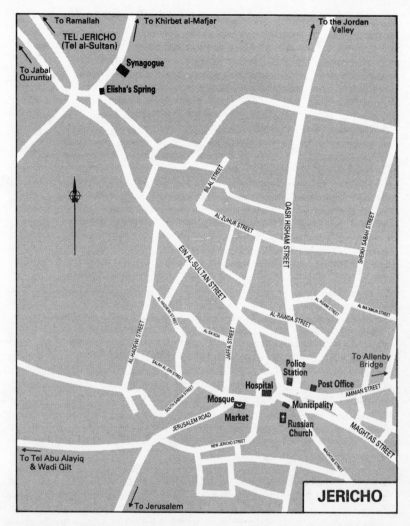

town and Tel Jericho. Prices and food are broadly comparable, so it's worth checking out where the best music is coming from. The first restaurant along the road is *Seven Trees* where, in a shaded outdoor garden, you can enjoy a full meal of *musakhan* or kebab for $10 or less, salad or omelette for around $3. Further along on the right, *Younes* serves oriental and international food – anything from *tabbouleh* to steak – and provides free bread, pickles, fruit and coffee with each meal. The *Beduin Tent* outdoor restaurant on the left, with its incongruous waterwheel, specialises in what they call *Beduin shishlik* – skewered pieces of lamb served on flat, oven-baked bread and onions. At the junction to Tel Jericho, the spacious and clean *Steak House* sells the usual salads and schnitzels (meat dishes around $6) and is rather quieter than the *Temptation Restaurant* opposite, which offers self-service salads ($4 for as much as you want) and assorted full meals. This latter is often crowded with groups off the tour buses.

Finally, you shouldn't leave Jericho without sampling Khalil Walaji's freshly squeezed **fruit juices**. His place is adjacent to Tel Jericho. Orange, grapefruit and pomella drinks cost $1, but it is definitely worth spending a bit more for the more exotic almond, date, apricot and walnut juices (around $2). You may even be treated to an improvised drum solo from the local talent. Whether it's the contagion of the drumbeat or the effect of the fruit juices, the whole show manages to get even the most starchy of European tourists clapping their hands and on their feet dancing.

Jericho's sole functioning **hotel**, *Hisham's Palace* (☎92-2414), is northeast of the main square, on the right of Ein al-Sultan Street. This rambling 1920s hotel is still imbued with the atmosphere of better days – you can imagine what it must have been like when it was a favourite gambling haunt of Jordan's King Hussein and his ministers. The now-empty swimming pool and garden at the back testify to busier and grander times. Nowadays you can get one of the 26 spacious and airy rooms with a balcony, private bathroom and hot water for as little as $7. If, as is most probable, you're one of few guests, you may even be able to get it cheaper. The management are more than happy to while away the long hours with you and share whatever is going. The *Park Hotel* (☎92-2386), further along the same road, is rumoured to open in the unlikely event of Hisham's being full.

Tel Jericho or Tel al-Sultan

Ancient Jericho is situated to the northwest of the modern town, a little over 2km from the centre. Standing on the ancient tel knowing that there are 10,000 years of previous civilisations under your feet can be an awesome sensation, an experience further enhanced by the magnificent view from the observation point; oasis greens against the backdrop of parched, stark desert.

From a distance, the **tel** (7am–6pm in summer, 8am–5pm in winter; admission $0.70, students $0.35) appears to be simply a huge mound of earth but, like others, it is actually the result of numerous settlements built upon the ruins of their predecessors. The first modern excavations were carried out in 1867. They were not a great success (an important stone tower was missed by inches) but ever since, archaeologists have been virtually queueing up to get their trowels into the ground. Today, the archaeological importance of the site is unquestionable. This is largely thanks to the late British archaeologist Dame Kathleen Kenyon, who began the most extensive dig at the site in 1952 and discovered the remains of 23 cities. She was the first to claim that Jericho provided evidence of the human transition from hunter to settled farmer. There are fascinating photographs in her book *Digging up Jericho* (Ernest Benn 1957). This is well worth trying to get hold of, as her discoveries are now sometimes hard to distinguish among the piles of earth and ditches littered with rubble and empty Coke cans.

One of the major archaeological discoveries here is the remains of a seven-metre-high **neolithic tower** that dates from around 7000BC. Its size and construction – with a central stairway – is unrivalled anywhere in the world for this period, and its position, just inside the walls, would have provided the city with an excellent defence against attackers. Just to the north of this lay the original shrine, the earliest structure at the site. The **city walls** that have been uncovered are later, dating basically from the Early Bronze Age (circa 2600BC). The sloping banks (glacis) of a fort from the Middle Bronze Age (circa 1400BC) would also have deterred invaders. Whether any of these walls are the ones which fell down when Joshua blew the trumpets is unclear, but a break in the occupation of the tel around the thirteenth century BC would accord with the Israelite invasion. The mud brick walls to the north of the tel are thought to date from a large scale re-occupation of the site in the seventh century BC.

What the neolithic inhabitants of Jericho may have looked like can be seen from the restored features of ten **skulls** on view at the Palestine (Rockefeller) Museum in Jerusalem. These seem to have been associated with some kind of cult of the dead: they were apparently kept inside the houses, perhaps the heads of dead ancestors. Their successors produced some remarkable pottery, such as the extraordinary vase in the shape of a human head dating from the Middle Canaanite period (1750–1500BC). This is also on display in Jerusalem, at the Israel Museum.

One reason why the ancient city of Jericho was originally established here is because of its proximity to a constant source of water – **Ein al-Sultan**. Opposite Tel al-Sultan, the spring still provides a lifeline for Jericho, gushing water at the rate of 1000 gallons per minute. This is distributed throughout the oasis by a complex system of gravity-flow irrigation. Early tradition identifies this spring with the one the prophet Elisha purified by throwing salt into it (*2 Kings 2:19–22*) and gives it its other name: Elisha's Spring.

Not far from Ein al-Sultan, to the right of the road leading to Hisham's Palace, a sign points to an ancient **synagogue**. Here, in the basement of a private Arab house standing in a grove of trees, you can see the beautiful mosaic floor of a fifth- or sixth-century synagogue. A rectangular building divided into three by two rows of columns, its floor is decorated with floral and geometric patterns. Beneath a *menorah*, the Aramaic inscription reads 'Peace Upon Israel'.

Khirbet al-Mafjar or Hisham's Palace

The splendid ruins of **Hisham's Palace** (Sat–Thur 8am–5pm, Fri 8am–4pm in summer, 8am–4pm and 8am–3pm in winter; admission $1.80) lie off the signposted road leading north from Tel al-Sultan, a pleasant two-and-a-half-kilometre bike ride past well-irrigated fields. One of the finest examples of Umayyad architecture in the country, the palace was built as one of a number of hunting lodges used by the Umayyad princes. When it was first discovered in the 1870s, it was described as the remains of a medieval monastery, showing just how tenuous archaeological assumptions can be. Stones from the ruins were used extensively in local construction work as late as 1927, but excavation and recognition of the site in the 1930s has prevented any further destruction.

Although the palace is named after Caliph Hisham Ibn Abd al-Malik, it was in fact designed by the caliph's high-living nephew and successor, al-Walid Ibn Yazid. Construction work began in 743AD but stopped a year later when Yazid was assassinated. The sumptuous palace was virtually levelled by an earthquake three years after that.

A small **museum**, on the right of the entrance, houses a collection of pottery found on the site, including pilgrims' flasks and jugs from the Umayyad and Abbasid periods. The most important finds, however, including huge sections of exquisitely carved stone and timber decoration, have been removed to the Palestine (Rockefeller) Museum in Jerusalem, where they are definitely worth a visit. Fortunately, enough has been left on site to see how grand the palace must once have been.

Through an imposing brick arch to the left of the entrance, magnificent walls stuccoed with arabesques surround a **courtyard** that would have been the general living quarters. In the northeast and southwest corners of the courtyard, steps led to an upper storey that was reserved for the imperial residence. The large, circular stone monument that dominates the central courtyard is thought to have been intended as a window. Two **mosques** were attached to the palace: the layout of the one adjacent to the southern wall suggests it was reserved for the caliph's personal use, while the larger of the two, northeast of the courtyard, was for public worship.

From the courtyard, a paved path leads to the imposing remains of the **bath hall** with its huge colonnade, swimming pool and exquisite pink-and-blue mosaic floor. Thirty-six mosaic panels in all cover the entire floor area, but only a few of these are on view – the rest are covered for their own protection. To the north of the hall is the palace's greatest treasure: a superb and undamaged **mosaic** forming part of the marble-edged dais in the *diwan* or reception hall. Apart from being arguably the finest mosaic in the region, it is also unique in that it follows no known contemporaneous school of design or influence. A huge apple tree – the Tree of Life – bears fifteen fruits, each representing a country under the rule of Sultan Abd al-Malik. The two gazelles beneath the tree on the left are diplomats or guests that have good relations with the kingdom and are therefore welcome. The gazelle on the right, however, representing a visitor who wishes the ruler harm, is savaged by the lion of revenge. The fine mosaic pieces are so tiny that the whole has a marvellously detailed, woven effect. The building housing the mosaic is labelled 'guest house'.

The Monastery of the Temptation

The climb up the bare, rocky slopes of Jabal Quruntul to the **Monastery of the Temptation** (7am–3pm and 4–5pm in summer, 7am–2pm and 3–4pm in winter) looks daunting, but in fact it's a trek of only 15 to 30 minutes (depending on how fit you are) and well worth the effort. The Greek Orthodox monastery lies about 350m above Jericho, perched on a rocky ledge about

3km northwest of the town. From the monastery, you get a bird's-eye view of the whole oasis and the Jordan Valley below.

The Arabic name of the mountain, **Quruntul**, derives from the Latin *Mons Quaranta*, meaning Mountain of the Forty. This is what the Crusaders called it in commemoration of the forty days Jesus spent fasting here, when he was tempted by the Devil: 'If thou be the Son of God, command that these stones be made bread. But He answered and said, it is written, Man shall not live by bread alone . . .' (*Matthew 4:3–4*). The present monastery was built at the end of the last century around a crude cave chapel that marks the stone on which Jesus reputedly sat during the temptation. The spot is another of the holy sites said to have been identified by Queen Helena in her pilgrimage of 326AD. Other sources, however, date the place only as far back as the twelfth century; this throws into some doubt the claim that some of the gold leaf icons in the chapel at the southern end of the building are of Byzantine origin. The rest of the structure is taken up with monks' cells.

If you're looking for some exercise, then you may be able to persuade the site custodian to let you continue along the path (barred by a gate) to the summit for an even higher view of the Jordan Valley and south towards the Dead Sea. The uncompleted walls here are from an unsuccessful attempt to build a church in 1874. A fortress known as **Doq** originally stood on the summit. Built by the Seleucids, who conquered Palestine in 198BC for a brief period, it was later taken over by the Hasmoneans (134BC). It was here that the Hasmonean leader, Simon Maccabaeus, was murdered by his son-in-law Ptolemy in yet another internecine power struggle.

Na'aran

About four kilometres northwest of Jericho are the remains of the Byzantine settlement of **Na'ran**. Here, a fifth century BC synagogue was excavated in 1918. Its elaborate and well-preserved mosaic floor includes commemorative inscriptions, geometrical designs containing flora and fauna and a zodiac.

Na'aran is situated by the springs of Ein Duyuk and Ein Nuwaiyymeh. The route of the aqueduct that brought water to Hisham's Palace can still be traced. The most impressive remnant is the fine arch spanning the *wadi* close to the springs, which is still in use today.

Tulul Abu Alayiq

At the entrance to Wadi Qelt, about 2km southwest of Jericho along the dirt road, is the Jericho of the Hasmoneans and later of Herod who constructed his winter palaces here.

Partly as a result of squabbling with the Hasmonean side of his family and partly as a result of Cleopatra's territorial aspirations, **Herod** was obliged to rent the estates of Jericho from the Egyptian queen, despite the fact that they formed part of his newly won kingdom. His mother-in-law, Alexandra, found favour with Cleopatra and consequently, in 35BC, Herod was forced to replace his candidate for the high priesthood with Alexandra's son, his brother-in-law, Aristobulus. A year later Herod had the unfortunate brother-in-law brought to Jericho and drowned in a swimming pool.

By 34BC, Mark Anthony's military campaigns were failing, and with the demise of the lovers' alliance in 30BC, the lands around Jericho reverted to Herod. At the beginning of his reign, Herod built a small residence where, according to the Roman Historian Josephus, he spent his final days in a state described as melancholy mad. After Herod's death, his slave Simeon supposedly burnt the palace to the ground, though there is no archaeological evidence to support either this or the reconstruction that Josephus attributed to Herod's son Archelaus.

Access to **the site** is not controlled, which means that it has suffered more than usual from the elements and from scavengers. A shortage of paths and signs means making the best you can of a scramble over assorted mounds of earth. Adjacent to the road, and not particularly well defined, is the outline of Herod's earlier palace, but the most interesting remains are 100m further north. The depression here once enclosed an ornate sunken garden fronted by a grand facade with narrow colonnades at either end. To the right, a large open area is thought to have been an artificial **pool**, which served to keep the whole place cool. A bridge, small portions of which can be seen on the northern bank, crossed the wadi and led to the main living quarters, a reception hall and the obligatory bath house. The frigidarium is the best preserved part of the complex. Unfortunately, much of the construction was in mud brick, which does not weather the passage of time too well.

To the northwest are the remains of the **Hasmonean Palace** which Herod incorporated into his later design. The Hasmonean foundations supported storerooms, a small villa and a *mikveh* (ritual bath), all surrounding the swimming pool where Herod may have drowned his brother-in-law. The water supply from Ein Duyuk was here supplemented by two additional aqueducts from the perennial springs within Wadi Qelt.

A short walk southwest along the ancient Jerusalem–Jericho road brings you to a strategic conical hill, **Tel al-Aqaba**, on the summit of which are the remains of another fortress built by Herod, which he named **Kypros** after his mother. He fortified the previous structure here and added the bath house which was supplied by cisterns from Ein Qilt. The fortress was used by the Zealots in the First Revolt against Rome (66AD), but the square building which you now see at the centre dates from the later Byzantine period. As the area is now used by the Israeli army, visits to the site must be arranged in advance with the military authorities.

East of Jericho: the Allenby Bridge

Four kilometres east of Jericho is the Palestinian-run **Boys Town Farm**, founded in 1951 to train refugee boys and orphans in farming skills. Its saline soil is treated with sweet water in order to support the dairy herds for which the farm is renowned. Milk and milk products from the farm are available in Jericho and in several shops in Jerusalem.

The main road east from Jericho to the **Allenby Bridge** over the Jordan river passes through a military zone and is only open to those who want to cross from or into Jordan and who hold permits to allow them to do so (see *Basics*). The checkpoint on the bridge (known as the King Hussein Bridge to all but the Israelis) serves as a reminder that Jordan and Israel are in an official state of war.

A couple of kilometres south of the bridge is the site where John the Baptist baptised Jesus in the Jordan River (*Matthew 3:13–17*). Formerly popular with pilgrims who came at the Feast of Epiphany to immerse themselves in the water, the site of the **Baptism of Jesus**, known as **al-Maghtes**, is now closed to visitors for military reasons. Several alternative sites are now used, above all one to the north, near to where the Jordan flows out of the Sea of Galilee.

travel details

The simplest way to visit towns and sites on the West Bank is from Jerusalem. Buses and *service* taxis are frequent, although all public transport may be disrupted by the *intifada*. Arab buses leave from either the Damascus Gate bus station or Nablus Road, Egged buses from the central bus station in Jaffa Road.

Driving

At present it is inadvisable to travel through the West Bank in a car with Israeli (yellow) number plates; even hire cars, distinguished by the green surround on the number plate, risk being stoned. If you want to hire a car with a blue West Bank number plate, there are a couple of firms on the ourskirts of Ramallah that may be able to help. For details, ask at any East Jerusalem travel agency.

Buses
From Damascus Gate

Bethlehem (every 15min; 30min); Hebron (10min; 1hr); Jericho (20min; 40min); Bethany (30min; 10min).

From Nablus Road

Ramallah (every 15min; 35min); Nablus (30min; 1hr 30min); Beit Hanina (15 min; 15min).

From Egged bus station

Hebron (every 30min 6am–8.30pm; 1hr) and Jericho (12 daily; 40min).

Service taxis

Service taxis to Bethlehem, Hebron, Jericho, Ramallah, Nablus and Gaza all leave from Prophets' Street near Damascus Gate whenever there are enough passengers.

CHAPTER THREE

TEL AVIV AND THE SOUTH COAST

Tel Aviv and its suburbs are home to almost a third of Israel's population. It's big: a sprawling modern city that is distinctly Israeli, its buildings jostling each other as if gasping for air. It's frenetic: the traffic jams on the roads and human crush on the pavements are unrelenting. It's brash, tacky and expensive. And at night it's loud and pushy. The sandy beaches, high-rise hotels and nightlife are packed with tourists washed up by package-tour hotel deals or visiting relatives on the coastal plain, and by Israelis on business or escaping the strictures of life elsewhere. As the financial, business, sporting and entertainment centre of the country, the city is endlessly on the move and has a remarkable ability to sap one's energy and patience.

Tel Avivians tend to sneer at Jerusalemites, incredulous that anyone could possibly prefer the conservativism and restrictions of the hill city to the pacy seaside sprawl. And if it has a saving grace it is that Tel Aviv raises a very tentative two fingers at the burgeoning religiosity and parochialism of the rest of Israel. While others sit around lighting candles on Fridays, Tel Aviv's Israeli population heads for the beach, the bar or the movies. If you start to OD on history and religion, then count your cash and give it a whirl.

Less than 2km south, the ancient town of **Jaffa** has managed to retain something of its ancient past, despite the ever increasing encroachment of the 'big city'. Although officially within the municipal boundaries of Tel Aviv, Jaffa is undeniably separate, not least because it is predominantly an Arab-Palestinian town with its own history, architecture and culture. There's a small working port, some attractive churches and mosques, a popular if somewhat touristy flea/antique market and some great restaurants. All of this is fighting a losing battle against development into chic boutiques, pretentious art galleries and expensive studio apartments, but for the moment it remains a great deal more attractive than Tel Aviv proper.

The communities which surround the conurbation are largely soulless dormitories for commuters into the city – about one million people travel through Tel Aviv's central bus station every day! **Ramat Gan, Petah Tikva** and **Rehovot** were established by European settlers in the late nineteenth and early twentieth centuries, but the ubiquitous three- and four-storey *shiku-nim* (communally run apartment blocks) thrown up wholesale all over the country since the 1950s have rendered them barely distinguishable from

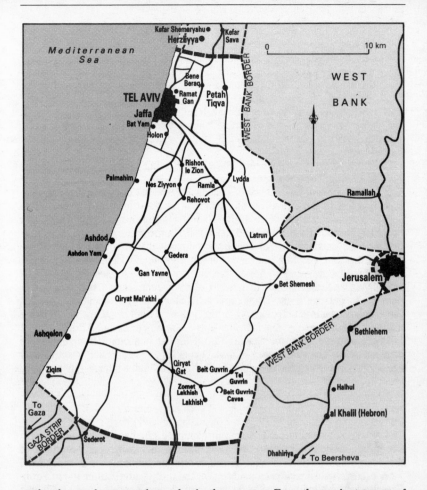

Mediterranean Sea

Kefar Shemaryahu • Kefar
Herzliyya • Sava

WEST BANK BORDER

WEST BANK

0   10 km

Bene
Beraq
TEL AVIV • Ramat   Petah
Gan   Tiqva
Jaffa •
Bat Yam •
Holon •

Rishon
le Zion
Palmahim •   Ramla   Lydda •
Nes Ziyyon •
Rehovot •

Latrun •

Ashdod •
Ashdon Yam •   Gedera •

Gan Yavne •   Bet Shemesh •

Ramallah •

Jerusalem

Qiryat Mal'akhi •

Ashqelon •   Bethlehem •

Ziqim •   Qiryat   Beit Guvrin •
Gat •   Tel
Zomet   Guvrin •
Lakhish •   Beit Guvrin
Lakhish •   Caves   Halhul •

To
Gaza   al Khalil (Hebron) •
GAZA STRIP BORDER
Sederot •

Dhahiriya • ← To Beersheva

WEST BANK BORDER

each other or from anywhere else in the country. Even the ancient towns of
Ramla and **Lydda** have had most traces of their important histories
ploughed under for *shikunim*. The sole consolation is a public transport
system which is efficient and cheap: it's easy to get to these places, equally
straightforward to leave again.

The **coast** south of Tel Aviv has similarly little to recommend it. Virtually all
pre-1948 habitation has been destroyed to make way for a couple of industrial
cities and a smattering of moshavim and kibbutzim: although the coastline
itself is attractive and for the most part undeveloped, the absence of important
biblical or historic sites keeps the area off most travellers' itineraries.
Accommodation is minimal and public transport, except between the main
towns, infrequent. If you're flush you can hire a car, but your money would be
probably better spent on travelling through the Negev Desert or in the north.

As you head down the coast there's nothing but sea to keep you busy until **Ashdod** and **Ashqelon**. The odd minaret or ruined building, standing as testimony to villages which have been wiped off the map, serve only to give the boredom a sinister edge. On the beaches there's a small surfing scene around **Palmachim**, and the ruins of the ancient port of **Jabneh** just to the south. **Ashdod**, the largest city on the coast, is a working port and naval base with virtually nothing to offer. **Ashqelon**, on the other hand, has a long history (as Asqalan), traces of which can still be seen. There are some good beaches, which are beginning to be exploited as a resort, but not much in the way of cheap accommodation.

Inland in the south, the **Ono Plain** is fertile but entirely missable. Apart from the usual kibbutzim and moshavim, the few small development towns such as **Qiryat Gat** have an air of depressing stagnation: there's nowhere to stay, nothing to do, and even the people who live there look permanently bored. The sole exception is **Beit Guvrin** (Beit Jibrin), whose ruins and caves are perhaps the least visited tourist site in the country.

If you are heading for Tel Aviv or the coastal plain in July or August, be warned that the **weather** can be extremely wearing. With upwards of 75 per cent humidity, the sticky climate can turn even the simplest tasks into an ordeal, make the dust and dirt seem even grimier than usual and cause tempers to get distinctly frayed. Frequent showers offer some respite, but there doesn't seem much point when you can never get dry. Unless you enjoy this sort of climate – or can afford to stay in an air-conditioned hotel – avoid Tel Aviv completely in the heatspells during the summer. Those extra five degrees of warmth can, however, make even Tel Aviv attractive when viewed from the freezing heights of Jerusalem in the middle of winter.

TEL AVIV

TEL AVIV is probably unique among Mediterranean cities in that its main streets are laid out parallel to the coast. This means that cooling breezes off the sea go absolutely nowhere. The modern city fathers have compounded their predecessors' lack of consideration for the Middle Eastern climate by allowing international chains to throw up multi-storey hotels all along the sea front. Now the early evening winds barely get beyond the first couple of streets, leaving the place as unbearable at night as it is during the day.

The reason for this original approach to city planning lies in Tel Aviv's history as the first Zionist city. The settlers came to Jaffa, Palestine's main port and pre-eminent town, and didn't like it. They also recognised that expansion was going to be essential if large numbers of Jewish immigrants were to be quickly absorbed. Looking around they saw that the dunes to the north were their only option. Farmers were not going to sell useful land to them and those that might would demand too high a price. So the main streets of the new town ran like tentacles starting in Jaffa and moving north. Once the process started nothing could stop it, and the first multi-occupancy, live-in sauna was born.

The city's rapid **expansion** (it was founded in 1909) followed the early successes of the Zionists. It was the centre of the *Yishuv* and housed the offices of the Jewish Agency and Jewish National Fund. New businesses established by incoming Europeans opened up here and the political, intellectual and artistic elites argued the toss in the cafés and restaurants. The British garrison found a home from home in Tel Aviv and the city's future was assured. By 1948, the city had grown to some 230,000 inhabitants, the vast majority of whom were new immigrants. In Hebrew, Tel Aviv means '**the hill of the spring**'; this was the name given to the Hebrew translation of Theodore Herzl's book *Altneuland* (Old-New Land) in which he sketched his vision of a Jewish State. In the book of *Ezekiel*, Tel Aviv was the place where the prophet had a vision of a collection of dry bones coming back to life on their return to *Eretz Yisrael*.

It was here, from Independence House on Rothschild Boulevard, that the declaration of the establishment of the **state of Israel** was proclaimed on May 15 1948 by the 'Provisional Government of Israel': Tel Aviv was the first capital. The move to Jerusalem was made in 1949, much to the chagrin of top level bureaucrats who had established themselves on the coast and didn't fancy the move uphill to a backwater. But Tel Aviv is still the centre of diplomatic activity – very few countries recognise Jerusalem as Israel's capital – and virtually every ambassador has stayed on the coast along with the defence ministry and the centres of Israel's fashion, commercial, culture and entertainment industries.

While the official histories still claim that Tel Aviv was built on 'uninhabited sand dunes', it soon started encroaching on **village land**. When the Palestinian inhabitants of Salama, Abu Kabir, Manshiyya, Sumayyil (Mas'udiyya), Jasmin, Sheikh Mu'annis and Jarrish were forced out during the 1948 war, Tel Aviv grew to cover them. Most were destroyed as developers moved in, but some parts can still be identified. The *Hilton Hotel* and neighbouring Independence Park were, for example, built over a Muslim cemetery; the headquarters of the *Histadrut* (Israeli Workers' Company and Trade Union Federation) are built on the lands of Sumayyil village; and the Arab architecture in the famous *Carmel Market* bears witness to its origins. Tel Aviv University was constructed over the land of Sheikh Mu'annis, and some of the original homes can be seen behind the campus. The few Palestinian students admitted have named their student paper *The Voice of Sheikh Mu'annis*.

Orientation

Tel Aviv is the hub of a vast urban sprawl which stretches down the coast from Herzliya to Rehovot. Like any big city it is initially intimidating. Most of what you'll want to see, however, falls within a small area bounded on the west by the Mediterranean, the east by **Ibn Gvirol Street**, the north by the **Yarkon River**, and the south by the **Central Bus Station**. Four streets just inland from the beach – **Allenby**, **Ben Yehuda**, **HaYarkon** and **Dizengoff** –

contain the majority of hostels, hotels, restaurants, airline offices and other everyday needs. Only the museums and a few of the embassies lie outside this area and these are all easily reached by public transport. Sandy **beaches** spread in front of the whole city centre, the main area bordered by Jaffa in the south, and the Marina and the large hotels in the north.

Buses and the Central Bus Station

The best way of getting about the city is by **bus**. A well developed network extends across Tel Aviv – the system runs from approximately 6am to midnight with a flat fare of $0.45 within the city – and with buses both frequent and reliable the only problem is coming to grips with their routes. The *Dan Transport Co-operative*, which runs the city's bus service, issues an excellent but infrequently available map. Get one from the **information kiosk** inside the central bus station or hassle them for the gen you need. Most routes run from one soulless suburb to another.

The **Central Bus Station**, not quite as central as the name implies, is the starting point for most city bus routes as well as for long distance services. You're probably going to spend quite a lot of time hanging around here, so you might as well get used to this, the most under-rated of Israeli tourist spots! The buses have long since burst the boundaries of the small bus station to cram every available space in all the surrounding streets. Pedestrian crossings are non-existent and all the roads around are a melee of kamikaze *sherut* drivers, buses apparently in the control of homicidal maniacs, and pedestrians – all vying for the few metres of tarmac between parked vehicles and street stalls.

The buses bring hundreds of thousands of customers a day to what has become one of the liveliest, and cheapest, **shopping** areas in the country. Hole-in-the-wall shops and street hawkers will get you anything from shirts to

BUSES IN CENTRAL TEL AVIV

#4 Central Bus Station, Allenby, Ben Yehuda; parallel to the coast.

#5 Central Bus Station, Allenby, Rothschild, Dizengoff, Nordau, Yehuda HaMaccabi (IYHA Hostel).

#10 City Hall via HaYarkon to Jaffa and Bat Yam; inwards via Ben Yehuda.

#25 Bat Yam through Jaffa, HaMelekh George, Shlomo HaMelekh, Ha'aretz Museum, Beit Hatefutsot (Diaspora Museum) to Tel Aviv University along Haifa Road.

#27 Central Bus Station, Petah Tikva Rd, Haifa Rd, HaAretz Museum, Tel Aviv University.

Routes **#4** and **#5** run almost continuously, and the others every 10 to 15 minutes throughout the day. Inter-city buses also run from the Central Bus Station – for information about these see "Travel details" at the end of this chapter.

An extra bonus for travel in the city centre are the taxi-like 9-seater **minibuses** which follow the #4 bus route, from the Central Bus Station along Allenby to the end of Ben Yehuda. A little more expensive than the buses, they have the distinct advantage that they can be stopped anywhere on these two roads and are a fast and convenient way of getting about the centre of the city.

sounds. The *falafel* are renowned, the nuts, seeds and other munchies good and cheap, and the down-to-earth cafés will supply a good copy of an Eastern European cake and great coffee. In recent years the central bus station bill of fare has expanded. Check out the sidestreets for pizzas, other varieties of oven-baked breads, stickier cakes and even the odd hamburger bar. There's a bustling fruit and vegetable market on the edge of the bus zone and several old-fashioned general stores where you can get groceries and other essentials. All of this makes the area – love it or hate it – one of the most vibrant places to hang out in Tel Aviv – which probably says more about the rest of the city than it does the bus station.

Of course, like most places in Israel, there's a story behind the story. As you leave Tel Aviv for Jerusalem you'll pass under a raised roadway. If you follow this round you'll discover that it comes to a dead halt in the middle of a residential area. This is all that exists of the modern bus station Tel Aviv has been promised for decades, halted abruptly by the bankruptcy of the construction company amid accusations of mismanagement and corruption. Meanwhile the bedlam around the bus station reaches new crescendos. If they ever do finish the new one, travel via Tel Aviv will only be marginally less stressful and thousands of great hustlers will be thrown onto the scrap-heap much to the detriment of the national image.

Taxis and trains

The **taxis** which patrol the city all day and all night are also a convenient way of getting about if you're stuck or in a rush. They're especially cheap if there's a group of you, and if you succeed in getting the meter switched on. If the driver refuses, you have the choice of accepting his price or getting another taxi – threats to report him to the police or the Israel Government Tourist Office are usually just laughed off. In Tel Aviv, the Israeli taxi driver has developed his (it's always his) lunatic art and reputation to its highest (or lowest) point.

There are two **railway stations** in Tel Aviv. The main **Central Railway Station**, adjacent to Haifa Rd, serves Jerusalem, Haifa and the north; the **Southern Railway Station** on Kibbutz Galuyot Street has only very occasional services to and from Jerusalem. See "Travel Details" on p.241.

Accommodation

Staying in Jaffa is arguably more pleasant, but Tel Aviv is handier, with dozens of **hostels** and **hotels** of widely varying price and quality. Only in July and August are you likely to encounter any difficulty finding a room: during these months the more popular hostels usually fill up by mid-afternoon. If you'll be arriving reasonably early then it's worth trying to book a room, but few if any of the hostels will hold a booking after 6pm.

Tel Aviv's hostels are slightly more expensive than those in Jerusalem or Eilat, but are also noticeably cleaner. Most of them offer mainly dormitory accommodation, but many of the hostels listed below also have single and double beds at a higher price. For a bed in a hostel you should expect to pay $4–8 a night, for a budget hotel room $20 for a double, $10–15 for a single.

The biggest cluster of hostels and cheap hotels is around the junction of **Allenby** and **Ben Yehuda** streets and below this junction towards the sea on **HaYarkon Street**. This area is also the main red-light district and therefore pretty seedy and – especially for women – unpleasant. Plans are slowly being executed to transform the area into a giant pedestrianised piazza, and when completed this will presumably drive the prostitutes out to other areas and reduce the considerable noise in the evenings. In the meantime, there are other hostels in central locations which tend to be safer and cleaner.

Sleeping on the beach in Tel Aviv is not recommended as muggings, thefts and harassment are alarmingly common. From the regularity of the thefts it would seem that a well organised gang patrols the beach for unsuspecting travellers. If you are really desperate, try to get to a beach as far north as you can – even the beach by the junction of Ben Yehuda and Dizengoff is a better option than the main Tel Aviv beach. The other alternative is the parks, of which HaYarkon Park is probably the best bet. People do also sleep in HaAtzma'ut Park (a gay cruising ground), but stories of harassment become more frequent.

If you arrive in Tel Aviv at the Central Bus Station with a back-pack and looking lost, you'll almost certainly be pestered by people offering accommodation and handing out leaflets. Their claims should be treated with a healthy degree of scepticism, since the better hostels don't usually need advertise in this manner.

The following are just some of the better places.

Hostels

The Greenhouse (201 Dizengoff St; ☎03-235994). Probably the best known and most popular of Tel Aviv's hostels. Very clean (almost too much so), pleasant rooms, nice rooftop bar, safe and well run. Beds from $7, single and double rooms also available, advance booking essential in the height of summer.

Hotel Yosef (15 Bograshov St; ☎03-280955). Clean – apart from the graffiti on the walls – friendly and informal. Popular with long-term travellers. Details of work opportunities available. Dormitory beds $5, space on the roof $3. Strict 1am curfew and male/female room arrangements.

The Top Hostel (84 Ben Yehuda St; ☎03-237807). Another popular hostel with excellent rooftop bar. Clean, friendly and informal. Dormitory beds $5. Strict 1am curfew.

The Gordon (corner Gordon St and HaYarkon; ☎03-22987). One of Tel Aviv's better hostels down by the beach, with clean, spacious rooms overlooking the sea. Dormitory beds $5. Cheap charter tickets to London or Egypt sold here.

Bnei Dan Youth Hostel (32 Bnei Dan St; ☎03-455042). Not central but clean, safe and air-conditioned. Rather strictly run. Bed and breakfast $9. To get there take bus #5.

Open Door Hostel (21 Trumpeldor St; ☎03-289445). Small, popular hostel with garden bar, laundry facilities ($3.20) and no curfew or getting up time. Dormitory beds $5.

Hotel Riviera (52 HaYarkon St; ☎03-656870). $6 for B&B in a ramshackle dormitory. Lively bar at the bottom of the building. Also a selection of doubles from $16 upwards.

Sandi Hotel (15 Allenby St; ☎03-653889). From $6. Watch out for the life-size model of a traveller at the entrance. Popular haunt of local 'working girls'.

The Hostel (60 Ben Yehuda St; ☎03-287088). Recent new owners intend to try and shake former bad reputation. A bit claustrophobic, but clean and central. Dormitory beds from $5, $16 for a double.

The Home (20 Alsheikh St, access from Allenby St; ☎03-656736). Neither clean nor particularly safe, this relic from the Sixties may appeal to the seasoned traveller. Policy of always finding space makes it a good option if the other hostels are full. Dormitory bed $4, floorspace $2.50

Hotel Galim (9 Allenby St; ☎03-655703). Dirty, dusty and downtrodden. Not surprisingly the place often has room, a good option if you're desperate.

Mash House (4 Trumpeldor St; ☎03-657684). Opposite the beach, offers cheap rooms and small apartments. Singles from $8, doubles $14, apartments from $22.

Cheap Hotels

If you're intending to book into a two- or three-star hotel for a few nights, you can often get cheaper rates, especially in the summer, by booking through a travel agent (see Listings). Below are some of the less fancy places.

Migdal David Hotel (8 Allenby St; ☎03-656392). Newly refurbished, the rooms are pleasant and the hotel staff friendly. Singles $20, doubles $28 including breakfast.

Ora Hotel (35 Ben Yehuda; ☎03-650941). Singles $23, double $32.

Dizengoff Square Hotel (2 Zamenhof St, just off Dizengoff Square; ☎03-296181). Often have special rates from $24 single, double $35.

Monopol Hotel (4 Allenby St; ☎03-657599). From $10 for a single room. Pretty average accommodation, but safe, clean and well situated.

Hotel Eilat (58 HaYarkon; ☎03-965368). Not particularly good value, and the hotel's religious air won't suit everyone. Singles $20, doubles $25.

Hotel Tamar (8 Gnessin St; ☎03-286997). Quiet area close to Dizengoff St. Singles from $10, doubles from $15.

The City

If you want to explore Tel Aviv then **Dizengoff Square**, at the southern end of Dizengoff Street, is as good a place as any to get a feel of the city. The area, *the* place to hang out between bars or before cinema performances, is a maze of pedestrian walkways which converge on a circular platform built above the traffic. It's also the centre for street musicians and entertainers – if you're thinking of busking yourself, this and Dizengoff Street itself are the best places. Bang in the middle of the square is an avant-garde, hi-tech water sculpture designed by Yaacov Agam – a leading Israeli artist. It is programmed to operate to music and like Dizengoff it's commercial, brightly lit and often broken down. The full 20-minute show takes place on the hour every hour except at 2 and 3pm. If you're bored and in the area, stick around and watch it.

Running north from the square, **Dizengoff Street** is a solid phalanx of cafés, restaurants and bars, broken only by stores selling clothes or expensive kitsch. Everybody in Tel Aviv seems to gravitate here, and strolling up and down is an entertainment in itself. For a good insight into Tel Aviv life park yourself in a street café and join the spectators in the parade of life.

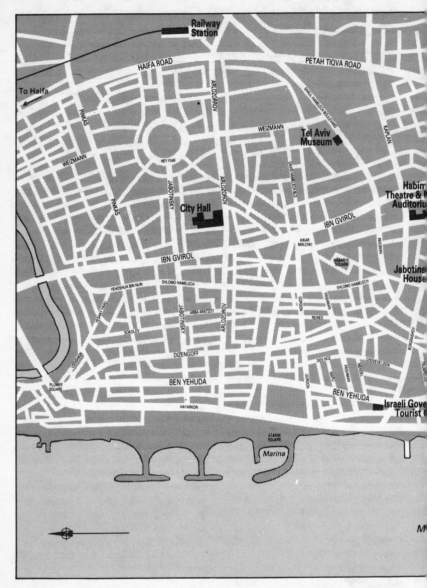

One block towards the beach, **Ben Yehuda Street** has a more conservative air. The restaurants are not quite so pretentious and are slightly cheaper
than those on Dizengoff, the atmosphere less frenetic and the people slightly
more sombre. Most of the major **airlines** have their offices on Ben Yehuda

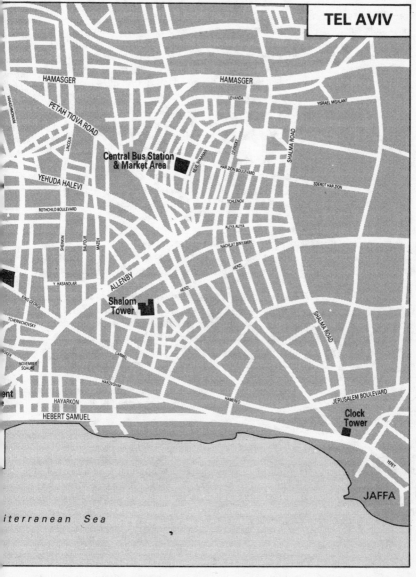

TEL AVIV

HAMASGER
HAMASGER
PETAH TIQVA ROAD
LEVANDA
YISRAEL MISALANT
HAMASGER/ALMA
LINCOLN
SHALMA ROAD
Central Bus Station
& Market Area
YEHUDA HALEVI
BER SHAMMAI
HAR ZION BOULEVARD
SDEROT HAR ZION
ROTHSCHILD BOULEVARD
LEVINSKY
TCHLENOV
SHENKIN
BALFOUR
MAZEH
ALIYA ALIYA
NACHLAT BINYAMIN
ALLENBY
HERZL
Shalom
Tower
Y. HASANDLAR
KING GEORGE
SHALMA ROAD
TCHERNICHOVSKY
CARMEL
HAKOVSHIM
NOVEMBER
SQAURE
ent
HAYARKON
HAMERED
JERUSALEM BOULEVARD
HEBERT SAMUEL
Clock
Tower
YEFET
JAFFA
iterranean Sea

and there are also a number of cheap **travel agents** which specialise in tickets for Europe-bound charters and cut price excursions to Egypt (see "Listings"). **Gordon Street**, which runs between Dizengoff and Ben Yehuda, boasts a number of up-market art galleries selling the work of contemporary

Jewish artists – both local and international – which are pleasant to browse around. Unless you're absolutely loaded you won't need the chequebook.

Further west, **HaYarkon Street** runs parallel to the beach, lined with flashy hotels. The *Sheraton* and the *Hilton* are the biggest, but with new rivals going up all the time the street often looks like a giant building site. You're unlikely to want to stay here, but the bars and cafés are no more expensive in the top hotels than on Dizengoff, and the plush upholstery makes a pleasant change from expanded plastic. Between the big hotels you can still find a number of older, boarding-house-style places as well as several car hire agencies, embassies and travel agents.

Kikar Namir is a dual level plaza in the shadow of the *Marina Hotel* on HaYarkon. With dozens of bars, restaurants and nightclubs within a minute or two's walk of each other, it's a hive of nocturnal activity, the places vying for custom with video screens showing the latest films and some good music videos. Many of them are enjoyable – but more so if someone else is paying.

Down below Kikar Namir is the Tel Aviv **Marina**. The haunt of the rich and famous, the marina is mostly off-bounds to the inquisitive tourist, but in any case it's little different from others on the Mediterranean. In the centre is an extremely popular fresh-water **swimming pool** (open every day, $5) with a large water slide. The marina is also the place to head if you fancy windsurfing, sailing or diving: several outfits offer tuition and equipment hire, again expensive.

At the end of HaYarkon, where the city's main thoroughfares meet, is the misnamed and shabby-looking **'Old Port'** area. Built only in 1936, it has long been abandoned by shipping, virtually all of which now uses the port of Ashdod, further south. Behind the Old Port, where HaYarkon, Ben Yehuda and Dizengoff meet, is the area known as **'Little Tel Aviv'**. Once the city's 'alternative' scene, with the requisite complement of artists and hangers-on, it has become wealthy and conventional, packed with high-priced restaurants and elegant offices. Nevertheless it has a pleasant feel, somewhat less tacky than the southern end of Dizengoff. Again, there are scores of bars, restaurants and clubs in this small area.

City Hall, at the side of a wide expanse of concrete known as *Kikar Malkhei Yisrael*, marks the old centre of Tel Aviv. An area which has become more fashionable over the last decade, the square is where most of the political rallies in the city are held. In 1982 almost 400,000 people – ten per cent of the population – gathered here to protest Israeli involvement in the Phalangist massacre of Palestinians in the Sabra and Shatilla refugee camps in Lebanon.

Following **King George Street** south from City Hall you pass the flashy shopping malls of the **Dizengoff Centre** on your right. Here you'll pay through the nose for goods which can easily be purchased cheaper in other parts of the city. Further down is **Jabotinsky House**, a high-rise block of offices that houses the *Jabotinsky Institute*, an organisation dedicated to preserving the memory of the early right-wing Zionist whose ideology spawned a number of anti-Arab terror groups and the philosophy which claims both sides of the Jordan River for the state of Israel. The current Israeli Prime Minister, Shamir, is a follower.

Magen David Square, another popular meeting place, is further along King George. On **Shenkin Street**, the first on your left, you can buy almost anything from books to wholefood. *Twentieth Century Books* is Tel Aviv's only left-wing bookstore – solidarity alone should take you there. You can also pick up (more) art and antiques in other stores, or for the historically-minded a stop at *Café Tamar* is obligatory. This used to be the hang-out of Israeli Labour Party hacks and assorted intellectuals and leftists in the days before a combination of TV and the lurch to the right took its toll. The café, though, right opposite the offices of *Davar*, the *Histadrut* newspaper, is still a meeting place for some segments of the Israeli left.

At the beginning of Shenkin Street lies **Shuq HaCarmel**, Tel Aviv's main market. A rich cacophony of styles, colours, cultures and traditions, its contents range from Eastern European delicatessens, household goods stalls, T-shirts, and cheap cassettes, to a vast assortment of fruit and vegetables and live fish and chickens. Most of the stalls are run by Palestinians from Jaffa, giving the market a Middle Eastern atmosphere, but also making it a focus for anti-Arab violence when trouble is in the air. Open Sunday to Thursday from sunrise to sunset, and on Fridays until late afternoon, the market has a tumultuous atmosphere similar to that of the bus station. Many of the best food bargains can be had late on Friday afternoon, just before the market shuts down for *shabbat*.

Just next to the entrance to *Shuq HaCarmel*, on pedestrianised **Nahalat Benyamin**, are a number of pleasant open-air cafés. Nahalat Benyamin, too, is an enjoyable place to stroll, safe for once from the terrors of Tel Aviv traffic. The shops are rather conservative and expensive, and a short way down are a couple of impressive-looking buildings with ornate balconies, wooden shutters and leaded and stained glass windows. These are dilapidated remnants of Tel Aviv's early architectural heritage – in most places they'd have preservation orders slapped all over them; here they are rapidly being replaced by the bland, low-rise blocks which pervade the country.

To the west of the market is **Kerem HaTeymanim**, the Yemenite Quarter, a characterful maze of narrow lanes and cramped buildings, with a collection of good cafés scattered among them. A little further south, **Neve Zedek** became in 1897 the first area to be settled by former Jewish residents of Jaffa. Its Arab-style houses, built almost on top of each other, went out of fashion for a while, but nowadays those which survived have become expensive again, and many have been renovated by artists and Israeli yuppies, transforming the whole area into a fashionable **artists' quarter**. The *Neve Tzedek Theatre* has an excellent and deserved reputation for experimental and avante-garde theatre (it was the first Israeli theatre to host a radical Palestinian production), and continues to stage cultural and musical events. If you're stuck in Tel Aviv for the evening you could do worse than check out their programme.

Nearby, the **Shalom Tower**, the tallest building in Israel, stands on the site of the *Herzliya Gymnasium* (High School) which was demolished to make way for the tower block in 1959. The only reminder of what was an impressive-looking building is a huge fresco by artist Nathan Gutman. For about $5 a lift will take you up to the 34th floor of the tower, where a café, observation point, and the best view in Tel Aviv await. At the base of the tower is a **wax museum**, devoted mainly to Israeli nationalist folk-history.

Allenby Street, which runs close by the Shalom Tower from the Central Bus Station to the beginning of Ben Yehuda, is the premier shopping street in Tel Aviv. Old photographs reveal a stylish, tree-lined boulevard, but today it's all rather drab, having been overshadowed by the brightly coloured multi-storey shopping centres which seem to be springing up everywhere. **Rothschild Boulevard**, by contrast, has managed to retain some of its Thirties charm, and an air of dignity somehow pervades its tree-lined pavements. At its northern end it converges on Kikar Habima where the **Habima Theatre**, the **Helena Rubinstein Pavilion** and the **Mann Auditorium** add a little cultural weight to an otherwise frivolous city.

Museums

Tel Aviv has a couple of genuinely interesting museums, and a series of exhibition centres and galleries masquerading as such. Most of them are primarily Zionist, so check out what you're going to see before you pay your money. They are, however, a good way to learn fast as the guides (human and literary) tend to be a lot more straightforward than the doublespeak of politicians and journalists.

Bet Hatefutsot (The Diaspora Museum)
(Tel Aviv University Campus, gate 2, Klausner Street, Ramat Aviv; Sun, Tues, Thur 10am–5pm, Wed 10am–noon, Sat 10am–2pm; no computer facilities on Sat, admission $2.50. Bus #6, 13, 24, 25 and 27.)
Not a museum in the strictest sense, but an assortment of maps, models, videos etc. which aim to illustrate the history of the Jews, their traditions, religion and settlement throughout the world. Particularly appealing is the massive **film library**, accessible via a personal video booth. From an introduction to the Hassidic way of life to an anthropological study of South American Jewry, there will probably be something to interest you. The museum has a replica of a synagogue and explains the origin of many Jewish traditions and religious practices. There is a computerised dictionary of Jewish family names through which you can trace your, or your friends', origins.
If you're pushed for time, the **Chronosphere**, a small domed theatre, provides a condensed view of the museum in slides and sound. Zealous guides are available if you have the numbers to form a group.

Ha'aretz Museum (also known as the Eretz Israel Museum)
(University Street; Sun–Thur 9am–4pm, Fri 9am–1pm, Sat 10am–2pm, admission $1.50, free on Sat.)
If you feel more at home in conventional museums then the Ha'aretz is for you – although again the wealth of exhibits is too much to cope with in one day. It's an ambitious and varied project, with the main museum acting as an umbrella for a number of smaller specialist collections. The most important of these is the **Glass Museum**, the circular green building at the top of the hill. As well as containing one of the finest collections of ancient glassware in the world, the museum also covers the history of glass-making from its

origins to the present day. **Other museums** within the complex are devoted to numismatics, folklore and ethnography, ceramics, the alphabet and the relics of the copper mines at Timna housed in the **Nechustan Pavilion**.

Adjacent to the complex is **TEL QASILA**, one of the few archaeological sites to have been preserved in Tel Aviv. Excavations have revealed evidence of occupation in the area for the past 3000 years, although the only substantial remains are the outlines of two **Philistine temples** from the twelfth century BC. Some scholars also believe there is evidence to suggest that this could have been the site of ancient Jaffa, or at least its port in the pre-Christian era.

The Tel Aviv Museum
(27 Sha'ul HaMelekh St; Sun–Thur 10am–10pm, Sat 10am–2pm and 7–10pm, admission $2.50).

An impressive collection of Impressionist and post-Impressionist artworks as well as permanent and temporary exhibitions of Israeli and Jewish artists and sculptors. The admission ticket to the museum also covers an annexe in the **Helena Rubinstein Pavilion** (6 Tarsat Boulevard). The museum's diary of events lists exhibitions, concerts, films, plays and dance programmes which are among the cheapest in an expensive city.

Hagannah Museum
(23 Rothschild Boulevard; Sun–Thur 9am–3pm, Fri 9am–12.30pm, admission $1.50, students $0.75).

Traces the development and military prowess of the pre-state Zionist militia of that name. After the creation of the state of Israel the *Hagannah* became the Israeli Defence Forces (IDF). An uncritical display of thousands of guns, mortars, hand grenades and more.

The Museum of the History of Tel Aviv-Jaffa
(27 Bialik St; Sun–Thur 9am–1pm).

A collection of photographs and documents tracing the brief history of Tel Aviv. The building itself, a wonderful 1930s structure, overlooks a dilapidated square which could be part of a set from a Hollywood film studio – actually it was Tel Aviv's first Town Hall – and is at least as interesting as the contents.

Independence House
(16 Rothschild Boulevard; Sun–Fri 9am–1pm, admission $2, students $1).

This is where the declaration of the establishment of the state of Israel was made on Friday May 14, 1948. The building, which was then used as the *Voice of Israel* radio HQ and the mint, has been converted into a giant memorial to this event. There are copies of the declaration on sale.

The Jabotinsky Institute
(38 King George St; Sun, Tue and Thur 10am–6pm, Mon and Wed 10am–1pm 6–8pm, Fri 10am–1pm).

Museum dedicated to the memory of Vladimir Jabotinsky (see *Jabotinsky Institute* above).

Beit Bialik Museum
(22 Bialik St; Sun–Thur 9am–7pm, Fri 9am–1pm).

This museum in the former home of the Israeli poet Haim Nacham Bialik has an exhibition of his books and writings.

Ben Gurion House
(17 David Ben Gurion Street; Sun–Thur 8am–2pm, Fri 8am–1pm; entrance free.)
The house of the former Israeli Prime Minister, David Ben Gurion, contains many of his possessions including his 20,000-volume library. A hagiographic film, *The Life of Ben Gurion*, is shown from Sunday to Thursday at 10am, 11am, noon and 1pm.

Etzel Museum
(Herbert Samuel Street, just before Jaffa).
The building itself, a well designed hi-tech structure inside an old Palestinian building, is the most interesting part of this museum. Yet another glorification of the 1948 war (*Etzel* was a right-wing guerilla group), replete with guns, mortars and scenes such as 'war hero having surgery on the battle f ield'.

Parks and beaches

When the concrete jungle starts to get too much, Tel Aviv offers a couple of parks a short bus ride north of the Yarkon River where you can remind yourself what greenery looks like, and some vast stretches of beach where you can join a few thousand others trying to escape.

Although the **beaches** of Tel Aviv are one of the great attractions for Israelis – and the sunset is invariably wonderful – they are really pretty grubby, overcrowded (particularly so on Saturdays) and, with the craze for smashing balls around in the game of *matkot*, hazardous places. The main beach runs parallel to HaYarkon Street for almost all of the city's two-and-a-half mile seafront. On the main drag there's little to differentiate any one spot from any other, except perhaps whether or not there's an on-duty lifeguard. Much of this beach has breakwaters a few hundred metres out to sea: these stop the larger waves and mean that you have to go a long way out for deep water.

The area closer to Jaffa has a slightly more pleasant backdrop than the large hotels which dominate the northern area. Though not exactly deserted, the quietest beach in the city is the one just east of the junction of Ben Yehuda and Dizengoff St, behind the *Tal Hotel*. The person-per-sand grain ratio is probably no different to that of Tel Aviv's main beach, but the atmosphere is less frenetic. If even this is too urbanised for you, head north to HERZLIYA – the beach at the suburb of BAT YAM, south of Tel Aviv, is really no more than a microcosm of the big city itself. The best beach near Tel Aviv is at KEFAR SHMARIYAHU, a wealthy suburb just north of Herzliya, about a half-hour bus ride away.

Of the **parks**, the most peaceful and pleasant is **HaYarkon Park**, to the west of the main road to Haifa, which has regular open-air concerts in summer (details from the IGTO or *Jerusalem Post*) and a small lake to row around. Nearer to the city centre, another small park starts at the corner of Kibbutz Galuyot and Herzl streets. This is dominated by **Peter's Church** – a reminder of the once strong Christian community in Jaffa. Other green escapes include **HaAtzma'ut Park** near the Hilton Hotel on HaYarkon and the small **Jana Wiener Park** at 260-258 Dizengoff Street.

Eating

There are hundreds of cheap cafés and *falafel* stalls scattered liberally throughout Tel Aviv, and if you patronise these you can eat cheaply and well, albeit a little repetitively. Restaurants, on the other hand, tend to be expensive and, on the whole, disappointing.

There are **falafel stalls** all over the city, but they concentrate in three main areas. The streets surrounding the Central Bus Station are probably the first you will encounter. Always well patronised and pretty good value, the only drawback here is the clouds of exhaust fumes which envelop the whole area. A second cluster can be found around the intersection where Allenby meets Ben Yehuda Street. Here there are also a number of cheap cafés where you can have anything from a morning coffee and *bureka* to a Hungarian goulash. The real king of the Tel Aviv *falafel* scene, however, has to be the self-proclaimed *Falafel Market*. To get there walk westwards down Tchernykovsky from Allenby and then take the first turning on your right. There are four stalls to choose from, all vying for customers by offering free tasters, and all allowing you to serve yourself from vast trays of *falafel* balls and accompanying salads. With mountains of food these stalls are highly recommended – especially if you're very hungry. They close at midnight: similar stalls around Dizengoff Square can't compete on quality, but they do stay open until at least 2am, ready to catch those leaving the late-night films and clubs.

As for **restaurants**, again there are plenty of cheap ones to serve the day-to-day demands of the local populace, but they seem to change so rapidly that recommendations are difficult. It's easier simply to head for the right areas and check out the alternatives for yourself. First of these is the **Yemeni Quarter**, a maze of small streets just east of the *Shuq HaCarmel*, where you'll find popular cafés and five-star restaurants alongside each other. Among the more consistent of the cheaper options are the functional and popular *Zarim Restaurant* (28 Nahali'el St), *Zion Gamliel Restaurant* (12 Peduyim St), and for the adventurous diner the unnamed café at 22 HaKovshim St. **Little Tel Aviv** also has plenty of restaurants popular with local people, on the whole slightly more upmarket and certainly less traditional. Here you should be able to find home cooking pretty much regardless of where home is, with a choice which runs from *Me & Me* pizzas to *Red Chinese* (both at the northern end of Dizengoff).

Walking south down **Dizengoff Street**, the choice gets wider and the prices higher with every block. *Pirozki* (265 Dizengoff) is an expensive Russian restaurant, *The Cherry Tree* (166 Dizengoff) does some tasty spinach quiches, *Cantina Pizzeria Capri* (107 Dizengoff) is self-explanatory, *Acapulco* (corner Dizengoff and Frishman) is a snack bar with South American leanings and *Batya* (corner Arlosoroff and Dizengoff) sells a variety of Hungarian goulashes, blintzes and other snacks. For fans of Indian food with a little money to spare, *The Indian Tandoori* (2 Zamenhof St, below Dizengoff Square) is excellent.

While nearby **Allenby Street** has neither the density or diversity of restaurants offered by Dizengoff, it does have some which, like the street itself, tend to be slightly less pretentious. For real Jewish cooking try the excellent *TIV Restaurant* (130 Allenby St) where a three-course meal will cost less than $6. Nearby, *The Habira* (46 Allenby St) serves traditional Eastern European kosher cuisine at reasonable prices. Another good Eastern European restaurant is *Goulash Corner* (108 HaYarkon).

The other main cluster of restaurants is in **Kikar Namir**. With prime seats overlooking the sea and the marina, these open-air restaurants and cafés are fairly reasonably priced although the food can be bland. The one real bargain is the eat-as-much-as-you-can *Safari Restaurant*, a good option when you've reached *falafel* saturation. Next door, *Chinatown Express* is poor and over-priced, but there are dozens of alternatives.

Health food and **vegetarian** places are only very slowly making an impact in Tel Aviv, though there are of course kosher dairy restaurants, mostly in the suburbs. Of the genuine vegetarian restaurants, the best is *Naturalist* at 59 Ben Yehuda: not especially cheap, but a varied and imaginative menu – try the *mujadara*, an Arab dish of rice and lentils. *Eternity* at 60 Ben Yehuda, run by a group of Black Hebrews, is probably Tel Aviv's only vegan restaurant. It has an interesting selection of snacks and main dishes at reasonable prices. *The White Gallery* (2 Habima Square), a healthfood café/mystical bookshop/meditation centre, is also a good option.

If you fancy a **late-night** feast there are a number of 24-hour bakeries and cafés. The most famous are in Jaffa, near the clocktower, but the *Bagel Shop* at 11 Pines Street, near Yavni'el Street, is also a regular stopping place for young Israelis returning home after a night out. Most of the bars on HaYarkon, open until the early hours, also offer a selection of snacks.

Drinking and nightlife

In complete contrast to Jerusalem, Tel Aviv takes its nocturnal activities seriously. Much of the nightlife revolves around the bar and restaurant scene, and with probably as many bars in Tel Aviv as in any comparable British or American city the choice is wide. As Israelis tend not to be large consumers of alcohol, most bars also serve coffee and a large selection of soft drinks: alcoholic drinks are expensive (and prices can vary wildly) so it might be sensible to join in. If there are any cheap watering holes then they are a closely guarded secret, though some places, especially newly opened bars, do have a 'Happy Hour' once or twice a week.

Styles, names and clientele change frequently, but the following seem reasonably permanent and congenial. All of them have a varied clientele of travellers, expatriates, locals and UN and MFO troops from Lebanon and the Sinai, play reasonable background music, sell light snack meals and are open into the early hours of the morning.

The White House, corner Frishmann Street and HaYarkon – the best travellers' bar in Tel Aviv.

The Terminator, 136 HaYarkon – popular and noisy.

The Gypsy, underneath Kikar Namir – raucous.

The Zula Bar, corner Dizengoff and Nordau.

The Gordon, Gordon Street between Ben Yehuda and Dizengoff – popular with Israelis.

M.A.S.H. House (More Alcohol Served Here), 275 Dizengoff Street. Very much geared to the expatriate community, with darts board and 'sausage, egg and chips'. Happy hour 5.30–7.30pm on Tuesday and Friday.

The Prince of Wales, Chen Boulevard across from the City Hall.

The Tent, 215 Ben Yehuda – occasionally has live music.

Live music

Over the last few years the Israeli music scene has been getting its act together as more and more international rock and jazz groups include Israel on their world tours. With the *intifada* keeping Israeli repression in the headlines, however, bands with an aspiration to a career in 'Live Aid' have started to drop out.

Only the most popular **Israeli bands** sell enough records to survive and the relatively small number of venues often means playing the same place time and time again. Live gigs are few and far between, and much of what you'll hear is highly derivative or straight covers of western 'pop'. Arab-style music (sung in Hebrew) is, however, increasingly popular with Sephardic Jews and a band called *HaBreira HaTivit* (Natural Choice), who blend Oriental and Western traditions to create an 'Israeli' sound are well worth seeing if you get the chance. Tapes are universally bootlegged and therefore very cheap. You'll never be far from a blaring radio, and you'll be able to pick up anything that takes your ear in the shops around the bus station (see "Music" in *Basics* section).

For most of the **big concerts** a section of HaYarkon Park is cordonned off and the bands play under the stars. There's some kind of performance in the park every week or two during the summer: check the *Jerusalem Post* for details. Tickets vary in price from $10–20.

Kolnoa Dan, 61 HaYarkon, a converted cinema, is another popular venue for local and small international bands, doubling as a fairly average disco most evenings. However, with quality bands a rarity, demand for tickets is keen, so don't expect to be able to simply turn up on the night when name groups are playing.

Other live music venues include:

Cassibar, 7 Mendele Street. The queen of the Tel Aviv punk and new wave scene. Play the latest from London and New York in congenial atmosphere and have live music most Fridays and the occasional midweek evening. Admission Fri and Sat $7, less during the week. Recommended.

The Rock Cafe, 92 Herbert Samuel. Live music most Mondays and Wednesdays in wine bar setting. Admission is free, but each person must order food to the tune of at least $8. Often has top Israeli bands.

Tzavta Club, 30 Ibn Gvirol. Owned by the kibbutz movement, has the occasional live event. One of Tel Aviv's better venues.

Dixieland, 270 HaYarkon. Jazz, recorded or live. Pleasant outdoor bar with reasonable prices and an extensive, but fairly expensive menu.

Shamain, Kikar Namir. Live jazz every Wednesday, very pricey bar.

Shablul, Dizengoff Centre. Serious jazz venue.

Bonanza Pub, 17 Trumpeldor St. Wednesday jazz nights.

Clubs and discos

Most young Israelis seem to prefer going to **discos** and **nightclubs**, especially on a Friday night. On the whole, the nightclubs tend to be stuck in the mid-Seventies disco groove, not having graduated to the diversity of sounds more common in London or New York. An exception is the excellent new *Soweto* on the corner of HaYarkon and Frishmann, with a wide variety of black music from reggae to soul, congenial atmosphere and low admission prices. Most popular with young Israelis is the *Coliseum*, the large domed structure in Kikar Namir, very flashy, crowded and expensive especially at weekends. Women get free entry a few nights during the week. Other popular places include:

Studio 73, 73 HaYarkon Street. Adjacent to the US Embassy and similar to the *Coliseum* except that drink prices are even higher.

Liquid, 18 Montefiore Street. Good place with a mixture of funk and new wave.

Penguin Club, 43 Ben Yehuda. Similar to *Liquid* and equally good.

Gordon, Kikar Namir. Cheapest place in town, with standard disco fare Friday and Saturday nights only.

Attractive, corner Dizengoff and Arlosoroff. Tel Aviv's only gay club. Sunday is women only. Latest music, popular with the younger crowd.

Film

Cinemas are plentiful, especially around Dizengoff Square, Ben Yehuda Street and King George Street. They show all the major international releases, sometimes before they reach London, and charge around $4.50 entry. On a Friday night the cinemas are open late with the last screenings in many at around midnight. For a run-down of what's on, see the Friday edition of the *Jerusalem Post*.

Theatre, dance and classical music

In cultural terms, Tel Aviv remains the capital of Israel, and enjoys a surprisingly diverse selection of events, though ticket prices can be high. For the best idea of what's on, see the Friday edition of the *Jerusalem Post*, *Tel Aviv Today* (available from the foyers of large hotels) or *Events in the Tel Aviv Region* produced by the IGTO.

Theatre is most sharply focussed around the modern *Habimah Theatre* (Kikar Habimah; ☎03-284102). Other venues include *Tzavta* (30 Ibn Gvirol St; ☎03-250156); *HaSimtah* (Old Jaffa); *Beit Leissin* (34 Weizmann Boulevard; ☎03-256222); and *ThY Studio* (1 Tveria Street; ☎03-726087). While most of the plays are performed in Hebrew, there are also performances in English from time to time.

Classical music reaches its crescendo during the **Israel Festival**, held annually in May and early June. At this time a number of major international orchestras and musicians perform in the festival's four main centres: Jerusalem, Tel Aviv, and the restored Roman theatres in Beit She'an and Caesarea. The rest of the year the *Israel Philharmonic* plays regularly in Tel Aviv and its sponsors are able to bring in virtuosi from all over the world. The main concert hall in Tel Aviv is the **Mann Auditorium** (Hubermann Street;

☎03-289163). Others include *ZOA* (Zionist Organisation of America) *House* (1 Frisch Street; ☎03-259341) and the Tel Aviv Museum (27 Sha'ul HaMelekh Street; ☎03-257361). Two other festivals whose events are well worth looking out for are the *Rubinstein Piano Competition* and the *Spring in Tel Aviv Festival*.

As for **dance**, both the *Israel Ballet Company* (which performs regularly at the *Habimah Theatre*, Kikar Habimah; ☎03-284102) and the *Israel Contemporary Dance Company* have a reputation for competence. The other main company is the *Batsheva Dance Company* (☎03-652479). Regular visits by overseas dance troupes help brighten the otherwise limited selection, and there should be some kind of contemporary dance or ballet performance on just about any night during the summer months. Information, again, from the *Jerusalem Post* and usual listings publications.

Suburbs and satellites

There's really very little reason to visit any of suburban Tel Aviv, which for the most part appears as an unending procession of characterless apartment buildings, known to locals as the 'bedroom suburbs'. Some of them have historic names or associations, but few have anything to show for it. If you happen to be on the wrong bus, though, or on your way in and out of the city, you'll pass through – and start to believe that the city goes on forever.

To the south beyond Jaffa, **BAT YAM**, ('Daughter of the Sea'), is easily accessible by suburban bus routes. It tries to portray itself as a new and exciting beach resort, but in reality is no more than an extension of Tel Aviv's beaches and hotels. Although the beaches are slightly quieter than Tel Aviv's they are still commercial, crowded and claustrophobic. The adjacent town of **HOLON** is a long series of nondescript residential blocks and light industry. Its only real claim to fame is that it has the only sizeable **Samaritan** population outside of Nablus – totalling about fifty families.

To the northeast of Tel Aviv, **RAMAT GAN** (Garden Heights) is the home of Bar Ilan University, but not too many gardens. The other main attractions in Ramat Gan are the **Safari Park** and the *Maccabiades* – a mini Olympic Games in which Jewish sportspersons compete every four years. The site of the games, the **National Stadium**, also hosts most of the country's large sporting events. Nearby **BENE BERAQ** is Tel Aviv's orthodox quarter, with a number of beautiful residential areas where East European-style houses are built around cobbled squares.

Beyond here, the urban sprawl extends almost continously to **PETAH TIQVAH** (whatever the maps might say), one of the first agricultural settlements established in Palestine by Jews from Europe. In its early days it was an important focus of the *yishuv* and home to many of its leaders. At that time, large sections of the secular Zionist movement were aggressively anti-religious: some are said to have deliberately horrified the orthodox at *Yom Kippur* by ostentatiously eating ham sandwiches in the middle of the town's central roundabout. Nowadays Petah Tiqvah is a major town with some industry of its own, but of very little interest as you pass.

East of here, if you're travelling towards Rosh Ha'ayin or Kibbutz Enat, you'll pass the remains of a sixteenth-century Turkish fortress on a hill to your left. The fortress sits on the remains of the biblical city of **Aphek**, later renamed **Antipatris** by Herod in memory of his father. The excavations are not extensive, but remains of the Bronze Age city wall have been exposed to the northwest of the site as well as elements of Canaanite, Herodian and Byzantine settlement. There are plans to turn the site into a park at some stage in the future, but for the present it's a case of hopping over the wall to gain entry.

Listings

Airlines *Air France* (1 Ben Yehuda; ☎03-5103040); *British Airways* (1 Ben Yehuda; ☎03-5101581): *El Al* (32 Ben Yehuda; ☎03-641222); *KLM* (35 Ben Yehuda; ☎03-662520); *TWA* (74 HaYarkon; ☎03-654255).

Airport International flights leave from Ben Gurion Airport, 22km southeast of Tel Aviv near Lydda. Egged bus #475 leaves from Finn Street near the central bus station every twenty minutes from 5.30am until 11pm. *United Tours* bus #222 leaves from the *Dan Panorama Hotel*, heading past the large hotels and the Central Railway Station on its way to the airport (Sun–Fri 4.15am–11.15pm). The bus journey is about 45 minutes. There is no regular shared taxi from Tel Aviv to the airport, but any private taxi will take you for around $30. For information on arrivals and departures ☎03-9712484.

American Express Poste restante and cheque services are available from the main office at 16 Ben Yehuda Street (☎03-222263; Sun–Tues and Thur 8.30am–1.30pm and 3.30–6pm, Wed and Fri 8.30am–1pm).

Banks and money exchange Bank branches are concentrated along Allenby, Dizengoff and Ben Yehuda streets. Most open Sun, Tues and Thur 8.30am–12.30pm and 4–5.30pm, Wed and Fri 8.30am–noon. A small black market thrives on Lileinblum and Shenkin Streets and along the beachside strip between the Ramada Hotel and Kikar Namir. The difference in exchange rates is rarely significant, but it's useful if you run out of money on Wednesday or Friday afternoons when the banks shut early.

Books *Steimatzky's* (103 Allenby St) are the largest stockers of English language books. A number of other bookshops on Ben Yehuda and Allenby streets also stock English books. For the best selection of left-wing books and current issues of *Al-Fajr* English edition check out *20th Century Bookshop* (7 Shenkin Street; ☎03-280761). Further down Shenkin Street are a number of other good second-hand bookshops.

Buses Inter-city buses to all parts of the country leave from the central bus station (for information ☎03-432414): check with the information counter for platform numbers. Local bus routes mostly start from the bus station or the streets around it. **Egged Bus Tours** (59 Ben Yehuda; ☎03-242271) are available to most parts of the country.

Camping gear Just about everything you could want can be got from either the *SPNI* shop (see "Hiking information", below) or *Lamtayel* (Dizengoff Centre; ☎03-286894).

Car hire Most of the larger car rental companies have offices on HaYarkon Street near the large hotels and Ben Gurion Airport. Discount vouchers are often printed in *Tel Aviv Today*. The main ones include: *Avis* (97 HaYarkon; ☎03-235608), *Eldan* (112 HaYarkon; ☎03-203366) and *Europcar* (148 HaYarkon; ☎03-247242).

Consumer advice *Israel Consumers' Association* (35 King George St; ☎03-285288). Open Sun–Thur 9am–noon.

Egyptian visas The visa department is open Sun–Thur 9–11am (but get there early as queues are long, the procedure is slow and they close promptly): you'll need your passport, two photos (there are booths nearby) and the fee (around $25). Return the same day – after noon – to pick up your passport and visa. Visas for the Sinai only can be obtained at the border. For visa information, ☎03-464151.

Embassies and consulates Britain (192 HaYarkon St; ☎03-249171/8); USA (71 HaYarkon St; ☎03-654338); Canada (220 HaYarkon St; ☎03-228122/5); Netherlands (4 Weizmann St; ☎03-257337/9); Australia (185 HaYarkon St; ☎03-243152); Sweden (4 HaYarkon St; ☎03-244121/2); Denmark (22 Bnei Moshe St; ☎03-440405/6); Norway (10 Hei Belyar St; ☎03-295207).

Emergencies Police ☎100, Ambulance ☎101, Fire ☎102.

Ferries *J Kassas Agency* (1 Ben Yehuda St; ☎03-664902) and *Mano Passenger Lines* (60 Ben Yehuda; ☎03-282121) both sell boat tickets to Athens (Piraeus), Rhodes and Cyprus.

Gay groups *Society for the Protection of Personal Rights* (PO Box 16151, Tel Aviv) is the main organisation to contact. They run a drop-in centre every Monday and Wednesday from 6 until 11pm at 23 Beit Yosef St. *The White Line* (☎03-625629) is an information service for gay people in Tel Aviv set up to provide 'information and a sympathetic ear'. The lines are open Sun, Tues and Thur 7.30–11.30pm.

Health food If it's pulses, grains or nuts you want, then the *Shuq HaCarmel* is easily the best place to go. For anything else you might need try *House of Grain* (214 Dizengoff; open Sun–Thur 9am–9.30pm; Fri 9am–1pm.

Hiking information The *Society for the Protection of Nature in Israel* (SPNI) (4 Hashfela St, near the Central Bus Station; ☎03-382501) has a large well-stocked shop crammed with information about hiking in Israel. You can also book onto one of their tours and buy camping gear.

Hitching If you want to hitch out of Tel Aviv, take a bus as far from the centre as possible. Progress can be slow as you'll be competing with hitching soldiers, who usually get priority.

Kibbutz offices *Takam* (also known as the *United Kibbutz Movement*; 82 HaYarkon St; ☎03-651710); *Kibbutz HaArtzi* (13 Leonardo Da Vinci St; ☎03-

253131); *Kibbutz HaDati* (7 Dubnov St; ☎03-257231) accept religious volunteers only. All offices are open Sun–Thur 8am–2pm.

Laundry 51 Ben Yehuda and 45 Bograshov St (Sun–Thur 8am–7pm; Tues and Fri 8am–1pm); 13 Allenby (Sun–Thur 7am–7pm; Fri 7am–2pm).

Listings Listings of most events in the city can be found in the *Jerusalem Post* (especially its Friday edition), *Tel Aviv Today*, which is available in the foyers of the main hotels, or in various publications from the IGTO.

Moshav offices *Moshav Volunteers Office* (5 Tiomkin St; ☎03-625806; Sun–Thur 9am–3pm, Fri 8am–noon).

Newspapers The best ranges of English and international newspapers and magazines are sold either around the bus station or at *Steimatzky's* (103 Allenby St).

Pharmacies *The Pharmacy* (132 Dizengoff) is central, or you'll find plenty of others along Allenby and Ben Yehuda streets, and in the Dizengoff Shopping Centre.

Phones International reverse charge calls can be made from the post office at 7 Mikve Yisra'el Street. To make an international call from a private phone dial 18 for the international operator. For directory information dial 14.

Police 221 HaYarkon (☎100)

Post office The main post office is at 132 Allenby, open Sun–Thur 8am–6pm, Fri 8am–2pm. The office to pick up poste restante mail is at 7 Mikve Yisra'el Street, open the same hours as the main post office.

Rape crisis Phone *Rape Crisis* (☎03-234314) open 24 hours or *Crisis Intervention* (☎03-234819) for telephone counselling.

Railway station Trains for Haifa and Nahariya leave from the Central Station (Arlosoroff St), for Jerusalem from Bnei Brak (at 8.15am daily). For further information ☎03-254271.

Taxis Pick them up almost anywhere in the city, and be prepared to hang on for dear life. The price on the meter goes up after 9pm.

Ticket agencies Tickets for all events in Tel Aviv (and around the country) can be bought from *Katros* (77 Ben Yehuda; ☎03-228880) or *Hadran* (90 Ibn Gvirol St; ☎03-248787).

Tourist offices The main IGTO branch is at 7 Mendele Street, off Ben Yehuda (Sun–Thur 8.30am–5pm, Fri 8.30am–2pm). They also sell tickets to the main cultural events in Tel Aviv.

Travel agents/student travel *ISSTA* (109 Ben Yehuda; ☎03-294654; Sun–Tues and Thur 8.30am–6pm, Wed and Fri 9am–2pm) offer cheap flights, information on hostels in Tel Aviv, tours of Israel, advice on ferries, buses and trains. There are scores of general travel agents on Ben Yehuda, many of whom offer cheap charter flights if you can leave at short notice. To find the best deals start at one end of Ben Yehuda and walk – most places advertise current fares in their windows.

Women's movement The Tel Aviv Feminist Centre at 82 Ben Yehuda is run
by the *Israeli Feminist Movement* (PO Box 3304; ☎03-234314/234917). Their
main project is the Tel Aviv Rape Crisis Centre, but they also organise
consciousness-raising groups and meetings. Women also meet informally at
Tzena VaRena bookshop and cultural centre at 14 Mazeh Street.
International Feminist Network (Israel Representative) c/o Yarron, 1
Stand Street, Tel Aviv (☎03-234144).

Work Finding work in Tel Aviv is rarely a problem. The hotel and building
industry are your most likely bets, although in the summer it's sometimes
possible to find work as a film extra. Hostels such as *Gordon's* and the *Top
Hostel* are often approached by local employers for temporary workers so it's
worth asking around there and directly in bars, restaurants and on building
sites. While technically illegal to work on a tourist visa, cases of official
harassment are few and far between.

Jaffa

*Few towns can rival Jaffa, with its gaily coloured houses towering amphi-
theatrically above one another up the steep slopes of its rocky promontory,
with its two wings of yellow sand-dunes stretching north and south along
the shore, and with its green belt of orange groves covered at one and the
same season with the gold of the ripening fruits and the snow of the new
blossoms.*

Sadly, much has changed since the nineteenth-century traveller who wrote so
enthusiastically of **JAFFA** passed this way. The town from which the oranges
were transported is a shadow of its former self, where tourists are shep-
herded to 'Old Jaffa', sanitised for their delectation, to the flea market and a
small fishing port. While each is interesting, there is an empty heart to this
once grand city as Israel continues to 'cleanse' it of its Arab history. In the
centre of Jaffa money has been spent to refurbish the buildings so that
wealthy artists may sell their wares to richer customers, in the Ajami Quarter
– where Palestinians still live – there is no state cash for crumbling homes
and indeed those who mend their own, or organise community workcamps to
fix others', face arrest.

The city's rapid decline – so rapid that it occurred almost overnight – was a
direct consequence of the 1948 war. Most of its population were forced to flee
when the town was conquered by Zionist forces and an ebullient, thriving city
was reduced to a ghost town. Its port, the main entry point into Palestine for
pilgrims for centuries, was immobilised. The orange groves which had made
its property-owning classes so wealthy stood neglected and were then
appropriated.

The past
If **history** repeats itself, then maybe Jaffa, which has been conquered no
fewer than 22 times, is a case in point. Stone Age artefacts (from around
5000BC) have been excavated in and around Jaffa and the early Canaanite

settlement was first conquered as early as 1468BC by Thuti, a general serving Pharaoh Thutmose III. From Thuti to the Israelis, Jaffa's list of rulers reads like a who's who of Middle Eastern and European powers: Egyptians, Philistines, Israelites, Assyrians, Persians, Ptolemaics, Romans, Crusaders, Turks, French, British and more, all had their hands on the city.

What attracted them all were Jaffa's strategic location, its natural harbour – perhaps the oldest port in the world – and an abundance of fresh water from nearby wells. All of these combined to give Jaffa a vital place in Middle Eastern **trade**. Serving Jerusalem and the major trade routes from the East, it was a favourite prey for pirates large and small, the most important prize in the Middle East. Well before the Israelis, other powers had sought to diminish this influence: one of the earliest economic blows came when Herod built Caesarea and diverted much of Palestine's trade there. It was several hundred years until, with the growth of Lydda in the ninth century and the subsequent building of Ramla, Jaffa recovered the ground it had lost. The Crusaders held the town twice, and in 1187 al-'Adil, brother of Salah al-Din, sold the entire population of the city into slavery after they had put up fierce resistance during the Muslim reconquest of Palestine. In 1345 the Mamluks razed Jaffa and filled in the port because of the threat of a new European invasion.

Under the Turks the port was re-opened, and Jaffa's bloodiest times came when it was captured from them by **Napoleon Bonaparte** in March 1799. After thirty hours of pillage and plunder the Arab garrison inside the city surrendered. Over 4000 prisoners were brought to the French camp, where Napoleon ordered them shot before the march on Acre. The city was left in ruins, its population decimated. By the middle of the nineteenth century, however, the town had once again entered a period of rapid expansion, fuelled by trade with western Europe. Local land owners had planted mulberry bushes some years earlier and by the end of the 1850s tons of raw silk were passing through Jaffa. The increased prosperity of villages in the hinterland rejuvenated commercial activity, and as the century continued growth was further boosted by the export of 'Jaffa' oranges and other agricultural produce and by the beginning of large-scale European tourism to the Holy Land. In 1886 over 1000 vessels passed through the port and over 100,000 boxes of Jaffa oranges were exported. The Jaffa–Jerusalem railway, the first railway in Palestine, was opened in 1892 and soon after the Jewish quarters of Neve Zedek and Neve Shalom, and the Palestinian Manshieh Quarter to the northeast of the town, were founded.

Up to the mid-nineteenth century Jaffa had been almost exclusively a Muslim-Christian town. Jerusalem rabbis, seeking to increase the Jewish population of their own city, had issued a *herem* (rabbinical interdict) which forbade Jews from settling in Jaffa. This was lifted in 1841, and as the century progressed Jaffa saw an increasing flood of European **Jewish immigrants**. Many of them stayed on the coast, particularly after the British conquest of Palestine and the League of Nations Mandate. Jaffa prospered too, but **political tensions** between Zionists and Palestinians were never far from the surface. The first major clashes occured in 1920, prompting a British commission of enquiry. Meanwhile the economic transformation of Palestine under

Britain and the introduction of new industries had stimulated the formation and growth of trade unions, radical political parties, progressive newspapers and a host of other social, artistic and cultural groups. Many of these were headquartered in Jaffa, which became a centre of resistance to the British during the **Palestinian Revolt** of 1936–39.

The **decline of Jaffa** as a port began with the Palestinian Revolt, although its limited space and rocky shore – necessitating the transfer of passengers and goods to small lighters for landing – had already begun to prove inadequate for modern shipping. When the rebellion brought it to a standstill for months the British, with the help of the settlers, used the opportunity to transfer trade to Tel Aviv and Haifa.

By **1948**, the population of Jaffa had risen to 100,000, making it the second largest Arab city in Palestine. The Zionists attacked even before the British had left. Menachem Begin's *Irgun* shelled the town with mortars captured from the British (they only relented when the local commander threatened to shell Tel Aviv in retaliation). One side of the town was left open and all but 3000 Palestinians fled. They were chased out by a mob of Tel Avivians – the *Irgun* in the van – who indulged in an orgy of looting and destruction. Israeli prime minister David Ben Gurion was later to describe the expulsion as a 'shameful and distressing spectacle', but neither he nor his successors were prepared to make any attempt at redress, and most of those 97,000 people and their decendants are still refugees today.

Their homes and businesses were taken over by opportunist Tel Avivians and later, in a more systematic way, the new Israeli government settled Jewish immigrants in the Palestinian homes. The port's decline continued – it was finally closed in 1965 – and the once impressive buildings fell into ruin, creating the atmosphere of shabbiness you see today. Only in the last decade has much been done to turn the tide, as one part of Jaffa has been extensively restored and turned into a fashionable 'artists' quarter'. The Palestinian population, meanwhile, has grown to over 15,000, most of them living in slum conditions while the boarded-up houses of Palestinian refugees are allowed to fall into ruin. They are now officially state property, but the Israeli authorities do not allow anyone to move into them. Families are forced to live in cramped, overcrowded conditions and face harassment and detention if they do anything about it. Similar repression applies to economic activities. A small industrial zone established by local residents to try and halt thirty years of decline was shut down by the Tel Aviv municipality on the pretext of lack of planning permission. Under the Israelis, almost all the streets in Jaffa have been renamed. We have used the new names as they are the ones on the signboards. Palestinians, however, will generally use the original street names. Be prepared for a little confusion.

The Town

Jaffa is less than thirty minutes walk along the seafront from Tel Aviv. Alternatively, buses #10, #25, #26 and #28 run frequently, arriving by the impressive 1906 **clocktower** on Yefet Street which marks the beginning of the town. Directly opposite, the slender minarets of the **Mahmudiyya**

Mosque provide an immediate contrast with the drab architecture of Tel Aviv. The mosque, like much of old Jaffa, was built in the early nineteenth century after the tremendous destruction of Napoleon's assault.

If you walk down from here towards the sea – past a series of fish restaurants – you'll find the simple **Museum of Antiquities Tel Aviv-Jaffa** (Sun, Mon, Wed and Thur 9am–1pm, Tues 4–7pm, Sat 10am–1pm) down a small lane, Mifratz Shlomo Street. Housed in the old Ottoman administration building, the museum displays archaeological finds from the immediate vicinity of Jaffa and assorted columns and other remains from Caesarea. It's worth a quick look, though inside everything is rather confusingly laid out.

Alongside the museum, a small path leads through the **HaPisga Gardens** to a small hill. On the far side, across a wooden bridge, is **Kikar Kedumin**, a square dominated by the **Greek Orthodox Monastery** and **Church of Saint Peter**. The church has a very attractive bell tower, and at the side of the square a small, well labelled excavation reveals remains dating from the third century BC to the third century AD. Not far away is the so-called **House of Simon the Tanner**, now a mosque. According to *Acts* (*9:36–43* and *10:5–23*) St. Peter stayed here after being called to the city and 'raising a godly woman', Tabitha, from the dead. To get to the house, follow the signs to the Old Port down the steps at the southern side of the Church of St. Peter. When the signs tell you to make a sharp right to the port, continue straight down the steps to the closed door at the bottom and ring for admission: you'll be shown round by an elderly guide. It's an attractive building even if there's absolutely no evidence of its authenticity.

From the nearby **lighthouse**, easily visible from Simon's House, you get a view of the port and the sea walls. A few hundred metres out to sea is **Andromeda's Rock**. According to Greek legend Perseus, son of Zeus, rescued Andromeda from the rock as she was being sacrificed to a sea monster. The grooves in the rock are said to have been made by the chains which tied Andromeda down.

Old Jaffa

The part of the city through which you have been walking is full of beautiful old buildings which make an interesting comparison with the architecture of Jerusalem's Old City, showing the continuity and development of architecture in Ottoman Palestine. Nowadays, however, **Old Jaffa** is thoroughly touristy: many of the houses have been converted into small galleries and studios, while some of the larger buildings house exorbitantly priced nightclubs and restaurants.

The **Israel Experience** – a multi-screen film presentation which can be viewed at almost any hour of the day or night in the well signposted building on Pasteur Street – seems to sum it all up. It has nothing to do with the 'Israel Experience' as endured by the people who put the building up, only the one the current occupiers would like you to see. Its lack of subtlety is only surpassed by its lack of honesty and substance. Gerald Kaufman, then British Shadow Foreign Secretary, saw the show during one of his trips to the Holy Land. He said, 'The 'Israeli Experience' is . . . a fraud. It did not begin to tell the truth about the land, but presented the state as its publicists wanted it to be seen; a colourful, picturesque, carefree, peaceful, prosperous, Jewish country, making steady progress and with no problems that could not be solved by hygienically white-coated scientists, laughable politicians, or nobly altruistic rabbis.' Given the choice between paying the $5 entry fee or having a drink down by the harbour, take the latter.

The other Israeli attraction which draws crowds to Jaffa is the flea market or **Shuq HaPishpeshim**. To get there take any of the streets to the left of the clocktower. Run primarily by Sephardi Jews, the market has several cheap eating stalls as well as the usual selection of trinkets and T-shirts. A lot of stores sell rugs and other orientalia, but there's also a wonderful selection of junk, from electric guitars to obsolete Palestinian passports, and old books and papers which make fascinating reading. Mixed in with the flea market is Jaffa's **antique market**, with a surprising amount of very high quality goods. Here, however, you're back in gold-card country again.

The harbour

The **harbour**, on the shore of Old Jaffa, is one of the most interesting sections of town. At the southern end it's still used by Palestinian fishermen, who set out daily to provide the fare for local restaurants; the northern section, nearer the Old City, is where the pleasure boats berth and Tel Aviv's yachting crowd drop anchor. Around them are the remaining shadows of Jaffa's illustrious maritime history – deserted berths and decaying warehouses. In its heyday the whole area was choked with ships from all over the globe. At the turn of the century ships were forced to anchor well offshore and passengers waded or were precariously rowed from ship to shore. Luggage was brought off by human chains of porters waist-deep in water. At this northern end some of the smaller warehouses have been converted into yachting supply stores, diving centres and art galleries. *Shorashim* (Roots) gallery produces original wood sculptures consisting of a complex series of moveable parts, which can be manipulated almost like a lump of clay. They're fascinating, but take $1000 with you if you think you might like to take one home.

Plans are currently afoot to complete the conversion of Jaffa's harbour into an upmarket yacht **marina**. Locals are vigorously opposed, fearing that soaring moorage charges will effectively end fishing in Jaffa, and with it much other economic activity.

Yehuda HaYammit Street runs back from the harbour to Yefet Street. On the right is the impressive, if not particularly ancient, **Franciscan Church of Saint Antonio**, one of the few churches still in regular use. Many were damaged in 1948, and lost the vast majority of their congregations. Even churches are not exempt from the prohibition on repairs and those which weren't damaged are now in a poor state. Just around the corner on Yefet St, the deserted **Coptic Church** is a good example. A few faded icons remain, but the windows were smashed and the interior is in disarray – almost as if proceedings had been interrupted in mid-service. Around the Coptic Church are a few other old church buildings and institutions, remnants both of Jaffa's Christian community and the building spree undertaken by the European powers in the final years of the Ottoman Empire.

Palestinian Jaffa

To see the Jaffa that people actually live in, walk south down Yefet Street. After a few hundred metres you'll come to a small tree-lined park which forms the centre of **Palestinian Jaffa**. Just south of the park is the **Arab Cultural Centre** at 71 Yefet St. The centre, founded by *al-Raabita al-Yafawi al-Arabi* (The League of Arab Jaffa) is a local community organisation which tries to lessen the effects of Tel Aviv Municipality's active neglect. If they are not over busy they may provide you with a guide – or at least pointers – to Arab Jaffa. *Al-Raabita* runs regular summer **voluntary workcamps** which last from seven to fourteen days. In exchange for your labour they provide board and lodgings with a Palestinian family, entertainment, and a political and educational programme.

Between Yefet Street and the sea is the main residential area, the **Ajami Quarter**. Most of it is depressingly squalid, and the area is scarred by the municipality's demolition of 'absentee' homes, but the architecture bears witness to its past and it is still possible to imagine the grandeur of the place at its height. Indications of the once thriving city are everywhere, with grand ambassadorial residences, deserted cinemas and schools standing uncomfortably amidst the mess. While some of the houses have been well maintained, the vast majority are slowly falling down, their owners incapable of raising the money to hold back the depredations of age.

If you're walking back to Tel Aviv along Herbert Samuel St, you'll pass the **Hassan Bek Mosque** after about ten minutes. Until 1948 this was the main mosque of Jaffa's **Manshieh Quarter**. The buildings which stood around the mosque were destroyed in the mid-1970s to make way for office blocks, hotels and a leisure park, and the mosque itself barely avoided the same fate when it was discovered that the brother of Israeli Labour Party leader Shimon Peres had received permission to convert it into a nightspot. The mosque, like many others in Israel, falls between two parts of the Israeli machine. The **Absentee Property Law**, passed in the early 1950s, took control of the building away from the local *Waqf* (Islamic trust). 'So God is an "absentee" too', was the ironic interpretation put on that Israeli move. At the same time, the propaganda machine made a lot of capital out of Israel's respect for religious buildings, so the new owners were unable to deliver the *coup de grace*.

In 1981 the Arab residents of Jaffa initiated the restoration of Hassan Bek. Finance came from Palestinian sources, and the energy and insistence of the youthful committee in charge provoked a crisis for those Israel had appointed to oversee Muslim affairs in Jaffa. Shortly after work began, an explosive charge demolished the mosque's minaret. The Israeli police are still investigating. Over the next couple of years, work on the mosque ground to a halt in a welter of court orders, arrests, rumours and recrimination. It picked up again in 1985 when *al-Raabita* took over and, if it's ever completed in the face of continuing obstacles, the mosque promises to be an impressive local architectural feature, as well as the focus of worship for Jaffa's Muslim population.

Jaffa practicalities

Just south of the Mahmudiyya Mosque are a number of outdoor **restaurants** serving superb locally caught fish and other seafood. A full meal may set you back $10–15, but it's well worth it. If you want something cheaper there are a number of take-away bakeries at the bottom of the Yefet Street hill selling delicious pizzas, pastries and breads. These are also good places to stock up with soft drinks and basic provisions. The *Tripoli Restaurant*, right next to the clocktower, serves tasty Middle Eastern food at reasonable prices. On the northern side of the harbour, the *Fishermen's Restaurant*, last on the quay right where the fishermen prepare their nets and unload their catch, is one of the cheapest places to eat local seafood.

If you want to **stay in Jaffa** there is only one option, the *Immanuel House Christian Hospice* (12 Beer Hoffman St; ☎03-821459). Built by the father of actor Peter Ustinov, the place is cheap, quiet and clean, but has a strict 11pm curfew.

SOUTH OF TEL AVIV

Heading south from Tel Aviv, the coastal road is fast but not very stimulating, bypassing the part of Ashdod, Ashqelon and everywhere else on the coast, before entering the **Gaza Strip**. Inland things are, if anything, even less exciting – from the major junction just outside Qiryat Gat, you can either head for Hebron on the West Bank, or south to Beersheva.

Rishon Le Zion and Yavne

Although on Tel Aviv's doorstep (only 8km south), the town of **RISHON LE ZION** has retained some individual identity because of its central role in Israeli wine production. Rishon Le Zion ('First in Zion') was founded in 1882 by ten immigrants from Russia, idealists from the pre-Zionist era who wanted to rediscover themselves and build a new life in the promised land. They failed, and in bankrupt desperation turned to the French philanthropist **Baron Edmond de Rothschild**. All Rothschild shared with the Zionists was a desire not to see Eastern European Jewish refugees settling in the west: he sponsored agricultural settlements all over the world, particularly in South America, and provided training and financial backing to his proteges. It was Rothschild's idea that Rishon Le Zion – and the northern settlement of **Zichron Ya'acov** – start producing wine, and he sent plants, experts and cash for cellars. The *Societe Cooperative Vignerome des Grand Caves* – which later became known as Carmel – was born. The cooperative currently has over 800 members who supply 85 per cent of Israel's wine grape crop.

The original **winery** is still working and there are occasional tours (Sun–Thur 8.30am–3pm). For $6 you get a walk round the factory, a tasting during which you can put away as much as you like, a small free sample bottle and the chance to buy more at cut prices. It's a pleasant enough way to while away a few hours if you like factories, or drinking. None of the wines are exactly world class but *Granache Rose*, for example, is good enough to fuel parties or simply impart bland Rishon Le Zion with a golden hue. The wine cellars are housed in the large building a couple of blocks south of the bus station. Any local will point it out if you get lost. Alternatively *Egged Tours* run a half-day **tour** that includes both the wine cellars and the **Weizmann Institute** in Rehovot. The tours leave Tel Aviv on Sunday, Monday, Tuesday and Thursday at 1.45pm (for more details ☎03-242271; if you have an *IsraCard* you can join this tour free).

Continuing south from Rishon Le Zion, **YAVNE**, site of the ancient city of Jabneh, is neither spectacular nor unusual, but it enjoys a certain notoriety as the site of Israel's first atomic research reactor – 4km out of town. Needless to say the reactor, built in 1960, is off limits to travellers. **Jabneh** itself has been settled for at least 2000 years, and in the past was an important religious centre – during the Hasmonean period it became a Jewish centre of learning after the destruction of the Second Temple, and later it was a Roman and Crusader stronghold and an important town during the early periods of Arab rule. All that remains of this rich heritage is a lone **Mamluk tower** that stands defiantly on a ridge a few kilometres south of the present town, the tomb of Maqam **Abu Hureira** (one of the Prophet Mohammed's companions) and an early church which was later converted into a mosque. Just north of town, where the Sorek River meanders into the sea, are the remains of the old port (now **YAVNE-YAM**). Its beach is used mostly by locals and is generally quiet; camping out here seems tolerated, though better from the safety of a group.

The **Ashdod junction**, a few kilometres south of Yavne, is an important public transport interchange. There are frequent buses to most main centres from here. **GEDERA**, just west of the junction, was founded, like Rishon Le Zion, by pre-Zionist Russians. Just outside the town is the destroyed Palestinian village of **KETERA** with ruins from both the Arab and Roman periods. Gedera's only claim to fame is that, in the late 1970s, the Israeli authorities destroyed an unlicensed house there. What was significant about the event was that it was owned by an Israeli Jew – the first, and so far only, time that this has happened (See the *Galilee* chapter). Interesting as this may be, it does not make Gedera worth visiting.

Ashdod

There has been human settlement around **ASHDOD** since the late Iron Age. After the Israelis destroyed the Palestinian town of **Isdud**, however, they merely constructed immigrant transit camps and the decision to establish the modern city wasn't taken until 1957. Ashdod was developed as a commercial port – it is now busier than Haifa – and as such is a must for anyone with a passionate interest in medium-sized freighters. Virtually all the town's 70,000 inhabitants depend on the **port** – tours of it are run by the Port Authority (☎08-528211, or contact the IGTO) – and the naval academy. Of the Canaanite settlement, or Isdud's history as one of the five main Philistine cities on the *Via Maris*, or of the battles in the area between the Crusaders and the Arabs, no trace remains. Indeed, the only thing of any antiquity left near Ashdod is the ruined **Qala'at al-Mina**, a tenth-century Fatimid castle.

Ashdod's **beaches** – with their commanding views of (and occasional spillage from) the oil terminal – are for domestic consumption only. The *Lido* has a small market on Wednesdays, the *Miami* doesn't, but at least the sand is soft and they're quiet except at weekends. There's a small **Tourist Information Office** in front of the central bus station which will provide details of the port tours, the beaches and the **Mediterranean Folklore Festival** which, before the *intifada*, was held every August in the evenings on the beach. Check who's appearing before making the trek to Ashdod; European performers are often reluctant to been seen on the wrong side in a war zone.

There is no cheap **accommodation** in Ashdod – although sleeping on the beach is no problem for men. The two hotels, *Hotel Orly* (22 Nordan St) and *Hotel Miami* (14 Nordan St; ☎08-522085) both charge upwards of $25 a night, and are often full during the summer months. The only 'sight' is the aforementioned **Qala'at al-Mina**: only parts of its four towers survive, so a visit does not take long. To get there take bus #5 from Ashdod central bus station and ask the driver to let you off at the site.

Ashdod to Ashqelon

The road south of Ashdod, with the sand-dunes of Ashdod on your right, is fast, flat and featureless. Four kilometres south of Ashdod, **TEL ASHDOD** was the centre of **Isdud** and site of the Philistine port. Get off the bus if you like old mounds, derelict Palestinian homes, fragments of pottery or archaeologists. Six kilometres further south is the kibbutz of **Nizzanim**, west of which are the unmarked remains of a settlement from the Persian Period (451–640BC) and remnants of a Byzantine church complete with mosaic and tomb. It's a pleasant walk as long as the day is not too hot.

Ashqelon

ASHQELON (ASQALAN), the most southerly town on Israel's Mediterranean coast, is perhaps unique in Israel in that the homes of its expelled Palestinian population have been neither destroyed, nor sanitised and commercialised. Instead there's a well preserved Palestinian heart – **Migdal** – which along with good beaches, a national park and a clutch of relatively cheap bars and cafés, makes the place worth a stop as you pass. The city is now making efforts to attract well-heeled tourists, but there is little accommodation for the less well off.

There has been a city at Ashqelon for 4000 years: its defeat after an uprising against Rameses II in 1280BC is depicted on the temple at Karnak in Egypt. Ashqelon was important because it served as a staging post on the vital Egypt–Mesopotamia trade route – a crucial source of water north of the Sinai. It was one of the five great cities of the Philistines and subsequently passed to the Assyrians, the Egyptians, the Babylonians and the Persians. During a period of Judaean belligerency in the First Temple period the city, then ruled from Tyre, sought protection from the Romans, a request which marked the beginning of Roman ascendancy in the city's affairs. Herod was born here and had a palace in the city. Despite being razed and rebuilt in the seventh century, Ashqelon enjoyed almost unbroken prosperity for six hundred years.

The city's strong defences allowed it to defy the first wave of European invaders in the Crusader period even though 10,000 Fatimid soldiers and civilians were slaughtered in front of its gates in 1099. Twelve years later, however, King Baldwin intimidated a weak Egyptian administrator, Shams al-Khalifa, into allowing a 300-strong force to take over the garrison. The Asqelanis were appalled and in a well coordinated revolt killed all the Europeans and Shams al-Khalifa. The Crusaders were not to retake Ashqelon · for another forty years when, as the last Fatimid bastion in Palestine, it finally fell in 1157. A mere 34 years later the great Salah al-Din retook the city and destroyed it to prevent the Crusaders' return. Richard the Lionheart was said to have gazed on the fires of the magnificent city from as far away as Jaffa. He did manage to hold the area briefly and built a fortress to replace the destroyed defences, but Salah al-Din again flattened the walls after forcing the English king out of Palestine in 1192. The Mamluk Sultan Baybars ripped the rebuilt city down yet again in 1270 to neutralise Ashqelon in the face of the threat of another European incursion. It was on these ruins that **Majdal** was constructed. Although never regaining its former opulence, Majdal did enjoy unbroken centuries of quiet prosperity until forty years ago.

Majdal was a centre of resistance to Zionist expansionism throughout the 1948 war, but it was only in 1950 that the new state implemented its plans to 'cleanse' the area of Palestinians. This they did by the simple expedient of piling the entire population into army trucks and driving them to the Gaza frontier in the wake of the thousands who had fled two years earlier. Like most of the southern part of the new state, Israeli Ashqelon was an economic backwater and the new inhabitants were, by and large, directed to live in it, rather than there by choice. But the settlement was important (Ashqelon was outside the borders set in the UN partition plan, and there was international pressure to allow its Palestinian population to return) and so considerable resources were devoted to its development. Responsibility for Ashqelon, perhaps aptly, was given to the South African Zionist Federation, whose largesse included the cost of building the Afridar neighbourhood. Much money also came from British Zionist sources. Today the Israeli population of the city has topped 60,000, while many of its former Palestinian residents still travel the short distance from the Gaza Strip to work here every day.

Arrival

Ashqelon is roughly divided into five **neighbourhoods**: Migdal (formerly the Palestinian city of Majdal), Afridar, Barnea, Zion Hills and Shimshon. They are well spread out and you'll have to take a bus to get from one to another. #13 travels from the bus station to the beach area; #4, #5 and #7 go from the bus station to Afridar, Migdal and Barnea and #3 and #9 will take you from the bus station to the National Park. There's an office of the **IGTO** in Zephania Square, Afridar (☎051-32412; Sun–Thur 9am–1pm, Fri 9–11.30am).

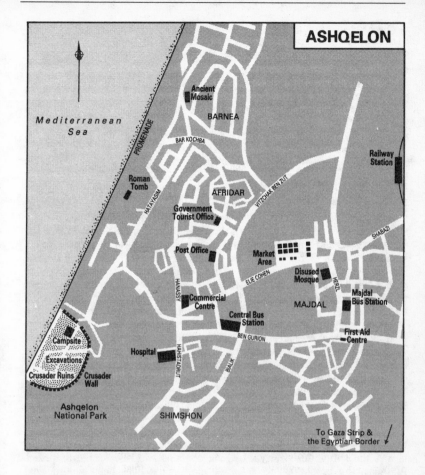

Most cafés and restaurants are in Afridar or the Commercial Centre, off Hanassi St; Migdal (also known as the 'old city') is rather run down, but has a reasonable market and some very cheap *falafel* kiosks; Shimshon, Barnea and Zion Hills are predominantly residential.

Finding **a place to stay** in Ashqelon is problematic if you're low on funds. The image the city is trying to foster is that of an upmarket tourist resort, so cheap accommodation is virtually non-existent. By far the least expensive is *Ashqelon Camping* (picturesquely sited near the beach inside the national park; ☎051-36777): to get there from the central bus station either walk to the southeasterly part of the city, or get bus #3 or #9 and ask the driver to let you off near the National Park. The site charges a standard $4.50 per person per night ($2.75 off-season), and if you don't have a tent you can hire caravans at $30 for a four-bed, $45 for a six-bed – less in the off-season (Oct–May) when bargaining is recommended.

The cheapest **hotels** are the *Ashqelon Hotel* (82 South Africa Blvd; ☎051-34188; from $15–30) and *Samson's Gardens* (38 HaTamar St; ☎051-34666; from $15–40). There is a wide variety of three- and four-star hotels situated on or near Delilah Beach offering accommodation for between $30 and $50. Alternatively the IGTO has a list of places where you can get a bed in a private home for $8 and up.

Sleeping on the beach is also commonplace during the summer, but you'd be well advised only to do so as part of a group, and to guard your valuables. A lot of campers congregate just south of the National Park which is far enough from the town centre to deter opportunist criminals.

Town and park

The heart of the old **Palestinian town** is Majdal Square, and this makes as good a place as any to start exploring. As in Jaffa the street names and the shop signs have been changed, but the Palestinian and Arab character of the district remains distinct. The old bus station, built in Jerusalem stone, is the best preserved building in the area – its size and solidity give some impression of the wealth and importance of the town the Israelis erased. To see the rest, Thursday, **market day**, is the best time to come, when the streets are packed and buzzing (although Monday and Wednesday are generally lively too). The main market is situated at the end of Herzl Street. If you intend to buy and cook your own food, this is by far the cheapest place to do your shopping, with mainly Moroccan and Iraqi stallholders offering a wide variety of vegetables, fruits, meats, poultry and fish.

Right at the end of Herzl Street, behind the *Paradise Restaurant* is the now disused **old mosque**. If you walk through the restaurant, or climb over the surrounding walls, you can enter its peaceful interior, now apparently used to store engine parts for nearby garages, while the minaret makes a convenient nesting place for local birdlife.

Of the other neighbourhoods, **Afridar** is the effective centre of the modern town, a concrete mesh of shops, banks, restaurants and bars. Its one attraction is the antiquities courtyard which contains two beautiful **sarcophagi**. Although the brochures don't say so these must have been moved from Philistine Ashqelon: the carvings on one depict the abduction of Persephone, daughter of Demeter, Goddess of Fertility; the other carries a battle scene between Greeks and Barbarians.

To the north of the centre, on Zvi Segal Road in the **Barnea** district, are the remains of two ruined **Crusader churches**, a sixth century **Byzantine church** and, on Jerusalem Boulevard, a **mosaic floor** from the same period. All of these, however, are so overgrown and neglected as to be barely recognisable. To get to Barnea, take bus #5 from Afridar or from the central bus station.

The National Park

Arguably a greater attraction than anything in downtown Ashqelon is the beachside **National Park**, site of **ancient Ashqelon**, a melange of archaeological remains, picnic areas, sand dunes and secluded beaches. Officially open Sun–Thur 8am–5pm and Fri 8am–4pm ($1.50 entry; ☎051-36444), the park is in practice freely accessible from the beach.

The early walls of the **Philistine port**, with magnificent columns, can be seen down by the beach. Nearer the centre of the park, a collection of **Roman** memorabilia has been collected from all over the area and is exhibited together in two displays: under Herod (who was born here) the town was spectacularly endowed with baths, fountains and colonnaded quadrangles. Remnants of one such quadrangle can be seen in the field near the cafeteria, along with hundreds of standing columns. There are also remains of Crusader and Byzantine churches, collapsed towers, esplanades and pillars scattered throughout the park. West of the cafe is a newly refurbished open-air auditorium. The municipality sponsors regular theatre and musical programmes here which are advertised in the IGTO. Trails to the venue are well-marked.

One of the most distinctive archaeological exhibits in Ashqelon is the third century AD **family tomb** (Sun–Fri 9am–1pm; Sat 9am–2pm; admission free) just outside the National Park on the way to Delilah beach. The outside of the tomb is decorated with frescoes of the god Pan playing his pipes, a naked boy gathering grapes, birds feeding, and stags, antelopes and dogs; a Gorgon's head runs down the main axis, possibly to ward off the evil eye. Discovered in a remarkably good state of preservation in 1936, the tomb is believed – from its decoration and quality – to have belonged to a wealthy Hellenic family.

Beaches

There is some 12km of beach around Ashqelon, with little to distinguish any one part – just sand and soft-drinks kiosks selling. **North Beach**, just inside the municipal boundaries, is the most secluded: popular for topless bathing but not covered by the lifeguards who patrol everywhere else. Moving south you come to **Barnea Beach, Bar Kockba Beach** at the end of Bar Kochba St, and a separate beach for religious bathers near the Roman Tomb. Just past the marina, **Delilah Beach** has three small islands a few hundred metres offshore – a good long swim if you're up to it. This is the most popular of the beaches, used by guests from the up-market hotels. Just by here is a small **theme park**, full of water slides, pools and the usual fairground rides, that's fun if you feel like that sort of thing. Beyond, the beaches continue into the National Park, the crowds dwindling the further you get. If all of them prove too crowded, as they can be at weekends, the beach at **Kibbutz Ziqim**, about five miles south, or **Palmachim**, not much further, are pleasant alternatives.

Eating and drinking

While the hotel prices seem designed to keep you away, you can **eat** cheaply and well at basic stalls and cafes throughout Ashqelon, particularly in Migdal. *Nissim Levy's Cafe* (Sun–Thur 7am–10pm, Fri 7am–3pm), at the bottom of the market towards the sea, is particularly recommended. There are also some of the cheapest *falafel* stalls in Israel on Herzl Street, south of the bus station. Numerous regular cafés, restaurants and bars are to be found in the same area.

Most of the more **upmarket bars and restaurants** are in Afridar. The open-air *Ma'adan Café*, opposite the IGTO with a sign in Hebrew only, is active seven days a week until the early hours, serving excellent pastries and snacks as well as more substantial fish meals and Moroccan dishes. Nearby you'll find *Burger Ranch*, the pricey *Forma Chinese Restaurant* and a number of popular bars. Busiest of the latter are *Bayit HaKfar* (The Village House), near the clocktower, and the *London Pub*, near the post office.

The other main concentration of bars and restaurants is in the central **commercial area** on Hanassi Street. *Diwana Restaurant and Pub* is an Israeli-style Indian place, which is at least different. There are a number of bars, a Yemenite take-away and a steak house in the same complex, and a couple of pizza parlours further down the street. The large **supermarket** on *Ben Gurion Street* is the cheapest in the vicinity. For ultra-cheap food this side of town try either the Egged Bus Station restaurant or the nearby *falafel* and kebab stalls.

As for **nightlife**, many of the large hotels have what pass for nightclubs. The *Cosmos Pub* at the *Ashqelon Beach Hotel* is popular; there are others at *Shulamit's Gardens* and the *King Sha'ul Hotel*. Culturally, Ashqelon is near the bottom of everybody's list. The *Rachael Cinema* (South Africa Street, Afridar; ☎051-31429) near the IGTO shows English-language films most evenings, and there's another cinema, *Esther* (☎051-22659), in the Zion Hills area. Little else happens – for details of occasional special events see the IGTO's *What's On in Ashqelon*.

Practicalities

Banks Most are located in Afridar (near the IGTO) or on Herzl Street in Migdal.

Buses Egged Bus Station (Ben Gurion; ☎051-22911 or ☎051-23807). Inter-city buses connect Ashqelon with Tel Aviv and Jerusalem at least every hour – look for the 'direct' buses, as many services stop frequently en route. You can also get a bus from here direct to the Rafah (Rafiah) border with Egypt.

Car hire *Eldan Car Hire* (corner of Ben Gurion Blvd and Herzl St; ☎051-22284). Check with the IGTO for the best local deals.

First Aid Magen David Adom (☎051-23333).

Hospital HaHistadrut Street (☎051-23131).

Pharmacies *Ashqelon* (Commercial Centre, Afridar; ☎051-34234); *Rom* (Hanassi St, opposite the Police Station; ☎051-27293); *The Chemist* (Kikar Golomb, Migdal; ☎051-22332).

Police The main police station is on Hanassi Street (☎051-34222).

Service taxis *Yael Daroma Taxis* (Zahal St, Migdal; ☎051-22334) go to Tel Aviv, Jerusalem and the Gaza Strip.

Taxis Central office opposite the Egged Bus Station.

Travel agent *Ashqelon Tours* (Civic Centre, behind the Egged Bus Station; ☎051-23651).

Beyond Ashqelon

The road which runs south from Ashqelon **into the Gaza strip** follows the line of the disused railway which once linked Aswan in southern Egypt with Turkey. Ten kilometres south of Ashqelon is **Kibbutz Yad Mordechai** – named after Mordechai Anwilewitz, the leader of the Warsaw Ghetto uprising. It has a museum dedicated to Jewish resistance in the Warsaw Ghetto and the Zionist military history of the Negev. The turning to the beach at **Kibbutz Ziqim** comes just before Yad Mordechai. The kibbutz doesn't like people to stay at the beach, so if you're planning on spending the night take whatever provisions you might need and walk a few kilometres away from the kibbutz itself. Continuing south, the road runs directly to the **Erez checkpoint**, the official point of entry for the Gaza Strip.

If you turn away from the coast just before Yad Mordechai, you'll embark on a rather laborious route **south into the Negev**. This is the land of stolen green fields and tiny settlements: there's virtually nothing else to see. **SDEROT**, a dozen or so kilometres south of the junction is named after the avenues of trees (*sderot* means avenues in Hebrew) planted by the Jewish National Fund (JNF). It's eminently missable. If you're hitchhiking you might want to get a cold drink, but that's about all the place is good for. Follow the road south, skirting the borders of the Gaza Strip towards RAFAH, and you'll end up at the Egyptian border. To get to **Beersheva**, follow the road east at the **Magen junction**. If you intend to hitch south make sure you have plenty of water, food for a day or so and warm clothes for the cold nights. There's little traffic on the roads and it's very easy to get stuck in the middle of nowhere.

INLAND AND THE ROAD TO JERUSALEM

The highway from Tel Aviv to Jerusalem runs out past Ben Gurion Airport, a fast main route which buses and taxis cover non-stop in less than an hour. If you want to visit the towns of Lydda, near the airport, Ramla and Rehovot, there are frequent buses and *sherut* taxis from the Central Bus Station in Tel Aviv.

Lydda

Twenty kilometres south of Tel Aviv, 50km northwest of Jerusalem, the town of **LYDDA** (referred to in Hebrew as **LOD**) was once among the most prosperous Arab towns in the country. Today, with the majority of Palestinians having been ousted after a massacre during the 1948 war, the city is neither wealthy nor enticing. It also has one of the most reactionary city councils in the country, and a certain notoriety as the only town in Israel which still has

Palestinian refugee camps. An active Palestinian cultural group – the *Sons of Lydda* – runs some community facilities and has regular workcamps to pave roads, improve drainage and prevent cemeteries being turned into waste dumps, but their work is at best limited. A tour of the city in the company of one of their number will allow you real insights into its history and current problems: otherwise Lydda has no aspirations to being a tourist stopping point and hardly any provision is made for the casual visitor.

According to the Bible, Lydda was founded by *Elpaal* son of Benjamin and, like Jaffa and Ashqelon, the city appears in records of Pharaoh Thutmose III. After the destruction of the second temple it became the seat of a small *sanhedrin* – a Jewish legal and administrative body – and a prominent religious seminary. Under the Romans it became known as *Diospolis* (the city of God) and later as *Georgiopolis* after St. George who, according to Christian tradition, was buried here. Georgiopolis was an important Crusader centre too, and many churches and other new buildings were constructed during their period in control.

A long history, then, but by local standards a relatively uneventful one until the British made Lydda into a district administrative centre and a central junction and depot for the Middle Eastern railway network. Its importance in the modern economy fostered the development of radical political movements and an active trade unionism among workers employed in the area's industries. One of the earliest confrontations between Palestinian workers and the British administration's pro-settler policies came when apartheid wage rates were introduced. In the early days of their administration the Mandate authorities undertook an extensive programme of public works, with ethnic quotas for the workforce. Zionist leaders prevailed upon the authorities to pay Jews at higher rates than Palestinian Arabs. A whole generation of Palestinian trade unionists cut their political teeth in the struggles against this racist policy, experience put to use in the 1936–39 revolt when Lydda was a centre of economic resistance. The brutality with which the British army suppressed opposition in the town and surrounding villages is still remembered by the older generation, and the revolt also had the effect of bringing significant numbers of Jewish immigrants to Lydda for the first time – the British needed strike breakers to keep the railways functioning.

During the 1948 war, the town occupied a vital strategic position for the Zionist forces as they moved towards Jerusalem. This at least is the excuse now used for **Plan Dalet**, by which the Arab population was driven from the region (though vital workers, especially those who operated the railway, were allowed to remain). The Zionists, led by a then unknown soldier called Moshe Dayan – later Minister of Defence – informed the local Palestinian population that if they congregated inside Dahamash Mosque they would be safe. Hundreds complied, and over eighty were machine-gunned to death. After incidents like this and reports of widespread looting and assaults by the Zionists, most of the Palestinian population fled in terror. Excellent accounts of these events can be found in Fawzi al-Asmar's *To be an Arab in Israel* or David Hirst's *The Gun and the Olive Branch*.

Among those who witnessed the atrocities was a 21-year-old medical student named **George Habash**, who went on to become one of the most important radical ideologists and leaders in the modern Arab world. He was prominent in the Arab National Movement, the revolutionary organisation which developed out of disillusion with Nasser's conservatism and which was to be so influential in the revolution in Yemen. After 1967 he founded and still heads the Marxist *Popular Front for the Liberation of Palestine* (PFLP), the second largest group inside the Palestine Liberation Organisation.

Lydda today

At first the Palestinian homes of Lydda were used by the new state of Israel to house immigrants, but as the town has grown the old has been left to decay and *shikunim* thrown up in faceless neighbourhoods around the city centre. Palestinian residents have been fighting for years for permission to live in the older houses and to renovate those they do hold. This has been stubbornly resisted by the housing authority, but there have been occasional successes. Around the railway station there is a small compound of houses built by the British for railway employees in an extraordinary pastiche of English cottage style. Behind them are two of the main refugee camps – areas where Palestinians are responsible for their own facilities.

Modern Lydda has almost 40,000 residents of whom over 5000 are Palestinian Arabs. The population is one of the most cosmopolitan in Israel: early settlers were primarily from other parts of the Middle East but since the 1960s large numbers of Georgians from the south of the Soviet Union and Cochinese from South India have been moved in to the town. The Palestinians too are from different parts of the country – as well as the original inhabitants who were spared expulsion by dint of their skills, there are refugees who have been here since they fled from surrounding villages in 1948, and significant numbers of Palestinian Beduin, driven here since by the poverty of the reservations in the Negev. This diversity of ethnic and cultural origin, however, is suppressed rather than celebrated. The Palestinians, Indians and Georgians retain some of their national dress, but their cultures are celebrated only in the home.

The architectural heritage is slightly more obvious, with remains from Byzantine, Crusader and Arab periods. The **Church of Saint George**, easily visible from the centre of the town, combines elements of all three. The first church on this site, built to house the tomb of St. George, was Byzantine, from around the sixth century. It was destroyed when the Crusaders conquered the town, rebuilt in the second half of the twelfth century, and later ruined again. The present Greek Orthodox church was built for the large Christian Arab community little over a hundred years ago, retaining an impressive mixture of influences: Byzantine apses, Crusader arches and Islamic columns. As you enter the church note the sculpture over the doorway, portraying St. George slaying the Dragon. Opposite is a wall with a large iron chain hanging from it: here those deemed to be insane were tethered overnight for St. George to effect a cure. Inside there's an extensive collection of Greek Orthodox icons, candle holders and richly decorated murals and paintings. The tomb of St. George itself is in the crypt – in its honour Palestinian Christians from all over the country celebrate St. George's Day (April 23) with a procession through the town and a mass at the church.

Next to the church is a mosque, **Jamia al-Omar**, which was built over part of the Byzantine church and is also dedicated to St. George, known as *al-Khadr* in Arabic. The founder's inscription over the entrance is dated 666 *Hijra* (1268AD), confirming this as one of the oldest mosques in the region. Opposite is a pleasant local café, popular with many of the older inhabitants of this Arab residential area.

The **Dahamash Mosque**, site of the Lydda massacre, is next to the bus station. Sealed off, it is slowly falling into irrevocable disrepair: some local people claim that the bloodstains of those who died can still be seen inside. At the back of the bus station, down an alleyway and through a housing estate, are the remains of the old Arab *khan*. Its extent gives a good impression of how important Lydda must have been both as a stopping point in the extensive regional trading networks and as a pilgrimage centre. The site has barely been maintained, however, and care should be taken when walking around it. In the town's **main square** are a number of cafés and food stalls grouped around another old *khan*, a bath house and Palestinian houses. Just north of the square is a large fruit and vegetable market.

On the road to Ramla, 4km east, a large Arabic inscription on an old **stone bridge** commemorates Sultan Baybars who built it. On either side of the inscription are leopards crushing a rat: the leopard represents Baybars' Arab army and the rat, the Crusaders. It was Sultan Baybars' campaigns in the thirteenth century which finally ended European Christian plans for Palestine.

Ramla

RAMLA, just a few kilometres from Lydda, has an equally rich history and rather more to show for it. Even so you're not likely to want to stay here – there's no cheap accommodation – and half a day is enough to see all you might want to see. Buses connect the city with Tel Aviv every fifteen minutes, Jerusalem every thirty minutes and the surrounding area at frequent intervals.

Founded in 716AD by **Caliph Abd al-Malik**, Ramla is relatively young by Palestinian standards, and claims to be the only town in Palestine founded by its Muslim conquerors. Deliberately promoted as a new regional capital – a dyeing industry was organised to ensure its prosperity – Ramla grew rapidly in the early years. Visitors in the ninth century remarked on its size and beauty and the importance of its markets and mosques: the dye works flourished and its products were sold to many of the finest cloth and carpet manufacturers in the Arab world.

In 1033 and 1067 earthquakes destroyed many of Ramla's finer buildings, and more damage was done by a fire in 1177 and in the battle between Salah al-Din and the Crusaders in 1187. In 1191, when **Richard the Lionheart** briefly held the city, its fortifications were destroyed by the retreating Arab forces. Returning to Arab rule under **Sultan Baybars**, Ramla again flourished and in the Middle Ages it became an important commercial centre on the road from Jaffa to Jerusalem.

Apart from a brief stay by Napoleon in the eighteenth century, Ramla spent the succeeding centuries in the relative peace of gradual decline, halted only in 1948. Like Lydda, it lay in the path of the Zionist advance on Jerusalem: here it was **Operation Dani** before whose calculated brutality the Palestinian population fled. Their houses were given to new Jewish immigrants, the majority of them from Yemen, North Africa and Iraq. Today Ramla has one of the most mixed Jewish-Arab communities in Israel with about 6,000 Palestinians and 32,000 Israeli Jews.

The Town

Israeli insta-architects are trying hard to make Ramla look like any other settlement with new buildings which are, to say the least, uninspiring. For the moment, though, enough of the architectural heritage survives – churches, mosques and secular Arab buildings – to lend the place more character than most of these inland towns.

Al-Jamia al-Kabir, the Great Mosque, is the grandest of them; handily located immediately outside the central bus station. Originally built by the Crusaders as St. John's Cathedral, it was converted into a mosque after the city was recaptured and is currently being renovated. The basic structure is a fine example of early Christian architecture, and there's superb Arabic calligraphy adorning the mosque. Best of all is the tall, slender minaret, among the most elegant in the country.

The Great Mosque stands on the fringe of a large, rambling *souq*, not that great as a market but still the busiest part of town and the place to go if you're after a cheap café snack or meal. On the far side of the *souq*, beneath the tall white tower, is the Franciscan **Church of Saint Joseph of Arimathea**. Christian tradition associates Ramla with biblical Rama – *Arimathea* in its Hellenised form – and the church commemorates one of Christ's earliest disciples, the owner of the tomb in which Jesus was laid after the crucifixion. The first church on the site was built in 1296, a second in 1750, but the current structure, as it architecture suggests, dates from the beginning of this century. Of the earlier churches little remains apart from a few walls and an intricate, faded mosaic; the adjacent **monastery** was built in 1750 but has been deserted since 1948. The three Franciscans who live next to the church are happy to take visitors around it and the older buildings; Father Jalil Attiye is a fascinating character with a good knowledge of the history of the area. The highpoint is a trip to the room where **Napoleon Bonaparte** stayed on his way to conquer Jaffa in 1799. The room itself is nothing special – a dusty white chamber with a few pictures of Napoleon adorning the walls and a rather uncomfortable-looking old bed – but the way up, through narrow passageways and up spiralling stairs, is an experience in itself.

A few hundred metres north of the church, at the end of Danny Mass Street (which branches off Herzl Street), the **Tower of the Forty Martyrs** is named for the forty companions of the Prophet Mohammed who, according to Islamic tradition, are buried on the site. A beautiful example of fourteenth-century Arab architecture, the six-storey, thirty-metre-high tower originally served as a minaret for **al-Jamia al-Abyad** (the White Mosque), which was destroyed by an earthquake in 1546. Unusual in that it is built on a square plan, the minaret is open irregularly, but if you're lucky the guard may open it for you to climb the 199 steps. Napoleon is said to have directed the siege of

Jaffa from the top which gives you some idea of the view! Around the tower are the remains of the mosque which in its heyday covered a massive 10,000 square metres.

Not far from here, close to the police station, just off Herzl Street in a garden on Hagannah Street, is the **Birket al-Azaqiah** – also known as the Pool of St. Helena. Once an underground cistern, this is one of two such Abassid constructions in Ramla, and it is thought that the original water was brought in by aqueduct. It too opens only sporadically, but if you are lucky you can rent boats to paddle round the complex.

Outside Ramla on the road to Jerusalem is the country's biggest high security jail, where political prisoners, among others, serve out their sentences in appalling conditions.

Rehovot

REHOVOT was founded in 1890 by pre-Zionist Polish settlers, enjoyed brief celebrity for its citrus growing prowess during the Mandate, and has now been thoroughly suburbanised by the overflow from Tel Aviv. Its only significant claims to fame are that here Hebrew with Sephardic pronunciation was first taught and, above all, that it is home to a prestigious scientific research establishment, the Weizmann Institute.

The **Weizmann Institute** (Sun–Thur 10.30am–3.30pm) is a twenty-minute walk from the bus station down Herzl Street. Named after Chaim Weizmann – the organic chemist who invented the industrial process for the mass production of acetone and was the first president of the state of Israel – the institute started life in 1934 as the Daniel Sieff Research Institute, the cash having been put up by the Marks and Spencer dynasty. Weizmann worked in the institute from 1936.

Weizmann was one of Zionism's early giants. He was the main lobbyist behind the 1917 **Balfour Declaration,** in which the British foreign secretary, Lord Balfour, promised British government support for a 'Jewish national home' in Palestine. This was in part repayment for Weizmann's acetone development, which played a vital part in the mass production of explosives during World War I. Weizmann was reactionary even by Zionist standards, however, and he lost influence in the *Yishuv* to labour movement politicians: the presidency, very much a ceremonial post, was offered to him in 1948 by way of a consolation prize. The Sieff Institute was renamed in his favour in 1949.

Nowadays over 2500 people are employed by the institute, which has ongoing projects in the fields of cancer research, astrophysics, immunology, solar energy and computer sciences. A free video show at the **Wix Auditorium** (the large building on your left as you walk through the main gates; Sun–Thur 11am and 3.15pm, Fri 11.15am) offers a full introduction to this work, and a free map and information sheet about events at the institute is available from the main entrance on Herzl Street.

After viewing the film, and perhaps visiting the massive atomic particle accelerator, you can stroll around the ornate, beautifully laid out **gardens,** reputedly the finest in Israel. Rumour has it that Meyer Weisgal, the

American Zionist who raised millions of dollars for the institute, was so proud of them that he used to spend hours there picking up rubbish. **Weizmann's House** in the institute grounds is an excellent example of 1930s European architecture, heavily influenced by Bauhaus. It has a peaceful library, an impressive art collection and what is said to have been Palestine's first private swimming pool. Weizmann himself is buried just outside.

If you're looking for something to **eat**, the covered **market**, on the corner of Bilu and Herzl streets, has the best and cheapest selection in town, or there's a cluster of reasonably priced restaurants further south on Herzl Street. Rehovot's only **accommodation** is at the *Margoa Hotel* (Maskovitz Street; ☎03-951303), which is neither cheap nor recommended.

Kibbutz Givat Brenner

The largest kibbutz in Israel, **Kibbutz Givat Brenner** is a short bus ride out of Rehovot. Founded in 1928 in memory of the writer Yosef Chaim Brenner, the kibbutz has grown to over 2000 inhabitants and runs three large factories – a fruit juice cannery, a metal casting operation and an arts and crafts workshop. The success of these and its agrobusiness is apparent from the obviously high standard of living enjoyed by its members and has moved Givat Brenner a long way from the kibbutz myth of pioneering socialism. With a large dining hall, community centre, fully equipped hospital, swimming pool and a sports centre the last thing that its members can complain of is austerity or hardship. Although it doesn't officially encourage tourists, there are almost always groups visiting, and they're used to people wandering around, so if you want to see a large kibbutz this might be your chance.

The Givat Brenner factories, fields and kitchens need a lot of cheap labour to turn a profit and there are often upwards of 75 volunteers employed here on a board and lodging and pocket money basis. With the *intifada* threatening the next-cheapest source of labour – Palestinians – there's probably room for more. The size of the kibbutz means that there is a large variety of cultural and sporting events and evening classes, so if you don't mind the exploitation it can be an enjoyable stay. For shorter-term visitors there are officially no facilities at all, although travellers can sometimes sleep on the roof of the tourist workers' dormitory if they can make a friend to take them under their wing. Buses from Rehovot run regularly to the junction leading up to the kibbutz – a ten minute walk from the main road. If you intend to travel to Tel Aviv from Rehovot, the wine cellars in Rishon Le Zion are on the way (see p. 223).

South: isolated sites

As you head south, central Israel becomes increasingly desolate. There are a few sparsely populated towns, kibbutzim and moshavim but virtually nothing between them, and little to stop for even at these, other than another cold drink as you press on towards Beersheva or Eilat. The only real interest lies in three isolated **archaeological sites** to the east of Qiryat Gat, well off the main road. Transportation – public and private – is sparse at best, so these and other archaeological and biblical sites are effectively off-limits unless you have a car or are prepared to spend a long time hitching. The other main hindrance is the lack of accommodation. Ashqelon on the coast has virtually the only cheap lodgings, although if you have a tent there are plenty of opportunities for freelance camping.

The road south from Tel Aviv, Rehovot or Ashdod meets the route inland from Ashqelon at the **Pelugot junction**, just outside Qiryat Gat. Pelugot, literally 'troops', was the scene of heavy fighting during the 1948 war and the ruins of the Arab village of **FALUJA**, where the fighting was centred, still stand southwest of the crossroads. Faluja earned a place in history when Egyptian troops – including an information officer by the name of **Gamal Abdl al-Nasser**, later President of Egypt – were trapped here for two months by the oncoming Zionist forces. The Egyptian troops were negotiated out of Faluja; the Palestinian villagers are still refugees. If you're continuing south, the main road to Beersheva and Eilat runs through here, traversed frequently by buses and bypassing virtually everything along the way.

Qiryat Gat

QIRYAT GAT, an industrial town of some 20,000 people, is the capital of the Lakhish region – a network of thirty Israeli settlements established in 1954. Although it's the only place of any size in the region, and easy enough to get to on regular buses from Ashqelon (slightly less frequent services from Tel Aviv and Jerusalem), there's really no reason to come: no accommodation, few bars or cafés, and limited bus connections to the surrounding sites. Nearby TEL GAT was thought to have contained the remains of Gath, one of the five main Philistine cities, but so far numerous excavations have failed to turn up anything of real significance

More interesting sites – Lakhish, Maresha and Beit Guvrin (Beit Jibrin) – are **east of Qiryat Gat** off the main road to Hebron. Buses are extremely infrequent: #011 leaves Qiryat Gat at 8am and 5pm, and buses back are at similarly inconvenient times. Hitching is possible, but traffic is sparse and most of the drivers are West Bank Palestinians who will probably mistake you for an Israeli and therefore not stop. You may have more than one long wait. Turn-of-the-century visitors to Beit Guvrin had to make an arduous four-hour journey from Jerusalem on horseback and, once there, needed permission from the local *sheikh* to explore. Permission which was frequently not granted. If you do get stranded, musing on the travails of tourism in an earlier age might help – then again it might not.

Lakhish

The first site you pass in this direction is **LAKHISH**, an ancient Canaanite city which, while not the most visually stimulating, is perhaps the most archaeologically important of the three sites. To get there take the small road south of the moshav of the same name for about 2km. The area had a thriving Canaanite civilisation for almost 2000 years until 'Joshua and the Israelites marched upon the city of Lakhish . . . took it on the second day, and put every living thing in it to the sword' (*Joshua 10:31–32*). After this conquest the city lay in ruins until fortified between 928 and 911BC by Rehoboam and grew to become the second most important city in Judah after Jerusalem.

Among archaeologists the site is known primarily as the source of the **Lakhish Letters** – which describe life in the city under Nebuchadnezzar, King of Babylon. Most of the artefacts from the site now rest in museums around the world and only the foundations remain. They are accessible, but they don't mean much to the untrained eye. The main things to look out for are the three-chambered **inner gate** as you enter the site, the largest in Palestine; the **palace area**, distinguishable by a large platform; and the **sacred area**, which is believed to be the first Israelite sanctuary. It still has a slightly raised altar dating from the time of Rehoboam. Very few cars travel the 3km from the main road to the site, so you may prefer to save your energies for Beit Guvrin. If you do decide to make the effort, there is an on-going dig and the archaeologists are usually happy to chat about their work and the site itself.

Tel Maresha and Beit Guvrin

Six kilometres further east, a battered orange sign points down a small, badly-maintained road to **TEL MARESHA** and the spectacular Beit Guvrin Caves. To get to Tel Maresha follow the road for just over a kilometre and then take the right-hand fork. Maresha, like Lakhish, was fortified by Rehoboam, and though never such an important town it became a prosperous commercial centre. During the third century BC it was a profitable centre of the Palestine-Egypt slave trade, and evidence of later, Hasmonean habitation has also been uncovered. Since most of the excavations have been filled in, however, there's little left to see.

To the west of the tel are some of the caves which make **Beit Guvrin (Beit Jibrin)** one of the most fascinating sites in the country. There are over 4000 artificial and natural caves in all, first used – and expanded – by a colony of Sidonians established here by the Ptolemies in the third century BC. Among the vast array of caves are burial chambers, olive presses, water cisterns, storage areas, dwellings and shrines. Most were robbed of everything of importance centuries ago, but it's still an explorers' paradise, with more caves constantly being discovered. To make the most of a visit you should equip yourself with a torch and wear old clothes and non-slip shoes: you tend to emerge covered in white dust from the soft chalk out of which the caves are carved.

Some of the more accessible caves can be reached by following the path which runs from the small swing-gate by the car park to the west of the tel. One of the first, about 200m from the gate (marked *07/01* by archaeologists), is thought to have been a giant underground **dovecote**. After crawling through the small opening you descend into a large cross-shaped chamber, its walls pitted with thousands of small holes arranged neatly in rows in which doves were bred to be sacrificed to the god Aphrodite. Slightly further west numerous other entrances hide dwellings, a water cistern, burial chambers and other caverns which are simply holes in the rock. While well trodden paths lead to many of them, none are marked: the best bet is to explore anything that looks interesting.

To the east of the tel is the most impressive of all the caves: a small **Sidonian tomb** with 41 burial compartments, quarried from brilliant white rock. The entrance to the tomb, just north of the car park, is slightly hidden by a large green bush. At the far end, the most important looking tomb is thought to be that of the chamber's creator, Apollophanes, and his family. Apollophanes was ruler of the Sidonian colony for 33 years and the tomb continued in use through to the first century BC. It's empty now, but some of the intricate rock carvings which adorned it during Apollophanes' reign have survived, as a counterpoint to less imaginative modern graffiti. South of the car park is the entrance to the smaller **Tomb of the Musicians**, named after a painting inside of a man with a flute and a woman playing a harp. This also dates from the Sidonian period.

If you go north towards the main road and take the first turning right, a small pot-holed road leads to another car park. From here a path heads east into a large pit, on the northeast side of which is the entrance to one of the most spectacular of a series of so-called **bell caves** dating from the fourth to the seventh centuries AD. In this region, a thin crust of hard rock covers vast chalk deposits. To get to the chalk, miners chipped away a small round hole in the hard rock and then quarried out the chalk beneath to produce large bell-shaped caverns, some over 300m high with spacious interiors that have the air of abandoned churches. The chalk dug here was roasted to produce mortar and plaster, and the vast number of bell caves in the vicinity – there are said to be over a thousand – bear witness to the importance of the commodity. After the Arab conquest of Eleutheropolis (see below) the caves provided materials for the building of Ramla.

At the junction to Maresha and the caves, below the kibbutz, you'll see the remains of **Beit Jibrin Castle**. Built by Fulk of Anjou in the twelfth century, the castle is recognisably a Crusader structure even in its current state of dilapidation. That it survives relatively intact is thanks to the Arab families who lived in it for generations, adding features such as the olive press. Remains of the Palestinian village of **Beit Jibrin** can be seen all around, especially among the kibbutz buildings: the old village school now serves as the kibbutz's administration block. Signs around the castle warn of 'falling stones' and 'danger of tick-borne disease' so visitors need to tread carefully: long trousers and sleeves should keep the ticks off. Behind the castle recent excavations have uncovered a small **Roman Amphitheatre**, but the better finds, including fine Roman and Byzantine mosaic floors, have been ripped up and taken to the Israel Museum in Jerusalem, leaving behind little more than dust.

This area was also the original site of ancient Beit Guvrin, which became the local administrative centre after Maresha had been destroyed by the Parthians. It was named Eleutheropolis by the Emperor Septimius Severus in 200AD, and during the Byzantine period was important enough to merit a bishop. The **kibbutz** here was originally founded in 1949 and rapidly went bust. In its new incarnation, it plans to develop facilities and encourage visitors to the surrounding antiquities. In one way this will be a shame, as one of the best things about a visit at present is precisely the lack of tour groups or tourist development. On the other hand if you can get someone from the kibbutz to guide you round, you'll probably get more from the caves. At weekends the kibbutz runs a small café, but there's nowhere to stay.

Bet Shemesh and the road to Jerusalem

If you continue **east from Beit Guvrin** the road winds its way through forests, Beduin camps and villages in the foothills of the West Bank on the way to HEBRON (see p.152). If you have the time, this is much the most interesting and scenic route **towards Jerusalem**. If you're in a hurry, however, a left turn almost immediately after Beit Guvrin will take you up to Bet Shemesh and the main Tel Aviv–Jerusalem road.

Founded in 1950 on the site of an old Jordanian army post, **BET SHEMESH** has little to offer beyond excellent connections to Jerusalem – buses leave at least every hour and there are occasional *sherut* taxis too. The town centre is about 1km from the main road and if you're hungry you'll find cafes, *falafel* stands and shops here: otherwise there's no reason to leave the bus stop. Until recently the main local employer was *Beit Shemesh Engines*, a manufacturer of jet engines for the Israeli warplane industry kept afloat by a considerable US subsidy. When in 1987 the US announced that it was no longer willing to subsidise the *Lavi* jet project, *Beit Shemesh Engines* lost most of its funding: the future of town and industry seems equally bleak.

A few kilometres to the west lies the biblical site (Bet Shemesh), after which the modern day town was named. Prosperous and important as the ancient city was reputed to be, however, Tel Bet Shemesh has surrendered little in the way of evidence. A rather more worthwhile detour is to **Soreq Cave**, just north of the Bet Shemesh junction in the **Absalom Nature Reserve**. Over 90m-long, and 80m-high in places, the cave is a well developed site with some impressive stalactites and stalagmites. Apart from the caves themselves, there is an informative audio-visual presentation on the geological history of the area.

travel details

Buses
From Ben Gurion Airport to Tel Aviv (every 20min 5am–11.30pm; 20min); Jerusalem (30min 6am–8pm; 30min); Haifa (40min 6am–8pm; 1hr 45min).
From Tel Aviv to Jerusalem (every 15min 5.30am–11.30pm; 45min); Haifa (express every 20min, local every 30min 6am–11pm; 1hr 45min); Ramla (30min 6am–10pm; 20min); Rehovot (20min 5am–10.30pm; 25min); Ashqelon (20min 5am–11pm; 1hr); Netanya (15min 8am–8.30pm; 20min); Nazareth (30min 6am–6pm; 2hr),Tiberias/Qiryat Shmona (hourly 6am–8pm; 2hr 30min/3hr 30min); Gaza (4 daily; 1hr 30min); Beersheva

(20min 6am–7.30pm; 2hr); Eilat (hourly 6am–5pm; 5hr); Cairo (2 daily; 10hr).
From Ashqelon to Jerusalem (every 30min 6am–6pm; 1hr); Beersheva (hourly 6am–7pm; 1hr); Rafah border (5 daily; 1hr).
From Ashdod to Jerusalem (7 daily; 1hr).
From Rehovot to Jerusalem (9 daily; 1hr) and Beersheva (30min 6am–11pm; 1hr 20min).

Train
To Jerusalem, departs daily 8.15am (2hr).
To Netanya, Haifa, and Nahariyya at least six departures daily (30min/3hr/4hr).

CHAPTER FOUR

HAIFA AND THE CENTRAL COAST

Haifa, Israel's third largest city, is the industrial and economic centre of the north. Climbing steeply from a jostling port to the airy peaks of the **Carmel mountain range**, it offers spectacular views over the Mediterranean. For many, the atmosphere is an ideal middle way between the frenetic buzz of Tel Aviv and the hidebound conservatism of Jerusalem: cooler and calmer than the former, livelier and freer than the latter.

The **Mediterranean coast** to the south is as varied as any: occasional enclaves of luxury, the odd downmarket resort, and a couple of fascinating archaeological sites. Above all though, there's a great deal of nothing, and much of the 100km shoreline from Tel Aviv to Haifa is entirely undeveloped, ideal if all you want to do is swim and sunbathe. It's covered in these pages from Tel Aviv northwards.

Herzliya, still on the fringes of Tel Aviv's sprawl, is a pricey resort, probably the nearest thing to South-of-France chic you'll find in Israel. There are excellent beaches, but you have to pay to get on to the better of them: walk up the coast, however, and you'll find plenty of free, empty sand. **Netanya**, the next place of any size, has aspirations to the same sort of classy resort status, but it's considerably more interesting, with a reasonably well-established town to add some weight to the hedonism, and one or two budget hotels.

Almost exactly halfway up the coast, around an hour's drive from either Haifa or Tel Aviv, is **Caesarea**, one of the most outstanding archaeological sites in the country. In the midst of the excavated remains of Herod's Roman city – amphitheatre, hippodrome, temples, port and, as ever, an impressive ancient sewage system – are the extensive ruins of a smaller Crusader town, its magnificent fortifications solidly threatening still. Beyond here is the least developed stretch of shore yet, interrupted only by the occasional kibbutz or moshav – the fishponds and bird sanctuary at **Kibbutz Ma'agan Mikhael** offer excellent opportunities to birdwatchers – or by small campsites such as **Neve Yam**. The one real blight on this landscape, just before Caesarea, is the **Hadera power station**, built on the site of the last Palestinian village to be destroyed in Israel.

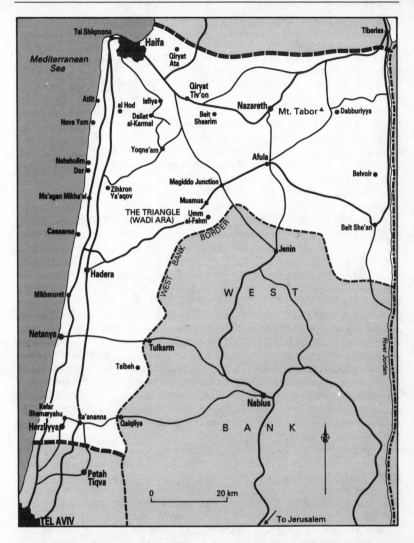

Inland, the southern half of the area covered in this chapter offers virtually nothing of interest, but setting out from Haifa there's some beautiful country and a number of interesting stopovers. Immediately south of the city, the picturesque plateaux of the Carmel range stretch for some 40km: much is given over to a large and undeveloped **national park**, but two large Druze villages, **Daliat al-Karmel** and **Isfiya**, are popular excursions, commercialised, but with a distinct atmosphere of their own nonetheless. **Ein Hod,** not far away, is a former Palestinian village taken over by an 'artists' colony' – a beautiful setting overrun by tourism.

East of Haifa, the road to Nazareth takes you past the catacombs of **Beit Shearim**, an important Jewish burial site during the first few centuries AD. **Nazareth** itself is something of a let-down. There are plenty of churches, but none of the romance which you might expect to attach to its famous name, and as an almost exclusively Palestinian town it's visibly impoverished – starved of the funds which elsewhere might be available to clean up its image. Still, the countryside around is attractive, especially if you head south into the **Jezreel Valley** towards the crossroads town of **Afula**. From here, or from Nazareth itself, you can head up towards the Sea of Galilee, past the site of Jesus' transfiguration at **Mount Tabor**. Back towards the coast, **Megiddo Junction** marks the site of **Armageddon** – a real place, much of which has been excavated. Beyond lies the area known as **the Triangle**, whose poor, overcrowded yet hospitable villages house the heaviest concentration of Palestinians in Israel. From Afula you can also travel south into the West Bank, or west to **Beit She'an** – site of yet more satisfyingly solid Roman remains – and the Jordan Valley.

NORTH ALONG THE COAST

Leaving the northern tentacles of Tel Aviv behind, you enter the broad agricultural stretches of the **Sharon Plain**. Transport here is fast and efficient, the main road and railway hugging the coastline – though rarely in view of the sea – all the way to Haifa. From the towns, buses and *service* taxis depart constantly, and even at smaller places you should never have to wait more than an hour. Hitching is always a good option too. Since it takes less than two hours to get from Tel Aviv to Haifa, virtually anywhere on the coast is an easy day trip. Unless you're heading for Nablus and the West Bank – roads cut across country from Herzliya and Netanya – there's little reason to stray from the shore. The first place you might consider stopping, barely outside the Tel Aviv city limits, is Herzliya.

Herzliya

Built in 1924 and named after Theodore Herzl, the original town of **HERZLIYA** has gradually come to be totally eclipsed by its more opulent suburb, **Herzliya Pituach**. If you come, this is where you'll spend your time too. Israel's premier up-market resort, its pay beaches, shorefront ice cream parlours, cafés, restaurants and hotels are patronised by wealthy Israelis, diplomats (many of whom have their residences around here) and the top end of the package tour market. It's not a place where you'll find a cheap bed or youth hostel, and since it's only a forty-minute bus ride from Tel Aviv or Jaffa is perhaps best treated as a day trip from there (*United Tours* bus #90 from Dizengoff Square to Shalit Square) or as a brief stopover on your way north. If you're really watching the pennies, bring along all the food and drink you'll need for the day.

When you arrive in Herzliya, get off the bus at the *Sharon Hotel*, just west of the main square. The main **beach** is directly in front of you, but officially you have to pay to get onto it. You may simply be able to walk in, but if not – and you're determined not to pay – walk north along the beach road to the Sidna Ali Mosque; access there is free. The #90 bus stops in **Nof Yam**, where the mosque is situated, before it gets to the *Sharon*.

Built around the turn of the century as a *caravanserai*, the **Sidna Ali Mosque** (no public access, but a striking clifftop situation looking down over the beach) now serves both as a mosque and a religious school. Just beyond, steps lead down to the sand: camping is permitted here, and during the summer the beach is overrun by school children, local scout and paramilitary youth groups and sometimes, it seems, virtually everyone in the country who owns a sleeping bag. For more tranquillity you can continue to walk up the beach for miles, and in the safety of a group there are plenty more places to camp. Not far past Sidna Ali, an enterprising beach lover has carved a house out of the sandstone cliffs, and in the summer runs a café which stays open late. It's not hard to track down – just follow the music which blares out for most of the day and early evening.

A little further (around 1km north of the mosque) is the ancient site of **Tel Arshaf**. Believed to have been a Canaanite setttlement dedicated to the Semitic god *Reshef*, it was later established as a port by the Greeks and renamed **Apollonia**. Most of the port has been overwhelmed by the sea, but parts of the city walls and some buildings are still clearly visible. In the twelfth century the Crusader Knights of the Cross built a small fortress, the remains of which can be explored about half a mile from the port. It was destroyed by Sultan Baybars in 1265 to dissuade the European invaders from coming back.

Netanya

NETANYA, some 20km further north, is not quite as expensive as Herzliya Pituach – but it would like to be. Founded by European settlers in 1928 as a farming village, it very soon became a small market town. With the collapse of the citrus industry in World War II it turned to diamond cutting and polishing, and to tourism. The mix has been remarkably successful: diamonds are still processed here in their thousands, and there's a thriving upmarket tourist industry. An interesting, and more recent, side-line is providing retirement and holiday homes for the kind of Zionist who sensibly made a packet in Europe or the US before 'giving it all up' to help 'build Israel' from a plastic beach chair while sipping overpriced drinks imported from the *galut*.

What makes Netanya more than an overblown version of Herzliya, however, is that alongside its beaches and garish, crowded hotels and restaurants survives an older, more interesting town, one with a sizeable diamond industry, a continuing role as an agricultural market centre, an elegant clifftop park, and above all the legacy of the local architects who in the 1940s and 1950s became turned on to **art nouveau**. Examples of their enthusiasm can

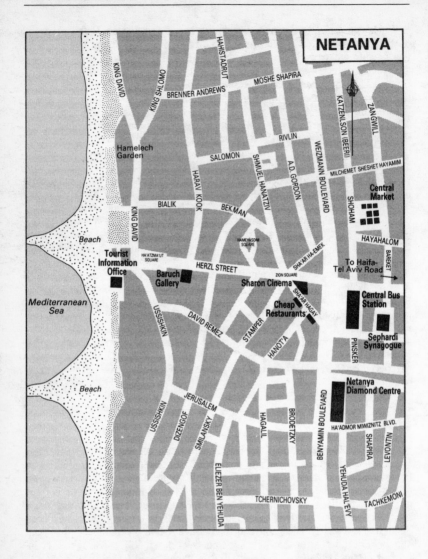

be seen everywhere, especially around the main shopping area, off Herzl Street. The elegance seems particularly impressive here as a contrast to the drab cubes of concrete everywhere else.

Arriving, you'll be at the central **bus station** on Benyamin Boulevard (☎053-37052; timetables posted near the information booth, last bus to Tel Aviv at 11pm). To get to the town centre and the sea, follow Herzl Street along to **HaAtzma'ut Square**. The square itself, full of nondescript bars and pizza places, is a good place from which to get your bearings, with the **IGTO** handily nearby, dishing out the usual array of maps and leaflets (Tues–Thur and Sun 8.30am–2pm and 4–7pm, Mon and Fri 8.30am–2pm; ☎053-27286). Most other services you may need are in the same area: the main **post office** at 59 Herzl Street (Sun–Tues and Thur 7.45am–12.30pm and 3.30–6pm, Wed 7.45am–2pm, Fri 7.45am–1pm); **bike rental** at 12 Nice Boulevard (☎053-28805); and a **launderette** just off the square opposite Bank Leumi.

Netanya has two cheap **hostels**, *Orit* (21 Hen Ave; ☎053-616818; $8, students $4) and *The Motel* (32 Jabotinsky St; ☎053-22634; $8 and up); and two reasonably-priced **hotels**, the *Hotel Rubin* (25 Ussishkin St; ☎053-23107) and the *Hotel Atzma'ut* (2 Ussishkin St; ☎053-22562). Both charge $16–24 single, $18–32 double, depending on the season and your bargaining skills. The IGTO can advise on availability of other accommodation and the prices (high) you can expect to pay. The crowded **beaches** are free (walk down the steps by the tourist office to get there), but don't try sleeping on them unless you want to run up against the local police. One **warning** if you do come: women alone in Netanya should be particularly careful, especially around the park, which has something of a reputation for harassment and muggings.

For good value **food**, try the stalls around the bus station: *Tzly Esh Café*, just to the east in the middle of Sha'ar HaGay Street, is easily spotted by its large yellow canopy and wooden bench seats. There are slightly more expensive places around Dizengoff Street and Zion Square – for a treat try the *Patisserie* at 6 Eliyahu Krause Street, off Smilanski – and glitzier bars and restaurants in and around HaAtzma'ut Square. The **market** on Zangwill Street can supply a wide variety of fresh produce if you want to make up your own picnic, or there's a **health food** store at 10 Herzl Street.

As for **entertainment**, Netanya's chief attraction after the beaches is the **Netanya Philharmonic Orchestra**, which performs each Tuesday night in July and August either in the Amphitheatre at *Gan HaMelech* or more usually in HaAtzma'ut Square. The rest of the year, they play on either the second or third Tuesday of the month. For more details on this, and other festivals in Netanya, contact the IGTO. There's also plenty of **sport**: **tennis** at the Elizur Sports Centre (Radak St; ☎053-38920); **bowling** at the Wingate Institute (south of Netanya; ☎053-96652); **windsurfing** at the Kontiki Club on Herzl Beach and **mini-golf** on Nice Boulevard. An annual **chess tournament** is held in May and June – open to all comers.

Elsewhere you can visit the various glittering **diamond centres**, filled to the brim with (mostly South African) gems, or the **Abir Brewery**, which offers free guided tours and the chance to sample a bit of its particular potion (open Sun–Thur from 10am; details from the IGTO). There are also a number of very expensive art galleries: *Baruh*, 4 Herzl St, *Kontiki*, HaAtzma'ut Square, and *Gallery 1*, 12 Krause St, generally have interesting exhibitions.

If you're intending to stay for a couple of days, you could make a day of a trip to the **Poleg Nature Reserve**, which starts 8km south of Netanya where the Poleg river meets the sea – but if time is short, Caesarea (see below) makes a better day out.

Netanya to Caesarea: Hadera

A little over halfway between Netanya and Caesarea, the **Hadera power station** towers above the plain, virtually the only landmark along the way. Beneath it lay the village of **Arab al-Mifger**, which in 1981 became the last Palestinian village in Israel to be destroyed – and marked the end of a heroic battle by a small group of people to save their homes.

Arab al-Mifger was a small Beduin settlement where for generations people had scraped a living from the sandy soil and the sea. It was so inconsequential that the 1948 war passed it by completely. When the reality of modern Israel finally arrived, in the form of the power station, it found a small place of less than 100 inhabitants, already cut off from the world by a four-lane highway. A few of the houses were breeze-block built, most were wood. Few had laid floors, none had electricity. But when the planners invited them to go, the villagers refused.

Ali al-Kaisi, like his neighbours, was a working man of little formal education but, because his house was slightly away from the rest of the village in the dunes, he became a national celebrity. It was his they bulldozed first. He rebuilt it. They put him in jail and bulldozed it again. He got out and rebuilt it. They jailed him for contempt of court. Ali was the barrack-room lawyer *extraordinaire*. He didn't know much about law, but his eloquence ran rings round Israeli prosecutors and judges alike. The police wrecked his home four times in all. He'd sit brewing tea over an open fire in front of whatever rooms he'd managed to salvage ("this firewood was part of my bedroom last week") and regale visitors with verbatim accounts of the latest court case or showdown with the cops.

When they finally buried his home under a coal hopper and gave Ali the simple choice of staying away from Arab al-Mifger or sitting in jail, the fight went out of the village. Ali gathered his kids, took a tent and went to live in the park opposite the Knesset – the seat of Israeli democracy. He held out there for another few months and it was the eviction from the park that finally broke him. In the years of struggle to save his home he became a Palestine-wide, and to a certain extent international, celebrity: he was the symbol of Palestinian attachment to their land and appeared on the posters of political parties who wouldn't let him within a hundred metres of their platforms. But in the end he failed and the power station went ahead: he lives now, all but forgotten, in a village in the Triangle where he subsists on the charity of friends.

There's been talk of cleaning up the river and of making a **park** around the power station – when Ali heard it, he tried to persuade the authorities to let the villagers stay on as 'local colour'. If that happens, he may yet win the last battle.

The town after which the power station is named, **HADERA**, lies inland a short way to the south. One of the main citrus growing centres in the Sharon Plain, Hadera is a largely residential town of very little interest to visitors. It is, however, a major transport junction, with regular buses heading inland through the Triangle towards Afula, a staging point on the way to

NAZARETH or TIBERIAS. There's an efficient bus station and regular departures, so no necessity to hang around for long.

Caesarea

Herod ordered the construction of **CAESAREA** – the second largest city in his kingdom – on the site of a Phoenician anchorage called Strato's Tower, to 'honour' Augustus Caesar. A fine career move for Herod, it was also a magnificent city: every contemporary account lauds the grandeur of its palaces, hippodrome and amphitheatre, and the two large aqueducts which kept Caesarea supplied with water were masterpieces of engineering. But by far the most spectacular part of the city was the harbour, in its day the finest in the eastern Mediterranean. Caesarea took ten years to build and the inaugural celebration in the first century BC became a four-yearly festival in honour of Augustus Caesar. After Herod's death, Caesarea became capital of the Roman province of Judaea, and the seat of the Roman Procurator, Pontius Pilate.

Judaism and Caesarea always had an uneasy relationship. It was here that the Roman policy of enforced Hellenisation of the country was devised, sparking off the **Jewish Revolt** of 66AD that culminated in the Roman seizure of Jerusalem and the destruction of the Temple. It began with rioting in the city during which, according to the Roman historian Josephus, 'the people of Caesarea massacred the Jewish colony, in less than an hour slaughtering more than 20,000 and emptying Caesarea of the last Jew'. As if to rub salt in the wound, Caesarea witnessed the execution, in 132AD, of the leaders of the Bar Kokhba revolt, among them Rabbi Akiva, a scholar famous for his teachings and writings on the *Mishnah*, the traditional laws which still govern the day-to-day lives of orthodox Jewry.

Nonetheless Caesarea was at this time and later an important Christian and Jewish centre: here Peter baptised the centurion Cornelius; and Paul was imprisoned for his heretical teachings (his trial and appeal to Caesar are detailed in *Acts 25* and *26*). In 640 Caesarea was captured by the Arabs, and under their guidance continued to prosper, as they developed both the harbour and the surrounding lands. What you see today, however, is largely a monument to the Crusaders. A few spectacular Roman buildings remain, but most of their stone-cutting labours were borrowed by successive rulers to adorn buildings up and down the country.

The Crusader era began in 1107, the year when most of Palestine fell under their dominion. In 1187, after the Battle of Hittin, Salah al-Din ousted the Crusaders, destroying much of the city. Over succeeding years the city changed hands five times, eventually being reconquered by the Crusaders in 1251 under the leadership of **Louis IX** of France. In a fourteen-year occupation, Louis managed to construct one of the most spectacular fortified cities in the Middle East, much of it still visible. A final conquest by Sultan Baybars brought all his work to nothing, though, as the city was destroyed and never again re-occupied.

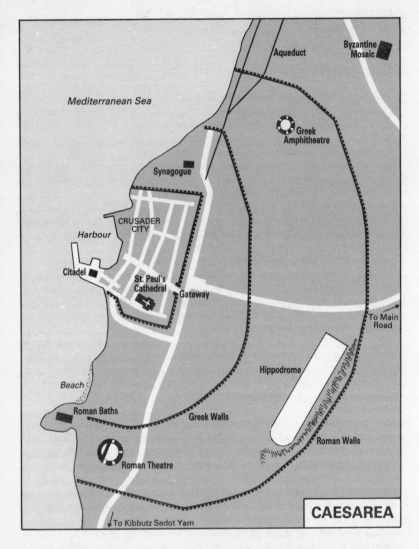

Mediterranean Sea

Aqueduct

Byzantine Mosaic

Greek Amphitheatre

Synagogue

CRUSADER CITY

Harbour

Citadel

St. Paul's Cathedral

Gateway

To Main Road

Hippodrome

Beach

Roman Baths

Greek Walls

Roman Walls

Roman Theatre

To Kibbutz Sedot Yam

CAESAREA

In 1878, the **Ottoman** rulers settled Muslim refugees from Bosnia nearby, establishing a farming and fishing village. Part of their land was bought up during the 1930s by the Palestine Jewish Colonisation Association – a land society founded by Baron Edmund de Rothschild to promote Jewish settlement – and nearby kibbutz Sedot Yam was established on it. The remaining Palestinian inhabitants were forced out when their village was obliterated in 1948. All that remains of it is the mosque beside the port.

The Site

Caesarea is probably the finest and largest archaeological site in Israel, with excellently preserved, visually stunning Roman and Crusader remains. Even rampant commercialisation, with souvenir stores, cafés, a disco, and relatively difficult access (at least by public transport) cannot take the shine off. The **site** (Sun–Thur 8am–4pm, Fri 8am–3pm; $1.50 admission to the main section) is easiest visualised as being split into three main areas: the northern sector, predominantly Crusader in origin; the southern sector, which is Roman; and the eastern sector, where you'll find the Roman hippodrome and the straggling fringes of the modern development of Caesarea.

The northern sector

The northern entrance is by the large Roman aqueduct and is dominated by the Crusader city, among the best preserved in the country. Before entering the fortress proper, follow the road north past the fortifications (towards the beach), where the **Roman aqueduct** offers a superb overview of the site and some idea of its scale. The aqueduct itself combines the work of two great Roman rulers, Herod and Hadrian. The western water channel, facing the sea, is Hadrian's work, built in the second century AD; the eastern side dates from the first century BC. Although the site is littered with rubbish and old mattresses, and the brick arches are half buried in sand, their presence remains majestic and familiar from dozens of travel agents' brochures. As you explore, you'll almost certainly be approached by local youths selling 'genuine Roman coins': fake, but good cheap souvenirs all the same. To the right of the aqueduct lie the remains of a fourth-century **synagogue** discovered by an expedition in 1956. It's only partially excavated, but the remains of the mosaic floor are clearly visible.

Back at the **Crusader City**, the impressive main gateway, flanked by two enormous Gothic towers overlooking the moat, is the work of Louis IX. In the process of revamping the city's fortifications, Louis also had the moat (now dry) constructed, strengthened the wall with an embankment, and added a large passageway at right angles to the old gate with an opening at its northern end. This served to break the approach of invaders, slowing them down and forcing them to pass beneath the defenders of the gate: to the same end, the bridge over the moat, supported by four pointed arches, passed in the shadow of the nine-metre-high tower. As you cross the bridge and proceed under the gateway, notice the hewn grooves in which the portcullis could be raised or lowered, and the sockets for the hinges of the iron doors. Within, the gateway is a beautifully proportioned structure with high vaulted interior supports made from smooth limestone.

Once inside the main gates you're confronted by a large collection of Roman, Arab and Crusader ruins. It's all a bit of a jumble, but everything is well marked and it's easy enough to identify the various periods. Perhaps the easiest place to start is the **Crusader Cathedral** dedicated to St. Paul in the main square: turn left and follow the walls around for about 200m. Built originally as a mosque in the early Arab period, the cathedral was taken over and substantially remodelled by the Crusaders, although the work was abandoned before completion because the vaults underneath started to crack. Excavations have revealed a finely proportioned building with a triple apse at the eastern end and a row of eight Corinthian columns bearing the cross of Richard the Lionheart (who recaptured the city from Salah al-Din's forces during the third Crusade). Adjacent is a second Crusader building, of which you can see the foundations and a small part of the upper structure.

Making your way up the broad road by the side of the cathedral, it is possible to get a sense of how each successive period reused, reworked and redesigned previous architectural styles. Statues taken from temples were smashed and used for stone by the Byzantines: floors of early Arab houses were used as the bases of later Crusader buildings; massive pillars of porphyry rock were hewn into rounded slabs for use as mill-stones; and most interesting of all, Roman columns were split in two and put to use as wall supports or door frames. Examples of this architectural reclamation can be seen as far afield as Acre, where Roman masonry from Caesarea is almost commonplace.

East of the small gate, past the rows of souvenir shops, the area around the **Crusader Citadel** is the most heavily commercialised at the site: the citadel itself has even had a restaurant built in (relatively tastefully done – and excellent value – but sacrilege nonetheless). From here there's a fine view of the Crusader city – only a fraction of the area of Roman Caesarea – and the surrounding coast. You can also get to the **beach**, though there's a steep entry fee (around $6): down by the Roman amphitheatre you can swim for free, but bathing is not allowed at the beaches immediately south of the Crusader city, where there's a dangerous undertow.

The southern sector

If you leave the Crusader city by the small side entrance and walk south along the old Byzantine road, you'll reach the **Roman Theatre** in around five minutes. Built into the side of a hill overlooking the sea, it has been heavily refurbished and is now used for ballets, concerts and operas, especially during the **Israel Festival**. Semi-circular and multi-tiered – and still scattered with ruined marble columns and capitals – the vast theatre illlustrates well the size and importance of Roman Caesarea. Here the entire community would meet, not just for theatrical performances but for trials, executions and other important civic matters. Excavations at the site began in the late 1950s, and when fully restored in 1961, the theatre was opened with a concert by the renowned Spanish cellist **Pablo Casals**. Just outside the entrance to the Roman theatre, buses stop on their way back to the main Tel Aviv–Haifa road.

Towards the east

East of the main site, the **Roman Hippodrome** was a racetrack with room for crowds of as many as 20,000 spectators. In the centre is an obelisk and nearby three granite pillars, all of which were used as 'horse frighteners'. Polished and turned towards the animals, they reflected a blinding beam which would 'scare them into speed'. Today there is little that will remind you of their original use, and modern Israel is rapidly encroaching on this part of the Roman city. Follow the signs to 'the site of the new Caesarea Shopping Centre', and eventually you will come to the new city, useful at least as a source of good cheap food.

Practicalities

If you want to **stay** at Caesarea there are two good possibilities a campsite and a kibbutz guest house – as well as a couple of expensive hotels at the beach. The cheaper options are both to be found at the *Kayet Veshait Camp Site* (run by Kibbutz Sedot Yam; ☎063-62928), 1km south of the Roman amphitheatre. The campsite costs very little, the guest house charges around $25 per person for bed and breakfast. Either offers a truly wonderful view out to sea. Camping on the beach is permitted, but it's definitely not recommended, as you're highly vulnerable to thefts: indeed there seems to be a chronic crime problem in Caesarea. Keep all your valuables with you all the time – car locks are no obstacle to local entrepreneurs.

Local **buses** to Caesarea run every hour, north and south, though for a wider choice and a faster bus it is best to try and get back onto the main Tel Aviv–Haifa highway.

Caesarea to Haifa

Leaving Caesarea, Haifa lies less than an hour to the north. Along the way are some fine beaches, and a couple of places worth stopping off if you're in no hurry.

Ma'agan Mikhael and Dor

About 5km north of Caesarea, **Kibbutz Ma'agan Mikhael** (☎063-90501) is one of the wealthiest kibbutzim in the country. It funds its own **bird- and wildlife sanctuary** (open daylight hours Sun–Fri) and a small natural history museum. The sanctuary is about 1km south of the kibbutz, set along the banks of a small river – a good site for migratory birdlife and large sea turtles are also occasionally seen. The sanctuary is easily visited in passing (or as a trip out from Netanya, Caeasarea or Haifa) but if you want to stay there's only a very expensive guest house or the *Bet Sefer Sadeh* (Field School) *Hostel*. This is a field study centre run by the Nature Reserves Authority and normally accommodates only pre-arranged groups and school parties on field studies: occasionally, however, they do allow individual visitors to stay. Alternatively, the campsite at Dor is just about within walking distance.

DOR lies 5km north along the beach – a beautiful, isolated walk. The campsite at **Moshav Dor** (☎063-99018), is about the first thing you'll reach, at the southern end of Dor's excellent beach. It can be crowded in summer, but it's a very pleasant place to stay: as well as tent space at $3 per person you can also rent three-person bungalows for $25. The moshav was built on the site of the destroyed Palestinian village of **Tantura**, which was famous for its murex: shellfish whose purple colouring was used as raw material by Haifa dye works. The **beach** itself is sheltered by four small, rocky islands which merge with each other at low tide and are the nesting place of terns and plovers. You can wade out to them when the tide is out.

At the northern end of the beach is the archaeological site of **Tel Dor**. Settled from the Bronze Age, Dor was described in Egyptian papyrus texts as 'a site of magnificence', and in the fifth century BC was the base of King Ashmanezer – a Canaanite from Sidon. Its zenith, however, came in the Hellenic period, when it was capital of an Assyrian province. **Temples** dedicated to Zeus and Astarte have been found at Tel Dor along with the remains of an early Byzantine church. The Crusaders built a fortress here – Castle Merle – whose sea-washed remains can still be seen. There is a large archaeological dig at Tel Dor through most of the summer, and one of its members will usually be happy to show you the key points. To volunteer on the dig, see "Work" in the *Basics* section.

Zichron Yaacov

Inland from Dor, **ZICHRON YAACOV** sits on a hill looking down over the coast. It's a sizeable place, but would be eminently missable were it not for the opportunity to visit the **Carmel-Oriental Wine Co.** (HaNadiv St, three blocks north of the bus station; ☎063-88643). The business was established in 1888, when Baron Edmund de Rothschild paid for the establishment of what was to become the best and largest vineyard in Palestine. A $2 walking tour (every half hour Sun–Thur 9am–3pm) introduces both the wine and the production techniques employed. The usual free samples of the product are your reward at the end. To find the winery get off at the central bus station, walk north along HaMeyasdim Street and turn right at HaNadiv Street. The Rothschild family tomb lies close by.

Neve Yam

Continuing up the coast, **NEVE YAM** was for many years a tranquil beachside campsite with superb sands and a pleasantly laid-back atmosphere. The beach is still there, but the ambience has suffered a little as more and more people have discovered the site and the beauty of its location. You can stay here at any time of year (☎04-942240), though the small shop is open only from May to October: since its limited stock is expensive anyway you'd be well advised to bring as much as possible with you. To reach the site watch out for the signs on the main Tel Aviv–Haifa coastal road – a couple of local buses go all the way to Neve Yam, but it's only a short walk from where through buses stop on the main road.

Immediately to the north, **Atlit Castle** dominates the small rock outcrop at the end of the beach. Dating from the Crusader period, this castle has had many keepers throughout its long history. Its present Israeli owners have built a naval port and a large prison nearby, which was used to detain Lebanese and Palestinian prisoners illegally brought from Lebanon at the time of the Israeli invasion of 1982. Needless to say inquisitive tourists are not welcome.

HAIFA

HAIFA, the third city in Israel, dominates the north of the country politically, socially and commercially. It's a working city (the Israeli aphorism 'In Jerusalem they pray, in Tel Aviv they dance, but in Haifa they *work*' has a lot of truth in it) and it's also a very attractive one, ranged steeply up Mount Carmel from the port.

The working side of town is based around a thriving port, supported by heavy industry and the railway: Israeli Haifans are proud of the 'Red Haifa' label – it's a stronghold of the Zionist labour movement. Haifa also claims a reputation as a 'tolerant' city. The most obvious signs of this liberalism are that three religious sects which claim a history of persecution – the Bahais, the Achmadians and the Carmelite order of monks – are based in the city, and that local buses run on the sabbath. On the other hand Palestinian aspirations count for no more here than anywhere else in Israel. In the 1950s Haifa was scarred by Jewish rioting as Sephardi Jews protested at Ashkenazi Jewish racism directed towards them.

From the port, the city climbs the slopes of the Carmel mountains, its residential areas more exclusive the higher you climb. From the top the views are terrific, and the cooling breezes sweeping along the range help make Haifa pleasantly temperate when everywhere else is sweating. The atmosphere is refreshing in other ways, too: as a large port Haifa is open to a wide range of outside influences that help offset the Israeli parochialism which plagues so many other towns. Most of the industrial base – an oil refinery, the largest grain processing plant in the Middle East and numerous other small industries – is located to the north, out of sight from all but the highest points on the mountains. The smell only gets through when the wind blows the wrong way.

History

Archaeological remains indicate that the area around Haifa has been inhabited since the Paleolithic period. A port was founded in the fourteenth century BC at a site east of the present city now known as Tel Abu Haram. In the early Christian era the area was a fishing centre, known for the production of purple dye extracted from the murex – a small spiny-shelled shellfish. By the eleventh century a local shipbuilding industry had developed, too, its progress interrupted by the **Crusader** invasion of 1099. Having all but destroyed the town and its population, the Crusaders proceeded to fortify and enlarge what was left: a small town very much overshadowed by Acre.

Over the following century Haifa was scrapped over like its more important neighbours: Salah al-Din recaptured the city in 1187 and destroyed the ramparts; Louis IX grabbed it back for the Crusaders; and in 1291 Sultan Baybars marched in, putting an end to the problem by destroying the place altogether. At the time of the **Ottoman conquest** in 1517, Haifa was little more than an impoverished village. In succeeding centuries, however, with the expansion of trade between Europe and the Orient, the port thrived.

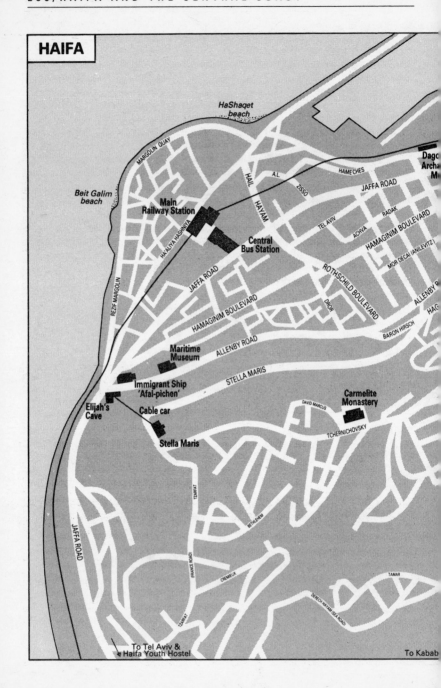

HAIFA

HaShaqet beach

Beit Galim beach

MARGOLIN QUAY

HAIL

A.L

HAMECHES

JAFFA ROAD

Dago
Archa
M

**Main
Railway Station**

HA ALIYA HASHNIYA

HAYAM

ZISSO

TEL AVIV

RADAK

ACHVA

**Central
Bus Station**

HAMAGINIM BOULEVARD

MOR DECAI (ANILEVITZ)

JAFFA ROAD

ROTHSCHILD BOULEVARD

ALLENBY R

HAG

REZIF MARGOLIN

HAMAGINIM BOULEVARD

DROR

BARON HIRSCH

**Maritime
Museum**

ALLENBY ROAD

STELLA MARIS

**Immigrant Ship
'Afai-pichen'**

**Carmelite
Monastery**

DAVID MARCUS

**Elijah's
Cave**

Cable car

TCHERNICHOVSKY

Stella Maris

TZARFAT

FRANCE ROAD

BETHLEHEM

CREMIEUX

TAMAR

JAFFA
ROAD

DERECH HAYAM (SEA ROAD)

TZAFAT

To Tel Aviv &
Haifa Youth Hostel

To Kabab

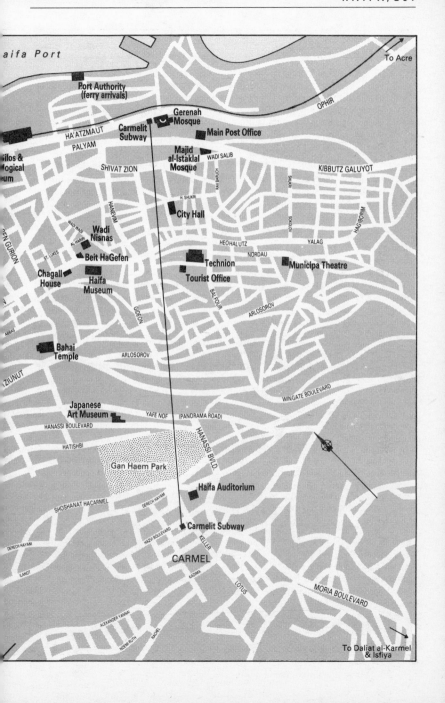

aifa Port

To Acre

Port Authority
(ferry arrivals)

OPHIR

Gerenah
Mosque

HA'ATZMAUT   Carmelit
Subway   Main Post Office

PALYAM

ilos &   Majid   WADI SALIB   KIBBUTZ GALUYOT
ogical   al-Istaklal
um   Mosque

SHIVAT ZION

H. SHUKRI

SHUKRI

HAGIBORIM

HANEVIIM

H. SHUKRI   City Hall

EN GURION   WADI WAS   HEOHALUTZ   YALAG
               AL HARIRI   Wadi   NORDAU
               Nisnas
ST LUKES   Beit HaGefen   Municipa Theatre
Chagall   Technion
House   Haifa   Tourist Office
            Museum

GIDEON

ABBAS   BALFOUR

Bahai   ARLOSOROV
Temple

ZIUNUT   ARLOSOROV

WINGATE BOULEVARD

Japanese
Art Museum   YAFE NOF   (PANORAMA ROAD)
HANASSI BOULEVARD

HATISHBI

HANASSI BULD.

Gan Haem Park

Haifa Auditorium

SHOSHANAT HACARMEL
DERECH HAYAM

Carmelit Subway

DERECH HAYAM   HAZVI BOULEVARD
                              KELLER
ILANIT   CARMEL
                KADIMA

ALEXANDER YANNAI   LOTUS   MORIA BOULEVARD

NOEMI RUTH   RACHEL

To Daliat al-Karmel
& Isfiya

In 1750 the city was conquered by **Daher al-Omar**, a Beduin who ruled the Galilee (see *Tiberias*). During the battle for the city, it was yet again destroyed; instead of rebuilding on the ruins, Daher al-Omar gave orders to construct a walled city in the area now known as *Haifa al-Ati'a* (Old Haifa) in Arabic (*Beit Galim* in Hebrew). Above it, a huge fortress was built. Finally, Haifa saw relative stability. In the mid-nineteenth century, overcrowding within the walls led a group of German Templars to begin building outside, establishing the **German Colony**, where Germanic influence can still be seen in Gothic spires and stairwells.

From then on, the city developed quickly. In 1905 Haifa's importance was assured with the building of a **railway** from Haifa to Damascus. Under the **British Mandate**, Haifa became the only significant working port in northern Palestine (a state encouraged by the British, as it allowed greater control of the area). In the 1922 census, the population of the city stood at 25,000: 17,000 Arabs and 8000 Jews.

Economic growth, however, coupled with escalating Zionist immigration, brought new tensions. It was from Haifa in 1935 that the elderly Syrian Sheikh Izzedin Qasim effectively set the **Arab Revolt** in motion by setting out for the hills of the West Bank with 800 men in a valiant attempt to overthrow the British forces and thus secure Palestine for the Palestinians. It didn't take long for the British, with the aid of a few reconnaissance planes, to track him down and force him into a hopeless battle. But although the fighting lasted only a few hours, its boost to Arab morale – and Qasim's martyrdom – far outweighed its military significance. The Arab Revolt may not have sprung directly from Qasim's rebellion – its causes, after all, were deeprooted – but for the first time armed rebellion had been used by Arabs in Palestine.

In May 1939, with Arab resistance finally crushed by the British army, it was the **Zionists'** turn to take to arms following the publication of a British government White Paper governing the numbers of Jewish immigrants coming into Palestine. By 1935 the number of legal immigrants had topped 60,000 a year, with Haifa their chief port of entry. Between 1936 and 1939 the number of illegal immigrants entering had also increased dramatically. But under the 1939 regulations, only 75,000 further refugees were to be admitted over a five year period. The Zionists reacted with violence. In November 1940 a small ship carrying 1900 refugees – the *Patria* – was blown up by the *Haganah* in an effort to highlight their opposition to British immigration policies. Two hundred and forty Jewish passengers died. In February 1942 the *Struma* carrying Rumanian Jews was turned away from the port: the ship sank with few survivors. The most successful Zionist propaganda coup came with the *Exodus*, which in 1947 arrived in Haifa crammed with Jewish survivors from European refugee camps. It was turned away, and eventually forced to return to Germany: an episode covered in every detail by the world's press.

With partition, Haifa was rapidly overrun by Zionist forces, and the majority of its Arab population driven into exile in Lebanon. Many of those who remain today, some five to ten per cent of the population, are refugees from rural parts of Galilee, who arrived later.

In its architecture, Haifa still bears the stamp of British occupation, although the suburbs are depressingly uniform concrete and the older, down-town residential quarters are falling into neglect. Perhaps another sign of the city's reputation for tolerance is the relative lack of racial segregation in hous-ing: *Wadi Nisnas* and *Kababir*, for example, are predominantly Palestinian areas, but far from exclusively so.

Orientation

Haifa is built on three levels: the **Port Area** at the bottom of the mountain, **Hadar** in the middle and **Carmel** at the top.

The **Port** area is split by two major thoroughfares – **Derech HaAtzma'ut** (Independence Way) and **Sderot HaPalyam** – that converge at **Faisal Circus**. From there, **Golani Brigade Road** follows the coast north towards Acre. Everything you'll need in terms of transport is by the port: the train station, the bus station and the beginning of the **Carmelit Subway** line. The area around the port is known locally as the **black market** area, though there's no sign of anything illicit.

Hadar, just up the hill from the port, is the business, shopping and enter-tainment centre, and by far the most crowded and animated section of the city. Its labyrinthine streets are dominated by good, cheap restaurants and shops.

The third and last level of the city is the prosperous, fashion-conscious **Carmel**. With its chic upmarket shopping and ritzy hotels, Carmel is Israel's northern centre of 'style'. It is also where Haifa's large student population hangs out. The parks – with stunning panoramic views – the outdoor theatres and trendy cinemas are generally packed-out.

Arrival and getting around

Arriving in Haifa by **bus** you'll be at the central bus station, which is also the hub for local bus services. It's built on two levels: arrivals at the top, depar-tures and most other services (information, luggage) at the bottom. Local buses pull up at the concourse in front. The main **railway station** is behind here (there's another at the port), connected by tunnel with the bus station and local bus departures. If you arrive by **ferry** you'll be in the middle of the port: once you've cleared customs (and perhaps visited the tourist office – see below), catch a bus right outside, or walk through to HaAtzma'ut Street.

For a free map and details of what's on in Haifa, the **IGTO** in Hadar is a good starting point (20 Herzl Street; ☎04-666521/2); there's a branch at the port, too, open only when a ferry docks. If you arrive at the central bus station the small **Municipal Information Office** near the queue for Jerusalem buses will help.

Haifa is easy to get around because of the unusual efficiency of the **local transport system**. For information on local buses, check with the Egged information booth in the central section of the bus station: the most useful routes are outlined below. Journeys tend to be slow, as the buses wind their

```
     USEFUL CITY CENTRE BUS ROUTES

#16 – Central Bus Station, Jaffa, HaAtzma'ut, Herzl, Arlosoroff, Geulla. About every
ten minutes.
#24 – Central Bus Station, Rothschild, Herzl, Arlosoroff, Geulla, Haifa University.
About every ten minutes.
#3a – Elijah's Cave, Jaffa, Herzl, Arlosoroff, Ramat Hadar, Central Carmel, Carmel
Youth Hostel, Haifa Tennis Centre. Every fifteen to twenty minutes.
```

way up the steep gradients. The **Carmelit Subway Line** is far quicker, but
closed for restoration until at least summer 1990. When it's going, trains run
every ten minutes from Paris Street, just off Jaffa Road in Hadar, up to
Carmel. You can buy tokens at every station.

Accommodation

There is only one cheap hostel in the centre of Haifa and a very limited
supply of cheap hotel rooms. The hostel is strictly run and evangelical, so
most travellers either pay the $10 to $15 for a hotel room, or head for the
excellent, but hardly central, *Carmel Youth Hostel*. Before paying the hotel
prices quoted you should try bargaining as most hoteliers will reduce prices
if business is slack.

In Hadar

Bethel Hostel (40 HaGeffen St; ☎04-521110). The hostel, mentioned above, charges $4
for a clean dormitory bed. Strict 10pm curfew and 7am wake-up call, run by enthusias-
tic Christian evangelists. To get there catch bus #22, #40 or #42 from the central bus
station.

Nesher Hotel (53 Herzl St; ☎04-640644). Clean and tidy, but with a very moribund
atmosphere. Singles $16, doubles $25.

Hotel Aliya (35 HaHalutz St; ☎04-663918). Clean, but hot rooms; basic but fairly pleasant. Singles from $10, doubles $20.

Talpiot Hotel (61 Herzl St; ☎04-673753). Less spotless than the former, but more popular with younger travellers and hence less austere. Single rooms $15, doubles $25.

Hotel Carmelia (35 Herzliya St; ☎04-521278) Slightly more upmarket, this place has all
the trappings you would expect from a three-star hotel, including higher prices.

In Carmel

Carmel has a lot to offer if you are prepared to pay what it costs to stay up
here. From the subway station on HaNassi Boulevard, walk up the road bearing right and in front of you will be the main Carmel junction of HaNassi and
Derech HaYam. The large and famous Gan HaEm (Mother's Park) is just
down the road. In this area are a number of large hotels.

Pension Wohlman (16 Derech HaYam; ☎04-818884). Pleasant place with middle-range
prices, but only five rooms.

Hotel Dvir (124 Yefe Nof Street; ☎04-89131). Overlooks the bay and the golden dome
of the Bahai Temple. Big and pricey, though the service is excellent.

Further out

Carmel Youth Hostel (4 km south of Haifa off the main Haifa–Tel Aviv road; ☎04-
531944, from $6). Bus #43 from the central bus station will let you off about twenty
minutes' walk away at the bottom of the road, or a taxi all the way will cost from $5 to
$10. A free uncrowded beach nearby, combined with the sea-views, landscaped lawns,
excellent food and nearby tennis and squash centres, make this a very pleasant place to
stay.

Qiryat Tiv'on Youth Hostel (12 Alexander Said St, Qiryat Tivon; ☎04-931482). Twelve
kilometres southeast of Haifa along the road to Nazareth, this is an option if everything
in Haifa is full. To get there take bus #74 or #75 from the central bus station and get off
at Qiryat Tiv'on. No curfew, or cooking facilities, but places to eat nearby.

The City

Haifa is not a city of great architectural delights, but it's an enjoyable place
simply to wander around. The **port** area, though it offers nothing very
specific to see, is perhaps the most atmospheric part of town, busy and
crowded. In **Hadar** the attractions are largely commercial – shops and businesses – while as you climb towards **Carmel** you increasingly come on the
views and the small parks which characterise the prettiest area of town.

If you spend any time in the city, perhaps visiting some of the sights
outlined below (all of them easily accessible on public transport), you'll pretty
soon get a feel for the character of its different neighbourhoods. An excellent
overview is provided by the free 2½-hour **tour of the city** run by the *Haifa
Tourism Development Association* (10 Ahad HaAm St; ☎04-671645) every
Saturday morning. It starts from the corner of Yefe Nof (Panorama Road) and
Sha'ar HaLevanon (Lebanon Gate) every Saturday at 10am. The HTDA guide
listing the main sights and their opening hours is available from the IGTO.

Taking some time out on the **beach** as you wander around is easy enough,
though the city beaches do tend to be dirty and crowded. Best of them is
HaShaqet (Quiet) Beach, not too far from the central bus station, reached
by walking down Hel HaYam Street. **Bat Galim** is covered with jagged
rocks. With more time to spare, you're much better off travelling southwards
to the beaches alongside the main Tel Aviv–Haifa road. The flashiest is
HaCarmel Beach; **Dado Beach** is much less commercialised. The open
beaches south of Dado are subject to treacherous currents, so you should
avoid swimming there.

The Bahai Temple and Archives Building

By far the most impressive and imposing complex of buildings in Haifa is the
Bahai Temple – whose shining golden dome is visible all over town – and its
adjoining **archives building**. The world centre of the Bahai faith, the temple
can be visited on HaTsionut Avenue (daily 9am–noon, garden until 5pm;
admission free; bus #22 from the central bus station or #23, #25 or #32 from
HaNevi'im St).

The **Bahai faith** was founded in Persia in the mid-nineteenth century by Mizra Husayn Ali (Baha' Ullah), a follower of the prophet al-Bab who had been executed for his belief that the prophets of all religions were sent equally to spread God's word. Baha' Ullah was persecuted in turn, and the religion was brought to Palestine by his son Abd al-Baha. All three of these figures are revered by Bahais as prophets, the equals of Jesus or Mohammed: Al-Bab's remains and those of Abd al-Baha now lie in the Persian Gardens near the Temple, Baha' Ullah's in the Bahai Gardens near Acre.

The golden-domed temple is huge and weighty: its Chiampo stone walls were cut and carved in Italy, the supporting columns are made from rose Bavento granite. With its classical dome supported on Arabic arches and columns, the building is an interesting combination of Europe and the Middle East. It fits well the faith's central message of the unity of all religions. The interior is lavishly furnished and decorated; the collection of ancient Persian rugs is impressive, the French chandelier which hangs over them grotesque. To enter, you should dress respectfully (no shorts or bare shoulders) and remove your shoes.

The temple is usually closed for three weeks in August, but even if you can't get in, the **Persian Gardens** which surround it merit the journey for themselves. Lush vegetation surrounds towering eucalyptus and delicate date palms; the views and the beauty of the buildings are a joy.

The **archives building**, across the road from the temple, is modelled on the Parthenon. The 1957 copy looks a lot sturdier than the original and you have to admire both the beauty of Greek architecture and the audacity of the designer who dared reproduce it. The inside of the building is closed to the public.

Just up the hill from the temple, a **Sculpture Garden** tucked away unassumingly on the right of the road contains the works of one of Haifa's leading contemporary artists, Ursula Malkin. It has been dubbed 'peace point' by the locals. Walk through the park to the lower left-hand exit and cross over the road to get to **'marriage bend'** – so named because of the constant flow of newlyweds who use the place as a backdrop to wedding photos.

Mount Carmel and the Carmelite Monastery

Mount Carmel, which dominates every view in Haifa, is as spectacular an observation point as you could wish. Its history goes back to Old Testament times, for this is one of two possible sites (the other is at al-Muhraqa, p.271) of the contest between monotheism and paganism in which the prophet Elijah is said to have challenged, and destroyed, the 'False Prophets of Baal' in the days of Ahab and Jezebel (*I Kings 18*). Legend has it that before the clash Elijah lived and meditated in a cave just below the present site of the Carmelite Monastery. Inside **Elijah's Cave** (summer Sun–Thur 8am–6pm, Fri 8am–1pm; winter Sun–Thurs 8am–8pm, Fri 8am–1pm; admission free) is a small altar which has become a shrine for Jews, Christians and Muslims alike. The cave is clearly visible from the main Tel Aviv–Haifa road and is surrounded by smaller caves which can also be explored. You can get to the site either via the road just behind the Maritime Museum (see below) or by walking down from the Carmelite Monastery. Admisson is free, and the caves are open in the summer Sun–Thur from 8am–6pm, Fri 8am–1pm; in winter Sun–Thur 8am–8pm, Fri 8am–1pm.

Above the cave is the nineteenth-century **Stella Maris monastery**, current home of the **Carmelite** order of Catholic monks. Founded in 1150, the monks have been forced to move several times, having been harassed by the authorities down the centuries, though given their Crusader origins and their collaboration with Napoleon during his 1799 siege (which led the Ottoman authorities to crack down on them) their unpopularity is perhaps understandable. In a tiny museum at the monastery, remains of earlier Carmelite centres are preserved along with a bizarre jumble of miscellaneous items which seem to have little to do with the Carmelites (entrance apparently at the whim of the monks). The church inside is a beautiful neo-Gothic structure whose stained glass windows depict Elijah's ascension to heaven in a chariot of fire. To enter the church and the museum you must dress conservatively: if possible try and attach yourself to a group of visiting pilgrims.

The monastery is open every day except Sunday (8.30am–1.30pm and 3–6pm; admission free). To get there take bus #25 or #26 from the Bahai Temple, or walk down from the Carmel district. Alternatively you could come up by the **cable-car** (Sun–Thur 9am–11pm, Fri 9am–3pm, Sat 4–11pm; one-way $1.50, round trip $2.50) which starts at the beach, past the bus station, and stops right next to the monastery: the views are great; the running commentary uniformative and for the most part unintelligible.

Palestinian Haifa: Wadi Nisnas and Kababar

The Arab quarter of **Wadi Nisnas** shelters in the heart of the commercial Hadar district: to get there head along Shabtai Levi Street towards the Haifa Museum. On the same side of the road as the museum you'll see a small stairwell, with steps leading down to a market. This is the heart of Wadi Nisnas, a crowded area with population of about 6000, which perhaps best preserves the feel of old Haifa – liberally dotted with mosques, churches and crumblingly impressive Arab architecture. The so-called melon market at the southern end of the wadi was the scene of some of the worst violence Haifa has seen when, during the Arab revolt, two bombs were exploded here (three weeks apart), killing 72 people in all. In general, however, Haifa Palestinians have co-existed relatively peacefully with their Jewish neighbours: though since the *intifada* there's a new tension in the air.

As far as Palestinian politics go, Haifa has established itself as an important centre of the Communist Party: *Al Ittihad*, the Arabic-language Communist Party daily is published here, and there's also a large Arab Cultural Centre, run by eminent Palestinian poet Samih al-Qassem.

Palestinians live throughout the city, but there's another important concentration high on the Carmel slopes in **Kababir**, the preserve of adherents of Ahmadism (a Sufi sect of Islam). In complete contrast to the cramped living in Wadi Nisnas, Kababir is a spacious suburb, established in 1836, with large houses and well kept gardens, so separate from its surrounds that it feels almost like a village. Many of the finer buildings escaped the ravages of subsequent wars and are very well preserved: pride of place goes to a large, richly decorated mosque completed in 1984. To get to Kababir take bus #3a, #22, #28 or #37 and get off at central Carmel. From here a short walk takes you to the Kababir area, on the peak of the hill overlooking Dado Beach. It is also possible to walk up to Kababir from the Carmel Youth Hostel, though it's a steep climb.

The Museums

Haifa Museum
26 Shabtai Levi Street (Sun–Thur 8am–2pm, Fri 8am–noon; admission free; ☎04-523255).

The largest of the city's museums is also in many ways its most disappointing – housed in the drab British Mandate headquarters and laid out with an extraordinary lack of imagination. The best is probably the ancient art on the top floor, with a substantial collection of Greco/Roman sculpture, some of it very fine. Up here too is a magnificent mosaic floor from the ancient city of Shiqmona – a forerunner of Haifa itself. Other collections cover Jewish ethnology – clothing, writings, and the minutiae of daily life – and modern Israeli art. In the evenings, the museum runs an entertainments programme which can be worth checking out.

The Tikotin Museum of Japanese Art
89 HaNassi St (Sun–Thur 10am–1pm, Sat 4–7pm; admission free).

By contrast with the above, the unpromising sounding Tikotin Museum is arguably the most rewarding and interesting in Haifa. The collection of nine-teenth-century prints and etchings occupies a replica of a traditional Japanese house: a single room divided by rice paper screens and narrow troughs. In its intimate relation between art and environment, it is a living example of the Taoist concept of art. Outside the museum is a small but beautifully laid out garden, a copy of the larger Naguchi Stone Garden at the Israel Museum in Jerusalem. The museum also has an excellent poster shop which sells repro-ductions of many of the prints on display at affordable prices.

Gan HaEm
(Sun–Thur 8am–4pm, Fri 8am–1pm, Sun 9am–6pm; $2).

Directly opposite The Tikotin, Gan HaEm park is home to three small museums, a zoo and reptile house, and an open-air theatre. Even without these it's a beautiful place to stroll, with lovingly tended lawns and a refresh-ingly peaceful air. The zoo and the museums – **Prehistoric** ('M. Stekilis'), **Natural History** and **Biological** – all concentrate on the indigenous life of northern Israel, particularly the Carmel Mountains.

Beit HaGeffen Arab/Israeli Cultural Centre
HaGeffen Street (Sun–Thur 10am–1pm; Fri and Sat 10am–noon; admission free).

A gallery, cultural centre and workshop for contemporary art, dance etc.

The Artist's House

Part of the same complex at 21 HaTsionut Street (Sun–Thur 10am–1pm and 4–7pm; Fri and Sat 10am–noon; ☎04-522355).

This hosts regular exhibitions of modern art. Both of the above are close to the Haifa Museum.

National Museum of Science and Technology

15 Balfour Street (Sun, Mon and Wed 9am–5pm, Tues and Thur 11am–7pm, Sat 10am–2pm; admission free).

A typical science museum, full of working models of mainly Israeli science and technology. The hands-on approach makes a change, at least.

Music Museum

23 Arlosoroff Street (Sun–Thur 10am–1pm, Sun and Wed 4–7pm, Fri 10am–noon; admission free).

Apparently little visited, the music museum displays ancient and modern instruments from the 'Fertile Crescent'. It gives the visitor some idea of the derivations of the instruments used by Palestinian musicians often seen in Jerusalem and the south.

National Maritime Museum

198 Allenby Street, below the Carmelite Monastery (Sun–Thur 10am–4pm, Sat 10am–1pm; admission free).

Largely devoted to models of ships built according to plans and paintings discovered in ancient tombs and palaces throughout the Middle East. They include: the first sea-going vessel from the reign of Pharaoh Sahure (2500BC); a Canaanite merchant ship (1400BC); the *Tarshish* ships mentioned in the Bible; and a series of Byzantine and Greco/Roman vessels. There is an excellent collection on maritime archaeology which includes three wooden Egyptian funerary boats dating from about 2000BC. The museum library is also open to the public.

Clandestine Immigration and Navy Museum

204 Allenby Street, just round the corner from the above (Mon, Wed and Thur 9am–3pm, Sun and Tues 9am–4pm, Fri 9am–1pm; admission $0.75).

The museum is divided into two parts, the first of which explores clandestine Jewish immigration into Palestine during the British Mandate. There are details of all the sailings (over 100,000 illegal immigrants arrived in 118 ships), a map showing the routes they took from Europe, and a full-size model of one ship to demonstrate conditions on board. Another exhibit contains articles from the Cyprus camps – where many of the would-be immigrants caught by the British ended up – and a display of belongings of camp inmates. No mention, however, of the ships blown up by the Zionists themselves. The rest of the museum is a straightforward display of Israeli naval power, with models and full-scale ships.

The Dagon Silo

Plumer Square (daily tour leaves Sun–Fri at 10am, from the main foyer; free).

On your travels around the upper reaches of Haifa you can't fail to notice an enormous fortress-like building with two huge towers situated on the shorefront. This is the Dagon Grain Silo – the largest granary in the Middle East – used to stock subsidised US wheat imports. On the tour you get a trip round the Archeological Museum of Grain Handling in Israel (*sic*) whose artefacts from 12000BC to the present day somehow manage to omit the whole of Palestine's Arab history. Eminently missable.

Railway Museum

40 Golani Brigade Road near the Dagon Silo (Sun–Thur 10am–1pm).

A tribute to the role of the railway in the development of Haifa: among the dusty exhibits are preserved some of the old British-built steamtrains which plied the now defunct Hejaz Railway.

Mane Katz Museum

89 Yefe Nof St (Sun–Thur 10am–1pm and 4–6pm, Sat 10am–1pm).

This little-known museum occupies the home of Mane Katz, an artist born in 1894 who worked in Paris, Vienna and the USA before retiring to Haifa in 1958. He studied and painted with Marc Chagall and Modigliani. The house contains Katz's collection of oriental rugs and religious artefacts from Jewish communities throughout the world, as well as his own expressionist paintings and sculptures. Very nearby is **Panorama point**, yet another famous viewing spot.

Technion Institute of Science and Technology and Haifa University

Haifa has long claimed to be the centre of Israeli higher education, and these two institutions are leaders in the country's quest for international academic recognition. Both are open to the public, and positively welcome visits from foreign students and travellers.

The **Technion** is split into two campuses: one in the Hadar district (Balfour and Herzl St), the other on Mount Carmel. The former is the older and more interesting of the two. Both have cheap student canteens. For information about tours around the Technion phone ☎04-292312. **Haifa University** is situated southeast of the Carmel district on the summit of the mountain near the beginning of the Carmel National Park. From its impressive 25-storey **Eshkol Tower**, you can see as far as the occupied Golan Heights, Rosh Haniqra and, on a clear day, the snow-covered top of *Jabal al-Sheikh* (Mount Hermon). The tower houses the students union, and normally has some kind of exhibition in its foyer. Regular, free guided tours are run by students between 9am and 2pm from the main building – follow the signs on the campus (call ☎04-240095 for details). To get to the campus take bus #24 or #37 from Herzl Street, or #92 from the central bus station.

Food, drink and entertainment

Places to eat in Haifa seem to match the city's character; plenty of straightforward food, but little excitement. Down around the **port**, the cafés and restaurants are aimed primarily at working people – good if you're after a reasonably-priced, filling meal. Two worthy Palestinian restaurants are *Abu*

Yusuf and the *Saleh Brothers Restaurant* on Paris Square (at the bottom of the Carmelit subway): both have a large selection of Palestinian food from the humble *humus* to *melukhia* – a spinach-like plant which turns into a sticky green broth when cooked, usually with meat. It's rare to find *mlochia* in a restaurant, so take your chance now. *Naim's* (6 Eliyahu HaNavi St) and *Restaurant Shichmona* (3 Nahum Dovrin St) in the market area serve good, cheap East European food. The central bus station has a reasonable cafeteria, and round about are some of the best *falafel* stalls in Haifa.

In **Hadar** the choice is slightly wider. Starting with basics, you'll find excellent *falafel* stalls around the junction of HaHalutz and HaNeviim streets. For Palestinian dishes, the best places are *Diab Brothers Restaurant* (6 Herzliya St) and *Ahalan WaSahlan Restaurant* (8 Herzliya St) – the latter gives students a ten per cent discount. Slightly further down the hill, in the Wadi Nisnas area, the streets are full of small cafés and low-cost restaurants. On Herzl Street you'll find cheap food at the cafeteria in the *Hamashbir* department store, or from the disappointingly unimaginative **vegetarian restaurant** at no. 30. For a bit more style try the *Ritz Self-Service Conditorei* (5 Haim St) or the *Beiteinu* (29 Jerusalem St), both of which offer the added attraction of art galleries exhibiting contemporary Israeli art.

Up in **Carmel** you're pretty much stuck with fast food if you hope to watch costs. Closely grouped along HaNassi Boulevard you'll find the Israeli-burger chain *MacDavid's* (no. 131), *Bagel Nash* (no. 135), serving bagels with hundreds of possible fillings, and the *Peer Pizzeria Via Veneto* (no. 130), a coffee house in the morning, a pizzeria the rest of the day. Carmel also hosts most of the city's best restaurants. Among the more reasonably priced of these are the *Chin Lung Chinese Restaurant* (126 HaNassi Blvd) and the dining rooms of the *Dan Carmel Hotel* (87 HaNassi Blvd) and the *Hotel Dvir* (124 Yefe Nof St).

Bars and nightlife

You don't come to Haifa for the **nightlife** – or at least not by choice. When there's a captive audience – sailors from the US Sixth Fleet for example – the **port area** becomes a seething mass of drunkenness and insistent pimps as the marines attempt to do for the black economy what their government does for the official one. Even when the docks are relatively empty the atmosphere down here is pretty sleazy: if you want to sample it head for HaAtzma'ut Street, where the *The London Pride* (distinguished by its lack of anything which remotely resembles London) and a few other plastic cafés and clubs form the centre of the scene.

Hadar at night is much more respectable, but also rather quiet. The busiest area is around Herzl and Arlosoroff streets, where crowds gather to stroll between the outdoor cafés. Among them are a couple of reasonably animated **bars**, including *Rodeo* (23 Balfour St), *Studio 46* (46 Pevsner St) and *The Place* (1 Hayyim St). In **Carmel** you've a wider choice, with numerous **pubs** around HaEm Park, HaNassi Boulevard and Tchernikovsky Street – plenty of them, and little to choose between. Busier than any of these in summer, however, are the **parks**, where locals spend the warm evenings hanging out and sometimes enjoying some organised entertainment. The Sculpture

Garden is one of the most popular places to have a drink and listen to some guitar playing.

If this all sounds too tame and the port too loud, then check out what's happening on the **beach**. On most summer nights you'll find some kind of entertainment laid on – discos, musical performances or rock videos. Dado Beach, for example, has a free, open-air disco most evenings. Zamir Beach also has a disco every Sunday from 8pm until late, and other happenings many weekday nights. For further details of the beach discos contact the IGTO, or if you're staying at the youth hostel ask the staff who often lead night-time sorties down to the beach themselves.

For **students**, the Technion Students Association (☎04-234148) promotes a varied cultural programme which you're welcome to join. Haifa University's *I.Q. Club* is open Friday and Saturday evenings; it only costs a few dollars, but you need a valid student ID.

Film and theatre

Two venues dominate Haifa's cultural scene: the *Cinemateque* and the *Haifa Auditorium*. For movie fans, the Cinemateque (104 HaNassi Blvd, Carmel; ☎04-383424) runs an average of three or four European and American **films** every night. Entry is quite reasonable and the one ticket allows you to sit through all of them if you want. The Haifa Auditorium (138 HaNassi Blvd, Carmel; ☎04-380013) is right next door. Here the programme is largely musical, with **classical concerts** throughout the year: you'll need to book in advance ($10–15) for the more popular events.

Smaller cultural centres include the *Zavit Café Theatre* (Jerusalem St, Hadar; ☎04-253641) and the small outdoor theatre in HaEm Park, both of which run weekend classical music evenings. **Theatre** is a major forum for dissent in modern Israel, and one of the most controversial playhouses is the *Haifa Municipal Theatre* (50 Pevsner St, Hadar; ☎04-670970), whose programme of modern works brings it into regular conflict with the municipality and the government. Most of the plays are of course in Hebrew, but it's worth scannning the *Jerusalem Post* for the latest political furore, and perhaps finding someone to go with you and translate. The Haifa Museum also has an evening programme of popular entertainment: they show a good selection of rock videos every Tuesday during the summer, for example.

For **information** on all these events contact the IGTO, who produce a monthly *What's On* advertising many activities, or take a look at the *Jerusalem Post* weekend supplement.

Listings

Airlines *Arkia* (84 HaAtzma'ut St; ☎04-643371, or at Haifa Airport ☎04-722220); *El Al* (80 HaAtzma'ut St; ☎04-670170); *British Airways* (84 HaAtzma'ut St; ☎04-670756).

Airport transportation *El Al* run an early morning bus service to Ben Gurion airport daily except Saturdays and holidays. For more details contact ☎04-670170. You can also get a *sherut* taxi from *Melia* (☎04-384667/9).

Banks You'll find bank branches throughout the city, but the main ones are down by the port along HaAtzma'ut Street and in the centre of Hadar. They follow normal Israeli banking hours: Sun, Tues and Thur 8.30am–12.30pm and 4–5pm; Mon, Wed and Fri 8.30am–noon.

Books *Steimatzky's* have three large outlets in Haifa – central bus station arcade, 16 Herzl Street and 82 HaAtzma'ut Street. For second-hand books try *Beverly Books* (7 Herzl St).

Emergencies ☎101.

Ferries The main agents for ferries to Cyprus and Greece are *Mano Shipping* (39/41 HaMeginnim St; ☎04-537227) and *J. Caspi* (1 Nathan St; ☎04-674444). Ferries leave early in the morning on Thursday and Sunday.

Gay information The Haifa branch of the *Society for the Protection of Personal Rights* (PO Box 45417, Haifa 31453; ☎04-257319) run a gay information hotline.

Hospitals Carmel Hospital (7 Michal St; ☎04-254321); Rambam Hospital (Bat Galim; ☎04-533111).

IGTO 16 Herzl Street (☎04-666521) offer the usual free maps and leaflets, as wells as the magazine *In and Around Haifa*. A branch office at the port is open to greet arriving ferries (Port building 12; ☎04-663988).

Municipality 14 Hassan Shukri St (☎04-640775).

Post office The main branch – for poste restante and international telephone calls – is in the port area at 19 HaPalyam St (Sun–Thur 8am–5pm, Fri 8am–1pm). Another large post office is on Haneviim St in Hadar (Sun–Thur 8am–8pm, Fri 8am–2pm).

Police 28 Jaffa Road (☎100).

Rape crisis centre PO Box 9308 (☎04-382611).

Sherutim The main termini for *sherut* taxis are: Tel Aviv/Jerusalem (10 Nordau St or 157 Jaffa St, next to the bus station); Acre/Naharriyya (16 HaNeviim St in the Hadar or Plumer Square downtown); Isfiya/Daliat al-Karmel (Eliyahu St, Sun–Fri 6am–6pm, on Saturdays from corner of Schmeriyahu Levin St and Herzl St).

Sports Squash (Kefar Zamir; ☎04-539160); tennis centre (Kefar Zamir; ☎04-522721); ice skating (Dakar St, Qiryat Mozkin; ☎04-750977).

Surfing *Surfboard Club* (south of Dado Beach; ☎04-521126).

Taxis *Kavei HaGalil* (1 HaHalutz; ☎04-664422) or *Mercaz Mitspe* (7 Balfour St; ☎04-662525)

Travel agencies *ISSTA* (28 Nordau St), the Israeli student and budget travel specialists, is the best place to start looking for cheap flights.

AROUND HAIFA

If you want to escape the city for a day, the only real choice, for anything more stimulating than lazing on the beach, is to head inland. North of the city the coast is heavily polluted by the industrial belt which spreads up to Acre; south, you get whipped onto the coastal road so quick you don't have time to think. Inland lie the mountains, with the scenic splendour of **Carmel National Park**; two much-visited Druze villages at **Isfiya** and **Daliat al-Karmel**; a revered holy place at **Al-Muhraqa**; and a colony of settler-artisans occupying the Palestinian village of **Ein Hod**. All these are accessible by public transport and walking or hitching, although the Carmel National Park is really best viewed from a car.

The Carmel Mountains

The Carmel range is topped by a long plateau which extends south from Haifa to HaHotem (The Muzzle). Triangular in shape, its two shorter sides, each 22km, meet in the east at al-Muhraqa, a rival to Haifa as the site of Elijah's battle with the priests of Baal. The gentle undulations, the natural forest and beautiful wild flowers (especially plentiful in the spring) lend the Carmel a special beauty. Much of this is given over to the **Carmel national park**, a vast area which in places provides visitors with trails and picnic tables, but that also has areas of real isolation where you can escape all this. Buses to the villages pass through, but if you really hope to explore the park you simply have to start hiking: a more satisfactory option is to have transport of your own.

Travelling to the two Druze villages is easy: there's a regular bus service (#92) which leaves from Haifa's central bus station; or *service* taxis, leaving during the day (6am–6pm) from the corner of HaAtzma'ut and Eliyahu HaNavi streets, at night (6pm–6am) from the corner of Shmeriyahu Levin and Herzl streets. From Daliat al-Karmel to al-Muhraqa there is no public transport, but hitching is easy and taxis not outrageously expensive.

Two Druze villages

The **Druze** are members of an Islamic sect founded in 1017 by Hamzah Ibn Ali. Most of them live in Lebanon or southern Syria, but there's also a substantial Israeli population, concentrated in two villages in the Carmel mountains. It's a tightly-knit and secretive sect, so secretive in fact that even among the Druze only a few initates know the full details of their religious mysteries or can participate totally in religious services: no conversion is allowed, nor any intermarriage with outsiders. Most remarkably, one of their guiding principles allows them to conform to the ways, and even profess the religion, of any people among whom they find themselves. It is probably this which has ensured their survival in modern Israel: many Druze even fight with the Israeli army.

ISFIYA is the first, and much the quieter, of the two Druze villages. Without the market or abundant commercialism of Daliat al-Karmel, Isfiya's attraction is that it has to a great extent survived as a living, working village. Still, the villagers are well aware of the money that can be made from the hordes of tourists, and over recent years a few shops selling oriental souvenirs, and a number of good restaurants, have opened. The restaurants in Isfiya tend to be cheaper and better quality than in Daliat al-Karmel – the best is the first restaurant on the right as you enter the village. There's also the *Stella Carmel Hospice* (at the entrance to the village; ☎04-222692), an Anglican hospice which is expensive at $18 a night, but welcoming and relaxing.

Five kilometres south, **DALIAT AL-KARMEL** is far more commercialised. As soon as you enter the village you can't fail to be struck by the profusion of colour. From Persian to Beduin rugs, brass coffeepots to large hooka pipes, the place seems on first impression to be one giant market for oriental goods. Apart from the tourist trade, however, villagers do still farm much of the local area. Tractors speed through the village, almost oblivious to the tourists casually walking around, and in the backstreets there's a surprisingly calm, rural atmosphere. It is this working side – and the friendliness of the villagers, especially if you try out some Arabic – which differentiates the place from just any other tourist trap. Saturdays are the busiest for the market, so you'll probably find it more relaxing to visit during the week: it's closed on Fridays.

Al-Muhraqa

If you take the road to the left at the end of Daliat al-Karmel's main street, and then turn left again at the next main junction, you'll arrive at **AL-MUHRAQA**, some 5km away. While the official al-Muhraqa guide book (available from the entrance to the church) argues strongly that this was the site of Elijah's battle with the Priests of Baal (*I Kings 18*), the setting of the confrontation – in which 450 priests of Baal were unable to match Elijah's feat of summoning fire from heaven to ignite a sacrificial bullock, and were subsequently executed – is far from certain. Al-Muhraqa's chief rival is Elijah's Cave in Haifa, an argument that's unlikely to ever be settled. Al-Muhraqa, regardless, is a delightful spot with spectacular views, a popular picnic area and a church commemorating Elijah's victory.

The **church** you now see is relatively recent. Construction by Carmelite monks began in 1867 but only the chapel (of a planned large monastery) was completed in the face of obstruction from the Turkish authorities. In 1883, the basis of the current building was completed, home to a small religious community. During World War I the site was much damaged, and its restoration was completed only in 1964. Nowadays, despite an estimated 150,000 visitors a year, the church and its surrounds have remained surprisingly tranquil, a popular site of veneration with Palestinian Christians. If you want to get into the spirit of things, then come on July 20, the Feast of Elijah, when local families camp out here in their hundreds: there's a small picnic and barbecue area, open all year round.

An interesting alternative to heading back the way you came is to **walk** down into the valley below. It's only about 3km (starting from the corner of the nearby car park) on a path marked by rocks striped red and black. Make sure you stick to the path, which is hard to follow in places, as if you try and find your own way you'll get stuck in the thick brambles near the bottom of the hill. At the bottom you can make for the youth hostel at Qiryat Tivon (see facing page). Buses run regularly back to Haifa and the surrounding area – there is a large bus stop at the junction past the garage.

Ein Hod

One of the best examples of the ghettoisation of art in Israel is the village and 'artists' colony' of **EIN HOD**. In the early 1950s a small group of Israeli artists settled in a deserted Palestinian village in a setting of extraordinary beauty. Crowning a small hill overlooking the Mediterranean, the sea views are offset by the classical simplicity of the Arab architecture and the dull greens of the nearby olive trees, provide a setting that most artists would envy. Ein Hod rapidly became one of Israel's leading artistic centres.

Today there are over 200 galleries and studios, as well as courses in everything from sculpture to needlework, and the village is packed with art of every imaginable kind, and – in summer at least – with coachloads of tourists. Some of the art is aimed squarely at this market, but there's serious work too, from traditional landscape painters to contemporary impressionists, potters to weavers, woodworkers to sculptors. You could spend hours browsing around the galleries – most of which are free – in the local museum, or simply taking it all in as you sit at one of the many cafés. In the small **Roman amphitheatre** near the *Artists' Inn Café*, Israeli rock groups perform most Friday evenings: if you go to this, remember that there'll be no public transport running by the time it's over.

All of this sounds pretty idyllic, but as so often in Israel there's a contemporary history to mar the idyll. Ein Hod was rare in that, unlike most pre-1948 villages, its buildings were not destroyed. And while most of the expelled villagers ended up in refugee camps, a small group stayed in the area, at first camping out in the surrounding woods, hopeful that once the hostilities had died down they would be allowed to return to their homes. From 1949 to 1952 they petitioned the government to be allowed to return. But all these requests were turned down: the government insisted that as they were not in their homes on the day the state of Israel was created, they had lost any rights to their property (under the Absentee Property Act). Their small encampment became semi-permanent as small concrete houses grew up; their protests, more vociferous over the years, have continued but to no avail. They are still there, regarded with scant sympathy by most of the current residents, but a permanent affront nonetheless.

To get to Ein Hod from Haifa take bus #202, #222 or #922 and get off at the Ein Hod junction on the main Haifa–Tel Aviv road. The village is twenty minutes' walk from the junction.

Haifa to Nazareth: Beit She'arim

The road from Haifa to Nazareth, a journey of just under 40km, runs through the Jezreel Valley: a quick journey, but a dry and dusty one. Just under half-way you can stop off at **QIRYAT TIVON** to visit the remains of the ancient city of Beit She'arim. From Haifa, bus #74 or #75 will take you to the centre of Qiryat Tivon: Beit She'arim is located in a large park 3km from here. If you want to stay, the **youth hostel** (12 Alexander Said St; ☎04-931482) on the way towards the site is a good option. They serve basic meals, or you'll find food stalls around Kikar HaZtiyonnut. Alternatively, there's a **campsite** just north of the village on the Haifa–Nazareth road. For recreation try the pleasant open-air swimming pool on Alexander Said Street between Kikar HaZtiyonnut and the hostel (Sun–Thur 9am–4.30pm).

BEIT SHE'ARIM (House of the Gates) is famous as one of the many seats of the **Sanhedrin**, the 71-member Jewish supreme judicial, ecclesiastical and administrative council in New Testament times. The Sanhedrin fled from Jerusalem to Bet She'arim after the failure of the Bar Kokhba revolt in the second century AD: having re-established themselves here, they were recognised by the Romans as the supreme Jewish authority. At Beit She'arim their most famous leader, Rabbi Yehuda HaNassi, undertook the task of setting down the *Mishnah*, the laws which governed the day to day lives of the Jews, which had previously been passed down orally (see *Tiberias*).

Rabbi HaNassi is buried here, and it's his burial that gives Beit She'arim much of its present significance, for it turned the town into a much sought after burial place, which developed a vast complex of **catacombs**. These are the main attraction of the site (Sun–Thur 8am–4pm, Fri 8am–3pm), housing an extraordinary number of tombs of wealthy Jews from all over the Roman world. In style they vary from caves with simple inscriptions to ornate mausolea, and the range of languages represented in the inscriptions gives some idea of the diversity of the people who chose this as their final resting place until 352AD, when the Romans destroyed the synagogue.

The most impressive of the tombs are in the area known as the **Necropolis**, near the car park, where more than 26 burial chambers have been excavated, although not all are open to the public. Among the most interesting are the family grave of Rabbi HaNassi (marked as tomb no. 14); tomb no. 1, a labyrinthine complex with 55 burial chambers and over 400 graves; and no. 20, which is the most elaborate of all the chambers and contains numerous richly decorated sarcophagi. Another of the catacombs has been turned into a small museum, with pictures and finds from the site to provide background to what you've seen.

The other chief aspect of the site is the **ancient town**, on the left of the road as you make your way down to the Necropolis. Nearest to the Necropolis are the remains of a second-century building, a collection of pillars and stone slabs thought to have been a traders' meeting place. The fourth-century olive press further up the road is impressive, but greatly over-shadowed by the remains of the synagogue at the top of the hill. Nearby there's a small café.

After Bet She'arim was destroyed in 352AD, during the suppression of a Jewish revolt against Byzantine rule, the town's Jewish population was virtually extinguished. Later an Arab village, SHEIK ABREIK, grew up in its place. The village was named after a local leader who performed a miracle in which he made bubbling water gush from a broken jug. The water, which formed a swamp, was said to possess healing powers, curing anyone who bathed in it. For this miracle the Sheik was proclaimed a saint.

Leaving Qiryat Tivon there are frequent buses on towards Nazareth, a scenic route through the **Balfour Forest** (a popular picnic site) and the Palestinian village of YAFA, which has a mixed (Muslim and Christian) population of over 6000 and contains within it the tel of Japhia, mentioned in the Bible and in ancient Egyptian documents.

Nazareth

NAZARETH, home of Mary and Joseph and the town where Jesus was brought up, has a name as resonant as any in Israel. Expect to be disappointed. For all the churches and Christian shrines which mark out the New Testament story, this is not an appealing city: under-funded, overcrowded and choked with traffic. Furthermore, despite the famous name, Nazareth actually saw little of Jesus as an adult – he moved on, to Galilee and Jerusalem, to begin his ministry and his miracles.

Modern Nazareth has some claim to fame as the largest Palestinian city in Israel, the capital of the Galilee and the home of many a Christian denomination and sect, and the centre still has some of the character of an Arab town, with its *souq* and narrow, winding streets, but for the most part this is lost behind the trappings of commerce. You should still visit, of course, if only for the multitude of churches, cathedrals and hospices, but it really doesn't need a great deal of time: nor does it cater particularly well to visitors. There is one great consolation: perched high on the mountainside overlooking the Jezreel Valley, Nazareth commands wonderful views from its many high points.

A brief history

Nazareth was relatively unimportant in antiquity and is first mentioned in the New Testament as the **birthplace of Mary**, the mother of Christ. Even this claim is the subject of scholarly debate: although Luke's gospel seems quite clear, many believe Matthew to imply that Mary and Joseph always lived in Bethlehem, a view they claim is supported by evidence from other sources. This hardly matters – Nazareth is not going to relinquish its claim, and all are agreed that the Holy Family settled here when they returned after the flight to Egypt.

At this time Nazareth was a small village of little fame or distinction, later destroyed during the Roman suppression of the Jewish revolt in 67AD. It was not until the Emperor Constantine built the town's first church in 326 that the site became a place of pilgrimage for Christians. In 1099 it was captured from the Persians by the Crusader Tancred, and it remained a Christian town until its capture by Sultan Baybars in 1263. Christians were then excluded from

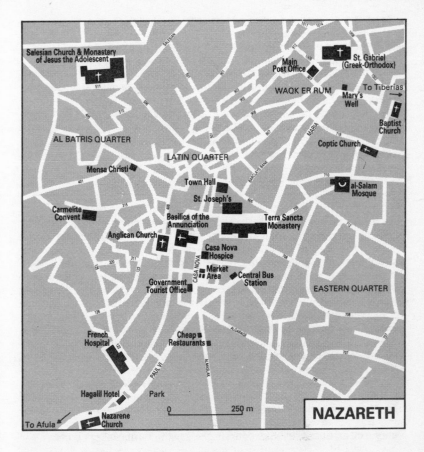

Salesian Church & Monastery
of Jesus the Adolescent

Main
Post Office

St. Gabriel
(Greek-Orthodox)

WAQK ER RUM

To Tiberias

Mary's
Well

AL BATRIS QUARTER

Baptist
Church

Coptic Church

LATIN QUARTER

Mensa Christi

al-Salam
Mosque

Town Hall

St. Joseph's

Carmelite
Convent

Terra Sancta
Monastery

Basilica of the
Annunciation

Anglican Church

Casa Nova
Hospice

Market
Area

Central Bus
Station

Government
Tourist Office

EASTERN QUARTER

French
Hospital

Cheap
Restaurants

Hagalil Hotel

Park

To Afula

Nazarene
Church

0   250 m

NAZARETH

the city until 1620 when Fakr al-Din agreed to sell back the remains of the
Basilica of the Annunciation to a group of Franciscans. From this humble
beginning the Christian community began to grow, until by the turn of this
century the majority of the population was Christian.

During World War I, Nazareth was chosen as the site of the headquarters
of the Ottoman army in Palestine, under German command. Seized by the
British in 1918, it was the district capital during the Mandate period, and an
important trading centre for the lower Galilee.

Under the 1947 UN Partition Plan, Nazareth was to have been part of the
Arab State of Palestine. On July 16, 1948, however, Israeli forces attacked the
city with the intention of forcing a mass evacuation of the Arab inhabitants.
That it remained a predominantly Palestinian-populated town was thanks to
the Canadian volunteer commander of the Israeli 7th Brigade, Ben
Dunkelman, who insisted that the order to evacuate be given to him in writing, which the Israeli chief of staff declined to do.

Today the population of Nazareth is around 40,000, the original Christian Arab population much swelled by the influx of Muslim refugees during and after the 1948 war. Overlooking the old town is **NATZERET ILLIT** (Upper Nazareth), which was established in 1957 with the intention of providing a Jewish presence in the area. Around 25,000 people live here, in a modern development of high rise blocks, government departments and shopping arcades. There are impressive views over the Jezreel Valley, but nothing much else. Taken as a whole, though, its grass-lined boulevards and plush recreational facilities provide a staggering contrast to the depressed town centre of Old Nazareth, and an instructive lesson in how the Israeli government feel happiest spending their money.

Getting about and finding a place to stay

It's easy to get lost in Nazareth, whose narrow streets wind over a series of hills, but it's generally equally easy to re-orient yourself by making your way to one of two main streets: Paul VI and Casa Nova. Most of the major sites are just off one or other of these. **Paul VI Street** runs right through the heart of town, changing its name to Maria Street in the east. The **bus station** is here – little more than a collection of bus stops along the side of the road – and if you walk west towards the great dome which sits atop the Basilica of the Annunciation you'll find the other main artery, Casa Nova Street, to your left. One hundred yards up here on the left-hand side, the local branch of the **Israeli Government Tourist Office** (☎065-71367) provides free maps and advice on the current accommodation situation. Amidst the souvenir shops which litter the sides of the road, and just before the Basilica of the Annunciation, a small street to the right takes you into the **market**.

There is no travellers' hostel in Nazareth, but many cheap Christian **hospices** have grown up to accommodate the thousands of pilgrims who visit every year: at busy times rooms can be hard to find, so it's worth phoning ahead, or checking with the tourist office, before you commit yourself to a long trek around. The most popular place is the *Casa Nova Pilgrims House* (Casa Nova St; ☎065-713670), opposite the Basilica of the Annunciation, which charges from $6 for a comfortable room with breakfast. Nearby, the *Convent of the Sisters of Nazareth* (Casa Nova; ☎065-54304) has dormitory beds, only $3 a night. Further up Casa Nova the *Freres de Betharram* (☎065-70046) and the *Sisters of Charles Barrameus* (☎065-54435) both charge about $10 a night. You pay for the level of comfort you will get so it's worth checking out the rooms or conditions before you accept anything. Most hospices have strict curfews and expect guests to be out early in the morning.

Nazareth **hotels** are considerably more expensive. Cheapest and most popular is the *Galil Hotel* (☎065-71311), about 300m west of the junction of Paul VI and Casa Nova, near the market. Pleasant, but hardly luxurious, the standard charge of $26 single or $40 double can usually be knocked down with a bit of bargaining. Second choice is the *Grand New Hotel* (St. Josephs St; ☎065-73020), not as central but slightly more luxurious for much the same price. Alternatively, since very little happens in the evenings here, you could treat Nazareth as a day trip, or series of day trips, from Haifa or Tiberias.

Food and drink

You're never far from something to eat in Nazareth, with dozens of **street stalls** and restaurants vying for tourist custom along Paul VI and Casa Nova streets. *Falafel*, uniformly good, is available almost anywhere – try the row of places just by the bus station for a start. There's also lots of *humus*. Nazarenes regard the small café on al-Maslach Street as the best: on the right-hand side about 100m down al-Maslach from the junction with Paul VI. Opposite, and again one of many, is an excellent place for Arab sweets. Its *kanafeh* is reputed to be the best in the Galilee, and a testament to its quality is the number of patrons who queue for take-aways on market day.

A number of good, reasonably priced **restaurants** cluster around the junction of Casa Nova and Paul VI streets. The *Astoria* is not the cheapest of these, but it does have an extraordinarily long and varied menu. The *Israel Restaurant* is also good value, but numerous others offer similar food at similar prices. Slightly more elaborate, but well worth trying out, is *Al Jeneenah Restaurant*, a large place popular for local weddings and celebrations. To get there walk up Paul VI Street to Mary's Well, where you should be able to see the restaurant about 50m from the main road. Look out for the faded red flag flying atop the local Communist Party headquarters opposite. Probably the liveliest place in Nazareth during the evening, the restaurant serves excellent food on its large open air verandah at very reasonable prices.

The Town

The *souq* and the traditional architecture of Nazareth make wandering the old alleyways an adventure. All the chief sights, however, are Christian religious places, including some exceptionally fine churches.

The most important of these, as well as the most impressive, historic and controversial, is the Catholic **Basilica of the Annunciation** right in the heart of town (Mon–Sat 8.30–11.45am and 2–5pm, Sun open only for mass). Said to be the largest church in the Middle East, it stands over the grotto where the angel Gabriel announced the forthcoming birth of Jesus to Mary. The current building dates from 1966, the fifth church to stand on this spot – remains of the earlier incarnations are preserved within. It's a spectacular structure on two levels (at the time the Catholic church was much criticised for spending so much here while the town itself lacked the most basic of amenities), adorned inside with murals, stained glass windows and a large collection of artworks from all over the world.

From the upper floor a side entrance leads towards the **Church of Saint Joseph**. Between the two churches lies a small, park-like plaza where remains of churches from the Byzantine and Crusader periods, and some excavations from earlier periods, are set amongst a collection of religious sculptures. It's an atmospheric and (for Nazareth) tranquil setting, beautifully set off by the facade of the **Terra Sancta Monastery** (closed to the public) along one side. St. Joseph's itself was built over a thirteenth-century Crusader church that is said to mark the home and workshop of Joseph, Mary's husband. This is little more than a cave: parts of the earlier church are also in evidence.

Opposite the front of the Basilica of the Annuciation (notice its great bronze doors engraved with the life of Jesus) a short street leads down to the very English-looking **Anglican church**, the home of the Church of England in Nazareth. Its vicar, Canon Riyah Abu al-Asal, is not only an impressive orator and theologian, but a major Palestinian political figure, secretary of the Progressive List for Peace, an Israeli-Palestinian party with a small representation in the Israeli Knesset. He is frequently here in person to show small groups of interested people around his church and give his views on peace in the region. You won't get to hear him outside Israel since he was banned from travelling abroad after some particularly forthright speeches to Christian communities around the world.

In the other direction, the **market** on Casa Nova is one of the few secular attractions of Nazareth. It's touristy, naturally, but it's also a working market, and still the place where much of the population of Lower Galilee does its buying and selling. Thursday is the main market day, but it's open every day of the week from around 8.30am until 5pm. In the centre of the market is the **Greek Catholic Church of the Old Synagogue** – the site where Christ preached and worshipped before becoming isolated from his fellow Nazarenes and his subsequent hasty departure from town.

Other sites are slightly further afield, and walking around you should be sure to keep an eye out for interesting architectural detail – and also for traffic. One of the most important visits for pilgrims is **Mary's Well**, the spot where the angel appeared to Mary as she was drawing water. To get there walk straight up Paul VI Street. To the left, two blocks from the large junction here, is **Saint Gabriel's** Greek Orthodox church. St. Gabriel's is a glorious jumble of a church, its walls elaborately frescoed and then covered in icons, the floor done out in intricately patterned marble. It's bursting with relics and religious objects of every kind, and seemingly populated by dozens of bearded elders trying to get donations for the church and proffering tales of the miraculous powers of the well's water. The spring which serves Mary's Well, connected to it by an aqueduct, is just outside: walk down the steps directly in front of the church's main entrance and you can view the tiny trickle of water from behind iron gates. Here there's a jug on a rope, with which you can draw some of the cool, fresh water and try out its miraculous properties.

To escape the noise and dust of the streets for a while, continue up Paul VI Street and you will find a small, rather neglected **park**, which makes a pleasant picnic spot. If you carry on up the hill you'll reach the less frenetic streets of Natzeret Illit, worth the walk if only to see how the other half lives. In the other direction you can climb from the centre of town to the **Salesian Monastery**, crowning a hill overlooking the whole of Nazareth. From the top, there's a fine view of town and the multitude of spires which adorn its skyline. Halfway between here and the centre, the plain Franciscan chapel of **Mensa Christi** (Table of Christ) is built around a large block of limestone said to be the table around which Jesus and the disciples met after the Resurrection.

Kufr Kanna

Just six kilometres northeast of Nazareth, the lively Palestinian village of **KUFR KANNA**, is said to be biblical **Cana**, the place where Christ turned water into wine at a wedding. To commemorate the miracle, the Franciscans built a church in 1880 over the remains of a house said to be the one in which the miracle was performed. Today thousands of tourists visit the village, coming, as the inscription on the church proclaims to '. . . adore the place upon which His feet trod'. The churches – there is also a Greek Orthodox one – are both particularly ornate, and the village friendly. You're unlikely to get lost – both churches are clearly visible as you enter the village – but if you do ask anyone, as the villagers are used to having tourists in their midst.

Today, Kufr Kanna is a mixed Christian and Muslim village with a population of about 10,000, traditionally living as farmers. Much of the village land has been confiscated, however, and the land alone can no longer support the villagers: after the latest confiscation, in 1976, protest demonstrations erupted in many villages in the Galilee with tragic results. In Kufr Kanna, a 15-year-old boy, Mehsin Hassan Taha, was killed by Israeli soldiers. To commemorate his death and the deaths of others that occurred at this time in other Galilee villages, *Yom al-Ard* – **Land Day** – is marked annually on March 30 in the occupied territories as well as within Israel's 1948 'borders'.

From Nazareth **buses** leave for Kufr Kanna every 45 minutes from Mary's Well, or you can get bus #431 from the bus station to Tiberias, and ask the driver to let you off at the village.

Mount Tabor

Mount Tabor, some 9km due east of Nazareth and at 588m the highest peak in the region, dominates the Jezreel Valley. A beautifully formed dome of a hill, it is also believed to be the site of the transfiguration of Christ. Jesus came to the mountain with Peter, John and James 'and was transfigured before them: and his face did shine as the sun, and his raiment was white as the light' (*Matthew 17, 2–3*). At the same time 'a voice out of a cloud' proclaimed Jesus the son of God. Since the fourth century pilgrims have been visiting Mount Tabor to worship, and churches and monasteries have been built to accommodate them.

Dominating the summit is the **Franciscan Basilica**, built in the 1920s on the site of earlier Byzantine and Crusader churches. Inside are artworks and frescoes depicting the transfiguration, while outside, from the ramparts of the older churches, the view is unparalleled. As well as Lebanon, Syria and Jordan, it is claimed that even the pinky hills of Saudia Arabia can be seen on a clear day. There is a **campsite** on the top of the mountain, which offers spectacular sunrises and sunsets, but no other facilities – so bring plenty to eat and drink if you plan to stay. You can get a **bus** to DABBURIYA, the splendid and rather affluent Palestinian village at the base of the hill, whence a small road leads to the summit. It's a pleasant and not overly strenuous walk up, particularly if you make it in time to catch the sunrise from the top, or you should be able to find a *service* taxi.

Nazareth to Hadera

The main road south of Nazareth, **Route 60**, is one of the most beautiful in the country. The descent from Nazareth into the Jezreel Valley, a steep and winding road, is an especially memorable journey whatever the time of year.

AFULA, 9km south of Nazareth, is the first town of any size the road passes through. The administrative and commercial centre of the region, the town's growing importance in the region can be witnessed by the new buildings going up everywhere. **Afula Illit**, a collection of tower blocks recently constructed on the hills above the town, is just the most recent stage in its expansion. The whole place, in fact, is a relatively recent creation. Begun in the 1920s, and originally popular with American Jews, its current population is more and more Sephardic in ethnic origin. In 1986 the town dominated the national press for a few weeks after some particularly nasty anti-Arab riots in which many Palestinians who happened to be in the town were badly beaten by racially motivated mobs. These incidents, and a number of overtly provocative mass rallies organised by Rabbi Meir Kahane, made the town the focus of counter-demonstrations by anti-racist Israeli liberals.

There's not a great deal to see here, but a good bus station provides onward transport to most parts of the country, and you can easily stop for just a couple of hours between buses. *Sherut* taxis, which ply from here to Nazareth, Haifa, Tel Aviv and other places en route according to demand, depart from a point just behind the bus station. Around here you'll find a number of cafés and *falafel* stands selling cheap food: if you want to stay in the area, the youth hostel at Ma'ayan Harod, on the road to Beit Shean, is the best option. To get there take bus #411 from gate 9 in the bus station and ask the driver to let you off at Ma'ayan Harod. The other options for accommodation are to backtrack to Nazareth or continue to one of the coastal towns.

Continuing towards Megiddo Junction, the contrast in land use is striking. Large open fields are mostly farmed by kibbutzim, most of which control vast tracts of land on which they can afford to utilise advanced farm machinery. The smaller fields, often no more than garden-size strips which together resemble a giant patchwork quilt, are usually the mark of the Palestinian farmer: after repeated Israeli government land confiscations in the last forty years, the land under the control of Palestinian farmers has decreased markedly.

Megiddo Junction, 10km southwest of Afula, is nowadays deceptively quiet. Historically, however, it was a vital crossing, a staging point for trading caravans and a strategic key for invading armies. Through here ran the ancient trade route from Egypt to Mesopotamia, a road which under the Romans became the Via Maris and which remained an important thoroughfare virtually throughout Palestine's history. Most recently, during the 1967 war, the junction was the focal point for supplies for Israeli army depots in the north and west of the country, less than 1km from what was then the

Jordanian border. The former barracks you can see on the hill near the junction are a reminder of more turbulent times. They're now used as a military prison which was the centre of much controversy during the Israeli invasion of the Lebanon in 1982, when, in contravention of international law, Palestinian and Lebanese prisoners were brought here from the Lebanon.

Head **west** (and slightly south) from the junction and you'll travel through the area known as the **Triangle**, and ultimately to Hadera (p.248). **Southeast** takes you to the **West Bank**, **northwest** goes past **Megiddo Archaeological Excavations** on the way to Haifa.

Armageddon

One kilometre north of Megiddo Junction along route 66, conveniently shielded by a small wooded area, are the **Megiddo Archaeological Excavations**. Megiddo, otherwise known as Armageddon (from the Hebrew *Har Megiddo* – the Mountain of Megiddo) is the supposed site, as proclaimed in the *Revelation* (*16, 16*), of the final battle between good and evil at the end of the world. You get little sense of impending disaster at the dusty site now, but it wasn't so badly chosen – the scene of innumerable battles over the strategic route from Egypt to the north, Armageddon also features in the Old Testament, wrangled over in the constant wars. As recently as 1918 there was a major battle here between British and Ottoman forces.

The earliest traces found at the site go back some 6000 years, and archaeologists have unearthed the remains of at least twenty cities built on the site (or rebuilt after destruction). The position of **Tel Megiddo** was strategic: not just overlooking the main transport artery, but also supplied by a good spring at the foot of the hill. It was a heavily fortified city with one major strategic flaw – since the spring was situated outside the city walls, water was likely to be cut off in times of siege. Around 600BC the inhabitants overcame this crucial weakness by engineering a 600m-long **tunnel** under the city walls to allow safe access to the spring. This architectural masterpiece is one of the central features of the site, still accessible by negotiating a steep spiral staircase.

Another worthy feature is the ancient **temple mount**, which the guides gleefully claim was the site of ritual sacrifice and public executions. All of it is easily accessible and well displayed. At the entrance to the site (open Sun–Thur 9am–5pm, Fri 9am–3pm; admission $1) there's a **museum** where artefacts and pottery discovered during the excavation of the mound are displayed. A model of the city as it may have been during the periods of Solomon and Ahab, circa 1000–600BC, is also on show. There is a small cafeteria serving snacks and cold drinks.

The road by the site of the excavations leads to **Kibbutz Megiddo**, a kibbutz traditionally popular with British volunteers. They're often prepared to take on more volunteers here, if you fancy staying on. The kibbutz is built on the site of the Palestinian village of **al-Lajun** (the Legion – so named because of the prescence there of a Roman army encampment), whose confiscated land was handed over to the *Hashomer Hatza'ir* Zionist movement for the establishment of a kibbutz in 1949. A few of the old buildings are still used by the kibbutz, whose 380 members, aligned to the left-leaning *Mapam*, survive on a mixture of farming and manufacturing jewellery and plastics.

Carry on up route 66 and you'll eventually reach Haifa. The last 15km of this journey, along the side of the Carmel Mountain range, is particularly picturesque.

The Triangle

East of Megiddo Junction, past the military compound, you enter the area known politically as the **The Triangle**: geographically as *Wadi Ara* in Arabic or the *Irron Valley* in Hebrew. This valley – through which the Via Maris ran – is home to over 60,000 Palestinians, a fact which to many Israelis is intensely problematic. The Jewish National Fund, a quasi-governmental body which controls most of the state land, writes in one of its publicity leaflets that 'Wadi Ara is like a spearhead aimed at the narrow backbone of densely-settled Jewish areas, making them vulnerable to hostile elements in the north and the northeast'. The JNF answer to the 'problem' of the Arabs in the area is to put money into Jewish settlements in the region, thus transforming the Triangle into 'an asset to Israel's security'.

To the Palestinians who live here, the Triangle (so-called because of a small triangular area which contains a large concentration of Palestinian towns and villages) represents an image of how an Arab Palestinian state might have been had it not been for the war of 1948 and the mass expulsions. Characteristically Middle-Eastern in atmosphere and appearance, the Triangle is delineated by the village of MUSMUS in the north, BARQUAY in the east and TAIBE to the south.

Coming from Megiddo the first village you will encounter is Musmus – the road passes straight through. Along both sides of it straggle houses built on columns in the local style. They're sturdy enough in fact, even if some of the older ones look perilously close to falling down. A few kilometres to the east is the junction to **UMM AL-FAHM**, a town tightly packed over the side of a mountain that marked the Jordanian border until 1967, and a much more worthwhile place to visit. With a population of over 25,000, Umm al-Fahn is known as one of the most politically active places in the country: many of its residents are key figures in the fight for Palestinian rights.

If you arrive by bus you'll be dropped at the bottom of the hill by an excellent restaurant, *al-Hilmi*, which serves good Arabic coffee and traditionally made Palestinian delicacies on a pleasant outdoor terrace. From here, *service* taxis make regular journeys to the town centre – wave down any that pass and eventually one will stop. The atmosphere in town is rather conservative, so to avoid hostility from the town's Islamic faction it's advisable to keep your legs and shoulders covered while you visit (women especially are expected to dress 'respectably'). The centre of town, little more than a collection of shops and offices, is marked mainly by the fact that the taxis all stop here: when everyone starts getting out, or when you see a large collection of taxis, you know you have arrived. If you're feeling energetic, you can also walk to the town centre in about 25 minutes.

The winding road which snakes its way up to *al-Markaz* (the centre) of the town will give you a feel of the place: a seemingly haphazard collection of houses broken only by small pot-holed streets and the occasional fruit or olive tree. As you climb, the streets become busier until at the centre there are crowds, and either side of the street is lined with cafés and coffee houses serving delicious sweets and pastries. Sitting in one of these cafés is as good a place as any to experience the pace and richness of life in the town. The old men in their white *Keffiyas* stooped almost double as they negotiate the steep roads contrast sharply with the swarms of young children who mill endlessly about. Local curiosity will probably be aroused by your visit so don't be surprised if you soon end up in a conversation with some of the local *shabab* (youth) – you will probably get a guided tour of the town and perhaps even a visit to a house.

Stay a few hours, or arrive at prayer time, and you'll be able listen to the chorus of the *muezzins* echoing their call to prayer across the hills. For a place its size Umm al-Fahm has a suprising number of mosques, whose minarets poke up into the skyline from every part of town. To appreciate them better, climb up to the hills at the top of the town, the point where the **West Bank** begins. Should you wish to stay longer here, check out the **summer workcamp** (see *Basics*) which usually has some foreign volunteers participating. The workcamp normally selects a few of the town's many urgent problems (the building of sewage channels or the resurfacing of roads) which can be completed in a few weeks. For details either contact the Municipality or enquire at the *Abna al-Balad Club* – a community centre linked to the Palestinian political party, Abna al-Balad ('Sons of the Village'). Both are near the centre of the town.

Heading on, there are frequent buses along the road at the bottom of the valley in both directions, so you shouldn't have to wait long whichever direction you decide to continue your journey. The Palestinian villages crowding the valley tend to be either Muslim or Christian: a distinction easy to spot from a distance by the presence of either a minaret or a church spire (just occasionally, both mark a mixed population). HADERA, down by the coast (p.248), is barely half an hour away.

Afula to Beit She'an

West of Afula, a busy road runs towards Beit She'an and the junction with the main road up the Jordan Valley, linking the West Bank with Tiberias. Buses and *sherut* taxis run frequently along this route. About halfway the **Ma'ayan Harod youth hostel** (☎06-531660) and a **campsite** are set back from the main road in beautiful surroundings by a huge natural swimming pool, popular with local families throughout the summer months. There's more swimming at the attractive park of **SAHNE** (renamed Gan HaShlosha by the Israelis in remembrance of three settlers killed here by a landmine in 1938) as you approach Beit She'an, where numerous lakes with underwater caves make a great place to cool off in summer. The park – also a good site for **birdwatching** – is open every day for a small fee: you'll see it signposted just east of **Kibbutz Hefzibah**. At the kibbutz a site known as **Beit Alfa** preserves the superb mosaic floor of a sixth-century synagogue, depicting the zodiac, assorted Jewish symbols and Old Testament events. None of these are far to walk from the main Afula–Beit She'an road, where you can easily pick up onward transport: the youth hostel can be reached directly from Afula on bus #35.

Before the outbreak of fighting in 1948, the thriving Palestinian town of **BEISAN** had a population of some 5000 Arabs. The battle for the town was initiated, as early as April of that year, with the Zionist occupation of key positions surrounding it. In early May, Beisan was completely besieged. The fall of Tiberias two weeks earlier and the evacuation of its people worried the town's residents, and those that could prepared to leave for the Jordan Valley, the only route out. On the night of May 11, the town came under heavy shelling, the following day it surrendered, and its inhabitants were piled onto trucks and forced to cross into Tranjordan. Today, **BEIT SHE'AN** is an unassuming place, visited if at all only as a stopover on the way from the West Bank to Tiberias, or en route to the superbly preserved **Roman theatre** and other remains at Tel Beit She'an. In this capacity it serves well enough. From the central bus station – a motley collection of bus stops overlooked by a Thirties-style terminal and café – all the main sites are well signed, and none is more than fifteen minutes' walk. There are plenty of *falafel* stands and cafés along the way if you get peckish.

First stop should be the **museum** (Sun–Thur 8.30am–3.30pm, Fri 8.30am–1.30pm), situated on the edge of town, which has an interesting collection of archaeological finds illustrating day-to-day life in the Roman city (the remains of the city are actually on the other side of town, past the old Turkish administration building). The other main place of interest in modern Beit She'an is the Byzantine **Monastery of the Lady Mary**. The building is disused and locked, but the keys can be got from the museum if you leave your passport or identity card as security. Now stranded in the industrial part of town, the monastery has some beautifully ornate mosaic floors dating back to the sixth century. The best is in the main hall, an intricately designed calendar which shows the twelve months of the year around the sun. You are almost certain to be alone as you explore, which adds greatly to the hushed atmosphere of a place which has apparently been abandoned for the past thousand years or so.

Tel Beit She'an

Much the most rewarding site, however, is **Tel Beit She'an** (Sun–Thur 8am–4pm, Fri 8am–3pm; admission $1.50), the remains of a Roman city on a site thought to have been first occupied as long as 8000 years ago. The earliest historical record of the town dates from the nineteenth century BC, when it appears in Egyptian records as one of the strongholds from which the Pharaohs controlled Palestine. Over the next centuries it changed hands repeatedly, becoming known as Scythopolis after being conquered by Alexander the Great; with the advent of Christianity, the Roman city became a Christian centre, eventually declining only after the Christian population fled before the Muslim conquests in the seventh century.

The **theatre**, an exceptionally impressive and extraordinarily well preserved example of Roman architecture, is the highlight and focus of any visit. Above the stage rows of stone benches climb up for at least a hundred feet, providing seating for an audience of around 4500 people. You enter through one of eight original tunnels, all of them still in immaculate condition. The only part of the theatre not to have survived, in fact, is the wooden roof which provided shade for the terraces; even here the niches for the wooden supporting joists can be clearly seen. Around the theatre other Roman buildings can be made out, and archaeological investigation is still going on all around: but nothing can match the exceptional presence of the theatre, which feels as if it could open for business again tomorrow. If you can, try to visit the site either early in the morning or late in the afternoon, avoiding the coach parties which tend to crowd out the middle of the day.

travel details

Buses

From Haifa to Jerusalem (every 40min 6am–8pm; 3hr); Tel Aviv (express every 20min, local every 30min 6am–11pm; 1hr 45min); Ben Gurion airport (40min 6am–8pm; 1hr 45min); Netanya (30min 6am–9pm; 1hr 20min); Hadera (30min 6am–11.30pm; 1hr); Acre/Nahariyya (20min 5am–11pm; 30min/1hr); Afula (30min 6am–9.30pm;1hr);Nazareth/Tiberias (30min 6am–8pm; 45min/1hr 30min); Safad/Qiryat Shmona (30min 5.30am–8.30pm; 1hr 30min/2hr 30min); Beersheva (7 daily; 4hr); Eilat (2 daily; 7hr).

From Netanya to Jerusalem (every 30min 6am–8pm; 2hr) and Tel Aviv (15min 6am–8.30pm; 20min).

From Nazareth to Afula (every 30min 6am–9pm; 20min); Tiberias (30min 7am–7pm; 45min); Tel Aviv (30min 6am–6pm; 2hr).

From Afula to Jerusalem (3 daily; 3hr 30min); Tel Aviv (30min 6am–8pm; 1hr 45min); Hadera (40min 6am–9pm; 1hr); Beit She'an (20min 6am–6pm; 40min); Qiryat Shmona (40min 5.30am–9.30pm; 2hr).

Trains

From Haifa to **Netanya** and **Tel Aviv** (2hr 30min/3hr), and to **Acre** and **Nahariyya** (30min/1hr) at least six departures daily.

Ferries

Twice weekly departures from Haifa to **Cyprus**, **Crete** and **Piraeus**. Also regular sailings to **Port Said**.

CHAPTER FIVE

GALILEE AND THE NORTH

Strictly speaking the **Galilee** stretches from Haifa in the south to the Lebanese border in the north, and extends eastward as far as the Sea of Galilee. The area covered in this chapter is slightly smaller, but it encompasses the essence of the Galilee, whose rugged terrain is some of the most excitingly scenic in Israel. Inland, it's extremely mountainous, with broad green valleys separated by sturdy peaks. In the plains the soil is richly fertile, and numerous kibbutzim and Palestinian farmers till their respective patches. The relatively high annual rainfall and moderate summer temperatures ensure almost permanent greenery, above all the swathes of olive trees clothing the hillsides – the very essence of the Mediterranean.

Most people come for the **coast**, whose standard-bearer, **Acre**, is among the most attractive Mediterranean towns in the country, certainly in terms of history. Its Arab Old City, a rich cacophony of architectural styles, is fascinating and packed with interest. Northwards, **Nahariyya** is very much a resort, but it's a stylish and unusually elegant one. From here to the Lebanese border **Ahziv**, **Rosh Haniqra** and the area slightly inland provide opportunities for days of idle wandering – and more excellent **beaches**.

Inland, Acre's counterpart is **Safad** in the east, one of the four Jewish holy cities. Built over the hills which characterise inland Galilee, it's another place of antiquity and charm. Between here and the coast, the mountains and the Palestinian villages which hug their flanks are the main attraction. In the north, the **Lebanese border** is as strategic today as it has always been: there are Crusader castles here and, a more recent style of defence, numerous kibbutzim and moshavim.

On a practical level, **transport** around the region is pretty straightforward: buses run frequently along the main roads and at regular, if not ideal, times to most of the out-of-the-way places. Organised **accommodation** is restricted to the coast and a few major towns inland, but much of the area is accessible to day trips. If you have a tent, or are prepared to stay outside, then so much the better – there are very few official campsites, but freelance camping is widely tolerated. The highlands of the **Tefen Plateau**, in central northern Galilee, are heavily wooded, and especially conducive to hiking and camping, though you'll need to take all your supplies with you.

For administrative purposes the Galilee is split in two, roughly along a line which runs east from Acre. **Upper Galilee**, the northern section, is much the more interesting and accessible. The mountainous greenery of the region alone gives it a feel which is very different from much of Israel, and this is amplified by the continuing Arab traditions, and a relatively high Palestinian population. In many ways life seems simpler and less rushed. It was a populous and prosperous region before 1948, but there are other reasons why the

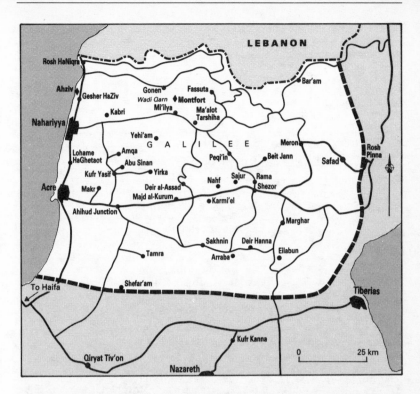

Galilee managed to retain many of its villages and its Palestinian identity. In part, since Galilee was taken by Israeli forces relatively late and there has been little Jewish settlement in the countryside – it was included in the 1947 partition plan as part of the proposed Arab state – the Arab population had the benefit of seeing what happened elsewhere and time to make plans to stay put. Then it was simply further from the centre of Israeli life – less attractive for settlers, less immediately in the eye of politicians.

Such was the Palestinian control over the Galilee in 1949 – physically and psychologically rather than militarily – that the Israelis felt it necessary to control the area with a military administration right up until 1966. In the 1960s, a conscious policy of the **Judaicisation of the Galilee** was adopted, and new settlements were planned and founded. But this has still gone much less far than in most of Israel. In other ways, however, the situation of Palestinians here is no better than anywhere else, and the struggle against land expropriations remains very much a live one. Palestinian villages may look charming and traditional, but many have no running water or electricity, and few enjoy properly maintained roads, schools or medical services – in stark contrast to their newly-built Jewish neighbours. As a traveller you will not bear the brunt of this frustration, but you shouldn't be surprised if you are engaged in political argument by Palestinians, and if you intend visiting their villages, it's as well to respect local sensibilities. A few words of Arabic can transform your welcome, although having lived within Israel's 'green line' for over forty years, all but the very elderly speak Hebrew, and most, excellent English.

Acre

Crusaders, Mamluks and Ottomans have left their mark throughout Israel and the occupied territories, but nowhere can visitors view and appreciate their influence more clearly than in **ACRE**. Above all, the attractive **Old City** retains the very essence of a Middle Eastern town with its gaggling *souq*, dusty streets, towering minarets and small port from which pastel-coloured fishing boats still sail. With a refreshing summer climate the city has masses of charm, character and, for a change, plenty of cheap accommodation.

Inter-city buses, *sherut* taxis and trains regularly connect Acre with most places in the country, and Haifa is less than 25km away: getting here is not a problem.

New Acre, surrounding the the Old City, grew after the creation of the state of Israel to house the influx of Jewish settlers. It includes a few older parts from which Palestinians were expelled in 1948, but most of the new town is typical 'Israeli modern' and no different from a dozen other places. This, though, is where you'll find most of the transport, many shops and services, and the best beaches.

With the contemporary life of the city existing amidst a mixture of Crusader and Islamic architecture, **history** is never far from your mind: the remnants of previous conquerors lie scattered around the old town like exhibits in a historical museum. Acre's heritage is under threat, however, as the municipality relentlessly renovates and 'improves'. While old Palestinian homes are crumbling and residents slowly being forced out, the area around the port is rapidly being transformed, with the planners not only giving permission for the most garish and brash night spots to open but also refusing to enforce licensing laws so that the music blares out until early morning, especially at weekends. Palestinians see these policies as part of a conscious design to get them out. The city fathers make little secret of their plans: 'Getting the Arabs out' has been a plank in the ruling bloc's platform in the past two elections and there are occasionally ugly racial confrontations in the town.

Acre in history

For a city that has seen no fewer than 22 civilisations come and go, no short history can ever really suffice. As early as the **Canaanite period**, its natural harbour gave Acre a vital strategic importance as an ideal point of entry into Palestine, an importance which was recognised by successive waves of rulers: Phoenicians, Persians, Greeks, Ptolemy II, Seleucids and Romans. In the seventh century AD the Byzantines presided over Acre's first economic boom and it grew further under the **Ommayad Caliphs** who developed the port as a supply and storage depot. However, the most important historical (and archaeological) legacies of the city, the ones that have most clearly survived to this day, are from its days as a **Crusader stronghold**, from the twelfth to the thirteenth centuries, and as a bustling **Arab port** from the sixteenth century until the British arrived after World War I.

The Crusaders took Acre as they pillaged and destroyed their way through the Levant in the early part of the twelfth century. They renamed it **St. Jean d'Arc** and, recognising the importance of the port to the viability of their hegemony over the Holy Land, began building the impressive fortifications and warren of underground passages and vaults which are still in evidence today. However the Crusaders' first reign over the city was short lived: in 1187, to the joy of the Arab populace, the Crusader defenders – vastly outnumbered and facing defeat – surrendered without a struggle to Salah al-Din.

It was immediately after the capture of Acre that **Salah al-Din** made what historians regard as the one error in his campaign to win back Palestine; he didn't march on Tyre. The fortified port a few hours march north of Acre was the Crusaders' last foothold in the region, and when he did move his army there a few weeks later Conrad of Montferrat had already arrived with reinforcements for the defenders. Securely ensconced, Conrad rejected Salah al-Din's offer of a peaceful surrender. Battle-weary and daunted by the fortifications protecting Tyre, Salah al-Din had little option but to withdraw. Four years later the Crusaders, under the dual command of Richard the Lionheart of England and King Philip Augustus of France, recaptured Acre. The stalwart resistance of the citizens behind the virtually impenetrable walls was an augury of the city's future. Once in possession it has proved down the centuries very hard to get the defenders out by siege.

For the next century, Acre was the capital of the Crusader kingdom and there was no real threat to their control. From here much of the Crusaders' spoil, especially the religious relics of the Holy Land, were shipped back to Europe. In the other direction came notables like **Francis of Assisi**, who passed through while on a pilgrimage, and **Marco Polo**, on his way east. In their tracks came a host of merchants trading with the orient, and Acre expanded rapidly. New outer walls were constructed to contain and protect the enlarged city. Only traces of these remain, but they originally enclosed an area three times bigger than the Old City. This relative calm, interspersed with minor squabbles about the succession to the throne of the Crusader kingdom, lasted almost exactly a hundred years. The Arabs, supported by the Egyptian Mamluks, were committed to the overthrow of Acre on conquering Palestine. When they arrived at Acre in 1291, the Crusaders, outnumbered by a factor of ten to one, were soon defeated.

Acre enjoyed over 450 years of stability under Arab rule – by far the longest uninterrupted peace in its history. In the eighteenth century, **Daher al-Omar** took the port, made it his capital, fortified it and built hostels and mosques (see *Tiberias*). He was assassinated here and the Ottoman Turkish rulers installed **Ahmed al-Jazzar** as local overlord in 1775. Known as 'the butcher' because of his cruelty, al-Jazzar continued rebuilding and restructuring the city – much of his work greatly enhances the city today. It was not long before the city was at war again. In 1799 it was attacked by **Napoleon**

Bonaparte, who made two attempts to capture the city (the second in 1801), but failed dismally. His plan was to open a trade route between India and Europe: his failure to capture Acre forced him to retire to Egypt and ended his 'eastern' campaign. Napoleon was defeated by a combination of the city's awesome defences and the diseases – cholera, malaria, dysentery – emanating from the swamps around the city, which took a heavy toll of his troops. **Napoleon's Hill**, an artificial rise thrown up outside the town as a place to station his cannons, provides a lasting reminder of that campaign, on the edge of town next to what is now a football ground. Less concretely, Napoleon left thousands of soldiers behind who were eventually absorbed into the local population. Some people ascribe the prevalence of blonde-haired, blue-eyed Palestinians in the Galilee to the genes of Napoleon's defeated army; others claim it is a legacy of the Crusaders.

Jazzar's successor, **Suleiman the Magnificent**, continued the work of restoration, but was eventually halted by the advancing armies of Ibrahim Pasha of Egypt in 1832. Eight years later the defeat of Ibrahim by the Ottomans reinstated Turkish rule of the area and the city. Over the next decade Acre declined in significance as Haifa grew. The city continued to be important in the economy of the northern Galilee, however, serving as a centre for the villages of the interior as it still does today.

Acre's last battle was in **1948**, when the Palestinian inhabitants held out for ten days against a heavily armed Zionist attack force. The battle for the Galilee was largely fought before May 15, the date when officially the British Mandate ended and separate Jewish and Arab states were supposed to be established. Haifa was taken on April 22 and Safad on May 11. Acre found itself encircled, with only the road to Safad open, and finally fell on May 18. Most of the inhabitants were driven, or fled, to become refugees in Galilee villages which survived. In 1948 the population of Acre was 4020, of whom 874 were Jewish; by 1965 there were 31,700 people living in the city, of whom 3500 were Arabs.

The two mainstays of the local Palestinian economy, commerce and fishing, are both being undermined by the municipality. Fishing has all but gone and plans are afoot to convert the port into a marina, thus closing it to Palestinian boats. The traders are surviving in their shops so far, but many of the buildings have deteriorated to a point where they are almost dangerous. Parts of the Old City have already been made squeaky clean (and Arab-free) and the walls are unlikely to be able to stop the process this time.

Arrival

Acre (*Acca* in Arabic and *Acco* in Hebrew) revolves around the Old City, but inevitably you'll arrive in the new. If you come in by bus you'll be at the **central bus station** on HaArba Street. To get from here to the Old City, turn left in front of the bus station and then take the first right down **Ben Ami Street**. Ben Ami is the main thoroughfare of new Acre, with most of the banks and cafés, so you'll almost certainly find yourself here again in the course of a visit. Two blocks down, turn right into Chaim Weizmann Street: follow this to the end and you will walk through a gap in the Crusader fortifi-

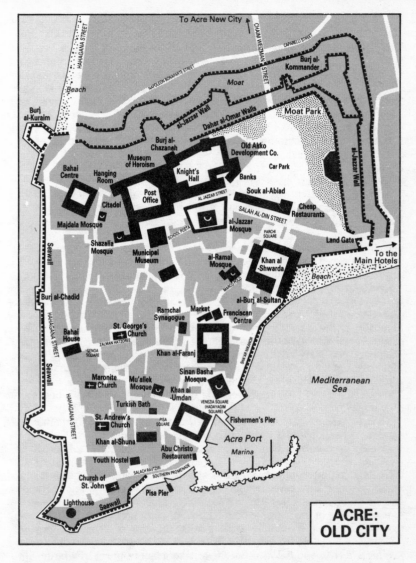

To Acre New City

Beach

Burj al-Kuraim

Moat

Burj al-Kommander

Moat Park

Bahai Centre

Hanging Room

Museum of Heroism

Burj al-Chazaneh

Knight's Hall

Old Akko Development Co.

Car Park

Banks

Citadel

Post Office

Souk al-Abiad

Majdala Mosque

AL JAZZAR STREET

al-Jazzar Mosque

SALAH AL-DIN STREET

Cheap Restaurants

Shazalia Mosque

Municipal Museum

SCHOOL PLAZA

PARCHI SQUARE

Land Gate

al-Ramal Mosque

Khan al-Shwarda

To the Main Hotels

Burj al-Chadid

Beach

al-Burj al-Sultan

Ramchal Synagogue

Market

Franciscan Centre

Bahai House

St. George's Church

GENOA SQUARE

ZALMAN HATZOREE

Khan al-Faranj

Mediterranean Sea

Maronite Church

Mu'allek Mosque

Sinan Basha Mosque

Khan al-Umdan

Turkish Bath

VENEZIA SQUARE (HADAYAGIM SQUARE)

Fishermen's Pier

St. Andrew's Church

PISA SQUARE

Acre Port

Khan al-Shuna

Marina

Youth Hostel

Abu Christo Restaurant

Church of St. John

SALACH RAYTZIRI

SOUTHERN PROMENADE

Lighthouse

Seawall

Pisa Pier

ACRE: OLD CITY

cations, past a large car park, and into a square near al-Jazzar Mosque. This is the start of the **Old City**. The **Israeli Government Tourist Office** is opposite the mosque in al-Jazzar Street; they sell a large pictorial map of the city which includes the area outside of the Old City, and will give details of any special events in the area.

The main *sherut* **taxi stand** is across the road from the bus station, and Palestinian *service* taxis serving the villages of central Galilee also stop around here. The **railway station** is one block east of the bus station on David Remez Street, the main road to the north. To get to the Old City from here, turn left outside the station and join Ben Ami Street at the small roundabout (Tel Acre Junction).

Once in the Old City, the only method of getting around is on foot. This, in any case, is much the best way to see it. It's not a large area, and walking lets you fully appreciate the splendour of the place. The main sites are all well signposted, and with the help of our map you should be able to navigate through the winding alleyways with relative ease – even if you do get lost you're never very far from a site or a signpost to put you back on course.

Accommodation

Places to stay are limited in number, but they always seem able to cope adequately with the demand, even in the height of the summer. Cheaper accommodation is almost exclusively in the Old City, more luxurious hotels are mostly in the newer part of town. If you prefer to **camp** there is a site at Ahziv, a 25-minute bus ride north of Acre. The large hotels on the beaches are less than welcoming to those who want to sleep on their doorsteps, so if you can't afford the hostel prices walk a few kilometres out of the town until you find a more secluded beach. The usual strictures about not camping alone, particularly for women, still apply.

The Old City has two main **hostels**, one of which is almost guaranteed to have room. If by some chance both are full, there are plenty of other rooms available in the Old City to which either of the hostels can direct you. The *Akko Youth Hostel*, just across from the lighthouse in the Khan al-Umdan Quarter (☎04-911982; B&B from $7.50), is a lovely old Arab building – once the palace of local Ottoman governors – and is easily the best place to stay in Acre. Run by a Palestinian couple, the hostel feels more like a family-run hotel, and although it can get very hot in the summer, its marble floors and wicker chairs adequately compensate for the close atmosphere. The *Clocktower Hostel*, also near the Khan al-Umdan, is smaller, cheaper (from $4) and more basic, but safe and popular with younger travellers.

New City **hotels** include the *Palm Beach Hotel* (HaAtmarin Beach; ☎04-912828) and the *Argaman Hotel* (Argaman Beach; ☎04-913755). At around $50 for a double room in the high season these are about the cheapest you'll find: the price buys considerable comfort and a beachside location. The *Nes Amin Guest House* (Nes Amin; ☎04-922566; around $40 double) is also an option if none of the above appeal. NES AMIN, just north of Acre, is an evangelical Christian community set up with the aim of bringing Jews and Christians together. To get there from Acre either drive up the main Acre–Nahariyya road and follow the signs or take a bus from HaArba Street. The mainly Dutch settlers at Nes Amin are devout Zionists to the extent that men serve in the local units of the paramilitary Border Guards. Their bad relations with the local Palestinian communities also stem from the fact that when they established the settlement they acted as middlemen in land deals; persuading Arabs to sell land to them as non-Israelis and then handing it over to local kibbutzim who had coveted choice plots but been unable to coerce the owners into parting with them.

The Old City

The main entrance to the Old City, Chaim Weizmann Street, passes through **walls** which have been built and rebuilt time and time again during the life of the city. Most of what is visible today is, in essence, either Crusader or Ottoman. Roughly speaking the foundations on either side of the Chaim Weizmann Street entrance date from the twelfth century: the upper sections were rebuilt in the eighteenth century under Daher al-Omar and Ahmed al-Jazzar. Exploring the walls – you can walk most of the way round, either on top or in the dried up moat – is an excellent introduction to ancient Acre, an appetiser for much of what you'll see within their compass.

The northeastern fortification is marked by the **Burj al-Kommandar**. This tower, of Crusader origin, is a superb vantage point, and more than once played a crucial role in the defence of the city. From here in 1799 al-Jazzar directed his troops to repel Napoleon. The cannons on top of the fortress are known as **Napoleon's Cannons**, but closer inspection reveals that although they are French, they weren't made until 1857. Following the walls to the south, you'll come to **Bab al-Ard** (Land Gate), one of three entrances into the Old City. Nowadays there's no way down to the street from this part of the wall, so to enter the City you have to walk almost all the way back up to Chaim Weizmann Street before steps lead you down to ground level.

At the end of Chaim Weizmann Street the road splits: right into al-Jazzar Street; left to Salah al-Din Street. Opposite this junction **Souq al-Abiad** (The White Market) is the only working covered market that survives in Acre: the others have long since fallen in disuse. Built by Daher al-Omar in the eighteenth century, it was restored by Suleiman Pasha in 1818 to include the small domes you now see. Today this small market has lost some of its former glory as the lure of the tourist dollar has changed much of its orientation: but the architecture is still fabulously simple and the atmosphere in many ways still medieval. The other end of this long, straight market emerges in Salah al-Din Street amid the crowds of **Parchi Square**, once Acre's commercial centre.

Al-Jazzar Mosque

Dominating the skyline of the Old City with its slender green and white minarets, **Al-Jazzar Mosque** is one of the finest surviving mosques in Israel. From Parchi Square, follow Salah al-Din Street towards its minarets. Built in 1781–82 by al-Jazzar, then Turkish governor of the region, the mosque complex has retained its original role as the administrative centre of the local *Waqf* (who administer to the local Muslim populace) and as a powerful focus for Acre's Palestinian community. A visit to the palm-tree-lined complex is highly recommended: it's open throughout the day except at Muslim prayer times.

The **entrance** to the mosque is in al-Jazzar street – you can't miss the main gate or the great flight of stone stairs that leads to it. At the gate you pay a small fee and have your dress inspected; the keeper will insist that you cover your head, and if you're wearing shorts will give you a piece of cloth to wrap around your legs. Inside, you emerge in a small courtyard in front of the mosque, whose serene atmosphere can have changed little since the place was built. On your left, the colonnaded **cloisters**, built of marble removed from Ashqelon and Caesarea, serve as a seminary for students of the *Quran* and as offices for the *Waqf*. To your right, an ornate **fountain** provides water for Muslims to wash before prayer. If you intend to go inside the mosque, you should remove your shoes.

On entering **the mosque**, note in the corners the names of the four caliphs who donated money for its building. The mosque's grandiose outer shell contrasts starkly with the simplicity of the decor within. Apart from the Quranic verses beautifully inscribed on the top of the side walls, it's an almost bare chamber, the absence of clutter lending a supremely tranquil air. Only a hair from the head of the Prophet Mohammed, proudly displayed, and the small wooden *minbar* from which the Friday sermons are delivered are allowed to disturb the simplicity.

As you leave the main mosque, a small building immediately to your left contains two small **tombs**: in the first is the body of Ahmed al-Jazzar, the creator of the mosque; in the other Suleiman Pasha, his adopted son. If you've time, the small garden within the complex makes a pleasant spot to sit and rest, watching the comings and goings. Recently a vast **underground water system** was discovered beneath the mosque. The entrance to this system is inside the mosque complex, and should soon be open to the public.

The Subterranean Crusader City

Opposite the main entrance to Al-Jazzar Mosque, in the **Subterranean Crusader City** (Sat–Thur 9am–4.30pm, Fri 9am–12.30pm; admission $2), excavations have revealed a vast complex of Crusader buildings. When they were built these were not actually below ground, but were buried after the Crusaders' defeat: on top, al-Jazzar built his citadel. What you see is only a part of the Crusader city, with the headquarters of the Knights of St. John, or Knights Hospitaller, and hence of the Crusader armies, as a centrepiece. Much more exists, but archaeologists, fearful of undermining the citadel above, have had to be content with revealing only a fraction. This is impressive enough.

The **entrance hall**, worthy of the entrance to a cathedral, has three large pillars protruding directly from the ground, indicating that the floor level in Crusader times was well below the ground that visitors currently walk upon. The staff in the ticket office, just inside the entrance hall, sell an interesting guide to the complex and are happy to answer questions and add their views on the place. As a general rule, the pictorial decorations on the pillars tend to be Crusader, the more elaborate, abstract designs Ottoman. The scale of the Crusader complex is apparent as soon as you enter one of the eight connected chambers so far revealed. The rooms just beyond the entrance are thought to be part of the Hospitaller complex; the seven enormous halls in the northern section were used by the seven '*Langues*' or national divisions of the Crusader orders.

The first major room you will come to is the **Knights' Hall**, a rectangular room supported by pillars with classical ornate brickwork, forming well preserved Crusader arches. After walking through the **Grand Maneir**, the administrative centre of the city which would have held the seat of the governor and his aides, you come to a small passage which leads through into the most impressive of all the halls. This enormous rectangular space is generally known as the **Crypt**, because before it was excavated you could look down into it from a window at street level. But it was actually a refectory, the knights' dining hall. As you enter, notice the heraldic *Fleur de Lis* cut into the stone of the supporting beams, with the name Louis VII and the date, 1184. It is, quite simply, a magnificent chamber, capturing the very spirit of Crusader architecture. From the hall – perhaps to ensure that revellers did not fall victim to enemies while weakened by too much food and drink – an **underground passage** provides a means of secret escape. A flight of stairs surrounding one of the large columns at the far end of the hall leads down to the passageway, which apparently dates right back to the Persian occupation. About 70m long, it gets smaller and smaller as you proceed, at times less than 1.5m high.

At the end of the passage you'll enter **the Post**, which has nothing to do with stamps and everything to do with its position guarding the city. The collections of rooms which comprise the post were used for a number of purposes: from assembly rooms for pilgrims arriving in the Holy Land to the wards of the hospital for which the Knights of St. John became famous.

During the autumn these underground halls, especially the Knights' Hall, provide venues for the **Acre theatre festival**. The festival is the largest fringe event in Israel and features the best of Israeli and Palestinian theatre groups – for details of the programme contact the IGTO. During the summer the Acre Theatre Group perform *Time Tunnel*, a short play about Acre during the Crusader and early Ottoman period. The play, informative and imaginatively done, takes the audience on a short tour of both this complex and its roots. The central message is conveyed through the medium of mime.

After emerging from the subterranean city you come to the **Municipal Museum**. The ticket which allows entry to the Subterranean City also gives access to this museum, housed in a former Turkish baths. The refurbished steam rooms and pools now contain many exhibits from Acre's Crusader and Arab past, although the major finds have been taken to museums in Tel Aviv and Jerusalem. The **citadel**, above the Crusader city, is also a museum; for details, see below.

Souqs and khans

If you go right at the entrance to the museum, past al-Jazzar mosque, a narrow street leads into the main commercial area of the **souq** at the junction of al-Jazzar and Weizmann streets. Alive with activity all day long (from around 7am), the *souq* is crammed with stalls overflowing with excellent fruit and vegetables: for once, prices seem to be fixed, so don't push too hard if traders refuse to bargain with you. Step off the winding main streets and you'll find quiet residential courtyards, surprisingly isolated from the activity around them. As you wander, you're likely to be approached by local youths offering their services as guides. If you pick, or are picked by, someone who speaks English, such company can be a real asset, full of interesting (if not always accurate) historical asides and, perhaps more fascinatingly, details of life in modern Acre. You may be asked to pay but none should charge much more than $5.

Heading down through the *souq*, towards the port, you'll pass the first of Acre's four **khans**, or caravanserais, on your left. The *khans*, large inns usually built around a central courtyard, provided accommodation for visiting caravans and merchants. Today, all four are well preserved, providing some impression of Acre as it was in its great trading days. **Khan al-Shawarda** overlooks the sea, and you can imagine the merchants who stayed here looking out, waiting for their ship to come in. The *khan*'s thirteenth-century tower, **Burj al-Sultan**, is still one of the town's great landmarks, pointing the way to Acre for arriving ships and for caravans making their way overland. On its walls you can still see the marks left by the masons who built it: each had their own unique symbol to sign their work. From here Marco Polo Street heads south, deeper into the heart of the market, past the **Ramal Mosque**. Built in 1704–5, this incorporated the foundations of a Crusader church into its structure, and on its southeast wall Crusader inscriptions can be found. One, written in Latin, reads: 'Oh, men who pass along this street, in charity I beg you to pray for my soul – Master Ebuli Fazli, builder of the church.' The mosque is now used as a Muslim scout hall and is open daily from 4 to 6pm, admission free.

Further down Marco Polo Street, past the bell-tower of a large, eighteenth-century Franciscan church now in use as a school, is the **Khan al-Franj**, the Khan of the Franks, or Crusaders. This is the oldest *khan* in Acre, established by Fakhr al-Din in 1600 to house a small group of French merchants, who during the sixteenth century had been given a trading concession in the town by the Mamluks in an effort to increase trade between Palestine and Europe. Later it became the place where most European merchants in Acre stayed (similarly, 'Franks' referred initially to the French, but came to be used as a general term for any European). Parts of the building incorporated a Clarissian nunnery – founded by Francis of Assisi – whose occupants committed suicide rather than surrender to the Mamluks when they captured the city in 1291. Crusader remnants can be found in the foundations and columns of the building, but as most of the *khan* has fallen into ruin these are hard to distinguish from the other fallen masonry. Two main entrances lead into a central courtyard, where the overriding impression is one of neglect and decay.

Head from the southern end of the Khan al-Franj towards the large, Italian-looking tower and you'll emerge in **Venezia Square**, a spacious cobbled area full of ice-cream sellers. All around are magnificent old facades. To your left, the white **Sinan Pasha Mosque** is the most recent of them, dating from the last century. It's a working mosque which doesn't particularly invite visitors, but on the other hand it doesn't turn them away either: ask the doorman at the top of the steps for permission to enter. Inside, a lush green courtyard, shaded by palm and eucalyptus trees, offers refreshing respite from the clamour without.

Dominating the other end of the square is the **Khan al-Umdan** (Khan of the Pillars), the second largest and best preserved of the *khans*. Built by al-

Jazzar in the eighteenth century, on the site of a Dominican monastery, it gets its name from the granite and porphyry pillars brought from Caesarea for its construction. Over the entrance rises a tall square **clocktower** (minus its clock in recent years) adorned by the Islamic symbol of the crescent moon and star. You used to be able to climb its winding staircase to the top, but in recent years it has been closed. It's worth checking to see if things have changed, though, because the view of the city and bay from up there is a great one. The tower was built in 1906 by Sultan Abd al-Hamid II to commemorate 'his glorious rule'.

As you walk through the main entrance beneath the clocktower and into the central courtyard, it is immediately obvious why the *khan* is famed for its pillars. The two-tiered quadrangle is a maze of colonnaded cloisters and blocked-off storerooms in a remarkable state of preservation (though sadly marred by litter). The lower level once consisted of storage areas and stalls where trade was carried out, with animals stabled in the courtyard; the merchants would have stayed in the rooms on the upper level. Right in the centre is a large trough for the animals, now sadly relegated to the status of dustbin.

The Pisan Quarter and the Port

From a second entrance in the *khan*'s southern wall, a small alleyway leads into **Pisa Square**. Just off the square is the smallest of the *khans*, the **Khan al-Shuna**, once the Inn of the Pisans. It's a ramshackle building in a run-down area: here many of Acre's Arab residents live in houses originally built during the Crusader period.

Beyond the *khans* lies Acre's **Port area**, still perhaps the most attractive part of the Old City. This is the best place to sample locally caught fish, as you watch the fishermen clean and repair their nets. It should be possible to arrange to go on a fishing trip with one of the local fishermen (you'll need to haggle over a price if this appeals), or less adventurously you can take a twenty-minute boat trip around the walls (departures throughout the day from the end of the pier).

From the port the walls curve around, past the the small white-stone **Church of Saint John** (dedicated to two British officers who fell at Acre in 1799 and 1940) and the lighthouse, to Hagannah Street. There are several other churches along Hagannah, or if you want to explore some of the Old City's residential areas virtually any of the small alleyways leading off here will do. About 300m from the port, one of these alleys leads to a small white **Bahai Temple**. This spot was an important meeting of the ways in medieval Acre, and it's still a good place to note interesting old architectural details.

Burj Kurajim and the Citadel

Walking northwards from the port along the sea wall, you can't help but be impressed by the scale and durability of the fortifications which protected the city from seaborne assault. The **Burj al-Kurum** (Tower of the Vineyards), the large tower which juts out into the sea at the end of the wall, is an Ottoman addition to the Crusader defences.

Facing inland here, the view is dominated by one of Acre's most impressive buildings, the **Citadel**. From the seaward side, a large ceremonial gate provides an entrance point into the complex, now renamed by the Israelis the **Museum of Heroism** (Sat–Thur 9am–4.30pm, Fri 9am–12.30pm; admission $1). Another of al-Jazzar's eighteenth-century improvements, the citadel takes as its foundations the Crusader buildings buried below. A massive and intimidating structure – its sheer size is its best feature – it served as a prison under both Turkish and British rule. One of its most famous inmates was the founder of the Bahai faith, Baha 'Ullah (see *Haifa*). Imprisoned here in 1868 for heresy, he was later transferred to what is now the Bahai Tomb, just outside Acre, to be placed under house arrest for his remaining years.

During the British Mandate, Acre jail was one of the most important in the country. Among the early Zionists held here, in the 1920s, was Vladimir Jabotinsky, one of the first Zionist theorists to openly call for armed struggle. Today the Museum of Heroism remembers more contemporary prisoners from the *Stern* and *Irgun* gangs which carried out attacks on both the Palestinians and the British in the years preceding the creation of the state of Israel. The **gallows room**, suitably austere and functional, lists the Zionists hanged by the British, and in the cells are the names of the prisoners they once held, and display cabinets giving more detail about their lives. However, this is a victor's history: in reality the gaol always held more Arab than Jewish prisoners, also convicted of fighting for their cause.

Much attention is given to 'one of Acre's most dramatic moments', an escape organised by *Irgun* and *Stern* in 1947 which freed over 250 prisoners. This incident was dramatised in the film *Exodus*, which was shot on location in the prison, and books on sale at the museum also retell the tale.

Back at the main entrance to the Citadel, Hagannah Street to the right heads out through the city walls, following the sea past some usually deserted beach. The first turning on your right, Napoleon Bonaparte Street, will take you back along the side of the city wall to the entrance of the Old City.

Eating, drinking and nightlife

When it comes to **food**, the Old City is again the place to head, for fresh fruit and vegetables from the market; *falafel*, *humus* and snacks from stalls and cafés; and succulent seafood from the port-side restaurants. The cheapest places are mostly in the northern part of the Old City, along Salah al-Din and al-Jazzar Streets: most serve both Arab and European dishes for around $2–6. In the winding streets of the *souq* there are also a number of good cafés around the Khan al-Franj and Venezia Square. The *Oudah Brothers Restaurant*, inside the Khan al-Franj is pricier than most, but excellent value. If all you want is a drink, try the Arab **coffee houses** just north of Khan al-Umdan. The haunt of (almost exclusively male) locals whiling the days away in games of cards, chess and backgammon, these serve delicious Arab coffee and mint tea.

The **restaurants** around the port are all rather more upmarket, but for what you get, none could be described as expensive. *Abu Christ*, right by the port, is something of an institution, with a reputation as the home of some of the best seafood in the north. Open from morning to midnight, it's a huge place, with over 500 seats, and great views over the bay towards Haifa. If you're saving money you can stick to salad, but that rather misses the point – freshly caught fish or squid from $10. *Abu Christ* is also a good place simply to sit and drink in the evening: it and the bars around the port are the liveliest places inside the Old City.

New Acre has if anything an even wider choice of places, but little of the atmosphere. Restaurants, cafés and bars, with a more European menu and higher prices than their Old City rivals, crowd on and around Ben Ami and Yehoshafat streets. The *Palm Beach* and *Argaman* hotels both have good restaurants and lay on night-time entertainment and **discos**.

Listings

Banks Most of the large banks are located on Ben Ami Street, between the intersection of HaArba and Chaim Weizmann. *Barclays* (al-Jazzar Street, in the Old City) has an efficient tourist service. If you get stuck for cash the intersection of al-Jazzar and Chaim Weizmann is the focus of a small black market.

Buses The central bus station on HaArba Street is the starting point for all intercity buses. A limited bus service also operates on shabbat, linking Acre with Haifa and Nahariyya.

Diving The Diving Centre (by the port) offers diving courses and, for qualified divers, the chance to go out and explore some of the wrecks just offshore. They'll also rent mask, fins and snorkel by the day.

IGTO On al-Jazzar Street, open Sun–Thur 9am–4pm, Fri 9am–12.30pm.

Police The police station is opposite the sea at 2 Ben Ami Street (☎04-910244).

Post office The main post office is at 11 Atzma'ut Street, just off Chaim Weizmann near the Municipality (Sun, Tues and Thur 8am–12.30pm and 3.30–6pm, Mon and Wed 8am–2pm, Fri 8am–1pm). The main post office has an international telephone centre and poste restante facilities. There is also a small post office in the entrance to the Subterranean Crusader City on al-Jazzar Street.

Service taxis *Kavei HaGalil* (HaArba Street, opposite the central bus station; ☎04-910111) operate *sherut* taxis to Haifa, Safad and Naharriyya.

Taxis *Acre Taxis* (HaArba Street; ☎04-916666).

Trains The railway station is on David Remez Street.

THE NORTHERN COAST

The flat coastal land north of Acre is known, with commendable simplicity, as the **Plain of Acre**. It's little over 20km from the city to the Lebanese border, an attractive drive up the coast. **Nahariyya**, just over halfway, is one of Israel's best beach resorts. Regular buses (#271) and trains link Acre and Nahariyya, and from there you can continue by bus to the border town of **Rosh Haniqra**. If you're planning a leisurely trip, there are a couple of places worth stopping on your way to Nahariyya.

The Bahai Tomb and Gardens

The first of these, just ten minutes from Acre by bus, right by the main road, is the Persian-style **Bahai Tomb and Gardens**. It was here – now a tranquil monument to the Bahai religion – that Baha 'Ullah was placed under house arrest after being freed from Acre Prison. He died here and was buried in the gardens. His ornate tomb and the displays of religious artefacts inside the nearby house have since become a shrine for members of the Bahai faith. The house (Fri–Mon 9am–noon) is really only of interest if you want to know more about the religion; the Gardens (daily 9am–5pm; admission free) are lush and peaceful, with welcome shade from the summer heat. To get there take the main Acre–Nahariyya road and get off when you see the sign '*Shammerat*' – any bus driver should know the place – from where the entrance is a short distance down a side road. Just before reaching this sign, you will notice some regal-looking gilded gates: these are open to members of the faith only.

Kibbutz Lohamei HaGeta'ot

Just a couple of kilometres further, **Kibbutz Lohamei HaGeta'ot** (Fighters of the Ghetto) has one of the largest holocaust collections in the country. Founded in 1949 by survivors of the concentration camps and ghettos of Eastern Europe, the centrepiece of the kibbutz is its museum (Sun–Thur 9am–4pm, Fri 9am–1pm, Sat 10am–4pm): 'a graphic exhibition of the life and culture of the European Jewish communities before their destruction by the Nazi death machine.' Inevitably it is a horrific and memorable experience, and with eleven halls on two levels has space to go into some depth documenting the struggles of these Jewish communities against fascism. This is the museum's particular focus, confronting the question of why the Jews failed to fight back and citing instances – especially the Warsaw Ghetto – where they did. It deserves some time.

You can't miss the museum as you pass on the main road, a large, austere and box-like building. Every year on *Yom HaShoah*, Holocaust Memorial Day, thousands of Israelis and visitors from abroad come to participate in the large memorial ceremony which takes place in the modern amphitheatre near the museum. A sombre event, the ceremony normally includes a dramatic production along the theme of 'From Destruction to Redemption'.

The kibbutz itself survives on an agricultural base, supplementing its income by farming fish and running the museum. With less than 300 members and generally around thirty volunteers, it seems wealthy and well equipped. If you have time, no one seems to mind visitors strolling around.

Next to the museum is the most accessible part of an Ottoman **aqueduct**, which runs from Acre to the Kabri Springs east of Nahariyya. The aqueduct, built by al-Jazzar in 1789, is extremely well preserved, although it was an obvious target for anyone attacking Acre. When Napoleon besieged the town, one of the first things he did was to destroy part of it near Acre. After the defeat of the French, Suleiman Pasha built a replacement which ran east of this one. Much of this survives too, but it's much harder to get to, with no access by road.

Nahariyya

Founded by German Jews in 1934, **NAHARIYYA**, Israel's most northerly beach resort, has a charm and sophistication that makes it one of the most pleasant in the country. Originally conceived as a dairy and poultry centre, its residents soon realised that the area's rugged coastline, with miles of glistening white sands, also made it an ideal tourist centre. Popular with Israelis and Europeans alike, the town has a marked European character: unlike many Israeli resorts, the prices aren't too outrageous either.

One of the town's main features is the River Gaton which flows – majestically in winter and spring, little more than a trickle in summer – right through its heart and down the middle of the main street. Its water feeds the towering eucalyptus trees which shade the central avenues. Planted by the first settlers in an effort to dry up the swamps which then acted as a breeding ground for malarial mosquitos, these have done their job well. You might still get bitten, but you won't catch malaria.

Practicalities

Arriving by bus you'll be right in the centre of Nahariyya on HaGa'aton Boulevard, the town's main street. The **railway station** is one block inland from here, the **Israeli Government Tourist Office** (Sun–Thur 9am–1pm and 4–7pm, Fri 9am–4pm; ☎04-922121) a short distance towards the sea, at the bottom of the Municipality Building in a little square on the left-hand side of HaGa'aton Boulevard.

Most of the better **places to stay** are nearby, especially along Wolfson Street, which runs off HaGa'aton directly oposite the *Egged Bus Tours* office at the bus station. Cheapest of these, and arguably the best value in town, is the *Rehayim Youth Hostel* at no. 6 (dorm beds $4.50; ☎04-920557). It has a pleasant outdoor patio and rents **bicycles** to residents for $3.50 a day ($4.50 to non-residents). You'll find several budget **hotels** down here too. The better of them include the *Motel Arieli* (1 Jabotinsky; ☎04-921076); *Kalman Hotel* (27 Jabotinsky; ☎04-920355); and *Hotel Beit Erna* (29 Jabotinsky; ☎04-920170). For most of the year a single room at any of these will cost $10–15, a double $15–20, but during July and August the prices rocket. In this midsummer peak period it can be hard to find anywhere to stay at all: if you do get a place expect to pay up to fifty per cent more. The same is true of the **rooms** available in houses with 'rooms to rent' signs outside. Many of these are very pleasant, and excellent value, but expect to pay up to $25 in the summer. At

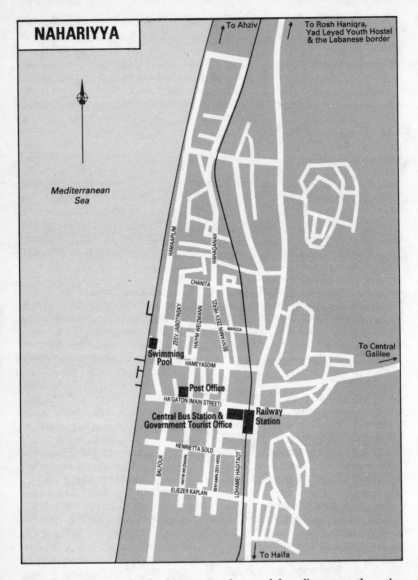

NAHARIYYA

To Ahziv

To Rosh Haniqra,
Yad Leyad Youth Hostel
& the Lebanese border

Mediterranean
Sea

HAMAAPILIM

HAHAGANAH

CHANITA

ZEEV JABOTINSKY

HAIYM WEIZMANN

BENYAMIN ZEEV HERZL

MARGOA

Swimming
Pool

HAMEYASDIM

Post Office

HA'GATON (MAIN STREET)

To Central
Galilee

Central Bus Station &
Government Tourist Office

Railway
Station

HENRIETTA SOLD

BALFOUR

HAIYM WEIZMANN

BENYAMIN ZEEV HERZL

LOHAME HAGITAOT

ELIEZER KAPLAN

To Haifa

other times it's worth checking out a few, and haggling over the price.
Sleeping on the beach is tolerated, though to avoid any hassle you need to
walk a little way out of the town.

If the hostels and hotels in Nahariyya are full, the nearest alternative is the
Yad LeYad Youth Hostel on the main Nahariyya–Ahziv road (☎04-921343; $10
a room). There are also two **campsites** nearby, one about 4km north at

Ahziv, just south of the national park, the other at the Kabri Springs, due east
of Nahariyya. For the former you can either walk up the beach or take bus
#22, for the latter take bus #43.

Places to eat are also plentiful and central; again HaGa'aton Boulevard is
the place to head. To start with, you'll find the usual selection of *falafel* stalls
and cafés here: the *Royal Café*, with good breakfasts, and *Lahmi Café*, both
near the municipality, are two of the most popular. For more substantial
meals try the local branch of the *Pizzeria Capri* chain, in Kikar HaBanim just
off HaGa'aton Boulevard, which has the virtue of being cheap, the *Chinese
Inn Restaurant* (28 HaGa'aton) or the Romanian *Donnau Restaurant*. And, as
ever, if you need a plain, nourishing meal and are short of cash, the *Egged*
restaurant in the bus station is hard to beat. The best place to buy your own
food for a **picnic** is the large *Supersol* supermarket, at the intersection of
HaGa'aton and Herzl streets.

At night everyone heads for the **bars** at the beach end of HaGa'aton, which
at weekends is closed to traffic and given over to revelry. There are a couple
of **nightclubs** behind the bus station; free admission, but outrageous prices
once you get in. The *Hod Cinema*, on Herzl Street, shows a variety of recently
released English-language films throughout the day.

Beaches

During the day, there's little to do in Nahariyya but go to the beach. The
most popular and central of them is **Galei Galil** – very clean and very
crowded, with a full-time lifeguard and an Olympic size outdoor pool.
Admission costs $2.50, and includes use of the volleyball and basketball
courts. South of Galei Galil is a section of free, unpatrolled sand and south of
this, another beach with a lifeguard, admission to which costs $2. North of
Galei Galil, there are a number of free beaches which tend to be less
crowded. If you want peace, continue walking north of Nahariyya until you
find somewhere secluded: the walk to Ahziv, 4km north, is particularly
recommended. These beaches have no lifeguards, and currents can be
strong, so take care when swimming.

Just about the only 'sight' in Nahariyya is the remnants of a 4000-year-old
Canaanite Temple, discovered in 1947. This lies about twenty minutes' walk
south of Galei Galil; a pleasant walk even if there's not a great deal to see
when you get there. The temple was dedicated to the fertility goddess
Asherah, which seems somehow appropriate in modern Nahariyya, which for
years has marketed itself as a **honeymoon** hideaway. During the Jewish festival of *Lag B'omer* – the only day in the six-week period following Passover
that Jewish couples are permitted to wed under Jewish law – you can see just
how successful the campaign has been. The hotels are full of young couples
and special activities are laid on by the municipality and local businesses.

Three **museums** in the Municipal building (Sun–Fri 10am–noon, Sun and
Wed also 4–6pm; admission free) offer a more cultural way of passing the
time, or shelter in the unlikely even of rain. The Municipal Museum has a
collection of archaeological finds from the area, the Modern Art Museum is
self-explanatory, though its collection is limited, and the Malacological
Museum houses a display of shells.

East of Nahariyya: springs and castles

Due east of Nahariyya, off the road to Ma'alot-Tarshiha, the **Kabri Springs** provide a relaxing setting for the *Kabri campsite* and a large, well-developed picnic area. The springs have provided cool, clear water for centuries: the Phoenicians were the first to build an aqueduct to divert it, and both Greeks and Romans followed suit. The Crusaders believed the water to have miraculous properties and well into this century it was bottled and drunk throughout Palestine: one 50-year-old guide book described it as 'the only thing to drink in Palestine: don't be put off by something "just as good" – it does not exist'. Nowadays most bottled water comes from springs in the Golan, but if you visit the spring you can still test its medicinal qualities. It is said to be especially good for digestive problems. The kibbutz which now occupies the site has erected a small monument to Jewish soldiers killed during the 1948 war.

You can get to the springs on bus #43, which runs from Nahariyya to the village of MI'ILYA, about 18km inland (the springs are less than halfway). Mi'ilya is the alighting point for **Montfort Castle**, a famous local beauty spot and the best preserved of three Crusader fortresses built to protect Acre. The walk up to the castle, on a hill above a particularly lush valley, is at least as great an attraction as the ruins themselves. Mi'ilya itself was the site of a second Crusader fortress, the **King's Castle**, but all that remains of this is a single hall on the edge of the village, facing west towards neighbouring TARSHIHA. From Mi'ilya to Montfort, follow the road that climbs towards the village of HILLA. After about 2.5km the road takes a sharp right and a little wooden sign points down a dusty track to Montfort. It's a further 1.5km from here to the castle, following the red and white posts which mark the trail. This is the most scenic part of the walk, through the wooded **Wadi Qurein** before a final scramble up to the ruins.

Montfort was built on the remains of a Roman fortress, a site acquired in the twelfth century by the Teutonic Order of Knights who called it **Starkenberg** (Strong Hill); Montfort is simply a French version of this name – in Arabic it is known as Qala'at al-Qurein. The Teutonic Order, of Germanic origin, was supported by the German Emperor Frederick II, and Montfort soon became their headquarters in the Holy Land. Its strategic importance to the Crusaders was small, but for the Teutonic knights it served as an administrative centre and a useful source of income: taxes collected from the local peasantry were enough to ensure its economic independence. Salah al-Din captured and damaged the castle in 1187, but it was reconquered, rebuilt and held out almost until the fall of Acre. Sultan Baybars besieged the castle for months in 1266, but was eventually forced to retire: six years later, however, his troops scaled the surrounding slopes and managed to tunnel a hole in the western wall. The Crusaders made a hasty retreat to Acre, and the castle was destroyed.

The remains of the castle consist basically of its tower, a large hall, and a chapel on the western side. A wine-press used here has been preserved, as has much of the elaborate sewage and water system: a maze of dams and aqueducts which ensured the comfort of the castle's residents.

If you want to return to Nahariyya by an alternative route, you have the option of descending on the north side and heading through the **Keziv Park** to the settlement of GOREN. On the way to the park, by the Keziv (*Qurein*) River, you pass a small, two-storey building of Crusader origin, perhaps part of a farm which supplied the castle with fresh food. Bus #25 runs from Goren to Nahariyya several times a day. Alternatively the main road, just north of the settlement is a good place to hitch from. The springs at the end of the Keziv River, at Ein Tamir, have large pools to bathe in: well worth the walk on a hot day.

The third of the Crusader castles, **Jiddin**, lies south of Montfort, near the settlement of YEHIAM. Neither the castle nor its surroundings have quite the appeal of Montfort, but the fabric has been more thoroughly explored: this castle too was destroyed at the end of the thirteenth century, but it was rebuilt in the eighteenth by Daher al-Omar, in a style true to the original. To get to Jiddin (Sun–Thur 8am–5pm, Fri 8am–4pm; admission $0.50) take the bus to Yehiam, from where it is well signposted.

Ahziv

The Keziv flows out to the sea 4km north of Nahariyya in the **Ahziv National Park** (daily 8am–7pm; admission $2.50), a stretch of manicured lawns and barbecue areas whose centrepiece is **Tel Ahziv**, the remains of a Phoenician port from the eighth century BC. There's a sheltered beach here, complete with changing rooms and showers.

The plaque outside the entrance to the national park is a classic of Israeli history-making. 'During the Talmudic period,' it proclaims, 'Ahziv had a flourishing Jewish community . . . In later centuries it declined into a coastal village'. In reality, Ahziv during the Talmudic period amounted to about 100 families: **Ahzib** (the Palestinian coastal village) had almost 10,000 residents until 1948.

Inside the park, most of the buildings are remnants from Palestinian Ahzib: beautiful white stone structures which have been transformed into restaurants and changing rooms. The focus for most visitors are the barbecue facilities provided by the Parks Authority: all you need to bring is some charcoal and food. Near the entrance to the national park is the **Ahziv Diving Centre** (☎04-926671), where you can hire snorkel, mask and fins for $6 a day.

Immediately north of the national park lies **AHZIVLAND**, a self-proclaimed 'Independent State'. In 1952 Eli Avivi came to Ahziv, fell in love with the place, and decided to stay. After leasing the land from the Israel Lands Authority he set up his own state, and for fifteen years lived like a hermit as the Israelis authorities repeatedly tried to oust him and get him to recognise their jurisdiction over the area. He spent ten days in prison on one occasion for relinquishing his Israeli citizenship and passport. Nowadays Ahzivland has become a respectable tourist attraction, and an effective truce has been declared: Avivi and the authorities still argue over his claims to the beach, but they seem resigned to allowing the oddity of Ahzivland for the time being.

The $2 admission fee to Ahzivland includes entry to a fascinating museum and a colourful little Ahzivland entry stamp in your passport outlining Avivi's territory, well worth taking your passport along to get. The **museum** occupies part of a house that belonged to an Ahzib notable before 1948; Avivi lives in the same building. The exhibits, all collected locally, constitute a unique historical document of human settlement in Ahziv, from Phoenician, Roman, Byzantine, Crusader and Arab artefacts to reminders of life in the Arab village: an old Singer sewing machine, baking bellows, ploughs, rakes and other paraphernalia of everyday life.

Volunteers are always needed to continue excavating the area and maintaining the extensive gardens. If you work for two hours you get to stay free. Otherwise, at his **hostel**, you pay $8 to sleep inside, $5 to stay outside. While the accommodation is not palatial, staying in Ahzivland will never be anything less than absorbing (though there been have complaints of sexual harassment at the site). Alternatively you can **camp** at *Ahziv Campsite* (☎04-921792), just by the national park. During the height of summer, expect to pay about $5 per night: bamboo huts are also available at $20 for a double or $36 for four. Just north of the campsite is the *Yad LeYad Youth Hostel* (☎04-921343; members $6, non-members $7), a large hostel right on the beach.

The other option for staying in the area is the guest house at **Kibbutz Gesher Haziv**, on the hill 1km inland from the national park. The kibbutz was founded to commemorate an incident in 1946, when fourteen *Hagannah* members were killed as the explosives they were installing to blow up a bridge were ignited by a British soldier's flare. The 'Night of the Bridges' (June 17, 1946), has since become part of the Zionist folklore of the area. The guest house is clean and comfortable, but pricey – it also has an excellent restaurant, and a large, open-air swimming pool accessible to non-residents when it's not too crowded.

Rosh Haniqra

ROSH HANIQRA is the most northerly point on Israel's Mediterranean coast: a small border crossing between Israel and Lebanon. Sitting across from the turmoils of Lebanon and less than an hour's drive from Beirut, its cliff-top views and peaceful ambience in no way reflect its geographical position. The white chalk **cliffs**, with their intricate maze of natural caves, are the main attraction here. At the top is an observation point from where you can see Haifa on a clear day, a reasonable self-service restaurant and a cable-car which runs down to the **caves** (Sun–Thur 8.30am–6pm, Fri 8.30am–4pm; admission $2, students $1.70). To visit the caves it's best to go early in the morning, as during the summer the queue for the cable-car can be almost two hours long. Though the caves are fun to visit, a wait of that length really isn't worth it: you've seen the lot in twenty minutes once you get down. You can go for a swim in the clear blue waters at the bottom of the cliffs – this is technically illegal, but more importantly it can be dangerous too, as the currents are notoriously strong. If you need to change money the souvenir shop will oblige, though the rates are not very good.

The **Lebanese border**, right outside Rosh Haniqra, looks real enough, but in practice is little more than a showpiece. The Israeli presence in South Lebanon since 1982 means that the whole border area is effectively under Israeli control. However, it is still a sensitive military area, so before you take any photos of the fence or the military you should ask permission. This may or may not be granted, but if you don't ask you may have your camera confiscated, or your film exposed.

EAST OF ACRE:
INLAND GALILEE

The main road east of Acre is one of the most picturesque in the country, encapsulating in a few kilometres all the beauty and ruggedness of the Galilee, from stunning mountain ranges to wide open plains. Leaving Acre, the route crosses the fertile coastal plain, passing a number of large, productive kibbutzim, until it reaches the slopes of **Mount Gamal** at the Ahihud Junction. Here lesser roads turn off right and left: to the left one traces the fringe of the highlands all the way up to the Lebanese border; to the right you can curl back round towards Haifa, past small strips of Arab-owned farmland. Straight ahead lies the Palestinian heartland of the Galilee, and the wooded mountains around Safad.

The road is well served by **public transport**. Buses run frequently along the road to Safad, and on to the Golan and Qiryat Shmona. It's easy enough to break your journey and continue by flagging down the next bus, or one of the *sherut* taxis that also ply the route.

Palestinian villages – Majd al-Kurum, Bi'na and Deir al-Asad

As you descend the far slope of **Mount Gamal**, you will notice groves of olive trees planted on either side of the road. These are owned by the residents of the villages of Majd al-Kurum, Bi'na and Deir al-Asad, many of whom left the country in 1948. Under Israeli Land Law, their property was automatically transferred to the state, so that while some of the groves are clearly cared for, others, belonging to the refugees, have been left sadly neglected. The remaining residents of the three villages have often offered to tend these groves, but the Israeli land authorities have consistently denied them permission to do so, preferring to leave the land unattended. **Olive harvesting**, around the end of September, is still done by traditional methods. The whole family will normally work for the period, with large cloths or nets placed on the ground to collect the olives which are knocked or shaken from the trees with the aid of a long pole.

The first village you pass is **MAJD AL-KURUM**, approximately 16km east of Acre. This place, which is reputed to be the site of Beit Kerem, a Jewish settlement mentioned in the Talmud, has a population of around 6000. If you simply want to get the feel of a Palestinian village, you can stop here and linger awhile in one of the cafés in the centre. The other two villages take a bit more effort to get to, but they're a great deal more attractive.

You'll see them first a couple of kilometres further on, where a small road climbs to the north. This winding way leads to the villages, and also divides them: Deir al-Asad, to the right, is Muslim, while Bi'na, on the left, is predominantly Christian. In recent years the distinction has become blurred as growing populations and shrinking land have forced each to straggle across the dividing line, but they remain reasonably distinct. Both are majestically sited high on the slopes of the **Tefen Plateau**. Most buses will continue along the main road, so to visit the villages you will have to either walk up the hill or stand at the junction and flag down a passing car like the locals.

DEIR AL-ASAD, Arabic for 'Monastery of the Lion', was founded, according to local tradition, in the early sixteenth century. The story of the village's conception reads like a fairy-tale, but it's by no means the strangest story you'll hear in the Holy Land. In 1516, so the legend goes, Sheikh Mohammed al-Asad set out from Safad on his donkey, and after many hours stopped near a well to pray and fill his water-skin. While he was praying, a lion killed his donkey, whereupon he took the saddle from the dead beast's back, put it on the lion, and continued on his journey. As he approached Nahaf (the village opposite Karmiel), he met the troops of al-Sinan Basha, who were travelling to Gaza and Egypt. After many of his horses, startled at the sight of the lion, had bolted in panic, Basha turned to the Sheikh and granted him a wish. Sheikh al-Asad pointed to the nearby monastery of **Saint Georges de Labeyne** and asked for the deeds to the monastery and its lands. These he was granted, and having expelled the monks, he founded and developed the village of Deir al-Asad on the ruins of the monastery.

Perched high on the slopes of the mountain-side to avoid using any of the precious agricultural land on the plain below, Deir al-Asad is typical of many of the surviving villages in the Galilee. Its agricultural base has all but disappeared, after a series of land seizures by the Israeli authorities, and today its residents form part of the pool of contract labour who travel daily to work in Israeli factories and industry. Its experiences during the **1948 war** are also fairly typical of the fate of Palestinian villages in the Galilee.

Before the major Israeli offensive in the region there were about 500 members of the *Arab Liberation Army* (ALA) operating openly in the Galilee highlands. However on October 29, 1948, after the second United Nations truce, when the Israelis launched **Operation Hiram**, the ALA retreated, leaving the villages undefended. The following day the *mukhtars* (village leaders) of Deir al-Asad and Bi'na went to the Zionist command post in the neighbouring village of al-Birwa (a Palestinian village taken in June 1948, after the first truce) and surrendered. Two days later Zionist forces entered the villages, collected all the arms, assembled the villagers in the village square, and searched the houses for members of the ALA. By mid-afternoon, having stood in the heat for most of the day, some of the villagers asked if they could go to the nearby well and collect water. The soldiers agreed, but those who left were, according to an eye-witness, shot by 'automatic gun-fire'.

Some of those who remained were taken prisoner, the rest were ordered to disperse. Many went into hiding in the hills above the village, and were allowed to return three days later. Others fled to Lebanon, spreading the news and panic as they went, and gathering more refugees from all the villages along the way. A UN investigation into the affair described the shootings as 'wanton slaying without provocation'.

Deir al-Asad was, and to some extent still is, famous for the quality of its **olive oil**. If you arrive during harvesting, you can buy some from the store that doubles as the village post office. The **mosque**, near the centre of the village, is a fine example of traditional local architecture, as indeed are the older parts of the village, east of the central square. Here, among remnants of early Arab and Crusader architecture, parts of the monastery of Saint Georges de Labeyne can still be seen: note the large circular rooms which make the inside temperature cool in the long hot summer months.

If the heat is getting to you and you're looking for some refreshment, try the café just above the village square, which serves a selection of pastries and even cold beer during the summer months. The walk to the top of the village provides some of the most breathtaking **views** in the country. To the south lies the Galilee region, with the tower blocks of Karmiel in the foreground, and to the west you can see the Mediterranean shimmering in the distance. On the road to the Tefen Plateau are rock-cut caves and tombs from the Byzantine period. These are now used by village herdsmen to pen goats and sheep.

Karmiel and beyond

Continuing along the main road, you will shortly pass the town of **KARMIEL**, off to your left. Established in 1964 with the aim of increasing the Jewish population in the Galilee (part of the 1960s plans to 'Judaicize the Galilee'), Karmiel today has a population of around 20,000 – a sizeable proportion of whom are new immigrants. It is considered to be a model development town; clean and relatively affluent, with an economy based on light industry and a large proportion of its inhabitants living in high-rise apartment blocks. None of this makes it particularly interesting to visit, but it's a convenient place to stop for a bite, with frequent buses and *sherut* taxis to Acre, Haifa and on towards Safad.

The centre of town, a few hundred metres from the main road, is marked by a large mural depicting the history of the Jewish people in Israel. Around it are the usual cafés and bars, with some particularly worthwhile *falafel* stalls just up from the bus station – a collection of bus stops around a large patch of grass. A post office, supermarket and banks provide other useful services. If you want to stay the night, the *Kalanit Hotel* (10 Nesiei Yisrael Boulevard; ☎04–983878) is the only place in town, and almost always has room, for upwards of $25 a night.

Beyond Karmiel the mountains become higher, with peaks of over 1200m to the north, and the upper slopes are liberally sprinkled with small villages. Two larger places, the Druze villages of SHEZOR and RAMA (see below) stand out. Some way to the south, on a road running parallel to this one (which you can reach by turning right at the next junction, right again and doubling back) are the three largest Palestinian villages in the Galilee: **DEIR HANNA, ARRABE** and **SAKHNIN**. Here, in 1976, protests about land confiscations erupted into a pitched battle between the Israeli army and the villagers which left nearly a dozen people dead. To commemorate this event, *Yom al-Ard* (**Land Day**) is marked every year on March 31. On this day, the Palestinian flag flutters from Arab villages across the country and a general strike is often called. If you have time to visit, these three villages, especially Deir Hanna, are scenic places with a quaint rural feel to them.

In the mountains between these villages and Karmiel are a number of small, isolated **Beduin settlements** which look as though the twentieth century has passed them by. Collections of tin huts, breeze-block houses and the occasional tent, they have few of the services enjoyed by their immediate neighbours. As in the Negev, the Beduin here are engaged in a complex dispute over land rights and demands for compensation for land already confiscated. The Israelis maintain that most of these Beduin settlements are illegal, and hence refuse them permission to build houses: from time to time the Israeli police come and demolish houses to underline their point of view. The Beduin claim that having lived in the area for at least as long as the State of Israel has existed (and in many cases having land deeds to prove it) the Israelis have no right to refuse them building permission on their land.

Rama to Tarshiha

At the junction to the village of **RAMA**, a large café/restaurant serves a variety of Arab salads and traditional dishes. Service can be slow, but if you're in no hurry the food is worth waiting for. The minor road which heads north here, to Tarshiha and on to Nahariyya, is a mountainous and beautiful one. There's little in the way of public transport, not much traffic at all in fact, but if you try to hitch you'll find a surprising number of the cars will stop. There are buses from Rama, but most go only as far as the Druze village of Beit Jann before turning round and coming back. The initial climb out of Rama, up punishing gradients to the **Tefen Plateau**, also makes a great hike if you're fit and adventurous. Take plenty of water, though, and however you travel leave early: there's nowhere to stay in any of the villages along the way.

BEIT JANN, perched high on the summit of Mount Meron commanding magnificent vistas of wooded hills, is the first of these villages. It is far less commercialised than the Druze villages near Haifa, but it's the views and the beauty of the countryside that really make a trip to Beit Jann worthwhile: there are numerous treks you can make from here to explore Mount Meron, and it's even possible to walk to Safad via the village of Meron on the far slope. To get to Beit Jann take the road to Tarshiha and turn right at the junction a few kilometres north of Rama.

Back on the main road to Tarshiha, a few kilometres north of the Beit Jann junction, the road passes through the village of **PEQI'IN**. This is a place where Arabs and Jews are said to have lived together continuously since the destruction of the Second Temple in the second century AD. Sadly, it's not much of an advertisement for interdenominational harmony – just one Jewish family remains, and a few questions about the acclaimed 'peaceful relations' between the village's different religious communities soon expose a bitter dispute about dividing the spoils that tourism has brought to the village: a dispute that recently hit the Hebrew press. Of the 4000 inhabitants, over half are Druze, approximately 1500 are Christian, a couple of hundred Muslim, and only around twenty are Jewish.

In the centre of the village the road forks, and there's a large café-restaurant on each side. The one on the left serves excellent snacks and will bake the *pitta* bread for its *labaneh* sandwiches in front of you. Druze *pitta* is very different from that served in most parts of the country – thin as paper and big enough to cover a large poster. The dough is first rolled and flattened until it is barely a millimetre thick, then thrown onto the roof of the oven (*taboon*) where it cooks in seconds, ready to be stuffed with herbs and fresh *labaneh*. The process is entertaining, the result delicious.

If you walk down the hill beside this café, you'll find a large map of the village with the various sites clearly marked. Most crowd into a small sector which represents the oldest part of town. The **synagogue**, a relatively new structure incorporating the remains of a second-century one, makes a good place to start (though you'll probably be asked to pay for the privilege). From here, follow the road down the hill past the Catholic church and the Druze *hilwe* (prayer hall), and you'll emerge in Spring Square, the centre of the old part of the village and a popular meeting place for young and old alike. Getting lost in the maze of streets around here is probably the best thing to do next, giving you time to appreciate the rural feel of the place. The villagers are friendly, especially if you can manage a few words of Arabic.

Not far out of the village, on the hill above the road as you come from Rama, is the cave to which **Rabbi Shimon Bar Yohai** is said to have fled from the Romans, with his son Elazar, after the Bar Kokhba revolt. Here, according to tradition, they lived for thirteen years, during which time the rabbi received daily visits from the prophet Elijah who instructed him in the mysteries of the *Torah*. These discussions provided the basis of the doctrinal texts in the *Zohar*, Bar Yohai's mystical work of commentary on the *Pentateuch* and the *Hagiographa*. He lived in the cave until his death, and was entombed in the village of Meron. To get to the cave, now a holy site, take the winding road up to the top of the village from the centre: a small synagogue nearby dates from the same period.

When you reach **TARSHIHA** you should find transport easier, with regular buses running west to Nahariyya. Tarshiha itself has a long history, and is believed to be the site of a Jewish settlement from Old Testament times. According to local Arab tradition, it is named after a holy Muslim recluse, **Shiha**, who after meditating on the summit of an adjacent mountain rose to heaven: the Arabic words, *Tar Shiha*, mean 'Shiha flew'. During the Crusader period the village was the site of fierce battles between Christians and Muslims and during the 1947–48 civil war it served as a stronghold of the Arab Liberation Army: their local leader is famed for having won a number of battles against the Israeli forces. Despite all this, modern Tarshiha is an unexciting little place, whose predominantly Christian population seem to share far more churches than they could possibly need.

Adjoining Tarshiha, and unusually forming part of the joint Jewish-Arab municipality of Ma'alot-Tarshiha, is the Jewish settlement of **MA'ALOT**. Founded in 1959 as a settlement for new immigrants, Ma'alot hit the headlines in 1974 when a PLO commando unit came over the Lebanese border and captured the school building, holding the teachers and children hostage. In the ensuing fight with the army, eighteen of the hostages were killed and seventy were wounded.

Rama to Safad

Beyond Rama, the Acre–Safad road begins a slow, heady climb. Four kilometres from Rama, the road divides: the left fork, **route 85**, goes down to the Sea of Galilee; the right fork, **route 18**, passes the Har Meron Reserve on its way to Safad. On the latter route, just before the Meron Junction, a signpost points down a small dusty road to the **tomb of Rabbi Shimon Bar Yohai** (see above).

If you have the time, this place deserves a visit if only for its bizarre atmosphere. For Sephardi Jews it's an important place of pilgrimage, and many come here with their entire families, sleeping on the floors of the surrounding buildings or camping out on the rough ground. Among the crowds wander vendors with large trays of sweets, biscuits and sandwiches – you take what you want from the tray, with a glass of juice or *arak* to wash it down. All of this takes place in a party-like atmosphere – the pilgrimage is a joyous occasion – which makes it feel as if you've stumbled into some giant religious holiday camp.

The main focus for pilgrims is a large, white multi-domed building: both a synagogue (the largest in the Galilee) and a shrine to the rabbi. Sitting on one of the walls at the back of the tomb, you can watch the action and take it all in. At the top of the hill overlooking the tomb is an ancient synagogue dating back to Roman times, and to the east of the parking lot you can see the remains of the settlement of **Meron** which date from the third and fourth centuries. They're well preserved and throw interesting light on the sophistication of these early Jewish communities. Walking around the site note the *mikveh*, ritual baths where the faithful washed before prayer, and the signs of the existence of ancient local industries.

The site is most interesting during the annual **festival of Lag B'Omer**, which takes place 33 days after the beginning of Passover (usually in May). Here, it commemorates the day that Rabbi Bar Yohai died, attracting large crowds of Orthodox Jews to dances and religious rituals. A number of sheep are slaughtered during the festival amongst the tents which accommodate the pilgrims, and a folk festival of traditional Jewish music provides entertainment. Underneath it all lies a deeply religious event, however, so if you go you'll be expected to dress, and behave, respectfully.

Not far away is the modern settlement of **MERON**, an orthodox religious place mainly run by Sephardi Jews. From here walks have been laid out by the Nature Parks Authority into the Har Meron reserve and up to the summit of **Mount Meron**, at just over 1200m the highest peak in the Galilee.

Safad

SAFAD (Safed, Tsfat, Zefat or Zfat) vies with Acre as the Galilee's top tourist draw. Here, according to the brochures, 'the hills and sky merge as nowhere else in the Holy Land'. And it is indeed a beautiful place, with stunning views from its hilltops, fine ancient Islamic and Judaic architecture, and an air of tradition appropriate to one of the four great Jewish holy towns. The tourist industry has also dicovered Safad's many attractions, but despite the prettification, and the art galleries selling prints of Orthodox Jews dancing traditional folkloric dances to coachloads of tourists, there are still plenty of secluded alleyways where life seems barely to have altered since the Middle Ages. And as a bastion of Jewish orthodoxy, Safad has not allowed the changes to go too far: you won't find many bars or discos here.

History

The hilltop position of Safad, with Lebanon to the north and the Sea of Galilee to the south, is a strategic one, but its first real historical significance came from about 60 to 70AD, when, like Tiberias, it became a haven for Jews during the revolts against Roman rule, and a centre of Jewish learning after the destruction of the temple. Most of what you actually see began to grow up almost a thousand years later, when the Crusaders conquered the town. It was a bloody period for Safad, and one which saw the Jewish community first decimated, then banished. When Salah al-Din reconquered the region, ransacking the newly built Crusader fortress, Jews were briefly allowed back. But it was another century – until the Crusaders were finally driven from their kingdom based at Acre – before any sort of stability came to the town.

This early town was, under Muslim control, a lively commercial centre, the capital of a province which included the Galilee and Lebanon. **Jewish** immigration began in earnest in the sixteenth century. After 1492 thousands of persecuted Jews fled the Spanish Inquisition, and many of them ended up in Safad. These were, on the whole, people of wealth and learning, and Safad, which by the end of the sixteenth century was a predominantly Jewish town, rapidly became known as an important centre of Jewish studies.

Numerous scribes and holy men lived in the town, amongst them **Rabbi Isaac Luria** (known as the Lion), and **Joseph Caro**, author of the seminal work on daily Jewish rituals, the *Shulhan Aruch*. Many others were drawn by the proximity of the tomb of Rabbi Bar Yohai at Meron, whose writings inspired the Cabbalistic ideas of Jewish mysticism for which Safad became renowned. At this time the first ever printed Hebrew text was made in Safad. Today Safad is one of four cities holy to Judaism, along with Tiberias, Hebron and Jerusalem.

By the nineteenth century the town's importance, and its population, had declined considerably: by now the inhabitants were roughly evenly split between Jews and Arabs, and over succeeding years the Jewish population continued to fall. Adding to this exodus were a series of earthquakes and attacks by the Druze in the nineteenth century, and Arab rioting in the early part of it. By 1948 less than 2000 of a total population of 14,000 were Jewish.

On the morning of April 16, 1948, the British commander declared that his forces would leave Safad on the afternoon of the same day. Following this withdrawal the Arabs occupied vital strategic sites in the town. But the capture of Tiberias and surrounding villages by the Israeli forces on April 24 had a demoralising effect on the Safad defenders and caused many of its inhabitants to flee the town. On May 6 the Israeli forces had reached Safad and by May 9 had occupied it. Today, Safad is an almost exclusively Jewish town.

Arrival

Safad straggles across three hills: atop the main one is the centre of town, while the districts of South Safad and Mount Canaan are built on adjacent peaks. The main streets of the centre run in concentric circles, descending from the fortress at the top of the hill. Chief of them is **Jerusalem Street**, whose loop takes in most of the important sites. Walking round its circuit, which takes no more than 15–20 minutes, is probably the best way to acquaint yourself with the layout of the place.

The **central bus station** (☎06-31122) is in HaAtzma'ut Square, at the lower end of Jerusalem Street. At the junction here another major thoroughfare, HaAtzma'ut Street, leads off towards Mount Canaan. Turn right at the bus station and a short walk up Jerusalem Street will lead you to the **IGTO** (23 Jerusalem St; ☎06-30633; Sun–Thur 8.30am–1pm and 4–6pm, Fri 9am–1pm), where you can buy a large colour map of Safad and pick up details of events, accommodation and tours around town. Most of your exploration will of necessity be done on foot, but there are local buses running out to South Safad and Mount Canaan. **Banks** and other businesses can mostly be found on Jerusalem Street; the main **post office** (Sun–Thur 7.45am–2pm, Fri 7.45am–noon) is on Aliyah Street below the Artists' Quarter.

Accommodation

Much of the accommodation in Safad takes the form of **rooms for rent** in private houses, sometimes a family's spare room, sometimes a purpose-built apartment. While demand is high during the summer months, you shouldn't have too much difficulty finding something. The simplest way to do this is to hang around the bus station until someone offers you a room – though you should always check it out before finally accepting, making sure that there are plenty of blankets, as Safad can be cold at night. Failing this, ask at the IGTO or go direct to any of the places mentioned below.

The best deal in town are the hostels run by **Shoshanah Briefer** (16 HaPalmach St, Artists' Colony; ☎06–793939). Facilities are good, and if some of the rooms are small and dark, you can't complain for $5 a night. These may not be open in winter. Other rooms can be found above all on Jerusalem Street near the IGTO, where you'll see 'Rooms for Rent' signs in a variety of languages.

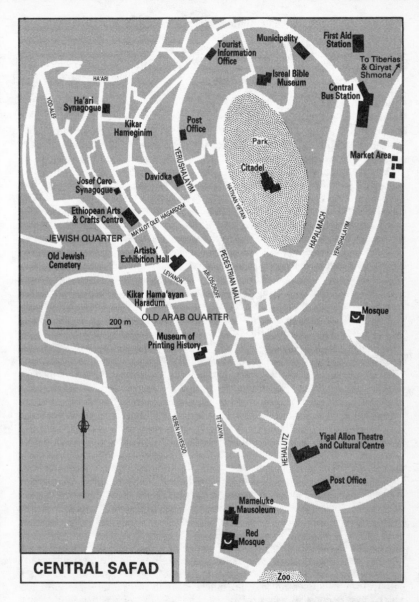

HA'ARI

Tourist
Information
Office

Municipality

First Aid
Station

To Tiberias
& Qiryat
Shmona

Isreal Bible
Museum

Central
Bus Station

YOD-ALEF

Ha'ari
Synagogue

Kikar
Hameginim

Post
Office

Park

Market Area

YERUSHALAYIM

Citadel

Davidka

Josef Caro
Synagogue

MA'ALOT OLEI HAGARDOM

HATNAN VETAN

HAPALMACH

YERUSHALAYIM

Ethiopean Arts
& Crafts Centre

JEWISH QUARTER

PEDESTRIAN MALL

Old Jewish
Cemetery

Artists'
Exhibition Hall

ARLOSOROFF

LEVANON

Mosque

Kikar Hama'ayan
Haradum

OLD ARAB QUARTER

0   200 m

Museum of
Printing History

KEREN HAYESOD

TET-ZAYIN

HEHALUTZ

Yigal Allon Theatre
and Cultural Centre

Post Office

Mameluke
Mausoleum

Red
Mosque

CENTRAL SAFAD

Zoo

On a more formal basis, there's a **youth hostel** and plenty of **hotels**. The *Youth Hostel Beit Binyamin*, on Weizmann Street (☎06-31086; members $8, non-members $9.50) is expensive compared to the private rooms, but at least it usually has beds. Located in newly-built South Safad, it's about twenty minutes' walk from the bus station: alternatively take bus #6, #6a or #7. Among the cheaper hotels the *Hadar Hotel* (Ridbaz St; ☎06-30068; singles from $15) and *Hotel Yair* (59 Jerusalem St; ☎06-30245; singles from $25) are good options. If you can afford upwards of $50 a night, the *Rimon Inn* in the Artists' Colony is the best hotel in town.

Food and nightlife

Hedonism is not one of Safad's strengths, and the **restaurants** are plain rather than exciting. One of the best of these is *Milu*, on the corner of Aliya Bet Street, with tasty Sephardi dishes. *Chabad House*, in the Jewish Quarter on Hatam Sofer Street, also serves traditional Jewish food for reasonable prices on an open-air patio with views over town. To get there walk up to the Davidka Canon Memorial, in memory of fallen Jewish soldiers, and take the stairwell down. Good take-away kebabs are served at *Stekia Haselah*, a few yards west of the bridge on Jerusalem Street, and of course there are the usual *falafel* stalls everywhere: try *Falafel Baruch*, just below the police station. If you're planning to cook your own food, Safad's **market** (open Tuesday and Wednesday in front of the main post office) offers the best selection. There is also a large supermarket on HaPalmach Street, near the bus station.

Decent offerings in the way of **nightlife** are even more scant, though there is one atmospheric bar, the *Tea House*, in the northern reaches of the artists' quarter. To get there walk up Jerusalem Street, go under the bridge and then take the first left. Between the bridge and the IGTO are a few other bars, none of which match the ambience of the *Tea House*. During the summer the artists' quarter can be reasonably lively in the evenings, with various public events organised by the municipality – plays, musical recitals, dance displays. For details of these contact the IGTO.

The Town

After a short time in Safad it will have become evident that the town's layout is far from conventional. The winding stairwells which run around the town make it all too easy to get lost. Eventually, though, you should find your way back to somewhere you recognise. It may help to visualise the town in three levels: the Citadel at the top; Jerusalem Street girdling the middle; the Artists' Quarter in the southwest and the Synagogue Quarter to the north as the lower level.

The Artists' Quarter

The **Artists' Quarter** (*Qiryat HaZtayarim* in Hebrew) is the most important surviving segment of the Arab town, its mass of cobbled streets and pastel blue-and-white houses full of atmosphere despite the rather twee galleries which now occupy so many of them. The area houses artists and crafts people from all over Israel, most of whom sell their work directly to the public. The sturdy, high-ceilinged old houses where they live and work, often with a well in the middle of the main room, are beautiful, and reason in themselves to visit.

The art itself is rarely that wonderful – all too many of the artists seem to simply pump out standard prints of the area, or works on Jewish themes, in order to make a living from tourists. There are private galleries everywhere, but many artists exhibit their work in the **General Exhibition Hall** (Sun–Thur 10am–1pm and 4–9pm, Fri 10am–1pm; small admission fee), which is clearly signed from the intersection of Jerusalem and Arlozoroff streets. Here you can buy pastiches of virtually any style you choose, as well as the occasional more original (and expensive) work. The exhibition hall occupies a former mosque which is still the subject of dispute between the *Waqf* and the gallery's owners: it was confiscated after 1948, and the Muslims argue that it should be restored as a place of worship.

Nearby is the imaginatively laid out **Museum of Art and Printing** (Tet Zayin Street; Sun–Thur 10am–noon and 4–6pm, Fri 10am–noon), which traces the history of book printing and binding in the Middle East, and identifies Safad as the centre of this industry during the sixteenth century. Exhibits and text illustrate how, in 1578, the first Hebrew book was published in Safad.

Walk south down Tet Zayin Street from here and you'll enter an area where for a while you can escape the coachloads of tourists. Near the end of this road are the **Red Mosque** and a **Mamluk Mausoleum**. These are two of the oldest buildings in Safad, the former dating from the thirteenth century, while the latter was constructed in the fourteenth as the burial place of Musa Abu Haj Eroktai, a ruler of the city. Beautiful structures suffering sadly from neglect, they have in recent years become makeshift galleries for artists. At the end of the street, opposite the junction with HaNassi, is a large **park** and a small childrens' zoo.

The Synagogue Quarter

Qiryat Batei HaKnesset (the Synagogue Quarter) lies to the north of the Artists' Quarter. To get there leave Jerusalem Street at Ma'alot Olei Hagardim (the 'central staircase' which used to divide the Jewish and Muslim quarters of the city) and follow it until you reach Beit Yosef Street. For the first of the synagogues walk down here until you get to Alkabetz Street, take the right-hand turning up a small stairway and continue under the arch. The HaAri synagogue will be on your right.

Starting with the *Zohar*, Rabbi Yohai's mystical interpretation of the ancient scriptures, which was written in nearby Peqi'in, Safad became a centre of Jewish **mysticism**. In its early forms this involved a belief that direct communion with the divine was attainable by contemplation and the observance of the commandments, the *mitsvot*, without the intercession of a Messiah. In the sixteenth century, when Safad became the haven for Jews fleeing the Inquisition in Europe, a more formal and messianic tone of worship was adopted. Rabbis who congregated in Safad became known as the 'Exiled'.

The main exponent of this exiled mysticism was a young rabbi from Egypt called **Isaac Luria**. Luria, who arrived in Safad in 1570 and died two years later at the age of 32, managed in his short life to overturn accepted rabbinical teaching. His message was that God had exiled himself after the physical creation of the world; the creation itself had gone astray, and that it was up to the Jews to redeem this catastrophe through an understanding of law and the cosmos. His teachings were the start of what became known as the *Kabbala* – or Cabbalistic – movement.

The **HaAri Synagogue** proclaims his immortality as do the rabbis who now worship there. It is a very simple building dominated by a large *Bima* (platform). Against the south wall is a beautiful ark, carved from a solid block of wood, which dates back to the time of Luria. For more information on Luria and his teachings, try latching on to one of the tour groups who frequently visit, or simply ask any of the rabbis or attendants – though be prepared for a long lecture.

The **Joseph Caro Synagogue**, just down the street from here, is the other great Jewish monument in the quarter. Caro, a founder of the *Kabbala* movement, was chief rabbi of Safad and author of the *Shulhan Aruch*, a lengthy work on the application of Jewish law to everyday life. The synagogue is more elaborate than the HaAri and looks out over the valley below. It is believed that the rabbis get divine inspiration from the setting sun, of which the synagogue provides a magnificent view. Inside are a number of ornate scrolls and books, including some of the earliest known printed copies of the *Torah*, and a number of *Torah* scrolls that were in use in Caro's day.

Nearby is an area known as the Spanish Quarter, where a small **market** sells handicrafts, Judaica and souvenirs. From here you can make your way to the main square of the synagogue quarter, where alleys lead off into a maze of cobbled residential streets, liberally scattered with lesser synagogues. Most of these are open to the public (there are 32 synagogues in all in Safad), though none are of the interest or importance of the big two. To the west of the Synagogue Quarter, off HaAri Street, a **cemetery** contains the graves of many of the famous *Kabbala* rabbis.

If you turn left at the main entrance to the Caro Synagogue, after a couple of hundred metres you'll come to the small **Ethiopian Folk Art Centre and Gallery** (Sun–Thur 9am–6pm, Fri 9am–noon). As its name suggests, the centre features the work of Ethiopian artists, many of whom arrived in Israel recently as part of the controversial *Operation Moses*, secretly airlifted out of Ethiopia. The small, semi-dilapidated building is indicative of the welcome given to the *Falashas* by their Israeli cousins.

Head down the main staircase nearby, turn right at the bottom, and you'll reach Safad's most interesting museum: **Hameiri House** (Sun–Fri 8am–2pm; admission $2). This examines the history of Jewish settlement in Safad, with a mass of everyday artefacts and documents to illustrate life over the last few centuries. Many of the objects are things which would be commonplace throughout the Middle East, but it provides interesting background and (accidental) insights – the description of the 'murderous' and 'barbaric' Arab population, for instance. If Jewish orthodox life interests you, call in at **Chabad House**, just below Jerusalem Street on Hatam Sofer Street. Its library, exhibition and guides aim to answer any questions you may have on Judaism in Safad. It also has a good restaurant.

The Citadel

Crowning the summit of Safad's hill, the remains of the Crusader fortress – the Citadel – are set in a small park. A stairway leads up here from Jerusalem Street. On the way, at the top of the first flight of stairs, is the **Israel Bible Museum** (Sun–Thur 10am–6pm, Fri–Sat 10am–2pm): a museum of art inspired by biblical scenes. Perched high above the town, the museum occupies the mansion of the last Turkish Pasha of Safad, an elaborate arched and colonnaded nineteenth-century confection that somehow provides an appropriate setting for the material. It's an interesting place with some fine works, especially the drawings of biblical characters by American Phillip Ratner, though by now you may find your capacity for art appreciation running low.

Of the **Citadel** itself, very little remains: just the odd foundation and wall. But the panoramas from the top are gorgeous, and the park around the walls, shaded by tall trees, offers escape from the heat and crowds. The fortress was originally constructed by King Fulk of Anjou in 1140, and handed over to the Knights Templar by Alamric I, King of Jerusalem, in 1168. Twenty years later, following the Crusader defeat at the Battle of Hittin, the fortress was destroyed. It was partially rebuilt when the Templars regained control of Safad in 1240, and under Mamluk rule the ramparts were again restored and the outer wall extended. In 1837 this citadel was almost completely destroyed by a series of earthquakes which hit much of the Galilee.

Today the most prominent structures are more recent, two memorials standing incongruously side by side. The first is a marble tablet bearing the names of Jews who died fighting for Safad in 1948; the second represents the extended hand of eternal life.

Near Safad: Bir'im and Iqrit

Perched high in the mountains northwest of Safad, a stone's throw from the Lebanese border, **BIR'IM** (BARAM) preserves ample reminders of both its distant and recent past. In contemporary Israel the village has become something of a *cause célèbre*, and has been the subject of legal controversy for almost forty years. On October 29, 1948 the Israeli army entered the village, and three weeks later its Palestinian inhabitants were ordered to evacuate to a neighbouring village 'for two weeks'. But at the end of this period the villagers were not allowed to return. In 1951 the villagers obtained an injunction from the Supreme Court against the military authorities, giving them the right to return. In response to this order, the military governor declared the area a 'security zone' to which entrance was allowed only by special permit. On September 16, 1953, the authorities demolished the village with aerial and artillery bombardment.

The 250 mostly Christian Palestinian families who lost their property and livelihood continue to fight to return to their homes, but are still unable to do so, although the security zone designation was cancelled in 1972. Some of their land was taken over in 1948 by **Kibbutz Baram**, part of the left-wing *Mapam* movement, and much of what remained became **Moshav Doveve** in 1963. You can still walk around the old village, where many of the bombed buildings are intact and the foundations of others are clearly visible. On most, slogans (in English, Arabic and Hebrew) calling for the villagers to be allowed to return are prominent. For the Israeli left, Baram remains an issue which frequently surfaces in the Israeli press: for most Palestinians, it is just one injustice among many.

The story of **ancient Baram** is the one the Israelis prefer to tell you when you actually arrive at the site: it has been restored by the National Parks Authority, whose leaflet on the history is available here. The centrepiece is a large, highly decorative synagogue built in the third century when a Jewish community grew up here after the destruction of Jerusalem. What you see is basically just the facade, a massive structure of brick and pillars which served as a covered entrance for worshippers. The leaflet sold at the entrance kiosk includes an artist's impression of what the rest of the synagogue would have looked like. All around, the site is richly scattered with other remnants from this and later periods.

IQRIT, a few kilometres east, has an almost identical political identity to Bir'im. Like their neighbours, Iqrit's villagers were moved for 'two weeks' and are still waiting to return. Their Supreme Court injunction, which saw 'no legal obstacle to the petitioners returning to their village', didn't stop the Israeli forces blowing up and destroying this Christian village on Christmas Day, 1951. Unlike Bir'im, Iqrit has no antiquities: just a couple of ornate churches and simple houses as poignant reminders in the half-demolished village.

travel details

Buses

From Nahariyya to Acre/Haifa (every 15min 5am–10.30pm; 20min/45min); Tel Aviv (2 daily; 2hr 30min); Jerusalem (3 daily; 4hr); Ahziv (hourly 6–9pm; 15min); Rosh Haniqra (6 daily; 30min).

From Acre to Karmiel/Safad (every 30min 6am–8pm; 30min/1hr).

From Safad to Tiberias (hourly 7am–6pm; 45min) and Rosh Pinna/Qiryat Shmona (30min 6am–8pm; 15min/1hr).

Train

From Nahariyya to Acre, Haifa, Netanya and Tel Aviv at least six departures daily (30min/1hr/3hr 30min/4hr).

CHAPTER SIX

TIBERIAS AND THE PANHANDLE

The **Sea of Galilee** – also known as Lake Kinneret (the lake of Gennaseret mentioned in the New Testament) and as Lake Tiberias – is one of Israel's major tourist sites, popular as much for a climate which is warm year-round as for its natural beauty and historical sites. Traditionally associated with events in the Gospels – it was here that Jesus walked on water – the freshwater lake is nowadays a thoroughly secular paradise, with beaches and watersports all around the shore, backed by hills that are a challenge to any walker.

The town of **Tiberias**, on the west side of the lake, is very much the centre of life, crammed with tourists from June to September and over every Jewish holiday. Within easy travelling distance of Tiberias are enough sites – churches, synagogues and mineral springs – to keep visitors engaged for weeks, with hotels, campsites, hostels and *kibbutzim* providing **accommodation**. The western and northern shores of the lake are busy throughout the year with tourists who take time out from their watery recreation to visit such biblical sites as **Capernaum**, **Tabgha** and the **Mount of Beatitudes**. The eastern side is far less spoiled and more pastoral: here, under the shadow of the Golan Heights, are the kibbutzim of **Ha'On** and **Ein Gev**.

From the northern end of the lake, the main road runs up into the area known as **the Panhandle or Finger**, thrusting towards the Lebanese border. It passes through **Rosh Pinna**, around the east of the **Hula Valley** and one of the country's main **nature reserves**, and on to the desolate border towns of **Qiryat Shmona** and **Metulla**.

Public **transportation** between the main towns is good; to explore less-frequented areas, though, you either need your own transport (hiring a bike is one way off the beaten track) or have to rely on hitchhiking. The **walk** around the lake, a distance of around 50km which can be completed in two or three days depending on your pace, is also a popular one. There are enough hostels and campsites to make this feasible, and in summer sleeping out can be a positive pleasure.

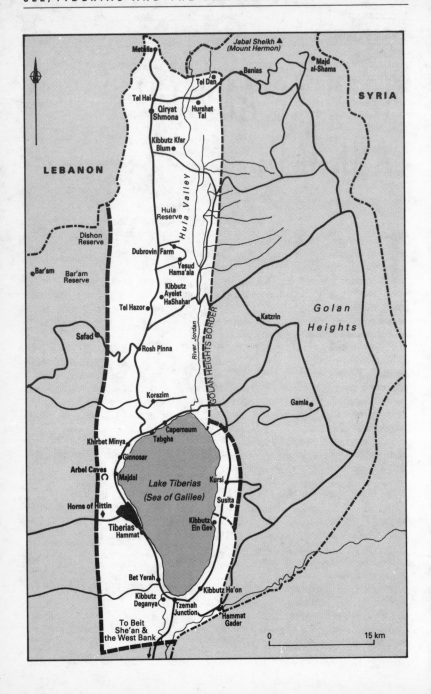

Tiberias

Tiberias, the capital of the Galilee, is Israel's premier northern tourist resort. Since it lies on the shore of the Sea of Galilee in the great **Rift Valley**, 200m below the level of the Mediterranean, it is always at least a few degrees warmer than the surrounding areas, warm in winter (average midday temperature 21°C, 70°F), very hot (average 35°C, 95°F) and humid in summer. The town itself has few notable historical or biblical sites – these are mainly to the north – but it is surrounded by glorious countryside and is ideal as a base for forays into the Golan and the north of the country. Although it is one of the four Jewish **holy cities**, its present day attractions are for those with more hedonistic pursuits in mind – water sports, sunbathing, eating and pubbing.

In the summer months and on Jewish holidays, Tiberias is packed with Israeli holidaymakers. The rest of the year the mood is calmer, the atmosphere more relaxing and hospitable. At any time, though, you'll probably be surprised by the brash commerciality of it all – there are very few reminders of the mixed Arab-Jewish town bustling with merchants and famed for the learning of its rabbis. Still, with the lake at its heart, the mineral springs to the south and the rugged isolation of the eastern shore within easy reach, Tiberias makes an ideal place to rest up and relax for a while.

Jewish scholarship

Tiberias was founded around 20AD by **Herod Antipas**, one of the sons of Herod the Great. Although his town, which he named after the Emperor Tiberius, had a magnificent synagogue and gold-roofed palace, Herod is said to have had problems in attracting more devout Jews and Christians to live here, perhaps because he had built the town over an old burial ground. Instead, so the story goes, Herod released all the petty criminals from his prisons and forced them to live here. The new city's growth was assured by the two Jewish revolts against Rome (66–70AD and 132–135AD), both of which passed it by virtually unscathed: many of the rabbis of Judaea and Jerusalem fled to the relative peace and safety of the lake city, and for several centuries Tiberias became one of the two leading centres of Jewish learning (the other being in Babylon).

Under the direction of **Rabbi Yehuda HaNassi** (c.135–217AD) studies that were to become central to Judaism were undertaken in Tiberias. The *Mishnah* – the detailed study of and commentary on the biblical texts – was codified around 200AD, incorporating the *halacha* (the oral law) and the teachings of the rabbis during the first two centuries AD that were in danger of being lost due to the Roman destruction of Judaea. In 220AD one of ha-Nassi's disciples, **Rabbi Yohanan ben Nappaha**, founded the Talmudic Academy of Tiberias. The scholars of the academy set about providing an extended commentary – the *Gemara* – on the work of their predecessors, which embraced the *halacha* along with the proverbs, parables, anecdotes and historical and biographical tracts. Together, the *Mishnah* and the *Gemara* that were compiled here constitute the *Talmud*. This **Palestinian Talmud**, completed around 400AD (and also known as the *Jerusalem Talmud*), is about one-third the length of the more authoritative **Bablyonian**

Talmud, compiled between 200 and 500AD in Babylon, where Jews had lived continuously since at least the time of Nebuchadnezzar.

The Talmudic academy saw a decline in the middle of the fifth century, but the Muslim conquest in the seventh century brought the Jewish community relief from three centuries of Christian intolerance. The Omayyad and Abbasid periods saw a spiritual renaissance among the Jews of Palestine, and again Tiberias was their religious centre. The Jerusalem Talmud was already completed, but work was done on collecting and editing the biblical commentaries known as the *Midrash*. There was also a linguistic revival: a new, more efficient system of vowelling the text of the Hebrew bible (*masorah*) was compiled between the seventh and eighth centuries in Tiberias. By the ninth century, the religious authority of the *ga'on* or president of the Tiberias Academy was recognised and accepted by Jews throughout the world; one of the Academy's tasks, for example, was to set the Jewish calendar for holy and other special days.

On a more mundane level, the Palestinian geographer and historian al-Muqaddasi, writing in 985AD, has left us a graphic if somewhat cynical description of life for the inhabitants of Tiberias at this time: 'For two months in the year they gorge themselves on the fruits of the jujube bush which grows wild and costs them nought. For two months they struggle with the numerous flies that are rife there. For two months they go about naked because of the fierce heat. For two months . . . they suck the sugar-cane . . . . For two months they wallow in mud . . . and for two months they dance in their beds because of the legion of fleas with which they are infested. It was said "the king of the fleas holds his court in Tiberias"'.

The Crusaders and after

In 1099, Tiberias was taken by **Tancred** who declared himself Prince of Galilee; it remained in Christian control until **Salah al-Din** routed the Crusader armies in the decisive battle at the nearby **Horns of Hittin** in 1187. The city was all but destroyed in clashes between the Crusaders and the Muslims during the twelfth century, but it revived under Turkish Ottoman rule, particularly during the reign of Sultan **Suleiman the Magnificent**. One of the many Jews who rose to high position at the Turkish court was a Portuguese banker and diplomat, **Joseph Nasi**. He became principal adviser to the Ottoman sultanate on European affairs and his influential position enabled him to secure the rights to Tiberias (in return for a minimal yearly remittance). Helped by his wealthy mother-in-law, Donna Gracia, Nasi rebuilt the walls of the town, set up a silk industry there and tried, unsuccessfully, to turn it into a Jewish enclave.

By the beginning of the seventeenth century, Tiberias (along with nearby Safad) was practically in ruins following repeated Beduin and Druze raids. The region revived only when it came under the rule of the remarkable Beduin leader, **Daher al-Omar**, sheikh of the Bani Zaidan tribe. Early in the eighteenth century, al-Omar set out to break Ottoman rule, and forced the Turks out of Galilee. He was to be the greatest of all the local rulers who set themselves up – at different times and in different parts of the country – to challenge Ottoman hegemony.

Daher al-Omar rapidly made himself master of Tiberias, Safad and the area between. In 1740, he built a fortress in Tiberias (today the *Donna Gracia* restaurant) and extended the city walls further north, using the large black basalt rocks that are still strewn around the town. Al-Omar's regime – he was a legendarily just ruler – brought security from Beduin raids and encouraged Muslims, Jews and Christians alike to migrate into his district. A friendship developed between him and Haim Abulafia, a rabbi from Smyrna, and the latter was encouraged to set up a Jewish community in Tiberias. Abulafia built houses in the city, a splendid synagogue, a bath house, shops and a press for sesame oil.

In 1749, when he was already 64 years old, al-Omar seized and fortified Acre and made it his capital. In an attempt to crush what was looking more and more like a stable, independent fiefdom, the Ottomans sent an army against him from Damascus in 1764, but to no avail. The Mamluk ruler of Egypt, Ali Bey, made an alliance with al-Omar and marched into Gaza while Daher moved south. After taking Jaffa and Ramleh, the allies headed north and even managed to take Damascus. But in 1773 the Ottoman Turks renewed their offensive, and al-Omar was finally killed two years later trying to flee his stronghold of Acre.

An earthquake in 1837 flattened much of northern Galilee including Tiberias, and it was not until the end of the nineteenth century that the city was resettled in any numbers. With the beginning of the **Zionist movement** and the founding of colonies in the region, the Jewish population of Tiberias once again increased, so that by 1917 there was a Jewish majority. A Christian missionary, Dr Torrance, who came to the country to convert Jews and Muslims alike, and whose opinions are probably less than impartial, described Tiberias at this time as a 'cesspool of intolerance riddled with disease'.

The **Palestinian Revolt** (1936–39) brought the factions into open conflict when the rebels – in retaliation for bombs which had been placed in public areas, killing scores of Palestinians – launched an attack on the Jewish Quarter of the town which left nineteen people dead. By March 1948, Palestinian and Zionist forces were engaged in full-scale fighting for possession of the city. At the beginning of April, the Zionists besieged Tiberias and cut it off from all contacts, splitting the old city (where most Palestinians lived) into two. The Arabs asked the British to break the siege and put the city under British protection. The British commander in charge of Tiberias announced that he would continue to be responsible for the Arab population for only three days: most Arabs used the truce to leave the city in a convoy escorted out by the British army. By April 19, Tiberias had become the first Palestinian town to come under Zionist control, even before the official British withdrawal on May 15.

Immediately before the occupation of 1948, Tiberias had had a population of 6000 Jews and just over 5000 Arabs: in the main, the Palestinian-Arab community lived down by the lake, and the Jewish population up on the hill in the area of Qiryat Shmuel. Today Tiberias is an entirely Jewish city: those Palestinians you do meet in the town are mostly working there, or just passing through.

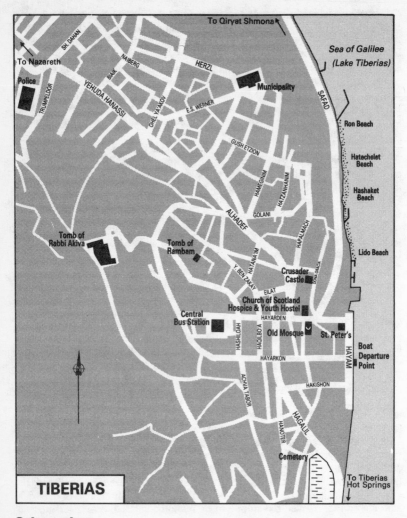

Orientation

Tiberias is still basically divided into **two parts**: the newer, upper city – **Qiryat Shmuel** – which is primarily residential; and the **Old City** down by the lake which contains all the action, antiquities and atmosphere. Two main streets bisect the downtown area. **Rehov HaYarden** leads from the **central bus station** to the lakeside; **Rehov HaGalil** cuts off it to the south, also curling round to end up on the shore. Practically everything that happens in Tiberias, and most of the places to stay, is located within the area bounded by these two roads.

From the bus station, it's a five-minute walk down Rehov HaYarden to the city centre, at **Kikar HaAtzma'ut** (Independence Square). The **IGTO** (☎06-720992; Sun–Thur 8.30am–6pm, Fri 8.30am–3pm) is at 8 Alhadef Street just off HaAtzma'ut – their publication *What's On in the North* is worth getting hold of if they have any left. HaYarden itself is lined with run-down shacks selling cheap *falafel*. The places don't look too appetising but the food tastes fine.

About a mile south of the Old City are the **Hot Springs**; north lie Majdal, Tabgha, the Mount of Beatitudes and Capernaum.

Accommodation

For such a small town, Tiberias offers a wide range of **accommodation**, from four- and five-star hotels by the lakeside, to cheaper hotels and hostels, as well as campsites and kibbutz holiday villages along the lakeshore roundabout. As you get off the bus at the central bus station, you'll probably be met by people offering rooms (many are fellow travellers who get free board in return for hustling up custom). These will generally be in the smaller hostels and they're worth following up, particularly if you arrive during a major Jewish holiday or in high season when cheap accommodation is at a premium, but make sure you're not going to be stuck somewhere too far from the action. Some of the more reliable, long-established budget possibilities are listed below.

If you want to **camp**, you'll find plenty of opportunities around the lake, where there are some 25 campsites in all: pick up a map from the IGTO office in Tiberias or, if you're approaching from the south, from the SPNI information booth in Zemah, where the road splits at the bottom of the lake. The closest site to the city is at **Kfar Hittim**, a short way inland.

Nahum Hostel (Tavor Street; ☎06-721505). Small hostel with friendly atmosphere. Beds from $4.50; roof-top bar serves good value breakfast and snacks and has an excellent view of the lake.

Maman Hostel (Atmon Street; ☎06-792986). The best by some way, with a secure and relaxed atmosphere, clean and comfortable rooms, and good facilities (including a verandah bar). Dormitory accommodation starts from $7; there are also some double rooms from $30 a night.

Hostel Aviv (HaGalil Street; ☎06-720031). Large, popular place with rooms off one long central corridor. Not the cleanest or most secure, but lively, with bar and verandah. Dorm beds from $5; double rooms available.

Yoseph Meyouhas Hostel (HaYarden Street; ☎06-721775). The official IYHA youth hostel. The impressive old stone building, and air-conditioned dormitories, make the niggling rules and extra charges bearable. Beds cost around $9; priority is given to IYHA members. A strict curfew (April–Sept 1am, Oct–March midnight) is enforced, and you must be out of the hostel between 9.30am and 1pm.

Castle Inn Hostel (on the wharf next to the Plaza Hotel; ☎06-721175). Clean, safe, sea views, but with a disco downstairs and most of the town's nocturnal activity happening nearby, it can be very noisy. Rooms from $9; midnight curfew and lockout from 1–4.30pm.

The Scottish Hospice (Safad Road, around the corner from the IYHA; ☎06-790144). Run by the Church of Scotland, this is situated in magnificent gardens and is one of the best places to stay in Tiberias – if you can afford $19 (bed and breakfast in a private room), or $6 for a dormitory bed. The hospice also serves tasty meals and is a stone's throw from the beach and the centre of town. It's also one of the few places you can get a copy of the latest *al-Fajr* newspaper.

Terra Sancta Hospice (on the wharf inside the Terra Sancta church; ☎06-720516). Quiet, characterful place popular with pilgrims. Beds from $5; no meals.

Galil Hostel (HaGalil Street; ☎06-791613). Small, clean and fairly pleasant; beds from $5.

Adina's Hostel (15 HaShiloah Street; ☎06-722507). Handy for the bus station, clean and tidy, with kitchen facilities. Beds from $5.

Panorama Hotel (19 HaGalil Street; ☎06-720254). One of the best of the cheap hotels, with double rooms from around $29 (possibly less out of season) for bed and breakfast, private shower and toilet. Some rooms have air-conditioning and sea views.

The City

Although there are remains of the Roman, Arab and Crusader periods scattered around and throughout Tiberias, the primary focus for visitors are the clear blue waters of the Sea of Galilee and in the evening the bars, restaurants and nightclubs. Apart from walking along the waterfront to catch the magnificent views of Mount Hermon and the Golan Heights across the lake, the sites worth visiting in the town itself are limited to the **tombs of the rabbis**, the **Crusader fort** and the **hot springs**.

The Tomb of Maimonides

Rabbi Moshe ben Maimon or Maimonides – known and venerated by Jews as **Rambam**, the initials of his name – was born in Cordoba, Spain, in 1135. He and his family fled the persecution there and went to Cairo where he devoted himself to Talmudic study, completing his first major work, *Commentary on the Mishnah*, in 1168. He earned his living by working as a physician and by 1185 had become personal healer to Salah al-Din. The written works of this remarkable scholar include not only an extensive correspondence but also medical treatises and major contributions to Judaism. The *Mishnah Torah*, completed in 1180, set out to codify and rationalise the Talmud and the rabbinical commentaries, and has been a seminal work ever since. In *The Guide for the Perplexed*, the last of his monumental works, finished a decade later and written in Arabic, Rambam attempted to link reason and scripture and to guide the devout for whom the 'Law has become established' but who are bewildered by certain 'equivocal, derivative or ambiguous terms'. His death, on December 13, 1204, was marked by three days of public mourning in Cairo and a public fast in Jerusalem.

According to legend, Rambam instructed his students that when he died, his coffin should be loaded on a camel (or donkey) and that wherever the animal stopped would be his burial place. This spot is marked by a small **stone tomb** on Yohanan ben Zakkai Street, at the end of HaGalil near the public garden. Walk towards the bus station, turn right into Ben Zakkai, and about 100m down, past the pitta bread factory, a path on the right leads to the tomb. Modest dress is expected of visitors to the tomb. Within the same serene enclosure are the tombs of **Rabbi Yohanan ben Zakkai**, who was one of the most eminent sages at the time of Jerusalem's destruction by the Romans and who founded the Yavne Academy, and of **Rabbi Eliezer ben Hyrcanus**, a leading second-century scholar.

The white-domed tomb of **Rabbi Akiva** is on the slope of the nearby hillside. Another second-century scholar who compiled commentaries on the *Mishnah*, Akiva acclaimed Bar Kokhba, the leader of the Second Revolt against Rome (132–135AD), as the messiah. After two years in hiding in the Gallilean hills, he was imprisoned and tortured to death. Near the Hot Springs to the south of Tiberias you can see the tomb of his pupil, **Rabbi Meir**, who is said to have been a miracle worker. Bonfires are lit around his tomb during the spring festival of *Lag b'Omer*.

The Crusader Castle

More concrete remains of the past are surprisingly few, and little survives from before the Crusader era. From that period, the most significant ruin is **Tancred's Castle**, approached by a black basalt stairway across the road from Lido beach. The steps are nineteenth-century, but the building to which they lead is the genuine article, a run-down Gothic fortress which now houses a few small art galleries and is home to a couple of local artists and artisans – nothing of any great quality, though.

Other Crusader relics face the Plaza Hotel down on the waterfront, chief among them the twelfth-century **Church of Saint Peter** (or Terra Sancta) whose apse is said to have been built in the shape of a ship's prow in honour of St. Peter's profession as a fisherman. Head along the pedestrianised seafront from here and then inland on HaYarden, and you'll see a modern commercial centre opposite the Church of Scotland Hospice. Inside, an open courtyard surrounded by cafés (and the biggest supermarket in Tiberias) contains the half-ruined eighteenth-century **Great Mosque**. It would make a great centrepiece to the square, but in fact it's boarded up, so at best you'll get a glimpse of the dusty interior through a broken window. This is about the only reminder of what the centre of town must once have looked like – but again, it's not the sort of history the current regime has any interest in promoting or restoring.

The Hot Springs

The hot mineral springs of Tiberias, 2km south of town on the coastal road, are perhaps the oldest known health baths in the world, created at the time of the great crack in the earth's crust that carved out the Jordanian **Rift Valley**. The curative powers of the springs have been noted by writers down the centuries and legends about them abound: one is that they date from the time of **Noah** and the **Flood** when the world was turned inside-out; another that **King Solomon** ordered demons to heat the water to cure his people; yet another that **Jesus** healed the sick here. Today, the waters have a well-established record in the treatment of arthritic and rheumatic ailments, and a less scientific reputation as a cure for infertility. The latter, though, is an ancient tradition: if a woman could stand the 60°C of the water, she was reckoned to be strong enough to stand childbearing, and if she sat on the stone lion in the **Ibrahim Pasha** pool, she would be granted her wish to conceive.

The buildings that house the baths still date in part from the time of Ottoman Turkish rule – Sultan Suleiman II built the original domed and vaulted bath house here in 1561. In 1783, Daher al-Omar is said to have granted religious freedom to the Jewish population of the city in return for their assistance in extending the baths. The present-day complex holds a series of indoor and outdoor **mineral** and **thermal baths**, mud-pack treatment rooms and a large new **swimming pool**. It also has a staff of doctors, physiotherapists and masseurs.

The baths in the older buildings, **Tiberias Hot Springs**, (Sun–Thur 6.30am–4pm, Fri 6.30am–1pm) are for those looking for treatment, while the ones in the **Tiberias Hot Springs Spa** (☎06-791967; Sat–Thur 8am–7pm, Fri 7am–1pm) in the new buildings are for relaxation. The water is distinctly slimy and doesn't smell too good (fresh water showers are provided to wash it off): a simple bath costs about $10, or you can treat yourself to a massage for around $14. There's also an expensive restaurant in the new complex. To get to the springs from Tiberias, either walk or catch bus #2 or #5 from the central bus station or HaGalil Street.

A few hundred metres across from the original three-domed bath house is the **Leham Museum** (Sun–Thur 8am–5pm, Fri 8am–4pm; admission $1) which describes the geographical and historical importance of the hot springs and of Tiberias under Roman rule. Nearby, a small park contains the excavated site of the ancient city of **Hammat** and the reconstructed ruins of the second-century **Hammat Synagogue** (Sun–Thur 8am–5pm, Fri 8am–4pm). The exquisite **mosaic floor** of the synagogue, depicting the **Ark of the Covenant** and a **zodiac**, was the work of Greek artisans. The zodiac reads from right to left; among the mythological characters portrayed are the Greek sun god, Helios, driving a chariot and, in the corners, four female heads each representing a season of the year. It's a beautiful piece of work, all the more interesting for the inclusion of 'graven images' (and Greek ones at that) in a Jewish place of worship. According to Moshe Dothan, the site's leading archaeologist, such figuration is acceptable because it is essentially a 'standing image of stone' (*Leviticus 26:1*) to which one must not bow down, rather than simply a mosaic floor.

The beaches

Almost all of the **beaches** in Tiberias are privately controlled, and charge a stiff fee (from $4 to $15) for access to a range of facilities including changing and shower rooms, kayak rentals, windsurfing, water-skiing, miniature golf, restaurants and discos. For a free swim you'll have to head some way north, or else cross the lake, and do without showers or changing rooms.

Of the places in town, **Lido Beach**, just north of the centre (admission $4), is about the best. It has a reasonably priced restaurant and by far the largest swimming area. Further north still are **Shell Beach**, **Quiet Beach** and **Blue Beach**, all of which offer comparable facilities. South of town there's a **municipal beach** ($2.50, about 15 minutes' walk), beyond which you begin to find places where there are no controls. Since there are frequent buses around the lake in both directions, it's easy enough to set off and simply get out when you find somewhere that appeals to you. To get across to the other side of the lake you could also take the **ferry** run by the *Kinneret Sailing Company*.

Eating and drinking

The speciality of the Sea of Galilee in general, and Tiberias in particular, is **Saint Peter's Fish**, an ugly looking character with marks beside its gills that were supposedly left by Peter's fingers when he picked it up. Nowadays, most of the fish come from the fish farms of nearby kibbutzim rather than the lake itself, but if you're camping and want to cook your own, it's still possible to buy them fresh from the **market** on HaGalil Street (closed Sat), or direct from local fishermen. Gastronomically speaking St. Peter's is no great shakes – rather bony and tasteless – but it's worth trying since you're here. Most local restaurants will serve you a St. Peter's fish, for prices starting around $10.

Restaurants worth checking out include *Bikos*, in the same square as the Great Mosque, *The Lido* on the beach at the bottom of HaYarden, and *Karamba*, a vegetarian restaurant and cocktail bar. The latter is one of the nicest places on the seafront, though not the cheapest, with birds singing in the trees above the tables and magnificent views out to sea. Another of the better places in town is **Chinese** – the *House Chinese Restaurant*, opposite the Lido Beach – complete with appropriate decor. The food is good, but not cheap.

Apart from the **pizza** and **falafel** stalls on HaGalil Street, there are in fact very few budget restaurants in Tiberias. One of the cheapest is *Maman*, a traditional Middle Eastern place on HaGalil opposite the Hotel Aviv: you'll find a similar, nameless, café/restaurant further south on the same street, opposite the Plaza Hotel, with enormous portions of good home-cooking (anything from *hummus* and a beer, to a roast chicken) at reasonable prices. If all you want is a hearty, filling meal, and you're not too worried about the surroundings, the Egged Bus Station Restaurant is also worth remembering.

Getting your own food together for a picnic is easy enough: the biggest and best **supermarket** in Tiberias is opposite the Great Mosque. If this is closed, there are a couple of others on HaGalil Street that stay open late; at least one of these is open on *shabbat*.

Finding somewhere to drink in the evening is no problem either. **Bars** cluster in three main areas within easy walking distance of each other: near the Great Mosque, on the seafront and just off HaBanim Street. There are dozens, but the best of them is probably *Karamba* (see above). Among the travellers passing through, the most popular form of evening entertainment seems to be sitting around in the **hostels**, most of which have bars open to non-residents. Hostels like *Nahum*, *Maman* and *Hotel Aviv* have particularly pleasant roof-top or verandah bars; if you feel like splashing out, the larger hotels on the seafront also have smarter bars and restaurants

Entertainment and nightlife

Tiberias hosts a number of **music** festivals which are well worth attending if you're around, and which add a little cultural weight to an otherwise commercial nightlife. The largest, the **Ein Gev Music Festival,** takes place at the 5000-seat amphitheatre in Kibbutz Ein Gev on the eastern shore during Passover week, and features visiting international orchestras and performers as well as the Israeli Philharmonic. The other main event is the **Sea of Galilee Festival,** held during the second week of July. This is primarily a folk festival, with music and dance from around the world. At other times a number of seafront folk and music events are organised by the local IGTO; ask at their office for details of all these, and other free events.

On a more regular basis, all the major hotels have **nightclubs** which standard, glossy disco fare; entrance alone will set you back around $7 on weekdays, $14 at the weekend, and drinks are invariably expensive. The most atmospheric **disco** (also one of the cheapest) is in the basement of what was once an old monastery and is now the **Castle Inn Hostel** on the seafront, next to the Plaza Hotel; admission is only $3.50 and drinks are reasonable, although the sound quality is terrible.

During the summer there are open-air discos on most of the **beaches** north of town: the most popular is at Blue Beach (from 8.30pm in summer; admission $7) where you can cool off in the sea between dances. Impromptu barbecues and beach parties are also a feature of Tiberias nightlife during the summer months.

Sports events

A number of annual sporting events also form an integral part of the Tiberias scene. The **International Tiberias Marathon** is held here every year in December; the **Trans-Kinneret Swim** takes place in late September from Ein Gev to Tsemach; the **Kinneret Cross-Country Walk** takes place every spring, the **Kinneret Bicycle Run** in May and the **Mount Tabor Race** in winter. Contact the IGTO for details.

Listings

Bike and camping gear rental *Gal–Cal* (Central Bus Station; ☎06-736278) rent bikes, tents, boats and camping gear.

Boat rental Ask at the harbour or at the Lido Beach; expect hugely inflated prices during the summer.

Boat trips The *Kinneret Sailing Company* (☎06-721831) runs ferries from Tiberias to Ein Gev (10.30am, noon and 1.30pm) and back (11.15am, 1.15pm and 3.30pm) and less frequently from Tiberias to Capernaum. The trip is enjoyable, but costs around four times as much as the bus.

Car hire There are dozens of car rental agencies, mostly located around the central bus station or near the IGTO on Alhadef Street: *Avis* (☎06-790898); *Eldan* (☎06-792233); *Hertz* (☎06-791822).

Emergencies *Magen David Adom*, First Aid station, on HaBanim Street (☎06-790111).

Police ☎06-792444.

Post office On the left-hand side of HaYarden as you walk from the bus station towards the lake.

Taxis *Galil* (☎06-720353); *Golan* (☎06-792888); *Kinneret* (☎06-722262/701515).

South of Tiberias

Heading towards Tiberias from the south, the cool blue waters of the southern end of the Sea of Galilee will excite even the most tired traveller after the long, hot and sticky drive up the **Jordan Valley Road**. At the **Tzemah Junction** at the lake's southern tip, the left fork leads to Tiberias (11km), the road to the right to the **east bank** of the lake and the **Golan Heights**. Setting out from Tiberias, the southern end of the lake seems somehow less inviting, suffering as it does from the ravages of Israeli land developers.

As you leave Tiberias, an ominous-looking fence about 1km south of the town encloses a complex of large water slides; the $15 entrance fee to **Luna Beach** (8am–5pm) is steep but allows you access to everything inside for as long as you like. There is a patch of free beach which you can get to by following the fence around to the left; the beaches further along the road towards Tiberias are cleaner and less rocky.

Seven kilometres further, near where the **Jordan River** leaves the Sea of Galilee, just before the Tzemah junction, lies **Kibbutz Deganya**. Deganya, birthplace of Moshe Dayan, was founded by Russian immigrants in 1910, and has grown so large that it has had to be divided into two sections: **Deganya Aleph** (A), the original part, is marked by a gutted Syrian tank at the gate, a reminder of the 1948 war when the settlers fought off the Syrians with molotov cocktails; **Deganya Bet** (B) is the newer extension of the kibbutz. Although set in beautiful, lush countryside, the current economic base of the kibbutz (like many others in the country) is industrial rather than agricultural – in this case, a diamond-tool factory.

For visitors, there are two small museums: a **natural history museum** devoted to the flora and fauna of the area, containing a rather macabre array of stuffed animals and even pickled human foetuses displayed in old-fashioned wooden cases; and an **archaeological museum** showing finds from the Kinneret region. Both museums are housed in **Beit Gordon** (Sun–Thur 9.30am–4pm, Fri 8.30–2pm, Sat 9.30am–noon; admission $2.50), named after A. D. Gordon, a leading Zionist thinker who preached return to the soil and the honesty of manual work. Gordon worked on the kibbutz until he died at the age of 74, although he never became a member of it. Next door to Beit Gordon is an **SPNI office**, which provides useful information about the local wildlife, and on camping and hiking around the lake.

Immediately before Kibbutz Deganya (coming from Tiberias) a sharp turn to the left leads down to the Jordan River; over the bridge, a small road leads to the spot where **Saint Peter** is said to have been baptised. This is now a popular place for group baptisms – especially since the *intifada* has made Jericho less popular with pilgrims – complete with souvenir shops and a café.

The eastern shore

Relatively unspoiled – at least in comparison to the western shore – the **eastern side of the Sea of Galilee** is bordered by acres of banana groves and date palms, and has a scent of remoteness which makes a journey around it feel like a real adventure. Travelling by public transport it can be: buses are infrequent (either hourly or two-hourly, according to the time of day and year); hitching very much a matter of luck, dependent on the seasonal flow of traffic. Cheap accommodation, too, is sparse, though there are plenty of campsites and a couple of fancy kibbutz holiday villages. However it's easy enough to pick out an individual site for a day trip (by bus or ferry) and return to the comfort of Tiberias in the evening. Probably the easiest way of getting around the lake is with a one- or two-day bus pass on Egged's Minus 200 Line which allows you to get on and off at 23 stops around the lake – details from the bus station or IGTO in Tiberias.

Hammat Gader (al-Hamma)

Starting at the southern end of the lake, from the **Tzemah Junction**, the first place of interest is **HAMMAT GADER**. This popular spa is not actually on the lake, but lies about 9km east of the southern tip, right at the Jordanian border and the former border with Syria – now the edge of the occupied Golan Heights. Perched above the waters of the **Yarmuk River**, the ancient hot water spring has been known since Roman times at least: as **al-Hamma** it was under Arab control until it was taken by the Israelis in 1967.

The spacious grounds of the spa complex include extensive and much reconstructed ruins of a Roman town – built around 200AD and destroyed by an earthquake in 900AD – with well-preserved **bathing pools** and a **theatre**. From more recent times, you can see the beautiful **minaret** of a disused mosque, now covered in graffiti. New attractions include an **alligator park** where, from a safe distance, you can watch the beasts swimming or sunning themselves. And of course there are health-restoring **sulphur baths**, a **health club** offering beauty treatments and massages, underwater **jacuzzis**, a cool water **swimming pool** and water slides, and a bar and restaurant. Entrance to the whole complex (☎06-751039; Sat–Thur 8am–4pm, Fri 8am–1pm) costs $8 during the week, $10 on weekends or holidays. Bus #24 from Tiberias bus station (gate 8) leaves for Hammat Gader at 8am, 9am and 10am, returning at 11am, noon and 2.15pm. If you can, visit during the week and avoid Saturdays when the place is packed with families and kids.

Kibbutz Ha'on

Following the coast road north from Tzemah Junction, you'll come to **Kibbutz Ha'On** after about five kilometres. The somewhat bizarre point of interest here is an **ostrich farm** (daily 9am–4pm; $4 admission includes access to the beach). The ostriches, originally from South Africa, are basically a tourist attraction, although some are occasionally slaughtered for their meat. Weird enough in this setting of date and banana plantations, the birds also have the unnerving habit of following you around as you visit, as if they imagine that they are the visitors, and you the spectacle.

Aside from the farm, the kibbutz has a pleasant **campsite** with 100 camping places (from $6), a **holiday village** (☎06-757555) with 42 air-conditioned rooms, a bar and restaurant, a disco and a minimarket (open Sun–Thur 8.30am–12.30pm and 5–7pm, Fri and Sat 8.30am–12.30pm).

Kibbutz Ein Gev

Further north, on the shore more or less directly opposite Tiberias, is **Kibbutz Ein Gev**, founded in 1937. Until 1967 the kibbutz was more or less directly in the line of fire of Syrian artillery on the Golan Heights, but it certainly doesn't feel embattled now. In fact it's a particularly wealthy kibbutz, which owns just about everything in the area (including the **ferries** which ply to and from Tiberias) and makes a living from fishing and from its vineyards, banana plantations and date groves. The kibbutz **amphitheatre** is the site of the annual **Ein Gev Music festival** (see Tiberias).

Buses (#18 or #21) run frequently from Tiberias to the **Ein Gev Holiday Village** (☎06-758027) where you can **camp** ($6), rent a **bungalow** for four ($10 per person) or, if you really want to do it in style, have an air-conditioned caravan ($20 single, $26 double, or $100 for six people for a week) which must be booked well in advance during the summer. The campsite is clean and well equipped with showers and toilets; there's also a lakeside restaurant that specialises, naturally enough, in St. Peter's fish.

Kursi

Not far beyond Ein Gev you enter territory which was Syrian until 1967. At **KURSI**, some 5km on, are the remains of the largest Byzantine **monastic complex** in the country (Sun–Thur 8am–5pm, Fri 8am–4pm; admission $1). Inside the walled and fortified monastery area is a restored fifth-century **church**, covered in mosaics of geometrical and floral patterns. An inscription over the entrance to the baptistry in the southeast corner of the complex dates the construction at 585AD; another room in the north contained an olive press, one to the south was a crypt, while others are thought to have been the monks' living quarters.

Kursi has been a place of pilgrimage since the fifth century because it is identified with 'the country of the Gadarenes' described by St. Mark *(5:1)*, where Jesus dramatically exorcised 'a legion of devils' from a man by sending them into a herd of two thousand swine that then 'ran violently down a steep place into the sea . . . and were choked' *(Mark 5:13)* – the story of the **Gadarene swine**. It is indeed a high place, as the view from here testifies: strategically important, too, when it was held by Syrian forces.

Immediately north of Kursi is **Samach Junction**, where a particularly scenic road winds its way up to the top of the **Golan Heights**. There are only a couple of buses a day in this direction, and other traffic is sparse, but if you've the time and the patience, it's an area worth exploring.

The view at **Ma'aleh Gamla Junction**, another 5km north, is even more impressive. Here the road to the Golan crosses a deep valley with spectacular **waterfalls**. The ruins of an ancient settlement at **Gamla**, on top of a steep hill resembling a camel's hump – *gamal* in Arabic – are thought to be those of a Jewish fortress town destroyed by the Romans during the First Revolt (66–70AD). A synagogue, two dykes, the city wall and watchtowers have been excavated on the site.

If you continue round the lake towards Tiberias, you'll cross the northern inlet of the Jordan River at the **Jordan River Park** (Park HaYarden).

North of Tiberias

Pleasant as the southern and eastern shores of the lake are, it's the area north of Tiberias which attracts most visitors, for here are concentrated the sites associated with the life of Jesus. Above all, it was at the Sea of Galilee that Jesus collected many of his disciples, and it was here that he walked on the water. The biblical sites – they include **Migdal**, **Tabgha**, the **Mount of Beatitudes** and **Capernaum** – are all beautiful places where, if you can avoid the crowds, history seems very close.

The Horns of Hittin

The first place of interest in this direction is neither biblical nor on the lake, but lies inland, to the north of the main road to Nazareth. Head in this direction and you'll see a long low hill – in fact an extinct volcano – with a peak at either end. These are the conspicuous **Horns of Hittin** (*Qarnei Hittim*), scene of one of the most important battles in the country's history, when **Salah al-Din** inflicted a decisive defeat on the **Crusaders**. A path from the road will take you to the top in less than half an hour.

In 1187 Salah al-Din's armies, with 12,000 archers, were camped at the southern end of the Sea of Galilee and on the heights above Tiberias, tempting the Crusaders to battle. On July 3 the bait was taken, and a Crusader force of 1200 knights and 16,000 infantry set out from Zippori, near Nazareth. Reaching the steaming valley at the foot of the Horns of Hittin the following morning, the heavily armoured Crusaders found the spring there dry, and moving east were caught with the sun in their eyes. They were met by the bows and lances of Salah al-Din's forces. Parched, unequipped for the heat and weighed down by their armour, the Crusader army was overwhelmed: by the end of the day vast numbers were captive, later to be sold into slavery, the True Cross had been captured and Crusader power in Palestine had been destroyed.

Mount Arbel

At the foot of the Horns of Hittin on the far side lies **NABI SHU'EIB**, the burial place of Moses' father-in-law, Jethro. Jethro is the first of the seven great prophets of the Druze, and the domed building which houses his tomb is the site of a Druze pilgrimage and festival every spring. Nabi Shu'eib lies at the end of a road through the Arbel Valley (Wadi Arbel), reached by turning right off the Nazareth road as you leave Tiberias.

To the right of this road is **Mount Arbel**, where the Maccabeans were defeated by the Syrians in 160BC. According to one Jewish tradition, this is also the place where the Messiah will appear and meet up with the Prophet Elijah and other noted sages. To mark this, a number of synagogues were built on and around the summit, the remnants of which are still clearly visible. It is thought that the remains of Jacob's children are buried near the main synagogue. The site has not been thoroughly excavated, so you have to look for the ruins among the swathes of yellow flowers that cover the place for much of the spring and summer. Mount Arbel can be approached from the other side via Majdal, through the canyon-like **Wadi al-Hammam**. If you don't feel like making the rather arduous climb right to the top to catch the view (Safad to the north, Tiberias to the southeast), you can explore the caves honeycombed up the rocky cliffs that served as hideouts for rebels in the Jewish revolts against the Romans – but be careful how you go.

Majdal and Ginnosar

Six kilometres north of Tiberias by the coast road, **Majdal** (Migdal) was the village known in the New Testament as **Magdala** – birthplace of Mary Magdalene. The ancient village was named after the tower (*migdal* in Hebrew) that once defended it, and was an important town right through to the Crusader era. In antiquity the local weaving industry was well known, and the robes worn by Jesus at the time of his crucifixion are said to have been made here. But modern Majdal was founded in 1910, and has little of interest beyond the beauty of its surroundings, an oasis of palm and eucalyptus trees.

The road north runs through the fertile **Valley of Ginnosar** that marks the border between the Lower and Upper Galilee. This is the *Land of Gennasaret* which Jesus and his disciples frequently cross in the New Testament: the **Galilee skull**, found in a cave in the valley in 1925, dates from around 100,000BC, the earliest evidence of human habitation in the region. **Kibbutz Ginnosar** lies at the heart of the valley about 5km from Majdal. Founded in 1937, the kibbutz is famed for its out-of-season fruits and vegetables, but today its main economic base comes from tourism – the four-star **Nof Ginnosar** guest house. It's a fancy, pricey place (around $40 for a single room, $60 for a double, B & B; ☎06-792161) with 170 air-conditioned rooms and a private beach providing kayaks, pedal boats and windsurfing. It is also one of the better kibbutzim to work on, as most volunteers are employed either in the guest house or in the neighbouring fields.

Nearby, during a period of particularly low water in 1986, a kibbutz member saw the remains of a **2000-year-old boat** protruding from the sands. The boat, which the mud had preserved in near pristine condition, was excavated by a team of marine archaeologists and now lies in a tank at the kibbutz where it is undergoing chemical treatment to preserve it. The fishing boat is believed to date from between 100BC and 100AD, and its discovery throws fascinating light on the fishing industry in biblical times. You can see it in the **Yigal Allon Memorial Museum** (Sun–Thur 8am–6pm, Fri 8am–5pm, Sat 9am–6pm).

Khirbet Minya or Hurbat Minnim

One kilometre north of Ginnosar, on the shores of the sea, are the ruins of the **Minya Palace**, one of the finest, and most neglected, examples of Omayyad architecture in the country. The palace was built by the renowned Caliph **Khalid Ibn al-Walid**, whose forces had routed the Byzantine army at the battle on the banks of the Yarmuk River (which joins the Jordan just below the Sea of Galilee) at the start of the Muslim conquest in 636AD. The large square structure has four round towers in the corner of each wall, some rising to ten metres; but the best of the place is inside, where there are remnants of a **mosaic floor** and, on the southern side, the oldest **mosque** in Israel, with a *mihrab* indicating the direction of Mecca. The former importance of the Minya complex is indicated by the fact that the Sea of Galilee was once known in Arabic as *Bahr al-Minya* – the Sea of Minya.

The easiest way to find the palace is to take the path beside the giant **Eshed Kinnarot pumping station**, easily visible from the road. The pumping station was built over **Khan Minya** – a caravanserai mentioned in writings of the seventeenth century.

Tabgha

TABGHA, not much further north, is where Christian tradition has, since the fourth century, located three important events in the life of Jesus: the multiplication of the loaves and fishes (*Mark 6: 35–44*), the Sermon on the Mount (*Matthew 5–7*) and the passing of leadership to Peter (*John 21*). At Tabgha – the name is an Arabic contraction of the Greek *Heptapegon* meaning 'seven springs', *Ein Sheva* in Hebrew – the main site is the **Church of the Multiplication of the Loaves and Fishes** (daily 7am–5pm). The original fourth-century church was built on the spot where the feeding of the five thousand is said to have taken place. Another church was erected over it in the fifth century, and its exquisite **mosaic floors**, discovered early this century, have been preserved within the modern, Byzantine-style church. Taken together, they form a unique example of early Palestinian church art. Many are simple geometric patterns, but between the columns of the nave is a startlingly exuberant riot of exotic birds – herons, doves, cormorants, ducks and geese – lotus flowers and even a snake; while in front of the altar (said to be the stone on which the miracle was performed) are depicted two fish on either side of a basket of loaves, beautiful in their simplicity.

The black basalt **Church of the Primacy of Saint Peter** (daily 8.30am–4pm), nearby, was built by the Franciscans in 1933, again on the site of a fourth century church. It encloses a flat rock said to be the table – the *Mensa Christi* – on which the resurrected Jesus offered a meal to his disciples ('As soon then as they were come to land, they saw a fire of coals there and fish laid thereon and bread' *John 21:9*), and where he conferred the primacy on Peter with the instructions 'Feed my lambs. Feed my sheep. Feed my sheep'. Near the church there is a rocky beach, and steps from which Jesus called out instructions to the disciples casting their nets. Below the steps are six double, heart-shaped blocks, sometimes covered by water, known as the **Thrones of the Apostles**. If you go for a swim, beware of the jagged rocks in the water.

The Mount of Beatitudes

Immediately north of Tabgha, set back from the lake, is the **Mount of Beatitudes**, the traditional site of the **Sermon on the Mount** (*Matt 5–7*). The octagonal chapel on the summit was built at the orders of Mussolini in 1937, its eight sides recalling the eight beatitudes or blessings (*Matt 5:3–10*). The seven virtues – justice, charity, prudence, faith, fortitude, hope and temperance – are represented in the pavement around the altar. The church, flanked by a pilgrims' hostel and an Italian convent, is, despite its popularity, one of the most peaceful sites in the country. Sunset is a particularly good time to visit, when the yellow chapel walls reverberate with the singing of white-robed monks seated around the altar. And the view of the Sea of Galilee from the top of the hill is probably the best in the area.

The ruins of an earlier, fourth-century church commemorating the Sermon on the Mount lie below, off the road just beside Tabgha.

Capernaum

The scenery along the road from the Mount of Beatitudes to **CAPERNAUM** (daily 8.30am–4.15pm; admission $0.75; modest dress required) is so gentle and beautiful that, if you have the time, you should try to walk. It's little more than 1km, though in midsummer heat even this can feel quite a trek. Capernaum, a Greek rendering of the *Kufr* or *Kfar Nahum* (the village of Nahum) which was referred to in the gospels as 'Jesus' own city', was the 'headquarters' of his Galileean ministry, where he lived, preached and performed miracles. There are two sites here: a nineteenth-century Franciscan **monastery** and, adjacent to it, the ruins of one of most famous synagogues in the country.

The **synagogue**, believed to date from between the third and fourth centuries, was built over an earlier one in which Jesus may have preached ('And they went into Capernaum and straightway on the Sabbath day he entered into the synagogue and taught' *Mark 1:21*). The Franciscans bought the site in 1894, cleared the ruins and later restored the Byzantine synagogue.

The synagogue consists of a prayer hall with a magnificent Roman facade and stone benches, with a column on the right which has a Greek inscription. East of the main hall, on the side of the lake, is an annexe with a grand carved lintel at the main entrance. The stone carvings inside the synagogue represent Jewish symbols – a palm, star of David, candelabra – and other less obvious figures, such as a wagon, an urn, eagles and a legendary animal which is half horse, half fish. In the courtyard are a huge, stone flour-mill and an olive-press, as well as carved stones from the ancient synagogue.

Beside the synagogue is the **Octagon of Saint Peter**, the remains of a very early church (probably before 500AD) beneath which have been excavated a number of still older houses. One of these was identified as Peter's house as early as the first century: archaeological evidence suggests that they were indeed fishermen's houses (mainly because of the number of fish hooks found in them).

Capernaum is a stopping place for **ferries** to the Lido Beach at Tiberias and across the lake to Ein Gev. The boat leaves Tiberias every morning for the round trip, at a cost of about $5, and heads back from here in the early afternoon. Check exact times at the pier. Continuing by **road**, you can either circle on around the east side of the lake, with roads providing access to the Golan Heights, or head back to Tabgha, where the road north towards Qiryat Shmona turns off.

Accommodation north of Tiberias

There are various places where you could camp as you head north from Tiberias, but little in the way of organised accommodation. The **Karei Deshe Youth Hostel** (about $5 a night; ☎06-720601), halfway between Ginnosar and Tabgha, does however offer at least one pleasant, reasonably priced option: it's within walking distance of either Ginnosar or Tabgha, or buses will stop on request. The hostel, originally a cattle ranch, is one of the best in the country, set in lush gardens (complete with peacocks), with its own private beach and a small campsite. If you want to cook your own food in the kitchen, bring provisions with you. This is one place where ringing ahead is definitely worthwhile. Quite apart from the fact that the hostel is often full, you may find that it no longer exists – the land on which it stands originally belonged to the German Church and promises have been made to return it.

A couple of alternatives can be found north of the lake, along the main highway from Tabgha. First of these is the **Vered HaGalil** riding stable (☎06-735785), where you can camp or sleep in the guest house (about $15, B & B), and use the opportunity to take a **horseback ride** (about $25 for a half-day tour) up into the hills or down to the Sea of Galilee. The stable is just east of the crossroads 6km from Tabgha. Further on, and far less attractive, there's a youth hostel in the former village school at the settlement of **Rosh Pinna** (☎06-937086; members $6, non-members $8). This almost invariably has space; to get there follow the signs from the centre of the settlement where the bus stops. From Rosh Pinna there are frequent buses west into Galilee and north to Qiryat Shemona.

The Galilee Panhandle

The narrow northern strip of eastern Israel is known as the 'Panhandle' or 'Finger'. It is dominated by the regional capital of **Qiryat Shmona** in the far north, but along the way both Tel Hazor and the Hula Valley make worthwhile stopovers. From Tabgha, the main road heads north to **ROSH PINNA**, where you can turn off for Safad (p.313). Rosh Pinna is a settlement founded by Rumanian and Russian immigrants in 1882, on land bought from the village of Ja'una. It's a useful point to change buses, with services north to Qiryat Shmona, west into Galilee and east to the Golan Heights – and there's a small airport for domestic flights – but unless you're staying at the youth hostel (see above) there's absolutely nothing to stop for.

Tel Hazor

As you come down from the hills into the Hula Valley, the site of **TEL HAZOR** is clearly visible from the road. This city was inhabited from the Bronze Age (around 2500BC) right through to the second century BC, and at least 21 separate settlements have been discovered. Like Megiddo (p.280), it lay on the main route from Egypt to Mesopotamia, and was an essential target for invaders from the north. The **Canaanite city** was among the most important of its age (eighteenth and seventeenth centuries BC), and in the Old Testament the city is mentioned as the capital of many pre-Israelite kings. It was conquered and burned by Joshua – 'And Joshua at that time turned back, and took Hazor, and smote the king thereof with the sword, for Hazor beforetime was head of all those kingdoms. And they smote all the souls that were therein with the edge of the sword, utterly destroying them: there was not any left to breathe: and he burnt Hazor with fire.' (*Joshua 11:10–11*) – and subsequently abandoned for a while. By the tenth century BC, however, a substantial city had once again grown up, and was fortified by Solomon, and then further strengthened by Ahab. This city was in turn destroyed by the Assyrians in the eighth century BC, and thereafter it never regained its former importance.

What you see, with so many superimposed levels, is slightly complex, but it remains impressive, and big. Among the highlights are the **Canaanite Palace**, approached by a broad ceremonial stairway. Over it a gatehouse and various defensive walls were constructed in the time of Solomon, and a large storehouse by Ahab. The **Citadel** dates basically from the time of Ahab, as does the impressive system for the supply of water. As at Jerusalem and Megiddo, this has been designed to allow access to water even when the spring outside the walls is cut off by attackers: in this case a shaft and tunnel system which leads to an underground pool. The steps have been restored to give access to this ancient underground chamber. The **Temple**, again built over remains of earlier temples, is also worth seeing. It dates from the time of the last Canaanite king, Jabin, and was destroyed when Joshua burnt the city.

Nearby, **Kibbutz Ayelet HaShahar** has a large guest house (☎06-730633) and a **museum**, at the entrance, displaying many of the finds from the site.

The Hula Valley

At the turn of the century most of the **Hula Valley**, from the Sea of Galilee to the foothills of the Golan Heights, was a vast swampland, attracting hordes of migratory birds. In the early 1950s work was started on draining and reclaiming vast tracts for farming use, but some of the original swamp and marsh does still survive and has been preserved in nature reserves. The largest of these is the thousand acre **Hula Nature Reserve** (Sat–Thur 8am–4pm, Fri 8am–3pm; admission $1.50), about halfway between Rosh Pinna and Qiryat Shmona. The wealth of wildlife in the reserve – from water buffalo to pelicans, wild boar to mongooses – is astonishing, so leave yourself the best part of a day to tour the whole area.

At the entrance to the reserve are a number of kiosks serving snacks and selling brochures for those who want help in telling the difference between a glossy ibis and a little egret. You can also rent binoculars here – well worth it if birdwatching is your interest. Access to the wildlife is provided by a network of trails that pass through the reserve, dotted with hides and observation huts. Getting to the reserve is relatively simple: buses pass by on the Rosh Pinna–Qiryat Shmona road at least every hour, and it's easy enough to hitch (or walk) the 2½km from the junction.

Just north of the Hula Reserve, **Dubrovin Farm** (Sat–Thur 9am–4pm, Fri 9am–2pm) has been renovated to show the lifestyles of early settlers in the area. If you have a car it might just be worth the detour, but it's not a terribly exciting attraction. Nearby **Kibbutz Kfar Blum** (☎06-94366) has a 46-room, three-star guest house with – among other facilities – an Olympic-size swimming pool, tennis courts, a sauna and kayaks that can be hired (at $9 per hour) for speeding down the nearby rivers. This predominantly Anglo-Saxon kibbutz is well known for its week-long **classical music festival** (tickets $10–15), which is held in April and features local and international musicians.

Qiryat Shmona and Tel Hai

QIRYAT SHMONA (the Village of Eight) was named after the eight Zionists who died in the nearby settlement of Tel Hai in 1920 (see below) and is still dominated by the Arab-Israeli conflict. Built in 1949 as a defensive settlement on the Lebanese-Israeli border, and as a *ma'araba* (transit camp) for predominantly *sephardi* immigrants, it is a natural target for cross-border attacks.

As towns go, it's about as unexciting as you could get – a collection of concrete blocks built with defence rather than aesthetics in mind. The only thing to recommend it is that it's a useful place to pick up transport around the area and into the Golan. The bus station, a few hundred metres east of the main road, marks the centre of town. From here shops, banks and anything else you might need are within a five-minute walk. If you do have to stay here, there's accommodation at the *North Hotel* (☎06-944705), but at $40 a head you're better off at the youth hostels in nearby Tel Hai, or back at Rosh Pinna

TEL HAI, 2km north of Qiryat Shmona, is a memorial to **Joseph Trumpeldor** (after whom one in ten streets in Israel seem to be named) and his seven companions, killed here in 1920. First settled in 1905 on land bought by Baron de Rothschild and named after the original village, *Khirbet Talha* – Tel Hai was taken over in 1918 by the socialist-Zionist *HaShomer* (guard) movement. Trumpeldor was one of the first Zionists to take to arms – having formed a Jewish force which fought alongside the British in World War I – and when he died fighting against Arab insurgents here, he became the first great martyr of the Zionist cause: his last words are said to have been 'it is good to die for our country'. The **cemetery** where Trumpeldor and his companions are buried is marked by a statue of a roaring lion and is a site of pilgrimage for thousands of young Israeli conscripts on the March 1 anniversary. A small museum nearby (Sun–Thur 8am–4pm, Fri 8am–1pm, Sat 9am–2.30pm; admission $1.50) tells the story of the battle in which they died.

Today, Tel Hai is part of **Kibbutz Kfar Giladi** (☎06-941414), which was also founded by the *HaShomer* movement (in 1916) and was temporarily abandoned after the Tel Hai incident. The kibbutz has a swimming pool, tennis courts and a three-star **guest house** with 150 rooms that sleep up to four people. Less expensive accommodation is available at the **Tel Hai youth hostel** (around $8; ☎06-940043), just off the main Qiryat Shmona–Metulla road (bus #20 or #23 from Qiryat Shmona). There are fine mountain views from many of the rooms in the 120-bed hostel.

Dan

Nine kilometres east of Qiryat Shmona, almost in the foothills of the Golan, are a number of nature reserves. **Hurshat Tal** is an ancient oak wood, known as *Shajarat al-'shara* (Wood of the Ten) in Arabic. The name is based on the legend that ten of Mohammed's companions, resting here, stuck their staffs into the ground to tie up their horses. From these staffs, the massive oak trees grew. The wood lies on the banks of the **Dan River**, one of the Jordan's three tributaries, and it's a great place to swim – the river here has been diverted into a large pool for that purpose. Just north of the entrance to the park (open daily; admission $2), the **Hurshat Tal camping ground** (☎06-940400) offers excellent pitches for tents (about $5) and bungalows which can sleep three, four or five.

Kibbutz Dan nearby also has a small nature reserve noted for its lush vegetation and location on the river – although swimming is not allowed here. One kilometre north through the reserve is the archaeological site of **TEL DAN** or *Tel al-Qadi* (Sun–Thur 8am–4pm, Fri 8am–3pm) which was a centre of the northern Israelite tribes during the First Temple Period. After the kingdom of David split into two in 1100BC, King Jeroboam (928–907BC) of the northern kingdom 'made two calves of gold' (*I Kings 12:28*), one of which he set up in Dan for the people to worship. Excavations here have revealed ruins from the Bronze and Iron Ages, including a ritual site, a magnificent tomb, city ramparts and gates. An arched gateway to the Canaanite city of *Leshem* or *Laish* (mentioned in Egyptian texts of the nineteenth century BC), was uncovered here in 1979. A guidebook to the site is available at the entrance to the nature reserve, where there's also a kiosk for refreshments.

Metulla and the Lebanese border

The town of **METULLA**, at the northern tip of the Galilee Panhandle, is the archetypal border town. Founded by Russian immigrants on land bought by Baron de Rothschild in 1896, its name is taken from the Arabic of the Druze village which stood here, *al-Mutalla'* or lookout. Metulla was temporarily evacuated after the Tel Hai battle in 1920, and at the end of the 1948 war found that most of its land in the **Iyun Valley** (*Marj 'Ayun*) was stranded on the Lebanese side of the border.

Although the landscape around Metulla is dramatic and the town itself – a collection of Swiss-style chalets – is pleasant enough, its attractions are few.

The refreshing mountain air and the plentiful apple orchards roundabout make a pleasant change for a while, but once you've filled your lungs, boredom can set in rapidly. The 'centre' of the town has a couple of hotel bars and restaurants that are frequented by UN personnel and Lebanese from across the border – good places to strike up conversation with Fijian soldiers and Lebanese merchants about what's happening on the other side.

Its location is the town's main claim to fame: less than a kilometre to the northwest is a border crossing, the so-called **Good Fence**, opened in 1977. The crossing was established after the residents of neighbouring Lebanese Christian villages sought medical attention in Israel because of fighting in the early seventies. Since then, there has been a flow of people from south Lebanon into Israel, and of Israeli goods and military personnel into Lebanon. However, the 'Good Fence' is only good to some: Lebanese who want to cross must have a relative active in the Israeli-backed South Lebanese Army (SLA). Every day, thousands of Lebanese cross the border to work as unskilled labourers in Israel and to earn wages that are meagre by Israeli standards but go a long way in a country whose economy, after years of civil war and foreign occupation, is in tatters.

Looking out over the fence from the **observation point** (a snack bar sells cheap *falafel* and hot dogs), the view of Lebanon is one of calm and normality. Yet you could be in war-torn Beirut in a matter of hours, or in the Syrian-controlled Beqa'a Valley in less than thirty minutes. The **Palestinian refugee camps** that Israel so regularly bombs are not far away either, mostly beyond the 40-mile security zone that Israel picked out for itself in the 1982 invasion of Lebanon – the so-called Peace for Galilee fiasco.

Today, the South Lebanon you can see from the border is effectively occupied territory, flooded by Israeli goods, by Israeli-funded militias and an estimated 1000 Israeli military personnel. The predominantly Shi'ite Muslim population of the south, who initially greeted the invading Israelis in 1982 as 'liberators', have since learned better and are now some of Israel's most bitter and most active enemies. Since Israel's casualties during the 1982 invasion proved unacceptably high and it was forced to withdraw most of its forces, Israel's proxy, the SLA, has found itself entrenched in a hopeless guerilla war with the Shi'ite population, adding yet another explosive dimension to the country's splintered factionalism. On a hill to the east of the crossing is **Beaufort Castle**, a major PLO stronghold until 1982. From here, the Palestinians bombarded Israeli border towns with Katyusha rockets.

According to the mayor of Metulla, it is 'possible' to cross the border and go visiting in South Lebanon. Don't do so unless you've a powerful death wish, however. Safer trips out of town include the spectacular eighteen-metre drop of the **Tanur Waterfall**, immediately south of Metulla. The waterfall is at its peak in spring, when its spray evaporates in the heat (*tanur* means oven) and pervades the area with a smoky mist. During the summer, even though the waterfall is reduced to a trickle, the main pool usually holds enough water to make it a good place for a cooling swim. Slightly further, to the east of the main road about 3km south, there's a second, smaller waterfall in the **'Ayun Nature Reserve** (Sat–Thur 8am–4pm, Fri 8am–3pm; admission $3). Here you'll also find a pleasant picnic area beside the 'Ayun River.

Metulla offers a couple of **hotels** – neither particularly good value – should you want to stay. The *Hotel Manara* (☎06-942361), near the municipal building, above the community centre, has double rooms from $15; *Yafeh Hotel*, next door, is more expensive. **Bus #20** runs between Qiryat Shmona and Metulla every hour.

travel details

Buses

From Tiberias to Nazareth/Haifa (every 30min 6am–8pm; 45min/1hr 30min); Tel Aviv (hourly 6am–8pm; 2hr 30min); Jerusalem (12 daily; 3hr 30min); Safad/Acre (hourly 7am–6pm; 45min/2hr); Qiryat Shmona (hourly 7am–10.30pm; 1hr 30min); Ein Gev (7 daily; 30min); Qazrin (hourly 7am–8pm; 1hr).

From Qiryat Shmona to Safad (every 30min 6am–8pm; 1hr); Jerusalem (6 daily; 5hr); Tel Aviv (hourly 6am–8pm; 3hr 30min); Banyas (2 daily; 20min); Qazrin (2 daily; 40min).

CHAPTER SEVEN

THE GOLAN HEIGHTS

I f you go on an Israeli guided tour of the Golan Heights, you'll be shown the bunkers formerly used by the Syrians and told how they used to bombard the Israeli farmers who were peacefully sowing the land of the kibbutz settlements around Tiberias. You will probably also be told how the Syrians intended to divert the water of the Jordan. Although the facts are true, what you won't hear is why this happened.

After the 1948 war, a number of demilitarised zones were established between Israel and bordering Arab countries: those along the Israeli-Syrian border ran at the foot of the Golan Heights. Under the terms of the 1949 armistice, neither side was to occupy this territory, which was policed by UN observers. The Israelis, however, decided to push their borders further east and, as elsewhere in the country, razed Arab villages and expelled their inhabitants, transplanted trees, built roads and, according to one UN official, 'developed a habit of irrigating and ploughing in stretches of Arab-owned land . . . beneath the glowering eyes of the Syrians'. Naturally enough, tension mounted and often flared into full-scale fighting, particularly during the sowing and harvesting seasons, and during the 1950s and 1960s, Israel carried out attacks against Syrian military positions on the Golan Heights. In April 1967, the Israeli government decided to cultivate all areas of the demilitarised zone. When, the day after the announcement, the Syrians began their bombardment, Israel sent in seventy jet fighters with napalm and explosives. Six Syrian planes were shot down, most of their fortified positions were hit, and many died. A month later, General Yitzhak Rabin (currently Israel's Minister of Defence) declared on Israel Radio that 'The moment is coming when we will march on Damascus to overthrow the Syrian Government.' The Arabs had to react. President Nasser of Egypt sent his forces into the Sinai, ordered the UN to withdraw from the Israeli-Egyptian frontier, and imposed a blockade of the Israeli port of Eilat. The incident marked the start of the June War of 1967.

During this war, the Israelis drove over 100,000 Syrians from the Golan Heights, to join Palestinian refugees in camps near Damascus. Of over a hundred villages in the region, only seven remain today, the rest having been demolished and their lands handed over to Israeli settlers. Now flattened slabs of concrete, the old houses' roofs, are all that remains of the villages. The population, the majority of whom are Syrian Druze, was reduced to 15,000.

In fierce battles with the Israelis during the October War of 1973, the Syrians broke through the Golan Heights; under the May 1974 Separation of

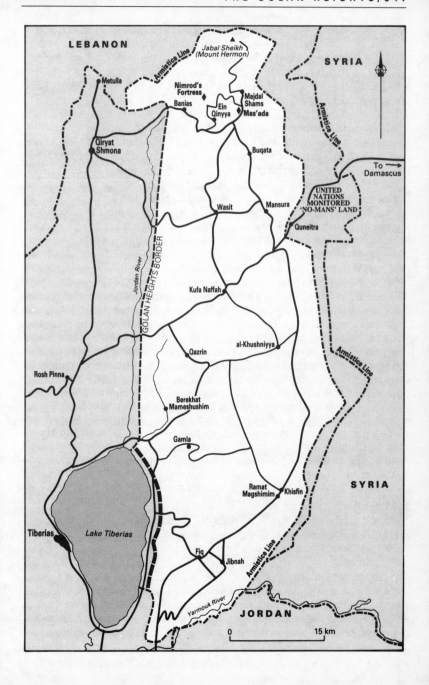

Forces Agreement, a section of the Golan was returned to Syria and a UN buffer zone established between the Israeli and Syrian forces. In December 1982, the Golan Heights were formally 'brought under Israeli law and legislation' – a euphemism for annexation – in contravention of international law and United Nations Resolution 242, according to which the Golan Heights are occupied territories.

Practical points: transport, tours and accommodation

The Golan is one of the few places in Israel not opened up to wholesale commercial exploitation. This makes it rewarding to explore, but poses problems when it comes to **getting around**. The region is served by only a handful of infrequent **buses**. Public transport to sites east of the Sea of Galilee runs from the central bus station in Tiberias, while the northern Golan is served by buses from Qiryat Shmona. With few cars touring the area, hitching can be slow and frustrating: hence the Golan is one of the few places that makes **hiring a car** a worthwhile investment.

A variety of **organised tours** operate in the area: *Egged Tours* have 1-day coach trips to the Upper Galilee and Golan from HAIFA ($37) and Tiberias ($22), and 2-day trips from Jerusalem and Tel Aviv (both $140); *Galilee Tours* also cover the Golan on 1-day runs from Jerusalem ($42), 2-day trips from Jerusalem and Tel Aviv that include the Galilee or Safad and Acre ($140), and 1- or 2-day tours from Tiberias ($22 and $115 respectively). For **camping trips**, try the *Society for the Protection of Nature in Israel (SPNI)*. Their 2- and 4-day nature tours to the Golan (from $70) are perhaps the best, taking in some of the more remote waterfalls and archaeological sites, and in summer usually including at least three swim spots a day – and a half-day's exhilarating inner-tube ride down the Hatzbani or Snir rivers. Other, more intimate tours are run from Tiberias by *Oded Shoshan* (☎06-721812), who has detailed military knowledge of the area but finds it hard to disguise his contempt for the Syrians who live here. A day's outing in a seven-seater taxi costs around $15.

As in the other occupied territories, the best way to visit the area is with local residents: the Syrians of the Golan are more than happy to talk to interested visitors. The Israeli tours may be practical and convenient, but entail putting up with David-versus-Goliath stories which today – post-Lebanon and the *intifada* – are wearing decidedly thin.

Accommodation in the Golan Heights is sparse: the only cheap hostels are in Qazrin and Hispin. The other option is to base yourself at one of the hostels at Qiryat Shmona, Rosh Pinna or around the Sea of Galilee, and make day excursions to the area. Alternatively, if you have a tent, or don't mind sleeping under the stars, you can spend the night in the **campsite** at Qazrin. Travellers have been known to sleep out in the bomb shelters scattered all over the Golan – but as there are still land-mines planted in the fields, it is advisable not to leave the main roads and definitely to avoid any fenced-off areas. But providing you take care, the Golan is a great place for **walking**: the SPNI has a good map which should see you through.

THE NORTHERN GOLAN

One of the most popular routes into **the Northern Golan** is the trip up to the summit of Mount Hermon – or **Jabal al-Sheikh** as it is known in Arabic. Route 99 heads northeast from Qiryat Shmona, crosses the 1967 border about a kilometre past Kibbutz Dan, and on to the ancient town of **Banyas**. From here, Route 989 leads through the *moshav* and ski-resort of **Neve Ativ** and the Syrian Druze village of **Majd al-Shams** to the snow-covered slopes of Jabal al-Sheikh. Bus #55 from Qiryat Shmona passes Banyas twice daily (1.10pm and 4.15pm), the last bus returning at noon. Buses back to Qiryat Shmona run more frequently from KIBBUTZ DAN, 5km to the east. It's easy to tell when you've crosssed into the Golan – barbed wire, military posts, bunkers and tank bridges mark the territory.

Banyas

BANYAS has two major claims to fame: its position on the road between Damascus, Tyre and Jerusalem made it a significant strategic site, and it is the main spring of the region's most important river – the **Jordan**. Here the Greeks built a cave-temple to Pan, the god of nature: the site became known as *Paneas*, its present name being the Arabic pronunciation. Herod dedicated a marble temple here to his patron, the Emperor Augustus, and the site was later inherited by Herod's son Philip, who built the city of Caesarea Philippi. To celebrate the capture of Jerusalem in 70 AD, Titus is said to have held games in which Jewish prisoners were thrown to wild beasts or forced to fight each other to the death.

In 1126 the **Assassins** obtained possession of Banyas. This sect of Shi'ite Muslims fought to establish a Shi'ite caliphate against the Seljuk Turks who ruled from Damascus. Their name in Arabic – the *Hashishin* – derived from the serenity with which the members disposed of their enemies in the knowledge that they themselves would be killed. Whether or not they were actually stoned on dope at the time is open to doubt. When the Crusaders arrived, the Assassins planned to assist them in taking Damascus, but the plot was discovered, members of the sect were massacred, and those who survived fled to Palestine. The Crusaders took over the strategic site of Banyas, and built a castle – Nimrod – in nearby **Subeibeh**. The small city reverted to Arab rule when it fell to Nur al-Din in 1164. When it was taken by the Israelis in 1967, the village had a population of around 200.

Banyas is now a **nature reserve**, its centrepiece being the **Cave-Temple of Pan** flanked by rock-cut niches where the Greeks placed statues of their gods. Above the cave is the supposed tomb of **al-Khader**, St. George, revered by Muslims and Druze. The church which once marked the spot was turned into a **mosque** many years ago, and is one of the few intact remnants of the Arab village. It's of particular religious importance to members of the Muslim Alawi sect, who live nearby.

Apart from the mosque and the temple, the most visible remains in the **park** (daily 8am–6pm; $1.50) are those of what was once the Syrian Arab village. Neither the ruined houses nor the fate of its former residents – now presumably somewhere in Syria – seem to worry the thousands who come to eat in the well laid-out picnic areas. Other ruins scattered around are those of the first century Roman city.

The highlight of any visit here must be the beautiful **Banyas waterfall** further up the hill – follow the sign at the side of the shrine or drive up the road through the town of Banyas. Once through the village, keep to the left, follow the signs to Majd al-Shams, and you will arrive at a car park with a small restaurant. The waterfalls are on your left: around them are several large pools which are great to swim in, although if you visit in summer, the waterfall may be no more than a trickle. Spring is the best time to be here, when the snows from Jabal al-Sheikh are melting and the mountainsides are swathed in lush vegetation.

Traveling east from Banyas to Jabal al-Sheikh, the road winds its way up into the mountains that dominate the skyline. Barbed-wire fences along the way warn that the land to your left and right is mined. Within safer walking distance, on the summit of a hill to the left, a 2km ascent to the northeast of Banyas, is the great fortress of **Subeibeh**, or **Qala'at Nimrod** – Nimrod's Castle, which commands an impressive view over the Galilee and the foothills of the Golan Heights. According to legend, the castle was built by one of Noah's descendants, 'Nimrod the mighty hunter'. The present structure, however, was clearly built by the Crusaders. Like Banyas itself, the site was given to the Crusaders' leader Baldwin by the Assassin sect in 1129, and the castle fortress built three years later. In 1157 Nur al-Din laid siege to Subeibeh, but only managed to take it in 1164. Later, it was restored by the Mamluks who used it as a prison.

Most in evidence today are the remains of its defensive towers and a large section of the outer walls. The square towers along the eastern wall belong to the original Crusader structure, and are interspaced with round towers added by the Muslims after 1164. To the north is a moat which attackers would have had to cross under fire from the overlooking towers, and a rectangular keep on the walls of which early Muslim paintings, now rather faded, were discovered. The approach to the fortress is up a steep, signposted path branching off the main Banyas-Neve Ativ road down below. Bus #55 runs here twice daily from Qiryat Shmona and will drop you off at the approach road.

The settlement of **NEVE ATIV** was established in 1969, the name being an acronym of four soldiers who died on the Golan. It was originally a *moshav shitufi* (with common production but separate family units), but was disbanded and replaced by the present *moshav* in 1971. The main income of the *moshav* is from tourism and from the **ski resort** that it runs on Mount Hermon. Here you'll find comfortable but rather expensive **chalet-style accommodation**, with double rooms from $22 (☎06-981333). The management will also advise on where to **camp** in the area.

THE DRUZE OF THE GOLAN

Before the 1967 war, the **DRUZE** in the Golan numbered around 100,000, representing 65 per cent of the total Syrian population. Since the Israeli occupation, their number has dwindled to about 15,000. The Druze broke away from mainstream Islam in the eleventh century and have since lived predominantly in isolated mountainous regions: large Druze communities exist today in the Mount Lebanon region in Lebanon, in Jebel Druze in Syria, and in the Galilee hills and the Carmel mountain range in Israel.

Many myths surround the Druze religion and the secretive rituals that only the chosen few can observe. The Druze are a religious sect stemming originally from the Shi'ites, but now are more closely linked to the Isma'ilis. They have been compared to Freemasons, which may or may not be true – the doors to their 'inner secrets' are tightly sealed. The more traditional Druze are distinguished by their dress: older men wear white head-dresses along with baggy trousers or *shirwaal*, and grow impressive moustaches.

Their close-knit, intensely loyal community has made the Druze a formidable force in the Golan. Unlike the Druze within the 1948 borders of Israel, many of whom serve in the Israeli Army, the Druze of the Golan will have nothing to do with the military and as little to do with the Israeli state as possible. On December 14, 1981 the Knesset voted to annex the Golan Heights, making its residents Israeli citizens subject to Israeli law – a status like that of Palestinians in East Jerusalem. In January 1982, the authorities' attempt to issue Israeli identity cards to the Golanis was met by a mass act of civil disobedience and the ID cards were ceremoniously burnt. The Golanis held a sustained and unanimous general strike and withdrew their labour in Israel.

The protest turned into a long and drawn-out battle of wits and stamina. The communities soon began to look after their own interests and food was shared amongst all the villages. Demonstrations erupted frequently, and bloody scenes of the army opening fire on unarmed crowds became a horrifyingly familiar sight. As the weeks dragged into months, the Israeli authorities concluded that the best way to break the strike would be to cordon off and isolate each of the four villages. No one was allowed in or out, and even food parcels sent by Israeli peace activists were turned back. After almost nine months, the authorities were forced to back down and agreed not to classify the Golanis as Israelis on their ID cards. The spirit of the strike is still very much alive in the villages, and demonstrations against Israeli occupation are commonplace. On a recent visit to Majd al-Shams, Prime Minister Shimon Peres was forced to flee the village as angry demonstrators pelted his entourage with stones.

Jabal al-Sheikh (Mount Hermon)

The climatic contrast between the snow-capped **JABAL AL-SHEIKH** and the plains of the Galilee down below is as extreme as you could get – half an hour after skiing on the summit, you could be swimming in the warm water of the Sea of Galilee. Jabal al-Sheikh – 'The Mountain of the Old Man' – is the highest mountain in the area, the peaks (held by Israel since 1967) being 2224 metres above sea level. Prices charged at the restaurant and ski-hire office (☎06-931103) on the summit are fairly high too – a complete outfit of skis, boots and pass will cost upwards of $35 per day. In theory, it's possible to roll around in the snow even in summer, although naturally in winter you're more assured of getting in some reasonable skiing.

The summit itself, spectacular and awesome, is a mesh of international borders, military no-go areas and serious-looking forward battalions – another place in the country where the political turmoils of the Middle East are painfully tangible.

Around Jabal al-Sheikh: Majd al-Shams, Ein Qinya and Mas'ada

Lying within the shadow of Jabal al-Sheik are four Druze villages, the largest and most important of which, **MAJD AL-SHAMS**, lies to the east, 1150m above sea level on the Syrian-Israeli disengagement of forces line. The road to the Hermon ski-slopes runs through the town, which itself is surrounded by snow-capped mountains.

The 10,000 residents of the village live primarily from the **apples** grown in the orchards in the valley below. In keeping with the socialist Ba'ath policies of the Syrian state, most cultivation is undertaken collectively, even though, under Israeli legislation, farmers are prohibited from planting new orchards without a permit. Large water containers in the fields give farmers a degree of independence from Israeli-controlled water supplies which, as in most parts of the country, are diverted to Israeli agricultural settlements, Arab farmers having only restricted access.

Many of the houses and shops in the village are decorated with ornate French-style metalwork, betraying the influence of Syria's former colonial master. The Syrian Eagle is also a common sight around the village, indicating where present-day loyalties lie.

With no hostels in the vicinity, it's only really possible to make a day visit to the village, but there are a few good cafés near the centre of town where you can watch the world go by and strike up conversations with the locals. As with all parts of the occupied territories, by far the best way to go is in the company of people who know, and are known in, the area. Any of the alternative sources of information (see *Basics*) can point you in the right direction, particularly the *Alternative Information Centre* in Jerusalem, who will also be able to put you in touch with the *Druze Initiative Committee* that is active inside Israel supporting Druze draft resisters. If you arrive in the village itself without having made any previous contacts, ask anyone to point you in the direction of the *League of Golan Heights University Graduates*, where you'll find someone who can fill you in on what's happening.

The nearest you can get to Syria is at the **shouting fence** just south of the village on the border. As in Rafah in the Gaza Strip, this place is the only way that the Druze of the Golan can keep in direct touch with their relatives and friends in Syria. With the aid of megaphones, the separated communities try to bridge the gap by shouting greetings and messages across the fence. From time to time, to impose collective punishment on the villagers under some pretext or other, the Israeli military will forbid even this minimum contact.

Ein Qinya

About 3km northwest of the Mas'ada junction (see below) is the tiny village of **EIN QINYA**, within which is a tel that reveals habitation in the early Bronze Age and the Roman-Byzantine period. It also contains a tomb believed to belong to the sister of al-Nabi Shu'eib – Moses' father-in-law Jethro, regarded by the Druze as a holy man. Across the stream south of the village is a new bridge built by the Israelis to replace one destroyed by retreating Syrian forces during the war of 1967. It's called the **Bridge of Friendship**, although whether the 600 villagers feel much friendship for their present occupiers is a moot point.

Mas'ada

South of Ein Qinya is the Druze village of **MAS'ADA**. Set on relatively flat land at the foot of Jabal al-Sheikh, it lies on the important road junction of Quneitra–Banyas–Majd al-Shams. The population of 700 are predominantly farmers working the mountain valley and ridges. The village has the Golan's central high school.

A couple of kilometres from Mas'ada is the perfectly round lake of **Birket Ram**. Herod's son Philip conducted an experiment here to determine the true source of the River Jordan. Josephus described the attempt:

> *To outward appearance the source of the Jordan is near Banyas, but in fact it issues from a pool known as the bowl, from where it follows to Banyas by an underground route . . . Formerly no one knew that the Jordan issues from the pool until Philip discovered it by practical experiment: He scattered chaff upon the water, and found that the chaff was brought down to Banyas, where it floated on the water.*

In fact, the chaff is said to have conveniently appeared in Banyas thanks to a diplomatic courtier. Source of the Jordan or not, the lake is a great area for a picnic or summer swim.

Beside the lake is the only restaurant in the area, *Birket Ram Restaurant*, usually packed with American and Israeli tourists. It also rents out rowing boats ($4 an hour) and sailboards ($6 for half an hour). From an observation point nearby you can see the delightful village **mosque** and surrounding area.

Four kilometres south of Birket Ram is the fairly large Druze village of BUQATA, with a population of over 2000. The road south from here leads to the modern-day Israeli settlement of Qazrin. On the way there's an interesting viewing point overlooking **QUNEITRA**, the former Syrian capital of the Golan. The town was returned to the Syrians in 1974; before 1967, it had a population of 30,000, but is now practically deserted. Despite Syrian efforts to repopulate the town, only a few former residents have returned, reluctant, presumably, to put themselves once again in the firing-line. The town borders on the UN-monitored no-man's land, and with a pair of binoculars or a telephoto lens, you can see the Syrian flag flying on the edge of town and the blue flag of the United Nations.

Qazrin

The Israeli settlement of **QAZRIN**, about 15km northeast of Lake Tiberias, is only a soulless collection of shops and identical houses, but as one of the few places in the Golan with a **hostel**, it's unavoidable for anyone wanting to stay in the area. The settlement was founded in 1974 and its inhabitants moved in three years later. It retained the name of the village that once stood on the site, which in turn was built on one of the oldest Jewish settlements in the Golan, dating from the third century AD. Excavations carried out in 1971 have uncovered the remains of a synagogue dating from that period, which had an ornate door lintel, vaulted rooms, water cistern, columns and pedestals engraved with Aramaic inscriptions and Jewish religious symbols. Clustered in the courtyard are everyday worktools collected during excavations of the site.

The **Golan Archaeological Museum** (Sun–Thur 9am–2pm, Sat 10am–2pm; $1) is at the northern end of town on Dalyat Street. Housing a collection of archaeological artefacts from the region, it's especially worth visiting if you haven't the time to explore the area fully. Near the museum are a swimming pool (Sun–Fri 9am-5pm, Sat 8am–4pm; $3), a supermarket, bank and post office. The handful of cafés in the central shopping arcade all vie for custom by showing videos.

As for **accommodation**, you have two choices: the **hostel** of the *Golan Field School*, run by the SPNI, and a **campsite**. The hostel is at the southern end of town and, if it's not packed with school kids, provides sleeping space for about $10. The field school is also a good source of information about the natural history of the surrounding area. The campsite has shower facilities and additional bungalow accommodation. A night here costs $3.50 for students, $6 for non-students; the registration office is open till 11am in the morning and from 6 to 9pm in the evening.

Gamla and Ya'ar Yehudiyya Nature Reserve

The main road south out of Qazrin meets Route 87 at the **Qusbiya** or **Kazrin Junction**. The road to the right passes through the peaceful Ya'ar Yehudiyya Nature Reserve and on down to the Sea of Galilee; left leads to the ancient ruins of Gamla and the spectacular Gamla Waterfall.

The walk to the **YA'AR YEHUDIYYA NATURE RESERVE** is a delight, as the countryside is magnificent, with rolling hills and streams set in an uncompromising calm. In the reserve, don't miss the natural **Hexagonal Pool** (Hebrew: *Brekhat HaMeshushim*), to the west of Route 87. This natural pool is enclosed by five- and six-sided basalt pillars, which were formed by the slow cooling of flowing lava after volcanic action. To reach it, follow the 3km track just north of the Yehudiyya Junction – there's a car park and often an ice-cream van marking the spot. If you have a tent it's possible to camp (illegally) in the reserve, but with no shops or restaurants nearby, you'll need to bring supplies along. On the eastern side of the main road are the remains of **Yehudiyya** itself, a Jewish settlement of the Roman-Byzantine period. These include another synagogue, with adjoining rooms, columns and capitals.

If you turn left at the Qusbiya Junction, after about 1km you'll come to a turning on the right signposted to RAMAT MAGSHIMIM. Follow this road until you pass a road to MOSHAV YONATAN on the left. Take the next turning right at Daliyot Junction to Gamla: with no bus service to the site, you either have to be a dedicated walker (or hitcher) or be driving to get here.

GAMLA, so called because the hill on which the ancient settlement lies resembles the hump of a camel (*gamal*), overlooks the Daliyot River, and is known as the 'Masada of the North'. Like the Dead Sea fortress, the occupants of this hilltop fort were besieged here for thirty days by Vespasian's Roman soldiers during the First Revolt of 66–69AD and, in the same spirit, chose suicide rather than surrender. According to Josephus, 4000 were killed in battle with the Romans and 5000 committed suicide by throwing themselves off the cliff.

Although the story of Gamla is indisputable, the layout of this particular site does not match Josephus' description, which fits better with that of Tel al-Dra near the village of Jamle in Syria, near the present border. But certainly this site was a Jewish fortress town; and that it was involved in battle is testified by the stone bullets found in the region. Excavations have revealed one of the oldest synagogues in the country, two dykes, a city wall and watchtowers.

The truly spectacular **Gamla Waterfall** nearby is the highest in the Golan Heights, and the sight of the spring waters gushing down the slopes of the Golan Plateau is worth the long hike here, particularly in the summer, when the pool is a delight to swim in (though beware of the jagged rocks.)

From Gamla, if you walk back to Daliyot Junction and turn right, you come to two Israeli settlements – **Ramat Magshimim** and **Haspin** – neither of which offer anything of much interest apart from a small **youth hostel** (☎06-763305) in the latter. Haspin was built on the Arab village of Khasfin by members of the *Bnei Akiva* religious movement, and is the regional centre for religious settlers. Guests intending to stay at the hostel must arrive before 4pm on Friday and may not leave until after the end of the sabbath. Meals can be bought from the canteen, and there's also a small supermarket in the settlement. The settlers here are devout Zionists who are firm believers in the Jewish settlement of the Golan – bring the subject up only if you feel like a fervent argument. **Buses** from Haspin to Qazrin run once a day and to Tiberias, 60km away, five times daily. Should you find yourself **camping** in the region, be on the lookout for snakes and scorpion spiders, especially the dangerous black ones.

A particularly scenic route out of the Golan is the road that runs south along the Syrian border, on the slopes of the valley leading down to the Yarmuk River. The scenery, of unbroken stillness and with relics from the 1967 war strewn along the way, makes for an interesting journey.

travel details

Buses
From Qazrin to Tiberias (hourly 7am–8pm; 1hr 30min); Qiryat Shmona (2 daily; 40min); Haspin (1 daily; 10min).

From Haspin to Tiberias (5 daily; 1hr).
From Jabal al-Sheikh/Banyas to Qiryat Shmona (2 daily; 20min).

CHAPTER EIGHT

THE GAZA STRIP

Wedged between Israel and the Sinai, the **Gaza Strip** is an artificial entity born out of the upheavals which accompanied the creation of the Israeli state. When the armistice lines were drawn between Israeli and Arab forces in 1949, only two areas of historic Palestine remained in Arab hands: the West Bank of the river Jordan and a 140km-square area of refugee-swollen territory around the port

city of Gaza that became known as the Gaza Strip. Originally administered by neighbouring Egypt, Gaza was seized and occupied by Israeli forces in the June war of 1967.

Today Gaza is Israel's Soweto. Massively overcrowded and underserviced, it is a home of sorts to some 650,000 Palestinians, most of them refugees and many still living in the shanty town misery of the Strip's sprawling **refugee camps**. The years of occupation have allowed Israel to reap enormous economic benefits from Gaza – the Strip provides Israeli industry with a plentiful supply of cheap labour and serves as a dumping ground for Israeli produce – but as in the West Bank, Israel refuses to sanction any kind of democratic opening for Gaza's Palestinian inhabitants.

Despite Gaza's extreme overcrowding, Israel has confiscated a third of the Strip's land area and handed much of it over, in contravention of international law, to Israeli **settlers**. By the beginning of 1988, Gaza's Palestinians were reluctant hosts to 2500 Israelis living in nineteen settlements. Some of these, perched crazily on top of sand dunes, resemble a cross between a prison camp and a caravan site, but the more established sites, notably in the **Katif bloc** in the south of the Strip, have all the trappings of middle-class suburbia – and ample helpings of razor wire. The population densities for Israeli settlers and Palestinians per square mile in Gaza are 52 and 7000 respectively.

Land seizures, economic control and an 'iron fist' response to all forms of dissent have turned Gaza into a political powder keg, and an eventual explosion was inevitable. In December 1987, four Gazans were killed in a traffic accident involving an Israeli military vehicle. Intitial protests at their deaths rapidly escalated into mass demonstrations as thousands of Gazans took to the streets to erect barricades and trade stones for bullets with Israeli soldiers. Within a week, the protests had spread to all areas of the Gaza Strip and the West Bank, and were being referred to as the *intifada* – the uprising.

Some history

Gaza's position on the crossroads between Africa and Asia has ensured it a history as troubled as it is long. Since biblical times, it has been fought over, invaded and occupied by nearly all the powers that have marched across the Middle East. Gaza rose to prominence as the chief port of the **Philistines**, and it was during Philistine rule that Samson, the jilted strongman, met his end. Legend has it that Gaza's **Great Mosque** is the site where the hirsute Hebrew pulled down the temple on himself and his Philistine captors.

Alexander the Great captured Gaza in 332BC and sold its 10,000 inhabitants into slavery. Over the next 300 years, Gaza developed into a cosmopolitan centre of Hellenistic civilisation. In 64BC it was captured by the **Romans** and 34 years later the Emperor Augustus handed it over to **Herod the Great**. During the third and fourth centuries AD Gaza was a religious battleground between the majority pagan population, who were reluctant to give up their pagan worship, and devotees of the new Christian cult. Finally in 395AD a Byzantine envoy, **Saint Porphyrus**, obtained a decree closing the temple of the local pagan god Marnas. For a while it seemed that Christianity was tolerated, if not properly established. In 570AD a Christian pilgrim to Gaza,

Antonious Martyr, called it '*A splendid and beautiful city, its men most honest, liberal in every respect and friendly to pilgrims*'.

Gaza fell early on to the **Islamic** conquests of the seventh century; it later suffered badly at the hands of the **Crusaders**, before they were booted out at the end of the twelfth century. In 1516 control of Gaza passed from the **Mamluks** to the **Ottomans**. Turkish rule of the city lasted 400 years, inter-rupted briefly by **Napoleon** in 1799 and by **Mohammed Ali** from 1831–40 during his revolt against the Ottoman Empire. In World War I, Gaza was the scene of a number of major battles and was severely damaged by British bombardment before **General Allenby** captured it from the Turks in 1917.

Under the **British Mandate** in Palestine, Gaza was a quiet backwater of the Southern District. Economically, it depended on its port (through which barley was exported to German breweries) and a handful of small industries. Having no real tradition of political activity, it was also less affected than other parts of Palestine by the tensions arising from the growth of political **Zionism**. After the **UN Partition Plan** sparked off a full-scale war in Palestine, many thousands of Palestinians who had been expelled from their villages along the coastal plain sought refuge in Gaza. Almost overnight, the population of the area trebled, putting enormous pressure on the **Egyptians** who found themselves administering the new Gaza Strip territory after the armistice lines had been drawn. Fearful of the instability so many dispos-sessed Palestinians might cause his fragile regime, Egypt's heavyweight despot King Farouk kept Gaza under tight and repressive control. However, despite Palestinian enthusiasm for the Egyptian Revolution of 1952 which toppled Farouk, there was little initial improvement in Gaza under Egypt's new leader, Gamal Abd al-Nasser. Members of the Muslim Brotherhood, Communists and other potential trouble makers were rounded up and detained in prison camps in the Sinai.

During the **Suez Crisis** of 1956 Gaza and Sinai were occupied by Israel for four months until American pressure forced a withdrawal. The conflict marked a watershed in Egyptian policy towards Gaza. Nasser had been impressed by unconditional Palestinian support for his anti-imperialist stance and began a liberalisation programme for the Strip. Attempts were made to revive the economy, Palestinians were placed in control of essential services and a Palestinian legislative body was created here. He introduced a Palestinian batallion to the Egyptian army and, after the creation of the **PLO** in 1964, its military wing, the **Palestine Liberation Army (PLA)** was stationed in Gaza. Military training was also made compulsory for secondary school students. These measures, together with impassioned promises to liberate Palestine from the 'Zionist entity', made Nasser enormously popular in Gaza – even among the hounded Communists.

Nasser's rhetoric, however, was no match for Israel's military might and Gaza was easily overrun during Israel's rout of the Arab armies in the **Six-Day War** of 1967. For the first years of Israeli rule there was fierce armed resistance by the different factions of the PLO: this was effectively crushed in the early 1970s by a ruthless counter-insurgency campaign which involved the destruction of thousands of homes and mass deportations of political activists.

Anxious to put a veneer of respectability on their occupation, Israel appointed a wealthy Gaza notable and pro-Jordanian 'moderate', Rashad Shawwa, as the mayor of Gaza City in 1970. Heavily criticised for accepting the post, he resigned two years later, only to be reappointed in 1975. He was deposed in the late 1970s for his opposition to the **Camp David Accords** (which Palestinians regard as a sell-out of their rights), and because he was a signatory to a statement supporting the PLO.

Throughout the 1970s and 1980s, the Israelis clamped down on all forms of political expression in Gaza, although in an attempt to reduce the influence of the PLO, they allowed the Muslim Brotherhood limited scope to organise – a policy which they have overturned by the mass arrest of Muslim activists during the *intifada*. On the economic front, land expropriation, heavy taxation and marketing restrictions led to the slow collapse of agriculture and industry in the Strip – and near total dependence on Israel for goods and employment.

In 1985, Israel stepped up repression in the occupied territories after the introduction of its 'iron fist' policy. It was met by a growth in voluntary and women's committees – semi-clandestine political organisations – and frequent demonstrations. Tension rose rapidly during 1987: the year opened with widespread protests, and in the summer a senior Israeli intelligence officer was assassinated. His death was followed by a spate of attacks on Israeli settlers and the killing of a number of Gazans in mysterious circumstances. By autumn, talk was of an impending eruption. When it did come, on **December 8th**, in response to a further four Palestinian deaths, its ferocity and scale took both Palestinians and Israelis by surprise. Initially spontaneous, the *intifada* quickly became organised by street and neighbourhood committees and began to take on new forms – strikes, boycotts and the resignation of government employees.

Gaza today

At the time of writing, the Strip is still in the grip of the *intifada* which, in spite of hundreds of deaths and countless arrests, shows no sign of dying out. Although you can take comfort from the fact that Palestinian hostility is reserved for the guys carrying the guns, there is no denying that the *intifada* has seriously disrupted life in the Strip. An **8pm–4am curfew** is currently enforced, and daytime curfews are imposed as a matter of course after any kind of major disturbance, particularly in the refugee camps. The whole Gaza Strip is frequently sealed off to the outside world for days at a time. In addition, **general strikes** are regularly called by the underground leadership of the *intifada* and are strictly observed, shutting down shops and paralysing transport in and out of the Strip: during such times, it's not possible to visit any part of the region. As in the West Bank, shop opening times are also restricted to three hours a day, from 9am to noon.

Having read all this, you're probably wondering what lure Gaza holds for the traveller. Years of political tension and turmoil have meant that there has never been a serious attempt to cater for outside visitors, or even to take steps to preserve sites and buildings of historic interest. Hence very few tourists ever venture into Gaza: the price of various handicrafts is lower than elsewhere and the beaches at the southern end of the Strip, some of the most beautiful on the entire coastline, are usually deserted. But few travellers make the effort of coming here to simply sightsee: it is as an opportunity to reach an understanding of the Palestinian side of the Middle East conflict that Gaza has most to offer. Gazans are hospitable and approachable, and if you're not the kind of person who shies away from political controversy, then a visit here can be a unique and memorable experience.

Understandably, the soldiers and poverty of Gaza are not the side of the country that the Israeli tourist authorities want you to see, and they'll do everything they can to discourage you from going. Best way to ensure that your visit is as trouble-free as possible is to avoid being here when **tension is running high** – on days of general strikes or political anniversaries, Palestinian or Israeli. Once in Gaza, seek advice if you want to travel outside Gaza City, especially to the refugee camps (see below).

There is a heavy military presence throughout the Strip and it's possible you may be stopped and asked to explain yourself. In this situation, adopt a business-like approach to the soldiers. Rubbing them up the wrong way can land you in trouble, and gushing friendliness will be viewed as suspicious by passers-by. Photographing soldiers (or military installations) could find you without a camera or worse. **Always carry your passport** and if you're visiting or being shown around by Gazans, don't give names or details – it can land your hosts in a lot of trouble*.

If you're unlucky enough to get caught in a **demonstration** (and violence can erupt at any time, especially in the environs of the refugee camps), don't be a voyeur. Feelings on both sides run very high, so move away as quickly as possible and get off the street at the earliest opportunity. Trouble often flares when schoolchildren are on their way to school in the early morning or leaving in the afternoon. The same goes for mosques at the end of midday prayers on Fridays. A good rule of thumb is to watch out for the black smoke of burning tyres and keep well away.

As a foreigner you can expect to attract attention in Gaza, especially from the younger school kids. Although it will be obvious to most people that you're not Israeli, it might be worth establishing this fact fairly early on. And if you do speak some Hebrew, Gaza is **not** the place to practice it. You might find kids greeting you with a Hebrew *shalom*, but as this is usually said with heavy irony, answer it with a forceful Arabic *marhaba*. Apart from this, language should pose you few problems in Gaza. Most young people and many of the older ones speak some English and will be very keen to practice it on you.

Gaza is very conservative and traditional Islamic values are strong – more so than the West Bank for example. Shorts and vests for men and above-the-knee skirts and sleeveless tops for women should not be worn. A scruffy appearance won't get you a very good reception either.

---

*Similarly, when you leave Israel you'll be questioned about where you've visited. To say you've been to Gaza will be a cue for rigorous interrogation, the purpose of which will be to get details of the Palestinians you came into contact with. To divulge such information may have serious repercussions for those concerned.

Getting to the Gaza Strip

The only **bus services** to the Gaza Strip are those ferrying in workers from Tel Aviv and Jaffa. These leave early in the morning and start returning mid-afternoon. The usual method of reaching Gaza is by *service taxi* which, before the *intifada*, used to run from the centres of major Palestinian cities in the West Bank. Your best bet is to go from East Jerusalem or Jaffa. Arab *service* taxis on inter-city trips are seven-seater Mercedes and begin their journey when all the seats are occupied. This can sometimes mean a long wait.

From Jerusalem, the best time to catch a taxi to Gaza is in the early morning or late afternoon. During the middle of the day, be prepared to hang around in the hot sun for more than an hour. You'll also be very lucky to get a taxi after sunset, summer or winter. Taxis leave from the taxi station opposite the Old City's Damascus Gate. Ask any of the drivers where the Gaza taxis are waiting, or just look for the white number plates of Gaza. Journey time is an hour and twenty minutes and costs about $5.

Service taxis **from Jaffa** are mostly used by Gaza workers returning home, and the best time to catch one is after 2pm. In the mornings, you can wait for hours for the car to fill up. Journey time is just over an hour and costs about $3.

A more adventurous way to get to Gaza is to take a bus to **Ashqelon** and get off at the main road junction on the north–south highway. From here you can join the Palestinian workers in trying to flag down a car with white Gazan number plates going south. You'll be expected to pay for the journey and will probably have to put up with clouds of cigarette smoke, but it's a good introduction to Gazans. Don't be surprised if your co-travellers or the driver think you've got into the wrong car by mistake – they're not used to picking up tourists.

A word of warning. It's not advisable to travel to, or in and around Gaza in a car bearing Israeli yellow number plates, or even a hired car with yellow plates framed by green. And don't accept a lift in any kind of military vehicle.

South to Gaza City

Nearly all the traffic entering the Strip from Israel does so from the north. There is a major roadblock and security check on the northern border – **Erez checkpoint** – which can cause frayed tempers and long delays in the after-noon rush hour between 3 and 5pm. It's likely that your car will be stopped by the military, in which case you'll be asked to show your passport and possibly explain why you're visiting Gaza. This used to be straightforward, but since the *intifada*, it's increasingly common for Israeli soldiers to refuse entry to outsiders, whatever their credentials.

The journey south from Erez to Gaza City is of interest only in as much as the transformation from the Israel you've left behind is so sudden and complete. Ordered fields give way to scrubby sand dunes, Beduin tents appear by the side of the road, and an odd assortment of carts and battered cars jostle for position in the rush south.

A few kilometres from the checkpoint there is a left fork – the Gaza bypass and the road to Egypt. Straight on is Gaza City. On the left in the distance, the Palestinian town of **BEIT HANOUN** marks the northeastern edge of the Strip, and if you keep a close lookout on your right you'll catch a glimpse of **Jabaliyya refugee camp** – the country's largest.

About 7km south of Erez, a large sign spanning the road welcomes you to Gaza in English, Arabic and Hebrew. Driving through the northern suburbs, you'll wonder what could possibly be welcoming about Gaza City. The roadside is lined with a series of blackened garages and workshops and behind these a crumbling brown maze of low buildings give some impression of Gaza's overcrowding and poverty.

Gaza City

If you're in a taxi coming from Tel Aviv/Jaffa, odds are you'll be dropped off in the first open area you come to, **Shujaiyya Square**. Jerusalem and West Bank taxis will pass by, swing up the hill by the fortress-like police station, continue for a couple of hundred metres along Wahida Street and come to a stop in **Palestine Square**, the bustling heart of **GAZA CITY**. On the north side of the Square is an upstairs café with an outside balcony – the perfect place for new arrivals to get their bearings, a cool drink, and generally observe the myriad comings and goings of Gaza's main square.

Orientation and transport

In recent years Gaza City has sprawled westwards towards the sea (which is about 3km from Palestine Square) but the historically interesting part of the city is remarkably compact and extends no further than a five-minute walk from the Square.

By far the most important street is **Omar al-Muhktar** (named after the Libyan revolutionary) which runs east to west from Shujaiyya down to the sea. You'll find most things you want along here: shops, banks, moneychangers and Gaza's cheapest hotel. The city's **central post office**, from where you can telephone, is on the corner of Wahida Street and Shujaiyya Square. Apart from Omar al-Muhktar and a handful of other roads, most streets in Gaza, especially in the older quarters, are unpaved and largely unnamed. Nowadays, though, you'll see Arabic painted onto the walls at the ends of street naming them after one or other local martyr killed during the *intifada*.

There is no reliable **bus service** in Gaza City, but economic stagnation and under-employment have produced a city of **taxi** drivers. Just about every car on the road is working as a *service* taxi which makes for cheap and frequent transport. All you have to do is stand by the side of the road in the direction you want to go and stick out your arm. Something is bound to stop within a couple of minutes. Tell the driver your destination and if he's going that way jump in. There's a fixed rate of $1 for anywhere in town which you should pay as soon as you get in. When you want to get out, tell the driver *aindak* or *min fadlak*.

From Palestine Square you can get cars easily to the sea (*al-baher*) or UNRWA's offices (*al-wikala*; see below). To get back to Palestine Square or Shujaiyya, ask for *al-balad*. If you want a taxi all to yourself, ask for a *special* and negotiate the price before you get in. You shouldn't pay more than $1.50 to anywhere in the city.

Taxis for the coastal road as far as Tel Aviv go from Shujaiyya. For everywhere else – Jerusalem, Beersheva, West Bank, Egypt and most places in the Strip – taxis start from Palestine Square.

Finding a room . . . and something to eat

There are only three **hotels** in Gaza, none of which is in the centre of town, and in two of which you'll quite probably find yourself the only guest. For the budget traveller, *al-Waleed* is the best bet. It's on Omar al-Muhktar Street, ten to fifteen minutes' walk from Palestine Square in the direction of the sea: expect to pay about $8 for dormitory accommodation. This has been open only erratically of late, so don't rely on it. More upmarket is the *Cliff Hotel* on the sea-front. Supposedly $35 a double in high season, $25 low, the management are so desperate for custom that they'll be open to some discreet haggling. To get to the *Cliff*, take a taxi to the seafront; from there, it's a left turn and a two-minute walk. Gaza's only other hotel is the *Marna House* (doubles around $30; ask in town for directions), hang-out of journalists, aid workers and Red Cross personnel. Even if you're not staying there, it's a good place to meet people and talk.

A hundred metres down the coast from the *Cliff Hotel* is Gaza's *UN Beach Club*. In theory, this complex of guest rooms, bar, lounge and games room is the exclusive reserve of UN officials and ex-pats, but you may be able to get a cheap room there if you plead desperation or can come up with a good story. Given the current political situation, the club's manager should be reasonably sympathetic. Bearing that same situation in mind, it would be madness to try and **camp or sleep rough** anywhere in the Strip.

Best place to start looking for **food** in town is west of Palestine Square, on and around Omar al-Muhktar, where small restaurants sell kebabs and chicken often grilled on pavement barbecues – as there are no menus, you'll have to point at what you want or ask what's going. Other inexpensive cafés serve *humus*, *ful* and *falafel*. Down by the **beach** you'll find the upmarket restaurants which specialise, sometimes exclusively, in fish. The best are the **Gaza Fish Restaurant** and **al-Fardous**, both on the coastal road a short walk south from Omar al-Muhktar. These are expensive by Gazan standards (about $10 for a two-course meal), but as with all restaurants in Gaza you'll have to establish beforehand how much the meal is going to cost. Some years ago the Muslim Brotherhood firebombed restaurants selling **alcohol** in Gaza and it's now almost impossible to get hold of. You might strike it lucky with beer at the beach restaurants but asking for booze anywhere else, apart from the *UN Beach Club*, will probably offend.

Since the *intifada*, Gaza's restaurants, and to a lesser extent the cafés, have been closed for days at a time. During Ramadan, food sellers are closed until after sunset.

About town

Sadly for such an ancient city, there are few historical sites in Gaza worth searching out. Rather it's the kind of place you should wander around at your leisure. Explore a few sidestreets and soak up the sights and smells of its vibrant street life: there's no danger here of the stuffed camels and souvenir sellers that have distorted much of the character of Jerusalem and Bethlehem.

A good place to start your wanderings is the **vegetable and spice market**. This is a small road, lined with stalls and usually crowded, running east from Palestine square, parallel to Omar al-Muhktar. At the end of the street is the **Great Mosque** or **Mosque of Omar**. Reputedly occupying the site of first the ancient temple of Marnas and then a Greek church, the mosque is actually a conversion of a Norman church built by the **Crusaders** in the twelfth century, and its round window and and solid square walls don't look typically Islamic. Much of the mosque was destroyed during a British bombardment during World War I and rebuilt in 1925. The interior is unremarkable but provides a wonderfully cool retreat from the midsummer heat. Look out for the marble pillars engraved with a Jewish *menora* (candelabra): this once excited speculation that the pillars were looted from a synagogue in Tiberias. Entrance to the mosque is at the end of the spice market: it can be visited daily except on Fridays and during daily prayers.

Turning left out of the mosque, you come to a small covered street on the left. This is Gaza's **gold market**, where merchants do a brisk trade from tiny booths hollowed out of the massive walls. Many of the customers are mothers of prospective bridegrooms, shopping for the obligatory rings and necklaces for their future daughters-in-law.

The gold market opens out onto Gaza's principle **money market**. Any one of the men clutching a thick wad of notes will happily exchange cash or travellers' cheques into whatever currency you want – and at a better rate than the bank. Walk left from here and on the other side of Wahida Street is an imposing stone building, known as **Napoleon's Fort** since the great man spent a couple of nights here on his way through town. It's now a girls' school, but try banging on the gates on a Saturday or during the summer months and the caretaker might show you around.

Definitely worth a visit is the fourth-century Greek Orthodox **Church of Saint Porphyrus**. From Palestine Square head east along Omar al-Muhktar Street until you reach the old **municipality building** on the left. Opposite, a street leads off into the **Zeitoun Quarter**. Take this and at the first junction bear left. An open gate and modern stonework signals the entrance to a complex which contains a courtyard, school, the priest's house and the church itself (ask for directions if you find yourself lost). The church is charmingly small and quaint but only the lower walls are original, the upper walls and roof having been added later. Like Gaza's other older buildings, the entrance is below ground level and the interior is as dark and ornate as any Orthodox church. If it's locked, the keys can be obtained from the priest's house opposite; he speaks reasonable English and is usually happy to show people round. It would be a shame to leave the Zeitoun, Gaza's oldest quarter, without a meander around its maze of tiny streets: home to many of Gaza's small Christian community, it contains some fine old homes in various states of noble decay, many with impressive carved wooden doorways.

Westwards towards the sea, Omar al-Muhktar has little of interest. Just past the square on your right are a number of workshops which sell cane furniture and on the right is Gaza's largest market, **Souq al-Fras**. There's not much to detain you here unless you're on the lookout for cheap vegetables or want a snap of Israeli settlers going shopping with their machine guns. Halfway towards the sea, you pass the massive brown walls of Gaza's **central prison**, jokingly referred to as Gaza's first university. A little further on, the road reaches **Midan Jundi** (Soldier Square), an oblong of sandy grass which not only boasts a reasonable souvenir shop but also the well-guarded residence of Gaza's military governor. The square gets its name from what used to be a statue of a Palestinian *feda'i* (freedom fighter) pointing north towards his lost homeland. The Israelis pulled it down in 1967 and now only the white base with its defaced Palestinian flag remains. Just down from the square on the right is a futuristic concrete fortress, Gaza's so-called **cultural centre**, built at enormous cost by the deposed mayor Rashad Shawwa. Its purpose is a mystery to everyone and years after completion, it has still not been opened.

Omar al-Mukhtar comes to an abrupt end just before the sea. The **beach** itself is not particularly attractive at Gaza (the best beaches are further south) but it's a fun place to be in the early morning when the fishermen come in with the night's catch. Some words of warning about the beaches. Firstly, all along the coast the beach is under a strict **dusk-to-dawn curfew**, so don't get tempted by that post-sunset stroll – odds are you'll be shot for it. Secondly, swimming for **women** anywhere in Gaza is not recommended unless you want to be an object of mass male curiosity. Finally, there are no **lifeguards** in Gaza. Each year the sea off Gaza claims a number of victims, and even strong swimmers may have difficulties with what can be a vicious undertow.

The Refugee Camps

It's arguable whether anyone could have devised a more ideal breeding ground for militancy and revolt than the vast **REFUGEE CAMPS** of the Gaza Strip. Established in the aftermath of the 1948 war by the Quakers and UNRWA (United Nations Relief and Works Agency – the organisation mandated by the UN to deal with the Palestinian refugee crisis), an estimated 350,000 Palestinians still live in Gaza's camps – reminders of an injustice which has yet to be righted.

The eight camps dot the length of the Strip and have developed into medium-size towns with their own schools, clinics and markets. In each, conditions remain appalling: spectacular overcrowding, sewage running freely through the streets and a high incidence of disease are the norm. Camp residents have also suffered the worst of Israeli repression, particularly during the clampdown of the 1970s and during the current *intifada*.

The Israelis are determined to get rid of the camps because they're both a political embarassment and a security headache. To persuade refugees to move into the resettlement projects which they've established next to the camps, the Israeli authorities refuse camp residents the right to improve or extend their homes. As most refugees have a fierce loyalty to these symbols of their cause, families will normally only leave the camps when conditions become unbearable. Once they've left, the refugees must sign an undertaking to destroy their homes.

Although a refugee camp isn't an obvious holiday destination, a visit to Gaza and an understanding of the Palestinian question would be incomplete without first-hand knowledge of life inside a camp. The most straightforward way to visit the camps is through **UNRWA**, who have a large office complex on Talatini Street (opposite the **Islamic University**) in Gaza City. It's best to arrange this by calling or visiting Maher Nasr, one of UNRWA's public relations officers (☎051-861195/98), at least a couple of days before you want to go, preferably longer. There is no charge for the trip but you should be prepared to make a **donation** to an organisation that is having to cut back on services because of budget deficits, and be sensitive to the tremendous pressure under which UNRWA are working. UNRWA tours concentrate on visits to their own institutions in the camps – kindergartens, clinics and the feeding centres where the poorest refugees receive monthly rations.

Visiting the camps with UNRWA should give you protection from any unpleasant encounters with the soldiers who patrol the camps (or the hordes of little kids who think all non-Palestinian outsiders are connected to the Israeli military and therefore a legitimate target for low intensity harassment), but it's no substitute for a tour with a Palestinian resident – if you get an offer don't hesitate to accept.

The nearest camps to Gaza City are **Beach (Shaati)** and **Jabaliyya**. Beach camp (population 38,000) is enclosed on two sides by Gaza City and is easy to reach, either by taxi from Palestine Square or by walking north along the coastal road. If you feel like jumping in at the deep end, visit Jabaliyya. Just north of Gaza City, this is the largest (population 60,000) and most militant of all the camps, with an Israeli military base at its heart. Taxis to Jabaliyya go from the top of Wahida Street, parallel to Palestine Square, and run to two different parts of the camp: **Faluja** and **al-Merkaz** (the Centre) – ask for al-Merkaz. The journey from Gaza takes about fifteen minutes and costs $0.40.

South from Gaza: Khan Yunnis

The road south from Gaza is reasonably good; unless you have an invite, there seems no reason to visit any of the middle camps which are situated just off the main road about 8–10km south of Gaza. Scenically, the road is dull – fields and orange groves line it for much of the way – but there's a quite perceptible change from the Mediterranean vegetation around Gaza City to the near desert scrub south of Khan Yunnis. And of course with deserts you also get camels and date palms – not exactly in abundance, but they're around.

Service taxis to the southern towns of **Khan Yunnis** ($0.75) and **Rafah** ($1), to the middle refugee camps of **Bureij** and **Nusseirat** ($0.40) and to **Deir al-Balah** and **Mughazi** ($0.50), all go from the taxi station in Palestine Square opposite **al-Ahli Hospital**. They are regular and frequent during daylight hours. The trip to Rafah on the **Egyptian border** takes about 35 minutes.

KHAN YUNNIS, the second city of the Strip, is 25km south of Gaza and about 4km from the sea. A market town for the agricultural produce of the surrounding villages, it is hemmed in on the west by a large refugee camp and some magnificent sand dunes.

The town itself can make no claims to magnificence. Architecturally, it has little to offer: its warren of narrow streets and the crumbling facades of nondescript buildings give it the look and feel of a poor Cairene suburb. For many years a stronghold of the Muslim Brotherhood, Khan Yunnis is so conservative that it makes Gaza seem positively cosmopolitan. Only rarely do you see women here who are not completely shrouded in black; there is no hotel in the town and only a handful of cafés around the town centre where you can sit down to eat.

However, Khan Yunnis is not without a saving grace or two. The **town square** (the drop-off point for taxis) is bordered by an impressive **khan** or fortress built in the thirteenth century by an obscure Mamluk official called Yunnis (hence the town's name), as a garrison for soldiers guarding pilgrims on their way to Jerusalem and Mecca. There's no tourist guide or literature, so take a look at your leisure. Inevitably someone will be at hand to show you round and practice their English. If you arrive here on a Wednesday morning, spend a couple of hours strolling about, or maybe just sitting and watching the **weekly market** on the left hand side of the *khan*: lots of colour and smells, and everything from fish to camels to be bargained for.

One thing not to be missed at Khan Yunnis is the **beach**. From the west side of the central square, walk a few metres north and you come to a left turning. This is **Sharia al-Baher** (Sea Street), which leads down to the sea; you can take a taxi from here or, better still, walk. It will take an hour or so at a leisurely pace, but there's a lot to see on the way. The road wanders up through the town for a few hundred metres, cuts through the camp which almost spills over onto the road, and then climbs the crest of a dune. From the top there's a wonderful view over the dunes and palms to the sea, unfortunately spoiled by the razor wire, radar balloons and gun turrets of the new Israeli **settlement** of **Neve Deqalim**, one of the largest in the Strip. You could try and get into the settlement to see what the settlers have say for themselves, but be warned that they tend to be surly and unwelcoming. Bear in mind also that being seen coming out of the place is not going to endear you to the local Palestinian population.

On the beach are a series of abandoned beach houses and a larger building which serves as a basic **café** and **restaurant** during the summer months. Apart from a few fisherman, the beach here is largely deserted on weekdays throughout the year. If you walk northward for a couple of kilometres, you'll come to the new Israeli complex of **Katif Beach** hotel and holiday village. This is threatened to be the beginning of an attempt by Israel's settlers and their right-wing backers in the Knesset to transform the southern section of the Gaza coast into the new 'Israeli Riviera'. *Gush Emunim*, the military settler movement, refers to this part of the coast as the 'Hawaii of Israel'. Bizarre as all this may sound, it has its own political logic: large-scale tourist development is seen as creating a stumbling block to Palestinian aspirations for self-determination in Gaza. If you do fancy a night in the *Katif Hotel*, be prepared to fork out $91, full-board.

Head south from Khan Yunis along a very attractive stretch of beach and you'll eventually reach Rafah.

Rafah

RAFAH, the border town with Egypt, can be reached easily from Gaza or Khan Yunnis. When you take a taxi, however, be careful to specify whether you want the **town** (Rafah *balad*) or the **border crossing** (*Musr*, ie Egypt) – the two are a few kilometres apart.

Rafah has nestled against the Egypt-Palestine border since the boundaries were drawn in 1906. A sleepy dust bowl of a place, its wide main street and ramshackle single-storey buildings could well double as the lot for a B-movie western. There are no hotels in Rafah and only a few kebab and *humus* stalls. What makes this archetypal one-horse town worthy of a visit is its **beach** and, more importantly, its border.

When Israel gave the Sinai back to Egypt as part of the Camp David peace treaty, they decided to draw the new border through the middle of Rafah – leaving a sizeable chunk of **Rafah refugee camp** in Egypt, dividing families and cutting houses in two. Despite international protestations and Israeli promises to reincorporate the thousands of Palestinians effectively deported to Egypt, words have yet to be matched by action. Every morning little dramas are acted out along the barbed wire border between the two halves of Rafah as messages are shouted across the gulf to family and friends on the other side.

Taxis to Rafah will drop you off at a junction in the middle of town. A few minutes' walk ahead of you is the border, while to the right is the road to the sea. You'll have no difficulty getting a taxi to the beach from here or, if you're feeling energetic, you could try and walk the 3–4km. The road passes by Rafah's huge refugee camp, a resettlement project for refugees sponsored by the Israelis, and a small Israeli settlement perched on a sand dune. As at Khan Yunnis, the beach at Rafah has an exotic backdrop of dunes and date palms and will not disappoint.

Once you've pottered around the beach, take a walk south to the **Swedish village** which nudges right up against the border. Constructed for refugee fishermen by the Swedish government in the 1950s, this tiny village still lacks piped water and electricity, but its inhabitants are very hospitable and it's a good place to while away the time over a chat and cups of mint tea.

CHAPTER NINE

NEGEV, THE SOUTH AND EILAT

T he **Negev desert** sprawls over the southern part of Israel from Beersheva to Eilat. This great arid triangle covers almost 10,000 square kilometres, over half the area of the state of Israel, but contains less than ten per cent of its population. To the east, the land falls sharply to the **Afro-Syrian Rift Valley**, one of the longest gashes in the rock crust of the earth, running all the way from Turkey, Syria and Israel through the Gulf of Aqaba to the Zambesi River in southern Africa. In the west, the Negev merges into the desert mountains of the Egyptian Sinai Peninsula.

While deserts generally conjure up images of endless rolling white sand-dunes and palm trees, the Negev is rugged and mountainous, with some of the most stunning landscapes in the country. The **northern Negev** is mostly composed of sandstone ridges criss-crossed with *wadis*. These are dry for most of the year, but can gush with occasional winter flash floods, explaining the seemingly incongruous roadside warnings to the unsuspecting traveller. The central Negev highlands – long, high ridges of sandstone, limestone, dolomite and granite running towards the southwest – offer the most dramatic scenery and are divided into two by the **Valley of Zin**. Here the landscape is broken by three giant craters, the largest and most spectacular of them being **Makhtesh Ramon**, on whose edge stands Mount Ramon, the highest point in the Negev. The southern Negev begins with the **Paran Plateau**, with imposing rock pillars on either side of its dry river bed. And at the southern tip, the **Eilat Mountains**, cut by gorges and bizarre geological formations, offer a fantastic variety of colours and shapes.

Traditionally, the inhabitants of the Negev have been the **Beduin**, but their semi-nomadic lifestyle has been all but destroyed by Israeli plans to develop the desert. They still constitute the majority of the population, but are on the whole confined to arid 'reserves' or soulless modern development towns. Despite the extravagant claims you may hear, Israeli development in the Negev remains confined to the scattered oases of kibbutzim and moshavim – around 150 of them in all – and most of these survive only with the aid of massive state subsidies. The most celebrated is the kibbutz of **Sde Boker**, home and burial place of the Israeli statesman David Ben Gurion.

There are two basic routes **through the Negev**. You can come down the shore of the **Dead Sea** – perhaps stopping on the way to bob about on the

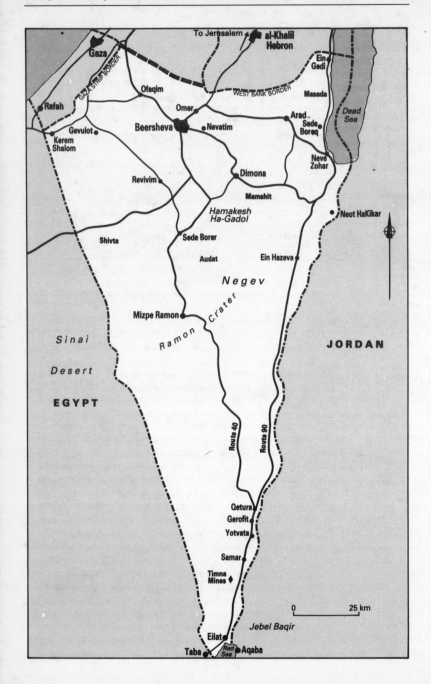

salty water's surface, to see the site of the discovery of the **Dead Sea Scrolls** at **Qumran**, to enjoy the fresh springs and natural beauty of **Ein Gedi**, or to see Herod's extraordinary castle at **Masada**, scene of Jewish martyrdom in the revolt against the Romans – and follow the Arava Valley, along the line of the Afro-Syrian Rift, all the way to Eilat. Or you can travel through the heart of the desert via **Beersheva**, the regional capital. Your reward in the south is **Eilat**, Israel's only outlet to the Red Sea and her most hedonistic resort, with year-round sun, great beaches, and some of the world's best diving on the Red Sea Reef. From here, if the desert still exercises a fascination, you can travel easily into the even vaster wilderness of the Egyptian **Sinai**.

THE DEAD SEA

The sudden appearance of the Dead Sea excites the astonishment as much as the admiration of the traveller who sees it for the first time; for this mass of water, limpid as crystal, with its azure mirror all sparkling under the rays of the sun, contrasts less with the frightful desert which surrounds it than the reputation which has been given to it in bygone days.

Father Barnabas Meistermann, *Guide to the Holy Land, 1923.*

The **Dead Sea** is indeed a pretty awesome sight. Four hundred metres below sea level, it seems to be trapped under an almost permanent blanket of eerie, airless, motionless heat. It is a place of superlatives: the lowest point on earth, the most saline body of water on earth, richer in oxygen than any place on earth, one of the hottest places on earth and certainly, one of the deadest. Individual reactions tend to be extreme too – you either love the place, or hate it. The name is said to have been coined by Christian pilgrims travelling in the area early in this century. Its other titles – *Yam HaMelach* (the Salt Sea) in Hebrew and *Bahr Lut* (the Sea of Lot) in Arabic – are equally appropriate: the former for obvious reasons, the latter because the sea was the setting for the destruction of Sodom and Gommorah, where Lot's wife was turned into a pillar of salt. The sites of these cities are now believed to be submerged in the shallow waters of the sea's southern end.

The Dead Sea is really more of a vast, enclosed lake than an open sea, its only inlet being at the northern end through the Jordan River. On the western shore stark and impressive rose-coloured cliffs contrast with dazzling white salt-flats, while across the water the mountains of Moab and Edom shade through an extraordinary range of purples and pinks as the sun crosses the sky. With no exit from the southern end, the only escape for the water is for it to evaporate, which it does at an incredible rate, leaving behind weird-shaped salt deposits on the surface, and in summer frequently bathing the whole area in an uncomfortable, sticky haze. The water that remains is so dense – twenty-five per cent of it is solids – that it is practically impossible to swim in; you simply can't get your feet beneath the water to kick. Instead you can bob about on your back, reading a newspaper at the same time if you want to pose for the inevitable photo, and then see the layers of salt crystallise on your skin as the water dries off in the heat. If the water gets into any cuts or grazes, or if it gets in your eyes, it will sting like hell – so watch out.

Over the years, the level of the Dead Sea has been gradually decreasing. It has dropped by seven metres so far this century. This is partly due to climatic changes, but the process has been accelerated by the increasing exploitation of the Jordan River. Already the sea is at times cut in half by the Lisan Peninsula, which juts out from Jordan (the southern half was always extremely shallow), and if the waters continue to recede at the present rate it is feared that it could disappear altogether in a few decades. One scheme proposed to solve this problem is to bring water by pipe and canal from the Mediterranean, at the same time using it to generate hydro-electricity and as a coolant in future nuclear power stations.

Although the sea is too saline to support any form of life, it is a vast reservoir of chemicals: potash, for example, is removed and used as a fertiliser. This commercial exploitation has been going on since the fourth century AD when Nabatean merchants sold bitumen to the Egyptians who used it for embalming. The spas and health resorts which dot the shoreline today use the waters to cure a variety of ills – skin diseases and arthritis are a speciality – while the beaches, hotels and hostels provide relaxation and entertainment for thousands of tourists every year.

A few kibbutzim and beach resorts apart, the Dead Sea's banks are very sparsely populated: if you come for any length of time you'd do well to bring some supplies with you to avoid being at the mercy of the one shop and the few restaurants, none of them cheap. The three main **beaches** on the Dead Sea come fully equipped with free shower facilities where you can wash off the slimy water before it turns to salt. Warm and pleasant during the winter when it is favoured by frozen Jerusalemites, the area becomes a steam bath during the summer, with temperatures regularly exceeding 40°C exacerbated by exceptional humidity – you'll need to bring water, sunglasses and a hat for protection.

Just one road runs through the area, sticking closely to the western shore all the way down: it starts in the West Bank at a junction not far from Jericho and runs from the northern tip to the southern extremity with only one minor road turning off, at Masada. **Buses** run frequently along this road, to and from Jerusalem, and you should never have to wait more than an hour for the next to pass. In the heat of summer, this can seem an extremely long time. If you do get stuck, hitching is generally easy, perhaps because drivers appreciate the difficulties involved in travelling around here. If you are driving, ensure that you fill up with petrol before setting out, as there are few petrol stations in the region.

Qumran and the Dead Sea Scrolls

Starting at the northern end of the sea, the first site of historical interest is **QUMRAN** (Sun–Thur 8am–5pm; admission $1.50) where the famous **Dead Sea Scrolls** were found. The story of the discovery has a mythical quality of its own. In 1947, a young Beduin shepherd from the Ta'amira tribe was looking for lost goats near the site of the **Monastery of the Essenes**, where a Jewish sect of the Second Temple period had built their community. At the

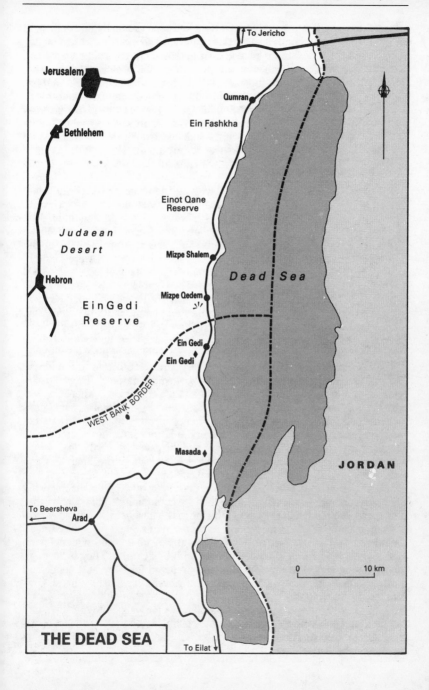

entrance to an ancient cave, he heard the stones he was throwing inside land on what sounded like pottery. On investigating, he found fifty cylindrical jars containing scrolls which are now known to date from the first century BC. The shepherd took a number of scrolls to the Sheikh of Bethlehem who, thinking they were Syriac writings, took them to a Syriac scholar. From there they passed to the Assyrian Archbishop in Jerusalem and then to an Armenian dealer in Bethlehem. Bethlehem at that time was under Arab control, but an archaeology professor at the Hebrew University, Eliezar Sukenik, was interested in the scrolls and decided it was worth crossing armistice lines, against military advice, to buy them. The scrolls are now housed in the **Israel Museum's Shrine of the Book** and at the **Rockefeller Museum** in Jerusalem.

The Dead Sea Scrolls themselves were written mainly on cleaned and treated animal hides, although fragments of papyrus and thin copper plate were also found. The ink used was a mixture of carbon and gum. The finished scrolls were then wrapped in linen and placed in clay jars of the distinctive Greco-Roman style of the period. The arid atmosphere of the desert contributed to their excellent preservation. Documents were found in eleven caves in all, one of which, in the south of the site, yielded some 40,000 fragments of biblical text. These included a complete seven-metre scroll consisting of 66 chapters of ancient scriptures agreeing with Greek, Latin and present day texts. Fragments of Leviticus dated to around 100BC predate all other existing Hebrew manuscripts by 1000 years. Except for the Book of Esther, there were parts of all the Old Testament books, as well as several Apocrypha works and documents relating to the daily life of the Essenes.

The **archaeological site of Qumran** lies barely 100m from the highway and consists, in the main, of the aforementioned 'monastery'. There are the remains of a tower, kitchens, dining hall and a 'scriptorium', where supposedly the scrolls were written. You can also see various cisterns, aqueducts and channels, evidence both of the importance of water in the desert, and of the role ritual bathing played in the life of the Essenes. At the far side of the site you can look out to the start of gorge and the caves where the first scrolls were found. The **Essenes** were a Jewish sect – rivals to the Pharisees and Sadducees – who first emerged around 150BC. This was their religious centre from then until 68AD, when it was destroyed by the Romans following the Jewish Revolt: it was at this time that the community's library and other treasures were hidden in the caves. The life of the Essenes did indeed resemble a monastic one. Their movement was a reaction against what they saw as the wealth and corruption of the Temple at Jerusalem, and aimed for an extremely simple life in strict accordance with biblical law. They believed in the imminent arrival of the Messiah, and prepared for it by abstinence and purity – in diet and lifestyle. This must, at any event, have been a harsh environment in which to live.

From the site there are numerous possibilities for walks into the surrounding Judaean Hills, with well marked routes taking you into the still and somewhat surreal desert. There's a small shop and cafeteria here, and any bus on the highway will stop if you signal it.

Oases: Ein Fashka and Ein Gedi

EIN FASHKA (or Einot Zuqim), the first and perhaps the best of the Dead Sea beaches, lies just 3km south of Qumran, a pleasant walk if you're not too heavily laden. A freshwater spring, whose waters tumble down from the hills, provides a refreshing alternative to the heavy waters of the Dead Sea and brings life to the barren surroundings, creating pools of lush vegetation. It also attracts wildlife – ibex and hyrax – and if not as spectacularly verdant as Ein Gedi (below), it's usually a great deal less crowded. Entrance is around $1, and well worth it. A cafeteria sells the usual snacks and drinks at reasonable prices.

As the road meanders on south, you'll pass more of these sudden bursts of life amid otherwise total desolation, each a sure sign of the existence of a spring. At regular intervals, too, you'll see signs indicating apparently non-existent bridges (curiously named 'Irish bridges') which mark the location of floodwater channels. During the winter, flash floods can pour down the Judaean Hills from Jerusalem and the surrounding area, instantly transforming the landscape, washing away everything in their path, and occasionally closing the road.

Twenty-five kilometres or so from Ein Fashka you leave the West Bank and enter territory which has been Israeli since 1948; a little further, roughly halfway down the sea, is the EIN GEDI Nature Reserve. With Masada this is the Dead Sea's most popular attraction, it's exciting enough to make it worth braving the occasional crowds. The spring here (Ein Gedi means Goats' Spring) has attracted people since the late Stone Age and was well known in biblical times. Here David hid in a cave when Saul was seeking to kill him, and here Saul acknowledged David as his successor (*I Samuel:24*). Various excavations scattered through the reserve recall this history, but it is the natural attractions which make Ein Gedi exceptional.

Turning down a seemingly insignificant track, you find yourself suddenly in a narrow *wadi* surrounded by lush vegetation. A series of well planned walking routes shows the difference a little water can make to the desert. A wide variety of vegetation grows all around, from sumptuous water plants to desert plants adapted to thrive in the harshest conditions. Dozens of hyraxes, small grey animals which look rather like badgers but have strange, hoof-like toes, appear to stand to attention at the mouth of the *wadi*, and there are herds of ibex too. Less likely to be seen are the leopards which signs warn you about at regular intervals: there are reputed to be thirteen of them prowling around in the undergrowth, and if you do meet one it would make sense to take heed of the notice telling you not to provoke it. A memorable one-and-a-half-hour walk leads along the course of Nahal David (David's Stream) to **David's Waterfall** whose waters crash over the rocks into a clear, cool pool where you can get some serious bathing done. Beyond here the trails get harder, climbing to other springs and caves, to a Bronze Age temple, and to **Tel Goren** and the remains of the biblical settlement, where a fourth-century synagogue has been excavated. Walking in the reserve, it is advisable to stick to the paths since some independent-minded ramblers have been known to almost get themselves killed clambering down slippery scree slopes. Further information, and maps, can be found at the Field School, near the entrance to the reserve.

If the area takes your fancy, **Ein Gedi Youth Hostel** (Beit Sarah), near the entrance to the reserve, is one of the best in the country. It offers dormitory and family accommodation, excellent cooked meals and a pleasant setting (members $7.30, non-members $8; check in 5–7pm, arrive early to be sure of a bed). One kilometre further along the main road, **Ein Gedi Beach** offers showers, a shop selling basics and a rather pricey self-service restaurant. There are also two shadeless **campsites** here, one has cabins and caravans to rent if you don't have a tent. The beach itself, stony and somewhat dirty, is particularly popular with West Bank Palestinians, especially on Fridays and holidays when barbecues blaze into action all over it. If you need luxury, and air-conditioning, there's a very expensive guest house at **Kibbutz Ein Gedi** nearby.

Masada

Eighteen kilometres beyond Ein Gedi, a minor road turns off to the left, to the ancient fortress city of **MASADA**. Perched high on the cliffs, Masada is one of the most spectacular sights in the country and the scene of one of its most dramatic episodes. Originally built by Alexander Jannaeus in the first century BC, it was reinforced by **Herod the Great** in 43BC and further improved throughout his reign. For Herod, never the most secure of rulers, it was above all a place of refuge, where he could sit out times of trouble behind impregnable defences. He built an elaborate system of dykes and channels which directed the rainfall, sparse in an area where rain sometimes does not fall for years, into twelve reservoirs hewn out of the mountainside. Enough water was thus caught as it cascaded down the hills from the west to make inhabitation of the fortress viable. These reservoirs, which you can still see, have a combined capacity of 40,000 cubic metres and once provided enough water for public and private baths to ensure the continuation of a lifestyle to which Herod and his fellow Romans were accustomed. More importantly, they would have allowed the defenders to withstand a siege for years if necessary.

The site is primarily known, however, for its role in the annals of Jewish history. In 70AD, when the **Jewish Revolt** against the Romans had all but failed, Jerusalem had been sacked and the Second Temple destroyed, this remote mountain top became the last pocket of Jewish resistance. It was occupied by a group of Zealots, just under a thousand strong, who had fled to Masada and were determined to fight to the death. For three years they held out but eventually, with the siege unrelenting, the enemy laboriously scaling the steep cliff and capture imminent, they preferred death to slavery and committed mass suicide. Or rather, they killed each other. First every man executed his wife and family with a sword. Then ten men were selected to put the other men to death. Finally, lots were drawn to determine the one who would complete the ritual slaughter, and then the survivor fell on his own sword. Just two women and five children, who had hidden themselves in a water channel, lived to tell the tale to the Romans, who broke through the following morning to find 960 bodies. This hopeless heroism is a potent symbol in modern Israel: today, every Israeli schoolchild and army recruit is taken up to Masada to absorb the lesson, the recruits taking an oath of allegiance that 'Masada must not fall again'.

The exposed remains at the site are magnificent in their rocky isolation. If you approach from the Dead Sea side, either by the appropriately named serpentine path or on the cable car, you'll enter through the east gate, having already passed some of the massive reservoirs on the way up. To your right are large storehouses, and beyond them, at the northern tip of the hill, Herod's fabulous palace. This exceptional construction clings to the cliff edge on three levels: at the top are the main living quarters with well preserved baths and a semi-circular terrace looking down over the lower levels; the central section, thought to have been Herod's summer residence, is enclosed by twin circular walls; at the bottom was a cloister-like open courtyard. From here, and indeed from vantage points all around the summit, the Roman wall surrounding the mountain, and some of the eight Roman army camps from which the siege was managed, are clearly visible. Heading back across the site from the palace, a synagogue built by the Zealots can be seen against the western wall, and there are a couple of ritual baths nearby. Further west, in the middle of the site, are Byzantine buildings and a church built when Masada was briefly occupied by a group of monks in the fifth century. Beyond these you come to the west palace and west gate (through which you'll enter if you come from Arad and up the Roman ramp). Here there are some fine Roman mosaics, and Zealot living quarters.

These are the highlights, but the whole mountain-top is liberally scattered with other remains of defences, baths and houses, all of them well labelled. A comprehensive and inexpensive booklet is available at the site, describing them in detail. As you wander, note that the painted black line that adorns most buildings divides the excavated walls from sections that have been reconstructed.

Masada is open daily from 4.30am to 4pm, and is linked directly by bus with Eilat, Jerusalem and Beersheva. There's a youth hostel at the bottom which is not recommended but, since it's the only accommodation for miles is often full (☎057-84349; check-in 5–7pm). If it is full they may allow you to camp outside and use their showers and restaurant; the other cafés and restaurants nearby are expensive. People used to sleep at the top to enjoy the magnificent sunset, but this seems strictly prohibited nowadays. The alternative is to stay at the hostel, get up extremely early and walk up to the site (just under an hour) in time for sunrise. This is a great experience, with the added advantage of letting you see the site while it's still relatively cool and uncrowded. When it gets hot, you can come down on the cable car, which runs approximately every fifteen minutes (Sun–Thur 8am–4pm, Fri 8am–2pm; admission and return cable car trip $6). Approaching from the west, a tarmac road leads to a Roman camp, where there's a ramp giving access to the summit.

South of Masada

South of the Masada junction the road passes the **Lashon (Tongue) Peninsula** where, in theory, it is possible to cross into Jordan on foot. Political reality, however, dictates otherwise, and it would be extremely foolhardy to try. The chief resort in the southern sector – indeed the biggest anywhere on the Dead Sea – is **EIN BOQEQ**, with an excellent beach and an army of three-, four- and five-star hotels. These are mostly full of package holidaymakers and charge the earth to casual visitors, but it's not a bad place to stop for a quick swim, with showers on the beach and plenty of bars and restaurants (even nightclubs in the hotels) which are open to non-residents.

Just 3km further the **Hamei Zohar Hot Springs** are the biggest and best-known of several mineral springs which have been used therapeutically since antiquity. Today the conditions treated here are mostly dermatological, though rheumatism and arthritis sufferers are also said to benefit from immersion in the sulphurous baths of the health spa followed by a dip in the Dead Sea. The smell of the sulphur can at times be overwhelming, ruining enjoyment of the excellent vegetarian restaurant next door. There are more springs, a campsite and a free beach at the otherwise unattractive **NEVE ZOHAR**.

Beyond Neve Zohar you rapidly leave the sea behind, travelling past **Mount Sodom** and the modern town which bears its name (where visitors are shown a pillar of salt said to be Lot's wife) and the vast mineral-extracting operations of the **Dead Sea Works**. From here on the road continues southwards to Eilat through the **Arava Valley**, gradually clawing its way back to sea level with the mountains of the Negev to the right and Edom, over the Jordanian border, to the left. With five hours to go before you reach Eilat and the desert scenery soon becoming monotonous, this is as good a place as any to catch a few hours sleep.

THE NEGEV DESERT

The popular myth that the Israelis have 'made the desert bloom' suggests that the area was previously devoid of human inhabitants and that it is now a hive of agricultural activity. Such beliefs have little basis in modern reality – the blooms are confined to isolated, heavily subsidised outposts – or in history. Over the years, the Negev has played host to a number of peoples and civilisations, characterised by alternating periods of settlement and desolation.

As early as the **Paleolithic** (Early Stone Age) period, about 10,000 years ago, hunters are thought to have lived off the plentiful wildlife which roamed the vast desert expanses. During the **Chalcolithic** (New Stone Age) period, in the fourth millenium BC, the area was extensively settled, with communities inhabiting the *wadis* around Beersheva. Hundreds of sites containing relics from this period have been and are still being discovered, and their contents are on display in museums around the country. Thereafter the

Negev was inhabited by nomadic tribes (from around 2000BC), Amalekites (1300BC) and Israelites until, in the tenth century BC, King David extended **Israelite** rule over the entire Negev. His son, Solomon, built a series of defensive forts and developed the famous copper mines at Timna. Solomon's southern port, Etzion Geber, is today's Eilat. After the Kingdom of David was split into Israel and Judah, the area was occupied by the Edomites until they too were expelled by the **Nabateans**.

This most impressive of ancient civilisations kept control of the Negev, and especially its important trade routes, from their mountain citadel at the Red City of Petra in Jordan for over a thousand years. Their ingenuity in adapting to the desert never ceases to amaze and can be witnessed in the impressive remains of their cities, whose sophisticated irrigation systems were adopted by later Roman and Byzantine inhabitants and in places are still used by the Negev Beduin today.

Nabatean power came most importantly from control of the burgeoning **trade route** between Africa, the Arabian Peninsula and the markets of the northern Mediterranean. They guaranteed safe passage to traders – dealing mainly in spices and perfumes such as frankincense, myrrh and aromatic gums from Arabia and Africa – and naturally took their cut as middlemen. Frankincense and myrrh were at this time treasures more valuable even than the gold which frequently accompanied them. They were used by many peoples in religious ceremonies and burial rites as well as for simple personal adornment. In the mines of Egypt, where the raw minerals were extracted, the workers were subjected to daily strip searches to ensure that no one was pilfering the precious materials.

Little is known about the exact origins of the Nabateans. Historians generally believe that they were originally nomads who migrated north from Arabia. Their civilisation was well developed; they had their own language and alphabet and left historical records in the form of thousands of inscriptions found on rocks from Arabia to Italy. Even after the decline of their trade routes, partly the result of the success of the Romans in diverting trade from the Negev to Egypt, partly a simple decline in the use of frankincense and myrrh thanks to the spread of Christianity, the Nabateans bounced back and developed highly sophisticated agricultural techniques, basing a new civilisation on farming and breeding livestock.

There are three sites in the Negev where well preserved remains of Nabatean cities exist: **Avdat**, **Shifta** and **Mamshit**. The most accessible is Avdat, situated on the main Beersheva–Eilat road. The most impressive (and naturally hence the hardest to reach) is Shifta.

The Beduin

From the Byzantine period on, the Negev was inhabited primarily by **Beduin** peoples, living as nomadic and semi-nomadic pastoralists and agriculturalists. During the period of Ottoman rule and under the British Mandate, the Beduin were effectively the sole inhabitants of the Negev. Many adopted increasingly sedentary modes of living, with rights to ancestral lands allocated among the 96 various tribes and sub-tribes. Today, the Beduin in the state of Israel constitute a significant and distinctive segment of the Palestinian community. The majority continue to inhabit the northern and central Negev desert.

On the eve of hostilities in 1948, the Negev Beduin numbered an estimated 80,000. More than two-thirds of this population fled or was expelled to Jordan and Gaza. The newly established state declared most of the Negev to be 'state land', imposing military rule on those who remained. In the early 1950s, these Beduin were rounded up and moved to a closed 'reserve area' in the northeastern Negev, ostensibly for security reasons. That area, between Beersheva, Arad and Dimona, is still the only region where Beduin are allowed to farm and freely graze their herds. Many tribes were relocated – 'temporarily' – from fertile lands to barren sites where, forty years later, they temporarily remain.

Today there are around 65,000 Beduin in the Negev, one third of them living in five Israeli-built settlements near Beersheva. Although the new towns have brought indoor plumbing, telephones and electricity, they have provided little in the way of a modern economic base, either in industry or in agriculture. The settlement of **Rahat** north of Beersheva, for example, has applied for industrial development status to enable investors to get government-subsidised loans, but such requests are consistently stalled. As a result, only 110 of the town's 15,000 residents were actually employed there in 1986.

Whilst the new towns become mere dormitories as people leave to seek daily work elsewhere – on kibbutzim or in Israeli industry – the Beduin have seen their traditional pastoral resources steadily eroded. Although the courts have recognised their traditional land claims, grazing land for sheep and goats has become increasingly scarce with the designation of large areas for military purposes or nature reserves and the spread of Jewish agricultural settlements. The building of the new Nevatim Air Force Base in the northern Negev, for example, forced the evacuation of 750 Beduin families from the Tel Malhata area to the new towns of **Kuseifa** and **Arou'ar**.

Meanwhile, the official response to the Beduin's request for recognised agricultural settlements of their own is consistent rejection. Beduin settlements in the Negev, no matter how large, are thus treated as illegal. Fruit, olive trees and crops planted by Beduin in ancestral land are regularly uprooted. Goats and sheep grazing on 'state land' are often confiscated by the notorious Green Patrol and can only be released from quarantine after the payment of large fines. Houses built without legal permits (which are only granted within the new townships) are demolished. Larger Beduin settlements, because deemed illegal by the authorities, are unable to obtain amenities such as electricity, roads or water supplies. Whilst the Negev's 150 Jewish kibbutzim and moshavim, housing some 59,000 people, use 254 million cubic metres of agricultural water a year, the allocation for Beduin agriculture is practically non-existent.

Financial aid, mainly from overseas, is readily available to new kibbutzim and moshavim in the Negev but there are no similar funds available to the Negev Beduin. A striking example of the contrast between Jewish and Beduin standards of living is the small settlement of **Abu Srihan**, just outside Beersheva some 200m from the affluent Jewish suburb of **Omer**. In Omer almost every house has its private swimming pool. In Abu Srihan, the Beduin temporarily relocated in 1951 live without electricity and with only one water tap. But at least that is better than **Segev Shalom**, southeast of Beersheva, which has no electricity, sewage system, telephone line or paved streets.

Despite all this, the popular image of the **Beduin** in Israel remains that of a rather quaint nomadic people, a relic of the past, to whom the modern Israeli state has brought the benefits of civilisation. Thus, you will be offered a visit to a 'Beduin tent' conveniently situated outside some tourist centre or other, to be shown how 'they' live, to partake of 'traditional' Beduin tea or coffee or to encourage you to buy Beduin handicrafts. Or you may visit exhibitions on Beduin culture, where an expert, invariably Israeli or western, will interpret and explain away this people as though they were some exotic but extinct species. What will not be said is anything about the actual situation of the Beduin today.

It can be difficult to meet Beduin other than those employed to serve coffee in tents at the various tourist centres, but if you make the effort, traditional Beduin hospitality is still very much alive, and genuine openness and interest on your part will often be reciprocated. To get beyond the sanitised image, try contacting the *Association for Support and Defence of Beduin Rights in Israel* (37 Hativat Hanegev Street, Beersheva; ☎057-31687), which attempts to raise public consciousness in Israel and abroad on the problems facing the Beduin.

Travelling in the Negev

Travelling in the Negev can be gruelling, especially in the heat of summer, and it needs to be undertaken seriously. The greatest danger is **dehydration**, which can occur quickly and imperceptibly. It's advisable to drink at least a gallon of liquid daily, preferably plain water: carry a canteen if you plan on hiking or spending time outside the cities. To avoid **sunstroke**, wear a hat or some other form of headcovering. Even those who are fortunate enough not to frizzle in the sun should protect exposed parts of the body either with a sunscreen or long sleeves and trousers. If you want a suntan, go and sit on a beach (where you should still be wary of the Middle Eastern sun), but don't attempt it in the desert. Sunglasses are also recommended to protect your eyes from the desert glare.

In general, you should set out on your trips early in the day and try to avoid being out or doing anything physically strenuous between noon and 3pm. Nights in the desert, on the other hand, can get extremely cold, so be sure to take some warm clothing, even in the summer. If you're planning to sleep out, a good sleeping bag is vital, but only do so in recognised sites as much of the area is under military control – and if the soldiers don't get you, the scorpions might!

Both for climate and scenery, **spring** is much the best time to travel. Like much of the country, the desert undergoes a profound transfiguration as the heat starts to take effect on the rugged terrain. During the winter, the northern area is full of brightly coloured flora: as this dies and fades away, the more familiar browns and yellows appear and the desert begins to look the way you always imagined it.

Getting about

There are in practice only two roads across the Negev: **Route 40**, south from Beersheva, and Route 90, south from the Dead Sea. The former is by far the more scenic, taking you through the winding foothills of the northern Negev to the ancient Nabatean city of Avdat and past the massive crater of Makhtesh Ramon. There are important kibbutzim along the way, too, at Sde Boqer and Mitzpe Ramon. **Route 90** also has its moments, but it follows the Arava Valley along the Afro-Syrian Rift virtually all the way to Eilat. Throughout this journey, the road runs sandwiched between the Jordan hills to the east and the Negev hills to the west. On the final **approach to Eilat** the two roads run together, passing two important areas of natural beauty, the Hai Bar Reserve and the Timna Valley National Park.

Buses from Tel Aviv, Jerusalem and Beersheva travel regularly along both these roads, stopping for refreshments en route, or there are *sherut* **taxis** from all the major cities in Israel. **Hitching** is possible but not advised – the scarcity of traffic in some areas and the punishing climate make it tough and potentially dangerous (especially in the summer, especially for women). If you have a **car**, so much the better: you'll have a great deal more freedom to stop where and when you want, and you'll be able to get to the more obscure sites.

With more time and inclination, there are numerous **package deals** around the Negev to choose from, from organised hikes to jeep trails, camel excursions to horse trips. The *Society for the Protection of Nature in Israel (SPNI)*, a non-profit organisation devoted to the preservation of Israel's natural resources, maintains four field centres in Eilat, Mitzpe Ramon, Kibbutz Sde Boker and Hatzeva in the Arava Valley, and offers a variety of trips. For further details, contact Yoav Nitzav at *Israel Nature Trails* (13 Helena HaMalka Street, Jerusalem; ☎02-249567) or the *SPNI* in Tel Aviv (4 Hashfela Street; ☎03-375063). For guided jeep and hiking tours, both in the Negev and Sinai deserts, try *Neot Hakikar* (36 Keren Hayesod, Jerusalem; ☎02-699385) with branches in Haifa, Tel Aviv (252 Hayarkon Street; ☎03-5463111) and Eilat (Sderot HaTmarim, Etzion Hotel; ☎059-71329). *Galilee Tours* (3 Ben Sira Street, Jerusalem; ☎02-246858) also do Negev trips, not cheap, but memorable. For camel tours, contact either the *SPNI* or *Camel Riders* (based in Eilat, ☎059-73218). If you intend to go on a desert hike, it is advisable to book through the *SPNI* in Jerusalem or plan it from Eilat.

Towards Beersheva: Arad and Dimona

Three roads converge on Beersheva **from the north**, one from Tel Aviv, Ashdod or Ashqelon via Qiryat Gat, one from Gaza, and the third from Jerusalem via Hebron and the West Bank. There's really nothing to stop for on any of them, though a small detour from the Qiryat Gat or Hebron roads could take you past **Lahav** and Laqiya (below). Approaching Beersheva **from the Dead Sea**, there are again three possible choices. The first, and perhaps the most scenic, is the small winding road that climbs from Masada to Arad, curving relentlessly up the side of the Arava Valley and providing some stunning views back over the Dead Sea and the Jordan Hills. The second choice is the main road to Arad from the junction at Neve Zohar; and the third goes via Dimona, leaving the Dead Sea road at the junction just south of the Dead Sea works.

From the north: Lahav and Laqiya

The northern limit of Beduin land is marked by **Kibbutz Lahav**, on the edge of the West Bank roughly halfway between the Qiryat Gat and Hebron roads. Originally a border settlement, the kibbutz has one of the largest pig farms in Israel and its members have built the **Joe Alon Centre** for regional and folk-lore studies. This contains an archaeological museum for finds from the region, an observatory, an ethnological collection which aims 'to preserve Beduin culture' and a natural history section for the area's fauna and flora. More enticingly, it also houses a **Museum of Beduin Culture** (Sat–Thur 9am–3pm, Fri 9am–noon; admission $2; ☎057-961597) which displays Beduin artefacts such as household utensils, traditional dress, jewellery and embroidery. You can ask for a guided tour, or attach yourself to a visiting group, to reap the benefits of a knowledgeable but rather patronising expert explaining how this unique culture worked and how it is disappearing under the pressure of modernisation. You can also ask to be shown a video on desert life, or sit with Saalem from the nearby township of Rahat in the tent erected outside the museum and drink a cup of strong coffee or sweet tea. The restored 'summer cave' of a *fellah* and a picnic area in the **Jewish National Fund Lahav Forest** can also be visited nearby.

A daily bus connects the kibbutz directly with Beersheva (leaves Beersheva 11.50am, returns 1.20pm), or you can hitch to one of the main roads and pick up buses there.

On the way from Lahav to the **Shoqet Junction** on the Hebron road you pass the Beduin settlement of **LAQIYA**. Here, in defiance of popular myth, Beduin have long lived in stone houses, farming and tending flocks. In 1952 the inhabitants were moved to the region of Arad, where many worked on the construction of the town, and they were only allowed to return to their original homes in the late 1970s, by which time the land had been designated state property. The contrast between the well irrigated kibbutz fields and Laqiya, across the road, is striking – only recently was the first water supply piped to the village.

Arad

ARAD, 30km west of Beersheva on the way to the Dead Sea, is one of the most likeable towns in the northern Negev. Vantage points around the town command fine views of the Dead Sea, the mountains and the multi-coloured desert and in the brochures you'll read that the air is famous for its cleanliness. Pollen-free, the atmosphere does indeed offer relief to sufferers of allergies like asthma and hay-fever, and to ensure that the environment stays pure, there is even a bye-law against the cultivation of plants which could cause allergies or factories which would create pollution (most of the population work at chemical plants or resorts down by the Dead Sea).

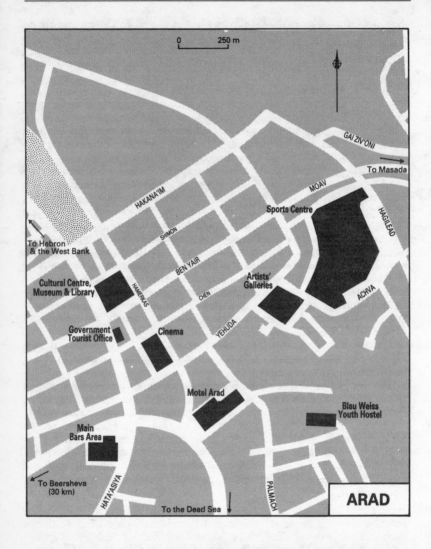

0   250 m

GAI ZIV'ONI

To Masada

MOAV

HAKANA'IM

Sports Centre

HAGILEAD

SHIMON

To Hebron
& the West Bank

BEN YAIR

Artists'
Galleries

ACHVA

Cultural Centre,
Museum & Library

HAMERKAS

CHEN

Government
Tourist Office

Cinema

YEHUDA

Motel Arad

Blau Weiss
Youth Hostel

Main
Bars Area

To Beersheva
(30 km)

HATA'ASIYA

PALMACH

To the Dead Sea

ARAD

On its own this would hardly make for a major attraction. But Arad is also a noticeably friendly town – the people who mill around the busy central square in the cool desert air seem more relaxed than the hardy types who inhabit other development towns in the area. And unlike most purpose-built desert towns, Arad has some soul. Why the architects struck lucky with this particular design – a plain North American style grid – is a mystery. But they did, and if nothing else Arad would be worth visiting as a rare example of Sixties success.

One of the advantages of Arad is that it is small. So a walk around the centre will soon reveal exactly what is on offer. With the Dead Sea only half an hour's drive away and frequent bus connections to Beersheva, Masada and Ein Gedi, it's a convenient and congenial place to spend a few days. For a map of the town and information on what you can do, go to the **IGTO** in the Central Square (Sun–Thur 9am–noon and 5–8pm, Fri 9am–noon; ☎057-958144). Cheap **accommodation** is available at the *Blau Weiss Youth Hostel* (Arad Street; ☎057-957150; members $3.50, non-members $4.50) east of the bus station, or at the *Arad Hotel* (6 HaPalmach Street; ☎057-957040), behind the police station. There's nowhere else cheap but if you prefer to spend a little more, there are a number of three- and four-star hotels, such as the *Margoa Arad Hotel* (hotel area; ☎057-957014).

Surprisingly lively, Arad even boasts a cinema (*Oron Cinema* in the Central Square) showing English-language films, as well as bars with live music and a sprinkling of reasonably priced cafés and restaurants. If you want a hard **drink**, try the *Public Bar* (just off HaTaasiya Street), which has live music, or the American style *Pub HaMidbar* nearby, both of which are open well into the early hours of the morning. The excellent *Konditorei Arad* serves thick, creamy cappucinos, beer and an array of continental cakes and sweets. This is just off the Central Square, near a number of cheap pizza restaurants.

The chief attraction nearby is **Tel Arad** (Sun–Thur 8am–4pm, Fri 8am–3pm), some 8km west of the new city. This hilltop fortress marks the site of biblical Arad which excavations have shown to be an important Caananite outpost, conquered by the Israelites as they entered their promised land. The most important of the remains are from the Israelite period, though there's plenty of evidence of later occupation, especially an Israelite temple from about the eighth century BC. This is quite unique, and provided important information about the religion of the early Israelites. The ancient city walls are also much in evidence, partially reconstructed, and there's a citadel and a maze of narrow streets delineating the residential quarters. You'll see the hill long before you get to it and, yet again, there are extensive views from the top.

Dimona

The town of **DIMONA**, about 25km southeast of Beersheva, has the dubious honour of being the site of Israel's Atomic Research Station and also, according to a technician at the plant*, the centre of Israel's nuclear weapons' industry. Say 'Dimona' to most Israelis and they immediately think of things nuclear. Despite the intrigue it is really not worth making the effort of getting here. In the flesh, Dimona is a depressingly stagnant place.

Originally built in 1955 as a residential area for workers at the Dead Sea chemical works – mainly immigrants from Tunisia – the development town is a maze of half-empty blocks of flats which give it a ghostlike atmosphere. Even local residents can summon little enthusiasm: one told us that the best way to see Dimona was from a distance. It might be a sociologist's dream, but it's not

* Hardly Israel's best-kept secret, this story was broken to the world in January 1987 via the London *Sunday Times* and their informant Mordechai Vanunu.

exactly welcoming to travellers: there are no hotels or hostels, though in the last resort the empty flats have been known to provide shelter for a night.

There are, however, at least two good reasons for travelling via Dimona. The first, on the main road 5km or so east, is the site of the Nabatean city of **MAMSHIT** (MAMPSIS; Sun–Thur 8am–5pm, Fri 8am–4pm). Built in the first century AD, the quality of construction ensured the town's survival when the Romans took control a century later. The Roman presence is still evident from the Latin inscriptions on the tombstones in the military cemetery. On the site, examples of Nabatean houses built around an open courtyard are clearly visible. Two churches from the Byzantine period (324–640AD), covering many Nabatean houses, are beautifully preserved and boast mosaic floors and baptismal fonts. The East Church is the oldest in the Negev area. In a nearby gorge, Roman engineers built three dams to collect water for the settlement and at **Maale Aqrabim** (Scorpions' Ascent) cut a stepped road in the steep cliffside to provide travellers' caravans with a smoother journey.

The second point worth stopping, only a few kilometres before Beersheva, is **NEVATIM**. While ostensibly no different from any other small desert village, its distinctive feature is that it is inhabited by Indian Jews. Originally from Cochin in Southern India, these people have kept many of their traditional customs and still wear Indian-style dress. Their brightly coloured saris, worn especially during religious festivities, contrast sharply with the dull colours of the surrounding desert. The main economic base of the village, a thriving flower-growing export business, ensures its continued existence.

Beersheva

BEERSHEVA is the City of the Patriarchs, birthplace and home of Isaac and Jacob. It was here that Abraham is said to have pitched his tent and dug the well at which he concluded a peace settlement with the Canaanite king, Abimelech (*Genesis 21:32*), thus giving the place its name, which means the Well of the Oath (an alternative translation is Well of the Seven, from the seven lambs handed over by Abraham when the oath was made). You might, then, expect the place to be replete with historical interest. You'd be disappointed. Although today it's the fourth largest town in the country and capital of the Negev, modern Beersheva has very much the feel of a small development town. The site of the ancient city has yet to be definitively discovered, and there are few other attractions to tempt you to stay more than a night or two. It is, however, a useful base for visits to the surrounding area.

Until the beginning of this century, Beersheva and its environs were controlled by local Beduin tribes for whom it was a trading centre and watering place, a crossroads for travellers from the Mediterranean to the Jordan River and for caravans moving north out of the desert. Under Ottoman rule it became the district and administrative centre for the Negev, with a new town – now the Old City – planned and built by the Germans during World War I. The town was the first in Palestine to be captured by the British under General Allenby on his northward advance in 1917. Witness to the heavy fighting can be seen in the **British War Cemetery** on HaAtzma'ut Street.

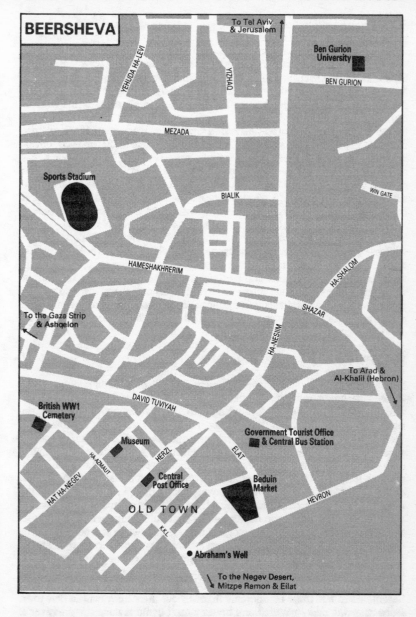

Nowadays Beersheva is a town of immigrants, with a population of 120,000 from over seventy countries, but the small Beduin community still has a relatively high profile, especially at the excellent weekly market.

The Town

If the biblical city has disappeared, Beersheva can at least boast the remarkable remains of a settlement dating from the Early Bronze Age, 1500 years before Abraham. Excavations have unearthed the underground dwellings of an agricultural people who produced beautifully crafted jewellery, baskets and pottery. The discoveries from this site, as well as others from the surrounding region and from later Biblical and Byzantine eras, are displayed in the **Negev Museum** (Sun and Mon 8am–2pm, Wed and Thur 8am–4pm, Tue and Fri 8am–1pm, Sat 10am–1pm; admission around $1;☎057-39105) on HaAtzma'ut Street in the centre of town.

The museum itself has an interesting and turbulent history. Originally a mosque, it was built in 1901 by the Ottoman rulers of Palestine for the 5000-strong local Muslim population. After Beersheva was taken by the Israeli forces on October 21, 1948, the mosque was used as a courtroom for several years before being turned into a museum in 1953. Today, it is the subject of a legal battle between the Beersheva municipality and the local Beduin community who, as part of a general campaign for their rights, want it restored to them as a place of worship. In the prevailing atmosphere this is unlikely to happen, the Israeli pretext for hanging on to the building being that the mosque's impressive minaret towers over an army camp conveniently erected just across the road and thus that it cannot be returned for 'security reasons'.

Contents aside, the mosque is well worth a visit for its architecture, with the Ottoman sultan's medallion over the main door, and the elegance of its setting in a small but beautiful park. The curator, Yehuda Govrin, is happy to show you around, which can be useful as hardly any information seems to be written in English. He also runs several archaeological digs in the area in which volunteers can participate in return for accommodation and two meals a day. The only qualifications needed, according to Govrin, are good health and a healthy interest. It is advisable to contact him beforehand at the museum rather than just turn up on spec, or to apply through the *Department of Antiquities and Museums* (*Ministry of Education and Culture*, Jerusalem) who act as a central agency for all excavations.

A rather different reminder of the past, and probably one of the best reasons to spend a night in Beersheva, is to be found in the **Beduin Market** (Souq al-Khamis) held every Thursday morning on the southern fringe of the old city by the junction of the roads to Eilat and Hebron. Some impression of what this market must have meant for the pastoral Beduin before the restrictions imposed on them by the creation of the Israeli state can be seen in the diminishing area set aside for livestock trading: camels, donkeys, sheep, goats and hens are still bought and sold here, even if some of the prospective buyers now come from nearby kibbutzim and moshavim to haggle over prices. And you can still buy a plethora of spices, incense, sweetmeats and 'orientalia', if not from the Beduin themselves, then from traders from the Gaza Strip and nearby West Bank towns who roll into town in the chilly air of the early morning in *service* taxis or beaten-up trucks.

Later on, most of the original market is squeezed out by Israeli stall-keepers selling everything from jeans to floor-mops, plastic jewellery to tape-recorders, and dominating proceedings by hawking their wares through megaphones from atop step-ladders. The market remains fascinating nonetheless, and if you've perfected the art of haggling, you can still come away with a bargain. If the prospect of attempting to beat down the price of a brass coffeepot from the eighty shekels the trader asked to the eighteen it was probably worth is too daunting, the experience is still one not to be missed. But get there early – the market starts at 6am – and be sure to check you're in the right place (there's a wholesale market nearby).

Another area worth a visit is the **Old City**, which today is the business centre of downtown Beersheva. As such it contains most of the restaurants, cafés and reasonable hotels. The liveliest section is **Smilansky Street**, known as the **Artists' Quarter**, with galleries for art and sculpture which stay open until midnight. The traditional site of **Abraham's Well** is on the Hebron Road on the outskirts of the Old City, near the market (Sun–Thur 8am–7pm, Fri 8am–2pm).

Practicalities

Beersheva's **central bus station** is a short distance to the northeast of the old city, and the **IGTO** (Sun–Thur 8am–5pm, Fri 8am–1pm; ☎057-36001/2/3) is directly opposite. To get from here to the centre turn left from the entrance, left again into Ben Tzui Street and walk up to HaNesim Boulevard – left here, straight across the main road, and you'll approach the old city. Alternatively you can catch a local bus outside the terminus. Most run to the centre via the market.

The only really cheap **place to stay** in Beersheva is the *Beit Yatziv Youth Hostel* (79 HaAztma'ut St; ☎057-77444; bus #13 from the bus station) just down from the museum on the corner of Herzl and HaAztma'ut. The hostel, which belongs to the IYHA, charges around $7 per night and has no curfew. If you intend staying check in early, as the 300 beds are often in demand from visiting school parties. A detailed list of **hotels** can be had from the IGTO: most charge between $10 and $20 per night, and none are particularly good. The better value ones include *HaNegev Hotel* (26 HaAzma'ut Street; ☎057-77026); *Hotel Arava* (37 Histadrut Street; ☎057-78792) and, perhaps the best, *Hotel Aviv* (Mordechai HaGetaot, off Keren Kayemet LeIsrael; ☎057-78059). You'll rarely have any problem getting a room at any of them.

Eating, drinking and nightlife

Restaurants and cafés in Beersheva are mainly geared to locals, with selection and price range reflecting the various communities. As ever, the cheapest and best food can be got from the **falafel stalls** on practically every street corner. The *King of Ful*, at the corner of Herzl and HaAztma'ut, is reputedly the best and you can munch your sandwich in the gardens of the old mosque which provides a relaxing setting for an afternoon siesta. Others include *Deliyahoo's Kiosk* (corner of HaAztma'ut and Hativat, near the Youth Hostel), the bakery on Sarah Street which is open 24 hours a day, and the multitude of stalls on Smilansky, Keren Kayemet and Herzl streets. And there is always the **cafeteria** in the *Egged Bus Station* for a hearty main meal. More upmarket alternatives include the *Bulgarian Restaurant* (Keren Kayemet LeIsrael) and Beersheva's elegant *Chinese Restaurant* (79 Histadrut; ☎057-75375).

Beersheva is not the place to go to looking for exciting **nightlife**. If you're staying for a night or two there are a few bars and cafés in Herzl Street and in the pedestrian precinct of Keren Kayemet, but most tend to be pretty soulless. Smilansky Street, a few blocks south of HaAtzma'ut, is marginally livelier, with bars and art galleries which stay open until at least midnight. The cowboy-style *Bar Nash* (15 Trumpeldor) has live **music** most nights of the week – not great, but loud and better than you might expect in Beersheva. Nearby are the 'bohemian' *Chaplin's Pub*, the *Piccadilly Pub* (at the end of Herzl Street) and a number of others. *Mandy's Nightclub* (57 Hadassah Street; open until 3am; $6 admission includes the first drink) plays mainly mainstream disco music to a predominantly young audience.

Listings

Banks Most are located in the centre of town and at the bus station. They will change travellers' cheques and foreign currency but be prepared to wait for ages in a queue.

Buses Egged buses run frequently to all parts of the country. For a detailed timetable, call bus station (☎057-74342).

Car hire *Avis*, Hebron Road (☎057-71777 or 33345); *Hertz*, New Rasco Centre (☎057-73878); *Gan Car*, 23 Ben Zvi Street (☎057-30983).

Emergencies Police, Herzl Street (☎100); Ambulance, Kaplan Square (☎101); Magen David Adom, First Aid, 40 Bialik Street (☎057-78333).

Hospitals Soroka Hospital, near Ben Gurion Street (☎057-77111); Kupat Holim regional clinic, Civil Centre.

Post office Main branch in HaNesim Boulevard (☎057-32510; Sun–Thur 8am–6pm, Fri 8am–2pm).

Travel agencies *A. Zakai*, 75 HaHalutz Street (☎057-77477); *Kopel Tours*, 44 Herzl Street (☎057-78860); *Negev Tours*, Passage Rasco (☎057-77421); *Teper Tours*, Passage Srul (☎057-34625); *Melia Tours*, 63 HaHistadrut (☎057-78012).

Sherut Taxis *Yael Daroma Taxi Co.* (Keren Kayemet LeIsrael; ☎057-39144) for transport to Eilat, Jerusalem and Tel Aviv.

Supermarket *Hypercol*, Ben Gurion Street (☎057-77297).

Swimming pools *Beit Yatziv*, Herzfeld Street; *Youth Pool*, Aliyat HaNoar Square (8am–6pm daily); *Desert Inn*, Tuviyahu Street (April–October; ☎057-74931); *GaleiHaNegev*, Yehuda Halevi Street; *Country Club*, Etzel Street (7am–6pm, May–Sept).

Taxis *Taxi Sinai*, 48 HaHistadrut (☎057-77525); *Taxi Mezada*, 45 HaAzma'ut (☎057-75555); Taxi Hazui, Nordau Street (☎057-39333).

Tours of Beersheva and the Negev are operated by *Egged Tours* at the bus station (☎057-75262). Sight-seeing and excursions with a chauffeur-guide can be arranged through the IGTO.

Around Beersheva

The most commonly accepted site for biblical Beersheva lies 6km northeast of the modern city at **TEL BEERSHEVA**. Here two successive circuits of city walls and gates have been discovered as well as shards from the Chalcolithic period. Outside the city gates lies a well 40m deep which archae-ologists suggest is the real Abraham's Well. Nearby, the **Man in the Desert Museum** focuses on the relationship between the desert environment and its human population, while the obligatory 'Beduin tent' houses a restaurant with 'Beduin folklore' entertainment, the cafeteria offers 'Beduin coffee' and snacks and at the gift shop you can obtain a variety of 'genuine' and, of course, 'Beduin' souvenirs. Reservations for a tour of the whole complex can be made at the Central Office, 33 Herzl Street, Beersheva (☎057-73308).

Next to Tel Beersheva and 5km east of Beersheva is the first of the five townships built in 1969 for the local Beduin, **TEL SHEVA**. The village was designed with high-walled courtyards separating the houses to provide their inhabitants with a degree of privacy, a style which met with little success. Most residents have preferred to build their own houses. As in the other modern townships designed to encourage the Beduin to settle, Tel Sheva has little in the way of industrial infrastructure or land for agricultural purposes. Consequently, it has the appearance of a ghost town during the day, when most of the population leave to find work in nearby Jewish towns and settle-ments as unskilled labourers. By way of contrast, the affluent Jewish suburb of **OMER** lies just 4km north. First established as a moshav in 1949 by a group of demobilised soldiers, it is today a prosperous town of around 3000 people.

South across the desert

Getting **to Eilat from Beersheva**, a distance of around 250km, is relatively easy. Buses run fast and frequently enough to allow you to jump off, spend a few hours somewhere, and continue your journey later in the day. Winding its way through the mountainous northern area, the desert road passes isolated Beduin settlements, kibbutzim and moshavim. Driving it can be a real experience, and even without a car hitching is far from impossible, although the irregular traffic can often make for slow progress. If you have the time, make the trip over a couple of days, staying overnight at Mitzpe Ramon or another settlement. The trip **towards Sinai** is considerably less tempting, but here too there are regular buses, and at Shivta there's a Nabatean/Byzantine site of outstanding interest.

At first the road is the same, south through the well manicured landscape of the northern Negev. But then the Eilat road turns off towards Sde Boqer (some buses run via the 1950s development town of YEROHAM): this is where the real desert begins.

Shivta

Although buses run all the way to NIZZANA on the **Egyptian border**, there's really no reason to go there – it's a grim little place and there's no onward public transport, although trucks do use this route. Off the road, however, about 20km from the border (50km from Beersheva) lies the Nabatean site of **SHIVTA** (SUBEITA; Sun–Thur 8am–5pm, Fri 8am–4pm). Not the most accessible of the Nabatean sites, it nevertheless can be reached by bus, getting off at the HORVOT SHIVTA stop and walking the final 5km from there, and it is well worth the effort. By car, of course, there's no problem.

Shivta's Nabatean builders developed a fascinating architectural structure in the first century BC to ensure the town's survival. To live in an area where the average rainfall is little more than 80mm per year, the whole city was planned as a giant reservoir to catch every drop of water that fell. The **reservoir** on the northern edge of the city, still plainly visible, collected the rain falling from the eastern slopes; and channels running either side of the streets directed more rainfall into the southern reservoir.

The town plan aside, what you actually see is Byzantine and later – the place continued to be inhabited well into the Arab period. Shivta had three important **churches** to serve a population which can never have been more than a few thousand. The south church, near the entrance, had a mosque built alongside in the seventh century. From here you can walk through the superbly preserved streets to the most impressive of the churches, the North Church, and near it the city **cemetery**, where ancient tombstones can be found.

If you are walking around the site, be careful where you go, as the surrounding area is a military zone. Equally, driving to and from the site, make sure you stick to the main road.

Sde Boqer

On the Eilat road there are scattered petrol stations, restaurants and roadside cafés, only a very occasional full scale settlement. The first of these oases, some 50km south of Beersheva, is **KIBBUTZ SDE BOQER**: famous as the final resting place of the Israeli statesman and first Prime Minister of Israel, **David Ben Gurion**. Always convinced of the need for more Israeli settlements in the desert, he became a member of the kibbutz in 1953, his own home providing an example to others. He died here 22 years later, at the age of 89, and was buried next to his wife on a hill overlooking the desert. The grave, commanding a magnificent view of the Valley of Zin, can be visited, as can their house (the **Paula and David Ben Gurion Hut**: open Sun–Thur 8am–3pm, Fri 8am–noon and Sat 9am–1pm; admission free) which has been left unaltered. The kibbutz also has a **zoo** full of Negev deer, swans and flamingos, and nurtures the **Ben Gurion University of the Negev**, established 3km south of the kibbutz in 1969 to encourage Negev development. The university houses the *Jacob Blaustein Institute for Desert Research*, a centre for comparative medicine, a health clinic, and the *Ben-Gurion Institute and Archives*, containing over 750,000 archives and documents related to Ben Gurion. These can be viewed with prior appointment.

If all this hero-worship becomes overpowering, you could alternatively continue southwards for approximately 15km to the junction for **EIN AVDAT** and an area of great natural beauty. Here the *wadis* Nafah, Abdeh, Mura and Fufra have been given the collective Hebrew name of **Nahal Zin**. A car park 1km from the road has signposts directing you to an observation post which offers panoramic views of **Ein Avdat Canyon** and its springs, which some identify as the place where Moses made water gush from a rock. If you are prepared to walk down to the bottom of the canyon, the **Ein Avdat Pools** are full of cool, clear water – a beautiful place for a swim after the heat of the desert.

Just beyond here, you reach the site of ancient Avdat.

Avdat

Sixty-five kilometres south of Beersheva, the site of **AVDAT** (Sun–Thur 8am–4pm, Fri 8am–3pm) is perhaps the best surviving testimony of the Nabatean civilisation. Founded in the third century BC, Avdat gets its current name from King Obodas II (30–9BC) who was buried in the township and was revered here as a god; this name was then Arabised to Abdah and finally Hebraicised to Avdat. When the Romans conquered the Negev they built an army camp nearby, and in the sixth century Avdat became a Byzantine monastic centre, with much new building. At this time the population is estimated to have reached around 3000. Once again most of what you see is from this era, but there are also some impressive relics of the Nabatean trading centre. Highlights include a handsome esplanade (the open area in front of the fortress where any attackers would be exposed to Nabatean fire) which was turned into a covered portico during the Byzantine period; a baptistry, church and the remains of a Byzantine Monastery; and an ancient spiral staircase. The rebuilt Nabatean pottery, complete with an original kiln and potters' wheel, gives some idea as to the scope and sophistication of the Nabatean civilisation.

As well as the buildings, there's fascinating evidence of Nabatean agricultural methods. A complex system of channels and dams ensured that none of the area's sparse rainfall or night dew was wasted, enabling the cultivation of wheat, barley, grapes and other produce.

If you are travelling direct from Beersheva make sure you are let off at Avdat archaeological site and not the Ein Avdat junction: the site itself, dominating its surrounds from a flat hilltop, is about an hour's walk from the main road and has been partially restored by the National Parks Authority. There's a small restaurant at the site but it's expensive – you'd be better off taking a picnic.

Mitzpe Ramon

MITZPE RAMON is a strange place. Perched high on the hills above the **Makhtesh Ramon Crater**, miles from anywhere, you can only wonder what draws its residents to come and settle here. Starting its life as a camp for workers building the nearby highway, it has become a support centre for the nearby military outpost, for the dwindling armaments factory and the developing local tourist industry. It is also a main centre of the reclusive **Black Hebrew** sect which came to Israel in the 1960s from the USA, mainly New York. Since their arrival, many believe they have been treated appallingly by the Israeli government. Charges of racism have been directed against the authorities who refuse to recognise their claim to be descendants of one of the tribes of Israel, and who have deported a number of their followers. In an effort to rejuvenate the fortunes of Mitzpe Ramon, regular air services are scheduled to link the town with the rest of the country and plans are underway to develop its tourist potential.

As the last urban area from Beersheva to Eilat, there are limited opportunities to **stay overnight**. The *Mitzpe Ramon Youth Hostel* in the centre of town (members $3.50, non-members $4.50) is a basic but friendly place which always seems to have room and offers kitchen facilities. The slightly upmarket *Nof Ramon Hotel* (from $12.50 per person) caters for those who prefer more comfort. The **Commercial Centre**, a handful of shops and bars, is closed on Saturdays, so make sure you get enough provisions to last through *shabbat*.

The main attraction here is the **crater** which has given the town its name. The largest of the three craters in the Negev, *Makhtesh Ramon* – over 300m deep, 8km wide and 40km long – provides naturalists with a particularly wide array of interest. There are over 1200 species of vegetation here, archaeological relics of ancient times including a Nabatean fort in the south, and a wealth of animal life – large predators, desert snakes and insects, as well as dinosaur fossils. A **Visitors' Centre**, on the western edge of the town, features exhibitions and slide shows, and offers further information on exploring the area. This is the first development in the planned expansion of the town's tourist potential: with a dry desert climate and comfortable temperatures thanks to the altitude, one suspects that in a few years Mitzpe Ramon will become a major centre for tourism. Meanwhile, the **Municipal Swimming Pool** (open Sun–Thur 9am–5pm, Fri 9am–4pm; admission $1.20) and an active **Cultural Centre** open almost every night provide a different sort of entertainment.

Beyond Mitzpe Ramon the road continues little changed, through country virtually uninhabited, until finally it joins the direct route down from the Dead Sea to run together down the **Arava Valley** for the final 70km into Eilat. In this last stretch are two more sites of considerable interest, both popular outings from Eilat: the **Hai Bar Biblical Wildlife Reserve** and **Kibbutz Yotvata**. For details of these see "Around Eilat".

EILAT AND AROUND

The southern Negev in general and **Eilat** in particular are very different from the rest of the country. Physically separated from the north – the nearest large town, Beersheva, lies almost 300km away – the region is distinct also in an almost complete lack of biblical or other antiquities. Eilat especially feels a child of the twentieth century. At the point where the southern Negev meets the Gulf of Aqaba (Gulf of Eilat to the Israelis), a bare 5km of coast separates Egypt from Jordan. Across this sprawls the resort of Eilat.

Over the last few years Eilat has become a popular package holiday destination, and **tourism** now provides the great majority of the city's income. The travel agents' enticements to cheap winter sun seem to have worked, and most people travelling around Israel call in at Eilat at some stage too. For Israelis themselves, this is the local version of the South of France – with the same free and easy atmosphere, good weather and bronzed bodies. Apart from the usual attractions of the beach – and there really is an extraordinary amount of sun here – there's also the desert, with its opportunities for wilderness hiking, there are magnificent opportunities for snorkelling and diving around the Red Sea reef, and for long-term travellers Eilat offers a real possibility of finding work. It is also perhaps the most straightforward point of entry into Egypt, with recently handed over **Taba** within walking distance.

Escaping the plastic sophistication of the resort is easy enough if you are into – and equipped for – solitary desert walking. On a more organised level there are a couple of worthwhile attractions along the road north, **Timna Valley**, **Hai Bar** and **Kibbutz Yotvata**, or you can take a trip of a day or two into the Egyptian **Sinai**.

Eilat

First impressions of **EILAT** suggest that tourism is the only reason for the town's existence. And they wouldn't be far wrong. But dig a little deeper and you can find more than this. If you have money, the sheer commercialism of the place is enjoyable in itself; if not, then the beauty of the setting, its ideal location as a staging post for sorties into the desert or the Egyptian Sinai, great swimming and a guaranteed tan are considerable compensation. The town is set on hills looking down over the Gulf, with beaches stretching out east to the Jordanian border (the main hotel strip) and to the south and west the port and then more beaches, less developed, stretching towards Egypt. The views from this strategic position are stunning: you can clearly see Egypt, Jordan and Saudia Arabia, while the deep blue of the Red Sea contrasts sharply with the pinky hills of Jordan and the more rustic heights behind the town. In a physical sense, if not a political one, you really feel yourself at the heart of the Middle East here.

Eilat's apparent modernity – you could accurately suppose that almost everything you see has been built within the last thirty years – does, however, hide a considerable history. The place was first revealed to the Israelites as they wandered through the Sinai after their expulsion from the Kingdom of Israel, and later King Solomon built a port called Etzion Geber here (*1 Kings 9:26*). After this had been destroyed in war, King Azzariah (785–733BC) rebuilt it as the port of Judah. In the internecine conflict which dogged the region over the following years, the port changed hands a number of times: it was renamed Berenice during the Hellenistic era, and then Aila by the Nabateans. During Roman times it became an important staging post when, in the third century, the Tenth Legion was moved here from Jerusalem. And after the demise of the Roman Empire, the Byzantine rulers created a citadel near modern Eilat that was the focal point of their

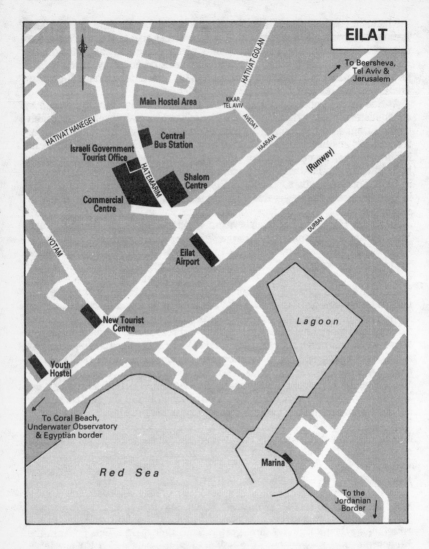

southern defence system. Remains of this are still visible, but nowadays they lie out of bounds on the Israel-Jordanian border.

In 1116, Baldwin I, then the Crusader king of Jerusalem, captured the port, and later the Arab presence was solidified with the erection of a fortress here by Salah al-Din. After 1588, however, Eilat was all but abandoned following the building of a new Turkish fortress east of Aqaba.

Not until the United Nations came to carve up Palestine did Eilat regain some strategic and political importance. The Zionist lobby fiercely argued for the inclusion of the town (Um Rashrash as it was then called) in the proposed Jewish State, since a Red Sea outlet giving direct access towards Asia was regarded as crucial to economic viability. After the declaration of independence on May 14, 1948, the movement of the Egyptian Army brought Eilat under Egyptian control. On March 11, 1949, Israeli forces, in **Operation Uvda**, reached the Red Sea and hoisted the Israeli flag.

At this time, Eilat was no more than a military outpost, but in the rush to consolidate such a strategically important location, the developers quickly began to build. The scramble for a firmer presence left little room for architectural and aesthetic considerations: the result was sturdy, but hardly pleasing to the eye. To complete the process of stabilisation, and to encourage both Israeli settlement and foreign tourism, Eilat was declared a tax-free zone in 1985. This means that the 15% VAT is waived, and should mean that prices in Eilat are noticeably lower than elsewhere. In practice it remains a relatively expensive town.

As far as **climate** goes, Eilat's claim to year-round sun is true enough. Monthly average temperatures range from 15.5°C in January to 33.4°C in August: but be warned that during the summer months, July and August especially, this can mean excessive heat, with mid-day temperatures well over 40°C. (A water bottle is essential equipment here, as drinks are expensive and few café owners are happy to serve plain water.) The only respite from the dry searing heat is the wind which blows, almost daily throughout the year, from the north-north-east along the Arava Valley; still known to local fishermen by its Arabic name, *Aylat*, this wind may well have given the town its name. Not surprisingly, rainfall is sparse. What little there is comes largely as flash storms during the winter months, so you can count yourself unlucky if you see any.

One final warning should be given about the **police**. In Eilat they are known to be particularly harsh on people getting drunk and causing 'a nuisance' in the streets, especially if they appear to be budget travellers. The British in particular have a bad name in this respect. Drug users, too, are harshly treated. The stuff is easy enough to come by here, but prison or deportation are real possibilities.

Arrival and orientation

Most people arrive in Eilat at the **central bus station**, a rather dilapidated, unmistakably Israeli-designed building – functional, but certainly not beautiful. Walk out of the bus station onto Hatmarim Boulevard and look left down the hill for your first glance of the Red Sea – an impressive sight, day or night. On the coast at the end of the road, **Eilat International Airport** is located almost bang in the centre of town – not where you'd have sited a runway if the residents' quality of life had been among your prime concerns.

Finding your way around Eilat is not difficult. The hills surrounding the town have conveniently limited the growth of the place and, wherever you are, provide an excellent reference point. Hatmarim Boulevard is very much the main drag, lined with shops and cafés and with the great shopping centres which characterise the town centre just off it. At the bottom

Hatmarim meets HaArava Road which runs through the town, past the Old and New Ports, and on to Coral Beach, Taba Beach and the Egyptian border. The **Israeli Government Tourist Office** is located in the **Commercial Centre**, off Hatmarim. Here you can pick up good advice on available accommodation, an entertainments guide to Eilat, and numerous other free maps and leaflets.

A few days in Eilat is quite enough to get to know it very well. Broadly speaking, the place can be split into four: the main body of the town on the side of the hill; the port areas below this to the east; a hotel zone containing the plusher hotels on the seaward side of the airport; and the North Beach area to the west by the Jordanian border. The centre of Eilat comprises little more than three shopping centres: the *Commercial Centre*, the *New Tourist Centre* and the *Shalom Plaza Centre*. These contain the vast majority of shops, restaurants and bars. Travelling east from the centre you will first pass the port area (out of bounds to tourists: it was from here that Israel purportedly shipped US arms to Iran in the 'Irangate' scandal), and then reach Coral Beach and Taba Beach on the way to the Egyptian border. This side of town is distinctly quieter, though regular bus and taxi services to the centre of Eilat ensure you're not entirely left out of the nightlife or amenities.

Accommodation

Eilat is popular all year round, but it still has distinct high seasons when **accommodation** may be harder to find and prices somewhat higher than usual. Particularly busy are the major Jewish and Christian holidays (Rosh Hashana, Pesach and Hanukka; Christmas and Easter) and the summer months of July and August when the town is overrun with Israelis. If you are planning to visit during any of these periods, you'd be well advised to book somewhere to stay in advance.

Most of the time, though, you've an exceptionally wide range of choice, from the ultra-smart and correspondingly expensive *King Solomon's Hotel* to the basic *Patio 830*, where a bed under the stars costs about $3.50, and just about everything else in between. Certainly cheapish hostels are plentiful (see below): arrive in Eilat by bus and you will normally be inundated by people offering hostel type accomodation. Much of this is fine, but some are overcrowded and overpriced, with notoriously aggressive hustlers. Don't agree to anything until you've seen the place.

Lists of the more expensive hotels and some private accommodation with Eilati families can be got from the IGTO at the *Commercial Centre*. Because package tours from Europe directly to Eilat are popular, these hotels are usually pretty well booked for most of the year. Some of the better, cheaper options are listed below.

If you don't want to pay at all, you'll find that **sleeping on the beaches** in Eilat has become commonplace over the years, and that while it's officially illegal, the police will normally turn a blind eye. The police, however, may prove the least of your worries. First of all, locals don't like it much, especially if you try dossing near the fancy hotels: some of the beaches near the centre of town are hosed down to clear them – normally at some godforsaken hour of the morning. In general, Taba Beach gets least unwanted attention from the authorities because it is out sight and mind of the plush hotels. North Beach is also popular, but for the best update on current conditions, ask others who are already settled in. And wherever you choose to sleep out, be very careful with your belongings and with your person, and stick close to others, preferably people you know. Tales of gear being ripped off abound and you may also hear of armed robberies and even rape.

Some of the better budget places to stay are listed below.

Central Eilat

HaShalom Hostel (HaNegev Street; ☎059-76544). One of the first hostels you will see if you arrive in Eilat by bus, this was originally built as a hotel but failed to get a licence – hence the slightly upmarket entrance and building. Relaxed atmosphere (where guitar playing ex-hippies seem particularly welcome), nice patio and video bar. From $5.60 for dormitory accommodation, single and double rooms also available. No curfew, but an 'inconvenience' charge of $0.50 if you come in after midnight.

Red Mountain Hostel (HaNegev Street; ☎059-74936). Next to the HaShalom, the hostel has a good bar with a 'play your own' music system, shows two videos a day in English, and is spotlessly clean. Prices for dormitory beds range from $6.25 to $9.50 upwards per night depending on the time of year. At the cheaper price, it is well worth the money.

The Village Hostel (HaNegev Street; ☎059-71311). Opposite the bus station: clean and pleasant, with barracks-style dormitory accommodation, TV room and bar. Prices start from $7.50 and include an Israeli breakfast.

Max and Merran Hostel (116 Simtat Ophirim St; ☎059-71408). Easy-going atmosphere, quiet and friendly. Strict midnight curfew keeps the peace, and if you don't mind this, $5 per person per night represents excellent value.

Patio 830 (☎059-76611). Phone ahead, and if there's room Dalia will come and pick you up from the bus station. A small converted house central enough to allow you to keep in touch with the town and distant enough (about 10 minutes' walk to the sea – which gives you an idea of the size of Eilat) to take you away from the brash commercial centre. Kitchen facilities and a washing machine provide the basics. Prices from $3.50 for a camp bed under the stars to $5 and up for a bed inside. A ten per cent discount is offered on production of this guidebook.

Eilat Youth Hostel (☎059-72358). In front of the New Tourist Centre towards the sea, the official youth hostel is clean, tidy and very helpful – the only snag is the curfew. $5.30 in winter, $5.80 in summer, plus a small daily membership fee for non card-holders.

Other hostels In the streets behind the bus station you'll find numerous other hostels for around $5 to $8 per night.

Dekkel Hotel (bottom of HaNegev; ☎059-74191). Just down from the central bus station and perhaps Eilat's cheapest hotel. The rooms are no better than some of the hostels, but the lush gardens and the hotel atmosphere may entice. Prices range from $20–23 single and $28–34 double, depending on time of year. Israeli breakfast and service included.

Etzion Hotel (Hatmarim Street; ☎059-74131). Three-star hotel in the Commercial Centre: functional and slightly sterile, but well situated for nightlife and boasts its own swimming pool. Full rates of $29 for a single room, $42 for a double (including breakfast) are expensive, but sharing can substantially reduce the cost. For four people sharing a double room, the price is $19 per person. Students get a ten per cent discount and in the low season prices can come down considerably.

North Beach

Sun Bay Holiday Village and Camping Site (☎059-73105). Beyond the hotels, right by the Jordanian border. Well laid-out complex with two types of accommodation: camping facilities or simple chalet-style huts. Camping space is reasonable at $3 per person per night, including shower and toilet facilities. The chalet-style accommodation can cost from $20 per room per night, depending on whether you want air conditioning: with four beds to a room this can also be excellent value. Always space for a tent, but the chalets are popular, so phone ahead. Restaurant/cafeteria open from noon until 9pm and well stocked supermarket five minutes' walk from the site towards the large hotels.

Coral Beach and east of Eilat

Almog Beach Camping Site (aka *Caroline's Camping*; ☎059-79272). Just past the new port, this large campsite rents out curiously designed semi-permanent tents at $10 per night single, $13 double. Again demand is high, so ring to check. Also, at $2.50 per person per night, the cheapest official place in Eilat to pitch your own tent. A café on site sells soft drinks, alcohol and basics.

Club Inn (Coral Beach; ☎059-79577). Ritzy complex across the road from the Coral Beach Marina. If you have the money, the low season rates of $80 (Thur–Sun) and $60 (Sun–Thur) for a villa capable of accommodating four people represent suprisingly good value. Included are pool, jacuzzi, multi-sports area and various bars and restaurants.

Yigal's Beduin Camping Site (☎059-76461). Opposite the Coral World Underwater Observatory, this represents the worst and best elements of Eilat. Like others in Eilat, it tries to attract tourists with coffee and a cosy chat with a 'real Beduin' in a 'real Beduin tent'. The shiny coffeepots and museum-like decorations are far from the hand-to-mouth existence experienced by most Beduin today. The campsite itself, which would seem more at home on a Pacific island, is however one of the most tranquil places in Eilat. There are about fifteen Hawaiian-style huts which can accommodate three or four persons: $11 single, $16 for two and $21 for three. A small cafeteria sells breakfast, drinks etc.

The Town

Beaches apart, the undoubted highlight of Eilat is **Coral World** (Coral Beach; daily 9am–6pm; admission $6), a Disneyland-style extravaganza which, for all the hype, is nothing short of amazing. Its chief attraction is the **underwater observatory** about 150m from the shore, and 6m below sea level. The observatory is built directly into the famous **Red Sea Coral Reef**, affording an unparalleled opportunity to view marine life in its natural environment without getting wet. Perhaps the most surprising thing, certainly for non-divers, is the sheer amount of marine life: brightly coloured shoals of exotic fish swim obliviously past the 360-degree observatory in a microcosm of tiered, multi-coloured coral – with the occasional human diver looking strangely awkward among them. This is something you should not miss.

Nearby, the **Red Sea Reef Tank** is the home of a seemingly infinite variety of exotic fish, corals and sea life. Also in the complex are three concrete seashore **pools**, embedded into the rocks bordering the sea, which contain specimens too large to be kept in a regular aquarium – sharks, giant turtles, and a large collection of vicious-looking stingrays. The **Aquarium**

and Sea Museum is fascinating too, with a comprehensive collection of Red Sea life. Each of the small tanks contains a whole world in itself: once you've taken in the fish, you begin to notice that what you thought were rocks are really living, moving corals and sea anemones. The darkened display of luminous corals in the museum is particularly good.

The Coral World complex has a reasonably priced cafeteria and supermarket where snacks, drinks and gifts can be bought. Don't be put off by its highly commercial atmosphere – it is well worth it. Alongside there's a sandy beach dotted with palm trees and bordered by waterfalls which provides a place for relaxation and sunbathing.

Other land-based attractions in Eilat are distinctly limited and, frankly, none are worth taking time out from the beach for unless your sunburn is so bad that you're forced to stay in the shade. There's a free **art gallery** at Beit Rubin (HaNegev Street; Sun–Thur 10am–noon and 5–7pm), with a rotating exhibition of mainly local Israeli art. The **Israel Palace Museum** (Sat–Thur 9am–noon and 4–10pm, Fri 9am–1pm; admission $2.50), in the hotel area next to the Caesar Hotel, presents a 'trip from the past to the present of the Jewish people' in the form of dioramas of waxworks dolls. Madame Tussaud's it's not.

At most times of year you'll find more excitement if you look up to the sky, for Eilat and the surrounding area is a **birdwatchers'** paradise almost as much as it is a marine biologists' one. Its position in the Afro-Syrian rift at the northern tip of the Gulf of Aqaba in the African-Syrian rift, puts it on one of the principal migration routes of European birds which winter in Africa. The main migratory periods are in spring and autumn – when ornithologists at times seem to outnumber beach bums – but there are thousands of birds here all year around. The **International Birdwatching Centre** has an information desk in the ritzy *King Solomon Hotel* by the Lagoon (open 5–9pm), where you can get up-to-date advice on where to go and what you're likely to see.

Beaches and watersports

There's sandy **beach** almost all the way around Eilat's shore, crowded close to town and around the hotel area of North Beach, less so as you head east towards Taba. Perhaps the classiest stretch of sand in Eilat lies in the sector which has now been handed over to Egypt: **Nelson's Village** (Taba Beach, admission $2–3), a wooden beach complex which looks like a set out of a spaghetti western. Egypt or not, you can still come here without any border formalities, as the frontier post remains (for the moment) where it used to stand beyond Nelson's Village and the *Sonesta Hotel*. The beach is clean and quiet and the small site has a large 'ranch' bar serving cold beers – to the accompaniment of live music on *shabbat* – and an open-air restaurant, *Cannibal's*, where you eat burgers, chicken or fish with your hands. They also serve vegetarian food at the bar.

If lying on the beach eventually starts to pall, there's no shortage of organised **watersports** to keep you occupied. Above all, you can get beneath the water, **snorkelling** or **scuba diving**. If you've been to Coral World you'll have some idea of what to expect on the reef, but getting down there yourself, away from the noise and out of sight of the concrete, is something else again. For absolute beginners, the Nature Reserve Authority has marked out several underwater trails in the **Coral Beach Reserve** (next to the Underwater Observatory), which anyone who can swim can follow. Prices for hiring equipment are modest and include access to Coral Beach. Experienced divers who hold an International Diving Licence can hire tanks, weights and the rest of the paraphernalia from the **Red Sea Diving Centre** (Coral Beach; ☎059-72788) for about $25 a day. Introductory courses for beginners are also available at $150 for a six-day course. Masks, fins and snorkels can be hired here at $3 per day. Other diving centres, which operate a similar price scale, include *Lucky Divers* (*Moriah Hotel*, hotel area; ☎059-75749) and the diving centre which operates from the Marina in the hotel area (☎059-72133).

Above the waves, opportunities for **sailing**, **windsurfing** and **boating** are plentiful. Organised boat trips range from the serene **glass-bottomed boats** (*Tour Yam*, New Pier, Coral Beach; ☎059-72111) to the less slick but perhaps more enjoyable yachts which operate from the Laguna in the hotel area. For around $20, you get a meal at sea and as much wine or beer as you can drink. The best windsurfing is from North Beach: *Andy and Elmar Windsurfing* for example. They charge around $6 per hour with a pick-up charge of $7 for those unlucky enough to get swept along too close to the Jordanian border and have to be towed back to dry land. A four-hour beginners' course will set you back about $38.

Eating and drinking

You may read in the brochures about the gastronomic delights served daily in Eilat, but in fact the **food** in general is overpriced and nothing to write home about. Candlelit restaurants abound for those willing to pay for 'romantic' moments, but there are few good cheap restaurants for those who want to dine out and still afford to eat the next day.

Unlikely as it may sound, the *Egged Bus Station Cafeteria* is highly recommended for a good, solid meal at least once during your stay in Eilat. Although the decor is more reminiscent of a school canteen, it is one of the few places in Eilat which serves traditional kosher Jewish cooking, and at some of the cheapest prices. Good for breakfast too.

The **New Tourist Centre** has the usual plastic hamburger places – *Miss Lucy* and *McDavid's* – or there's more interesting **fast food** around the top of Hatmarim Boulevard: *falafel* stalls such as *Tubul Falafel*, a bakery over the road serving pizzas and pies, and shops which sell hot dogs and delicious cheese or potato *burekas*. **Pizza** can also work out fairly cheap: try *The Pizzeria* (hotel area), *Le Festival* or *Pizzeria Am Shalom* (both in the Shalom Plaza Centre). Also in the Shalom Plaza Centre is the good value American-style *Pancake House*.

If you want to spend more on a meal, the choice is endless. When you're hungry, the numerous **'eat all you can'** restaurants are worth trying. One of the best is the busy *Fisherman's House* on Coral Beach (noon–midnight), with a selection of salads and fish, good atmosphere, and no pressure to move on. Others include *New York, New York* (99 HaAlmogim Street) where for $8 you can gorge yourself on an extensive array of Jewish/Polish food. The free listings magazines available from the IGTO and hotel lobbies usually carry advertisements, and often discount vouchers, for a number of these set-price restaurants.

More **upmarket**, perhaps the best restaurant in Eilat is the atmospheric *Pago Pago*, a floating restaurant which lies serenely in the Laguna on North Beach (daily 6pm–3am). In fact this needn't be outrageously expensive, but once you start it usually turns out that way, so bring the plastic. You can also come here for a drink in the bar. Another pricey but stylish place is the vegetarian *Galletino* (174 Eilot St; ☎059-73578; 6pm–2am), with quality modern art on the walls and a distinctly nouvelle menu.

Bars in Eilat fall broadly into two categories: there are the glossy hotel and restaurant bars where cocktail-sipping tourists hang out; and there are some surprisingly earthy pubs popular with local workers and long-term travellers. Of the latter, try the *Red Lion Bar* (in the New Tourist Centre), a popular haunt of English travellers which tends to attract trouble; *The Tavern* (nearby and similar); the *Peace Café* (HaAlmogim Street) which spills out onto the road in the summer and has a far more laid-back atmosphere; the *Hard Rock Café* (Eilot Street), a British-owned pub which serves pints of lager and the best sausage, egg and chips you are likely to get in Eilat; and the *Tropicana* (upstairs in the Shalom Centre) which has a happy hour and gives everyone a free drink at 9pm every evening. Most of these have loud music and videos.

The less glossy bars down by the hotel area include the *Yatush Barosh* bar (literally 'gnat in the head') overlooking the Marina, which is cheap, has good music and a good selection of vegetarian food, and *Rhapsody in White*, a floating island on the North Beach side of Eilat. If you are staying at Coral Beach try *My Pub* (opposite the Coral Beach Marina) which serves snacks and stays open until 6am.

Nightlife

Nightlife in Eilat basically involves a drink, a romantic meal, and afterwards maybe a **disco** – all of them thoroughly predictable, most attached to the big hotels. The better ones include *Le Prive* (Industrial Zone; 10.30pm–4am; first drink $6); the *Maestro Nightclub* (Commercial Centre; 11pm–6am; first drink $6); the classy *Disco-Americano* (at the *Americana Hotel*; free, but drinks very expensive); or the *Club Inn* (Coral Beach, varying prices) which sometimes offers live entertainment at a not unreasonable cost.

The only **cinema**, *Cinema Eilat* (Commercial Centre, next to the post office), shows fairly recent films most nights of the week. More interestingly, the **Phillip Murray Cultural Centre** (Hatmarim Boulevard; ☎059-72257; daily 5–11pm) puts on a variety of jazz, classical, rock and theatre performances. Games such as chess and backgammon are available at the cafeteria free of charge. For details of the above and any ad hoc cultural activities, contact the IGTO.

Listings

Airlines *Arkia* (Shalom Plaza Centre; ☎059-72110); *El Al* (Shalom Plaza Centre; ☎059-75180).

Banks Most are open Sun–Thur 8.30am–12.30pm, Sun–Tue and Thur also 4–5.30pm, Fri 8.30am–noon. You'll find branches above all in the Commercial Centre and the New Shalom Centre. *Bank Hapoalim* and *Bank Leumi* have special tourist facilities, which considerably speed up the transaction process – remember to take your passport.

Bike rental Try *Red Sea Sports Centre* (Coral beach; ☎059-71846) or at the lagoon in front of the *Queen of Sheba* hotel (hotel area).

Books Good selection of books at *Steimatzky's Bookshop* in the Egged Bus Station facing Hatmarim Boulevard and *Book Bar* (15 Almogin St; ☎059-74211). Most large hotels also have a small bookstall.

Buses and tour tickets *Egged Bus Station* (Hatmarim Blvd; ☎059-75161), regular bus service and tours; *United Tours* (New Tourist Centre; ☎059-71720), daily tours all over Israel and into the Sinai; *Johnny Desert Tours* (Shalom Centre, 2nd floor; ☎059-76777), a variety of popular desert tours; *Neot Hakikar* (Commercial Centre, facing Hatmarim Blvd), tours, walking, diving, by jeep and by coach into the Sinai and Negev deserts, highly recommended; *Galilee Tours* (*Neptune Hotel*, hotel area; ☎059-74720), big and well organised; *Geographical Tours Ltd* (*Moriah Hotel*, hotel area; $059-72151), also big; *Tour Yam Ltd* (Marina, hotel area; ☎059-72436), boat trips on the Red Sea.

Camping gear *Camping Shop* at *Almogin Camp Site*, Coral Beach.

Car rental While all the major international companies are represented in Eilat, the cheapest are *Eldan Rent a Car* (HaArava Street, Shalom Plaza Centre; ☎059-74027) and *Europa Car* opposite the airport (HaArava Street; ☎059-74178).

Egyptian Consulate 34 Dror Street (☎059-76115). Open Sun–Thur, visas issued on day of application for $10–25 depending on nationality. When you get near you should see the Egyptian flag flying from the top of the building.

Emergencies Police ☎100, Ambulance ☎101. First aid posts on Hatmarim Boulevard and several of the beaches.

Hospital Yotam Rd (☎059-72301 or ☎059-73151).

Information IGTO in the Commercial Centre off Hatmarim Blvd (Sun–Thur 8am–6pm, Fri 8am–1pm; ☎059-72268 or ☎059-76737), exceptionally well stocked with brochures, advice and help with accommodation. Also a municipal information centre in the *Neptune Hotel* (hotel area; Sun–Thur 8am–10pm, Fri 8am–5pm, Sat 9am–1pm and 5–10pm; ☎059-74233).

Laundry *Gill Laundromat* (corner of Eilot and Hatmarim Blvd), open Sun–Thur 8am–1pm and 4–7pm, Fri 9am–1.30pm.

Pharmacy *Eilat Pharmacy*, Eilot Street (☎059-75002).

Phones International phone boxes can be made at *Bezek* in the Commercial Centre (Sun–Thur 8am–2pm and 7–10pm, Fri 8am–1.30pm). Reverse charge calls can also be made from the public telephones at the front of the post office.

Post office Main post office in the Commercial Centre, facing Hatmarim Boulevard, is open Sun, Tue and Thur 7.45am–12.30pm and 4–6.30pm, Mon and Wed 7.45am–2pm, Fri 7.45am–1pm.

Supermarket *Supercolberg*, Hatmarim Boulevard, the Commercial Centre (Sun–Thur 8am–10pm, Fri 8am–2pm, Sat 10am–10pm).

Travel agents *Peltours* and others in the Commercial Centre.

Work Eilat is probably the best place in Israel to find casual or temporary work. The burgeoning tourist industry is in constant need of cheap labour, skilled and unskilled, and while wages are low, most people who look seem to come up with something. No agency exists to find these (strictly speaking illegal) jobs, so the obvious first step is to tour the hotels and restaurants and ask. Turnover is constant for jobs done by travellers who tend to leave after a few months. In addition try the marinas, especially the boats which specialise in day trips. While the wages here are even worse than most, and the hours long, being out on the water does have its appeal. The second major job market is casual labour, especially in the summer, for employment on a day-to-day, week-to-week basis. Early morning (about 6am) at the *Peace Café* (Almogin St) is fast becoming the meeting place for workers and prospective employers. If you do get work, fellow employees can be a good source of information about the Israel not usually seen by the tourists.

Around Eilat

If you intend to hire a car at some stage of your visit to Israel, then Eilat is probably the place to do it, giving you the opportunity to explore the desert at leisure. Unfortunately, you cannot take an Israeli hire car into Egypt. The sites below are, however, all accessible on tours from Eilat, and a couple can be reached without too much difficulty by regular bus.

Timna Valley National Park

Timna Valley National Park lies 28km north of Eilat (daily 8am–4pm; admission $1), a vast area of awesome desert landscape where copper has been being mined for almost six thousand years. Excavations began here around the turn of the century, and have uncovered evidence of mining from the Early Bronze Age and a particularly strong Egyptian presence from around 1400BC. Recently, mining has returned to the area, although the new mines remain out of bounds and out of sight for visitors.

Immediately inside the main gate is an **information area** where maps, illustrations and text explain the ancient techniques of copper mining and smelting, techniques remarkably similar to many modern-day methods. You

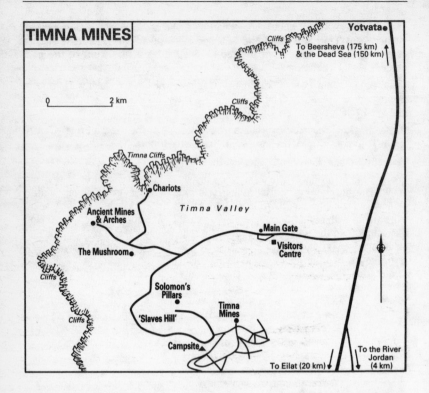

TIMNA MINES

can also pick up information about the hiking trails and the main attractions in the park. Perhaps the area's most striking feature is the rugged rockface which hems in the large crater-like valley, an isolation that evokes vivid pictures of the conditions and lives of those early miners. The valley floor is arid and stained red by the rich mineral deposits, and in the cliffs are carved **rock drawings**. You can discern Caananite warriors on their ox-drawn chariots, and a multitude of ibex and oryx, animals now all but extinct in this region.

The greatest of the natural wonders are **King Solomon's Pillars**, at the southern end of the park towards the artificial Timna Lake. Two great red pillars of rock, they protrude from the valley wall like the entrance to some vast prehistoric cathedral. Railed off nearby are the remains of the **Temple of Hathor**, an Egyptian shrine dating from the fourteenth century BC.

Several companies run tours to Timna Valley from Eilat (try *Egged* or *United*), or you can get a bus up the Arava Valley as far as the track leading to the park, and hike 3km from there to the entrance. Once inside, however, walking is not a particularly attractive prospect – the various attractions are widely scattered, and it's very hot. With a car you can drive between them, or you could consider hiring a bike in Eilat and spending a few nights camping in the valley. A rough, free campsite by Timna Lake provides fresh drinking water and toilet facilities; it's crowded during the day when the tours roll in, but eerily quiet at night. A small snackbar sells the basics during the day, but if you intend to stay for a while, bring provisions with you to save money.

Hai Bar Biblical Wildlife Reserve and Kibbutz Yotvata

Some 40km north of Eilat, the **Hai Bar Biblical Wildlife Reserve** is a safari-park-style reserve with over 450 native animal species on show in their natural habitat. Some wander freely throughout the complex – oryx, addax and other antelope-like animals, ostriches – others, including large cats, wolves, hyenas and other predators roam in spacious enclosures. Many of these animals are otherwise extinct or close to extinction in the Negev, where centuries of hunting has taken its toll. All of them are mentioned in the Bible at some stage (hence the 'biblical' reserve); and the place gives some idea of the size of the animal population in biblical times, and perhaps helps to explain how early human populations were able to survive here. The reserve is easy enough to reach by bus, right by the main road, but you can only go round it in a vehicle; if you wait at the entrance, you may find someone with space who is prepared to take you round. Again, though, if you don't have transport of your own, it's easier to take a tour.

On the same site as the Hai Bar Reserve is the **Nature Reserves Authorities Visitors' Centre** (Sun–Thur 8am–4pm, Fri 8am–1pm, Sat 10am–2pm; admission $1, joint admission for both $1.75). Here the archaeology, geography, geology, flora and fauna of the area are demonstrated through pictures, exhibitions and an audio-visual presentation. By the road is a cafeteria belonging to **Kibbutz Yotvata**, where the kibbutz's famed dairy products are sold – any of the fourteen different kinds of yoghurts, milk drinks and ice-creams are very refreshing and heartily recommended. Yotvata itself, little over 1km to the north, offers tours of its **regional dairy centre**, where again the highlight is sampling the end product. It's a popular kibbutz with volunteers, especially during the winter.

If you are planning to stay in the area, then **Yee'lim Holiday Village/ Campsite** (200m from the road by the cafeteria) is your best bet. Owned by **Kibbutz Grofit**, 8km north of the site, Yee'lim offers caravan accommodation at $26 per night for two, $20 single, and camping from $4.50 per head. The village has a dining room, clubhouse with bar and TV, a swimming pool with water slides, and at least makes a change from Eilat: at night especially, it is drowned in the stillness of the desert. From here, you can arrange to visit Kibbutz Grofit.

Into Egypt: the Sinai

The triangular **Sinai Peninsula**, lying between the continents of Africa and Asia, has been the battleground of four wars between Egypt and Israel. After the war of 1948, it became the ceasefire line between the two countries; in the 1956 Suez war it was captured by Israeli troops but returned to Egypt after a UN agreement to keep the **Straits of Tiran** open to Israeli shipping; in 1967 it was again occupied by Israel; and in the Yom Kippur/Ramadan War of

1973, the Egyptians crossed over the **Suez Canal** on the western edge of the desert in an attempt to retrieve the area.

The bulk of the Sinai, however, remained in Israeli hands until the **Camp David Accords** in 1979 assured the return of most of it to Egypt. The only bit that was left – **Taba** – took ten years of lengthy and bitter negotiations for Egypt to retrieve. Taba was handed back to Egypt on March 15, 1989. Once you step over the border and see just how small and apparently insignificant the area in dispute is, it becomes clear that the struggle over who was to keep Taba was more about financial and ideological than strategic considerations. All that's there are the luxurious five-star **Sonesta hotel** and **Nelson's Village**; apart from the expensive restaurant and beach facilities on offer here, there's little to do other than go for a swim or visit the quite unspectacular concrete platform that was erected in the middle of nowhere for the handing-over ceremony.

Travelling into the Sinai from Israel requires a **visa**. A **Sinai-only** visa is obtainable at the Israeli border-crossing at Taba, but if you intend to travel on to the rest of Egypt, a regular Egyptian visa must be obtained **in advance**, either from an Egyptian consulate in your country or in Tel Aviv or Eilat. The Sinai-only visa costs $6 and is valid for one week; travel on it is limited to the Aqaba Coast – Taba, Nuweiba, Dahab and Sharm al-Sheikh – and the area of **Saint Catherine's Monastery**.

The **Sinai Desert**, bordered to the east by the Gulf of Aqaba and to the west by the Gulf of Suez, offers some truly spectacular and varied scenery. Clear blue seas, coral reefs, open sandy beaches and oases contrast with spiky black and sandstone mountains, deep canyons and wide expanses of sand-dunes. The Sinai is populated by nomadic Beduin who depend primarily on their herds of camels and goats, but increasingly make a living from the thriving tourist industry in the region.

The Taba-Sinai **border crossing** is fairly straightfoward but can be tedious, with frustratingly long waits on both sides. This makes the one-day **tour of Saint Catherine's** organised by *Neot Hakikar* – the easiest way to take a quick look at the Sinai – something of an ordeal, with more time spent sitting at border posts and on buses than actually at the sites. If you're short of time, however, even this fleeting glimpse of the splendid desert monastery is worth it. The tour entails setting out at 6.30am for a dawn drive to the border. On the Egyptian side, you are transferred to a couple of minibuses which drive down the Red Sea Coast to the oasis of Nuweiba where the buses mysteriously disappear, guide and all, to be replaced by one large tourist bus. When you finally pull up at St. Catherine's two hours later you have a bare twenty minutes to elbow your way through the other groups of camera-clicking tourists at the **Greek Orthodox Church** before it closes. With a bit of luck, you may catch glimpses of the superb collection of icons and Bibles. This is followed by a fleeting visit to the site of **Moses' burning bush** and a glance at **Saint Helena's Church** before being piled back on the bus and speeding off to **Zeituna**, for a salad lunch and a drink.

Then you're on your long way back, with a stop at the grave of **Nabi Saleh** at the meeting of the ancient trade routes across the desert. After another stop at the strategic **Coral or Pharaoh's Island** where the Crusaders built a castle to 'safeguard' pilgrims travelling from Jerusalem to St. Catherine's, levying a tariff on Muslim traders on their way to and from Jordan and Saudi Arabia, it's back in the bus to the border for another tedious bout of bureaucracy and finally back to base.

Despite this, the Sinai is not to be missed. *Neot Hakikar* run a variety of other more leisurely tours, from one to seven days, including a dawn climb up **Mount Sinai** (where Moses received the Ten Commandments), camping at the oasis of **Dahab**, diving and snorkelling in the coral reefs of the **Red Sea** and camel treks across mountain ranges. And St. Catherine's Monastery deserves more time than the day-trip allows. If you want to travel independently and spend longer in the Sinai, there's a fairly regular **bus service** from Taba. Air-conditioned buses run twice daily to Cairo (at 10am and 2pm), a journey of nine hours. These stop at Nuweiba and St. Catherine's Monastery. Less luxurious buses run at 1pm and 3pm from Taba to Sharm al-Sheikh, via Nuweiba and Dahab. There are also seven-seater *service* taxis from Taba to St. Catherine's, Nuweiba, Dahab or Sharm al-Sheikh, and a *service* direct to Cairo along the new, 425km road, a journey of around five hours. **Hitchhiking** is not a good idea as traffic is sparse and the heat is punishing. It is advisable to take some food reserves for longer stays, although there are reasonable and cheap restaurants in each town.

travel details

Buses
From Beersheva to Hebron/Jerusalem (every 30min 6am-8.30pm; 30min); Qiryat Gat/Jerusalem (30min 6am-8.30pm; 40min/2hr); Tel Aviv (20min 6am-7.30pm; 2hr); Haifa (7 daily; 4hr); Ashqelon (hourly 6am-7pm; 1hr); Gaza (2 daily; 1hr); Arad (hourly 6am-10pm; 45min); Dimona (30min 6am-6pm; 30min); Eilat (hourly 7.30am-6.30pm; 3hr).
From Arad to Masada/Dead Sea (7 daily; 30min).

From Eilat to Jerusalem (6 daily; 5hr); Tel Aviv (hourly 6am-5pm; 5hr); Haifa (2 daily; 6hr); Taba (7daily; 15min).

Planes
Eilat is the one place in Israel to which you might consider taking an **internal** flight, with daily *Arkia* shuttles to Jerusalem and Tel Aviv. Scheduled **international** flights go to Frankfurt and London, and to other destinations in high season. These flights are free of airport tax.

PART THREE

THE

CONTEXTS

THE HISTORICAL FRAMEWORK

Palestine was in a very real sense the crossroads of the ancient world. Its political fortunes were – and are – determined as much by external factors as internal ones, as the strengths and alliances of its neighbours waxed and waned. The great and densely populated Egypt of the Pharaohs lay to the south; a string of small countries – Edom, Moab, Ammon and Gilead – lay to the east; wealthy Assyria and Babylonia flourished on the Tigris and Euphrates rivers in the distant northeast, and to the immediate north were the powerful states of the Amorites and Mitanni. For several hundred years the Hittites dominated Asia Minor to the northwest, west lay Crete with its splendid culture and across the strait of the Hellespont was the land later known as Greece.

The ancient Land of Canaan, as Palestine was first known, lay uneasily between all these – the route between them, and for most the only access to the Mediterranean Sea. By taking and holding this crossroads, any one of them could bar the others and thus gain supremacy. Canaan was therefore constantly invaded and conquered as nation after nation tried first to get a foothold, then to gain complete control, then to establish a political claim to Palestine and make the claim stick.

THE CANAANITE PERIOD

Human habitation of the region stretches back about 50,000 years. For the first 30,000 years or so, the inhabitants lived in the open during the warm, dry summers and in caves during the cold, wet winters. The **Canaanites** were then known by the name of the towns or valleys in which they lived – the Jebusites, for example, came from **Jebus** (Jerusalem). About 20,000 years ago the Canaanites started to settle, and to build houses with beautifully painted and polished floors, mostly near water sources. The discovery of soft copper in about 4000BC transformed their culture and over the next thousand years, they learned to combine it with tin to make **bronze** for hard and durable tools and weapons. In the early Bronze Age they built massive walls to encircle and protect their towns – such as Beisan, Jericho, Jebus and Megiddo – and started trading with Egypt and Babylonia.

THE EGYPTIANS

The earliest recorded foreign rulers of Canaan were the powerful **Pharaohs** of the First and Second Egyptian Dynasties who made the country a colonial possession around 2800BC. A thousand years later, the Hebrew (or Habiru) tribesman named Abram (later **Abraham**) came up from Babylonian Chaldea and drifted into Canaan, the period historians believe to correspond with the Patriarchal Age of the Bible.

Although the Pharaohs continued to claim Canaan as part of their empire, they were gradually ousted as the northern, nomadic **Hyksos** shifted south; their empire lasted from the eighteenth to the twentieth century BC, and thousands of their inscribed seals have been found all over Palestine.

Around 1550BC, the Egyptians drove the Hyksos out and held on to the crossroads for the next 130 years. The rebellious **Pharaoh Akhenaten** (and Queen Nefertiti) reigned in the fourteenth century BC; correspondence between him and the kings of various Canaanite cities in the **Tel al-Amarna letters** describes the threat posed by the Habiru tribesmen – the descendents of Abraham. But when Akhenaten lost control of his empire (supposedly because of his heretical belief in monotheism), the weak and divided city-kings of Canaan were unable to impose independent control. Instead the **Hittites** moved in from Asia Minor with a new war weapon – iron. They took the land of the Amorites (Syria), then Canaan. Egypt under Ramses II (the Great) reoccupied the southern part of the Canaanite corridor about 1290BC. Ninety years later, the Hittite Empire was wiped out, their cities burned by invaders referred to in Egyptian records as 'Sea Peoples'. It is about this time too that, according to the book of *Exodus*, the Habiru or Hebrews, who had migrated to Egypt through famine, escaped from there to the Sinai desert. More than 600,000 people, led by Moses, are said to have left Egypt and, over forty years, made their way towards the grasslands of Canaan. There is, however, no mention of this in otherwise highly detailed Egyptian records; neither is there any archaeological evidence of this event to date.

THE PHILISTINES

Canaan now had Egypt still trying to maintain its hold from the south, with the Amorites closing in from the north, the desert tribes (including the Hebrews) from the east and the **Philistine** sea-farers from the west. The Philistines and the Israelites were in constant battle with each other, but the feather-crowned Philistine warriors were stronger than the bearded Israelites (as they are depicted in historical records of the time), managing to capture the Israelites' most holy object – the Ark of the Covenant – at Eben-Ezer and to enslave them ('and the Lord delivered them into the hands of the Philistines forty years' *Judges 13:1*). The Philistines' one lasting mark on the country is their name; it ceased to be known as Canaan and became Philistia (Palestine). The Philistines settled in the coastal strips, but neither they nor the Israelites were able to conquer the native inhabitants behind the walls of their cities.

The cultural accomplishments of the Philistines were markedly superior to those of the Israelites: they were well organised in a federation of five city-states and were adept in using iron, not only for chariots, shields and swords but also for making iron-tipped ploughs, while Philistine ships and camel caravans maintained commercial links with countries bordering the Mediterranean and Mesopotamia.

The **Israelites** were much influenced by the Canaanites and Philistines. Since they were a semi-nomadic people, they had little agricultural or architectural expertise, or even political organisation, but rather adopted the institutions of their settled neighbours. However, territorial rivalries kept the factions apart and, since the Israelites never wholly conquered Canaan, the cultural and religious distance between them and the Canaanites was preserved; yet Israelite religious practice at the time had more in common with Canaanite rites than with later post-Roman Judaism.

THE HEBREW PERIOD

The Philistines posed both an economic and a military threat to the Israelites. In order to unite the Hebrew tribes against them, the prophet Samuel appointed **Saul** as king. His reign, however, lasted only twenty years until about 1000BC. Saul's successor, **David**, finally took the fortified Canaanite town of Jebus (Jerusalem) completed Saul's task of defeating the Philistines, conquered Canaan and eventually also the eastern neighbours of Edom, Moab, Ammon and Gilead. He set up an independent kingdom and ruled for forty years (seven as a city king at Hebron and 33 at Jerusalem).

David's son **Solomon** ruled for a further 33 years; his **Temple** in Jerusalem was built between 957 and 950BC. Essential to the construction was Solomon's maintenance of his father's alliance with Phoenician King Hiram of Tyre, who supplied the builders, the masons, the famed cedars of Lebanon and other commodities for it. On Solomon's death in 928BC, the 73-year-old kingdom fell apart and split into two hostile factions – the tribes of Judah and Benjamin formed the **kingdom of Judah** in the south, the remaining ten tribes forming the **kingdom of Israel** (Samaria) in the north. Weakened by domestic quarrels and corruption, they were not strong enough to withstand the Egyptians who invaded Judah from the south and destroyed Jerusalem.

Al-Hadad of Syria annexed part of the northern kingdom, then formed an alliance with it against Judah. Judah appealed to the **Assyrians** who needed no second invitation; they swept north, taking the Phoenician trading ports of Tyre and Byblos by 740BC. By 722, they had completely obliterated the whole of the northern kingdom of Israel (many Israelites fled or were taken to Babylon, those who remained became known as the Samaritans), laid Judah under tribute and became rulers of Lower Egypt. The smaller kingdom of Judah survived for more than a century after the fall of Samaria. But in 600BC, the Assyrian empire was defeated by **Babylon**. In 586BC, King Nebuchadnezzar came from the east, invaded Judah, looted Jerusalem, burned its Temple and palaces, and exiled the people of Judah to Babylon.

THE PERSIANS

In 538BC, the conquering **Persians** from further to the northeast took over the Babylonian Empire, and Palestine with it. The Persian emperor, Cyrus the Great, allowed the Judaeans in Babylon – now known as Jews – to return to Jerusalem. Only a minority chose to leave, however, as by now they were well established in Babylon, with their own distinct commercial, political and religious institutions. The small community in Jerusalem, under the leadership of the prophets Haggai and Zechariah, built a smaller and more austere **Second Temple** – known as the Temple of Zerubbavel after the local Persian governor – which was completed in 515BC. The vast Persian empire lasted for 200 years.

THE GREEKS

Next to invade was Alexander the Great, who led a Greek army through the Middle East as far as Persia, taking Palestine in 332BC. The rich civilisation of the Greeks provided sculptors, architects, scientists, mathematicians, poets and philosophers. Their influence in Palestine was considerable: young and eager Jews learned new ideas which departed from tradition, infuriating their elders.

When Alexander died in 323BC, his Middle East empire was divided between two of his generals – Ptolemy, who acquired Egypt, and Seleucus, who got Syria. Initially ruled by the **Ptolemies**, Palestine fell to the **Seleucids** in 198BC. This division brought weakness and, between 167BC and 141BC, the Jews of Palestine, led by the three Maccabean brothers, revolted against the Hellenisation of their

culture. The victory of the **Maccabeans** over the Seleucids consolidated the dynasty of the priestly **Hasmonean** family who embarked on a programme of military and religious expansion which extended to the whole of Palestine, the Golan and the east bank of the Jordan. Internecine struggles weakened the Hasmoneans, however, and this Jewish attempt at independence was short-lived.

THE ROMANS

In 63BC, a real power in the shape of **Rome** arrived from the west. General Pompey took Jerusalem and an Edomite named **Herod** was set up as a puppet king over what became the Roman province of Judaea. The hated Herod levied taxes, impressed labour and commissioned enormous and expensive public works, including rebuilding and refurbishing the Temple in Jerusalem.

Although Herod was an astute politician, he is renowned for his cruelty toward rebels and rivals (he murdered his Hasmonean second wife Mariamne and their two sons). For the people of Palestine, the period of Roman rule under local puppet kings and procurators was a brutal one. There were numerous uprisings, but lack of unity frustrated attempts at liberation. The Jewish population was split into two main political factions: the **Sadducees**, a conservative, priestly and privileged class who held onto their position by obedience to Rome, and the **Pharisees**, who believed in strict adherence to the Jewish law, and in the coming of the messiah. The ministry of **Jesus** that was later to have such an impact on the world, was at the time an attempt to unite Palestinian society. It was for his refusal to recognise any other than divine power that Jesus was betrayed to the Romans by the High Priest Caiphas.

The provinces of Judaea fought two bloody but unsuccessful **revolts** against the Romans. The first revolt, in 66AD, culminated in the destruction of Herod's Temple (70AD) by Titus, the son of the Roman Emperor Vespasian. Bands of Zealots, however, continued to hold out against the Romans in their fortresses, above all at **Masada**, which became the last to fall in 73AD. Six decades after the fall of the Temple, there was a second revolt (135AD), led by Simeon ben Kosiba (Shimon Bar Kokhba). This time Jerusalem was completely razed by Hadrian who built a Roman city, Aelia

Capitolina, over its ruins and banned Jews from living in or even entering the city. Official Jewish connection with Jerusalem thus came to an end in 135AD, although pockets of Jewish culture survived elsewhere, above all in the Galilee.

THE BYZANTINE ERA

In 330AD Emperor **Constantine** succeeded in reunifying the Roman Empire after a period of division, and moved its capital to the Greek city of Byzantium (Constantinople), ushering in Byzantine rule in Palestine. **Christianity** became the official state religion, and many sites associated with Jesus were identified and consecrated for the first time, with the building of churches and monasteries and an influx of pilgrims into the country. Much of the local population converted to Christianity at this time, but restrictions placed on Jews and Samaritans led to the Samaritan revolt in 529AD. In 614AD the Persians attacked from the east; their conquest lasted fourteen years.

THE EARLY ARAB PERIOD

Palestine was taken by the Arab followers of the Prophet Mohammed at the battle of Yarmuk on August 20, 636AD; two years later, Muslim armies took over the entire Byzantine Empire of the Middle East. The **Caliph Omar** (638–644AD) made Jerusalem the capital of the Arab realm of Palestine, and in the course of the seventh century the Mosque of al-Aqsa was built in the city. Because of its associations with the Prophet, Jerusalem became the third holiest site in Islam (after the mosques of Mecca and Medina) and a place of pilgrimage.

The country's Muslim rulers interfered very little with the internal life of the Jewish or Christian communities whose members had freedom of movement and worship, and were able to occupy significant administrative and economic positions. 'Above all', according to Israeli historian and politician Abba Eban, 'life under Arab rule offered wide scope for creative spiritual energies'.

Many Canaanites, who through all the changing sovereignties and much diluted by foreign blood still formed the backbone of the rural population, converted to the Muslim faith. The language became Arabic, the architecture

Islamic, the population Arab. From this time until the end of World War I, apart from the relatively brief Crusader period (1099–1291), Palestine was under Muslim rule, although the power centre shifted from Damascus under the Omayyads (661–749), to Baghdad under the Abassids (750–969) and to Cairo during Fatimid rule (969–1071). In 1071 Palestine became part of the empire of the Seljuk Turks who ruled in Persia, Iraq and Anatolia.

THE CRUSADERS

At Clermont in November 1095, Pope Urban II called for the 'liberation' of the Holy Land from Muslim rule. Spurred by the desire for revenge for the loss of Byzantium and by stories of the persecution of Christians in Palestine, such a crusade offered an opportunity for high-born younger sons to seek wealth, adventure and divine approval at one and the same time. Setting out from different parts of western Europe, the army of **Crusaders** took Jerusalem in 1099, massacring its Muslim and Jewish inhabitants. The Europeans maintained their domination for less than 100 years, until **Salah al-Din** (Saladin) led his Muslim armies from the mountains of Kurdistan in the northeast, defeated the Crusaders at the battle of Hittin on July 4, 1187, and ushered in the **Ayyubid dynasty** (1187–1247). Pockets of Crusaders remained during this period (in Acre, for example) and after the death of Salah al-Din in 1193, cities such as Jerusalem, Bethlehem and Nazareth were returned to Crusader rule by Sultan Malik al-Kamil. But in 1244 the Crusaders were finally ousted from Jerusalem. The next to descend on Palestine were the Khwarizmians (Tartars), followed by the Mongols from still further east under Hulagu Khan, grandson of Genghis Khan.

THE MAMLUKS

In 1248 the Ayyubid dynasty was replaced by that of the **Mamluks** of Cairo. In Palestine the Mongol army was defeated at Ayn Jalut in 1260 and, by 1291, the Crusaders had been ousted from their final stronghold at Acre and were finally expelled from the Middle East. During the Mamluk period (1248–1517), many religious, educational and legal institutions were established in Jerusalem, which became a centre of pilgrimage and learning.

THE OTTOMANS

The **Ottoman Turks** defeated the Mamluks in 1517, conquered Egypt itself, and extended their rule along both sides of the Mediterranean. Sultan Suleiman the Magnificent took charge in Palestine and rebuilt Jerusalem where his great walls stand to this day. Ottoman rule, which lasted until 1918, gave Palestine its longest period of peace yet; but the price was one of economic stagnation. As long as their cut came in the form of taxes and other duties, the rulers cared little for what went on. By the end of the nineteenth century the Ottoman Empire was crumbling and increasingly corrupt and tyrannical. By the start of World War I, the Palestinian population was ready to revolt.

In the meantime, another element was being added. **Jews** had played little part in the political history of Palestine since their dispersion in 135AD. The indigenous Palestinian-Jewish community, known as the *Yishuv*, were mainly religious Jews, living primarily in the holy cities of Jerusalem, Hebron, Safad and Tiberias. During the nineteenth century, however, Jews seeking refuge from pogroms and anti-Semitism in eastern Europe and Russia obtained the permission of the Ottoman rulers to immigrate to Palestine – to make *aliyah* (literally, going up). The first Zionist colony – the town of Petah Tikva – was established in 1878, but the first major wave took place in 1882.

In central Europe, the **Zionist movement** was gaining momentum; in 1896 Theodor Herzl wrote his seminal work *Der Judenstaat* (The Jewish State) which called for the establishment of a Jewish state in either Palestine or Argentina. A year later, the World Zionist Organisation held its first congress in Basle, and declared its aim 'to create for the Jewish people a home in Palestine ...' In 1901, the Jewish National Fund (JNF) was set up to finance the purchase of land for Jews in Palestine. Eight years later saw the founding of Tel Aviv, north of the Palestinian city of Jaffa. By the outbreak of World War I, subsequent waves of immigrants had raised the Jewish population of the country to 60,000, less than ten per cent of the total. The overwhelming majority were Palestinian Arab, a little over ten per cent of them Christian, the rest Muslim. Nevertheless, the Zionists' slogan, 'A land without people for a people without land', remained convincing to western ears for many years to come.

THE END OF THE OTTOMAN EMPIRE

During **World War I** Turkey sided with Germany against Britain and France. The Arab subjects of the Ottoman Empire, by now seeking independence, joined with the Allies to fight their Turkish rulers. In return for their contribution to the allied war effort, the British undertook to recognise and support the independence of the Arabs in the Arabian Peninsula, Palestine, Transjordan, Syria and Iraq. But behind the scenes, something else was cooking. According to the secret Anglo-French deal of 1916 (the **Sykes-Picot Agreement**), Britain and France would divide the defunct Ottoman Empire between them, with Palestine placed under an 'international administration' of some sort.

Meanwhile, Zionist leaders were pressing high British government officials for their support for a Jewish homeland in Palestine, stressing the strategic advantages to them of having an ally in the Middle East which would be, in Herzl's words, '... a portion of the rampart of Europe against Asia, an outpost of civilisation as opposed to barbarism'. The argument was convincing to the supreme imperialist power of the time: on November 2, 1917, British Foreign Secretary Balfour signed the **Balfour Declaration** which stated that 'His Majesty's Government view with favour the establishment in Palestine of a national home for the Jewish people, it being clearly understood that nothing shall be done which may prejudice the civil and religious rights of the existing non-Jewish communities'. To reassure the Arabs, however, an Anglo-French declaration was issued a year later, promising 'the complete and definite emancipation of the Arab peoples ... and the establishment of national governments and administrations deriving their authority from the initiative and free choice of the indigenous populations' – a promise clearly betrayed in Balfour's memorandum of 1919 in which he wrote: 'in Palestine, we do not propose even to go through the form of consulting the wishes of the present inhabitants of the country ...'

Palestine was occupied by allied forces under the command of General Allenby in 1918. By the end of World War I, Jewish immigrants had managed to acquire about two percent of Palestine and, with the second *aliya* at the turn of the century, more and more Palestinian peasants were resisting being ousted from their lands.

THE BRITISH MANDATE

After the defeat of Germany and its Turkish ally, the Ottoman Empire was dismembered. The earlier agreement for the internationalisation of Palestine was nullified and in April 1920 Britain was mandated by the League of Nations to control Palestine. The terms of **the Mandate** included, among others, responsibility for 'the establishment of the Jewish National Home' and approval of Jewish immigration, referring to the Palestinian population of the country simply as 'non-Jewish communities'. Acquisition of land and mass Jewish immigration, directed by the Jewish Agency, raised Jewish land holding to five per cent and the Jewish population to seventeen per cent by 1929. Between 1930 and 1939, substantial numbers of European Jews chose Palestine as a refuge from Nazi terror in Europe, so that by 1939 the Jewish population constituted almost a third of the whole.

For Palestinian Arabs, this burgeoning Jewish National Home meant dispossession from their land and a violation of promises of independence. Having no formal political organisation at the start of the Mandate, their resentment was expressed by a series of violent protests, the first of which was in 1920. Each subsequent revolt – in 1921, 1929 and 1933 – was followed by a commission of enquiry that found that the Palestinians had good cause for concern. Eventually, from 1936 to 1939, there was a full-scale **Palestinian Revolt**. A series of strikes brought the country to a stand-still; roads, railways, telegraph and telephone lines, oil pipelines and other government property were sabotaged, and both the British and the Zionists came under armed attack. The British responded by authorising the Jewish Agency to bring in several thousand new immigrants and enrolled 20,000 Jews into the police being used against the 'rebels'. Members of such armed groups as *Haganah*, *Irgun* and the *Stern Gang*, some trained by British officers, launched operations against the Palestinians.

The Palestinian Revolt precipitated the termination of the Mandate. A British Royal Commission of 1937 concluded that 'the situation in Palestine has reached a deadlock. We cannot . . . both concede the Arab claim to self-government and secure the establishment of a Jewish National Home.' Its solution was to end the mandate and partition the country. Both sides rejected partition. A White Paper in 1939 then proposed a unified state in which both Jews and Palestinian Arabs would share in government.

By the start of World War II, the Palestinian nationalist movement had been firmly suppressed and the Zionists began looking to the US for political support. With worldwide revulsion at the Nazi persecution of European Jewry at its height in 1942, the Zionists (at the Biltmore Conference) demanded unlimited Jewish immigration into Palestine and the establishment of a Jewish state in Palestine, and announced plans for organising a Jewish army to confront the British policy of a unified Palestine. Meanwhile the British were attempting to impose far tighter restrictions on immigration to Palestine, strictures which were met with vastly increased illegal immigration and added to the already rife tensions and hostility. The Jewish campaign against the British escalated and reached a climax with the bombing of the **King David Hotel** in Jerusalem, which housed the offices of the Government Secretariat and part of the military headquarters: 86 Arab, Jewish and British public servants were killed. Further commissions of enquiry, conferences and negotiations proved futile; finally, after thirty years of rule in Palestine, Great Britain admitted defeat, concluding that 'the only course now open to us is to submit the problem to the judgement of the United Nations'.

PARTITION

Palestine was a land of violent strife when the question was taken up by the **United Nations** in February 1947. The United Nations Special Committee on Palestine (UNSCOP) agreed on the termination of the Mandate and independence for Palestine, and also asked the UN to deal with the plight of European Jewry. Thus in a sense partition involved the shifting of a

European problem to the Middle East. The Holocaust was not, of course, a Palestinian problem. But the UN could not ignore its consequences and while the world reacted in horror as the full scale of Nazi atrocities emerged, many European countries closed their doors to Jewish immigrants altogether, and nowhere in the world was prepared to accept Jews on a scale large enough to accommodate those made refugees in Europe.

The proposal put forward was to **divide Palestine**: the plan allocated the Palestinians – some seventy per cent of the population who owned ninety per cent of the land – just under half of their own country, the hilly territory in the east; the Jewish state would cover 53 per cent, including the most fertile land in the west. After intense negotiations and pressure, the General Assembly approved the partition of Palestine (**Resolution 181**) on November 29, 1947. The Zionists accepted the partition plan, but the Palestinians, on being asked to agree to their own dispossesion, perhaps not surprisingly rejected it. Between November 1947 and January 1948, an estimated 2000 people were killed or injured in Palestine. Britain announced it would withdraw all its forces and terminate the Mandate on May 15, 1948. The Zionists had succeeded in driving out the British, but there still remained the Palestinian Arabs.

In order to make 'Palestine as Jewish as England is English', the indigenous Palestinian population had to somehow disappear. The head of the Jewish Agency at the time, Joseph Weitz, wrote in his diary: ' . . . there is no room for both peoples together in this country . . . The only solution is a Palestine without Arabs . . . And there is no other way than to transfer the Arabs to the neighbouring countries . . . not one village, not one tribe, should be left.' These words, written in 1940, find an ominous echo in the statements of some present-day Israeli Knesset members. The Palestinians were 'encouraged' to leave not only by being dispossessed of their land and livelihood, but also by massacres such as that at Deir Yassin. Five weeks before the expiry of the British Mandate, on April 9, 1948, a combined force of *Irgun* and *Stern* murdered 254 Palestinian villagers, an act which official Zionist leaders condemned but which fitted in well with official purpose. By May 15, Zionist forces numbered over 30,000 well-armed and trained troops; the forces sent to Palestine by five Arab states, after the proclamation of the State of Israel, numbered some 15,000 ill-equipped men.

ISRAEL

The Israelis used the opportunity afforded by the 1948 war to take an additional twenty per cent of Palestinian territory, including half of Jerusalem. By the time the Armistice Agreements were signed in 1949 almost eighty per cent of Palestine was controlled by the Israelis, 385 Palestinian villages had been destroyed and some 750,000 Palestinians had been driven out of their homeland and become refugees. The remainder of the land, on the west bank of the Jordan river (including the east half of Jerusalem), was annexed by the renamed Hashemite Kingdom of **Jordan**. The United Nations armistice line along the battlefront dermarcated Israel from Jordan until 1967 and became known as the **'green line'**. Despite UN resolutions stating that those Palestinian refugees who wished to should be allowed to return home, the Israelis have never allowed them to do so. By contrast, in July 1950, the Israeli parliament (the Knesset) passed the **Law of Return**, giving every Jew the right to settle in Israel.

Since 1948, the country has suffered four more major wars: in 1956, 1967, 1973 and 1982. In **1956**, France, Britain and Israel attacked Egypt in order to try and reverse the nationalisation of the Suez Canal by President Nasser and to curb the growth of Arab nationalism. Israeli troops reached the Suez Canal but were forced by the UN and the superpowers to withdraw to the 1948 borders.

In the 1960s a new element was added to the region in the form of an organised Palestinian resistance movement, now known as the Palestine Liberation Organisation (**PLO**), established in 1964 in Jerusalem under the leadership of Ahmed Shukairy. On January 1, 1965, the first military operation against Israel was launched by *Fatah* – the main body of the PLO.

In the **'Six Day War'** of June 1967, Israel defeated the armies of Syria, Jordan and Egypt and acquired territory three times its size. Israel now occupied the remainder of Palestine: the West Bank (including East Jerusalem which was annexed three weeks after the war), the Gaza Strip and Sinai, and the Syrian Golan

Heights. More Palestinian villages were destroyed and a further 200,000 Palestinians crossed the Jordan river to become refugees, some for the second time. As in 1948, the Israelis made it illegal for anyone (apart from limited family reunification cases) to return.

In October **1973** war (the Yom Kippur or Ramadan war) again broke out between Israel, Egypt and Syria. The Egyptians crossed the Suez Canal and retook the east bank of the canal, breaking through Israel's defensive Bar-Lev Line. Israel's defeat in the 1973 war brought about negotiations between the two countries and following Egyptian President Sadat's visit to Israel in 1977, the **Camp David Accord** was signed by Israel, Egypt and the US. The peace treaty led to the staged withdrawal of Israeli forces from Sinai, finally completed in March 1989 with the return of Taba to Egypt.

Egypt's separate peace with Israel did not, however, bring peace to the area. In **1981**, Israel formally annexed the Syrian Golan Heights, which it had occupied in 1967, and the following year invaded Lebanon. While the declared aim of the invasion was to stop attacks on Israel's northern border, the unofficial purpose was to destroy the PLO and drive the organisation out of Lebanon – it failed in the former and succeeded in the latter. On this occasion Israel's heavy casualties, and the massacres in the Palestinian refugee camps of Sabra and Shatilla, brought about serious domestic disquiet, and a widening split in Israeli society led eventually to the withdrawal of the Israeli army.

Palestinian opposition to military occupation has been growing steadily since 1967. Over half of the West Bank has been expropriated for Israeli settlements in two major phases: 1968–1977 under the Alignment government, and 1977–1984 under Likud. By 1985, the number of settlers in the occupied territories was over 50,000. In December 1987, Palestinian resistance intensified and erupted into the **intifada**.

On November 15, 1988, the PLO took a major step towards a possible settlement, for the first time accepting a two state solution, and UN Resolution 181 (over partition). In a speech to the UN, Yasser Arafat recognised Israel's 'right to exist in peace and security'. At the same time the PLO declared an independent **State of Palestine**, which has to date been recognised by the majority of member states of the United Nations. These include the USSR and China, though not the US or Britain. The EEC has called for a peace conference at which both Israel and the PLO would be represented, and for restriction on trade with Israel until there is freedom of movement for Palestinian agricultural exports. Meanwhile the US government is also now prepared to meet the PLO and, perhaps most tellingly, has moved closer to their distinction between terrorism (anti-civilian activity) and armed struggle (attacks on military targets): the PLO has renounced terrorism but not armed struggle. All of this has, of course, had little effect on official Israeli policy, particularly at a time when the government survives only with the support of ultra-right and religious parties. Nevertheless most senior Israeli politicians would accept that they cannot survive without US support. No end to Israel's problems or the occupation may realistically be in sight, but the *intifada*, and the changes it has brought about in international and local opinion, has made the last couple of years perhaps the most significant since 1948.

RELIGION IN THE 'HOLY LAND'

Israel, within its 1948 boundaries, is a Jewish state; its population is 85 per cent Jewish. But the 'Holy Land' is also the home of some of the most revered sites of all three great monotheistic religions, and as in many other parts of the world, religious fundamentalism – Jewish, Christian and Muslim alike – is on the increase. Almost everywhere you go, and particularly somewhere like Jerusalem, you'll be struck by the sheer number of berobed representatives of the three main religions. All have their own holy sites, and many of the most important are sacred to all three, often sources of contention between them and between factions within them.

For Jews, the principal place of prayer is the Western or **Wailing Wall** of the Temple Mount in Jerusalem; for Christians, the **Church of the Holy Sepulchre** in Jerusalem and the **Church of the Nativity** in Bethlehem; for Muslims, **al-Aqsa Mosque** and the **Dome of the Rock** in Jerusalem. As well as the 'big three', there are other religious groupings – the **Druze** (see p.351), **Bahais** (see "Haifa"), **Samaritans** (see "Nablus") – to complicate matters further. All have their own various laws, rituals, times and ways of worship, dress and holidays, and you're bound to run into some during your visit. In practice this means that opening times at the various sites will vary, that some place you wanted to visit will be closed for a festivity or fast, that what you are required to wear will be different . . . The best advice is to be prepared for all eventualities, and to keep an eye on the time of year and month and day of the week.

JUDAISM

The fundamental tenet of Judaism is belief and trust in a single, eternal and invisible God who created the world (5749 years ago). The most sacred text of Judaism is the **Torah**, primarily the five books of Moses or *Pentateuch* (*Genesis, Exodus, Leviticus, Numbers* and *Deuteronomy*), as well as other religious teachings. According to tradition, the *Torah* is both historical record and divine law, and a complete guide to human life.

Unlike Christianity and Islam, Judaism does not date its beginning from a specific event. According to the Old Testament, **Abraham** was the founder of monotheism, and this belief was continued by his son Isaac, and Isaac's son Jacob (later Israel). It was **Moses**, though, who was the lawgiver; it was to him that the **Ten Commandments** were given on Mount Sinai after the exodus of the Hebrew tribe from Egypt.

Many of the characteristic ideas and institutions of Judaism, however, emerged during the **Babylonian exile**, between the destruction of Solomon's Temple by Babylonian King Nebuchadnezzar (586BC) and the **return** of the Judaeans – now called **Jews** – under Cyrus the Great some 48 years later. The Babylonian exile marked the beginning of the Jewish **Diaspora** or dispersion, since many Jews remained in Babylon which, in late antiquity and the Middle Ages, had one of the largest and most important Jewish communities in the world. In Babylon, much of the Hebrew Bible was rewritten, codified, annotated and completed; the ancient Hebrew alphabet – which the Samaritans still use – was replaced by the Aramaean one with which Hebrew is written today. After the return, Persian Emperor Cyrus ordered the rebuilding of the Temple and the essentially tribal law of Moses became the rule of the **priests** and the institutions of the Temple.

After the destruction of the Second Temple in 70AD and the razing of Jerusalem after the Second Revolt in 132–135AD, the centre of Judaism moved to the Galilee and Mesopotamia. The **rabbis** (Jewish scholars and religious authorities) codified and elaborated the traditional teachings; two such compilations – the **Talmud** – emerged. The vast Babylonian Talmud was compiled between 200 and 500AD in the rabbinic academies of Babylon where Jews had lived continuously at least since Nebuchadnezzar's time; the second version, less complete and authoritative and often wrongly called the Jerusalem Talmud, was compiled predominantly in Caesarea,

Tiberias and Sepphoris. Both have the same starting point, each being a form of commentary on the **Mishnah** which was codified in Galilee around 200AD.

The most important centres of the Diaspora in the Middle Ages were Muslim Spain and France, until the **Spanish Inquisition** resulted in the expulsion of over 100,000 Jews from Spain and Portugal at the end of the fifteenth century. The term **Sephardim** encompasses those who left either as Jews or as conversos (forcibly converted), as well as their descendants. Many of them went to Palestine and settled in Safad in the Upper Galilee, which became an important centre of learning, particularly during the Ottoman period. In many parts of Christian Europe, Jews were restricted to separate, often closed quarters – **ghettos** – and their lives were subjected to strict regulation, including a ban on following certain professions.

In Eastern Europe in the eighteenth and nineteenth centuries, Judaism was split by the new **Hassidic** movement which placed the emphasis on piety and prayer as opposed to the scholasticism of the Talmudic academies. The *Hassidim* maintained their identity, and still do, by their dress – black hats, long coats, sidelocks (*pay'ot*) and beards – while the less orthodox were more in favour of integrating into the societies in which they lived.

Anti-Semitic **pogroms** (attacks on Jews and Jewish property) in the late nineteenth century led to a mass exodus of Jews from Poland and Russia, culminating in the Nazi **holocaust** during World War II in which many old European communities were destroyed and six million Jews perished in concentration camps. Today, the largest Jewish community outside Israel is in the USA (six million), with sizeable communities in most western European countries.

While orthodox Judaism asserts the supernatural authority of the Torah and **halakha**, this is today challenged by **reform** Judaism (which began in Germany in the early nineteenth century) which attempts to adapt traditional Judaism to the modern world. The reforms include many of the ritual laws, acceptance of modern biblical criticism, services in languages other than Hebrew, and full equality for women, even women rabbis.

JUDAISM IN ISRAEL

The Jewish inhabitants of Israel are subject to the jurisdiction of the Chief Rabbinate in matters concerning **kashruth** (dietary laws), opening hours on *Shabbat* and other holidays, and marriage and divorce. Since there is no civil marriage and divorce in Israel, members of different faiths cannot marry under Jewish law. There are two **Chief Rabbis**, for the Ashkenazi and Sephardi communities. Under the **Law of Return**, all Jews have a right to settle in Israel. This law has raised the 'Who is a Jew' question; according to a strict interpretation of the law, only those born to a Jewish mother or who have converted to Judaism according to the *halakha* are Jewish. This comes into conflict with a sizeable body of people, particularly in the US, who have converted through liberal or reform synagogues. The controversy hit the headlines recently when Ethiopian Jews – the **Falashas** – were airlifted into Israel and once there, were told they had to go through 'reconversion' according to halakhic law.

The Orthodox lobby in Israel is influential: the **National Religious Party** holds the balance of power in the Knesset and other religious groupings, such as **Gush Emunim** and **the Faithful of the Temple Mount**, are at the forefront of the settler movement, backed by the Orthodoxy. Both Chief Rabbis have recently declared that the *halakha* forbids the giving up of any part of the Land of Israel to non-Jews, even if it means overruling the supreme law that the saving of life takes precedence. However, some ultra-orthodox Jews – the **Haredim** and **Neturei Carta** – oppose the State of Israel altogether, believing that it is blasphemous, and that there cannot be a truly Jewish state until all Jews practice the **mitzvot** (duties) and thereby bring about the coming of the Messiah.

CHRISTIANITY

Christianity is based on the teachings of Jesus Christ, which had their origins in Judaism. Central to Christianity is the belief in the **Trinity**, the **Incarnation of Christ** and the **Resurrection**, as well as in Christ as the son of God and the **Messiah** prophesied in the Old Testament. Jesus was a Jew, born in Bethlehem in the last years of the reign of Herod the Great. He taught in synagogues in the Galilee, gathering around him **twelve disciples** who accompanied him to Jerusalem where he was arrested and executed – **crucified** – according to Roman practice.

Despite persecution under Nero and later emperors, Christianity spread rapidly through the Roman Empire. The belief was first taught orally by the **Apostles** but was later written down in the four **Gospels** of Matthew, Mark, Luke and John. The Gospels, together with the *Acts of the Apostles*, the *Epistles* and the *Book of Revelation*, constitute the **New Testament**, which covers a period from the birth of Jesus to the spread of Christianity and was written between 50 and 100AD. Five patriarchates were established – in Antioch, Alexandria, Constantinople, Rome and Jerusalem – whose leaders (patriarchs) claimed that their descent from the Apostles gave them the authority to disseminate correct doctrine.

In the early centuries of Christianity, Palestine was a hive of activity as hermits came to the desert to follow in Jesus' footsteps. At first living in isolated caves, they soon attracted followers and disciples, and founded desert hermitages that were the precursors of the **monastic** movement in Europe and elsewhere. The desert monasteries became important centres of study, and in them biblical texts were translated, copied and annotated.

In the fourth century AD, Emperor **Constantine** legitimised Christianity and declared it the state religion of the Roman Empire. Constantine's establishment of his new capital, Constantinople, led to a growing polarisation between the **Eastern Orthodox Church** and the **Roman Catholic Church**. In the fifth century AD, the Syrian and Egyptian churches, which were under Byzantine occupation, broke away from the Eastern Church to form **Oriental Orthodoxy**.

Despite the collapse of the Western Empire, western Christianity spread vigorously, but the Orthodox Church became increasingly isolated until finally, in 1054, a formal separation from the Roman Catholic Church took place. A second major schism took place in the sixteenth century when the **Protestant** churches broke away from Rome, a movement basically against the wealth and simony of the established church towards a simpler form of worship, but with political roots too in the growing power of the northern European nations.

Thus there are four major branches of Christianity: **Eastern** and **Oriental Orthodoxy** in the East, and **Catholicism** and **Protestantism** in the West. Eastern Orthodoxy is composed of the Greek, Russian, Serbian and Bulgarian Orthodox churches; each has its own patriarch but all recognise the seniority of the Ecumenical Patriarch of Constantinople. Oriental Orthodoxy comprises the Armenian, Coptic (Egyptian), Ethiopian, Indian and Syrian Orthodox Churches, which do not follow Constantinople. Catholicism is primarily the Roman Catholic (Latin) Church but includes Eastern and Oriental Christians, such as the Maronite and Melkite Churches (see below) which keep their own liturgies but come under the jurisdiction of Rome. The Protestant churches embrace a multitude of varied and sub-divided denominations.

Under Muslim rule from the seventh century AD, the Christians of Palestine, many of whom had converted under Byzantine rule, were free to practise their faith, most remaining Christian until around the eleventh century when conversion to Islam increased. In the twelfth century, the western European **Crusaders** invaded Palestine, temporarily ousted the Orthodox Primate from Jerusalem and installed a Latin bishop. With the defeat of the Crusaders, the Orthodox Church regained its place but Catholicism had established a foothold in the country. Later Catholic missionaries encouraged local Christians to detach themselves from the indigenous Orthodox Churches and to come under the patronage of the Papacy. Two Catholic Churches developed: the **Roman Catholic (Latin)** and the **Greek Catholic (Melkite)** (with Greek rites but under Rome). From the fourteenth century until the establishment of Israel in 1948, some ten per cent of Palestinian Arabs were Christian, but due to the exodus of Palestinians, the number has dropped to below three per cent. There is now a higher percentage of Palestinian Christians outside the country than in.

CHRISTIANITY IN ISRAEL

The vast majority of **Palestinian Christians** are members of the three major churches: the Greek Catholic or Melkite, the Greek Orthodox and the Roman Catholic. The Greek Catholics live mostly in the Galilee area and come under the jurisdiction of the Melkite Archbishops; the Greek Orthodox, mainly in the Jerusalem area, are under the Greek Orthodox patriarch who claims direct descent from St. James, the first bishop of Jerusalem.

Whilst the patriarchs and bishops of the Melkite Church are entirely indigenous Palestinians, the hierarchies of the Greek Orthodox and Roman Catholic Churches have traditionally been dominated by Greeks and Italians. The European influence can be clearly seen in icons and paintings in Palestinian churches, almost all of which depict Jesus and the Virgin Mary as blonde and blue-eyed, even though they were both indigenous Semites. The Via Dolorosa (see *Jerusalem*), among other sites, is also largely a figment of European imagination. This century, however, there have been moves to bring Christianity back home: in January 1988, a Palestinian Arab, Michel Sabbah, was appointed Latin Patriarch of Jerusalem.

On top of these major divisions, there are a plethora of denominations from all over the world. In addition to the 2000-strong **Armenian** community (Catholics and Orthodox) in Jerusalem, there are also smaller congregations of Maronites, Copts, Ethiopian and Russian Orthodox, Syrian Catholics and Syrian Orthodox. Many newer churches also claim rights to the holy sites; these include Anglicans, the Church of Scotland, Seventh Day Adventists, Quakers, Mennonites, Mormons and Jehovah's Witnesses. A more recent phenomenon is the arrival of fundamentalist, **born-again Christians**, mostly North American, who believe that the state of Israel is the fulfilment of biblical prophecy. These Christian Zionists now have a 'Christian Embassy' in Jerusalem to spread the message – one of their main aims is the conversion of Jews.

A number of prominent Palestinian intellectuals and nationalists, both outside the country (such as George Antonius, Philip Hitti, Edward Said, George Habash and Nayif Hawatmeh) and in, are Christians: Canon Riyah Abu al-Assal of Nazareth is General Secretary of the Progressive List for Peace (PLP); Reverend Shehadeh N. Shehadeh is chair of the Haifa-based Committee for the Defence of Arab Land, and Reverend Elias Chacour was

the founder of the Peace Research Centre in Ibilin.

Islam, which in Arabic means submission to God, originated in 622AD in what is today Saudi Arabia. The essential creed of Islam is that there is one God, Allah, and that Mohammed is his prophet. The basis of Islamic belief and practice, and the source of its legal and social system, is the **Quran**, containing the divine revelations received by the **Prophet Mohammed**. The Quran consists of 114 **suras** or chapters, arranged according to length and written in classical Arabic. One of the *suras* (number 17) describes Mohammed's **night journey** from Mecca to **Jerusalem** in the company of the archangel Gabriel, where he prayed and then ascended to heaven. It was towards Jerusalem that Muslims first directed their prayers, and although this later changed, Jerusalem has remained the third holy site of Islam, after Mecca and Medina, and has long been a place of Muslim pilgrimage. The revelation which prompted the change of the **qibla** (direction of prayer) is set out in the second *sura* of the Quran, which established the **Ka'aba** in Mecca (Saudi Arabia) as the religious centre to which all Muslims have turned in prayer ever since. Mohammed claimed **Abraham** and his son Ishma'el as founders of the Ka'aba and of Arabian monotheism, thus predating and independent of both Judaism and Christianity.

Mohammed was born in 571AD in Mecca and worked for a merchant for whom he travelled along trade routes as far north as Damascus. He became disillusioned with the multiple idolatries of Arabia, with the exclusiveness of the Jews, and with the ritual and doctrine of the Christians. But the new monotheistic faith that Mohammed introduced into his native city of **Mecca** met with opposition and persecution so that, in 622AD, he and his followers were forced to flee to **Medina**. It is from this event – the **Hijra** – that Islam is dated. Seven years after the *Hijra*, the new code of social justice had gained such influence that Mohammed was able to return to Mecca as a powerful political leader. After the Prophet's death in 632AD he was succeeded by four **caliphs** (successors). It was under the third caliph, Uthman, that the revelations which had been preserved by Mohammed's followers were collected.

Not long after Mohammed's death, the spiritual leadership of Islam became a source of contention. The first three caliphs were all related to Mohammed by marriage, but the fourth, Ali, was not only the Prophet's son-in-law but also his cousin. A substantial minority – the **Shi'ites** – supported Ali (*Shi'at Ali*) and broke away from the mainstream **Sunni** Muslims. The Shi'a believe that the **Imam** is a divinely appointed ruler who possesses super-human qualities, whereas for the Sunni Muslims, the ruler is responsible for the administration of justice through the **shari'a** (Islamic law) and for the defence of the realm of Islam. One of the offshoots of Shi'a Islam is the sect known as the **Assassins,** who bear a remarkable resemblance to the suicide commandos of the Shi'ite Hizballah operating out of South Lebanon today.

In the seventh and eighth centuries, Islam extended through the Middle East and North Africa, later spreading to sub-Saharan Africa, India, China, Southeast Asia, parts of Russia and the Balkans and Spain. Islam was brought to Palestine in 638AD by the first caliph, Omar Ibn al-Khattab, and the land lay under Muslim rule for the next 1300 years, interrupted only by around eighty years of Crusader dominance (1099–1187).

Islam shares a number of beliefs with Judaism and Christianity, accepting the Books of Moses and the Gospels of Jesus as parts of divine scripture which, however, is definitively revealed in the Quran. There is no formally organised church or priesthood, but there are **five fundamental duties** which a Muslim must perform: to adhere to the central article of faith in the One God Allah and his Prophet, Mohammed; to observe the **five daily prayers** at set times which are recited facing Mecca; to fast during the month of **Ramadan**; to pay a special tax (**zakaat**) for charitable purposes; and to make the **pilgrimage** (*haj*) to Mecca at least once, if possible. Friday is observed as the sabbath and, as in Judaism, meat must be legally slaughtered (*halal*). Pork is also forbidden, as is alcohol.

PALESTINIAN MUSLIMS

The Muslims of Palestine are predominantly of the majority Sunni branch of Islam, with their own religious institutions. The **Supreme Muslim Council** consists of a president (*Ra'is al-'Ulema*) and four members, two representing the district of Jerusalem, one Nablus and one Acre, who are elected by an electoral college for a period of four years. The council, based in Jerusalem, has authority over all Muslim **waqf** (pl *awqaf*) property and *shari'a* courts. The *awqaf* are Muslim religious endowments, whose property is dedicated to charitable uses; the *waqf* committee in Jerusalem has authority over all *awqaf* in Palestine. The **shari'a** courts, each of which is presided over by a **qadi** or judge, have exclusive jurisdiction in matters such as marriage, divorce and inheritance and can adjudicate in matters concerning *waqf* properties.

The *waqf* administers the Muslim holy sites of the Dome of the Rock, al-Aqsa Mosque and other Islamic institutions in Jerusalem, and is regularly in dispute with the Israeli authorities about jurisdiction over the properties. It has been involved in legal battles to stop archaeological excavations under the sanctuary in Jerusalem which threaten the buildings above, as well as with the Faithful of the Temple Mount who want to limit their authority and ultimately to rebuild a Jewish temple on the site where the Dome of the Rock now stands. For the Muslims of Palestine, whether devout or otherwise, the holy sites in the country are symbolic of their identity, and threats against the sites are felt as threats against themselves.

With the rise of Islamic fervour in Shi'ite Iran, and especially with the success of the Shi'ite population of South Lebanon in making life for the Israeli army there unbearable, the Muslim lobby in Palestine has grown. Religious groupings have recently been elected onto student unions at West Bank universities, and the influence of Islam in already conservative areas, such as the Gaza Strip, is on the increase. During the *intifada*, the influence of the Muslim Brothers – in the shape of **Hammas** – has been growing, whilst staying within the main body of Palestinians under the leadership of the United National Leadership of the Intifada.

BOOKS

There are possibly more books written about Israel and Palestine than about anywhere else in the world, and certainly too many to list here. They range from early travel writings to ancient and modern histories, religion and archaeology, the whole spectrum of politics, and some fiction in translation. And, of course, the earliest written 'guide book' to the Holy Land (and the western world's all-time best seller) is the Bible; whether you take it to be historical fact or fiction, it certainly makes interesting reading as you visit the sites.

The Israeli view of Israeli history and society is widely available anywhere, and any branch of *Steimatsky's* in Israel will have a wide range of this and Israeli fiction. Perhaps the easiest way of assimilating these views is through the writings – especially the autobiographies – of Israeli politicians: Golda Meir, Menahem Begin, Moshe Dayan. There are also a number of pot-boiler historical novels, like Leon Uris's *Exodus*, James Michener's *The Source* or Chaim Potok's *Wanderings*. The list which follows is basically an 'alternative' reading guide, to books which may be harder to find but are worth the effort, presenting the country in a different light.

GENERAL BACKGROUND

Peter Mansfield *The Arabs* (Penguin £3.50). A clear, perceptive and wide ranging introduction to the Arab world, starting from the beginning of Islam and ending in the 1970s, with sections on individual countries.

George Antonius *The Arab Awakening* (Capricorn Books, US). One of the best historical accounts, considered a classic, of the origins and development of the Arab national movement from the nineteenth century to World War I, covering Ottoman rule, through the Arab Revolt and British involvement in it (Lawrence of Arabia), ending with the British and French mandates in the Middle East.

Edward Said *Orientalism* (Peregrine £6.99). This heavyweight but extremely important book, written by Palestinian-born Professor of English and Comparative Literature at Columbia University in the US, sets out to show how the West discovered, invented and sought to control the East. The wide-ranging study covers nineteenth-century western authors, travellers, politicians, linguists and archaeologists who were caught in the trap of racism and colonialism, and shows how the myths and prejudices then created have lasted until today.

Rana Kabbani *Europe's Myths of Orient* (Pandora £4.95). Along similar lines to Said's work, Ms Kabbani unravels the erotic fantasies and myths which western travellers, painters and poets built up about the East. Starting with the Crusaders and on through the Victorians, she shows how the East was portrayed as sexually voracious and thus intellectually and morally inferior.

Amin Maalouf *The Crusades Through Arab Eyes*, translated from French by Jon Rothschild (Al-Saqi £6.95). Lebanese writer and journalist Amin Maalouf has used the writings of contemporary Arab chroniclers of the Crusades to retrace two centuries of Middle Eastern history that is normally presented only from a European point of view. The conclusion of this well written and fascinating book is that present-day relations between the Arab world and the West are still marked by the battle that ended seven centuries ago.

Abba Eban *Heritage: Civilization and the Jews* (Weidenfeld & Nicolson £14.95). British-educated Israeli statesman, diplomat and scholar, Abba Eban, charts the history of the Jews from the time of Abraham to the establishment of the modern state of Israel. Illustrated with objects from museums around the world, Eban examines the Jewish influence on civilisation throughout the ages. The book was recently made into a nine-part television documentary.

Ilan Halevi *A History of the Jews: Ancient and Modern*, translated from French by A.M. Berrett (Zed £7.95). Halevi grew up in Israel, now lives in Paris, and is PLO representative to the Socialist International. His history of the Jewish people is as wide-ranging as Eban's but starts from a political interpretation of the Roman occupation and the decline of Temple authority through to the Zionist settlement of Palestine in this century. Halevi's style takes some getting used to, but it's worth the effort.

Maxime Rodinson *Cult, Ghetto, and State: The Persistence of the Jewish Question*, translated from French by Jon Rothschild (Al-Saqi £5.95). In a collection of essays, Marxist theoretician Rodinson addresses such issues as the survival of the Jewish people, whether they are a people or a nationality, the ideological foundations of Zionism and the form of anti-Semitism. Also hard-going, but rewarding to work at.

ARCHAEOLOGY

Jerome Murphy O'Connor *The Holy Land: An Archaeological Guide from Earliest Times to 1700* (Steimatsky, widely available in Israel). This clearly written and illustrated guide, by a New Testament professor and priest in Jerusalem, is a good book to take along on trips. The sites are laid out in alphabetical order, accompanied by historical and archaeological accounts that do not presuppose prior knowledge of either.

Kathleen Kenyon *The Bible and Recent Archaeology* (British Museum £9.95). Dame Kathleen Kenyon, who died in 1978, was among the foremost modern Palestinian archaeologists and especially noted for her excavations at Jerusalem and Jericho. In this book she summarises the changes in interpretation of the Bible over the last forty years, based on the results of recent archaeological discoveries. Illustrated by drawings and black-and-white photographs of excavation sites, this is one for the more serious student of archaeology.

Yigael Yadin (ed) *Jerusalem Revealed: Archaeology in the Holy City 1968–1974* (Israel Exploration Society). A collection of articles by such eminent Israeli archaeologists as the late Benyamin Mazar, this well presented and illustrated book reveals the major excavations

undertaken at several locations in the Old City of Jerusalem, and shows how they add to our knowledge of the city's Jewish, Christian and Muslim history.

PERSONAL TESTIMONY

Fawzi al-Asmar *To be an Arab in Israel* (Frances Pinter). Lively personal account, by journalist, poet and political activist, born in Haifa in 1937, of life in Palestine from the establishment of the Israeli state to his release from prison in 1970.

Fawaz Turki *Soul in Exile: Lives of a Palestinian Revolutionary* (Monthly Review Press £9.95). Excellent personal account from a Palestinian perspective.

Raja Shehadeh *The Third Way: A Journal of Life in the West Bank* (Quartet £5.95). The author, a Palestinian lawyer and founder of *al-Haq* human rights organisation, charts his personal experience of daily life in the West Bank. The title comes from the Treblinka concentration camp: 'Faced with two alternatives, always choose the third'. For Shehadeh, this third way is to be *Samid*, steadfast in the face of occupation.

Elias Chacour *Blood Brothers* (Chosen Books, US). Chacour is pastor of the Melkite Church in the village of Ibilin, and studied the Bible and Talmud at the Hebrew University. Born in Bir'im, a border village from which the population was expelled, Chacour urges reconciliation between Arabs and Jews.

Felicia Langer *An Age of Stone*, translated from Hebrew by Isaac Cohen (Quartet £12.95). One of the few Israeli lawyers who works defending Palestinians in the occupied territories, Ms Langer was born in Poland and came to Israel in 1950. Her book deals with the period from 1979 to 1988 and describes the rise of militarism in Israel and the deteriorating moral climate since the invasion of Lebanon in 1982.

Amos Oz *In the Land of Israel* (Flamingo £3.99). One of Israel's foremost novelists interviews a cross-section of Israelis and Palestinians to record their views on the conflict.

David Grossman *The Yellow Wind*, translated from Hebrew by Haim Watzman (Picador £3.99). The account of this Israeli novelist's journey into the West Bank in 1987 caused a sensation when it was published, and was described as 'the most valuable contribution of all the millions of words produced by Israel to mark the anniversary of the Six Day War'. Grossman talks with both Palestinians and Jewish settlers, and exposes his own moral dilemmas.

David Shipler *Arab and Jew: Wounded Spirits in a Promised Land* (Bloomsbury £5.95). Shipler, correspondent for the *New York Times*, also interviews a cross-section of Palestinians and Israelis across the spectrum of religious and political convictions.

Beata Lipman *Israel: The Embattled Land. Jewish and Palestinian Women Talk About Their Lives* (Pandora £5.95). Another 'journey of discovery', this time focussed on Palestinian and Israeli women of all ages and viewpoints, Ms Lipman's interviews are particularly interesting for the light they throw on how the situation of women is changing and how they experience the conflict, although her own lack of position does not enable her to draw the disparate voices together.

Ingela Bendt and James Downing *We Shall Return: Women of Palestine*, translated from Swedish by Ann Henning (Zed £5.95). These interviews with Palestinian women in the refugee camps of Lebanon describe the impact that expulsion from their country and the emergence of a resistance movement has had on them.

CONTEMPORARY POLITICS

Edward Said *The Question of Palestine* (Routledge). One of the best historical accounts of Palestinian-Israeli conflicts, written from the Palestinian point of view. In *After the Last Sky* (Faber £6.95), Said combines his eloquence with the photos of Jean Mohr.

Edward Said and Christopher Hitchens (eds) *Blaming the Victims* (Verso £8.95). A collection of essays by Palestinian, Israeli and American authors showing how the facts about the Palestinian exile have been distorted, how Palestinian claims to a home have been dismissed and their very existence denied.

Henry Cattan *The Palestine Question* (Croom Helm £25). The author is a Jerusalem-born international jurist, who was a lecturer at the Jerusalem Law School and represented the Palestinian Arabs at UN debates in 1947 and 1948. Divided into five parts, the book exam-

ines the background to the Palestinian question, the emergence of Israel, the five wars (including the Sabra and Chatila massacres), the problems specific to Jerusalem and ends with a study of the various peace solutions.

Naseer Aruri (ed) *Occupation: Israel Over Palestine* (Zed £9.95). A collection of 17 articles written by people who live or have worked in the area and who have first-hand knowledge of life under occupation. Subjects dealt with include history, law, Israeli settlements, judicial rights, economics, Palestinian women, education and politics.

Rosemary Sayigh *Palestinians: From Peasants to Revolutionaries* (Zed £6.95). A 'people's history' recorded from interviews with camp Palestinians in Lebanon, from the period of the British Mandate, through the uprooting and the new reality of living as refugees, to the growth of the Palestinian resistance movement.

Abdallah Frangi *The PLO and Palestine*, translated by Paul Knight (Zed £5.95). Dr Frangi, a Palestinian born in Beersheva and member of the Fatah Revolutionary Council, explains the PLO 'from within', detailing the organisation's development, military units, medical, social and cultural institutions, as well as its relations with western European states.

Simha Flapan *The Birth of Israel: Myths and Realities* (Croom Helm). Fascinating and eye-opening book by the late Israeli writer, publisher and peace activist (who founded and was editor-in-chief of *New Outlook*) sets out to debunk widely accepted myths about the foundation of Israel.

Benny Morris *The Birth of the Palestinian Refugee Problem* (CUP £12.95). Born and educated in Israel, and diplomatic correspondent of the *Jerusalem Post*, Morris bases his revealing study on recently declassified Israeli, British and American state documents, party political and personal papers. He traces the stages of the 1947–49 Palestinian exodus, particularly from Haifa, Jaffa, Lydda and Ramle, as well as from the Upper Galilee and northern Negev, analyses its causes, examines Israel's decision to prevent refugees returning and looks at the fate of abandoned villages.

Michael Palumbo *The Palestinian Catastrophe* (Quartet £6.95). Like Benny Morris, Palumbo uses archive material from the US, Europe and Israel, as well as the testimonies of

Jewish veterans, to tell how the Zionists implemented Ben Gurion's plan to 'expel the Arabs and take their place'.

Uri Davis *Israel: An Apartheid State* (Zed £6.95). This in-depth study by prominent anti-Zionist Israeli academic, former lecturer and research fellow at the universities of Bradford, Durham and Exeter, looks at the official structures of the Israeli state, particularly such organisations as the Jewish National Fund and the kibbutz and *moshav* movements, and shows how ninety per cent of the country is defined as land which only Jews can lease or cultivate. See also *The Jewish National Fund* and *Debate on Palestine* (edited by Fouzi al-Asmar, Uri Davis and Naim Khader; Ithaca £2.50).

Amos Elon *The Israelis: Founders and Sons* (Penguin £3.50). Elon, a prominent Israeli journalist and representative of the liberal Israeli intelligentsia, traces the history of his country, showing how the ideals of the founders 'have floundered in the reality of war and violence', and how Zionism led to the development of the Palestinian nationalist movement.

Jon Rothschild (ed) *Forbidden Agendas: Intolerance and Defiance in the Middle East* (al-Saqi £6.95). An illuminating collection of articles from the journal *Khamsin*, divided into five sections: oriental Jews in Israel; women; Lebanon; religion; and dialogue.

Shlomo Swirski *Israel: The Oriental Majority*, translated from Hebrew by Barbara Swirski (Zed £7.95). Dr Swirski's study of the history and present role of Oriental Jews as Israel's underclass is an important contribution to a little publicised aspect of Israeli society. The first part looks at economic and social aspects while the second, based on interviews, allows the non-Ashkenazi majority to speak for themselves.

Tony Clifton and Catherine Leroy *God Cried* (Quartet £15). Coffee-table essay about the siege of West Beirut by Israeli forces in 1982 and the defence of the city by Palestinian and Lebanese fighters. The accompanying photos manage to be horrific and beautiful at the same time.

Jacobo Timerman *The Longest War: Israel in Lebanon*, translated from Spanish by Miguel Acoca (Vintage, US). Timerman was a prominent journalist, editor and publisher in Argentina until his arrest by the military authorities there in 1977; on his release, he moved to Israel, only to be shocked and outraged by Israel's invasion of Lebanon in 1982. He visits Lebanon and there witnesses the carnage inflicted by the Israeli forces, joins anti-war demonstrations inside Israel and tries to understand how his adopted country has become an aggressor.

Rafael Mergui and Philippe Simonnot *Israel's Ayatollahs: Meir Kahane and the Far Right in Israel* (Al-Saqi £6.95). An analysis of the growth of Jewish extremism in Israel, through interviews with its leaders.

Uri Avnery *My Friend, The Enemy* (Zed £7.95). A leading Israeli journalist and member of Knesset, Avnery also crossed into Lebanon during the Israeli invasion and became the first Israeli politician to meet with PLO leader Yasser Arafat. This is his story.

Alan Hart *Arafat: Terrorist or Peacemaker?* (Sidgwick & Jackson £13.95). Another journalist who met with Arafat, Hart has been a foreign correspondent for both ITN and the BBC. This biography of Arafat and history of the PLO is based on his interviews.

Alain Gresh *The PLO: The Struggle Within*, translated from French by A. M. Berret (Zed £8.95). *Le Monde* journalist Alain Gresh wrote the bulk of this comprehensive history of the PLO in 1983, with an update bringing it up to June 1987, before the *intifada* and the landmark PNC meeting in December 1988; nevertheless, the study is illuminating for an insight into how the PLO works and how it has changed since its inception.

Pauline Cutting *Children of the Siege* (Heinemann £12.95). The British doctor whose experience working in the Palestinian refugee camps of Beirut made the headlines when she managed to contact the BBC to let the world know what was happening, recounts what it was like for her and the Palestinians in Burj al-Barajneh under siege, running short of food and medical supplies. A harrowing story of courage and comradeship.

David Hirst *The Gun and the Olive Branch: The Roots of Violence in the Middle East* (Futura £2.50). Undoubtedly the best historical survey of the Palestinian-Israeli conflict, written by a *Guardian* journalist, clear, detailed and well researched, beginning with the seeds of conflict in 1882 and ending with Arafat's historic address to the United Nations in November 1974.

Noam Chomsky *The Fateful Triangle* (Pluto £8.95). Distinguished American linguist and scholar deals with American policy towards and involvement in Israel.

Maxime Rodinson *Israel and the Arabs* translated from French by Michael Perl (Croom Helm £14.95). First written in 1968, with a postscript of 1970, Rodinson's work is a bit outdated but still relevant. He examines Jewish and Arab nationalism, Israel's first decade, the rise of Arab socialism and the Arab-Israeli conflict.

David Gilmour *Dispossessed: The Ordeal of the Palestinians* (Sphere £2.95). This Oxford-educated British author's book is in three parts: the first looks at Palestinian society before 1948, the second deals with the new Diaspora, and the last section deals with resistance, the PLO, Lebanon and relations between the international community and Palestine.

Institute for Independent Social Journalism *Our Roots Are Still Alive* (Zed £1.75). Lively and beautifully illustrated book, aimed as an introduction to the Palestinian-Israeli conflict.

Jonathan Dimbleby *The Palestinians* (Quartet £5.95). When this prominent and respectable British TV journalist first brought out this book ten years ago, it was something of a milestone. His message, that the Palestinians did exist, do exist and will exist, is by now common knowledge, but the book with its great photos by Donald McCullin, still remains a worthy testimony.

Sarah Graham-Brown *Palestinians and their Society 1880–1946* (Quartet £4.95). Beautifully produced photo-essay documenting the social and economic life of Palestinians through Ottoman and British rule.

Paul Cossali and Clive Robson *Stateless in Gaza* (Zed £5.95). Both writers worked in the Gaza Strip, as a development worker and teacher, and interviewed a cross-section of Palestinians living there who describe, among other things, life under occupation and resistance to it, the development of the women's movement, the role of the UN, and working conditions in Israel.

POETRY AND FICTION

Emile Habibi *The Secret Life of Saeed, The Pessoptimist*, translated from Arabic by Salma Jayyusi and Trevor LeGassick (Zed £3.95). Emile Habibi, editor of the Haifa-based Arabic

daily, *al-Ittihad*, is also a superb novelist and satirist. Saeed, the hero (or anti-hero) of this wonderfully funny and painful book, is a Candide-type character, gullible and wise at the same time, who somehow manages to walk the tightrope of contradictions of being a Palestinian citizen of Israel.

Soraya Antonius *The Lord* and *Where the Jinn Consult* (Hamish Hamilton £10.95). Two blockbuster novels set in Palestine at the end of the British Mandate, packed with characters and fast-moving action against a backdrop of struggle.

Sahar Khalifeh *Wild Thorns* (Al Saqi £3.95). Ms Khalifeh was born in Nablus and is a lecturer at Bir Zeit University. Another book that has been overtaken by the *intifada*, it paints a rather gloomy picture of Usama's return to the West Bank, only to find that most of his friends and family seem to have adjusted to life under occupation. Despite this, the characters and situations ring true, and the novel is an interesting one.

Anton Shammas *Arabesques* (Viking £11.95). Shammas is a Palestinian from within the pre-1967 borders of Israel who made the headlines by writing in Hebrew. This is a translation of his first novel.

Amos Oz *My Michael, The Hill of Evil Counsel, The Black Box, Elsewhere Perhaps* (Flamingo £2.50–£3.99). Amos Oz has gained some acclaim as one of Israel's finest prose writers. The first novel, set in Jerusalem of the 1950s, tells the story of a marriage that goes wrong; the second is a group of three stories that take place in Jerusalem during the British Mandate. Although his characters seem at times a little flat, the books do offer an insight into Jewish concerns and aspirations in the early days of the Israeli state.

Amos Kenan *The Road to Ein Harod* (Al-Saqi £3.95). Kenan, an Israeli-born journalist, was a member of the *Stern Gang* but later founded the Israeli-Palestinian Peace Council. His novel, in the form of a political thriller, takes place after a military coup in Israel. An Israeli member of the opposition makes his way out of Tel Aviv and heads for Kibbutz Ein Harod, the centre of resistance. On the way, he meets an Arab 'going beyond Ein Harod' and the two, although bitter enemies, are compelled to travel together through a landscape of violence and impending doom.

Simon Louvish *The Therapy of Avraham Blok* (Heinemann £9.95), *City of Blok* (Collins £11.95), *The Death of Moishe-Ganef* (Heinemann £9.95). Having spent his youth in Israel and now living in London, in the first two books Louvish portrays the surreal chaos of Israel, and specifically Jerusalem, through the eyes of the film-maker that he is. His myriad characters rush, tumble and collide with resurrected figures from the past in a wonderfully funny, and often tragic, confusion of madness. The third novel, set in London and Jerusalem, is a hilarious 'whodunnit' satire, with innocents caught up in Mossad murders, plots and intrigues in the country and abroad.

Yehuda Amichai *Selected Poems* (Penguin £5.99). English translations of some of the best works of perhaps the best contemporary Israeli poet. Well worth a look.

A. B. Yehoshua *Continuing Silence of a Poet: collected short stories* (P. Halban £11.95), *Five Seasons* (Collins £12.95), *Late Divorce* (Harvill £10.95). An Israeli novelist deals with the contradictions and tensions of Israeli society, particularly within the Jewish community.

Mahmoud Darwish *Selected Poems*, introduced and translated by Ian Wedde and Fawwaz Tuqan (Carcanet Press). Selections of excellent poetry by Darwish, a Haifa-born Palestinian member of the PNC, including such classics as *Identity Card*, *Letter from Home* and *To My Mother*.

Mahmoud Darwish, Samih al-Qasim and Adonis *Victims of a Map* (Al-Saqi £6.95). A bilingual anthology of new poetry by Darwish, al-Qasim, a Druze from the Galilee, and Adonis, a Syrian poet.

A. M. Elmessiri (ed) *The Palestinian Wedding* (Three Continents Press £7.95). A bilingual anthology of some of the best contemporary Palestinian resistance poetry. The authors include Mahmoud Darwish, Samih al-Qasim, Tawfiq Zayyad, Rashid Hussein and Fadwa Tuqan.

Howard Schwartz (ed) *Elijah's Vision and other Jewish Folktales* (Penguin £6.95). A collection of short stories and folktales from throughout the Jewish diaspora, from fifth-century Babylon to nineteenth-century Poland. In the same series *Arab Folktales* (tr. Inea Bushnaq; Penguin £6.95) includes some traditional stories from Palestine, though very much in the Orientalist mould.

GUIDES, ANCIENT AND MODERN

Palestine has always been a popular place of pilgrimage, and hundreds of books have been written about travels here. Listed below are some of the more interesting of the old ones – mostly out of print, but often available in libraries or secondhand bookshops, especially those of Jerusalem and Tel Aviv – along with some relevant special-interest guides.

Polunin and Huxley *Flowers of the Mediterranean* (Hogarth £9.95). Not specific to Israel, but the best field guide you'll find.

Hollom, Porter, Christensen and Willis *Birds of the Middle East and North Africa* (Poyser £14). The best published for this region.

Heinzel, Fitter and Parslow *The Birds of Britain and Europe, with North Africa and the Middle East* (Collins £8.95). Less full on Israel than the above, but with the advantage of covering all Europe.

Bemert and Ormond *Red Sea Coral Reefs* (Routledge £30). All you ever wanted to know about the Red Sea reefs – and more.

Baedeker *Palestine*. The guide no early twentieth-century traveller would be seen without. Originals are available – though early ones are valuable – and there's also an American abridged reprint, *Baedeker's Historical Palestine* (David & Charles 1985, $17.50).

Thomas Hodgkin *Letters from Palestine* (Quartet £11.95). Reprinted letters of a colonial civil servant travelling in Palestine between 1932 and 1936.

Fr B. Meistermann *Guide to the Holy Land.* (OFM, 1923). One of many from this prolific writer on the Middle East, with some perceptive description.

Cook's Travellers Handbook *Palestine and Syria* (London, 1929). One of the best of the early travel guides, packed full of quirky tips and sometimes bizarre information.

Luke and Roach *The Handbook of Palestine and Syria* (Macmillan, 1930). The official government issue handbook for Mandate officials. Good on history and archaeology, and full of arcane information such as the number of goats in Safad.

Canon J.E.. Hanauer *The Folklore of the Holy Land* (London, 1907), *Walks about Jerusalem* (London, 1907). Both are readable, enjoyable and surprisingly relevant.

WRITERS ON ISRAEL AND PALESTINE

Israeli and Palestinian writers take much of their inspiration from the tensions between their peoples and the contradictions in their society. Below, two short stories and two poems give some impression of the sort of writing the country inspires.

WHEN THE JERUSALEM NIGHT LIT UP

AKRAM HANNIYEH, *short story writer, was editor of* al-Shaab *Arabic newspaper in East Jerusalem until he was deported from Israel in December 1986.*

The author

The child shouted: Look!

It was nearly ten o'clock at night. The night of a hot summer's day. A day of Ramadan. In the squares and alleyways and steps leading to Damascus Gate, in the small gardens huddled against the walls and the nearby streets within the Old City and outside it, thousands of people pursuing new rituals connected with Ramadan nights in Jerusalem were gathering.

They sat on iron benches in the small gardens, on the edges of pavements, on the green grass, on the stone steps descending to Damascus Gate. An uninterrupted stream of human beings surged in and out of the gateway. Whole families emerged in search of a breath of fresh air, men made for the Haram* to perform the Ramadan evening prayers, women walked out with their sons and daughters and children, young men roamed the streets, all coming from different towns and villages.

They spread out everywhere, in front of the cafés, shoe shops, clothes shops, sweet shops and humus shops whose doors stayed open until midnight, in front of the roving vendors of soft drinks, of sesame-seed bread, of cooked corn cobs, of turmus beans, in front of hawkers

---

*Haram: The third most holy sanctuary in Islam, containing al-Aqsa Mosque and the Dome of the Rock.

who only appear on a night such as this to put pieces of carpets and hand-made rugs, woollen blankets and clothes, children's toys and household utensils on the iron railings separating the small huddled gardens from the large sidewalks.

The child shouted: Look!

Nobody heard him. His voice was lost amidst the din of firecrackers and fireworks with which the youngsters were amusing themselves, amidst short bursts of laughter from members of the families sprawled out on the grass and from the mouths of young girls flirtatiously scolding the young men pestering them in the streets, amidst the cries of the vendors and the hooting of cars searching for passage through the throngs that crowded the main streets, the sound of songs coming from cafés and cassette shops within the walls, the smell of sweets and grilled meats and perfume and incense, and amidst the clamour of thousands of people who had come from different regions to this small spot in search of a breath of air and a moment of joy on a long Jerusalem night.

Look! shouted the child.

But nobody paid him any attention as he tugged at the dress of his mother busy talking to a friend of hers about a young man looking in their direction whom she had learned was thinking of becoming engaged to her daughter who was sitting beside her looking discreetly in the direction of the young man, her smile giving her away.

It was a night of the full moon. Stars studded the clear black sky. And the patrols did not stop moving at the top and bottom of the streets.

Suddenly . . . there was light.

In a matter of moments, the night vanished. The darkness and blackness dissolved. Gone were the moon and the stars, the lights of mosques and churches, of electric garlands hung on the walls, of street and car lamps, of restaurant candles, illuminated signs, traffic signals, houses, shops and television screens, of the searchlamps of army patrols and border guards and police. Jerusalem was bathed in light.

It fell gently on the walls and houses and people. It surprised men at evening prayers in the mosques, mothers persuading their children it was night and time for sleep, men making love with their wives and others on their way to starting their nightshift, a young man sneaking off into a darkened alleyway with a foreign tourist, a boy writing nationalist slogans on one of the walls, a flower used to opening at nighttime, people selecting dishes for supper in restaurants, agreeing on appointments and jobs for the following day, boys and girls studying for secondary school exams, journalists and printers who had prepared most of the material for the next day's issue and prostitutes who had come to Jerusalem in search of clientele for the long night.

Dreamily, gently, refreshingly, fell the light.

It drowned with tenderness the people and huddled houses and walls, the mosques and churches and cars and streets. The sky looked like an impetuous woman who had stripped off her black cloak, had put on a robe of pure transparent blue and had lain down to bathe in the cascade of light, a light that shone so that daylight drowned the city though there was no sun in the sky.

The child shouted: Look!

But nobody listened to him for terror had gripped them.

Shouts rang out. Short shouts expressing fear and alarm of something unknown and mysterious, sounds of bewildered weeping, the wailing of women who had begun slapping their faces in dismay, of young girls who had started weeping, tears of fear flowing from their eyes, of children who did not understand what was happening and began crying wildly. Everything stopped moving. Cars. Selling and haggling. Praying. Talking. Innocent pestering and love making. Invocations rose up in the name of Allah, in the power of Allah, seeking refuge in Allah, asking mercy from Allah, from the Prophet Mohammed, from Jesus and from the Virgin.

An elderly man said: It's a divine miracle in blessed Ramadan.

A bearded young man in the courtyard of the Haram said: It's a warning from Allah for us to return to His religion and teaching.

A woman still sitting on the grass trembled as she said: What is happening is a good omen. Let us wish for what we want, since the doors of heaven have opened for us.

A woman from between her copious tears answered: But it is not Leilat al-Qadr* tonight.

---

*Leilat al-Qadr: The night during Ramadan when the Holy Quran was revealed.

A young man trailing a beautiful girl along Salah Eddin Street shouted: It's a natural phenomenon. It's a white night, like the white nights that are known in some Soviet republics and other states.

A pretentious young man said: It's most likely the explosion of an atomic bomb.

A girl in fear shouted: What's happening? God have mercy on us!

Look! Look! Look! the child was shouting furiously, crying and pointing to the top of the wall over Damascus Gate. Some noticed his shouting and urgency and alerted others. Everyone looked towards the wall ... and a deep silence fell.

On top of the wall, a few meters above the massive gateway, was the source of the light. From between one of the openings that separate the symmetrical tapering stone blocks on top of the wall, rose the daylight. It was just possible to make out what was happening amidst the cascades of delicate light. There stood a man, hands folded on his chest, and from him emanated the luminous threads, spreading light and day and blue.

A man crying called out: It's my son whom the Jews killed.

A woman surrounded by her children shouted: It's my son who died a martyr in Lebanon.

A man overwhelmed by the strangeness of what was happening proclaimed: It's the awaited Mahdi.

An elderly woman said: It's my son lost in exile.

A young man said decisively: It's my brother held in prison.

Another said: It's a saint of Allah on this blessed night.

A child came to the front through the crowd: It's my father who is away in prison.

A woman making the sign of the cross said: Blessed Virgin, it's Jesus, Jesus my saviour.

A young woman, who did not try to hold back her tears, trembled as she whispered: It's my beloved. I recognise him. He's my knight ... for whom I've waited so long. He has come, he has come.

The squares and steps and gardens and pavements and streets and roofs of buildings and houses received more and more people drawn to the source of the light. The soldiers drew their weapons at the ends of the streets and on the rooftops of high buildings watching, confused and wondering.

When the three, the man, the young girl and the child, went up to the top of the wall where the man of light was, complete and utter silence fell and we saw them cross the gateway, vanish briefly, then appear on top of the wall as they approached the man of light. Everything was perfectly clear. The child came first, then the girl, then the man. We could see amidst the cascades of soft light a smile on the lips of the man of light as he turned to receive them. Then he spoke to them.

The eyes of the gathering crowd strained to see what was happening. Jerusalem was bathed in a sea of light and silence and anticipation. Until the bullets roared.

The child
I was the first to see him.

I was beside my mother watching the fireworks when I saw him move on top of the wall above Damascus Gate. I shouted: Look! to alert my mother for I was wondering why the man had climbed to such a high place. But nobody paid any attention to me or my shouts until the light rose from the man.

I was the first to climb up to him. I felt he resembled my father who has been away for years and whom my mother says has gone on a journey. My mother let me go to Damascus Gate and climb the steps towards him and when he saw me, he opened his arms and lifted me up and clasped me to him. Behind me were the girl and the man who had come up. He began talking to me as I showered him with questions. Until the bullets roared.

The girl
He has come at last.

God, could my dreams have come true like this? Or haven't I been dreaming at all?

I have waited for him so long, so long. They said to me: He will not come but I was sure he would be on time. I did not cut my hair knowing he loves it as black and long as the nights in which he used to walk. I would perfume myself every night and open the window of my room waiting for him to leap through it, having evaded the soldiers' rifles. I waited for him to come to throw myself into his arms, run my fingers through his hair and wipe the sweat of the long journey from his brow.

Before the child shouted: Look! my heart was thumping as I walked with my girl friends near Damascus Gate to buy clothes from the shops there. And when the light dawned, I found myself looking up towards the top of the wall and saw him. He was looking at me. I felt embarrassment amidst my pleasure and joy. I ran my hand over my hair and dress, wanting to be beautiful, like he should see me. Making my way through the gathering of terrified, surprised people to go up to him, I felt I was running on green silvery ground.

I was behind the child when we reached the top of the wall. I felt I was floating on a coloured cloud in the sky above the city. I did not feel embarassed when I rushed towards him and embraced him. He put out his hand, stroked me on the shoulder and wiped a tear from my eye. We began to talk ... until the bullets roared.

The man
It's him. How could I ever forget him? It's not possible to forget a beautiful lifetime gone by. It's him. I felt he was looking at me, so I smiled and waved to him and found him returning the greeting.

That was immediately after the light broke out, taking me by surprise. I was sitting with my wife and son on the ground in the small garden huddled against the wall of Damascus Gate. I recognised him from the first moment. And how could I forget him, lifelong companion, comrade and friend?

Whilst the people were muttering and shouting and running, with the light flowing over them suddenly on this night, I stood up to look at him immediately after I heard the child shouting: Look! and pointing to the top of the wall. I found myself pushing through the throngs amidst the tears of the women, the apprehensive silence of the men and the crying of the children, until I reached the gateway and looked up at him on high and greeted him and he returned the greeting.

He said: Come up, and I found myself entering the gateway and climbing up towards him. I was captivated by the lure of the strange, beautiful moment. I could hardly believe myself. It was him. Climbing the stone steps towards him amidst the festival of light and human beings gathering everywhere and amidst the eyes glued to the wall, I did not ask myself how it was possible for him to be here.

The daylight was brilliant. It's him. My friend whom I haven't seen for so long. I saw him only in pictures, in the eyes of his mother when she cried for him and in the eyes of his beloved as she fought back the tears and declared that he was not dead.

That was during the long years of war in Lebanon. He fought savagely in one of the positions defending the camps. He and his company were steadfast many a long day until the position fell. It was said at the time that all had died fighting and that the enemies had brought a bulldozer that dug a deep ditch and threw their bodies into a communal grave. His mother cried for a long time, but his beloved did not believe it and when the two of them, mother and beloved, went together to Lebanon, none of his comrades confirmed he had really died fighting. Some said perhaps he had fallen prisoner to the enemies, some others said perhaps he had stolen out to join one of the fighting groups in the south. But, during the month she spent in Lebanon, his mother persisted in going every day to the communal grave. She would sit in a plot of land on which had been placed a masssive tombstone indicating the site of the communal grave. She would spend long hours in silence, except when drawn into conversation with other women who had come in belief that their sons, or husbands, lay in that grave.

I was sure he was not dead. It is hard for hateful death to snatch away all that abundance of life, all that light. Hard for death to destroy his smile and pealing laughter. And here I see him before me, comrade of my childhood, youth, adolescence and manhood. Here he stands on top of Damascus Gate and from him comes the light, sweeping away the darkness from the sky of my sad city.

I reached the top of the wall and walked quickly towards him. His smile welcomed me. The light radiated from him gently, tinged with cold breezes. I stood beside him. It's him, him. I turned around and caught sight of the throngs of gathering people, wondering where his mother was, where his beloved.

The child and the girl who had come with me were standing beside him. I had a short conversation with him. Until the bullets roared.

The man of light

You should not have been surprised and confused when you saw me.

I had to appear in this place and at this particular time.

When I saw you congregating in these squares and streets on this night in search of fresh air, laughter and a moment of joy, I had to appear. When I saw faces I knew, that had come from all towns and villages and camps, the laughter of children mingled with cares as evident as the deep wrinkles on the foreheads of the men, with the looks of anxiety and apprehension in the eyes of the mothers, with the sweat of fatigue and exhaustion pouring from the bodies of the young people, and with the life which reveals its secrets slowly in the laughter of beautiful girls, I had to appear in this place and at this particular time.

I am not precisely him whom you saw. But I am him, in one form or another. I am neither angel nor devil. I am you. I emerged when you created the festival of colours on this long night. Thus all know me. I am the one you remembered, but not exactly. I am a synthesis of your meeting. I was born when you saw me light up Jerusalem. But it is not my first life. Before it, I lived many lives in other ages.

Tonight I am the man who stood on high upon the wall above Damascus Gate. I did not know him before I took possession of him and passed into his body. I did not choose him, he did not choose me. But I had to be him tonight, before your vast gathering in this place.

I have a family in this city. I will knock at their door. The voice of my father will come to me faintly asking: who is it?. The door will open slowly with an irritating creak. He will find me before him coming from exile and sadness and waiting. He will embrace me and cry a lot. My mother will collapse. She will kiss me a lot, clasping me to her in disbelief. I will sit amongst my brothers and sisters surrounded by warmth. They will bring me hot supper. We will laugh a lot and cry a lot. My parents will talk about a lifetime which passed quickly. They will restrain themselves and hide their pains and ailments. I will tell them much about my exile and sadness and death.

I have children in this city. I will go to their families and plant a kiss on the forehead of each one of them as they sleep. They will wake up and shout with joy. They will jump up and cling to me, questions and laughter bursting from them. I will give them the presents I brought from distant towns and I will tell them stories of the sad tired knight until they sink into sleep.

I have a beloved in this city. I will leap over the roofs of the small huddled houses until I reach her window. I will find it open and jump inside. I will find her before me. I will hold her beautiful body tightly to me. I will kiss her mouth with longing and passion and rapture and drown in the sea of her goodness and the smell of her body. I will run my fingers through her long black hair and I will put out my hand to wipe the tear that leaps from her eyes. I will take her in my arms, kindling desires like a wild gypsy song. I will say to her: I will sow in you a child as beautiful as you.

I have friends in this city. I have acquaintances, memories, secrets and stories which the walls and gardens remember. I lived here many times before I lived this night.

I was that Canaanite farmer who planted the first olive seedling in this land and changed the face of the earth which grew more radiant and splendid. I was that simple soldier who fought against the invasions and I was that worker who carried stones to build this wall on which I am standing. And I returned at other times to repair it.

I was that fellah who threw the first stone at the first boat of strangers which landed on our shores in 1882 for I saw on their faces no signs of people looking for refuge or peace. And the stone is the same stone which your children throw today at the military patrols.

I have been born many times and I have died many times. I have been killed many times by enemies, and by brothers. I have a grave enclosing me in Amman, another in Damascus, another in Beirut, yet another in the south and in . . .

And here I am today before you. The man, me, climbed the wall and stood where I stand. I took possession of him and the light burst forth. This is my time, your time, the time of joy, the time for closed doors to open, for horses to shatter their chains and whinny in the open fields, for birds to break open their cages and fill the sky. It is our time, our colour, our day, our night. You are here together, so here I am, here the light.

When the child and the girl and the man climbed up to me, you too came up with your glances. I felt that I knew each one of you very well, just as each one of you felt you knew me, knew the man who had climbed up to the top of the wall and stood as if waiting for me to take possession of him, for the light to break out.

We were having a conversation and had begun to recall shared memories, when the bullets roared.

The author
When the bullets roared, shattering the silence of the city, nobody understood what was happening. The incandescence of the emanating light held everyone spellbound, but when the commotion happened on top of the wall, when the child screamed and the girl started to cry, and then the man of light fell hanging onto a stone, it was clear to all what had happened. The soldiers occupying the roofs of the buildings had turned torrents of gunfire on him.

The child
When we heard the sound of the bullets, he indicated to us to lie on the ground and drew me towards him, shouting reassuring words. And when the bullets hit him, he did not cry out. He looked at me, blood pouring from his body, then pointed to a piece of cloth which had been there beside him the whole time, and asked me in a trembling voice to bring it. So I crawled forward and brought it.

The girl
I was saying to him: Promise me you won't go away again, and he was smiling as he listened, his eyes filled with a glow of confidence and trust that enveloped me until the bullets roared. We turned round in terror. He indicated to us to bend down behind the blocks of stone on top of the wall. I clung to him and when the bullets hit him, he quickly put out his hand to my mouth to prevent the scream which almost came out, and pointed to a piece of cloth heaped beside us which the child was fetching. The blood was pouring from his chest, but he was more beautiful than ever.

I said to him: I will wait for you.
He said to me: I will not be away long.

The man

I believe he was on the point of asking me about his mother and about his beloved, when the bullets rained down on him. He leaned on me when he was hit in the chest. I said in answer to the question he did not ask: They are both well, both awaiting your return. When he fell to the ground, it was as if a garden of flowers opened, as if new green pastures covered the stone of the walls. I found he was whispering some words which I could just make out. Was he saying to me: Reassure them. I will return?

The man of light

They fired the bullets. They could not stand the light. The blood exploded from my body which was standing on top of the wall. The man collapsed slowly. The child and the girl and the man clung to him. I found my hand showing the child the piece of cloth lying beside us. It was my new death. I went far away. The body of the man whom I had possessed and whom I did not know before, remained laid out in its place. The soldiers continued firing. I went away after your gathering had called me and brought me back to my city to be born in the body of the man who climbed the wall carrying a piece of

cloth which he placed beside him. Do not search for me. I will return. I will return. Search for me in the body of men like that man, inside them. Then will the light burst forth.

The author

The firing and raging of the patrols and running of soldiers and screams of terror and tumult amongst the gathering throngs continued. The people surged forward, the carts and stalls of the roving vendors were overturned, the sobbing of the women and children was unrestrained. And light drenched the city. Then we saw them.

The child was standing in the same place the man of light had stood. It was not possible to see more than his head and chest. It appeared that the girl and the man were standing beside him. They were holding up a piece of cloth, raising it slowly ever higher and higher.

Jerusalem was bathed in the sea of delicate dreamy light that burst forth from it and from the sea of people gathering everywhere. Refreshing breezes wafted from all directions. And the flag fluttered on high.

Akram Hanniyeh tr. Shirley Eber

THE TASTE OF MULBERRIES

HAVAH HALEVI *is a former member of Kibbutz Gan Shmuel. She is now an active member of the Israeli peace movement.*

The name of the village was Sarkas, which probably refers to the former origin of its inhabitants, Circassians, who came, I would not know how, to the Middle East and settled here*. Anyway, when I came to know the village, all of its inhabitants were Palestinian Arabs. In fact, I never came to properly know the village; I was never there, though this is only half the truth, and I shall return to that later.

In our eyes, the eyes of children four or five years old, the village was represented by two women: Khadija and Hanifa. Maybe they were more courageous than the rest, or maybe they

served as something like the 'Foreign Office' of the village. They often walked about in the kibbutz, and as far as I can remember they were mainly preoccupied with the picking of khubeiza (mallow) leaves which grew in wild abundance along the roadside. When we asked

*After the Russian conquest of Circassia from the Ottomans in 1878, many Circassian clans and families loyal to the Ottoman regime emigrated to various countries throughout the Ottoman empire. The Ottoman Sultan Abd al-Hamid extended his support to the Circassian settlement and made lands available to them in Palestine, inter alia. Today there are two Circassian villages: Kufr Qanna in Lower Galilee and Rihaniyya in Upper Galilee. The attempt to settle Circassians in the northern Sharon in the coastal plain, where they established the village of Sarkas, failed, and the original Circassian inhabitants were gradually replaced by native Palestinian Arabs. In 1947, the village population totalled some 400 inhabitants.

why they pick the khubeiza we were told that the Arabs cook the leaves and eat them. And so, the first thing I ever knew about Arabs was that they eat khubeiza. I also knew, of course, that they ride on camels, since the camels used to pass through the kibbutz and occasionally camp there; I knew that they ride on donkeys along the white road which probably stretches up to the very end of the world. But at that time there were in the area also British soldiers (the Mandate), and Australian soldiers (WWII), and thus it was imbedded in my consciousness that Eretz Israel consists of us, as well as passers-by: Arabs, British, Australians . . .

About that time they all disappeared, and I really did not notice their disappearance all that much. Of course, the departure of the British was accompanied by much talk on the radio and in the yard of the kibbutz. But as to the fact that Khadija and Hanifa ceased to show up – well, there are many events that pass through the universe of any child, and he or she accepts their appearance as well as their disappearance as a matter of fact. Later I came to know that the village was destroyed by bulldozers, and I was a little scared. And then I forgot, and many years passed before Sarkas again emerged before my eyes as a place where people lived.

The destroyed village was made into the kibbutz garbage dump. I do not know who was the first to discover that in the midst of the ruins and the dust and the stench there remained a mulberry tree. A huge mulberry tree which, in summer, produced huge mulberries: black and deliciously sweet. The mulberry trees in the kibbutz were grown on much water and their fruit was therefore somewhat watery, and anyway they were much too high to climb on. But this mulberry tree was low, spreading wide and heavily laden with fruit, to the deep delight of a little girl who was rather quiet and clumsy and who loved mulberries. And thus, every Saturday, we would go on pilgrimage to the mulberry tree, stand around it for hours and eat of its fruit and return home with hands and faces blackened by the dark dye of mulberry sap. Never, not once, while standing there among the ruins and the dust under the scathing sun, did we talk or think about the inhabitants of Sarkas who lived here: where were they? where did they go? why?

From the distance of 15 years of difficult political development, I watch this group of children devouring mulberries in the midst of a destroyed village, and I just cannot comprehend: how? where from this utter blindness?

For many years, I would walk on Saturdays to Sarkas. At times with company. At times alone. Now Sarkas was no longer embodied in Khadija and Hanifa. Now Sarkas was reduced to the stench of the kibbutz garbage dump and the mulberries in summer. On either side of the road to Sarkas, there were sabr cacti hedgerows, but today they have all disappeared, except in books and in Arab villages where they still remain. In summer, the sabr would bring forth their fruit and raise masses of tiny red and orange flags glued to their rounded green flagpoles in a summer festival. And when the sabr fruit was ripe, the Arab women would appear out of nowhere, fill their big tin containers with the red and orange fruit, and walk away. Today I remember these Arab women and I ask myself: where did they come from? who were they? were they exiled inhabitants of the village? And in the evening, when they eat the fruit that they had gathered or when they sell it at the roadside, do they feel the taste of their lost homes?

But at that time I did not think of them in the least. The Arabs were something whose temporary provisional existence was eternal. They pass along the white road on a donkey-cart, emerging out of somewhere, going on to somewhere else. Only once, for some reason . . . There was a big scout night game, a sort of test of courage. I hid behind the sabr hedgerows and waited for my pursuers to pass by. I sat there in the dark for a long time, quietly. I was not afraid. And all of a sudden they were with me. The women of Sarkas. Women who pick khubeiza along the roadside. Women with long knives who steal wheat of the fields of the kibbutz. Women with the water cans and the bundles of dry wood on their heads. Slowly, slowly, they slipped by on their bare feet, black and silent. Their round outline, like the sabr cacti leaves, merged into the darkness around, silent.

Today, there stands on the site a huge plant for the processing of agricultural products. An exemplary cooperative venture. And the hill? The hill of the village of Sarkas, where is it?

The entire area was levelled down and around the huge factory, orange groves were planted, and there is not one single cut stone left as testimony. Yet, I remember, I testify.

In 1961, a very young woman from Kibbutz Giv'at HaSheloshah married an Arab youth who was employed on her kibbutz. The kibbutz refused to allow them to remain there, and they applied to join 'my' kibbutz. The debate on whether they were to be admitted or whether they were not to be admitted lasted over one and a half years, and shook the kibbutz in a way that no other subject ever did before or since. The debate cut across families, and brought sons to rebel against their parents, brothers against brothers, husbands against wives. The leadership of the HaShomer HaTza'ir kibbutz federation was called to present its position (opposed) and threats of leaving the kibbutz over the matter were voiced in both camps. In the end, the 'mixed couple' was not admitted to the kibbutz. Both camps were already tired of endless debates and rows. In a bitter discussion which I (who supported their admission) had with one of the leading opponents, he told me: "Do you know that Rashid is a son of the village of Sarkas? Do you think he can live here, raise his children here, always see across the street the mound which was his village, and not think anything?"

At that moment, together with the scorching sun and the dust, I felt in my mouth the taste of the mulberries, and I understood what homeland means, and also, for the first time, vaguely and at a distance and a little bit afraid, I understood that this homeland, the homeland of songs and of school textbooks, is simply the taste of mulberries, and the smell of dust, and the moist earth in winter, and the colour of the sky, and that is it a homeland not only for me, but also for Rashid Masarwa. At that very moment, in the midst of the heated discussion, the taste of mulberries and the shock, I remembered one fearful memory.

It was towards the end of the 1948 war, after we had won the war and defeated the Arab armies and had a state of our own. We were lying in bed. Eight children in the children's house. It was night. From the distance, we heard a heavy and rumbling noise. It was not very far away, but one could clearly hear that the noise did not come from inside the

kibbutz. And the noise went on and on and on. I asked what this protracted, continuous noise was, and one of the children told me that two kibbutz members had gone with bulldozers to Sarkas to destroy the houses of the Arabs. In real fear of Arab revenge, I asked: "But what will the Arabs do when they come back and see that we have destroyed their homes?" Then he answered: "This is why we destroy their homes, so that they will not come back."

I knew then that the matter was lost. The home of Rashid was destroyed in order that he should not return. In order that he, his mother in the long black robe who walks erect with a bundle of wood magnificently balanced on her head, and all his brothers and sisters who run barefoot on the stones, should not return. And still now they will not let him come back.

In December 1972, the entire country was shaken with what was dubbed in the press as the 'affair of the espionage and sabotage network'. Some 30 Arab youths and six Jewish youths, Israelis, were arrested on charges of forming a 'sabotage organisation' operated by the Syrian intelligence whose object was 'to damage the security of the state'. One of the Jewish detainees, a youth aged 26, was a son of 'my' kibbutz. Another detainee from the Arab village of Jatt, was a youth named Mahmoud Masarwa. In his defence speech, he stated:

'The honourable court, your honourable judges,

My father was born in the village of Sarkas, near Kibbutz . . . in the vicinity of Hadera. My father was the son of a peasant. In 1948 he was removed from his land, expelled by force. Their lands were confiscated. Their homes were destroyed. On the site, a factory for the kibbutz was built. My father was compelled to go out and seek work as a labourer in order to feed his family. We went to live in such a tiny house, 12 people in a space of two by three metres. In 1957, I remember this quite well, one year after the Sinai war, my father told me and my brother who sits here (in the courtroom): "Go out to work in order that you at least help me finance your studies . . .".' (Quoted from the official court protocol).

"My brother who sits here in the courtroom"!

His brother who sat there was Rashid Masarwa who, in 1961, applied to be admitted to the kibbutz together with his Jewish wife. It was Rashid Masarwa who told the members of the kibbutz: "I want to live here as a loyal kibbutz member like everyone else, but I want my children to know that their father is an Arab, and I want my children to know the Quran, and I want them to celebrate all the Jewish holidays, but also know what is Ramadan, and that their grandfather and grandmother will come to visit them here in the kibbutz, and that my children will also go to the village to be with their grandfather and grandmother in the holidays."

Now he is sitting here, Rashid Masarwa, and watches his brother being sentenced for wanting to take by the force of arms what he himself hoped to gain by application and consent, and all the brotherhood among the nations in the world could not be of any avail to them.

In Ramleh Central Prison, the son of the dispossessing kibbutz and the son of the dispossessed village meet again. Only one youth, one Udi Adiv, from that kibbutz, resolved in his mind to cross the road. But the world has no space to accommodate the naive. And if prisoners in jail do dream – both prisoners, no doubt, see in their dreams the colour of the sky, and perhaps they also savour the taste of mulberries.

Havah Halevi tr. Dr Uri Davis

ON THE TRUNK OF AN OLIVE TREE

TAWFIQ ZAYYAD, *born in Nazareth in 1932 is one of the leaders of the Israeli Communist Party, Rakah; he is a member of Knesset and in 1977 was elected mayor of Nazareth.*

Because I do not weave wool
Because each day I am subject to detention orders
And my house is subject to police calls
To searches, to "cleanses"
Because I am unable to buy paper
I will carve all I feel
Carve all I conceal
On an olive tree
In the courtyard
Of the house

I will carve my story and the chapters of my tragedy
And my sighs
On my grove and on the tombs of my dead
I will carve
All the bitterness I have tasted
Wiped out by the sweetness to come

I will carve the number of each title deed
Of our land plundered
The site of my village and its boundaries
The houses of its people demolished
My trees uprooted
Every wild flower crushed

The names of those who are expert
At shaking my nerves and bringing me down
The names of the prisons
Every type of manacle
Clamped around my hand
The files of my guards
Every curse
Rained on my head

I will carve:
Kufr Qassim, I will not forget
I will carve:
Deir Yassin, rooted in the memory
I will carve:
We have reached the peak of tragedy
It has found us and we have found it
And yet, we have reached it

I will carve all the sun relates to me
And what the moon whispers to me
And what the lark reports to me
On the well which
The lovers have deserted

In order to remember
I will remain steadfast and carve
All the chapters of my tragedy
And all the stages of the catastrophe
From the molehill
To the mountain
On the olive tree
In the courtyard
Of the house

Tawfiq Zayyad tr. Shirley Eber

CONCERNING HOPES

MAHMOUD DARWISH *was born in 1941 in al-Birwih, east of Acre, a village wiped out in 1949. He was jailed and restricted before moving to Beirut and since 1972 has been a member of the Palestine National Council.*

Don't tell me:
If only I were a bread seller in Algeria
I'd sing with a revolutionary!
Don't tell me:
If only I were a cattle herder in Yemen
I'd sing of the uprisings of time!
Don't tell me:
If only I were a café worker in Havana

I'd sing of the uprisings of the sad!
Don't tell me:
If only I were a young porter in Aswan
I'd sing to the rocks!

My friend!
The Nile will not flow into the Volga
Nor the Congo or the Jordan into the Euphrates!
Each river has its source, its course, its life!
My friend! Our land is not sterile
Each land has its day of birth
Each dawn, its date with revolution

Mahmoud Darwish, tr. Shirley Eber

ECOLOGY OF JERUSALEM

YEHUDA AMICHAI *was born in Germany in 1924, an Orthodox Jew, and settled in Palestine in 1936. He is now arguably Israel's leading poet, with a growing international reputation.*

The air over Jerusalem is saturated with prayers and dreams
like the air over industrial cities.
It's hard to breathe.

And from time to time a new shipment of history arrives
and the houses and towers are its packing materials.
Later these are discarded and piled up in dumps.

And sometimes candles arrive instead of people,
and then it's quiet.
And sometimes people come instead of candles,
and then there's noise.

And in enclosed gardens heavy with jasmine foreign consulates,
like wicked brides that have been rejected,
lie in wait for their moment.

Yehuda Amichai tr. Chana Bloch and Stephen Mitchell

LANGUAGE

Although both Hebrew and Arabic are official languages, who speaks what, when, where and to whom can be a minefield as bewildering to an outsider as other more directly political issues. Not surprisingly, Hebrew is the dominant language, widely used and spoken within the pre-1967 borders. Arabic is generally regarded by Israelis as a second-class language, used by most only when swearing or giving orders to Palestinian workers – or when serving in the army in the occupied territories.

Many Israelis speak languages other than Hebrew, determined by their or their parents'

country of origin. Thus, many *ashkenazi* Jews may know western languages such as English, French or German, or Yiddish – the language spoken by European Jews in the 'diaspora'. Some ultra-orthodox *ashkenazim* continue to speak **Yiddish** rather than Hebrew, since they regard it as blasphemous to hold daily intercourse in the holy language of the scriptures. *Sephardi* Jews often retain a knowledge of Arabic or Persian or other 'eastern' language and may speak the Ladino spoken by Jews in the 'east'.

Palestinians from inside the 'green line' know Hebrew as a learned language, and most speak and read it fluently. It is usually important in their jobs and many will follow the Hebrew-language press and media, which is far less heavily censored than Arabic publications. But Arabic is the mother-tongue which Palestinians on both sides of the 'green line' speak at home and amongst friends.

In the occupied territories many people speak and understand Hebrew, particularly the young, and especially those who have found themselves on the Israeli employment market. But for them it is the language of occupation and visitors to these areas, (as, to a lesser degree, to the Arab villages of the Galilee or amongst Beduin in the Negev) are advised not to practice their Hebrew there. Attempts to speak even a few words of Arabic, however basic, are usually greeted with delight and given every encouragement.

NUMBERS

	Hebrew	Arabic		Hebrew	Arabic
1	ekhad	wahid ١	18	shmona esray	tamantaash ١٨
2	shtayim	itneen ٢	19	tsha esray	tisataash ١٩
3	shalosh	talata ٣	20	esrim	ashreen ٢٠
4	arba	arba ٤	21	esrim ve-ekhad	wahid w-ashreen ٢١
5	khamaysh	khamsa ٥	22	esrim ve-shtayim()	itneen w-ashreen ٢٢
6	shaysh	sitta ٦	30	shloshim	talateen ٣٠
7	sheva	sabaa ٧	40	arbaim	arbaeen ٤٠
8	shmoneh	tmaniya ٨	50	khamishim	khamseen ٥٠
9	taysha	tisaa ٩	60	shishim	sitteen ٦٠
10	eser	ashara ١٠	70	shivim	sabaaeen ٧٠
11	ekhad esray	hidaash ١١	80	shmonim	tamaneen ٨٠
12	shtaym esray	itnaash ١٢	90	tishim	tiseen ٩٠
13	shalosh esray	talataash ١٣	100	maiya	meeya ١٠٠
14	arba esray	arbataash ١٤	200	matayim	meetin ٢٠٠
15	khamaysh esray	khamastaash ١٥	300	shalosh maiyot	talata meeya ٣٠٠
16	shaysh esray	sittaash ١٦	400	arba maiyot	arba meeya ٤٠٠
17	shva esray	sabataash ١٧	1000	elef	alf ١٠٠٠

HEBREW

Yes/No	ken/lo	First/last/next	ha-rishon/ha-akharon/ha-shaini
Please	bevakasha		
Thank you	toda raba	Today	ha-yom
You're welcome (response)	al lo davar	Tomorrow	makhar
		Yesterday	etmol
Hello	shalom	What time is it?	ma ha-sha'a?
How are you?	ma shlomkha (m)/ shlomekh (f)?	How much is that?	kama zeh?
		It's too much	zeh yoter midai
Fine, thank you	beseder	I want something . . .	ani rotzeh (m)/rotzah (f)
Goodbye	shalom		mashehu
See you	lehitra-ot		
Good morning	boker tov	. . .cheaper	. . .yoter zol
Good evening	erev tov	. . .better	. . .yoter tov
Goodnight	laila tov	. . .bigger/smaller	. . .yoter gadol/katan
Sorry	slikha	Do you have (anything) . . .	yesh lekha (mashehu) . . .
Never mind	ain davar	There is/is there? . . .	yesh/yesh? . . .
What's your name?	aikh korim lakha (m)/ lakh (f)?	There isn't . . .	ain . . .
		I don't want . . .	ani lo rotzeh (m)/rotzah (f)
My name's . . .	korim li . . .	I don't understand	ani lo meveen(m)/ meveena (f)
Do you speak Hebrew?	ata medaber Ivrit?		
A little . . .	ktsat . . .	I'm tired	ani ayaif (m)/ayaifa (f)
What's that in Hebrew?	ma zeh be-Ivrit?	. . .hungry	ani re'ayv (m)/re'ayva (f)
		. . .thirsty	ani tsamay (m)/tsmaya (f)
How do you say . . . ?	aikh omrim . . . ?	Everything's OK	ha-kol beseder
Where is . . . ?	eifo yesh . . . ?	Let's go	yalla
. . .a clean hotel	. . .malon naki		
. . .a restaurant	. . .misada	kilo	kilo
. . .the bus station	. . .eifo takhanat ha-autobus	half	khetzi
		quarter	reva
. . .the taxi to . . .	. . .ha-sherut li . . .		
. . .the post office	. . .ha-do'ar	Saturday	shabbat
. . .the toilet	. . .ha-bait shimush	Sunday	yom rishon
Left/right/straight on	smol/yemin/yashar	Monday	yom shaini
Near/far	karov/rakhok	Tuesday	yom shlishi
Here/there	po/sham	Wednesday	yom revi'i
When . . . ?	matai . . . ?	Thursday	yom khamishi
. . .is the bus	. . . ha-autobus	Friday	yom shishi

Phrasebooks and courses

Modern Hebrew is a language created in the 1920s from biblical Hebrew, with the addition of words from European languages. Since it was necessary to teach a standard language to successive waves of immigrants into the new country, there is no shortage of phrasebooks, course books or *ulpanim* – Hebrew language courses. Good phrasebooks include *Say it in Hebrew* and *Berlitz Hebrew for Travellers*, both widely available. The standard course book is *Elef Milim* which provides you with a basic 1000 words. Many *kibbutzim* run *ulpan* courses, offering half-day studies and half-day work. There are also Hebrew classes in town-based *ulpanim*, such as Ulpan Akiva (Green Beach Hotel, POB 256, Netanya, ☎053-52312/3) which runs a variety of residential courses ranging from twenty weeks to 24 days, that cost between $4000 and $900! External fees, including tuition, are $630 for the eight-week summer course, $330 for the 24-day course, with meals at the hotel costing about $10 per meal.

The Hebrew University and *Ulpan Etzion* in Jerusalem also teach Hebrew. For further information, contact the IGTO or the Ministry of Education.

ARABIC

In the phonetic system below, everything is pronounced. kh as the ch in loch; gh as a guttural g.

Yes/No	aiwa/la shukran	Here/there	hoon/hoonak
Please	min fadlak (m)/fadlik (f)	When . . . ?	imta . . . ?
Thank you	shukran	. . .is the bus to	. . .el-bus ila
You're welcome (response)	afwan	First/last/next	el-awal/el-akhir/et-tani
		Today	el-yom
Thank you (for food)	sallim idaik (m)/idaiki (f)	Tomorrow	bukra
(after eating)	ammar	God willing	insha Allah
Hello	marhabah	Thank God	el hamdu lil-lah
Hello (response)	marhabtain	What time is it?	ad-eesh es-sa'a?
Hello (formal)	assalamu aleikum	How much is that?	ad-eesh hada?
How are you?	keef halak?/shu akhba- rak? (m) keef halik?/shu akhbarik? (f)	It's too much/ expensive	hada ktir/ghali
		I want something . . .	bidi aishay . . .
Fine, thank you	mabsut/mnih (m) mabsuta/mniha (f	. . .cheaper	. . .arkhas
		. . .better	. . .ahsan
Goodbye (leaving)	bi-khatrak (m)/-khatrik (f)	. . .bigger/smaller	. . .akbar/asghar
Goodbye (response)	maa salameh	Do you have (anything) . . .	fi 'andak (aishay) . . .
Good morning	sabah el-kheer		
Good morning (response)	sabah en-nur	There is/is there . . .?	fi/fi . . .?
		There isn't . . .	ma feesh . . .
Good evening	masa el-kheer	I don't want . . .	bideesh . . .
Good evening (response)	masa en-nur	I don't understand	ana mush fahim (m)/ fahmeh (f)
Goodnight	sayeedeh	I'm tired/unwell	ana taaban (m)/ taabaneh (f)
Sorry	aasif (m)/aasifa (f)		
Never mind	maalesh/baseeta	. . .hungry	. . .jawaan (m)/ jawaaneh (f)
What's your name?	shu ismak (m)/ismik (f)?		
My name's . . .	ismi . . .	. . .thirsty	. . .atshaan (m)/ atshaaneh (f)
Do you speak Arabic?	btehki Arabi?		
A little . . .	shwaiyeh . . .	Everything's OK	kulshay tamaam
What's that in Arabic?	shu hada bil-Arabi?	Let's go	yalla
How do you say . . . ?	keef bitool . . .	kilo	kilo
Where is . . . ?	wain fi . . . ?	half	nus
. . .a good hotel	. . . otel mnih	quarter	rub'
. . .a restaurant	. . . mataam		
Where is the bus station	wain mahatat el-bus	Saturday	yom es-sabt
		Sunday	yom el-ahad
. . .the service to . . .	. . .es-service ila . . .	Monday	yom el-itneen
. . .the post office	. . .el-bareed	Tuesday	yom et-talaata
. . .the toilet	. . .el-hamam	Wednesday	yom el-arba
Left/right/straight on	shimaal/yemin/dughri	Thursday	yom el-khamees
Near/far	areeb/bayeed	Friday	yom el-juma'

Arabic phrasebooks and courses

Whilst different from the Modern Standard Arabic found in most English-Arabic phrasebooks, Palestinian Arabic does bear some similarities to it. There are no phrasebooks specifically geared to Palestinian Arabic, but if you scour the bookshops, particularly in East Jerusalem, you may be lucky enough to come across a large green book, simply called *Lessons in Spoken Arabic*, by Y.Elihai, and even luckier to find the cassettes that go with it, or *Let's Speak Arabic*, a beginner's course by Omar Othman. Both of these are course books rather than phrasebooks, but are highly recommended. Others, rather more Egyptian-based, are *Getting By In Arabic* by Salah el-Ghobashy and Hilary Wise, which comes with two cassettes and has a useful quick reference word list; *Colloquial Arabic of Egypt, Syria, Iraq and Saudi Arabia*, by DeLacy O'Leary, shows its outdated, orientalist bent in such 'useful' phrases as "Boy, do not beat your donkey"! *Berlitz Arabic for Travellers* is as good as any of the standard phrasebooks.

If you're serious about learning and have the time, both Bir Zeit University and the Hebrew University run summer courses. *Ulpan Akiva* (Green Beach Hotel, POB 256, Netanya, ☎053-52312/3) runs a 12-day residential course in spoken Arabic for English speakers in January, costing $750 per person for accommodation is a double room, $600 in a room for 3–4. If you can organise a group of five or more English speakers, the management can also lay on a course at a 'mutually convenient' date. The *Martin Buber Centre for Adult Education*, in the Mount Scopus campus of the Hebrew University, holds five-week spoken Arabic courses for English speakers, costing around $100. During the breaks, activities and meetings are arranged between these students and Hebrew speakers learning Arabic and Arabic speakers learning Hebrew. The *Christian Information Centre* at the Jaffa Gate in the Old City of Jerusalem is a useful source of further information on courses and has been known to run its own.

A HEBREW AND ARABIC GLOSSARY

HEBREW

AIN/EIN Water spring or source

ALIYA Immigration of Jews to Palestine/Israel
First aliya 1882-1903
Second aliya 1904-1918
Third aliya 1919-1923

AZTMA'UT Independence

BEIT House

BEIT KNESSET Synagogue

DEREKH Way or major road

DIASPORA Jewish dispersion or exile from historic Palestine

ERETZ YISRAEL (lit. The Land of Israel) often meaning "Greater Israel"

GALUT The Jewish diaspora or dispersion

GAN Garden or park

GEMARA Commentary on the Mishnah, including parables and anecdotes

GUSH Bloc, as in Gush Emunim (Bloc of Believers), Gush Etzion (Etzion Bloc)

HAGANAH Underground Jewish fighting force established before 1948

HASSID (pl. Hassidim) Ultra-orthodox Jews

HISTADRUT Zionist labour federation

HOF Beach

HURVA Ruin

IRGUN (Zvi Le'umi) Underground pre-1948 terrorist organisation

KABBALA Jewish mysticism

KACH Right-wing party advocating expulsion of Palestinians etc.

KASHER/KOSHER Food prepared according to Jewish dietary law

KFAR Village

KIBBUTZ (pl. Kibbutzim) Communal settlement based mainly on agriculture

KIBBUTZNIK Member of a kibbutz

KIKAR Square, of town or village

KNESSET Israeli Parliament

LIKUD Ruling right-wing party in the Knesset

MA'ABARA Absorption camp for new Jewish immigrants

MA'ALE Ascent

MAGEN DAVID Star of David

MAGEN DAVID ADOM "Red Star of David" = Red Cross

MALON Hotel

MENORAH Seven-pronged candelabra, associated with the festival of Hanukah

MIKVEH Jewish ritual bath

MISHNAH Legal codification of basic Jewish law — the Halakha

MOSHAV Cooperative village combining collective and private farming

MOSHAV SHITUFI Cooperative village with private housing but collective farming

NAHAL Agricultural/military settlement operated by army unit

NEVE Fertile dwelling place

PALMACH Striking arm of the Haganah

QIRYA Town or suburb

REHOV Street

SDERA (pl. Sderot) Boulevard

SHALOM ACHSHAV Peace Now protest movement

SHERUT (literally, service) Seven-seater communal taxi

SHUQ Market

SIMMON (pl. Simmonim) Telephone tokens

STERN GANG Splinter of the Irgun

TALMUD Interpretation and elaboration of the Mishnah and the Gemara

TEL Artificial mound created by layers of ancient settlements

TORAH The five Books of Moses or Pentateuch

ULPAN Intensive Hebrew school

YA'AR Forest

YAD Memorial

YESH GVUL (literally, There's a Limit) Movement against conscription in the occupied territories

YESHIVA (p. Yeshivot) Jewish religious seminary

YISHUV Jewish community in Palestine prior to establishment of Israel

ARABIC

ABU Father

AIN/EIN Water spring or source

ASSIMON (pl. Assimonim) Telephone tokens

BAB Door or gate

BALADIYYEH Municipality or town hall

BET/BEIT House

B'IR Well

BURJ Tower

CALIPH Muslim rulers, successors to the Prophet Mohammed

DAR House

DEIR Convent

EMIR Prince or commander

FATAH Acronym for Palestine Liberation Movement, the main faction of the Palestine Liberation Organisation (PLO)

FEDA'I (pl. Feda'iin) Freedom fighters or guerillas

FELLAH (pl. Fellahin) Farmers, agricultural workers

HAJ Pilgrimage to Mecca

HAMMA (pl. Hammat) Hot spring

HAMMAM Hot baths

HARAM Holy sanctuary or precinct

HARA Area or quarter of a town or village

HATTA (or KEFFIYA) Headress worn by men

HIJRA Dating of Muslim calendar from Mohammed's flight from Mecca to Medina

INTIFADA Palestinian uprising in the occupied territories

JEBEL/JABAL Mountain

KHAN Caravanserai or inn for travellers and traders

KHANQAH Sufi hostel or hospice

KHIRBE Ruins

KUFR Village or hamlet

MADRASA School, formerly only for religious studies

MAJDAL Tower

MASHRABIYYA Lattice-work window, usually of wood

MASTABA Stone bench

MIDAN Square, of town or village

MIHRAB Prayer niche in the Qibla wall of a mosque

MINBAR Pulpit for sermons in a mosque

MUEZZIN The one who calls Muslims to prayer from the minaret of a mosque

MUFTI Expounder of Islamic law, leader

MUKHTAR Village leader

NABI Prophet

PASHA Turkish high-ranking official

QADI Muslim judge

QAL'A Fort

QASR Palace

QIBLA Direction of prayer for Muslims, ie. Mecca

QURAN Muslim holy scriptures

RAMADAN Muslim month of fasting

RAS Summit

RIBAT Pilgrims' hostels

SHARIY'A Muslim law

SHARIA' Street or road

SEBIL Drinking fountain

SERVICE Seven-seater communal taxi

SHEIKH Term of respect for learned, or old, man (Sheikha, for a woman)

SHI'A Muslim followers of the Prophet Mohammed's son-in-law, Ali

SOUQ Market, usually covered

SUFI Muslim mystic

SULTAN Ruler

SUNNI Majority Muslim followers of the Omayyad and Abbasid caliphs

SURA Chapter of the Quran

TALA'A Ascent

TARIQ Way or path

TAWLEH/SHESH-BESH Backgammon

TEL Mound

TURBA Tomb or graveyard

WADI River bed

WAQF (pl. Awqaf) Trust or endowment set aside for charitable or religious purposes; organisation administering such property

ZAWIYYA Living quarters for Muslim holy 'men'

INDEX

Acre 288
Afula 280
Ahziv 305
Airport Security 4
Al-Bireh 165
Al-Jib 165
Al-Muhraqa 271
Allenby Bridge 192
Arad 383
Armageddon 281
Artas 150
Ashdod 224
Ashqelon 225
Avdat 393
Ayun Nature Reserve 344

Bahai Tomb 300
Balata 169
Banks 9
Banyas 349
Basilica of the Annunciation 277
Beduin 379
Beersheva 386
Beisan 284
Beit Guvrin 239
Beit Jala 146
Beit Jann 310
Beit Sahur 145
Beit She'an 284
Beit She'arim 273
Beitin 167
Ben Gurion Airport 5
Bet Shemesh 241
Bethany 178
Bethlehem 138
Bethlehem University 137
Bethphage 179
Bir Zeit University 168
Bir'im 319
Books 426
Buses 12

Caesarea 249
Camping 17
Cana 279
Canada Park 129
Capernaum 339
Carmel Mountains 270

Christianity 422
Church of the Nativity 141

Dabburiya 279
Daliat al-Karmel 271
Dan 343
Dead Sea 371
Dead Sea Scrolls 372
Deir al-Asad 308
Deir Yassin 127
Desert monasteries 147
Dhahriyyeh 160
Dheisheh 150
Dimona 385
Directory 36
Dor 253
Druze 351

Eilat 395
Ein Boqeq 378
Ein Fashka 375
Ein Gedi 375
Ein Hod 272
Ein Qinya 353
Emmaus 128
Entertainment 28
Erez checkpoint 361

Food 18

Galilee 286
Gamla 355
Gay life 32
Gaza City 362
Gaza refugee camps 365
Gaza Strip 356
Getting Around 12
Getting there 3
Ginnosar 337
Glossary 446
Golan Heights 346
Good Fence 344
Good Samaritan Inn 180

Hadera 248
Hai Bar Wildlife Reserve 407
HAIFA 255–269
    Accommodation 260
    Arrival 259
    Bahai Temple 261
    Eating 266
    History 255
    Information 259
    Kababir 263
    Listings 268

Map 256
Mount Carmel 262
Museums 264
Nightlife 267
Stella Maris Monastery 263
Transport 259
Wadi Nisnas 263
Halhul 151
Hammat 330
Hammat Gader 334
Health 9
Hebron 152
Herodion 146
Herzliya 244
Hisham's Palace 189
History 413
Holidays 26
Horns of Hittin 336
Hotels 16
Hula Valley 341

Information 10
Insurance 10
Iqrit 320
Isfiya 271
Islam 424

Jabal al-Sheikh 351
Jabaliyya 362
Jacob's Well 173
Jaffa 217
Jalazoun 168
Jericho 184
JERUSALEM 41–125
  Accommodation 52
  Airport 51
  Al-Aqsa Mosque 89
  Al-Haram al-Sharif 86
  Al-Tur 97
  Armenian Compound 62
  Armenian Quarter 61
  Ben Yehuda 104
  Buses 51
  Calvary 66
  Cardo 84
  Chain Gate Street 74
  Christian Quarter 68
  Church of the Holy Sepulchre 65
  Citadel 60
  City of David 100
  Cotton Merchants' Market 79
  Damascus Gate 63
  Dome of the Rock 88
  Dung Gate 81

East Jerusalem 93
Eating 114
Ein Karem 112
Ethiopian village 67
Gethsemane 99
Gihon Spring 100
Gilo 112
Hadassah Hospital 111
Hebrew University 111
History 44
Holidays 43
Information 50, 121
Islamic Museum 92
Israel Museum 108
Jaffa Gate 57
Jaffa Road 104
Jesus' tomb 67
Jewish Quarter 80
Kidron Valley 99
Knesset 109
Last Supper 101
Listings 122
Mahane Yehuda 103
Mamluks 73
Map: general 48
Map: Old City 58
Mea She'arim 106
Monastery of the Cross 109
Mount Herzl 109
Mount of Evil Counsel 110
Mount of Olives 96
Mount Ophel 99
Mount Scopus 111
Mount Zion 101
Museums 95
Muslim Quarter 73
Nablus Road 94
New Gate 69
Nightlife 118
Old City 56
Orientation 46
Palestinian culture 120
Religion 42
Rockefeller Museum 95
Russian Compound 105
Settlements 112
Souq Khan al-Zeit 64
St Stephen's Gate 70
Stations of the Cross 71
Strikes 43
Talbieh 107
Tariq al-Wad 77
Taxis 50

Temple Mount 86
Tours 47
Trains 51
Via Dolorosa 71
Wailing Wall 82
West Jerusalem 103
Yad Vashem 110
Yemin Moshe 106
Joseph's Tomb 173
Judaism 421

Karmiel 309
Kastel 126
Khan Yunnis 366
Khirbet Minya 338
Kibbutz Deganya 333
Kibbutz Ein Gev 335
Kibbutz Gesher Haziv 306
Kibbutz Givat Brenner 237
Kibbutz Kfar Blum 342
Kibbutz Lahav 383
Kibbutz Lohamei HaGeta'ot 300
Kibbutz Ma'agan Mikhael 253
Kibbutz Sde Boqer 392
Kibbutz Yotvata 407
Kibutz Ha'on 334
Kufr Kanna 279
Kursi 335

Lakhish 238
Language 442
Laqiya 383
Latrun 126
Lesbian life 32
Lifta 126
Literature 432
Lydda 231

Ma'alot 312
Maale Adumim 180
Maimonides 328
Majd al-Kurum 307
Majd al-Shams 352
Majdal 337
Mamre 152
Mamshit 386
Maps 11
Mar Elias 136
Mar Saba 148
Mary's Well 278
Mas'ada 353
Masada 376
Media 24
Megiddo 281
Meron 312

Metulla 343
Mi'ilya 304
Mitzpe Ramon 393
Monastery of St George 180
Monastery of the Temptation 190
Money 8
Montfort 304
Mount Arbel 337
Mount Gerizim 174
Mount of Beatitudes 339
Mount Sinai 409
Mount Tabor 279

Na'aran 191
Nabi Musa 183
Nabi Samwil 165
Nabi Shu'eib 336
Nablus 170
Nahariyya 301
Nazareth 274
Negev 378
Netanya 245
Neve Ativ 350
Neve Yam 254

Opening hours 25

Peqi'in 310
Petah Tiqvah 213
Phones 23
Police 31
Post 23

Qazrin 354
Qiryat Arba 159
Qiryat Gat 238
Qiryat Shmona 342
Qumran 372
Quneitra 353

Rachel's Tomb 137
Rafah 368
Rama 310
Ramallah 162
Ramla 234
Red Tape 7
Rehovot 236
Religion 421
Rishon le Zion 223
Rosh Haniqra 306
Rosh Pinna 340

Safad 313
Sahne 283
Sakhnin 310
Samaria 175

Samaritans 174
Samu'a 159
Sea of Galilee 321
Sebaste 175
Sexual harassment 31
Shechem 173
Shepherds' Field 145
Shilo 169
Shivta 392
Sinai 407
Sinjil 169
Sleeping 15
Solomon's Pools 150
St Catherine's Monastery 408
St Theodosius 148
Subeibeh 350
Surif 151

Taba 408
Tabgha 338
Tarshiha 311
Tel al-Sultan 188
TEL AVIV 196–217
  Accommodation 199
  Arrival 197
  Bat Yam 213
  Beaches 208
  Ben Yehuda Street 202
  Buses 198
  Dizengoff Square 201
  Eating 209
  Kikar Namir 204
  Listings 214
  Map 202

Museums 206
Neve Zedek 205
Nightlife 210
Old Port 204
Parks 208
Petah Tiqvah 213
Ramat Gan 213
Shalom Tower 205
Shuq HaCarmel 205
Suburbs 213
Taxis 199
Tel Hai 342
Tel Hazor 341
Tel Maresha 239
The Triangle 282
Tiberias 323
Tiberias Hot Springs 329
Timna Valley 405
Tomb of the Patriarchs 157
Trouble 30
Tulul Abu Alayiq 191

Umm al-Fahm 282

Visas 7

Wadi Qelt 180
West Bank 132
West Bank settlements 150
Work 33

Ya'ar Yehudiyya Nature Reserve 354
Yavne 224

Zichron Yaacov 254